COMPANY LAW

FUNDAMENTAL PRINCIPLES

Fourth edition

Stephen Griffin LLB, M.PHIL

Professor of Law,
University of Wolverhampton

Chapter 12 on Insider Dealing
contributed by Michael Hirst LLB LLM,
Professor of Law,
De Montfort University

Chapter 15 on Insolvency Procedures
contributed by Peter Walton LLB PHD,
Principal Lecturer in Law,
University of Wolverhampton

PEARSON
Longman

Harlow, England • London • New York • Boston • San Francisco • Toronto
Sydney • Tokyo • Singapore • Hong Kong • Seoul • Taipei • New Delhi
Cape Town • Madrid • Mexico City • Amsterdam • Munich • Paris • Milan

Pearson Education Limited

Edinburgh Gate

Essex CM20 2JE

England

and Associated Companies throughout the world.

Visit us on the World Wide Web at:
www.pearsoned.co.uk

First published 1994
Second edition published 1996
Third edition published 2000
Fourth edition published 2006

ISBN-13: 978-0-582-78461-1
ISBN-10: 0-582-78461-1

British Library Cataloguing-in-Publication Data
A catalogue record for this book is available from the British Library

Library of Congress Cataloging-in-Publication Data
Griffin, Stephen.
  Company law : fundamental principles / Stephen Griffin.—4th ed.
    p. cm.
  Chapter 12 on insider dealing contributed by Michael Hirst; chapter 15 on insolvency procedures contributed by Peter Walton.
  Includes bibliographical references and index.
  ISBN 0-582-78461-1
  1. Corporation law—England. 2. Corporation law—Wales. I. Hirst, Michael, 1954– II. Walton, Peter, 1965– III. Title.

KD2079.G75 2006
346.42′066–dc22

2005053547

10 9 8 7 6 5 4 3 2 1
10 09 08 07 06

Typeset in 10/12pt Sabon by 35
Printed and bound by Henry Ling Ltd, Dorchester

To Donna.
Thanks for being my wife and best friend
for the last twenty years.

CONTENTS

PREFACE

Company law has always been a fast-moving legal subject but in the five years since this work was last published the subject's momentum has been that of a runaway train – travelling down a very steep incline. The subject area has expanded and developed in many key areas. Increased legislation and other regulatory measures, EC regulation, significant case law development, and proposals for structural and procedural reform backed up by two White Papers, have all played their part.

At times, company law is a technical and complex subject but it is also an interesting and dynamic area, lively, sometimes controversial, a subject in which diverse opinions are abundant in the representation of its academic debate. Representing a vast subject area, the topics contained within this book concentrate their attention on areas of corporate law which represent common constituents of the UK undergraduate/postgraduate company law courses.

In common with the previous three editions of this work, the fourth edition is designed to encourage and assist a student's understanding and perception of the fundamental principles of company law. I have made every effort to write this book in a style which is clear and unambiguous, yet at the same time I have sought to maintain a substantive degree of academic analysis and debate in its presentation. The book is significantly longer than previous editions, a fact which may be explained by the expansive growth of the subject area and also by my own desire to inject more analysis, depth and debate into the work.

I have endeavoured to state the law as of 1 May 2005. However, at the proof stage I was able to include a brief discussion of the decision of The House of Lords in *National Westminster* v *Spectrum Plus* (reported on 30th June 2005). The case is discussed in Chapter 13.

Stephen Griffin

ACKNOWLEDGEMENTS

I wish, as ever, to express my sincere thanks to my wife, Donna, for her understanding nature and patience. To my children, Vicky and Emily, for their support and laughter. To my friends and colleagues for their kindness and tolerance. Special thanks to Michael Hirst for revising Chapter 12, and to Peter Walton for lending his insolvency law expertise to the book by writing a new chapter (Chapter 15) on Insolvency Law Procedures.

Finally, I would like to thank my publishers for their patience, help and assistance; special thanks go to Lissa Matthews, Michelle Gallagher, Rebekah Taylor, Nicola Chilvers, Heather Palomino, Joe Vella and all at Longman/Pearson.

TABLE OF CASES

TABLE OF STATUTES AND STATUTORY INSTRUMENTS

INTERNAL RULES AND REGULATIONS

TABLE OF EUROPEAN AND INTERNATIONAL LEGISLATION

REGULATIONS

INTERNATIONAL LEGISLATION

1

THE LEGAL CHARACTERISTICS OF A REGISTERED COMPANY

INTRODUCTION

This chapter seeks to explain the fundamental legal characteristics of a company registered with a limited liability status. It examines the historical roots of the modern registered company and analyses the landmark decision of the House of Lords in Salomon v A Salomon Ltd [1897] AC 22. *The chapter concludes by briefly considering future developments in the field of company law.*

THE LEGAL CONSEQUENCES OF INCORPORATION

A company may be perceived as an artificial entity in the sense that it is but a vehicle, occupied and controlled by its management and membership, steered by the former in the pursuit of business goals. The human constituents of the company will ultimately determine the route that is to be taken by the corporate enterprise. Nevertheless, in law the artificial nature of a company is ignored to the extent that a company registered in accordance with the provisions of the companies legislation (currently the Companies Act 1985) is, as from the date of its incorporation, a body corporate (s 13(3), CA 1985). As such, the registered company is a separate legal entity; it possesses rights and is subject to duties in much the same way as a natural person. For example, a company may sue and be sued in its own name and will be liable to pay its own form of tax, i.e. corporation tax.

In addition to a registered company's separate legal identity, the vast majority of registered companies are incorporated with a limited liability. (Note that a company may be registered as an unlimited company: see Chapter 5.) A company may be limited by shares or by guarantee. (Unless otherwise stated, this book will concentrate on the former; for a brief discussion of companies limited by guarantee, see Chapter 5.) Limited liability means that a member of a company will cease to incur a liability to contribute to the debts of the company once the shares held by that member have been fully paid for, that is, the nominal value of the share has been paid to the company (price of share when first issued). A registered company with a limited-liability status is therefore responsible for its own actions and will be predominately liable for its own debts, where its debts exceed the extent of its membership's limited liability.

The immediate result of a company's incorporation is the creation of two independent bodies: the company and its membership. The membership of a limited company take shares in the company. The shares held represent a member's interest in the company. The nature and extent of this interest will determine the member's right to participate in dividend payments as well as a member's right to participate in the decision-making policy of the company (discussed further in Chapter 9). Subject to any prohibition contained in a company's constitution, a shareholder may freely sell or dispose of his shareholding interest. In respect of the company's existence, it is quite irrelevant that the identity of its shareholders may change. A company's legal existence is not dependent upon the survival of individual shareholders. Accordingly, a company is said to have perpetual succession.

The legal rights and duties of shareholders, in respect of their relationship with the company and fellow shareholders, are determined by the company's constitution (see Chapter 5). Despite the fact that a person may have exclusively owned the property and assets of a business prior to its incorporation as a registered company, the property vested in the company belongs to the company; a shareholder has no right of ownership in respect of the company's property or assets. For example, in *Macaura v Northern Assurance Co* [1925] AC 619, a timber merchant converted his business into a registered company; the timber merchant held the majority shareholding. The property of the newly incorporated company was destroyed by fire and the merchant sought to recoup his loss by claiming against his insurance company. Although the property was insured, the insurance policy was held in the merchant's name. As the merchant no longer owned the property to which the claim related, the property having been transferred to the company, the insurance company was held not to be liable in respect of satisfying the claim. On the incorporation of the business, the insurance policy should have been transferred into the name of the new owner of the property, namely the company (see also *Re Lewis Wills Trust* [1985] 1 WLR 102).

Although one person may in effect control and execute the affairs of a company by occupying several positions in the corporate structure – for example, an individual may be the majority shareholder, the company's managing director and at the same time the company's sole employee – such a person is not to be regarded as the company. The company is a separate legal entity: see e.g. *Lee v Lee's Air Farming* [1961] AC 12 and *Barakot v Epiette Ltd* [1998] 1 BCLC 283.

While a company holds its property and assets for the ultimate benefit of the associated rights of its membership, a member of a company may still be convicted of theft from the company in which he is a member, notwithstanding that the member in question holds all or substantially all the shares in the company: see e.g. *Attorney-General's Reference (No 2 of 1982)* [1984] 2 WLR 447 and *DPP v Gomez* [1993] AC 442.

The principal advantage of incorporating a business is undoubtedly the limited liability attached to the company's human constituents coupled with the favourable status that the public (often mistakenly) affords to a limited liability concern. The principal disadvantage of incorporation is a loss of privacy for the business. Unlike unlimited partnerships (discussed in Chapter 5), registered companies are subject to many disclosure requirements.

Disclosure requirements

Disclosure is a regulatory requirement that is imposed on companies for the general benefit and safeguard of the public interest. Information relating to the functioning and financial state of a company offers a degree of transparency, enabling investors and creditors to have an opportunity to obtain knowledge of a company's business functions. Public disclosure requirements are imposed by the companies legislation and are made to Companies House (where registration documents, registers, etc. are kept). The disclosure requirements include the basic registration procedures (see Chapter 3), compiling and maintaining registers such as the members and directors register, details of changes to the constitutional structure of the company, copies of all the special or extraordinary resolutions passed by the general meeting of a company and information of a financial nature.

Disclosure of information of a financial nature

In accordance with ss 363 and 364 of the Companies Act 1985, every company must complete an annual return (report of company's affairs); this must be filed with the Registrar of Companies, at Companies House. In addition to the annual return, all companies must submit a directors' report for each financial year (s 234, CA 1985) which will include matters such as the development and business activities of the company and the amount (if any) which the directors recommended be paid as a dividend. The White Paper (2002) proposed the replacement of the current content of the directors' report. In the case of small companies the report would be replaced by a short supplementary statement and for larger companies by means of an Operating and Financial Review (discussed in Chapter 20).

A company must also provide an annual report of its accounts that must provide a 'true and fair' view of the company's financial affairs (see Schs 4 and 4A, CA 1985), albeit in the case of small and medium companies the return of the accounts may be in an abbreviated form (discussed further in Chapter 20). Section 242 of the Companies Act 1985 provides that the annual accounts must be accompanied (where applicable) by an auditor's report (discussed further in Chapter 20).

THE HISTORY OF THE REGISTERED COMPANY

The concept of the registered company was born of the mid-nineteenth century and as such company law is a comparatively modern legal phenomenon. Nevertheless, prior to the mid-nineteenth century, business associations existed in such a form whereby they may be properly described as ancestors of and necessary catalysts to our present system of company law.

The chartered joint stock company

Chartered joint stock companies were developed in the seventeenth century, largely as a result of the expansion in the world shipping trade, examples of which included the East India Company formed as a joint stock company in 1612, the Massachusetts Bay Company formed in 1629 and the Hudson's Bay Company formed in 1670. A sophisticated form of a partnership concern, the joint stock company was created by royal charter and comprised an association of members; each member contributed capital towards specific trade ventures. The charter often provided the association with monopolistic rights in specific trades. In addition, the joint stock company was deemed to have a separate legal identity and in some cases the privileges attached to the company included a limited liability status, although this latter privilege had to be specifically provided for in the charter. A member of a joint stock company would take shares in the concern in proportion to his initial contribution towards the company's stock.

The growth in joint stock companies mirrored an expansion in the number of share dealings. By the early part of the eighteenth century speculation in share values had become another means by which the gentry could amuse their gambling instincts. One such company in which the speculative fervour thrived was the South Sea Company. This company was founded in 1711 with the objective of obtaining a monopoly of trade with the colonies in South America. The company prospered and, in an ambitious attempt to expand its wealth, entered into a venture whereby it proposed to purchase the national debt. The company proposed to buy out government creditors or to persuade them to take shares in the South Sea Company in exchange for their claims on the national debt. In an attempt to secure this transaction members of the government and other high-ranking officials were rewarded with shares in the company. The rationale behind this venture was that the national debt was a profitable high interest-bearing loan. Confidence in the South Sea Company's proposals escalated. In 1719, the year in which the company had offered to purchase the national debt, a £100 share in the company was quoted at £136, whereas by mid-1720 the share price had reached £1000. The surge of confidence in the South Sea shares resulted in a general increase in share dealings and a speculative boom in the general value of share prices of other companies. Unfortunately, many companies with dubious corporate objectives, many of which had been formed by purchasing charters of long extinct companies, thrived as a result of the general acceptance by naive investors that a company share could do nothing but escalate in value.

The subsequent collapse of the South Sea Company led to the panic selling of shares, the resulting general collapse in markets was inevitable, fraudulently conceived companies were prosecuted, members of the government who had been involved in the share dealings fell from grace, and Parliament, in an attempt to curb the improper use of the corporate form, passed the so-called Bubble Act of 1720. The purpose of this Act was to prevent share transactions other than those involving the shares of companies that had been granted powers by individual Acts of Parliament or those with legitimate charters. The new Act imposed a stricter regime on the ability of businesses to trade as companies. The South Sea bubble episode was the first speculative boom and crash in British history, although it was certainly not to be the last.

Unincorporated associations

The decline in the popularity of the corporate form as a business medium continued until the start of the nineteenth century. The nineteenth century witnessed an increase in the number of companies created by individual Acts of Parliament; such companies were basically large trading concerns. The expense of incorporating by this method was extremely prohibitive of smaller business ventures. However, despite the growth in statutory companies – these included concerns such as banks, canal companies, railway companies, etc. – by far the most popular form of business organisation at the time was the unincorporated association, formed under a trust deed (the deed of settlement), whereby members of the association would, in a similar way to joint stock companies, invest capital in an association and in return take shares in the association. Yet, unlike joint stock companies, the property and assets of the association were not held by the business as a separate legal entity. Trustees who could sue and be sued on behalf of the association held the property and assets. The principal disadvantage of the unincorporated association was that the members of these businesses did not have a limited liability status. In addition, the right of members freely to transfer shares in the associations remained undoubtedly questionable under the provisions of the Bubble Act, an Act that was not repealed until 1825.

The Joint Stock Companies Act 1844

The Joint Stock Companies Act 1844 gave birth to the first form of registered company. As a result of the 1844 Act, a company could be incorporated by a registration procedure as opposed to incorporation by royal charter or by an individual Act of Parliament. Under the Act, companies could be incorporated by registration providing the company had more than 25 members. The 1844 Act also created the Registrar of Companies with whom particulars of registered companies had to be lodged. Despite the creation of the registered company, the 1844 Act did not confer limited liability on the membership of these companies. Limited liability was, at that time, seen as a means by which undercapitalised concerns might exploit the corporate form to the detriment of creditors and the investing public.

Limited liability

The Limited Liability Act of 1855 allowed companies with at least 25 members, each holding shares to the minimum value of £10, with at least one-fifth fully paid up on the share, to incorporate with a limited-liability status. Prior to the Act the ability to grant a limited-liability status to a small business enterprise had been the subject of much discussion and severe reservations that centred around the fear that general limited liability would result in undercapitalised concerns to the detriment of creditors and the general public interest (see e.g. the report of the Royal Commission on Mercantile Law and the Law of Partnership in 1854).

In accordance with the 1855 Act, a company was required to have not less than three-quarters of its nominal capital subscribed and the word 'limited' added to its name. Liability was (as it still is today) limited to the nominal value of the share. The 1855 Act was incorporated into the Joint Stock Companies Act 1856 which required an obligation on the part of a company to have and register constitutional documents, namely the memorandum and articles of association (these in effect replaced the deed of settlement). In addition, and to encourage smaller business enterprises to register as companies, the 1856 Act removed the restrictions relating to the minimum amount of capital to be contributed by members of a company and also reduced the minimum number of members required for the purposes of incorporation from 25 to seven members. The companies legislation was consolidated into the Companies

Act of 1862. The desire to encourage incorporation was fuelled by acceleration in business activity inspired and generated by the industrial revolution.

THE JUDICIAL ACCEPTANCE OF THE COMPANY AS A SEPARATE LEGAL ENTITY

In relation to the incorporation of large established business concerns, the judicial interpretation of the Victorian legislation, in its recognition of the registered company as a separate legal entity, was generally accepted without much dissent. Providing a large business concern was registered in accordance with the companies legislation, it was taken that it could benefit from the advantages of incorporation; see e.g. the House of Lords' decision in *The Princess of Reuss* (1871) 5 LR 176, a case in which the existence of an enterprise properly incorporated as a limited-liability company under the Companies Act 1862 was unsuccessfully challenged on the basis that its membership was comprised of 'foreigners'!

Nevertheless, despite the general judicial recognition of the separate legal existence of the larger registered company, the judicial acceptance of smaller registered companies, often incorporated with only one substantial shareholder, was a matter of some uncertainty. It had been perceived by many that the 1862 Act raised a presumption, in providing that a company should be incorporated by at least seven members, that the said members would all offer a significant contribution towards the company's capital, a presumption not realised in the case of many small private companies. The incorporation of small 'one-man type' businesses had at the start of the 1860s been rare, but towards the end of the nineteenth century the incorporation of small businesses dramatically increased to the extent that by the start of the twentieth century the small incorporated concern represented an overwhelming majority of all registered companies.

The case heralded as the one which finally established the applicability of the registered company as an acceptable and valid form of business medium for small businesses was *Salomon* v *A Salomon Ltd* [1897] AC 22 (however, it should be noted that earlier examples of the judicial acceptance of the ability to incorporate small businesses do exist: see e.g. *Re George Newman & Co* [1895] 1 Ch 674 and *Farrar* v *Farrar* (1889) 40 Ch D 395).

The facts of the *Salomon* case were as follows. The proprietor of a small but successful leather business, a Mr Salomon, incorporated the business as a limited company in accordance with the registration provisions contained within the Companies Act 1862. Section 6 of the 1862 Act provided that seven or more persons together could incorporate a business, provided that it was associated for a lawful purpose. The seven subscribers to A Salomon Ltd were Mr Salomon, his wife and their five children. The company, A Salomon Ltd, purchased Mr Salomon's business in a solvent state for a consideration to a value of approximately £39 000. Mr Salomon received 20 000 fully paid-up £1 shares, an issue of debentures to the value of £10 000 (a debenture acknowledges a loan or other credit agreement between the company and its creditor and is normally secured against the assets of the company; in Salomon's case the debenture was secured by means of a floating charge (floating charges are discussed in Chapter 13)) and took the remainder of the sale price in cash. The remaining members of the family were each allotted a £1 share in the company.

Unfortunately, A Salomon Ltd did not prosper. Mr Salomon's debentures were transferred to a Mr Broderip in return for £5000; this amount was then pumped back into the company by Mr Salomon. Despite further efforts on the part of Mr Salomon to keep the company afloat, less than a year after its incorporation, the company fell into an insolvent state. The company could not meet Broderip's debenture interest payments and, fearful that his investment would be lost, Broderip sought to realise his security (the floating charge) by appointing a receiver. The company, which had other creditors, was subsequently put into liquidation. The liquidation (resulting, ultimately in a sale of corporate assets) of the company's assets realised sufficient funds to meet the company's debt to Broderip but not the debts owed to the company's other creditors who, unlike Broderip, had no secured interest (debentures).

In the High Court (heard as *Broderip* v *Salomon* [1895] 2 Ch 323), the liquidator admitted the validity of Broderip's prior claim to be repaid from the company's assets: as holder of a secured loan he had priority. Nevertheless, the liquidator counter-claimed that the company (and therefore the company's unsecured creditors) was entitled to be reimbursed by Salomon personally. The trial judge, Vaughan Williams J, agreed with this contention. Whilst admitting that upon its registration a company was a legal entity, distinct from its corporators, the learned judge opined that A Salomon Ltd (the company) was no more than an agent of its principal, i.e. Mr Salomon. As such, the principal was responsible for the debts of its agent. The basis for the agency argument was that the company was a mere alias of its founder and had not been formed in accordance with the true spirit of the 1862 Companies Act. Vaughan Williams J believed that the 1862 Act, in its requirement for 'seven persons associated for a lawful purpose' should be interpreted to mean seven persons with a *bona fide* intention of participating in a trading venture, and not, as in the present case, a company which, in reality, was akin to a one-man business.

On appeal, the decision of Vaughan Williams J was upheld, although in the Court of Appeal's opinion the correct analogy between the company and Mr Salomon was that of a trust relationship: the company held its property on trust for its beneficiary, Mr Salomon. As such, the creditors of A Salomon Ltd were entitled to a claim against Mr Salomon through the company. As at first instance, the Court of Appeal recognised that A Salomon Ltd, in complying with the registration provisions of the 1862 Act, had been validly incorporated as a separate legal entity. However, the court would not recognise that the liability of A Salomon Ltd should be divorced from that of its founder, Mr Salomon, because in common with the High Court it agreed that in relation to the requirements of incorporation, the correct interpretation of the Companies Act 1862 was that the seven persons who became members of the company should participate in the venture, rather than having but a nominal and superficial interest.

Notwithstanding that the business had been profitable prior to its incorporation, Lindley LJ was of the opinion that the manner in which the company had been formed indicated that it had been created for an illegitimate purpose, that it was 'a device to defraud creditors' (at p 339) and as such was therefore contrary to the terms of the 1862 Act because it was not associated for a lawful purpose. Indeed, in the Court of Appeal's opinion the company's illegitimacy stemmed from the fact that it was in reality a one-man company. Lopes LJ stated:

'If we were to permit it to succeed, we should be authorising a perversion of the Joint Stock Companies Act. We should give vitality to that which is a myth and a fiction . . . To legalise such a transaction would be a scandal.' (at p 341)

The House of Lords, in reversing the decision of the Court of Appeal, rigorously denied the assertion by the lower courts that a company could not be formed by one dominant character together with six other persons divorced of a substantial interest in the business venture. According to the House, the statutory language of the Companies Act 1862 (s 6) was clear. A company could be incorporated providing it had at least seven members, irrespective of whether all seven members made a substantial contribution to the company.

Although both the High Court and the Court of Appeal recognised that A Salomon Ltd, having complied with the registration provisions of the 1862 Act, was a corporate entity, they had not contemplated the fact that once incorporated the company could not be considered as anything other than an independent entity, totally separate and distinct from its founder, Mr Salomon. The House of Lords' interpretation of the separate legal identity of a company was, in respect of A Salomon Ltd, absolute. Lord Macnaughten stated thus:

'It may be that a company constituted like that under consideration was not in the contemplation of the legislature at the time when the Act authorising limited liability was passed; that if what is possible under the enactments as they stand had been foreseen a minimum sum would have been fixed as the least denomination of share possible; and that it would have been made a condition that each of the seven persons should have a substantial interest in the company. But we have to interpret the law, not to make it; and it must be remembered that no one need trust a limited company unless he so please, and that before he does so he can ascertain, if he so pleases, what is the capital of the company and how it is held.' (at p 46)

His lordship then went on to state:

'The company is at law a different person altogether from the subscribers to the memorandum; and though it may be that after incorporation the business is precisely the same as it was before, and the same persons are managers, and the same hands receive the profits, the company is not in law the agent of the subscribers or trustee for them. Nor are the subscribers as members liable, in any shape or form, except to the extent and in the manner provided by the Act.' (at p 51)

The House of Lords in considering the agency and trust arguments of the lower courts concluded that both were contradictory to the view that the company was a separate legal entity. The finding of an agency or trust relationship would have rendered as illusory the limited liability of the company's majority shareholder, Mr Salomon. The finding of an agency or trust relationship would have meant that Mr Salomon would have been personally liable for the company's debts. Lord Herschell said of the decisions of the lower courts:

'It is to be observed that both courts treated the company as a legal entity distinct from Salomon and the members who composed it, and therefore as a validly constituted corporation . . . Under the circumstances I am at a loss to understand what is meant by saying that A Salomon & Co Ltd is but an alias for A Salomon.' (at p 42)

Lord Halsbury remarked:

'Once the company is legally incorporated it must be treated like any other independent person with rights and liabilities appropriate to itself, and that the motives of those who took part in the promotion of the company are absolutely irrelevant in discussing what those rights and liabilities are.' (at p 30)

A problem for unsecured creditors?

One of the most worrying implications of the *Salomon* decision is that a trader in incorporating a business will not only be able to obtain the advantage of limited liability but, in addition, could also ensure by taking debentures in the company that he had a first call on the assets of the company, should the company become insolvent. In theory, this problem should be limited because if a founding member of a company was to take debentures in the enterprise his secured interest would be registered and as such any future creditor of a company would have the opportunity to check the register of company charges to discover the existence of the charge; should a creditor fail to check the register he would nevertheless be deemed to have constructive notice of a registered charge (company charges and priority interests are discussed in Chapter 13). Yet, commercial expediency dictates that small trade creditors are unlikely to expend time and money on making such checks. Therefore, the decision in *Salomon* may be said to place unsecured trade creditors in a perilous position in respect of an ability to seek the repayment of sums due by the company in priority to a member's claim where that member's claim is secured by a debenture (however, note that in such circumstances specific statutory provisions may attempt to remove the shield of limited liability: see Chapter 18).

THE REGISTERED COMPANY INTO THE TWENTY-FIRST CENTURY

While many statutory changes have occurred in the field of company law since the creation of the registered company – for example, a private limited company may now be incorporated with just one member, and a public company with two members – the skeleton of the Victorian legislation remains as a definite characteristic of modern company law. Indeed, incorporation by the process of registration, the recognition of a company as a separate legal identity and the ability to incorporate with a limited-liability status are characteristics at the very heart of modern company law (now regulated by the Companies Act 1985 and related legislation).

The birth of the registered limited liability company was and remains a means by which businessmen can limit the risk of investing funds into a business enterprise. Encouraging the growth and expansion of companies is of the utmost importance to the national economy because successful companies generate wealth and employment. Indeed, limited liability has been a stimulant to economic expansion. From the time of its introduction it has encouraged capital to be aggregated for investment purposes.

Nevertheless, while in the nineteenth century loan funds for small to medium-size entrepreneurs were not readily available and thus the aggregation of capital through the medium of the company was a means to enhance the value and potential of a small business, in more modern times this position has not been so apposite. As part of the twentieth century's credit boom, the availability of business loans has, in small private companies, deflated the need for the aggregation of capital. Therefore, in the context of a private company, a limited-liability status may no longer be viewed as a clear advantage in the funding of the enterprise. In addition, in private companies comprised of very few members and where the majority of the membership are also directors of the company (the position in the vast majority of private companies), the advantage of limited liability may, in one real sense, be artificial because large creditors of the enterprise are likely to demand personal guarantees of the members/ directors to secure the repayment of debts. To this end, should the company become insolvent, the company's human constituents will gain little from having traded the enterprise as a limited liability company. The principal advantage for trading as a private company will (in addition to possible tax advantages) be that, unlike an unlimited enterprise, small trade creditors/customers of the company will not ordinarily be able to lay claim against the shareholders and/or directors in respect of their personal assets.

In relation to public companies, limited liability offers greater protection to the company's shareholders and directors where, unlike private companies, the expectation of personal guarantees is less obvious in the wake of security represented in the form of substantive corporate assets. Further, unlike the private company, the ability of the public company to offer shares to the general public, with no liability attached to the share once fully paid, may be an advantageous method of raising substantial amounts of investment capital.

The European Union

Where appropriate, individual chapters of this book will deal with the impact of European law on UK company law. The said impact has been particularly noticeable in respect of laws related to capital and financial dealings but many other areas have also been touched by the incoming tide of European regulation.

The UK became a member of the European Community in 1972. The UK's membership was implemented in accordance with the European Communities Act 1972 (in force from 1 January 1973). Since 1992, the pillars of the European Community have collectively become known as the European Union (EU), so established by the Treaty of Maastricht in 1992. The EU is, of itself, a political entity without law-making powers. Of the constituent elements (pillars) of the EU, the European Community, the EC (formerly named the European Economic Community) determines Community laws.

With an objective of paving the way for a greater degree of understanding and cooperation between the member states of the EU, in respect of community trade and the freedom of movement of goods, capital and workers, the freedom of establishment, the mutual recognition of companies or firms and transnational mergers, the EC has strived to bring about a harmonisation programme of national company laws.

The spirit of the harmonisation programme is based on principles contained in Art 54(3)(g) of the EC Treaty. More recently and largely in response to the recommendations of the Commission's High-Level Group of European company law experts, the European Commission, in May 2003, devised a schedule for future action in the area of company law with specific reference to harmonising the areas of corporate governance, directors' duties, directors' liabilities and corporate structures.

The process for harmonisation is principally pursued by Council Directives. In principle, a Directive is binding on all member states but only as to the result that it seeks to achieve. Therefore the national legislature must implement the Directive into its own legislation in whatever form and by whatever method is deemed appropriate (see Art 189(3) of the EC Treaty). While a Directive may afford some flexibility in the manner in which it is implemented, by contrast, if a provision of EC law is prescribed by a regulation, the regulation will be deemed to be directly applicable.

Reform, the CLR review and the government's response

In the last decade, company law has been subject to a significant and at times overwhelming number of consultation reports issued by both the Law Commission and the DTI's Company Law Review (CLR). The CLR was set up in 1998 and ran for a period of three years in which proposals for an extensive procedural reform of most areas of company law was proposed. The CLR, in producing ten consultation documents, examined and expanded many of the Law Commission proposals. The CLR culminated in the Final Report of 2001, 'Modern Company Law for a Competitive Economy'. In 2002, the government responded to the findings of the CLR and produced a White Paper, 'Modernising Company Law' (Cm 5553). In some respects, the 2002 White Paper was disappointing, given that its scope was less extensive than issues raised by the CLR consultation exercise. The White Paper (2002) concentrated its attention on specific core themes, e.g. the formation and regulation of small companies, disclosure rules, shareholder meetings, codifying directors' duties and share capital. The White Paper was split into two parts; part I presented a summary of matters which were then, in part II, translated into the draft clauses of a Companies Bill.

In May 2004, the Department of Trade and Industry (DTI) published a further consultation document, 'Company Law: Flexibility and Accessibility'. The consultation document reaffirmed the government's intention to introduce legislation (a) to reform specific company laws, and (b) to simplify and restructure the content of existing laws. To this end it is likely that any reforming legislation will not take the form of a new consolidating Companies Act, that is, to replace the existing 1985 Act. Instead it is envisaged that reforming legislation will be contained in a number of smaller Acts supplemented by secondary legislation that will add to, or attempt to simplify, the existing provisions of the 1985 Act. For company lawyers and students of company law, the government's chosen method of introducing a staggered system of reforming legislation (especially of the secondary type) will do little for the clarity and certainty of the subject area.

On 17 March 2005 the government published a second White Paper, 'Company Law Reform' (Cm 6456). This second White Paper resembles but builds upon the content of the earlier White Paper (2002). Draft Bill clauses are included for a number of the areas (see Chapter 7 of the White Paper (2005)). Chapter 1 of the White Paper (2005) sets out a summary of the proposed key aims and themes of the proposed future legislation, which include the following:

- enhancing shareholder engagement and a long-term investment culture. To encourage the concept of enlightened shareholder value by making clear that directors must promote the success of the company for the benefit of its shareholders and in doing so take account of both the long-term and short-term, and wider factors such as employees, effects on the environment, suppliers and customers

- introducing a statutory statement of directors' duties to clarify their responsibilities and improve the law regulating directors' conflicts of interest

- relaxing the prohibition on provisions which prevent auditors from limiting their liability, while delivering further improvements in the quality of the audit

- enhancing the rights of proxies

- facilitating the use of e-communications

- ensuring a more transparent regulatory system of company law for smaller companies by, for example, providing better-adapted default articles (the current 'Table A') for private companies, simplifying decision-making (formalities concerned with meetings and resolutions) and the rules relating to share capital and abolishing the requirement for private companies to have a company secretary

- abolishing the requirement for a company to have an authorised share capital

- enabling a single person to form a public company

- streamlining the rules on company names and trading disclosures.

Where appropriate, commentary on the aforementioned proposals will be considered and analysed in the remaining chapters of this book, together with points of discussion and interest in relation to the reforms advanced in the White Paper (2002), the CLR exercise and Law Commission reports.

Suggested further reading

Historical development of company law from 1825

Gower *Principles of Modern Company Law* (6th edn) (Sweet & Maxwell, 1992), Chapters 2 and 3

Foxton (2002) 118 LQR 428

Santuari (1996) 17 Co Law 281

Ireland in John Adams (ed.) *Essays for Clive Schmitthoff* (1983), p 29.

The European Union

Sheikh (2003) 24 Co Law 362

O'Neill (2000) 21 Co Law 173

Company law reform

See the DTI website: **www.dti.gov.uk** (for electronic versions of the White Papers and CLR reports).

2

THE COURTS' ABILITY TO DISLODGE THE CORPORATE VEIL AT COMMON LAW OR IN EQUITY

INTRODUCTION

A company is regarded as a distinct legal entity with a separate existence from its membership and management team (see Chapter 1). The independent legal status of the corporate entity is said to cast a veil between the company and its human constituents, 'the corporate veil'. Although the following chapter will illustrate that case law examples and statutory exceptions (discussed further in Chapter 18) exist to dislodge the corporate veil, it must be stressed from the outset that a company's separate legal existence represents a fundamental and essential characteristic of company law which, save for exceptional circumstances, is unlikely to be impugned.

In the majority of situations in which the veil is dislodged under common law or equity, it is merely pierced (as opposed to being totally removed) with the purpose of imposing some form of liability against a company's shareholders and/or directors. Where the veil is not completely removed, the separate legal existence of the company will subsist. In other instances, for example, those concerned with groups of companies, the corporate veil may be completely removed, to the extent that individual corporate entities (subsidiary companies) will be treated as but a division of another corporate entity (the holding company); in such cases the holding company will be merged with its subsidiaries, and the group of companies will, for all practical purposes, be treated as one economic entity, as opposed to a collection of different corporate entities.

DISLODGING THE CORPORATE VEIL

Although the judiciary has universally accepted the principle of a company as a separate legal entity, an entity that is divorced from the interests of its membership and management, the courts, in exceptional instances, have dislodged the corporate veil. Notwithstanding the general reluctance of the courts to depart from the principles enunciated in *Salomon* v *A Salomon Ltd*, the effects of the case law exceptions have been more acute than the statutory exceptions (see Chapter 18). While the majority of the statutory provisions impose some form of penalty on a company's human constituents, they normally do so without denying the separate legal responsibilities of the company. In contrast, the case law examples generally penetrate deeper and in some instances may have the effect of lifting the corporate veil in its entirety, thereby abandoning the identification of a company as a separate legal entity.

Dislodging the corporate veil in times of national emergency

When the nation is at war or finds itself in some other serious political or economic conflict, it may be expedient for the court to dislodge the corporate veil to protect the nation's interests. This example of the judicial piercing of the corporate veil is obviously limited in terms of its potential application, being dependent upon a state of hostility between the UK and some other nation. The justification for interfering with the corporate veil is primarily concerned with invoking a substantial penalty against individuals who have a significant connection with an enemy state. For example, the corporate veil may be lifted to prevent the payment of moneys from companies registered in the UK to the 'enemy' state or citizens of that state, as seen in the case of *Daimler* v *Continental Tyre & Rubber Co* [1916] 2 AC 307. Here, the Continental Tyre Co sought to enforce a debt owed to it by Daimler. The membership of the Continental Tyre Co was comprised of German nationals. As the UK was at war with Germany, the House of Lords (reversing the decision of the Court of Appeal) refused to sanction the enforcement of the debt. In doing so, and despite the fact that Continental was registered in the UK, the House refused to recognise that Continental was an entity that was independent from its membership (see also *The Polzeath* [1916] 32 TLR 674, *Bank voor Handel en Scheepvaart NV* v *Slatford* [1953] 1 QB 248).

Dislodging the corporate veil in cases of fraudulent abuse

The ability to disturb the corporate veil may be justified where the formation and subsequent existence of a company constitutes a fraudulent abuse of the incorporation process. The fraud exception deems the incorporation of the company to be a sham, a façade. To justify this exception a company must have been incorporated for an improper and illegitimate purpose. Ordinarily, the fraud exception will operate where the underlying motive for incorporation was to enable the company's human constituent(s) to impugn a pre-existing obligation with a third party. In such cases the court may recognise the existence of the corporate entity but may nevertheless pierce the corporate veil to prevent individuals involved in the illegitimate activity from escaping a liability that otherwise would have been enforceable had the individual(s) concerned not sought to hide behind the company's separate legal status. Indeed, in *Salomon* v *A Salomon Ltd*, had the motive for the company's incorporation been of a fraudulent character, the case would have had a different outcome. The evidence in *Salomon* suggested that although Mr Salomon had overvalued the price of his pre-incorporated business, the overvaluation had not been of a fraudulent character. As Lord Macnaughten remarked:

> 'If, however, the declaration of the Court of Appeal means that Mr Salomon acted fraudulently or dishonestly, I must say I can find nothing in the evidence to support such an imputation.' (at p 52)

Clearly, Mr Salomon had done everything possible to keep A Salomon Ltd afloat, including disposing of his debentures and using his own personal funds to inject capital into the company.

From the *Salomon* decision, it is therefore important to note that the motive behind a company's incorporation may be highly relevant in determining whether the corporate veil may be dislodged to impose a liability on the members of a company. For example, in *Gilford Motor Co v Horne* [1933] Ch 935, Mr Horne (H) entered into a contract with Gilford Motor Co by which he agreed to abide by a restrictive covenant which provided that should he leave Gilford's employment he would not solicit their customers. On leaving Gilford's employment H, through nominees, formed a company through which he impliedly sought to escape the terms of the restrictive covenant. The court held that the company was a 'sham', an alias of H, and as such an injunction was granted to enforce the covenant. The restrictive covenant was enforced against both H and the company, that is, the company's corporate existence was not denied although the company's corporate veil was pierced to recognise H's personal culpability for the breach of the restrictive covenant. In effect, H had formed the company as a fraudulent device to evade the terms of the restrictive covenant in order to escape the terms of a pre-existing contractual obligation entered into with the Gilford Motor Co.

A further illustration of fraud in this context is provided by *Jones v Lipman* [1962] 1 WLR 832, in which a Mr Lipman (L) sought to escape specific performance of a contract entered into for the sale of land. L attempted to evade the contract by transferring the land in question to a company that he had recently incorporated. It was held that the incorporation of the company was but a device to evade L's contractual responsibility and as such specific performance of the sale of land was granted against both L and the company. Once again, the company's corporate existence was judicially recognised (in so far as the order was granted against the company), although the company's veil was pierced to the extent that the court recognised L's personal culpability in relation to this deceit.

In respect of a holding company–subsidiary relationship, it should be noted that in *Adams v Cape Industries* [1990] Ch 433 (discussed further below) the Court of Appeal could find no legal objection where the corporate structure of a group of companies had been used to ensure that any **future** legal liability, so attached to the group enterprise, would fall on a subsidiary of the holding company, rather than on the holding company itself. In other words, it would appear quite legitimate for a company to eliminate the risk of being held potentially liable for pursuing a future course of conduct by transferring risk-bearing activities to an existing subsidiary company over which it, the holding company, maintains control, notwithstanding that the conduct in question may carry a high risk of failure.

Although the Court of Appeal considered that the manipulation of a group structure was a legitimate means for a holding company to evade liability, it must be said that it is difficult to substantiate the acceptance of such a manipulation as anything other than a blatant abuse of the incorporation process. Accordingly, it is regrettable that it has been afforded a legitimacy which would appear to be both unwarranted and unjust, especially in a case where the transfer of risk is a blatant attempt to evade a highly foreseeable risk as opposed to, say, a risk that is no more than of a speculative nature. Indeed, following the reasoning in *Adams*, it is likely that a holding company could actually incorporate a new subsidiary company with the objective of evading a potential liability, notwithstanding that the probability attached to the occurrence of that future liability may, to the knowledge of those in control of the holding company, be very high. Following on from this reasoning, an individual could incorporate a company to evade a potential future liability where the said liability was not connected to any pre-incorporation obligation.

Therefore, while, on the basis of the fraud exception, the motive for a company's incorporation may be most relevant in determining whether the corporate veil should be dislodged, it does not always follow that an improper motive will always render the incorporation to be a sham, a façade. A more recent example of the dislodgement of the corporate veil on the premise that a company constituted a sham, a façade, is the decision of Morritt VC in *Trustor AB* v *Smallbone* [2001] 1 WLR 1177. Here, the defendant (D), the managing director of the plaintiff company, Trustor (T), transferred, in breach of his authority and duty, substantive sums of money from T's account to another company, Introcom Ltd (I Ltd). D, although not formally appointed as a director of I Ltd, was nevertheless the company's controlling mind. I Ltd held trust funds of which D was a beneficiary. The funds transferred from T to I Ltd were primarily used to make payments to D's wife and another company controlled by D. T sought the return of the moneys misappropriated by D. While I Ltd was, itself, a constructive trustee (discussed further in Chapter 17) and therefore liable for the return of the funds, D was held personally liable for their return on the premise that I Ltd was a sham, a façade, a vehicle used by D to collect the misappropriated funds. D had sought to override his obligation to repay the funds to T by attempting to hide behind the corporate veil of I Ltd. (See also, *Buckinghamshire CC* v *Briar* [2003] Env LR 25.)

Dislodging the veil to establish a controlling interest/ an economic entity

Although the following discussion of controlling interest will concentrate on the establishment of an economic entity in a holding company–subsidiary relationship, it should be noted that companies under the control of a dominant person or persons (as opposed to a dominant holding company) may be viewed as constituting an economic entity: see e.g. *Creasey* v *Breachwood Motors* [1992] BCC 639 (discussed below).

Dislodging the corporate veil to establish an economic entity removes the corporate veil of the subservient company, merging that entity with the dominant entity (holding company or individual), thereby constituting a single economic entity. An economic entity may be deemed responsible for the activities of both the dominant and subservient parties. Although there are clear examples of the courts' acceptance of an economic entity, it should be stressed that following the decision of the Court of Appeal in *Adams* v *Cape Industries*, this particular exception to the *Salomon* principle has been severely eroded in the sense that the qualifying characteristics deemed necessary to establish a dominant company's (individual's) control over the subservient entity must now amount to control warranting the finding of an agency relationship (discussed further below).

In seeking to establish an economic entity in relation to a holding company–subsidiary relationship it must be pointed out that a group relationship does not in itself imply that the group can be regarded as one economic entity. Further, it does not necessarily follow that a company, which is a wholly owned subsidiary of its holding company, will be classed as but a division of the holding company and therefore part of one economic entity.

Prior to *Adams v Cape Industries*, the method for establishing that a group of companies was in reality one economic entity was somewhat vague but a number of cases (discussed below) suggest that an economic entity could be established where the holding company exerted a substantial degree of control over the affairs of the subsidiary company, to the extent that the holding company controlled and dictated the corporate policy of its subsidiary.

Establishing the necessary degree of control prior to Adams v Cape Industries [1990] Ch 433

In *Holdsworth & Co v Caddies* [1955] 1 WLR 352, a dispute arose over a managing director's (X's) service contract that had been entered into with a holding company. X alleged that the holding company had breached the contract following its decision to exclusively restrict X's managerial duties to a subsidiary company. X contended that he could not, as a result of his employment contract with the holding company, be employed by its subsidiary because, applying the *Salomon* principle, the subsidiary was a distinct and quite separate legal entity from the holding company. The House of Lords (Lord Keith dissenting) ruled against X on the premise that, in terms of economic reality, the subsidiary was but a division of the holding company. The subsidiary was wholly owned by its holding company, the holding company appointed all of the subsidiary's directors, and, further, it was in a position whereby it was able to dictate the subsidiary's corporate policy. Accordingly, the House of Lords in lifting the corporate veil of the subsidiary company merged the legal entities of the holding company and its subsidiary to constitute one economic entity.

Similarly, in *Scottish Co-operative Wholesale Society v Meyer* [1959] AC 324 the House of Lords found that the economic reality of a group relationship was such that the corporate veil of the holding company's subsidiary should be lifted to create one economic entity. In this case the subsidiary company was not wholly owned by its holding company; however, the holding company did control the corporate policy of the subsidiary. The corporate veil of the subsidiary was lifted to enable a Dr Meyer (M), a minority shareholder in the subsidiary, to obtain relief under s 210, CA 1948 (this section of the Companies Act has since been replaced by s 459, CA 1985: see Chapter 24).

M sought an order for the holding company to purchase his shares in the subsidiary company at a fair value. To succeed with this action, M had to establish that the company of which he was a member (i.e. the subsidiary) had conducted its affairs in a manner that was oppressive to his shareholding interest. However, the oppression complained of was the holding company's positive policy of running down the subsidiary company; the subsidiary company had, in the eyes of the holding company, become surplus to requirements. The holding company controlled a majority of the voting shares in the subsidiary and appointed a majority of the subsidiary's directors. The said directors had failed, due to their inactivity, to prevent the subsidiary's decline. For M's claim to succeed the corporate veil of the subsidiary had to be lifted so that the oppressive conduct of the holding company could also be interpreted as oppressive conduct in relation to its subsidiary, that is, the holding company and subsidiary had to be merged into one single economic entity.

The House allowed M's claim, although it must be observed that Lord Morton (and to a lesser extent Lord Denning) expressed reservations in relation to the ability of the court to lift the corporate veil of the subsidiary to merge it into an economic entity. Lord Morton preferred to rest his decision on the fact that the directors of the subsidiary had 'conducted' the subsidiary's affairs. (However, note the decision in *Nicholas* v *Soundcraft Electronics Ltd* [1993] BCLC 360: here the Court of Appeal confirmed that, in appropriate circumstances, a holding company could be held responsible for conducting the affairs of its subsidiary. This case is discussed in Chapter 24.)

Another leading case example of the courts' finding of a single economic entity is the decision of the Court of Appeal in *DHN Food Distributors Ltd* v *Tower Hamlets LBC* [1976] 1 WLR 852. The case involved a group of three companies. The holding company, DHN, traded from premises owned by its subsidiary company, Bronze Ltd. The third company in the group operated a transport business for the sole benefit of DHN. The litigation in this case occurred when Tower Hamlets Borough Council ordered that the land upon which the business premises of the group were located (land registered to Bronze Ltd) be made the subject of a compulsory purchase order. In accordance with the terms of the order, compensation was payable to the owner of the land (i.e. Bronze Ltd) and for any disturbance to the landowners' business. As Bronze Ltd did not carry on an independent business, the Council claimed that this latter form of compensation was not payable. The Court of Appeal unanimously disagreed. Lord Denning opined that the three companies should, for all practical purposes, be treated as one entity and that a technical rule of company law, the separate legal identity of each company in the group, could be disregarded, where, as in this case, the ownership and control of the two subsidiary companies were completely in the hands of the holding company, the two subsidiary companies having no independent existence. Shaw LJ was of the same opinion. However, it should be noted that Goff LJ was more reluctant to justify his decision in favour of DHN on the basis of the existence of an economic entity. Instead, Goff LJ rationalised his decision in favour of the DHN group by concluding that Bronze Ltd held the property in question on trust for DHN, with the effect that DHN held an equitable interest in the property, a beneficial interest which was sufficient to entitle it to compensation for the disturbance to the group's business interests.

Establishing the necessary degree of control post Adams v Cape Industries

As a result of the case of *Adams* v *Cape Industries* [1990] Ch 433, a company's (or an individual's) ability to control the overall policy structure of another company is unlikely, of itself, to be sufficient to justify the lifting of the corporate veil. Indeed, it is now probable that the courts will be most reluctant to depart from the principles enunciated in *Salomon* v *A Salomon Ltd*, based solely on the premise that a holding company controls the corporate policy of its subsidiary. To dislodge the corporate veil of the subsidiary, the courts have demanded something more: namely, in addition to a holding company's control over the policy structure of its subsidiary, the finding of a façade is required in relation to the incorporation of the subsidiary company.

The requirement to establish a 'façade' may be traced to the case of *Woolfson* v *Strathclyde Regional Council* 1978 SLT 159. Here, the House of Lords, in upholding a decision of the Scottish courts, refused to dislodge the corporate veil even though the *Woolfson* case bore many similarities to the facts encountered in *DHN Food Distributors Ltd* v *Tower Hamlets LBC*. Indeed, the House of Lords doubted whether the Court of Appeal's decision to dislodge the corporate veil in the *DHN* case could be properly justified.

Although the respective cases of *Woolfson* and *DHN* were in many respects similar, it should be pointed out that in *Woolfson* there was never any holding company–subsidiary relationship; rather, this case was concerned with an individual's control over a group of companies. The individual in question, Mr Woolfson (W), held 99.9 per cent of the shares in Campbell Ltd (C Ltd). C Ltd carried on a retail business in a chain of shops, three of which were owned by W and the other two by Solfred Ltd (S Ltd), a company in which W held two-thirds of the shares; his wife held the remaining shares in S Ltd and the remaining 0.1 per cent of shares in C Ltd.

The dispute in this case arose when the local council acquired the shop premises in accordance with a compulsory purchase order, the terms of which provided that compensation was payable for disturbance to an occupier or to an owner-occupier but not to an owner who was not an occupier. C Ltd occupied the premises and W Ltd and S Ltd sought further compensation for disturbance on the grounds that with C Ltd they formed one single economic entity (i.e. they sought compensation as owner-occupiers). However, although the three businesses were associated under the dominant influence of W, unlike the *DHN* case, the three businesses were not completely controlled by one entity; indeed the House of Lords distinguished the *DHN* case on that basis. In reaching its decision to refuse to merge the three business enterprises into one economic entity, the House of Lords concluded that the corporate veil should not be dislodged in relation to a group enterprise, save in cases where the relationship between a group of enterprises was a façade. However, the House of Lords did not elaborate upon the meaning to be attributed to the term 'façade'.

In *Adams* v *Cape Industries* [1990] Ch 433, the Court of Appeal, in following the House of Lords in *Woolfson*, and its own decision in *Bank of Tokyo Ltd* v *Karoon* [1987] AC 45, confirmed that a strong economic link between a group of companies could not in itself justify the merging of a group of companies into one economic entity. The facts of the Adams case were as follows. The holding company, Cape Industries plc (Cape), was involved in the asbestos industry. Cape was an English company with a mining subsidiary in South Africa and a wholly owned marketing subsidiary (NAAC) in the USA. As a result of working with asbestos, employees of NAAC suffered serious illnesses and sought damages (the Tyler 1 action) against NAAC. NAAC was obliged to pay $5.2 million in compensation. Although NAAC was obliged to pay this compensation, in effect the cost of the action fell on the Cape group. To prevent the incursion of any further liability against the Cape group in the USA, NAAC was put into liquidation.

The American marketing base of the Cape group was nevertheless continued by another company, CPC, which, whilst not a subsidiary of Cape, was nevertheless set up with substantial financial support from the Cape group. CPC operated from the premises previously occupied by NAAC. CPC's managing director, who was also its majority shareholder, had previously been the managing director of NAAC. A Liechtenstein-registered company, AMC, controlled by the Cape group, acted as Cape's agents in the American market; in effect AMC were middle-men in the relationship between Cape and CPC.

Shortly after NAAC's liquidation, a second series of actions were successfully commenced in the American courts by former employees of NAAC (Tyler 2 action). The Court of Appeal was called upon to determine whether the judgments in favour of the American employees were enforceable in the UK against Cape. Cape argued that any liability attributable to NAAC had been extinguished following NAAC's liquidation and that Cape itself could not be made party to proceedings in the USA because it no longer had any presence in the USA. Further, Cape contended that, notwithstanding its own removal from the USA, any responsibility attached to NAAC or CPC should rest with those companies as distinct and separate legal entities. The plaintiffs contended that NAAC and CPC were part of one economic entity, namely the Cape group, and that Cape was therefore still present in the USA, through CPC.

In finding in favour of Cape, the Court of Appeal denied the validity of the distinct entities being part of one economic entity. This denial was understandable in respect of the relationship between Cape and CPC, in so far as CPC was not even a Cape subsidiary. However, the court's finding that NAAC had not been a part of one economic entity, with Cape at its head, was a much more debatable proposition. The court conceded that Cape controlled the general corporate policy of NAAC; the holding company determined the subsidiary's expenditure and financial policy. Nevertheless, the court opined that the subsidiary was an independent entity in so far as NAAC was not totally dependent on Cape. NAAC managed the day-to-day running of its own business: for example, it was allowed to enter into business contracts and employ its own staff. In denying the existence of an economic entity, the Court of Appeal took the view that control, in the sense of justifying a conclusion for the recognition of an economic entity, meant absolute control in a manner whereby the subsidiary was an alias of the holding company, a mere façade.

The Court of Appeal gave two examples of what it considered to justify a finding of a façade. The first example was the relationship between Cape and AMC, which was one of agency, AMC having been exclusively created for the purpose of carrying out its master's instructions. Yet, the finding of a façade in this particular relationship did not assist the plaintiffs because AMC had not been involved in the running of the asbestos factory, nor had it been present in the USA. The second example was the case of *Jones v Lipman* [1962] 1 All ER 442 (discussed above). Therefore, the court's guidance as to the definition of a façade would, in relation to a group of companies, indicate that an entity will be properly described as a façade where it was created on the pretext of a lack of any corporate independence of its own, it was created as an agent, a mere alias for its master or, alternatively, where it was a device created to exploit the corporate form to satisfy an improper or illegitimate/fraudulent purpose.

The Court of Appeal, in reaching its decision in *Adams*, undertook an extensive review of the authorities related to circumstances in which the corporate veil had previously been dislodged in a group relationship. In doing so, the court distinguished cases such as *Holdsworth* v *Caddies, Scottish Wholesale Co-op Society* v *Meyer* and *DHN Food Distributors Ltd* v *London Borough of Tower Hamlets*. According to the Court of Appeal the said cases allowed a group of companies to be merged into one economic entity on the premise that the wording of a particular statute or contractual provision had, in such cases, been of a type which necessarily justified the treatment of a parent and subsidiary company as but one unit.

However, the Court of Appeal's explanation is suspect. It is contended that the cases cited by the Court of Appeal indicate that justifications (namely the control of corporate policy) independent from the wording of a particular statutory or contractual provision had first to be established before the corporate veil was dislodged. Once the corporate veil had been pierced, then, and only then, could the particular statutory or contractual provision be applied. Accordingly, it may be said in respect of such cases that the removal of the corporate veil allowed a particular statutory or contractual provision to be applied. Contrary to the Court of Appeal's interpretation, the specific wording of a statutory or contractual provision did not, in itself, justify the courts in piercing the corporate veil to establish an economic entity. Further, if one considers the group relationship in, for example, *DHN Food Distributors Ltd* v *London Borough of Tower Hamlets*, would this case not fall within the *Adams* concept of an agency relationship?

Finally, it is to be noted that the draft Ninth EC Directive was concerned with the conduct of groups of companies and in part sought to impose an element of responsibility on holding companies in respect of the actions of their subsidiaries. The proposal for the draft Ninth Directive was introduced in 1984 but was never formally adopted and it would now appear lost. Given the rigidity of the common law position, the said loss may be considered unfortunate.

Agency

In accordance with the decision of the Court of Appeal in *Adams* v *Cape Industries* the ability to establish an agency relationship between a holding company and its subsidiary will facilitate a finding that the holding company (the principal) is responsible for the actions of its subsidiary (the agent). An agency relationship equates to a façade in respect of establishing an economic entity. Yet, although an agency relationship may establish the existence of an economic entity, it must be observed that in terms of pure theory an agency relationship creates no disturbance to the subsidiary's corporate veil because to establish an agency relationship one must have a principal and an agent, that is, two distinct legal entities. Therefore, as a legal concept, agency is not a device which dislodges the corporate veil, albeit, notwithstanding the theory, the finding of an agency relationship between two distinct entities will result in the same effect as if the corporate veil had been lifted, namely the principal will be liable for the actions of its agent.

In the context of an agency relationship between corporate entities, agency may be tentatively defined as a relationship which is based upon the express or implied consent of both the subsidiary company and its holding company, whereby the subsidiary company is made subject to the holding company's control and will and to the extent that the subsidiary conducts its business affairs for the ultimate benefit of the holding company. (See, for example, the judgment of Lord Pearson in *Garnac Grain Co Inc* v *HMF Faure and Fairclough Ltd* [1968] AC 1130 at p 1137.)

To establish an agency relationship in a group relationship it is therefore crucial to prove that one dominant company exerts absolute control over the affairs and actions of another company. For example, in *Adams* v *Cape Industries*, Cape's relationship with NAAC was not considered to be an agency because Cape did not completely control its subsidiary. NAAC employed its own staff, rented its own warehouses, occasionally purchased asbestos on its own behalf, earned its own profits and paid USA tax. The control argument also defeated the claim that CPC should be regarded as Cape's agent.

In *Smith Stone & Knight Ltd* v *Birmingham Corp* [1939] 4 All ER 116 (the issues in this case were almost identical to *DHN Food Distributors Ltd* v *London Borough of Tower Hamlets*, discussed above), an agency relationship was established in a group relationship on the premise that the subsidiary company was a mere tool working for the ultimate benefit of its holding company. By contrast, in *Kodak* v *Clarke* [1902] 2 KB 450 the court denied the existence of an agency relationship between an English holding company and its overseas subsidiary because the English company, which held 98 per cent of the subsidiary's shares, never attempted to interfere with the management of the subsidiary.

In determining an agency relationship, it must be stressed that it does not necessarily follow that a wholly owned subsidiary will be regarded as the holding company's agent: see e.g. *Gramophone & Typewriter Ltd* v *Stanley* [1908] 2 KB 89. Conversely, it does not follow that an agency relationship will not be present in a situation where the subsidiary is not wholly owned. For example, in *Re FG (Films) Ltd* [1953] 1 All ER 615 the court was called upon to determine whether a film made by an English registered company was a British film as defined by the Cinematograph Films Act 1938, s 25(1). The English company (FG Films) that claimed to have made the film had a share capital of 100, £1 shares, 90 of which were held on behalf of an American company that financed the film in question. Vaisey J held that the participation of the English company in making the film was so small as to be negligible; it had acted as a nominee of and agent for the American company. The film was therefore deemed not a British film, but one that had been made exclusively under the control of the American company.

It is to be observed that the discussion of agency has thus far concentrated its attention on the group relationship without any mention of whether an individual shareholder/director of a company may be considered to be in a position to control the activities of the company to the extent that the company is in effect the agent of the shareholder/director. The feasibility of any suggestion of an agency relationship between an individual and the company that he/she controls was clearly rejected in *Salomon* v *A Salomon Ltd* (discussed above). Nevertheless, in *IRC* v *Sanson* [1921] 2 KB 492, Lord Sterndale (at p 503) observed that in an appropriate case it may be possible to establish an agency relationship between a majority shareholder and a 'one-man type company' under his/her absolute control. The validity of such a contention is clearly based on the premise that if a company is dominated and controlled by an individual in a manner which would be described as an agency relationship had the individual been a holding company then why should the individual–company relationship not be described as one of agency? The answer to this question is, in theory, far from obvious. Nevertheless, any affirmation of the existence of an agency relationship between an individual and a company under his/her control, must be seriously doubted, other than perhaps in a situation where the individual controlled more than one company – in effect, where the individual acted as the human equivalent of a holding company. (Consider this suggestion in relation to the cases of *Woolfson* v *Strathclyde Regional Council* (discussed above) and *Creasey* v *Breachwood Motors Ltd* [1992] BCC 639 (discussed below). However, note *Yukong Lines Ltd of Korea* v *Rendsburg Investments* [1998] BCC 870, discussed below.)

Notwithstanding that a company may be dominated and controlled by an individual shareholder in a manner akin to a holding company's dominance over its subsidiary, to permit a finding of agency as between a single company and its controlling shareholder would be to challenge the very heart of corporate law. Many small companies are one-man type concerns, the alter ego of the controlling shareholder, controlled and dominated in a manner akin to an agency. This type of company is incorporated because of the perceived business incentives provided by the separation of identity and responsibility between the individual and corporate entity. While such incentives are beneficial to the individual (although the benefits are often exaggerated), the incorporation of a company may, in the expectation of future growth and expansion, be of future benefit to the economy and general public interest. To deprive an individual of such incentives would be to eliminate any benefit attached to the current incorporation process. Obviously, one must guard against the improper exploitation of the incorporation process and to this end the corporate veil of a small private company may be dislodged in circumstances where its incorporation was of a fraudulent or other improper nature.

Removing the corporate veil for justice's sake?

The ability of a court to lift the corporate veil has thus far been considered in the light of circumstances (the accepted headings) which may be indicative of the existence of a state of national emergency: a fraud, or an agency relationship. The aforementioned circumstances may be viewed as giving rise to specific exceptions to the judicial acceptance of a company's separate legal identity; alternatively they may be seen as masking the fundamental justification for denying the preservation of the corporate veil, namely to prevent injustice, a perversion of the corporate form.

In order to substantiate a claim that principles of justice determine the judicial disturbance of the corporate veil, it is necessary to decide whether the case examples relating to dislodging the corporate veil, hitherto examined, may be explained in terms of the application of equitable principles. Do the circumstances which invoke the disturbance of the corporate veil point to one primary justification for the disobedience of the principles enunciated in *Salomon* v *A Salomon Ltd*, a justification based upon the interests of justice, or are the specific accepted instances of dislodging the corporate veil based upon rigid and self-contained rules?

In attempting to answer the above question it is important to note that, prior to the Court of Appeal's judgment in *Adams v Cape Industries*, the courts had shown a general reluctance to define a specific set of accepted instances in relation to when the corporate veil could be dislodged. Indeed, Lord Denning advocated that a court's power to lift the corporate veil should be viewed as a discretionary power as opposed to a tool which could only be employed in set defined circumstances: see e.g. Lord Denning's judgments in *Littlewoods Mail Order Stores Ltd v IRC* [1969] 1 WLR 1241 and *Wallensteiner v Moir* [1974] 1 WLR 991. In the *Littlewoods* case, Lord Denning stated:

> 'The doctrine laid down in *Salomon*'s case has to be watched very carefully. It has often been supposed to cast a veil over the personality of a limited company through which the courts cannot see. But that is not true. The courts can and often do draw aside the veil. They can and often do pull off the mask and look to see what really lies behind.' (at p 1254)

If the courts do possess a general discretion to draw aside the corporate veil, then such discretion gives validity to the view that the individual merits – the justice of a case – may ultimately justify a court in disturbing the corporate veil. Indeed, in *Re a Company* [1985] 1 BCC 99, 421 Cumming-Bruce LJ was adamant that:

> '. . . the cases before and after *Wallensteiner v Moir* [1974] 1 WLR 991 show that the court will use its powers to pierce the corporate veil if it is necessary to achieve justice irrespective of the legal efficacy of the corporate structure under consideration.' (at pp 99, 425)

However, in *Adams v Cape Industries* the Court of Appeal forcefully denied that the corporate veil could be disturbed by considering issues relevant to the justice of a case. For example, Slade LJ opined that:

> 'If a company chooses to arrange the affairs of its group in such a way that the business carried on in a particular foreign country is the business of its subsidiary and not its own, it is, in our judgment, entitled to do so. *Neither in this class of case nor in any other class of case is it open to this court to disregard the principle of Salomon v Salomon & Co Ltd* [1897] AC 22, *merely because it considers it just to do so.*' (at p 513) (emphasis added)

Notwithstanding that in *Adams v Cape Industries*, the Court of Appeal unequivocally denied that issues of justice could form the basis of a decision to dislodge the corporate veil, the first instance judgment of Richard Southwell QC, sitting as a deputy High Court judge in *Creasey v Breachwood Motors Ltd* [1992] BCC 639, attempted to reassert the belief that the underlying justification for lifting the corporate veil could, if necessary, be couched in terms of equitable considerations.

The facts of the *Creasey* case were as follows. The plaintiff, a Mr Creasey (C), was dismissed from a company, Welwyn Motors Ltd (W), where he had worked as the company's general manager. W carried on its business at premises owned by Breachwood Motors Ltd (B). The two directors of B were its only shareholders; the same two individuals were also the only directors and shareholders of W. Therefore, although there was no holding company–subsidiary relationship between W and B, the two companies were related, in so far as the control of both was in the hands of the same persons (by analogy see *Woolfson v Strathclyde Regional Council*, discussed above).

As a result of his employment being discontinued, C commenced an action against W for wrongful dismissal. However, before proceedings could be brought against W, the company ceased trading (after about one year's business activity). B took over all of W's assets and paid off W's trade creditors, with the exception of C's claim for compensation. B carried on the business (sale of Saab motor cars) as previously undertaken by W, and traded under the name of Welwyn Saab, from W's former premises. C's solicitors continued to communicate with solicitors acting on behalf of W, who were in effect acting on B's instructions. B's solicitors claimed that the existence of W as a separate legal entity could, as a result of its informal takeover by B Ltd, no longer be substantiated and as such they considered it pointless to offer any particulars of defence to C's claim for unfair dismissal. Nevertheless, at the initial hearing for the unfair dismissal claim, an order was made in favour of C. Shortly after the hearing, W was struck off the Companies Register pursuant to s 652 of the Companies Act 1985 (i.e. for not carrying on any business). As the effect of the order was to end the legal existence of W, C's solicitors successfully applied to have W substituted by B as the defendant to the order made in favour of C. B appealed to the High Court; the grounds for the appeal included the contention that, as both W and B were separate legal entities, it therefore followed that B, in accordance with its distinct legal identity, could not be made responsible for the compensation payable to C.

B failed in its appeal. The court, in removing the corporate veil of W, considered W to be but part of B. Therefore, B was *prima facie* deemed responsible for the payment of the compensation order in favour of C. However, in a quest for justice between the parties the court decided that B should be given the opportunity to defend the action for wrongful dismissal. In reaching his decision to remove the corporate veil of W so as to merge that company with B, thereby creating a single economic entity, Richard Southwell QC first considered whether W could properly be regarded as a façade so as to meet the requirement expounded in *Adams* v *Cape Industries*. However, the evidence of the case was not conclusive of the finding of a façade, as there had been no fraud in relation to the incorporation of the company (although note, was it not possible to substantiate a finding of agency?). In *Creasey*, the corporate veil was lifted for justice's sake. Richard Southwell QC, opined that:

> 'The power of the court to lift the corporate veil exists. The problem for a judge of first instance is to decide whether the particular case before the court is one in which that power should be exercised recognising that this is a very strong power which can be exercised to achieve justice where its exercise is necessary for that purpose, but which, misused would be likely to cause not inconsiderable injustice.' (at pp 646–7)

The decision of Richard Southwell QC was subsequently followed in *The Tjaskemolen* [1997] CLC 521. Here Clarke J, in referring to *Creasey*, stated as follows:

> 'That case is thus an example of piercing the veil where assets are deliberately transferred from A to B in the knowledge that to do so will defeat a creditor's claim or potential claim, even if that has not proved to be the purpose of doing so. The judge in that case would have regarded the case as even stronger if the purpose of the transaction was to defeat the creditor's claim. I agree with the reasoning in *Creasey*.' (at p 529G)

Nevertheless, despite the equitable and commonsense conclusion reached in *Creasey*, subsequent decisions of the English courts have, in reaffirming the lengthy and powerful comments of the Court of Appeal in *Adams* v *Cape Industries*, sought to deny that individual issues of justice may, in appropriate cases, facilitate the removal of the corporate veil. For example, in *Re Polly Peck International plc (No 3)* [1996] 1 BCLC 428, Robert Walker J opined that lower courts should not seek to expound the concept of justice as a means by which the corporate veil could be disturbed. In *Ord* v *Belhaven Pubs Ltd* [1998] 2 BCLC 447, the Court of Appeal condemned the reasoning applied in *Creasey* in no uncertain terms, stating that the case should no longer be treated as authoritative.

The issues involved in *Ord* v *Belhaven Pubs Ltd* were very similar to those that had arisen in *Creasey*. In *Ord*, the plaintiffs took a 20-year lease of a public house from the defendant (B) based on B's representation of the pub's turnover and profitability. B was a subsidiary within a group of companies controlled by Ascot Holdings plc (A). The plaintiffs alleged serious misrepresentations and breach of warranty and claimed damages in tort and contract. The action progressed slowly. Prior to the trial of the proceedings the group of companies restructured with the result that B no longer retained any substantial assets. Given that B was left with no assets, the plaintiffs applied for leave to substitute A for B.

At first instance, the deputy High Court judge (Judge Alton) allowed the application for substitution. Judge Alton based her decision on the economic unity of the group and the control that A exerted over the group. The learned judge concluded that it was unjust to permit B to take advantage of the reconstruction to avoid a contingent liability. The Court of Appeal in reversing the first instance decision applied the principles of law enunciated in *Adams* v *Cape Industries* and concluded that the defendant company could not be construed as a mere façade in so far as the transfer of B's assets was undertaken without any intention to harm the plaintiffs. The court held that the motive for the reconstruction had been based upon an understandable business decision undertaken as a consequence of a decline in the property market. The court found that the decision of Judge Alton, in removing the corporate veil, had been one based upon a misconception that the veil could, in just and equitable circumstances, be removed in a situation where there was a strong economic unity between a group of companies. Hobhouse LJ, in giving the judgment of the Court of Appeal, stated:

> 'The approach of the judge in the present case was simply to look to the economic unit, to disregard the distinction between the legal entities that were involved and then to say: since the company cannot pay, the shareholders [the holding company (A)] who are the people financially interested should be made to pay instead. That of course is radically at odds with the whole concept of corporate personality and limited liability and the decision of the House of Lords in *Salomon* v *A. Salomon & Co Ltd*.' (at p 457)

In rejecting the decision in *Creasey*, the Court of Appeal has sought to remove the judiciary's discretion to remove the corporate veil in circumstances where the economic realities of a given situation are, when coupled with issues of justice, indicative of a finding that the corporate veil should be removed for the purpose of protecting the interests of an innocent third party. In *Creasey*, it is submitted that the removal of the corporate veil was a just and reasonable exercise of the court's discretion and as such it is submitted that the case should have been distinguished by the Court of Appeal rather than overruled. Although the factual circumstances of *Creasey* were similar to *Ord* v *Belhaven Pubs Ltd*, there was, nevertheless, a significant difference between the two cases. In *Ord* there were strong economic reasons to explain why the assets were transferred away from B; indeed, the Ascot group may have been prejudiced if that transfer had not been undertaken. However, in *Creasey*, the justification for the transfer of assets appeared far less significant, because a failure to transfer the assets would have been unlikely to cause prejudice to the shareholders of Breachwood Motors Ltd; that is, the motive for the transfer of funds in *Ord* may have been justifiable and indeed, understandable, whereas the motive for the transfer of the assets in *Creasey* appeared far more suspect.

Yet, in accordance with the decision of Toulson J in *Yukong Lines Ltd of Korea* v *Rendsburg Investments* [1998] BCC 870, it would appear that where, in a group relationship, a transfer of funds takes place from one company to another for the purpose of avoiding the incursion of a contingent liability by the transferor, then any improper motive in relation to the transfer of such funds should be ignored in respect of considering whether, at common law, the corporate veil of the transferor may be dislodged. Briefly, the facts of this case concerned the repudiation of a charterparty agreement. The defendant company (D) had transferred the vast majority of its funds to L, funds which may have been used to meet any liability resulting from a breach of a charterparty agreement entered into with the plaintiff (P). The funds had been transferred from D to L on the actual day of the charterparty's repudiation. The issue in the case was whether the agreement had been entered into with the plaintiff on behalf of D by its brokers (M), or whether Y, an individual who held a majority shareholding in both D and M, should (together with L, a company controlled by Y) be held liable for the repudiation of the agreement as undisclosed principals (i.e. was D merely an agent of Y and L). As an alternative to contending that Y and L should be held liable as undisclosed principals (the agency argument), the plaintiff contended that the corporate veil of D could be dislodged on the basis of the fraud exception, or in accordance with the decision of Richard Southwell QC in *Creasey* v *Breachwood Motors Ltd*.

In respect of the fraud argument, this was defeated on the premise that the charterparty was not entered into with a view to defeating any pre-existing obligation (unlike, for example, *Gilford Motor Co* v *Horne*, discussed above). In relation to the agency argument, the learned judge, in purportedly following *Adams* v *Cape Industries* and in distinguishing *Smith Stone & Knight Ltd* v *Birmingham Corporation*, concluded that an agency agreement could only be established where the relevant parties consented to the agreement. In this case, Toulson J found no such consent, because Y had signed the charterparty agreement in his capacity as the managing director of M on behalf of D. In effect, Y had signed the agreement as an agent of M and not as its principal or indeed as the principal of D. There was no express consent in respect of an alleged agency agreement. However, what of implied consent based upon Y's control of D? Indeed, it is interesting that the learned judge appeared to rule out the significance of implied consent, despite the fact that in *Adams* v *Cape Industries*, the absolute control of one company by another (implied consent via the concept of control) was cited as an example of a façade/agency relationship, that is, Cape's control of AMC (however, in *Yukong Lines Ltd* control was vested in an individual, i.e. Y). In relation to the justice issue, the case of *Creasey* v *Breachwood Motors Ltd* was distinguished, albeit that the grounds given by Toulson J for doing so were somewhat vague, relating primarily to the fact that, in *Creasey*, unlike the present case, there had been a total transfer of the undertaking.

Summary

Following the Court of Appeal's decision in *Adams* v *Cape Industries*, the courts' ability to dislodge the corporate veil is now limited to cases involving an 'enemy corporation' or where the incorporation of a company is classed as a façade. A façade is identified in a situation where a company's incorporation was for a fraudulent or illegitimate purpose: for example, where a company was formed to defeat a pre-existing statutory/contractual obligation. A façade will also exist where, in a group situation, the holding company controls a subsidiary company to the extent that the control amounts to an agency relationship. Any exception based upon the justice of a particular case, would now appear to be very much in the shadows. While the disadvantage of the justice approach is its dependence on the judicially perceived merits of an individual case, a dependence which may lead to uncertainty in the development of the law, the rigidity of the rules expounded in *Adams* v *Cape Industries* may, in future, lead to an unreasonable and unjust conclusion in situations where the corporate form is used as a shield to protect a holding company (or individual) in a situation where that protection is unwarranted and where the protection of the corporate form prejudices the rights of an innocent party.

LIABILITY IN TORT

Where a director of a limited liability company causes the company to be involved in a tortious act, the normal presumption of liability will be against the principal (the company). The said rule is in accordance with ordinary agency principles as between the director and company. Liability will not be expected to fall on the agent (the individual officer): see e.g. *Rainham Chemical Works Ltd* v *Belvedere Fish Guano Ltd* [1921] 2 AC 465. Nevertheless, in exceptional circumstances a director may be deemed to be personally responsible for the commission of the tortious act. The director's liability may be as a joint tortfeasor or it may be a distinct liability. The ability to impose personal liability against a director will be dependent upon establishing that he/she exhibited a personal as opposed to a corporate competence for directing or procuring the wrongful act.

In instances where the tort in question is of a fraudulent character, thereby involving a dishonest intention on the part of a director, the director, being personally responsible for the commission of the tort, will not be permitted to escape the consequences of his own fraudulent conduct notwithstanding that such conduct is, for the purposes of liability, also attributable to the company for which he acts. The said position was affirmed by the House of Lords in *Standard Chartered Bank* v *Pakistan National Shipping Corporation* (No 2) [2002] 3 WLR 1547 (see also *MCA Records*

Inc v *Charly Records* [2003] 1 BCLC 93 and *Koninklijke Phillips* v *Princo Digital Disc* [2004] 2 BCLC 50). In *Standard Chartered Bank*, the House of Lords emphasised that, in cases involving the tort of deceit, a director could not escape personal liability on the ground that he acted in the course of his employment. As Lord Hoffmann remarked:

> 'No one can escape liability for fraud by saying "I wish to make it clear that I am committing this fraud on behalf of someone else and I am not to be personally liable".' (at p 1154)

In cases involving negligent as opposed to fraudulent conduct, the ability to establish a director's personal liability in tort will be dependent upon complying with the principles of law set out by the House of Lords in *Hedley Byrne* v *Heller & Partners Ltd* [1964] AC 465. As such it will be necessary to establish a special relationship between the plaintiff and tortfeasor (director). Having established that relationship, it will be necessary to ascertain whether the director assumed a personal responsibility for the negligent acts and whether the plaintiff relied upon that assumption of responsibility. For example, in *Fairline Shipping Corp* v *Adamson* [1975] 2 QB 180, although the plaintiff entered into a contract with a company, a director of that company was held to be personally liable for the performance of a negligent act in so far as the director conducted the negotiations with the plaintiff on a personal as opposed to a corporate footing: for example, by personally writing to the plaintiff, as opposed to writing *qua* director on company note paper. The court held that the director had created a clear impression that he was to be personally responsible for carrying out the performance of the contract with the plaintiff.

By contrast, in *Trevor Ivory Ltd* v *Anderson* [1992] 2 NZLR 517, although the director of a company negligently advised the plaintiffs in relation to the manner by which a product, supplied by the company, should be used, the director was held not to be personally liable for the negligent advice, in so far as in his dealings with the plaintiff, the director had always acted *qua* director: that is, he had never sought to deal with the plaintiff other than as an agent of the company.

The evidence to substantiate a claim that a company director should be made personally responsible for the company's commission of the negligent act must be little short of overwhelming, a fact illustrated by the decision of the House of Lords in *Williams* v *Natural Life Health Ltd* [1998] 1 BCLC 689. In *Williams*, the plaintiffs entered into a franchise scheme operated by Natural Life Health Ltd (N Ltd). The plaintiffs were, in part, induced into entering into the scheme by the company's marketing brochure that contained misleading statements falsely alluding to the company's expertise in, for example, product knowledge, finance, management techniques and marketing. However, and of more relevance to the claim, the plaintiffs relied upon projected figures which had been drawn up by the company and which had misleadingly projected a profit of £30 000 for the first 18 months of trading. In reality, the plaintiffs made a loss of £38 600 for that period. Following the commencement of proceedings N Ltd, originally the sole defendant to the action, was put into liquidation. Thereafter, the plaintiffs' claim was pursued against M, the company's managing director and its majority shareholder. M's role in the franchise agreement, albeit of an indirect nature, had been a considerable one. Indeed, the company's own purported expertise in franchising was exclusively based upon M's own personal experience of the franchise business. The plaintiffs had relied upon the projected figures for their franchise as a result of M's personal proficiency in the franchise business. M was clearly the principal driving force behind the company.

Following the first instance judgment of Langley J [1996] 1 BCLC 288, the Court of Appeal concluded that a director could only incur personal liability in special and exceptional circumstances. However, the circumstances of this case were such that M was held personally liable. Hirst LJ, in delivering the leading judgment of the Court of Appeal, analysed the legal principles derived from the decisions of the House of Lords in *Hedley Byrne* v *Heller & Partners Ltd* [1964] AC 465 and *Henderson* v *Merrett Syndicates Ltd* [1995] 2 AC 145. In harmony with the views expressed by Langley J, Hirst LJ asserted that the ability to establish an assumption of responsibility was devoid of any necessity to ascertain any form of personal dealings between the parties. Accordingly, Hirst LJ observed that personal liability could be imposed against a director for a negligent act where it was evident that he/she was an instrumental figure in the ordinance of the wrongful act, albeit that his/her involvement and relationship with the plaintiff was of an implied as opposed to an express nature. M's role in the franchise agreement had been a considerable one and as such it was held that there had been, on M's part, an implied assumption of personal responsibility, a responsibility that extended beyond his capacity as a director of the company.

On appeal to the House of Lords, the decision of the Court of Appeal was reversed, notwithstanding that the House accepted that it was patently evident that the respondents relied upon negligent advice. The House found that the responsibility for the negligent act resided in the company and not in M and resolved that the Court of Appeal had misapplied the principles enunciated in *Hedley Byrne & Co* v *Heller & Partners Ltd* and *Henderson* v *Merrett Syndicates Ltd*. Lord Steyn, in giving the judgment of the House, stressed that the internal arrangements between a director and his company could never be the foundation of a director's personal liability in tort. Lord Steyn considered that the evidence of the case before him was akin to that represented in *Trevor Ivory Ltd* v *Anderson*. Although the company had relied almost exclusively on M's personal expertise, such expertise was never marketed or advanced otherwise than under the company's corporate umbrella. While M viewed and impliedly approved the financial projections for P's franchise business, M never sought to play an active role in their preparation, nor had he ever expressly held himself out as having done so. Further, in dealings with the company, the respondents had not identified M, other than as a part of the company. Lord Steyn remarked (at p 435) that Hirst LJ had been wrong to surmise that:

'the relevant knowledge and experience was entirely his *qua* Mr Mistin (M), and not his *qua* director.' ([1997] BCLC 131 at p 153)

Lord Steyn concluded that in so far as M had held himself out at all times as the managing director of a limited company, it followed that on his part there had never been an assumption of personal responsibility.

In accordance with the common law's strict desire to uphold the independent legal status of a corporate entity, the decision of the House of Lords in *Williams* v *Natural Life Health Ltd* is, to say the least, of a conforming nature. The decision confirms that a company director's personal liability in tort may never be presumed on the premise that the director held a dominant position in, or was an integral part of, the company's directing mind. Further, the decision of the House of Lords expounds the principle that, notwithstanding that a director may be portrayed by his company as the instrumental figure in respect of any given business venture, the director will not be presumed to have assumed any personal responsibility for that venture other than where he himself expressly or impliedly affirms an assumption of personal responsibility.

Notwithstanding the House of Lords' decision in *Williams* v *Natural Life Health Ltd*, it has been suggested (*obiter*) in a subsequent Court of Appeal judgment, namely *Lubbe* v *Cape plc* (unreported, 30 July 1998), that it may be possible to impose tortious liability in a case where a negligent act was committed by a subsidiary company acting under the directions of its holding company. Indeed, in a group relationship there would appear to be no logical reason, where the subsidiary undertakes the performance of a negligent act at the direct bequest of its holding company and the conditions laid down in *Hedley Byrne & Co* v *Heller & Partners Ltd* and *Henderson* v *Merrett Syndicates Ltd* are met, why the holding company should not be deemed responsible for the commission of the tortious act in its capacity as a shadow director of the subsidiary company (the characteristics of a shadow director are discussed further in Chapter 16).

The primary issue in the *Lubbe* case involved a dispute over the jurisdiction in which a claim in negligence should be made, namely South Africa or England. (It is to be noted that the House of Lords subsequently adjudicated that the case could be tried in the UK: see *Lubbe and Others* v *Cape Plc* [2000] 1 WLR 1545.) The action was commenced by a number of ex-employees of a South African company engaged in the asbestos industry. The said company was a subsidiary of Cape plc (C). The plaintiffs sought to advance their claim in the English courts on the ground that C (an English registered company) was responsible for the negligent acts, notwithstanding that the tortious acts had been perpetrated in South Africa. The plaintiffs alleged that C should be deemed responsible (or its individual directors) in so far as it exercised *de facto* control over its subsidiary, decisions relating to the policy and management of the subsidiary having been taken in England and not in South Africa.

The Court of Appeal concluded that the plaintiffs had established that there was a case to answer in the English courts and that C itself (or the individual directors) could, if the allegations were substantiated, be liable to the plaintiffs. Establishing liability would be dependent on the plaintiffs' ability to prove that C controlled the operation of the South African subsidiary. Interestingly, the Court of Appeal defined control in much broader terms than in *Adams* v *Cape Industries*, by providing that control equated to a need to prove that the directing mind of C (its directors and senior personnel) were responsible for the decisions which led to the business in South Africa being carried on in a negligent manner, that is, in terms of its corporate policy and instructions to the local workforce. Here, control did not have to be substantiated on the basis that Cape controlled the day-to-day implementation of those policies and instructions. If, in future cases, such obiter comments were to be followed, the result would be quite startling: tortious liability could be established in circumstances where a holding company directed and controlled the corporate policy of its subsidiary without the need to establish that the group relationship was, as defined in *Adams* v *Cape Industries*, one of a façade. However, it is suggested that, while such a transformation in the law would be both logical and equitable, the resulting radical departure from the principles set forth in *Adams* v *Cape Industries*, will render the likelihood of such a transformation to be most improbable.

DISLODGING THE CORPORATE VEIL BY STATUTE

The Companies Act 1985 permits a company to be incorporated with a separate legal identity and limited liability. However, specific statutory provisions may, in instances where the statutory provision is clear and unambiguous in its intention to disturb the corporate veil, interfere with the privileges normally associated with incorporation (see the general comments of Lord Diplock in *Dimbleby & Sons Ltd* v *NUJ* [1984] 1 All ER 751 at 758).

Disturbing the veil to impose liability by statute

Where a statutory provision purports to allow a disturbance of the corporate veil, its effect will normally be to pierce the corporate veil for the purpose of imposing a liability on a human constituent of the company; the veil will not be completely removed. It is to be observed that legislation specifically concerned with the taxation of companies is usually interpreted in a manner so as to prevent the use of the corporate form as an instrument for tax avoidance: see e.g. *Firestone Tyre & Rubber Co* v *Lewellin* [1957] 1 WLR 464.

The overwhelming majority of statutory provisions that have a capacity to dislodge the corporate veil are employed for the purpose of curbing and penalising the delinquent conduct of company directors involved in the management of insolvent companies. Liability may be imposed against a director, for example, to contribute towards the debts of a company. Here the corporate veil will be dislodged in the sense that as a separate legal entity a company would normally have an absolute responsibility to discharge its own debts and liabilities. The statutory provisions that target the delinquent activities of company directors are specifically dealt with in Chapter 18.

Although the statutory examples of dislodging the corporate veil are predominantly concerned with matters relating to the delinquent activities of company directors, nevertheless, there is one example of a statutory provision which purports to dislodge the corporate veil for the purpose of imposing a liability on a company shareholder, namely s 24 of the Companies Act 1985. This provision provides that if a company, other than a private company limited by shares or guarantee (private companies are now exempt from the provision as a result of the Companies (Single Member Private Limited Companies) Regulations 1992), carries on business for more than six months with less than two members then any person who (a) was a member of the company during that time, and (b) knew it was carrying on business with less than two members, will be jointly and severally liable with the company for the company's debts during the aforementioned requisite period. This statutory provision is very rarely invoked and as a result of the now legitimised 'one-man company' the likelihood of it being applied in the future is even more remote. (For an example of a case (pre-implementation of the 1992 Regulations) in which the provision was applied, see e.g. *Nisbet* v *Sheperd* [1994] 1 BCLC 300.) The section, in imposing liability on the company in addition to an individual shareholder, does not completely remove the corporate veil, although where applicable it does seriously disturb the corporate veil by upsetting a shareholder's claim to limited liability.

Examples of general statutes that disturb the corporate veil

Section 157(1) of the Environmental Protection Act 1990 (EPA)

This provision disturbs the corporate veil in so far as it provides that any director, manager, secretary or other similar office holder of a company, or a person who was purporting to act in any such capacity, who consented or knew of, or was negligent of the fact that an offence had been committed under any provision of the EPA by the company, will (together with the company) be guilty of that offence. The EPA was implemented to regulate and control, amongst other matters, pollution, waste disposal, genetically modified organisms and hazardous substances on, over or under land.

The Employment Rights Act 1996 (ERA)

Although the case of *Lee* v *Lee's Air Farming Ltd* [1961] AC 12 establishes that a majority shareholder/director of a company can, for the purposes of an insurance contract, be regarded as an employee of the company, UK employment legislation may, in some respects, appear to contradict such reasoning. For example, in *Buchan* v *Secretary of State for Employment* [1997] BCC 145, a shareholder (B) with a 50 per cent holding in a private company was, following the company's liquidation, denied what he perceived to be his right as a full-time employee of the company, namely a claim for a redundancy payment and arrears of wages. Notwithstanding that B had been paid an annual salary, had paid tax and national insurance contributions, he was denied the status of employee in so far as the ERA was construed in a manner whereby a person in control of a company and who was able to prevent the passing of a motion to dismiss him was not to be regarded as an employee. However, by contrast, in *Secretary of State* v *Bottrill* [1999] BCC 177, the Court of Appeal denied the validity of a test based upon whether the claimant was the 'controlling shareholder' of the company. Here, the court upheld a decision of the Employment Appeal Tribunal (EAT) to the effect that a sole shareholder, who was also a director of a company, could be regarded as an employee for the purpose of recovering redundancy payments under the ERA. The Court of Appeal dismissed the Secretary of State's appeal on the premise that there was no one simple test to determine the status of an employee and that the ERA did not itself specify any such test. The court held that the determining factor in the *Buchan* case – namely a director's influence over voting rights so as to prevent his own dismissal was only one factor which should be considered, amongst a number of other factors, in each individual case. Accordingly, no one factor could be taken to be conclusive. The court found that the employment tribunal had been correct in its conclusion that there was a genuine contractual relationship between Mr Bottrill and the company. Lord Woolf MR, in giving the judgment of the court, stated:

'The first question which the tribunal is likely to wish to consider is whether there is or has been a genuine contract between the company and the shareholder. In this context how and for what reasons the contract came into existence (for example, whether the contract was made at a time when insolvency loomed) and what each party actually did pursuant to the contract are likely to be relevant considerations. If the tribunal concludes that the contract is not a sham, it is likely to wish to consider next whether the contract, which may well have been labelled a contract of employment, actually gave rise to an employer/ employee relationship. In this context, of the various factors usually regarded as relevant (see, for example, Chitty on Contracts 27th ed. (1994) para 37-008), the degree of control exercised by the company over the shareholder employee is always important. This is not the same question as that relating to whether there is a controlling shareholding. The tribunal may think it appropriate to consider whether there are directors other than or in addition to the shareholder employee and whether the constitution of the company gives that shareholder rights such that he is in reality answerable only to himself and incapable of being dismissed. If he is a director, it may be relevant to consider whether he is able under the Articles of Association to vote on matters in which he is personally interested, such as the termination of his contract of employment. Again, the actual conduct of the parties pursuant to the terms of the contract is likely to be relevant. It is for the tribunal as an industrial jury to take all relevant factors into account in reaching its conclusion, giving such weight to them as it considers appropriate.'

Although, as stated by the Court of Appeal, each case must be decided on its own merits, it may be possible to distinguish the cases of *Buchan* and *Bottrill* on the basis that, in the former case, the shareholder/director worked for the company without the benefit of a service contract, whereas in *Bottrill*, the director/shareholder worked under the terms of a service contract. It is to be noted that the reasoning applied in *Bottrill* was followed by the Court of Appeal in *Sellars Arenascene Ltd* v *Connolly* [2001] EWCA Civ 184 (unreported, 2 February 2001).

Suggested further reading

Samuels [1964] JBL 107

Pickering (1968) 31 MLR 481

Smithoff [1976] JBL 305

Whincup (1981) 2 Co Law 158

Dee (1986) 7 Co Law 248

Rixon (1986) 102 LQR 415

Ottolengui (1990) 53 MLR 338

Griffin (1991) 12 Co Law 16

Mitchell (1999) 3 CFILR 15

3

THE PROMOTION AND FORMATION OF A COMPANY

INTRODUCTION

The purpose of this chapter is to examine the procedures and rules relating to the promotion and formation of a limited company. Prior to obtaining a certificate of registration, the promotion of the company must be undertaken. This chapter analyses the legal principles involved in the promotion process and the validity of contracts entered into by persons acting for or on behalf of a company prior to its legal incorporation. This chapter also considers the registration provisions contained in the Companies Act 1985; compliance with registration procedures is essential if a company is to obtain the benefits and status of a limited liability company.

THE PROMOTION OF A COMPANY

Although the companies legislation has never sought to provide a definition of the legal characteristics that identify a promoter, the promoter is nevertheless essential to the creation of a new corporate entity. To establish that a person acted as a promoter of a company, the case law in this area is indicative of the necessity to show that the person concerned contributed some essential element towards the incorporation of the company. The level of contribution may be substantial (e.g. the negotiation of the purchase of business premises) or, on the other hand, it may be less extensive (e.g. a person may be deemed a promoter by organising the appointment of a company director). In *Whaley Bridge Calico Printing Co v Green* (1879) 5 QBD 109, Bowen J was of the opinion that in deciding the question of whether a person could be properly described as a promoter, the court should bear in mind that:

'The term promoter is not a term of law but one of business, usefully summing up in a single word a number of business operations familiar to the commercial world.' (at p 109)

The promotion of a public or large private company is likely to be undertaken by a professional agency, but, where a small business is to be incorporated, the promotion will normally, although not exclusively, be carried out by the owner of the pre-incorporated business.

The promoter's duties

A promoter cannot be considered to be an agent or trustee of the company that he undertakes to promote, because prior to incorporation the company has no legal existence. Nevertheless, a promoter occupies a position that the courts have recognised as one that is liable to abuse and one which should therefore be subject to fiduciary duties. A promoter's fiduciary duties are similar to those owed to a company by its directors (for a discussion on directors' duties, see Chapter 17). A promoter, in common with a director, is also subject to the common law duty to exercise reasonable care and skill in the performance of his duties.

As a consequence of the promoter's assumed fiduciary position, a promoter must make full disclosure of any personal interest that is related to the promotion process. Accordingly, the promoter must disclose whether he obtained a profit as a result of the promotion of the company concerned. For example, in *Gluckstein* v *Barnes* [1900] AC 200, a syndicate of businessmen purchased the Olympia Exhibition Hall in West London from a company in liquidation, for a sum of £140 000. The syndicate then promoted a company which subsequently purchased the hall for £180 000. On the public issue of the company's shares the prospectus disclosed the purchase profit of £40 000. However, the prospectus failed to disclose that in addition to purchasing the Olympia Exhibition Hall, the syndicate had also purchased certain secured debts of the insolvent company, namely debts secured against the insolvent company's assets. The syndicate purchased the secured debts for £20 000 and on the realisation of the insolvent company's assets made a further £20 000 profit on that purchase. The House of Lords held that the syndicate, the promoters of the company, were liable to account to the company for the amount of the undisclosed profit, that is a sum of £20 000.

Disclosure of a promoter's personal interest in the promotion of a company must be made to the company. At one time it was thought that disclosure to the company would only be satisfied by disclosure to a full and independent board of the company's directors: see e.g. *Erlanger* v *New Sombrero Phosphate Co* (1878) 3 App Cas 1218. However, the *Erlanger* case was decided before the decision of the House of Lords in *Salomon* v *A Salomon Ltd* [1897] AC 22, in which the disclosure of the balance between the true value of Mr Salomon's business and the overvalued price paid by the company (that Mr Salomon promoted) was found to have been made to the company's shareholders but not to an independent board of directors. As a consequence of the decision of the House of Lords in *Salomon*, it is sufficient for a promoter to satisfy the disclosure duty by making disclosure to those who have invested in or are about to invest in the company, that is the company's shareholders or potential shareholders: see e.g. *Langunas Nitrate Co* v *Langunas Syndicate* [1899] 2 Ch 392.

Where a promoter fails to disclose any benefit obtained as a result of entering into a contract that is related to a company's promotion, the contract, whilst not void, will be voidable. The company, if it is successfully to rescind the contract, must not delay in avoiding it; neither must its actions, nor for that matter its inactivity, be construed as indicative of the ratification of the contract. The restitution of the subject matter of the contract must be possible, although, where it is not, the court may order financial adjustments to be made between the parties.

Much of the relevant case law in relation to the extent and enforcement of a promoter's duties is rooted in the mid to late nineteenth century, a time when it was quite a common practice for newly incorporated companies to offer shares to the general public. The duties imposed on promoters were a means by which investors could be protected from any fraudulent attempt on the part of a promoter to obtain undeclared and unwarranted profits from the promotion of what was often an unknown and untested business entity. In today's world the vast majority of public issues take place as a result of established private companies electing to become public companies. As such, the likelihood of fraud is less probable. Nevertheless, the protection of the investing public is still necessary, especially in the context of protecting the public interest from offers for company securities that may contain untrue or misleading information (see Chapter 11).

PRE-INCORPORATION CONTRACTS

Prior to incorporation, the promoter(s) of a company will usually be required to enter into contractual agreements appertaining to the future needs of the pre-incorporated company. However, until a company is incorporated it will not exist as a separate legal entity and therefore cannot be bound by contracts made in its name or on its behalf: see e.g. *Natal Land & Colonisation Co* v *Pauline Colliery Syndicate* [1904] AC 120. A company, even after its incorporation, cannot expressly or by conduct retrospectively ratify or adopt a contract made in its name or on its behalf: see e.g. *Re Northumberland Avenue Hotel Co* (1886) 33 Ch D 16. Neither may a company claim to have adopted a pre-incorporation contract by including the terms of the contract within its articles: see e.g. *Browne* v *La Trinidad* (1887) 37 Ch D 1. Indeed, the only method by which a company may take the benefit of a pre-incorporation contract is by entering into a new contract with the party with whom the promoter dealt (i.e. a novation). Evidence of the existence of a novation may be found where the re-negotiation of the terms of the original pre-incorporation contract has resulted in the express or implied creation of a new set of obligations between the company and the other contracting party: see e.g. *Howard Patent Ivory Manufacturing Co* (1888) 38 Ch D 156. It should be observed that neither the company nor the party with whom the promoter originally contracted is obliged to enter into a new contract following the company's incorporation.

However, following the Court of Appeal's decision in *Rover International Ltd* v *Cannon Film Sales Ltd* [1988] BCLC 710, where a pre-incorporation contract is entered into, moneys mistakenly paid by the subsequently incorporated company to a third party in the mistaken belief that the pre-incorporation contract was binding, may be recovered as against the third party. In addition, the court may grant a *quantum meruit* award to the company for services provided during the period in which the company was under the mistaken belief that the pre-incorporation contract was valid. Equally, the aforementioned remedies may be awarded against a company in circumstances where a third party mistakenly believed that the company with which it had contracted had been incorporated at the time of the contract and, as a consequence of the mistaken belief, paid moneys to the company or performed services for that company.

The liability of a promoter

Prior to its legal incorporation, a company does not possess the legal capacity to enter into a contractual relationship. Therefore, where a promoter enters into a contract for or on behalf of the unincorporated company, is the promoter to be regarded as having entered the contract as a principal, and can the promoter sue or be sued on the contract in his own name?

Before the UK's accession to the EC in 1972, common law rules exclusively determined whether a promoter could be regarded as a principal to a pre-incorporation contract. The common law rules operated on the basis of a technical and artificial distinction, related to the manner in which the promoter had signed the contract. Where a promoter entered into a contract signing the contract as the company's agent, or on behalf of a company, the promoter could be held personally liable on the contract: see e.g. *Kelner* v *Baxter* (1866) LR 2 CP 174. On the other hand, where a promoter entered into a contract by signing the contract using the company's name and merely added his own name to authenticate that of the company's, then, following *Newborne* v *Sensolid* (*Great Britain*) *Ltd* [1954] 1 QB 45, the promoter would not be regarded as a principal to the contract and would hence escape any personal liability for a purported breach of the contract's terms. The contract would be classed as having been made with a non-existent entity and as such would be declared a nullity. However, it should be noted that where a contract was declared a nullity a promoter could still incur liability for breach of warranty in a situation where the promoter, in authenticating the contract, did so as a director of the company. By authenticating the contract with his own signature, expressed to represent the signature of a director of the unincorporated company, the promoter would misrepresent his authority because at the time of signing the contract the company had no legal existence and therefore had no validly appointed directors: see e.g. *Collen* v *Wright* (1857) 8 E & B 647.

As a consequence of the UK's entry to the EC, the UK was obliged to implement Art 7 of the First Company Law Directive. As a result of the UK's implementation of Art 7 the artificial distinction in the rules of common law, as applicable to pre-incorporation contracts, were eradicated. Article 7 provided:

> 'If, before a company has acquired legal personality (i.e. before being formed) action has been carried out in its name and the company does not assume the obligations arising from such action, the persons who acted shall, without limit, be jointly and severally liable therefor, unless otherwise agreed.'

Article 7 was implemented in the form of s 9(2) of the European Communities Act 1972, which subsequently became s 36(4) of the Companies Act 1985 and which is now (as a result of s 130(4) of the CA 1989) s 36C(1) of the Companies Act 1985. Section 36C(1) is expressed in the following terms:

> 'A contract which purports to be made by or on behalf of a company at a time when the company has not been formed has effect, subject to any agreement to the contrary, as one made with the person purporting to act for the company or as agent for it, and he is personally liable on the contract accordingly.'

In accordance with s 36C(2) of the Companies Act 1985, s 36C(1) will apply:

(a) to the making of a deed under the law of England and Wales; and

(b) to the undertaking of an obligation under the law of Scotland as it applies to the making of a contract.

The wording of s 36C(1) is akin to its predecessor (s 36(4), CA 1985), the statutory language of both being derived from s 9(2) of the European Communities Act 1972.

The effect of s 36C(1) is to render a promoter personally liable on a pre-incorporation contract, irrespective of whether the promoter signed the contract in the company's name or on behalf of the company.

One obvious difference between Art 7 and what is now s 36C(1) of the Companies Act 1985 is that, whilst Art 7 expressly states that a company, once formed, may 'assume the obligations' contained within a pre-incorporation contract, s 36C(1) does not. While the party with whom the pre-incorporation contract was made may agree to enter into a new contract with the company (a novation), the new contractual obligation cannot be deemed an assumption of the obligation contained in the pre-incorporation contract; the present position subsists despite the fact that in 1962 the Jenkins Committee (Cmnd 1749) recommended that companies should be given the statutory power to adopt pre-incorporation contracts.

Where s 36C(1) is applicable, its effect is to remove the technical distinctions found in the common law prior to the UK's implementation of the EC First Company Law Directive. Indeed, in *Phonogram v Lane* [1982] QB 938, Lord Denning stated that the distinction between cases such as *Kelner v Baxter* and *Newbourne v Sensolid* had been 'obliterated'. The almost unbelievable facts of *Phonogram v Lane* were as follows. A company, to be named Fragile Management Ltd, was to be formed for the purpose of managing a musical band known as 'Cheap, Mean and Nasty'. The plaintiff, Phonogram Ltd, agreed to finance the group to the sum of £12 000, a sum which was to be payable in two instalments. The first payment was sent to the defendant, the group's manager, in anticipation of a recording contract being entered into within a specified time period; the money was to be returned if the contract had not been completed within the time period. For administrative reasons, the cheque was made payable to Jelly Music Ltd – the defendant was a director of that company. The defendant, at the request of the plaintiff, signed the financial agreement 'for and on behalf of Fragile Management Ltd'.

The management company (Fragile Management Ltd) was never incorporated. The plaintiff sued the defendant for the return of the first instalment (i.e. £6000). The defendant contended that the then relevant legislation, s 9(2) of the European Communities Act 1972, only applied (in accordance with the French translation of Art 9) to a company already in the course of formation (Fragile Management had never been in the course of formation). The defendant also argued that in accordance with s 9(2) personal liability could only be imposed where a person had contracted as the company's agent; on this point the defendant argued that, as Fragile Management had never been formed, there could be no principal for which an agent could act. Notwithstanding the defendant's protestations, the Court of Appeal held that the wording of s 9(2) of the EC Act 1972, and not the French translation of Art 9, was to be applied; and in accordance with the interpretation of s 9(2) the defendant was deemed personally liable to account to the plaintiff for the sum in question.

Avoiding section 36C(1) of the Companies Act 1985

For a promoter to avoid the threat of being made personally liable on a pre-incorporation contract, an express statement excluding the promoter's liability must be included within the contract (so held in *Phonogram v Lane*). Despite the theoretical possibility of the appearance of such a clause, it would be most unlikely to be incorporated into the contract given that its practical effect would be to prevent the party with whom the promoter dealt from seeking specific performance or damages for non-performance or non-compliance with the terms of the pre-incorporation contract (i.e. neither the company, once incorporated, nor its promoter would be liable).

The judicial interpretation of section 36C(1) of the Companies Act 1985

Section 36C(1) of the Companies Act 1985 deems that a person who purports to contract for a company which, as of the date of the contract, was not then formed may, in relevant circumstances, be made personally liable on the contract. Somewhat surprisingly the section does not specifically state that a person who purports to act for the company (the promoter) is also endowed with the right to enforce the terms of a pre-incorporation contract. However, following the decision of the Court of Appeal in *Braymist Ltd* v *Wise Finance Co Ltd* [2002] BCC 514, the promoter will, in accordance with basic contract law principles, be permitted to enforce the terms of the contract.

Given a wide, but nevertheless plausible, interpretation of s 36C(1), the possible application of the section would not appear to be exclusively confined to the standard type of mischief against which it is aimed, namely a promoter's ability to escape personal liability in respect of pre-incorporation contracts. Indeed, the section may be interpreted, if one construes the term 'formed' to mean legally incorporated, as potentially applicable to any situation whereby a person contracted on behalf of a company which, as of the date on which the contract was made, was not, for whatever reason, legally incorporated in accordance with registration procedures. However, the judicial interpretation of s 36(4) of the CA 1985 and its predecessor, s 9(1) of the European Communities Act 1972 (the wording of both are akin to s 36C(1), CA 1985), has adopted a restrictive stance in respect of the applicability of the legislation, a fact which is illustrated by the following three decisions of the Court of Appeal.

The first of the three cases, *Oshkosh B'Gosh Inc* v *Dan Marbel Inc Ltd* [1989] BCLC 507, involved the acquisition of an off-the-shelf company, which in 1979 was acquired under the name of Egormight Ltd. In 1980, the company passed a resolution to alter its name to Dan Marbel Inc Ltd. As a result of an administrative oversight by the company, a certificate confirming that the company's name had been changed was not issued until 1985. Yet, from 1980 onwards, the company (the first defendants) traded as Dan Marbel Inc Ltd.

The plaintiff, a creditor of the company, commenced an action against the second defendant, a director of the company, for the non-payment of debts. The action was commenced against the second defendant on the premise that s 9(2) of the European Communities Act 1972 was applicable. The plaintiff contended that he had entered into contracts (on which the debts arose) with the second defendant, who acted on behalf of a company (Dan Marbel Inc Ltd), at a time when that company had not been formed. Strictly speaking, that assertion was correct. Dan Marbel Inc Ltd had not been incorporated until 1985. Nevertheless, the Court of Appeal concluded that s 9(2) of the 1972 Act was not applicable, in that the company with which the plaintiff traded had been formed and was not merely in the process of formation. While the Court of Appeal conceded that the company had been trading under an incorrect name, the court could not appreciate how s 9(2) of the 1972 Act could be successfully pleaded unless the company, as under its first name, was a completely different entity from the company under its second name.

The Court of Appeal reached its conclusion notwithstanding that the company traded under the name of Dan Marbel Inc Ltd at a time when that specific company was without legal existence. Although the second defendant purported to enter into a contract on behalf of a company structure that was in existence at the time the contract was made, the company structure in question was not specifically identifiable with a company named Dan Marbel Inc Ltd; the company registered under the name of Egormight Ltd – an off-the-shelf company – would most probably have had a completely different constitutional framework to that of Dan Marbel Inc Ltd: different directors, objects, subscribers, etc. The two differently named companies were not, in terms of corporate theory, the same entities. (An action under s 108(4) of the CA 1948 – now s 349(4), discussed in Chapter 18 – was also commenced against the second defendant; this action failed on the basis that the relevant instruments had never been signed and as such they were outside the ambit of s 108(4).)

The second of the three cases, *Badgerhill Properties Ltd* v *Cottrell* [1991] BCLC 805, concerned a director of Badgerhill Properties Ltd, a Mr Twigg (T), who had entered into two contracts with a Mrs Cottrell (C). The contracts related to building work that was to be carried out by two different businesses; Badgerhill Properties Ltd in fact controlled both businesses. At the end of both contracts the company's name had been misrepresented as Badgerhill Property Ltd, instead of Badgerhill Properties Ltd.

C alleged that the building work had been carried out in an unsatisfactory manner and claimed damages totalling a sum of £80 000. As Badgerhill Properties Ltd was in a poor financial state, C pursued an action against T under s 36(4) of the CA 1985 on the premise that T had entered into contracts on behalf of a company at a time when the company, Badgerhill Property Ltd, had not been formed. However, the Court of Appeal refused to apply s 36(4) on the premise that the contracts were not entered into with a non-existent company, Badgerhill Property Ltd, but rather by the businesses controlled by a genuine company, Badgerhill Properties Ltd, a company that had been formed. Woolf LJ stated that:

> 'The only relevance of the name Badgerhill Property Ltd appearing on the contractual documents was that it was an indication that the businesses were not being conducted by Mr Twigg personally but by a company and the name of that company was Badgerhill Property. It was not therefore a situation where Badgerhill Property had purported to make the contract.' (at p 813)

However, despite the Court of Appeal's findings, the non-existent company, Badgerhill Property Ltd, was, by the appearance of its name on the two contracts, representing itself to be in control and responsible for the businesses operated by Mr Twigg. Theoretically, Badgerhill Property Ltd and not Badgerhill Properties Ltd would have been ultimately responsible for a breach of the contracts entered into by the businesses.

The final case example is *Cotronic (UK) Ltd* v *Dezonie* [1991] BCLC 721. In this case the plaintiff company commenced an action for the recovery of a sum of money in respect of building work carried out in its capacity as sub-contractor to a company called Wendaland Builders Ltd (W1), a company controlled by the defendant, a Mr Dezonie (D). D contended that the debt owing to the plaintiff was outstanding as a result of a failure on the part of the owner of the property (O) to make payment for the work provided. As a result of O's failure to settle the debt, D commenced third-party proceedings against O.

At first instance, D succeeded in the claim for the third-party proceedings against O. O appealed on the premise that at the time of entering into the contract with W1 that company had ceased to exist; at the time of the contract the company, unknown to D, had been struck off the Companies Register. O argued that, as it was impossible to contract with an entity which had not been in existence at the time the contract was made, the contract must have been a nullity and thus void.

In defending this claim, D contended that s 36(4) was applicable so that D should be allowed to sue O for a breach of the contract in much the same way as D could, given different circumstances, have been personally liable to O under the terms of s 36(4). D's contention as to the applicability of s 36(4) was based on the fact that, after becoming aware that W1 had been struck off, he had formed and incorporated another company, Wendaland Builders Ltd (W2). Therefore, in effect D was a person who had entered into a contract on behalf of a company that had, at the time of the contract, not been formed.

The Court of Appeal concluded that D was not entitled to rely on s 36(4), although he was entitled to a *quantum meruit* award (a monetary claim against O for the building services provided). In reaching its decision, the court stated that it was impossible to argue that D had entered into the contract for the benefit of company W2, for at the time of making the contract D never had any intention to form company W2; therefore, the contract could not have been made on behalf of W2. As Dillon LJ stated:

> 'At the time of the . . . building agreement no one had thought about forming a new company at all. Accordingly it is not possible to say that the contract purports to be made by the new company.' (at p 723)

Yet, despite the apparent logic of Dillon LJ's words, the Court of Appeal's decision in *Cotronic* may be criticised in the sense that D actually made the contract on behalf of Wendaland Builders Ltd. As the contract could not have been made on behalf of W1, for at the time of the contract W1 had no legal existence, it must have been made for a company which, at the time of the contract, had not been formed, namely W2. Therefore, as with the two previously discussed Court of Appeal decisions, it is at least arguable that the case facts of *Cotronic* were technically within the ambit of s 36(4), especially if one construes the term 'formed', so used in the section, to mean legally incorporated.

Notwithstanding the above arguments, the Court of Appeal's construction of the statutory language of the section now represented by s 36C may be defended as rational in that it is difficult to imagine the section having been designed to impose liability on individuals who enter into contracts with the genuine intention of contracting for or on behalf of a registered company that had been formed in accordance with the registration procedures, but which had mistakenly used an incorrect representation of its name. (Although by analogy consider the stricter approach taken by the judiciary in relation to the construction of s 349(4) of the CA 1985, discussed in Chapter 18.)

The application of the common law principles

Where the court finds that s 36C(1) is not applicable to the factual situation of a given case, the potential liability of the person who entered into a contract in the name of or on behalf of a company may still fall to be determined by common law principles. As previously discussed, the common law principles created a distinction between, on the one hand, a promoter who signed the contract as agent for or on behalf of the company and, on the other hand, a promoter who signed the contract in the name of the company. However, in the cases of *Badgerhill* and *Cotronic*, the Court of Appeal, in seeking to apply the common law principles, relied upon the observations of Oliver LJ, who in *Phonogram v Lane* [1982] QB 938 remarked:

> 'Speaking for myself I am not convinced that the common law position . . . depends on the narrow distinction between a signature "for and on behalf of" and a signature in the name of a company or association. The question I think in each case is what is the real intent as revealed by the contract? Does the contract purport to be one which is directly between the supposed principal and the other party, or does it purport to be one between the agent himself, albeit acting for a supposed principal, and the other party? In other words, what we have to look at is whether the agent intended himself to be a party to the contract.' (at p 945)

The Court of Appeal, in applying Oliver LJ's comments to the factual situations found in *Badgerhill* and *Cotronic*, concluded that in both cases the relevant contracts had been made with an intention to bind a company and not the individuals who purportedly acted on behalf of the company.

THE REGISTRATION PROCEDURE

The incorporation of a company must be conducted in accordance with the registration provisions contained in the Companies Act 1985. Provided that the registration procedures are followed, and the object of the incorporation is for a lawful purpose, s 1(1) of the Companies Act 1985 (amended as a result of the UK's implementation of the EC Twelfth Company Law Directive by s 3A of the Companies Act 1985) allows any one or more persons to form an incorporated company with or without limited liability by subscribing their name(s) to a memorandum of association (the memorandum of association is discussed in Chapter 4). A single member company may only be formed as either a private company limited by shares or a private company limited by guarantee. The registration of a company involves the delivery of the following documents (together with a registration fee) to the Registrar of Companies:

- the company's memorandum of association;
- the company's articles of association signed by the subscriber(s) named in the memorandum (it should be noted that a company may be registered without a formal set of articles, in which case the statutory model of articles found in Table

A of the Companies (Tables A–F) Regulations 1985 will be deemed to take effect as the company's articles);

- a statement giving particulars of the company's first director(s) and secretary. (Such persons must consent so to act in the capacity prescribed by the particulars. It is to be noted that where a company has a single director that director cannot also act as the company's secretary – discussed further in Chapter 16.) The statement must also specify the address of the company's registered office;

- a statutory declaration by a solicitor engaged in the formation of the company or a person named as a director or secretary of the company to the effect that the statutory requirements relating to registration have been complied with (s 12(3), CA 1985). (If the company is a public company the declaration must provide that the nominal value of the allotted share capital is not less than £50 000 and that the amount paid up on this sum represents not less than one-quarter of the nominal value.)

Proposals for future reform

Government proposals contained in Part A2 of the White Paper, 'Company Law Reform' (2005) (together with the prior recommendations of the earlier White Paper (2002) and the Company Law Review's (CLR) Final Report (2001)) do not distinguish between a single person's ability to incorporate either a private or public company (i.e. the incorporation of a single member public company will be permitted).

Although the White Paper (2005) does not seek to alter the specific content of the information required in respect of a company's registration, it is to be observed that, for the most part, information currently contained within the memorandum will be required to be placed in an 'application for registration' (see clause A9 of the White Paper (2005)). In effect, the memorandum will completely lose its current significance (discussed further in Chapter 4). Indeed, clause A8 defines the new form of memorandum in quite 'pathetic terms', as follows:

(1) A memorandum of association is a memorandum stating that the subscribers

   (a) wish to form a company under this Act, and

   (b) agree to become members of the company and, in the case of a company that is to have a share capital, to take at least one share each.

(2) The memorandum must be in the prescribed form and must be authenticated by each subscriber.

In accordance with clause A9 of the White Paper (2005), it is proposed that (i) the memorandum, (ii) an application for registration, and (iii) a statement of compliance, must be delivered to the Registrar for the purpose of completing the registration procedure.

The Electronic Communications Act 2000

The Electronic Communications Act 2000 permits companies to submit registration documents electronically (amongst other matters it also permits companies to communicate their annual report and accounts to shareholders by electronic means). Electronic incorporation is basically a process of registration via e-mail with appropriate attachments (the memorandum and articles and other registration forms, etc.) being sent to and processed electronically by Companies House. It is envisaged that the electronic system will greatly improve the efficiency of the registration process and speed up the present system.

The refusal to register a company

Prior to the issue of a registration certificate, the Registrar of Companies must be satisfied that the requirements of the statutory registration procedure have been complied with (s 12(1), CA 1985). For example, the Registrar may refuse to register a company where its proposed objects (contained in the memorandum) are illegal or contrary to public policy. (It should be noted that a trade union cannot be registered as a company under s 10(3) of the Trade Union and Labour Relations (Consolidation) Act 1992.)

A case example of the Registrar's refusal to register a company can be found in *R v Registrar of Companies, ex parte More* [1931] 2 KB 197. Here, the Registrar refused to register a company because its objects provided that it was to sell lottery tickets in England, on behalf of an Irish lottery; at that time it was illegal to sell lottery tickets in England. The decision of the Registrar to refuse to register a company is, however, subject to judicial review and the Registrar's decision may be reversed. For example, in *R v Registrar of Companies, ex parte Bowen* [1914] 3 KB 1161, the Registrar refused to register a company under the name of 'The United Dental Service Ltd' because the company, in pursuing a dentistry business, was seeking to operate with unregistered dentists. The Registrar objected to the incorporation on the basis that the title of the company's name implied, in its use of the word 'dental', that the dentists employed by the company would be registered dental practitioners. However, the Registrar's decision was reversed on the basis that the word 'dental' did not necessarily imply that the dentists employed would be registered. (It should be noted that regulations made under s 29 of the CA 1985 now stipulate that a company wishing to be registered with a name which includes the word 'dental' must first obtain the approval of the Registrar of the General Dental Council.)

THE CHOICE OF A COMPANY NAME

A company's name must be stated in its memorandum, and the name with which a company is registered must not be one that is already included in the index of registered company names (s 26, CA 1985). The Registrar of Companies is not responsible for checking the companies name index prior to the registration of a company; that responsibility falls upon the person in control of the company's promotion process. Section 28(2) of the Companies Act 1985 provides that within 12 months of a company's registration the Secretary of State is permitted to direct a company to change its name in circumstances where the choice of name was the same as or too similar to the name of a company already listed on the register.

The passing off action

Where the Secretary of State refuses to exercise his discretionary powers under s 28(2), a company which is already in existence may nevertheless challenge the adoption of a name by a newly incorporated company by means of a passing off action. The passing off action is a common law remedy. In the case of a business name, the action may be pursued by any enterprise, be it an incorporated company, a partnership or a sole trader. An action may be commenced in circumstances where a newly formed business adopts the name of an existing enterprise or a name that is similar to an existing enterprise. In addition, it must be established that the defendant is engaged in a similar type of business activity to the plaintiff. The general preconditions for any passing off action were set out by the House of Lords in *Reckitt & Colman Products Ltd* v *Borden Inc* [1990] RPC 341. Lord Oliver described the characteristics as follows:

> '. . . – no man may pass off his goods as those of another. . . . the plaintiff in such an action has to . . . establish a goodwill or reputation attached to the goods or services which he supplies in the mind of the purchasing public by association with the identifying "get-up" (whether it consists simply of a brand name or a trade description, or the individual features of labelling or packaging) under which his particular goods or services are offered to the public, such that the get-up is recognised by the public as distinctive specifically of the plaintiff's goods or services. Secondly, he must demonstrate a misrepresentation by the defendant to the public (whether or not intentional) leading or likely to lead the public to believe that goods or services offered by him are the goods or services of the plaintiff. Whether the public is aware of the plaintiff's identity as the manufacturer or supplier of the goods or services is immaterial, as long as they are identified with a particular source which is in fact the plaintiff. . . . Thirdly, he must demonstrate that he suffers or, in a quia timet action that he is likely to suffer, damage by reason of the erroneous belief engendered by the defendant's misrepresentation that the source of the defendant's goods or services is the same as the source of those offered by the plaintiff.' (at p 406)

The case of *Ewing* v *Buttercup Margarine Co Ltd* [1917] 2 Ch 1, provides an excellent example of a passing off action in the context of a corporate name. Here, the plaintiff commenced a passing off action against an incorporated company which had been named the Buttercup Margarine Co Ltd and which had been formed to operate a wholesale and retail business in margarine. The plaintiff also operated an unincorporated dairy products business which specialised in the wholesale and retail sale of margarine; the business operated under the name of Buttercup Dairy Co. Although the plaintiff had its principal business activities in Scotland, whereas the defendant operated in southern England, the passing off action succeeded. The Court of Appeal opined that the reputation of the plaintiff enterprise was clearly exploited by the defendant company's choice of name and business activity. (See also *Halifax plc* v *Halifax Repossessions Ltd* [2004] BCC 281.)

MISCELLANEOUS RESTRICTIONS AND OBLIGATIONS IN RESPECT OF THE USE OF A COMPANY NAME

● Section 26(1) of the Companies Act 1985 prohibits the insertion of the following words: limited, unlimited and public limited company (or their Welsh equivalents) into a company's name, otherwise than at the end of the company's name.

- Where the Secretary of State is of the opinion that the use of a specific name may constitute a criminal offence, the use of that name may be prohibited (s 26(1)(d) and (e), CA 1985).

- If the Secretary of State considers that the use of a company name would imply a connection with HM government, or any local government authority or agency, the Secretary of State may refuse to allow the company concerned to register the name in question (s 26(2), CA 1985 and s 2(1), Business Names Act 1985).

- A business concern is restricted from adopting a name governed by the terms of the Business Names Act 1985. The prohibited names are listed in the Company and Business Names (Amendment) Regulations 1992; such names may only be used where written permission has been obtained from the government body or other association responsible for the protection of the name in question.

- In accordance with s 349 of the Companies Act 1985, a company will be liable to a fine where it fails legibly to make mention of its name (including its limited liability status) in all its business letters, notices, invoices, receipts, letters of credit, bills of exchange, cheques and other instruments where the same confer a monetary obligation on the part of the company.

- A company's registered name must clearly and conspicuously be affixed or painted on the outside of every office or other premises from which it conducts its business. A company (and every officer of it who is in default) that fails to do so will be liable to a fine (s 348, CA 1985). The abbreviation 'Ltd' for a private limited company and 'plc' for a public limited company will suffice (for the purposes of ss 348 and 349, CA 1985) as will the abbreviation 'Co' to represent company. The word 'and' may also be represented by the abbreviation '&'.

- A business which represents itself (in the last word of its name) to be a limited liability company when in fact it is not a limited liability company is liable to a fine (s 34, CA 1985).

THE SECRETARY OF STATE'S ABILITY TO ORDER A COMPANY TO CHANGE ITS NAME

In accordance with s 32 of the Companies Act 1985, the Secretary of State has the power to order a company to change its name within a period of five years from the date on which the offending name was first registered. The company may, within three weeks of the Secretary of State's direction, apply to the court in an attempt to have the direction set aside. The Secretary of State may exercise this power when he/she is of the opinion that the use of the name resulted, or could have resulted, in a misleading indication of the business activities of the company – misleading to the extent of causing harm to the public interest. The provision was subject to its first judicial consideration in 1997, in *Association of Certified Public Accountants of Britain* v *Secretary of State for Trade and Industry* [1997] 2 BCLC 307. Here Jacob J held that it is for the Crown to establish that a company's name offends the statute. The learned judge, in formulating a legal test, concluded thus:

'. . . what the court has to do is to decide on the evidence whether the name of the company gives so misleading an indication of the nature of its activities as to be likely to cause harm to the public. It is not sufficient to show that a name is misleading; a likelihood of harm must be shown too. In many cases the latter will follow from the former, but this is not necessarily so: it is difficult to imagine harm, for instance, if a company called Robin Jacob (Fishmongers) Ltd in fact carried on a business of bookbinding.' (at p 311)

It should also be observed that where a company's name is obtained by means of deception, the Secretary of State may also, within a five-year period, compel the company in question to alter its name (s 28(3), CA 1985).

Where a company is, for whatever reason, compelled to change its name, it must do so by passing a special resolution in compliance with s 28(1) of the Companies Act 1985: see e.g. *Halifax plc & Ors* v *Halifax Repossessions Ltd & Ors* [2004] BCC 281. The economic dangers inherent in a company having to change its name may be serious. For example, after a few years of trading under a specific name, that name may have become associated with the company's product range to such an extent that a change in corporate name may result in a failure by the general public to associate the product with the newly adopted name of the company, a factor which may adversely affect the company's image. Further, if a change in name is ordered, costs will be incurred in changing company documents, signs, advertising logos, letterheads, etc.

THE CERTIFICATE OF INCORPORATION

A company is legally incorporated following the issue of a certificate of incorporation. The certificate of incorporation identifies the company, registered by its name and allotted serial number, and is conclusive of the fact that all the requirements of the statutory registration procedures have been complied with (s 13(7), CA 1985). The certificate is also conclusive of the status of the company registered; therefore, if the certificate provides that a company is registered as a public limited company then the certificate is conclusive of that matter.

A company, having obtained a certificate of incorporation, is permitted from the date of the certificate to enter into business activities as a registered company. For example, in *Jubilee Cotton Mills Ltd* v *Lewis* [1924] AC 958, a company's certificate of incorporation was incorrectly dated 6 January 1920, notwithstanding that the certificate had not been signed by the Registrar until 8 January 1920. Nevertheless, the House of Lords held that an issue of shares made by the company on 6 January was valid. Although a mistake was made in respect of the date of the company's incorporation, the certificate's date was, in law, conclusive proof of the fact that the company's incorporation took effect from 6 January 1920.

Except in a case where the Crown (which is not bound by s 13(7), CA 1985) challenges the legality of the objects for which a company was formed, the legal existence of a company cannot be challenged once the certificate of incorporation is issued. An example of the Crown's ability to challenge the objects of a company is found in *R* v *Registrar of Companies, ex parte Attorney General* [1991] BCLC 476. The case involved a company which had been formed with objects which sought to establish a prostitution business. Although the Registrar had previously refused to register the company under the names of 'Prostitute Ltd', 'Hookers Ltd' and 'French Lessons Ltd', the company was finally granted its registration under the name of Lindi St

Clair (Personal Services) Ltd. Despite the fact that the company had overcome all the procedural requirements for registration, its objects were clearly contrary to the public interest. As such, the court held that the Registrar had erred in granting the company its registration certificate and accordingly the company was struck off the companies register.

Where the Crown successfully brings proceedings to strike a company off the companies register, the company's existence is retrospectively denied. In law, the company will be regarded as an enterprise that never attained incorporation in accordance with the registration provisions of the companies legislation. Therefore, any outstanding contractual obligations incurred by the business whilst it was on the companies register will be rendered void: that is, a contract cannot be enforced against a party, where that party never attained a legal existence or capacity. (Although this type of situation may be within the theoretical ambit of s 36C(1) of the CA 1985, the judicial interpretation of s 36C(1) would clearly be dismissive of such an action (discussed above).)

The Crown's ability to commence proceedings to strike a company off the register may be harmful to creditors and the practice must be questionable, especially when an alternative course of action is available under s 122(1)(g) of the IA 1986, whereby a company registered with illegal objects may be wound up on just and equitable grounds: see e.g. *Re International Securities Corporation* (1908) 99 LT 581. To allow the company to be wound up under s 122(1)g would provide the company's creditors with an opportunity to make a claim against the company's assets. It should be noted that the Crown's powers would also seem contrary to the EC First Company Law Directive (Art 12(3)), which provides that:

> 'Nullity shall not of itself effect the validity of any commitments entered into by or with the company, without prejudice to the consequences of the company's being wound up.'

Commencement of business

A private company may commence business from the date of its incorporation, whereas a public limited company must, prior to the commencement of its business, wait until it has received a trading certificate (s 117, CA 1985). Where a public company commences business prior to the receipt of a trading certificate any party with whom the company dealt will nevertheless be protected; the contract will not be set aside. However, the company and any officer in default of the provision will be liable to a fine.

Off-the-shelf companies

A registered company may be purchased from an agency specialising in the sale of what are commonly known as 'off-the-shelf companies'. An off-the-shelf company is one that has been incorporated in accordance with the registration provisions provided by the Companies Act, normally having a minimal share capital (usually two £1 shares), the ultimate purpose for its incorporation being its subsequent sale. The advantage to a prospective purchaser of an off-the-shelf company is the speed, relatively low cost and ease by which a business can attain a corporate form. On the payment of a fee (to the agency supplying the off-the-shelf company – usually between £200 and £300) the relevant transfers of shares and company's registers will be conveyed to the purchasers of the company. Notification in the change of address of the company's registered office, company directors and secretary, will then be made. The new shareholders of the company may also, if they so wish, change, in accordance with relevant statutory procedures, the company's name and make any other amendment to the company's constitution as they see fit: for example, they may wish to change the contents of the company's articles or memorandum.

Suggested further reading

Promoters and pre-incorporation contracts

Prentice (1973) 89 LQR 518

Green (1984) 47 MLR 671

Griffiths (1993) 13 LS 241

Savirimuthu (2003) 24 Co Law 196

Company names

Watts and Walsh (1996) 18 EIPR 336

4

A COMPANY'S MEMORANDUM AND ARTICLES OF ASSOCIATION

INTRODUCTION

The constitutional structure of a company is governed by its memorandum and articles of association. This chapter commences by examining the company's memorandum and the powers available to a company to alter clauses contained therein. It moves on to consider the format of a company's articles and the so-called statutory contract created by s 14 of the Companies Act 1985. In considering s 14, the chapter examines the powers available to both the company and its membership to enforce and alter obligations created by the articles, then considers government proposals to reform the constitutional structure of a company. The chapter then moves on to consider a company's power under s 9 of the Companies Act to alter its articles. Finally, it considers contractual agreements other than those created by s 14: for example, membership/shareholder agreements.

THE MEMORANDUM OF ASSOCIATION

The memorandum of a company is primarily concerned with the regulation and outward appearance of the company in its dealings with third parties. Section 3 of the Companies Act 1985 empowers the Secretary of State to specify by statutory instrument the standard form of memorandum to be adopted by a company. For example, Table B of the Companies (Table A–F) Regulations 1985 prescribes the form of memorandum for a private company, whereas Table F prescribes the form of memorandum for a public company. With the exception of certain compulsory clauses, the provisions contained within Table B and Table F are not mandatory.

Where a provision in a company's memorandum conflicts with one contained in the company's articles, then the provision in the memorandum will take preference: see e.g. *Welton v Saffery* [1897] AC 299. However, where a provision in a company's memorandum is unclear, reference may be made to the company's articles in an attempt to clarify the ambiguity. In accordance with s 2(7) of the Companies Act 1985, a company may not alter the conditions contained in its memorandum unless the purported alteration is permitted by a provision of the Companies Act 1985 (discussed below).

Compulsory clauses

Section 2 of the Companies Act 1985 provides that the memorandum of a company limited by shares must contain certain obligatory clauses. The obligatory clauses must include the following information:

(a) the name of the company (discussed further in Chapter 3);

(b) the situation of the company's registered office, i.e. whether the company is situated in England and Wales, or, specifically, Wales or Scotland. The exact address of the registered office does not need to be provided, only the jurisdiction;

(c) the objects clause of the company. The objects of a company state the business or other activities for which the company is incorporated (discussed in Chapter 7);

(d) that the liability of the company's membership is limited (s 2(3), CA 1985). The memorandum of a public company must specify that the company is a public limited company (s 1(3)(a), CA 1985);

(e) in the case of a company having a share capital, the company's memorandum must specify the amount of share capital with which it proposes to be registered and also the manner by which the share capital is to be divided into shares of a fixed amount (s 2(5), CA 1985). A subscriber to a memorandum must take at least one share in the company. The exact number of shares taken by a subscriber must be shown against the subscriber's name (s 2(5), CA 1985). In respect of a public limited company, s 11 of the Companies Act 1985 prescribes a minimum share capital requirement for the company. At present this figure is fixed at an amount of not less than £50 000 (s 118, CA 1985). (Share capital is discussed further in Chapters 9 and 10.)

The alteration of the compulsory clauses

A company may, where permitted, alter the compulsory clauses of its memorandum in the following ways:

(a) **Name**. A company may alter its name by means of a special resolution (s 28(1), CA 1985). It should be noted that a change in a company's name does not affect any rights or obligations incurred by the company whilst operating under its previous name: see e.g. *Oshkosh B'Gosh Inc v Dan Marbel Inc Ltd* [1989] BCLC 507 (discussed further in Chapter 3).

(b) **Jurisdiction**. The Companies Act 1985 does not contain any power to allow a company incorporated in one jurisdiction (for example, a company having its registered office in England and Wales) to move that office to another jurisdiction (for example, to move its registered office to Scotland). As such, if a company wished to move jurisdiction it would have to undertake the arduous task of having to completely re-register itself as incorporated within the new jurisdiction. However, it is to be noted that the government's White Paper, 'Company Law Reform', proposes to change this position (see clause A36).

(c) **Objects clause**. Section 4 of the Companies Act 1985 permits the members of a company to alter the company's objects clause by means of a special resolution. It should be noted that, by s 5 of the Companies Act 1985, a member who did not vote or consent to a resolution which seeks to alter the company's objects clause may, providing they hold at least 15 per cent of the nominal capital of the company, apply to the court to challenge the purported alteration. The court has the power to invalidate the alteration or accept it in whole or part.

(d) **Status.** Where a company acts in accordance with the relevant provisions of the Companies Act 1985, a company may change its status. A private company may become a public company and vice versa, etc. (discussed further in Chapter 5).

(e) **Share capital.** A company may alter its share capital in a number of ways. The methods and requirements for an alteration of a company's share capital are specifically dealt with in Chapter 10.

Alteration of other clauses within the memorandum

Except for the aforementioned powers to alter the compulsory clauses of its memorandum, or unless a power to alter a clause is specifically provided for by a distinct provision of the companies legislation, a company may not (subject to one exception) alter any clause within its memorandum. The stated exception is that any provision within the company's memorandum which could have been legitimately contained in the company's articles may, by virtue of s 17 of the Companies Act 1985, be altered by the passing of a special resolution. If a company seeks to entrench a clause that could have been validly contained in the articles within the company's memorandum and exclude the operation of s 17, it must specifically provide that the clause cannot be altered.

THE ARTICLES OF ASSOCIATION

A company's articles of association are primarily concerned with matters related to the internal affairs of the company. For example, a company's articles will normally contain clauses governing the regulation of general meetings (discussed in Chapter 21), the appointment, regulation and powers of company directors (discussed in Chapter 16), class rights attached to shares, share capital and dividends (discussed in Chapter 9).

Following a company's registration, the Registrar of Companies must be provided with a copy of the company's memorandum and articles. A company may register its own distinct set of articles (s 7, CA 1985) but if it chooses not to do so then, by s 8(2) of the Companies Act 1985, the company's articles will be determined by reference to the model form of articles found in Table A of the Companies (Tables A–F) Regulations 1985 (Table A articles). Where a company registers its own set of articles and a regulation is excluded by the articles but is contained within the Table A articles, reference will be made to the Table A articles to determine the absent matter.

Where a company adopts the Table A articles, the format of the Table A articles in force as of the date of the company's registration will regulate the company's internal affairs. Therefore, a company incorporated prior to 1985, having adopted Table A articles, will, unless the company has subsequently altered its articles, have articles based on the format of Table A of the 1948 Companies Act.

Any provision within a company's articles that is inconsistent with the memorandum of the company or the provisions of the Companies Act 1985 will be invalid. For example, in *Re Peveril Gold Mines Ltd* [1898] 1 Ch 122, the Court of Appeal held the terms of a company's articles to be invalid in so far as they provided specific conditions concerning a shareholder's ability to petition for the winding up of a company, conditions which were contradictory to those stipulated by ss 79 and 82 of the Companies Act 1862 (now governed by s 122, IA 1986).

THE WEIGHTED VOTING CLAUSE

Although a clause contained in a company's articles will be invalid where it seeks to override a provision of the companies legislation, it is nevertheless acceptable for a company to insert a clause into its articles for the purpose of enhancing the voting rights of any given member of the company in a specified situation. Accordingly, a weighted voting clause may, in a practical sense, be adopted to make it virtually impossible for a company to pass a resolution in accordance with a provision of the companies legislation.

The concept of the weighted voting clause was approved by the House of Lords in *Bushell* v *Faith* [1970] 1 All ER 53. This case involved a small domestic company with a membership comprised of a brother and two sisters; each member held 100 shares. After a series of disagreements between the members, an extraordinary general meeting was called whereupon it was proposed to remove the brother from his directorship of the company. After the meeting, the sisters claimed that the brother had been validly removed by a resolution that had polled 200 votes for dismissal as against 100. The brother disagreed on the basis that the articles of the company included a clause (Art 9) which provided:

> 'In the event of a resolution being proposed at any general meeting of the company for the removal from office of any director, any shares held by that director shall on a poll in respect of such resolution carry the right to three votes per share . . .'

Applying Art 9, the brother claimed that his sisters had failed to secure the vote to dismiss him, i.e. by 300 votes to 200. At first instance, Ungoed-Thomas J found that the brother had been validly removed by the resolution. Ungoed-Thomas J took the view that Art 9 was invalid, because it infringed the statutory power to remove a director by an ordinary resolution (a vote passed by a bare majority). However, both the Court of Appeal and House of Lords (Lord Morris of Borth-y-Gest dissenting) overruled the learned judge; the validity of Art 9 was upheld. In giving its approval to the weighted voting clause the House of Lords emphasised that, as the clause was solely concerned with the allocation of a company's voting rights and as Parliament had never sought to fetter the right of a company to issue a share with special rights or restrictions, it would be quite wrong for the courts to interfere in this matter.

Therefore, although a weighted voting clause may, in a practical sense, have the effect of restricting the ability of a company to pass a particular type of resolution, it does not offend against the terms of the companies legislation; a company's ability to exercise any statutory power by the passing of a requisite resolution remains unfettered – that is, theoretically, the company may still, by a requisite majority (either by ordinary or special resolution), pass the necessary resolution. Yet, the theory is overridden by the practical effect of the weighted voting clause. The effect of a weighted voting clause will, on a resolution to which the clause applies, prevent the requisite majority of votes being cast to pass the resolution. Only in a most bizarre case, where on a matter governed by the weighted voting clause, the holder of the clause decides to vote in agreement with the other voting members, will the effect of the weighted voting clause be defeated.

THE CONTRACTUAL NATURE OF SECTION 14

Section 14 of the Companies Act 1985 provides:

> 'Subject to the provisions of the [Companies] Act the memorandum and the articles when registered bind the company and its members to the same extent as if they respectively had been signed and sealed by each member, and contained covenants on the part of each member to observe all the provisions of the memorandum and of the articles.'

The wording of the current s 14 provision has undergone little transformation over the years; its wording may be traced back to the Companies Act of 1856. Prior to the Companies Act 1985, s 20 of the Companies Act 1948 adopted the exact same language now found in s 14. Although s 14 is applicable to both the memorandum and articles, the controversy surrounding its interpretation has largely been in respect of provisions contained within a company's articles. The controversy has been in relation to the extent by which the provision exerts a contractual agreement.

Although the wording of s 14 stipulates that the articles and the memorandum, when registered, bind the company and its members, the section only provides that the articles and memorandum are binding 'to the same extent as if they respectively had been signed and sealed by each member'. There is no mention of the fact that the company as a separate legal entity is bound as if it had signed and sealed the articles and memorandum. As such, the section fails to recognise the company's separate legal capacity to 'sign and seal' the memorandum and articles. One consequence of this statutory omission is that a debt due to the company from one of its members may be enforced as a specialty debt within a limitation period of 12 years, whereas a debt due from the company to one of its members will only be afforded a limitation period of six years: see e.g. *Re Compania de Electricidad de la Provincia de Buenos Aires Ltd* [1980] Ch 146.

Although the courts construe a company's articles as a commercial/business document (see e.g. *Tett v Phoenix Property Ltd* [1986] BCLC 149), it is clear from the reported cases that s 14 cannot be interpreted as conferring an equality of rights and obligations which one would normally expect to flow from the law of contract. Notwithstanding the 'business efficacy' rule the so-called 'statutory contract' embodied in s 14 is not liable to be set aside on the grounds of misrepresentation, mistake, undue influence or duress. Moreover, absent terms cannot be implied into the memorandum or articles.

For example, in *Bratton Seymour Service Co Ltd v Oxborough* [1992] BCC 471 a company involved in the management of a housing development which comprised a number of properties, sought rectification of an agreement (contained in the company's articles) by which an occupier of property within the developed site, a shareholder of the company, had agreed to contribute a pre-determined sum of money for the maintenance of specified parts of the common land attached to the developed property. The company claimed that the rectification of the agreement would accord with the true intentions of the parties, namely that the shareholder concerned should be liable to contribute to all parts of the common areas of the developed property and not just those areas of common land specified in the agreement. The Court of Appeal unanimously held that the rectification of the agreement would be inconsistent with the statutory nature of a company's articles. If the articles were to be rectified, then the alteration of the articles needed to be in accordance with the statutory procedure for alteration, namely in accordance with s 9 of the Companies Act 1985 (discussed below). Dillon LJ stated that:

> '... the articles of association of a company differ very considerably from a normal contract ... It is thus a consequence as was held by this court in *Scott* v *Frank F. Scott (London) Ltd* [1940] Ch 794, that the court has no jurisdiction to rectify the articles of association of a company, even if those articles do not accord with what is proved to have been the concurrent intention of the signatories of the memorandum at the moment of signature.' (at p 474)

In relation to the possibility of a court admitting intrinsic evidence to vary the terms of a company's articles, Sir Christopher Slade commented thus:

> 'If it were to be admissible, this would place the potential shareholders in a limited company, who wished to ascertain their potential obligations to the company, in an intolerable position. They are in my judgement entitled to rely on the meaning of the language of the memorandum and articles of association, as such meaning appears from the language used.' (at p 476)

However, it is to be noted that although intrinsic evidence cannot be admitted and absent terms cannot be implied into the memorandum or articles, in some cases terms may be so vague as to require 'interpretation' in a way which gives them sense and clarity: see e.g. *Folkes Group plc* v *Alexander* [2002] 2 BCLC 254.

Obligations enforceable by a company under section 14

Obligations contained within a company's articles that seek to regulate the relationship between the company and its membership are enforceable by the company. An oft-quoted illustration of this fact is provided by *Hickman* v *Kent and Romney Sheepbreeders Association* [1915] 1 Ch 881. The case involved a provision in the Association's articles which provided that disputes between the membership and the Association had to be referred to arbitration. It was held that a member of the Association was not entitled to commence court proceedings against the Association without first submitting the dispute to arbitration.

The case of *Borlands Trustee* v *Steel Bros* [1901] 1 Ch 279 provides another example of a company's ability to enforce the terms of the articles. In this case a provision in a company's articles stated that the company might at any time give notice to a member, not holding a senior management post in the company, whereby that member would be obliged to transfer ordinary shares to persons holding senior management posts. The court found that this provision was enforceable by the company as against any member of the company not holding a senior management post.

A company may also rely on provisions in its articles to deny the existence of an alleged internal contractual relationship. For example, in *Kerr* v *John Mottram Ltd* [1940] Ch 657 a member of a company sought specific performance against the company for the sale of shares, a sale which had apparently been agreed at an extraordinary meeting of the company. Nevertheless, as the minutes of the meeting failed to verify such an agreement it was held that the existence of the contract could be denied. This decision was justified on the basis that the articles of the company provided that the minutes of any company meeting would be conclusive evidence of the business of that meeting.

However, following the decision of His Honour Judge Weeks QC (sitting as a judge of the High Court) in *Exeter City AFC Ltd* v *The Football Conference Ltd & Anor* [2004] BCC 498, the line of cases (such as *Hickman* (above)) which suggest that there is an absolute requirement on the part of a member to abide by the terms of the articles (in favour of the company) must be subject to a major qualification; the qualification being that an arbitration clause, or any other type of restrictive clause contained within the articles, will not necessarily preclude a member of a company from commencing court proceedings to override the effect of the restrictive clause. However, for a member to succeed, the said proceedings must relate directly to the enforcement of a statutory right.

The *Exeter City* case concerned the financial decline of Exeter City AFC (E). E was a member of the Conference League (C) and the Football Association (FA). The said organisations were incorporated companies. E was insolvent and was made subject to a Company Voluntary Arrangement (CVA) (explained in Chapter 15). Under the terms of C's articles, E was compelled, in the repayment of its debts, to favour a particular set of creditors. If the said preferred creditors were paid in full, the FA and C had the right to exercise discretion in favour of the club to allow it to continue playing football in the Conference League. The said preferred creditors did not include the Inland Revenue, to which E was in debt. If E abided by the terms of the articles the Inland Revenue would not be paid the sums due and as such they sought to have the CVA revoked. However, if the CVA was revoked, E would be wound up. E therefore needed to resolve its predicament by attempting to escape from the requirements of the articles and did so by presenting a petition under s 459 of the Companies Act 1985 (see Chapter 24), alleging that the affairs of the C/FA were being conducted in a manner which was unfairly prejudicial to E's interests. The C/FA sought a declaration under s 9 of the Arbitration Act 1996 for a stay of the s 459 proceedings, to compel E to comply with the articles. In refusing to grant the stay, the learned judge concluded that both a right to petition to wind up a company and the right to present a petition under s 459 were statutory rights, conferred on every single shareholder. Compliance with such rights amounted to a condition of incorporation under the Companies Act 1985 and therefore outweighed any requirement on the part of E to, in this instance, be compelled by the terms of C's articles.

Obligations enforceable between members inter se

Although the obligations created by s 14 may be viewed as creating a quasi-contractual relationship between a company and its membership, s 14 fails to indicate whether obligations contained within the articles are directly enforceable between members *inter se*: can one member sue another to enforce an obligation? Indeed, on a literal construction of s 14, it would appear impossible to enforce obligations which affect the rights or liabilities of members *inter* se, other than in accordance with the internal management principle associated with the rule in *Foss* v *Harbottle* (see Chapter 23). Thus, the member would have to enforce the right against his/her fellow member through the company, and in effect the company would pursue the action on behalf of the member: see e.g. *MacDougall* v *Gardiner* (1875) 1 ChD 13. Accordingly, the wrong would only be corrected where the board of directors or a majority of the membership decided that the company should enforce the right. Support for the view that a member cannot directly enforce obligations against a fellow member is to be found in the *obiter* comments of Lord Herschell in *Welton* v *Saffery* [1897] AC 299. His lordship remarked:

> 'It is quite true that the articles constitute a contract between each member and the company, and that there is no contract in terms between individual members of the company; but the articles do not any less, in my opinion regulate their rights *inter se*. Such rights can only be enforced through the company.' (at p 315)

Despite such comments, in specific circumstances a member may be able to directly enforce obligations against a fellow member without the need to pursue the action through the company. The principal justification for allowing a membership action is that the company should not become involved in what would essentially be a dispute between its members; namely, the company should not be involved in unnecessary litigation. Support for this view may be found in cases where pre-emption rights have been enforced between members of a company. Pre-emption rights are those contained within a company's articles which provide that if a member wishes or is compelled to sell his shares, he/she must first offer them to existing members of the company: see e.g. *Rayfield* v *Hands* [1960] Ch 1.

However, it should be noted that membership disputes involving obligations which were created entirely outside the framework of the internal corporate relationship are not enforceable in accordance with s 14 in so far as such disputes are not concerned with the constitutional rights of the membership. For example, an obligation involving an independent trading transaction between two members of a company would not be enforceable, even in a situation where the purported dispute was regulated by the terms of the company's articles: see e.g. *London Sack & Bag Co Ltd* v *Dixon & Lugton Ltd* [1943] 2 All ER 767.

Obligations enforceable by the membership against the company

Much of the controversy associated with the interpretation of s 14 concerns the extent by which obligations, contained within a company's articles, may be enforced by the membership of the company against the company. If s 14 created a mutual set of contractual rights as between a company and its membership, it would follow that all the provisions of the memorandum and articles would be enforceable. However, as previously discussed, s 14 is peculiar in that its contractual effect is not in accordance with what one would normally expect to flow from the law of contract. In *Hickman* v *Kent and Romney Sheepbreeders Association* [1915] 1 Ch 881, Astbury J opined thus:

'The wording of [s 14, CA 1985] is difficult to construe or understand. A company cannot in the ordinary course be bound otherwise than by statute or contract and it is in this section that its obligation must be found. As far as the members are concerned, the section does not say with whom they are deemed to have covenanted, but the section cannot mean that the company is not to be bound when it says it is to be bound, as if etc., nor can the section mean that the members are to be under no obligation to the company under the articles in which their rights and duties as corporators are to be found. Much of the difficulty is removed if the company be regarded, as the framers of the section may very well have so regarded it, as being treated in law as a party to its own memorandum and articles.' (at p 897)

While the courts' interpretation of s 14 limits the enforcement of rights conferred on the membership of a company, the exact scope of this limitation is unclear. Nevertheless, one class of obligation for which there is no dispute as to a member's right of enforcement is the class of obligations regarded as pure membership or insider rights. Such rights are common to all the members of any given class of shares. Examples of insider rights include:

- the right of a member to insist that, once a company has declared a dividend, the dividend should be paid in accordance with the terms of the articles (see e.g. *Wood v Odessa Waterworks Co* (1889) 42 ChD 639);

- the ability of a member to enforce a right to a share certificate (see e.g. *Burdett v Standard Exploration* (1899) 16 TLR 112);

- on the winding up of a company, after the company has paid its creditors, a member's right to a return of capital (see e.g. *Griffith v Paget* (1877) 6 ChD 511) (note that a class of preferential shareholders may have priority to a return of capital over other shareholders: see Chapter 9);

- on a valid transfer of shares, the right of a member to have his/her name entered in the register of members (see e.g. *Re British Sugar Refining Co* (1857) 3 K & J 408).

Another commonly perceived example of an insider right is the entitlement of a member holding voting shares in a company to exercise his or her vote at company meetings in any way and for whatever purpose he or she so chooses. The leading authority on the enforcement of the right to vote at a company meeting is *Pender v Lushington* (1870) 6 ChD 70. In this case the articles of a company, the Direct United States Cable Co Ltd, restricted the total voting rights available to its members to the extent that for every ten shares held, a member was entitled to one vote. Irrespective of the number of shares held, no member was entitled to more than 100 votes. The plaintiff (Pender) transferred a number of his shares in the company to nominees who were to use the voting rights attached to support a resolution that would have had the effect of indirectly benefiting the interests of a rival company in which Pender had a substantial interest. In so transferring the shares, Pender would ensure that many more than the 100 votes he was personally entitled to would be cast in favour of the resolution. At the meeting at which the relevant motion was to be voted on, the chairman of the company disallowed the votes of Pender's nominees with the result that the resolution was lost. The Court of Appeal held that the votes attached to the shares of the nominees had been improperly rejected. Jessel MR was of the opinion that:

'In all cases of this kind, where men exercise their rights of property, they exercise their rights from some motive adequate or inadequate, and I have always considered the law to be that those who have the rights of property are entitled to exercise them whatever their motives may be for such exercise.' (at p 75)

While the ability of a member of a company to exercise a right to vote is an example of an obligation which the courts will normally enforce in accordance with s 14, a view confirmed by the House of Lords in *Carruth* v *Imperial Chemical Industries* [1937] AC 707, it should be noted that a member's entitlement to enforce a right to vote may be lost where a resolution to which the vote relates is concerned with a matter of internal procedure, as opposed to a substantive issue affecting the constitutional rights of the membership. For example, in *MacDougall* v *Gardiner* (1875) 1 ChD 13, a company meeting was held with a view to the plaintiff proposing a motion to dismiss the company's chairman. The company's deputy chairman presided over the meeting and accepted a vote on the show of hands (one vote per member) to have the meeting adjourned. As a result of the proposed adjournment, the plaintiff demanded a poll (recorded vote entitling votes to be cast in accordance with the number of shares held). Although the plaintiff demanded the poll in accordance with the terms of the company's articles, the poll on the motion to adjourn the meeting was refused.

In refusing to accept that the plaintiff had been wrongly denied the right to a poll vote, the Court of Appeal emphasised that the plaintiff's action was concerned with an internal procedural irregularity of the company. The procedural wrong (decision to refuse a poll vote) was a wrong committed against the company and not an infringement of the plaintiff's personal rights of membership. The court considered the action to have been ill conceived. Baggallay LJ remarked:

'I apprehend that it is not the practice of the court to make declarations of so utterly useless a character as is here asked.' (at p 27)

Although the Court of Appeal clearly rejected the plaintiff's claims, in doing so it surely ignored the underlying principle at issue in the case: namely the ability to enforce the right to vote in accordance with the terms of a company's articles. Had the poll vote been concerned with the actual motion to dismiss the chairman, as opposed to a motion to adjourn the company meeting, it is most likely that the outcome of the case would have been a different one. The decision in *MacDougall* v *Gardiner* may be a dangerous precedent to follow in that it most certainly distorts the protection of a basic membership right, the right to vote (but note that the decision in *MacDougall* was followed in *Cotter* v *National Union of Seamen* [1929] 2 Ch 58).

Perhaps an even more exceptional example of the court's ability to refuse a member's entitlement to vote is to be found in *Standard Chartered Bank* v *Walker* [1992] BCLC 603. In this case the court was asked to grant an injunction to restrain a member (W) from exercising his right to vote on a motion that had two linked purposes. The member held a substantial but nevertheless minority holding in a public limited company. The first purpose of the motion was to enable a consortium of banks to instigate a rescue package on behalf of the company; the second sought to remove W from his directorship of the company. The two purposes were advanced as one motion; therefore, if the first purpose failed, so would the second, and *vice versa*. As it was almost certain that W would use his votes to block the ordinary resolution required to pass the two-part motion, the court, casting off its normal reluctance to involve itself in the internal management of a company, granted an injunction to prevent W from exercising his right to vote.

Although the court's decision may be defended on the premise that the grant of an injunction served to protect the very existence of the company, for without the rescue package the continued existence of the company would have been unlikely, it is difficult, if not impossible, to reconcile the decision with the principles enunciated in *Pender* v *Lushington*.

Unenforceable membership rights

Although obligations contained in the memorandum or articles and identified as 'insider rights' or 'pure membership rights' are enforceable by the membership of a company, other obligations relating to members' rights are generally regarded as unenforceable; such rights are referred to as 'outsider rights'. Outsider rights are obligations that do not correspond to the collective constitutional rights of any given class of shareholder. Nevertheless, an 'outsider right' may be indirectly enforceable in a situation where the enforcement of that right occurs as a consequence of the enforcement of an 'insider right' or directly enforceable in a situation where the outsider right is supported by an independent contract (i.e. other than the statutory contract represented by s 14). It should also be noted that while an 'outsider right' is not directly enforceable in accordance with s 14, the 'outsider right' may nevertheless constitute what is termed a membership interest and as such may, if it is infringed, permit an action under s 459 of the Companies Act 1985 (see Chapter 24).

The acceptance of the generally held view that an 'outsider right' is not enforceable in accordance with s 14, owes much to the comments of Astbury J who, in *Hickman* v *Kent and Romney Sheepbreeders Association Ltd* [1915] 1 Ch 881, laid down three principles of law which he considered governed the provision. These principles have been quoted with approval in many subsequent cases in which the issue of 'outsider rights' has arisen: see e.g. the Court of Appeal's application of the said principles in *Beattie* v *E & F Beattie Ltd* [1938] Ch 708 at p 714. To return to the comments of Astbury J, he stated:

'First that no articles can constitute a contract between the company and a third person; secondly, that no right purporting to be given by an article to a person, whether a member or not, in a capacity other than that of a member, as for instance a solicitor, promoter, director, can be enforced against the company; and thirdly, that articles regulating the rights and obligations of the members generally as such do create rights and obligations between them and the company respectively.' (at p 900)

The inspiration for the above comments may be found in cases such as *Eley* v *Positive Government Security Life Insurance* (1876) 1 ExD 88 and *Browne* v *La Trinidad* (1877) 37 ChD 1. In *Eley*, the articles of the company provided that the plaintiff (E) was to be appointed as the company's solicitor for the duration of his life. E was also a member of the company. The Court of Appeal held that E could not enforce the right to lifelong employment as the company's solicitor because the obligation to maintain E in that position was one which did not affect the constitutional rights of the shareholding body; the obligation was unrelated to rights commonly held by the members of the company.

In *Browne* v *La Trinidad*, the plaintiff (B) made an agreement that was incorporated into the company's articles, whereby, in consideration for the sale of his property to the company, B would become a member of the company and would also be appointed as a director of the company for a minimum period of four years. Although, in accordance with the terms of the sale transaction, B was appointed to a directorship in the company (B never became a member of the company), B was removed from his directorship before the minimum specified period had expired. The Court of Appeal held that, even if B had become a member of the company, the right to hold a directorship was not a right common to the membership; rather it was an outsider right and as such was unenforceable (see also *Re Tavarone Mining Co* (*Pritchards case*) (1873) 8 Ch App 956).

The indirect enforcement of 'outsider rights'

A person who is not a member of a company will not have any right to enforce obligations contained within s 14. Clearly there is no privity of contract between a company and a non-member of the company and, although the general law of privity has been significantly altered by the Contracts (Rights of Third Parties) Act 1999, s 14 of the Companies Act 1985 is specifically excluded from the ambit of the 1999 Act. Therefore, an obligation contained within the memorandum or articles which purportedly confers some form of right on a non-member of the company will be unenforceable. However, where a member of the company holds the 'outsider right', the right, whilst unenforceable in respect of the generally accepted interpretation of s 14 may, in certain circumstances, be held to be indirectly enforceable.

In decided cases where outsider rights have been indirectly enforced, the right in question has usually been one associated with the management functions of a company: for example, the right may be associated with the powers and functions of an organ of the company (the board of directors or the general meeting) or a constituent part of an organ of the company. For example, in *Quinn & Axtens* v *Salmon* [1909] AC 442, a member and managing director of a company successfully enforced a term of the company's articles associated with the exercise of rights attached to the office of the company's joint managing directors. The facts of the case were as follows. The company's articles provided that any one of the two appointed managing directors of the company could, in certain circumstances, veto a decision of the company's board of directors. In accordance with the terms of this provision, the plaintiff sought to exercise his right of veto. The veto was ignored by the company, as a result of which the plaintiff sought an injunction to prevent the company from acting otherwise than in accordance with its articles. The managing director pursued the matter as a member of the company (*qua* member) and succeeded in obtaining the injunction. The House of Lords, affirming the decision of the Court of Appeal, held that the company, in seeking to discard the obligation, was in effect attempting to bypass rules on the decision-making process of the company in a manner which would have had the effect of altering the articles contrary to the statutory procedure (i.e. by the passing of a special resolution (see s 9, CA 1985)). It should be emphasised that the enforcement of the managing director's right was pursued *qua* member, for, in accordance with s 14, only a member of the company may enforce the rights contained within the articles.

Other case examples which illustrate the indirect enforcement of outsider rights include *Pulbrook* v *Richmond Mining Co* (1878) 9 ChD 610 and *Imperial Hydropathic Co* v *Hampson* (1882) 23 ChD 1. In both these cases the articles of the relevant companies contained provisions that sought to restrict the ability of the company to dismiss its directors. In both cases the Court of Appeal held that the restrictions were enforceable by the directors, suing in their capacity as members of their respective companies. (Note that these cases were decided prior to the implementation of s 303, CA 1985 which precludes any constitutional fetter on the general meeting's right to pass an ordinary resolution to remove a director. However, also note that a director of a private company may still be entitled to relief, *qua* member, where the court considers his/her dismissal to have been unfairly prejudicial: see s 459 of CA 1985, discussed in Chapter 24.)

A more modern example of the indirect enforcement of an 'outsider right' may be found in *Rayfield* v *Hands* [1960] Ch 1. Here, Vaisey J held that a member of a company was allowed to enforce a provision of the company's articles that compelled the directors of the company to purchase the member's shares. Vaisey J held that the directors, whilst in a strict sense outsiders, were, as members of the company, bound by the provisions of the articles. (See also *Re Harmer* [1958] 3 All ER 689, where the directors of a company, in pursuing an action as members of the company, obtained a remedy for oppression under s 210, CA 1948.) (Note that this provision is now represented by s 459, CA 1985.)

Academic theories that have sought to explain the cases involving an enforcement of an outsider right, have resulted in three different lines of thought. The three theories may be identified in the following manner:

Theory A

A member of a company has the right to enforce any obligation contained within the company's memorandum or articles irrespective of whether the right is an 'insider' or 'outsider right'. However, the member must sue *qua* member.

Theory B

A member of a company has the right to enforce any obligation contained within the company's memorandum or articles, irrespective of whether the right is an 'insider' or 'outsider right'. However, the member must sue *qua* member and the enforcement of the obligation must constitute something more than the enforcement of an internal irregularity.

Theory C

A member of a company has the right to enforce obligations contained within the company's memorandum or articles. Nevertheless, where the member seeks to enforce an 'outsider right' he can only do so where he sues *qua* member and where the right is essential to the proper functioning of the company or an organ of the company. The right in question must relate to the ability of a company to function within the constitutional framework of its own regulations and regulations imposed upon it by statute.

It should be made clear that any attempted reconciliation of the academic theories in relation to outsider rights is a difficult, if not improbable, task. It must be remembered that the case law in relation to s 14 is, to say the least, often obscure, portraying a level of inconsistency which stems from the very nature of a provision that fails to specify the extent of its contractual effect. However, it is submitted that a common factor in seeking to explain those cases in which outsider rights have been enforced is the fact that the so-called outsider right has been construed as an essential constituent of a pure membership right. Such an explanation is more akin to Theory C (outlined above). Take *Eley* v *Positive Government Security Life Insurance* (1876) 1 ExD 88, for example: although those who support Theory A or B (see above) would contend that the outsider right in question, the right belonging to the company's solicitor, was unenforceable because it was not pursued *qua* member, it is submitted that a more logical explanation for the failure to enforce the article was because the right could not be related to one commonly held by the membership; the right belonged to the solicitor in a personal capacity. By contrast, in *Quinn & Axten* v *Salmon* [1909] AC 442, the failure to enforce the managing director's power of veto would have affected a membership right ('insider right'), namely to have the business decisions of the company dealt with in accordance with the terms of the company's articles to the extent that, if the right had not been enforced, the terms of the company's articles may have been flaunted in a manner which would have affected the rights of the entire membership.

Proposals for future reform

In June 2001, the CLR issued its final consultation report. The 'Final Report' followed on from a series of consultation documents issued by both the CLR and the Law Commission. In the context of a company's constitution, the 'Final Report' largely accepted the recommendations of its earlier (1999) consultation document, 'Modern Company Law for a Competitive Economy – Company Formation and Capital Maintenance'. On the whole, and unless otherwise indicated, the recommendations have been adopted into the government's White Paper (2005) (following on from the White Paper (2002)). The White Paper's (2005) proposals are as follows:

● The White Paper 2005 retains the concept of the memorandum and articles, albeit the significance of the former (see Chapter 3) is significantly reduced, to the extent that, in effect, the company's constitution will be determined by the terms of the company's articles. Indeed, clause A27 of the White Paper (2005) provides that provisions that would have previously been included in the memorandum (other than those contained in clause A8 of the White Paper, discussed in Chapter 3) are taken to have been transferred to the articles. Prior to the White Paper (2005) it had been proposed that for companies formed under the new legislation, the memorandum and articles should be abandoned in favour of a single constitutional document, albeit that the document would broadly have corresponded to the current format of the company's articles.

- In accordance with para A18 of the White Paper (2005), the current Table A will be subject to substantial modification (confirming the recommendations of the earlier 2002 White Paper at clause 2.4 and the CLR). It is proposed that distinct model articles will be drawn up for both public and private companies. An illustrative draft of the model articles for private companies was alluded to in Part 8 of the White Paper (2005). The illustrative draft is constructed in a far less detailed and complex manner than the current Table A articles; no doubt with the intention of promoting a more accessible and less regulatory system for both the shareholders and directors of private companies.

- The White Paper (2005), in approving the recommendations of the earlier White Paper (2002) and the CLR's Final Report, provides that the membership of a company will be permitted to entrench specified provisions of the company's articles by, for example, requiring that specific clauses may only be changed by the unanimous consent of the members or a percentage of members greater than that required for a special resolution.

- The White Paper (2005) provides that in relation to registering details concerning share capital, the same will no longer need to incorporate an authorised share capital clause.

- Companies will still be obliged to register an objects clause which will be contained in the company's articles (see para A39, White Paper 2005). However, the objects of the company will not restrict the company's contractual capacity in the company's dealings with third parties (discussed further in Chapter 7). It is to be noted that the 'trading certificate' requirements will still apply for public companies.

- In accordance with the recommendations of the CLR's Final Report (clause 7.34) it was suggested that the effect of s 14 of the Companies Act 1985 should, in its application to the constitution of a company, be given full contractual force in a manner favoured by Theory B (discussed above). Further, members of a company would be capable of enforcing the terms of the constitution against fellow members. It is interesting to note that the findings of the Final Report were quite contrary to those of an earlier Law Commission report (1997, Report No 246); a report which recognised the potential problems associated with the interpretation of s 14, but one which considered that no real hardship was being caused by the provision (at p 105). It is submitted that the CLR's proposals are to be favoured in so far as the quasi-contractual nature of the current s 14, although having generated much academic interest and debate, is unnecessarily obscure and complicated. Indeed, it is suggested that to permit the contractual relationship so favoured by the CLR would in fact accord with the true and intended spirit of s 14. However, despite the welcomed recommendations of the CLR, it is to be noted that the White Paper (2005) intends to make no specific reform in the context of the contractual effect of the current s 14 (see clause A40).

THE POWER TO ALTER A COMPANY'S ARTICLES

By s 9(1) of the Companies Act 1985, a company may alter a provision in its articles by passing a special resolution, namely by a three-quarters majority vote of those members who are entitled to vote at general meetings. Alternatively, if Table A articles are adopted (Table A 1985, art 53), the articles of a company may be altered by the written consent of all the shareholders without the need to convene a company meeting to pass the requisite special resolution (see *Cane* v *Jones* [1981] 1 All ER 533). Indeed, even if Table A, art 53 is not adopted, then, as a result of the introduction of s 381A of the Companies Act (introduced by the Companies Act 1989), it is now permissible for a private company to pass any form of resolution, to include one which purports to alter a company's articles, by way of a written resolution (discussed further in Chapter 21). It is to be noted that the White Paper (2005) suggests, in terms of future reform, that the membership of a company should be permitted to entrench specified provisions of the company's articles by, for example, requiring that specific clauses may only be changed by the unanimous consent of the members or a percentage of members greater than that required for a special resolution.

A company may not alter its articles where the effect of the alteration would be inconsistent with the terms of the company's memorandum or with a provision of the companies legislation. For example, in accordance with s 16 of the Companies Act 1985, a company may not, without the prior consent of its members, alter the terms of its articles (or memorandum) to increase its members' liability (also note the restrictions on a company's ability to alter the class rights of its members (see Chapter 9)). Therefore it follows that any regulation or article of a company, which seeks to fetter a company's ability to alter its articles in accordance with the statutory power of alteration, is invalid. In *Allen* v *Gold Reefs of West Africa* [1900] 1 Ch 656, Lindley MR stated that:

> 'The company is empowered by the statute to alter the regulations contained in its articles from time to time by special resolution and any regulation or article purporting to deprive the company of this power is invalid on the ground that it is contrary to statute.' (at p 671)

Determining a valid alteration

To alter a company's articles, the alteration must comply with requirements formulated by the courts to safeguard minority interests. As such, an alteration of a company's articles must not be retrospective in its effect: see e.g. *Swaeby* v *Port Darwin Mining Co* (1899) 1 Meg 385. Here, the Court of Appeal held that the directors of the company could not, by a subsequent alteration to the articles, be deprived of fees already earned by them under the terms of the company's original articles.

Of more general significance is the rule which requires an alteration of a company's articles to have been made *bona fide* for the benefit of the company as a whole. This rule is necessary to prevent a three-quarters majority of the membership adopting an article by which the majority could seek to gain an advantage, at the expense of the minority of the membership. At first sight this rule may be seen as an exception to a basic principle of company law, namely that a shareholder should be able to exercise his vote in the manner he/she pleases. However, strictly speaking, the rule does not curtail this basic principle; it does, however, enable the court to challenge a vote when its outcome is considered to be contrary to the interests and benefit of the company as a whole.

The exact meaning of the term 'the benefit of the company as a whole', in respect of its relevance to determine the validity of an alteration of a company's articles, is unclear. As it may be difficult to measure benefit in relation to the company as a commercial entity, one isolated from the interests of those persons who actively participate in the company's business affairs, a more realistic interpretation of the term 'the benefit of the company as a whole' may be to consider the interests of 'the shareholders as a whole'.

To determine whether an alteration of a company's articles is *bona fide* for the benefit of the company, the courts have generally adopted a two-part test. The first part of the test is subjective and seeks to determine whether a three-quarters majority of shareholders, in seeking an alteration to the terms of a company's articles, did so with the honest belief that the alteration would benefit the company as a whole (benefit the shareholders as a whole). The second part of the test is objective in nature and requires the court to consider whether the alteration of the company's articles was undertaken in good faith without any intention of producing a discriminatory effect on minority interests. Due to the general reluctance of the courts to interfere in the business decisions of a company other than where there is an obvious instance of bad faith, the majority of the decided cases emphasise the importance and predominance of the subjective element of the test: see e.g. *Shuttleworth* v *Cox Bros & Co Ltd* [1927] 2 KB 9 and *Rights & Issues Investment Trust Ltd* v *Stylo Shoes Ltd* [1965] 1 Ch 250.

While the effect of an alteration to a company's articles may cause some disadvantage to minority interests, disadvantage in itself is not sufficient to warrant a declaration that the alteration was invalid. For example, in *Allen* v *Gold Reef* [1900] 1 Ch 656, the articles of a company were altered to allow the company to have a 'first and paramount lien' for debts owing by any member of the company upon all shares held in the company. Prior to the alteration the lien extended only to shares that had not been fully paid up. In fact, the alteration of the company's articles affected only one member of the company, the said member being the only holder of fully paid up ordinary shares. The Court of Appeal upheld the validity of the alteration on the grounds that it was beneficial to the company as a whole. Although the practical effect of the alteration was to disadvantage a single shareholder, the alteration did not, in a theoretical sense, have a discriminatory effect, given that its terms applied equally to all members who held fully paid up ordinary shares.

In applying the objective part of the test, the court must divorce itself from a consideration of the personal motives which may have influenced a three-quarters majority of the membership to accept the proposed alteration. The court must weigh up the advantages and disadvantages of the alteration and in doing so consider the effect of the alteration in relation to the rights of those who claim to have been prejudiced. However, the court must balance the interests of the minority against the potential benefit which the alteration may have been calculated to have on the company as a whole. An example of the factors to be considered in the application of the objective test is found in *Greenhalgh* v *Arderne Cinemas* [1951] Ch 286, where Evershed MR stated that:

'. . . the case may be taken of an individual hypothetical member and it may be asked whether what is proposed is, in the honest opinion of those who voted in its favour, for that person's benefit.' (at p 291)

Evershed MR went on to state that the alteration would be impeached if:

'. . . the effect of it was to discriminate between the majority shareholders and the minority shareholders, so as to give the former an advantage of which the latter were deprived.' (at p 291)

However, the above interpretation of the objective test is not without a fundamental flaw, namely, its application would be highly improbable in a situation where a company's membership was split between two opposing factions of the company's membership – that is, where there was no middle ground, no hypothetical member. (By analogy, see *Clemens* v *Clemens Bros Ltd* [1976] 2 All ER 268, discussed in Chapter 21.)

In cases where the courts have applied objective considerations to adjudicate upon a proposed alteration of a company's articles, the alteration has been set aside on the premise that its intended effect was aimed at producing an inequitable division in rights as between holders of the same class of shares. For example, in *Dafen Tin Plate* v *Llanelly Steel Ltd* [1920] 2 Ch 124, a company altered its articles to give members who held a majority stake in the company an absolute right to purchase the shares of any minority shareholder. The reason for the alteration was to prevent a minority shareholder, who had transferred business interests to one of the company's competitors, from retaining his membership of the company. Whilst the motive behind the alteration may have been for the benefit of the commercial entity, the terms of this alteration were too wide. The alteration had the effect of permitting members holding a majority stake to expel a minority shareholder without valid excuse.

The above case may be contrasted with *Sidebottom* v *Kershaw, Leese & Co* [1920] 1 Ch 154, where the alteration of a company's articles was deemed valid notwithstanding that its effect was also to allow the directors of the company to purchase the shares of any member of the company. However, unlike *Dafen Tin Plate*, the amended article expressly specified that the purchase of a member's shares could only take place in a situation where a member carried on a competing business.

A further case example of the court invalidating a proposed alteration of a company's articles is *Brown* v *British Abrasive Wheel* [1919] 1 Ch 290. Here, the company sought to alter its articles to compel a minority holding of two per cent to sell its shares to a group of majority shareholders who held the remaining 98 per cent of shares in the company. The reason for the proposed alteration was to encourage the majority to inject more capital into the company with the objective of saving the company from liquidation: the majority shareholders had promised to inject the necessary capital providing the minority were compelled to sell their shares. Astbury J held the alteration to be unjust, the learned judge commenting as follows:

'I find it very difficult to follow how it can be just and equitable that a majority, on failing to purchase the shares of a minority by agreement, can take power to do so compulsorily.' (at p 297)

While the alteration may have been unfair in relation to the interests of the minority, it is nevertheless questionable whether the potential survival of the company was, in this instance, more important than the interests of a very small minority holding (by analogy, see e.g. *Standard Chartered Bank* v *Walker* [1992] BCLC 603).

Finally, it should be noted that, where an alteration of a company's articles results in a membership interest being subjected to unfairly prejudicial conduct, it may be preferable for the member to pursue an action under s 459 of the Companies Act 1985 (see Chapter 24). By analogy, it is interesting to note that the Privy Council, in *Caratti Holding Co Pty Ltd* v *Zampatti* (1978) 52 ALJR 732, held that a clause in a company's articles which permitted a majority shareholder to purchase the shares of a minority shareholder at par value, when the share value was greatly in excess of the par value, was oppressive to the minority's interest (dealt with under a provision akin to s 459, CA 1985). Indeed, a minority shareholder's task of seeking to establish grounds for an action for unfairly prejudicial conduct may be a less daunting proposition than attempting to substantiate a finding that the alteration of articles was not conducted *bona fide* for the benefit of the company as a whole.

ENFORCEABLE OBLIGATIONS, WHICH FALL OUTSIDE THE SCOPE OF SECTION 14 OF THE COMPANIES ACT 1985

Directors' service contracts

A member of a company (or indeed a non-member) may enter into a separate enforceable contractual agreement with the company, the terms of which would have been unenforceable as outsider rights had they been included within the company's memorandum or articles. A typical example of a separate enforceable contractual agreement which, had it been contained within the company's articles, would have been viewed as giving rise to outsider rights, is a director's service contract. An independent service contract will allow a director to pursue an independent claim for damages in a situation where the company breaches the terms of the agreement. It should be noted that where a director's service contract is silent as to a specific matter (for example, the length of the service contract), the relevant term may be implied into the independent service contract if it was included within the company's articles (see e.g. *Re New British Iron Co, ex parte Beckwith* (1898) 1 Ch 324 and *Read* v *Astoria Garage (Streatham) Ltd* [1952] Ch 637).

It should be observed that the appointment of a person to a directorship is not, in itself, evidence of an independent contract between the director and company (see e.g. *Newtherapeutics Ltd* v *Katz* [1991] Ch 226), although upon being appointed to a directorship, the newly appointed director will be bound by the provisions of the company's memorandum and articles even where the director is not a member of the company: see e.g. *Re Anglo Austrian Printing & Publishing Union* [1892] 2 Ch 158, where Bowen LJ stated:

'. . . the company puts forward the terms of the articles as the terms by which it will be bound; and the director by becoming and acting as a director of the company accepts that position.' (at p 168)

In circumstances where a director has a separate service contract and terms of the company's articles are impliedly incorporated into the service contract, a valid alteration of the company's articles will have the effect of altering the implied terms of the service contract, therefore, the new terms of the articles will be impliedly incorporated into the director's service contract. For example, in *Shuttleworth* v *Cox Brothers & Co Ltd* [1927] 2 KB 9, the company's articles provided that its directors were to be appointed for life unless they were disqualified from holding office in any one of six prescribed ways. The company's articles were subsequently altered by adding a seventh and more general discretionary power of removal. A director, to whom the seventh condition was applied, sought a declaration that the alteration was invalid in so far as it had a retrospective effect on the terms under which he was appointed to hold office. In upholding the company's ability to invoke the seventh condition and thereby dismiss the director, the Court of Appeal concluded that the new condition had been validly introduced to alter the articles (by special resolution) and therefore governed the terms of the director's service contract; the director had no grounds for complaint. While giving the appearance of a retrospective alteration, here the alteration had not (as, for example, in *Swaeby* v *Port Darwin Mining* Co) sought to deprive the director of an existing and specified right but rather sought to expand upon the pre-existing conditions for the dismissal of all directors.

Where, however, a director's service contract expressly contains terms which are also included within the company's articles, an alteration of the articles will not have the effect of altering the terms contained within the director's service contract. In such a case the terms of the service contract remain separate and severable from those contained within the altered articles.

Remedies for a breach of an independent contract

Where the terms of an independent contract seek to exclude the company from exercising a statutory power (for example, the alteration of the company's articles), can a company breach the agreement and impugn the existing contractual obligation? Should an agreement purporting to exclude the company from exercising a statutory power be declared invalid, or should the agreement be valid only to the extent that a breach of its terms will render the company liable to a claim in damages? Alternatively, is it possible to restrain a company, by means of an injunction, from acting in accordance with the terms of a statutory power where to do so would place it in breach of the terms of the independent contractual obligation?

In seeking to answer the above questions, first, it is important to stress that a company cannot include a term in its articles which would allow it to forgo its right to alter its articles. However, other than where a statutory power (see e.g. s 303, CA 1985) specifically provides that its effect cannot, in any way, be impugned by the articles or **otherwise** (i.e. by a separate contractual agreement), it would appear legitimate for an independent contractual agreement to include a provision which purports to restrain a company from exercising a specified statutory power. For example, an independent contractual agreement could legitimately provide that the company is prohibited from altering a term of its articles: see e.g. *Punt* v *Symons & Co Ltd* [1903] 2 Ch 506.

However, will a breach of the contractual agreement give rise to the usual remedies associated with a breach of contract? In *Punt* v *Symons & Co Ltd*, the remedy for the breach of the agreement was restricted to a claim for damages. Nevertheless, in *Baily* v *British Equitable Assurance Co* [1904] 1 Ch 374, the Court of Appeal, in distinguishing *Punt* v *Symons & Co Ltd*, implied that the remedy for a breach of such an agreement should not be so restricted. Cozens-Hardy LJ stated:

> '... It would be dangerous to hold that in a contract of loan or contract of service or contract of insurance validly entered into by a company there is any greater power of variation of the rights and liabilities of the parties than would exist if, instead of the company, the contracting party had been an individual. A company cannot by altering its articles, justify a breach of contract.' (at p 382)

Although the decision of the Court of Appeal was subsequently overturned by the House of Lords ([1906] AC 35) on the basis that there was not in fact a contractual agreement to the effect that the company would not alter its articles, it is to be observed that the House of Lords did not seek to challenge the findings of the Court of Appeal in respect of its conclusions relating to the effect and consequences of a breach of the independent contract. Indeed, the Court of Appeal's findings were followed in *British Murac Syndicate* v *Alperton Rubber Ltd* [1915] 2 Ch 168, where an injunction was granted to prevent a proposed alteration of a company's articles.

However, in *Southern Foundries Ltd* v *Shirlaw* [1940] AC 701, the House of Lords came to the conclusion (albeit in *obiter* comments) that an injunction should not be granted to prevent a company from altering its articles, notwithstanding that the company would be in breach of a contract by acting on new articles; a breach which could, however, be remedied by an award of damages. Indeed, it is submitted that the approach adopted in *Southern Foundries* represents the correct interpretation of the consequences attached to a breach of a contractual agreement which purports, by implication, to preclude a company from exercising its right to exercise a statutory power. Accordingly, a company should not be prevented from breaching the contractual obligation in that it should not be prohibited from acting in accordance with a statutory power, a power of which the other contracting party should be aware. Nevertheless, a company should not be allowed to breach a contractual obligation without fear of the imposition of some form of penalty: it should in such a case be made liable to a claim in damages.

MEMBERSHIP AGREEMENTS

In addition to those terms of a company's articles which purport to regulate the relationship of members *inter se*, the shareholders of a company may lawfully bind themselves by way of an independent membership agreement, to act or vote in a specific way on issues governed by the terms of the agreement: see e.g. *Greenhalgh* v *Mallard* [1943] 2 All ER 234.

A membership agreement is a common feature in small private companies and usually purports to bind the entire or a substantial majority of the existing membership of the company. The agreement seeks to regulate matters of internal management with the effect that members who are a party to the agreement agree to act and vote on specific issues in a predetermined way (see *Breckland Group Holdings Ltd* v *London & Suffolk Properties* [1989] BCLC 100, discussed further in Chapter 22).

Although an effective membership agreement (i.e. one which comprises a majority of the company's membership) affords a degree of certainty as to the outcome of issues governed by the terms of the agreement, the terms of a membership agreement may prove to be a handicap where, for example, a member, as a party to the agreement, refuses to sanction/vote on a motion to pursue a matter that would otherwise contradict the terms of the agreement. For example, with the passage of time, a majority of members who are party to a membership agreement may consider that a term contained therein should no longer be pursued, thereby rendering it essential to dispense with its continued adoption. However, if just one member who is a party to the agreement disagrees, it may be possible for that member to enforce compliance with the disputed term by way of an injunction, a situation that could clearly be contrary to the company's interests.

The effectiveness of a membership agreement, in terms of its ability to influence the outcome of any given vote, will clearly be dependent on the number of members who are bound by its terms. Problems relating to the validity of a membership agreement may arise in a situation where the vast majority of a company's membership are bound by an agreement, the effect of which may, in practice, effectively prevent the company from exercising statutory powers: for example, the statutory power to alter the terms of its articles by the passing of a special resolution, or the removal of a director by the passing of an ordinary resolution.

In *Russell v Northern Bank Development Corporation Ltd* [1992] 1 WLR 588, the House of Lords upheld the validity of a membership agreement by which all five (current) members of the company were bound. The five shareholders contracted in a membership agreement to refrain from voting to increase the company's share capital, save in a situation where all parties consented in writing to the increase. When, subsequently, the board of the company proposed a motion to increase the company's issued share capital, one of the members challenged the motion's validity on the premise that to vote in favour of it would contradict the terms of the membership agreement. The four shareholders who were in favour of the motion counter-claimed for a declaration that the membership agreement was invalid because its effect was to restrict the company from exercising a statutory power to create further capital.

The power to alter the company's memorandum, in respect of the company's capital clause, was governed by Art 131(1) of the Companies (Northern Ireland) Order 1986 (a copy of s 121(1), CA 1985). In accordance with this statutory power the company was permitted to alter its share capital if it was authorised to do so by the terms of its articles. Article 1 of the company's articles adopted the regulations contained in Part II of Table A in Sch 1 to the Companies Act (Northern Ireland) 1960. Regulation 44 of Table A (a copy of reg 32 of Table A Companies (Tables A–F) Regulations 1985) provided that the company could increase its share capital by means of an ordinary resolution.

Although the House of Lords, overruling the decision of the Court of Appeal (MacDermott LJ dissenting) [1992] BCLC 431, recognised that the membership agreement would have been invalid if it had been contained in the company's articles, it formed the opinion that the agreement was separate and distinct from the company's articles (confirming the view expressed by MacDermott LJ in the Court of Appeal). The membership agreement was construed as one of a purely personal nature. Lord Jauncey, expressing the unanimous opinion of the House, quoted with approval (at p 593) a passage from Lord Davey's judgment in *Welton v Saffery* [1897] AC 299, namely:

> 'Of course, individual shareholders may deal with their own interests by contract in such a way as they may think fit. But such contracts, whether made by all or some only of the shareholders, would create personal obligations, or an *exceptio personalis* against themselves only, and would not become a regulation of the company, or be binding on the transferees of the parties to it, or upon new or non-assenting shareholders.' (at p 331)

However, in so far as the membership agreement sought to bind the company (the company was also a signatory to the agreement), the House held the agreement to be as obnoxious as if contained in the company's articles. The company had in effect agreed not to exercise its statutory powers for a period that would last for so long as any of the members who were a party to its terms remained shareholders of the company. Nevertheless, as the membership agreement between the company's shareholders was found to be independent and severable from the purported agreement with the company, the agreement, in so far as it affected the rights of the shareholders *inter se*, was held to be binding. Further, the House of Lords confirmed that an injunction could be sought as a remedy to a purported breach of a membership agreement (contrast *Southern Foundries Ltd* v *Shirlaw* [1940] AC 701, discussed above).

The significance of the decision of the House of Lords in *Russell v Northern Bank Development Corporation Ltd* should not be underestimated. Although a company or the future membership of the company is not bound by the membership agreement (however, future members could sign up to the agreement), the practical effect of the House of Lords' decision is one which restricts the company, through the membership, from acting in accordance with its statutory powers. While the fetter on the company's ability to act in pursuance of a statutory power is of a temporary nature, that is, for so long as those party to the agreement commanded a sufficient majority of votes, the effect of the obstruction distorts the intention of the relevant companies legislation, a result which shares some similarity with the application of a *Bushell* v *Faith* weighted voting clause (discussed above). A motion to pass a resolution or an act that is contrary to the terms of a membership agreement should be agreed upon by all who are a party to the agreement. However, note that the resolution or act may succeed without any formal consent where, in applying the *Duomatic* principle (see Chapter 21), all of the members who are party to the agreement informally agree that it should so succeed: see e.g. *Euro Brokers Holdings Ltd* v *Monecor (London) Ltd* [2003] BCC 573.

Therefore, the inherent danger of the decision in *Russell* is that it opens up the possibility of a member, a party to the membership agreement, seeking an injunction to prevent other members of the agreement acting in accordance with the requirements of a statutory power. Indeed, the statutory framework within which companies operate may be rendered subservient to the terms of a membership agreement. Moreover, in an extreme case, a company may become a slave to the terms of a membership agreement thereby existing in an isolated independence from the statutory framework into which it was born. Finally, it is submitted that a far more logical, albeit more passive, remedy for a breach of a membership agreement would be for an aggrieved shareholder to pursue an action for damages or seek some other form of redress under s 459 of the Companies Act 1985 (discussed in Chapter 24).

Finally, it may be implied from *Exeter City AFC Ltd* v *The Football Conference Ltd & Anor* [2004] BCC 498 (discussed above) that a distinct contractual agreement between the members of a company cannot, however, exclude the right of a member to exercise his/her statutory right to present a winding up petition or petition for relief under s 459 of the Companies Act 1985 (i.e. seeking relief for conduct unfairly prejudicial to his/her membership interests: see Chapter 24). In effect, where the terms of a membership agreement attempts to exclude a member's aforementioned statutory rights, then, while technically the pursuit of the statutory right may breach a term of the membership agreement, the term of the membership agreement, in so far as it seeks to restrict the statutory right of the member, would be deemed redundant. Also consider *Union Music Ltd & Anor* v *Watson & Anor* [2004] BCC 37, discussed in Chapter 21, where it was held that the court's power to call a company meeting pursuant to s 371 of the Companies Act 1985 could not be disturbed by the terms of a shareholder agreement.

However, should not the breach of the membership agreement still give rise to an independent claim for damages by that part of the membership which seek compliance with the term that offended the statute? By analogy, consider those cases in which damages have been awarded in circumstances where a company breaches a contractual obligation with a third party by, for example, exercising the statutory power to alter the terms of its articles: see e.g. *Southern Foundries Ltd* v *Shirlaw* [1940] AC 701 (discussed above).

Suggested further reading

The contractual effect of s 14, CA 1985

Theory A

Gregory (1981) 44 MLR 526

Theory B

Wedderburn [1957] CLJ 194 and [1958] CLJ 93

Theory C

Goldberg (1972) 35 MLR 362 and (1985) 48 MLR 158

Prentice (1980) 1 Co Law 179

Alteration of articles

Rixon (1986) 86 MLR 446

Independent contracts and membership agreements

Sealy [1992] CLJ 437

Davenport (1993) 109 LQR 553

Shapira (1993) 109 LQR 210

Griffin [1993] NLJ 589

Savirimuthu (1993) 14 Co Law 137

Riley (1993) 44 NILQ 34

Ferran [1994] CLJ 343

McGlynn (1994) 15 Co Law 301

5

THE CLASSIFICATION AND STRUCTURES OF COMPANIES AND OTHER TYPES OF BUSINESSES

INTRODUCTION

This chapter examines the various types and structures of corporate entities and the rules applicable to altering the corporate status of a company. The relationship between a holding company and its subsidiaries – the group relationship – is also investigated. The chapter also undertakes a brief analysis of various types of business structures other than that represented by the registered company. The chapter concludes by considering proposals to reform the structures of private companies.

CORPORATE STRUCTURES

Although registered companies make up only about 40 per cent of the UK's population of business structures (when combined, partnerships and sole traders are by far the most common form of business medium) the registered company, incorporated following compliance with the registration procedures laid down by the Companies Act 1985 (or previous Companies Acts), is the standard and most common type of corporate entity. While s 716 of the Companies Act 1985 provides that a company may be formed in pursuance of an Act of Parliament (other than by the Companies Act 1985) or, alternatively, by royal charter, today the latter two methods of incorporation are rarely adopted. Companies granted corporate status by royal charter are normally institutions with either charitable aims or objectives relevant to the public interest: for example, the British Broadcasting Corporation (BBC).

Registered companies

A company registered in accordance with the provisions of the Companies Act 1985 will take one of the following forms:

- a public company limited by shares;
- a private company limited by shares;
- a private company limited by guarantee; or
- a private company that is unlimited.

Prior to 22 December 1980, it was possible to register a fifth type of company, namely a private or public company limited by guarantee and with a share capital. While it is no longer possible to register this type of company (see s 1(4), CA 1985), a company registered prior to 22 December 1980, as a company limited by guarantee and with a share capital, may still operate in that form.

Public companies limited by shares

A company which proposes to operate as a public company must, as from 1980, be specifically registered as a public limited company. A public company must have at least two shareholders and two directors; a private company need only have one shareholder and one director. Before a public company can trade it must be registered with a minimum share capital (currently £50 000).

Prior to 1980, a company was classified as a public company if (a) it had a membership in excess of 50, (b) the general public could subscribe for its shares, and (c) no restriction was placed on the transferability of its shares. The pre-1980 position, which had survived since the Companies (Consolidation) Act 1908, was altered by the Companies Act 1980, which implemented the EC Second Company Law Directive. The Directive, which was adopted on 13 December 1976, established a requirement to create a formal distinction between the identification of public and private companies. As a result of the implementation of the Directive, a public company must be identified (at the end of its name) as a public limited company ('plc' will suffice).

In accordance with s 1(3) of the Companies Act 1985, any company which is not registered as a public company is construed to be a private company. Unlike a private company, a public company may offer its securities to the general public. Whilst a public company is entitled to offer its securities to the general public, it is not bound to do so, but, where its shares are so offered, it has the option of applying to have them listed for dealing on the stock exchange (see Chapter 11). Unless a public company registers a specific distinct form of articles, they will take the form of the Table A articles prescribed by the Companies (Tables A–F) Regulations 1985. A public company's memorandum should follow the format of Table F of the Companies (Tables A–F) Regulations 1985.

Private companies limited by shares

Private companies limited by shares represent the vast majority (approximately 98 per cent) of all limited companies registered in the UK. Many private limited companies are small concerns and the shareholders of such companies are often the major participants in the management of the company. These small concerns may usually be classified as domestic/family type companies and/or companies formed as a result of the incorporation of a small unincorporated business. The relationship between the shareholders of a small private company may ordinarily be viewed as one built upon mutual trust and confidence and with this in mind the courts have, where applicable, developed flexible attitudes in the application of company law to small private companies. The said attitudes are positively influenced by equitable considerations and are closely related to partnership law principles.

Although the vast majority of private companies are small concerns, there is no legal compulsion on the part of a successful private company to re-register itself as a public company. Indeed, the shareholders of a large and successful private company may wish to retain its private limited liability status in order to exert control and influence over the company's destiny, rather than risking the possibility of losing a controlling interest in the company by altering its status to that of a public limited company. Unlike a public company, a private company cannot offer its securities to the general public (s 81, CA 1985).

The format of a private company's articles will usually follow (but they are not compelled to) the statutory prescribed format of Table A of the Companies (Tables A–F) Regulations 1985. A private company's memorandum should follow the format of Table B of the Companies (Tables A–F) Regulations 1985.

Private companies limited by guarantee

While the vast majority of private limited companies are limited by shares, a private company may be limited by guarantee. With a private company limited by guarantee the company's memorandum will provide that the members of the company will be liable to contribute a fixed sum of money, the amount guaranteed (usually a nominal sum, e.g. £1) towards the debts of the company, should the company be wound up. A member's fixed sum liability cannot be altered and continues during the term of the membership of the company or, where the company's liquidation occurs, within a year of the member having left the company (see s 2(4) of the CA 1985 and s 74(2) of the IA 1986).

The form of articles and memorandum adopted by a company limited by guarantee is prescribed by Table C of the Companies (Tables A–F) Regulations 1985. With a company incorporated before 1980, the company may have been incorporated with a share capital, in which case the form of articles and memorandum is prescribed by Table D of the Companies (Tables A–F) Regulations 1985. The most appropriate type of company to be registered as a private company limited by guarantee is one with a charitable or non-profit-seeking objective, such as a local club or association. Ordinarily the company will not have any shareholders and therefore any profits made by the company will not be distributed as dividend payments. The members' capital (amount of guarantee) is kept in reserve and may be called upon in the case of the company's liquidation. Unlike the uncalled share capital of a company limited by shares, the sums of money guaranteed from the company's members are not deemed to be assets of the company and therefore cannot be used as a means to repay or secure any of the company's debts.

A company limited by guarantee is not compelled to include the word 'limited' after its name if it satisfies s 30 of the Companies Act 1985, in which case it will also be exempt from having to send lists of members to the Registrar of Companies. To be exempt under s 30, a company must have issued a statutory declaration to the effect that it is a private company limited by guarantee with objects that promote commerce, art, science, education, religion, charity or any type of profession. The company's constitution must state that any profits, or any other income, will be used to promote the company's objects and not be paid to members. Further, it must state that if the company is wound up, its assets will not be divided amongst its members but instead be transferred to another body or organisation having similar objects.

The unlimited company

The unlimited company is a separate legal entity; it is a private company and possesses the characteristics of a corporate entity. While an unlimited company may have a share capital (here the company's articles and memorandum is prescribed by Table E of the Companies (Table A–F) Regulations 1985) the members of an unlimited company do not have the advantage of limited liability.

In many respects an unlimited liability company will be regulated by the companies legislation in a manner akin to a limited liability company. However, while unlimited companies must, as with limited companies, prepare accounts for the benefit of their members, they are not required to file the accounts at Companies House, save in a situation where the company is a subsidiary of another company that has a limited-liability status. Further, because the members of an unlimited company are ultimately responsible for the debts of the company, should it be wound up, an unlimited company is not to be subject to the rules and disclosure requirements in respect of the maintenance of share capital.

A private unlimited company is similar to a business partnership concern. However, unlike a partnership, the creditors of an unlimited company cannot ordinarily sue the company's individual members for the repayment of business debts. In order to compel members of an unlimited company to contribute towards the payment of the company's debts, it is necessary for the creditors of the company to seek an order for the company to be wound up.

On the winding up of an unlimited company, the members' contribution towards the repayment of the company's debts will be in accordance with the terms of the company's memorandum or articles. Where the memorandum or articles have not specified a procedure for such contributions, calls are made equally upon all the contributories; if a member cannot meet the terms of his contribution, the other members of the company will be obliged to make good this loss.

TYPES OF COMPANIES

Single member companies

The Companies (Single Member Private Limited Companies) Regulations 1992 (SI 1992/1699) came into force on 15 July 1992 to comply with the EC Twelfth Company Law Directive, which was adopted on 21 December 1989. The regulations give effect to the birth of the single member private limited company. At present, the single member may be either a natural person or a legal person, that is, the single member may be a corporate entity. The regulations provide that, in the absence of any express provision to the contrary, any enactment or rule of law applicable to a private company limited by shares or guarantee which has two or more members, will apply with such modification as may be necessary for companies formed by one person or with only one person as a member (reg 2(1)).

Although Art 2(2) of the Directive makes provision for individual member states to lay down special regulations or sanctions to prevent the possible abuse of the single member company as a corporate form, the UK has thus far decided against imposing regulatory conditions, save for the provision that a single member company may not be registered as a public company. However, government proposals contained in the White Paper, 'Company Law Reform' (2005) (together with the prior recommendations of the (2002) White Paper, 'Modernising Company Law', and the proposals of the Company Law Review's (CLR) Final Report, 'Modern Company Law for a Competitive Economy'(2001)), propose to allow the incorporation of a single member public company.

The community interest company

Following on from a government consultation exercise launched in 2002, a new type of company, the 'community interest company' (CIC), was created by Part II of the Companies (Audit, Investigations and Community Enterprise) Act 2004. The Act received Royal Assent on 28 October 2004 with the main provisions on CICs intended to be brought into force on 1 July 2005. The government's intention in introducing the CIC is to increase (although not necessarily replace) the existing forms of social enterprises such as charitable companies and industrial and provident societies, with an ultimate objective of expanding and improving the transparency of the social enterprise sector. The government fears that without the CIC the sector may be unable to achieve sustainable financing and therefore the flexibility of the company form will hopefully improve this condition and encourage and reassure investors that their investments will be used for the good of the community.

CICs will largely be regulated by the companies legislation but are tailored to the needs of non-profit social enterprises and are to be placed under the supervisory control of an independent Regulator. Social enterprises which are expected to consider becoming CICs include those geared to promoting public services: e.g. providers of community care services. However, s 35(2) of the 2004 Act provides a rather general definition, namely:

> 'A company satisfies the community interest test if a reasonable person might consider that its activities are being carried on for the benefit of the community.'

As CICs are formed as limited companies (by shares or guarantee) they will take the benefits of a limited liability status but, as with any other type of limited company, they will be subject to the disclosure and reporting requirements imposed by the Companies Act 1985. Unlike existing registered charities, CICs will not to be afforded any special tax concessions, a fact that may deter many organisations from choosing this type of business structure. In addition to complying with the usual registration requirements for a limited liability company, a CIC must comply, and continue to comply during its lifetime, with specific 'community interest rules'. For example, a CIC must:

- Ensure that profits or financial assets are not ordinarily distributed to its members or investors during its lifetime and on winding up. A CIC may issue shares upon which a capped dividend may be paid, the capped amount to be decided by the CIC Regulator.
- Together with the annual accounts, a CIC must submit an annual 'community interest report' to the CIC Regulator. The community interest report must give a detailed account of the activities the company has undertaken in pursuit of its community interest objectives.

At first sight, the creation of the CIC would appear to be an admirable social objective. The government's desire to promote, help and expand a sector of the community that is primarily concerned with serving the public interest should be applauded. However, although an admirable objective, is the creation of the CIC really the way forward? The existing voluntary organisations and charities already have established structures, rules and levels of transparency which, although not perfect, are surely as effective as those represented by a limited liability company. While the government intends to expand the social enterprise sector it is conceivable that the promotion of the 'implied competition' within the sector may in fact dilute the numbers and diversity of existing voluntary organisations. Indeed, does the creation of this new form of 'business' warrant an annual expenditure by the government (taxpayers) relating to the administration and regulation of the CIC, of an estimated £500 000 (figure based on government calculations)? Clearly the answer to this question will depend upon the success of the CIC and its general effect on the stability of the social enterprise sector.

The open-ended investment company

In accordance with s 262 of the Financial Services and Markets Act 2000 (superseding the Investment Companies with Variable Capital Regulations 1996 (SI 1996/2827), which came into force on 6 January 1997) it is possible to create what is termed an open-ended investment company (OEIC). The purpose of this type of company is strictly limited. Members purchase shares in the OEIC, which is then responsible for managing a portfolio of investments on their behalf. An OEIC may issue more than one class of share and it is possible for the shares to be traded on an investment exchange. The shareholders of an OEIC are permitted to request that their shares be redeemed or purchased by the OEIC at a fair price calculated in accordance with the amount of shares held in proportion to the then value of assets held.

The partnership company

Partnership companies are defined by the Department of Trade and Industry (DTI) as private or public companies that share a common characteristic of having employees who hold a substantial proportion of the company's shares. The DTI considers that the meaning of the term 'substantial holding' should vary from company to company, albeit that it should constitute a shareholding of at least 15 per cent. Provision will be made for such a company under s 8A of the Companies Act 1985 (inserted by s 128, CA 1989). Under s 8A(1), the Secretary of State will, by regulation, be able to prescribe a Table G containing articles of association applicable to a partnership company although Table G will be optional.

OTHER FORMS OF BUSINESS STRUCTURES

The limited liability partnership

Legislation to establish a new business structure, the limited liability partnership (LLP), was passed in the form of the Limited Liability Partnership Act 2000 (supplemented by the LLP Regulations 2001). The Act was brought into force on 6 April 2001. This new business structure is applicable to a business which wishes to retain the benefits of trading as a partnership but at the same time wishes to take advantage of a limited-liability status.

In accordance with the draft Bill (published in 1998) the ability to create a limited liability partnership had been restricted to specific regulated professions such as firms of accountants and solicitors, the same having championed the cause for the creation of LLPs as a means of protecting the personal assets of partners from an increasing number of litigation claims in relation to alleged malpractices in the performance of their professional services. However, the said restriction was waived; the 2000 Act is potentially applicable to all business partnerships comprising two or more members.

The LLP is a distinct legal entity, a body corporate (s 1(2), LLP Act 2000). Accordingly, its members have no personal liability for the acts or obligations of the LLP except as provided by statute or under the general law. Therefore, where an LLP becomes insolvent, its assets and not those of its members will be used to discharge its debts. A member will have no liability to contribute to the repayment of the debts of the LLP save where the member had previously agreed to contribute a guaranteed amount. The members, as agents of the LLP (s 6(1), LLP Act 2000), owe duties to the LLP of a type and nature similar to those owed by the directors of registered companies and minority members will be able to avail themselves of provisions such as s 459 of the Companies Act 1985.

Yet, an LLP is taxed as a partnership and not as a company and its internal structure remains more identifiable with a traditional partnership: for example, it has no share capital and therefore a member's income is not in the form of dividend payments. As an LLP has no share capital it is not subject to the capital maintenance rules. Although an LLP has no memorandum or articles of association akin to those of a registered company, it is obliged to register an incorporation document which in effect is similar in content to a company's memorandum, although without the inclusion of an objects clause. Therefore, absent of an objects clause, an LLP has an unlimited capacity to enter into a contract or other transaction (s 1(3), LLP 2000). Further, although absent of a set of formal articles in the manner prescribed for a registered company, the members of an LLP are obliged to enter into an LLP agreement, the purpose of which is to regulate the relationship between the members and the LLP and the rights of the members *inter se* (s 5(1), LLP 2000).

The price to be paid for an LLP taking the benefits of a limited-liability status relates to compliance with the requirements and safeguards of the companies legislation, compliance in a manner akin to that of a registered company. Accordingly, financial and other information will need to be filed on a regular basis: for example, an LLP will be obliged to file accounts, an annual return with the Registrar of Companies and a register of charges will need to be kept. Further, the delinquent activities of members of the partnership are subject to similar sanctions to those imposed against company directors: for example, wrongful and fraudulent trading and disqualification (discussed in Chapters 18 and 19). In respect of wrongful trading it is to be noted that s 214A of the Insolvency Act 1986 (introduced by the 2001 Regulations) is specific to an LLP. This provision provides a liquidator with the right to 'claw back' **any** withdrawals of assets from the LLP which were made by a member(s) within the two years prior to the commencement of liquidation in a situation where the member(s) knew or had a reasonable ground to believe that at the time of withdrawal, or as a consequence of the withdrawal, the LLP was unable to pay its debts and as such the member(s) knew or ought to have concluded that there was no reasonable prospect of the LLP avoiding liquidation.

In effect the LLP is a version of a registered company in all but name and absent of a share capital, a version which has been expensively tailored to suit the needs and requirements of a small group of professionals with perhaps an objective more inclined to the protection of the interests of the said professionals than the general public interest. The advantage of the limited-liability status of an LLP, together with the possible taxation advantage to its members, may make this form of business medium a highly attractive proposition, especially with those firms who can afford the compliance costs of the legislation and who view themselves to be most at risk from potential litigation claims.

Business partnerships

A business partnership is a relationship between persons carrying on a business in common with a view to profit (s 1, Partnership Act 1890). With a partnership business, the property of the business belongs to its members and not the actual partnership business. A partnership, unlike a registered company, is not a separate legal entity, although it may sue or be sued using the partnership name. Although the Limited Partnership Act 1907 allows a member of a partnership to attain a limited-liability status, a partner with such a status is precluded from taking an active role in the management of the partnership firm and therefore, other than for a 'sleeping' partner, the 1907 Act will have little application. Unlike a registered company, a partnership is contractually bound by an agreement entered into on its behalf by any of its members. For a company to be bound by a contractual relationship, its agents must have been authorised to act by the company's board of directors (see Chapter 8).

In contrast to a company, a partnership does not have perpetual succession. A partner's interest in the partnership business is a property right and, whilst this right may be transferred, the transferee will not be admitted as a member of the partnership firm without first obtaining the consent of the partnership's existing members. The acceptance of a new member into the partnership will have the theoretical effect of dissolving the old partnership, that is, by creating a new one. Where a member leaves a partnership, the retiring member (or his estate) must be paid his share of the partnership business. Again, the partnership in such a case will theoretically be dissolved, although in practice the partnership will, with the consent of the remaining partners, continue its existence.

In an attempt to raise finance, a partnership may seek contributions from its partners in a manner acceptable to all of the partnership members. A partnership may raise funds from outsiders and the partners acting collectively may give security for loans in the form of the partnership's assets. It must be noted that a partnership's ability to grant security over its assets is subject to statutory restrictions that prevent individuals and partnerships from creating floating charges over fluctuating assets (the nature of a floating charge is discussed in Chapter 13). Partnerships are further handicapped in respect of raising finance in so far as the majority of business partnerships are permitted to have 20 members only. Exceptions to this rule do exist: the exceptions include firms of solicitors and accountants (see s 716, CA 1985).

One of the principal advantages of forming a partnership business as opposed to the creation of a registered company is that a partnership business does not have to comply with the many formalities required of a registered company. However, it should be noted that the current trend in legislative policy, aimed towards the deregulation of private companies, may weaken the partnership's advantage in respect of the formality rules.

Reform

In November 2003, following a consultation exercise, the Law Commission and Scottish Law Commission published a final report relating to the reform of partnership law (Cm 6015, Law Com No 283). The report recommended that there should be a new Partnership Act, with a principal objective of creating partnerships as distinct legal entities, a reform aimed at removing the rigidity and potential complexity arising from a change(s) in the constitution of the partners of a firm. The report also recommended that the Act should provide a code (similar in objective to Table A, Articles for registered companies), the terms of which would be applicable to the internal governance of partnerships but subject to an individual partnership's ability to vary the terms of the code. In May 2004, the Department of Trade and Industry issued a further consultative document in respect of the Law Commission's proposals for the reform of partnership law.

EUROPEAN STRUCTURES

The Sócietas Europaea

As a result of EC Regulation (2157/2001) (and its supplementing Directive (2001/86)), legislation to create a new European Company structure (the Sócietas Europaea (SE)) was introduced into the UK by the European Public Limited-Liability Company Regulations 2004 (SI 2004/2326) which came into force on 8 October 2004. The idea behind the creation of the European company was originally conceived in the late 1960s with a draft statute proposing the creation of an SE first adopted by the EC Commission in 1989.

The SA is an available corporate vehicle for at least two commercial bodies with operations in more than one member state. An SE may be created as a European public limited liability company registered in one of the member states, provided it has a minimum share capital of €120 000. The SA will be governed by the terms of the regulation and more especially the applicable corporate laws of the member state in which it is registered. If registered in the UK, the SA will therefore be governed by the terms of the regulation but will primarily be regulated by the UK companies legislation as applicable to plcs.

Although the commercial bodies involved in forming an SE must ordinarily have their registered offices in the EU, there is an option in the regulation under which their head offices need not be in the EU provided there is a real and continuous link with a member state's economy. The UK has taken advantage of the said option. There are five ways in which a SE may be created, namely:

- *By merger*: Two or more public limited companies or existing SEs may merge to form an SE provided at least two of them are governed by the laws of different member states.

- *A holding SE*: Two or more private or public limited companies (including existing SEs) may form an SE by promoting the formation of a holding SE. The companies promoting the formation must become majority-owned by the SE. At least two of the companies must be governed by the laws of a different member state, or for two years have had a subsidiary company governed by the laws of another member state or had a branch in another member state.

- *A subsidiary SE*: Two or more companies, firms or other legal bodies formed under the law of a member state may form an SE by subscribing for its shares. At least two of the companies or firms must be governed by the laws of a different member state or for two years have had a subsidiary company governed by the laws of another member state or had a branch in another member state.

- *Subsidiary SE formed by another SE*: An existing SE may itself form another SE as a subsidiary company, in which it may be the sole shareholder.

- *Plc transforming to become an SE*: An existing plc registered in the UK may transform itself into an SE registered in the UK if the plc has for two years had a subsidiary governed by the laws of another member state. This process does not involve the winding up of the plc or the creation of a new legal person in the form of an SE.

Providing an SE has been registered for at least two years, it may, with the approval of its general meeting (by the passing of a special resolution), convert itself to become a plc.

An SE may operate under either a one-tier or two-tier management system; in the UK that system will typically be the one-tier system. Under the one-tier system a board of directors will manage the SE. By contrast, in the two-tier system (e.g. in Germany) a secondary board supervises the work of the principal management board (a system of internal governance). However, the supervisory board does not exercise management powers.

The creation of the SE is perhaps more a success in terms of its political as opposed to practical achievement. Its birth has been time-consuming, bureaucratic and expensive, taking over 30 years to reach a somewhat tepid goal.

European Economic Interest Groupings

The 1985 EC Regulation No 2137/85, allows UK businesses, corporate or otherwise, to enter into an agreement of cooperation with a business or businesses in other member states. An agreement of this nature creates a European Economic Interest Group (EEIG). The purpose in creating the EEIG system was to facilitate cooperation between businesses located in different member states. The businesses, which together form an EEIG, become its members although an EEIG may not exert control over the business activities of any individual member of its EEIG grouping. An EEIG has a separate legal personality but, unlike a registered company, the members of the EEIG are liable for the EEIG's debts: that is, it does not possess a limited-liability status. An EEIG cannot invite investment from the public.

The registration documentation of an EEIG must include objects which seek to promote economic cooperation between its members, although an EEIG must not, in its individual capacity as a separate legal entity, seek to make a profit. An EEIG is not required to have a share capital nor does it need to file annual accounts or reports. Where an EEIG is registered in the UK, the UK companies legislation, in so far as it is applicable to the EEIG, will regulate its affairs (see the European Economic Interest Grouping Regulations 1989 (SI 1989/638)).

GROUPS OF COMPANIES

Although each individually registered company is a separate legal entity, responsible in law for its own actions and liable for its own debts, it is quite a common feature of the UK's corporate structure to find companies which are tied to a group structure. At the head of the group of companies will be the holding company. A company which is directly or indirectly under the control of the holding company is termed a subsidiary company. The importance of the holding company/subsidiary relationship is apparent in a number of provisions contained within the Companies Act 1985 and related legislation. Where appropriate, such provisions will be considered within individual chapters of this book.

A holding company/subsidiary relationship is legally defined by s 736 of the Companies Act 1985 (as amended by s 144, CA 1989). Section 736(1) provides that a company is a subsidiary of a holding company if:

- the holding company holds a majority of the voting rights in the company; or
- the holding company is a member of the company and has the right to appoint or remove a majority of the company's board of directors; or
- the holding company is a member of the company and controls alone or in agreement with other shareholders or members of the company, a majority of the voting rights in the company.

In addition, a company will be classed as a subsidiary of a holding company where that company is a subsidiary of another company that is itself a subsidiary of the holding company. For example, company A will be a subsidiary of company Y where company A is a subsidiary of company B which is itself a subsidiary of Y. A company is classed as a wholly owned subsidiary of another company if its shares are exclusively owned by the holding company and/or the subsidiaries of the holding company, or persons acting on behalf of the holding company and/or its subsidiaries (s 736(2), CA 1985).

For the purposes of s 736(1), s 736A(2) of the Companies Act 1985 provides that, in calculating voting control, the 'voting rights' are those rights held by the shareholders (or members where a company does not have a share capital) in relation to their ability to vote at general meetings on all or substantially all matters. The right to appoint or remove a majority of the directors in accordance with s 736(1) is defined by s 736A(3) as the right to appoint or remove directors holding the majority of voting rights at board meetings on all or substantially all matters. A company is treated as having the right to appoint a person to a directorship (of the subsidiary) if the appointment necessarily follows from that person's appointment as a director of the company, or where the company itself holds the directorship.

The amendments made to s 736 by the Companies Act 1989 have rightly transformed the emphasis for determining the existence of a holding company/subsidiary relationship away from a previous reliance on whether control existed as a consequence of a holding company holding more than a 50 per cent share of another company's equity share capital. Prior to the amendment of s 736, the holding company/subsidiary relationship could have existed in a situation where the holding company did not have voting control in the subsidiary: that is, whilst holding more than 50 per cent of a company's equity share capital, the equity share capital of the company may have been divided into shares carrying different voting rights to the extent that a 50 per cent holding of the share capital did not necessarily equate to a 50 per cent control over voting rights. Conversely, a company, prior to the amendment to s 736 could have escaped being classed as a holding company by holding less than 50 per cent of the company's share capital, notwithstanding that it may still have controlled the company's voting rights. Thus, the amended s 736, in its adoption of voting control as the principal criteria to determine the holding company/subsidiary relationship, is more realistic in its approach to determining the question of control. (It should be noted that under s 736B, CA 1985, the Secretary of State has a power to amend ss 736 and 736A, CA 1985.)

The membership of a holding company

A subsidiary or a subsidiary's nominee is not permitted to be a member of its holding company and any allotment of shares to the subsidiary from its holding company will be void (see s 23(1), CA 1985, introduced by s 129, CA 1989). The general prohibition contained in s 23(1) is, however, subject to the following exceptions:

- a subsidiary which was a member of its holding company on 1 July 1948 is permitted to continue as a member of the holding company;

- a company which was not a subsidiary of any other company prior to the enactment of s 144 of the CA 1989 but which, as a result of s 144, is now classed as a subsidiary company, may also retain its membership of its holding company;

- s 23(1) of the CA 1985 is not applicable where the subsidiary or its nominee holds shares in the holding company in the capacity of a personal representative or trustee. However, this exception will not apply where the holding company or subsidiary has a beneficial interest under the trust (s 23(2), CA 1985). An interest in the holding company's shares, held only by way of security for the purposes of a transaction entered into by the holding company or subsidiary in the ordinary course of business, which includes the lending of money, will be disregarded for the purposes of determining whether the holding company or subsidiary is beneficially interested;

- the general prohibition contained in s 23(1) does not apply where the subsidiary is concerned as a market maker. A market maker is a person who holds himself out and is permitted by a recognised investment exchange, other than an overseas investment exchange, as willing to buy and sell securities in accordance with the rules of the exchange (s 23(3), CA 1985). It should be noted that as a consequence of the Companies (Membership of Holding Company) (Dealers in Securities) Regulations 1997 (SI 1997/2306) market makers have, in respect of the Stock Exchange Electronic Trading Service (SETS), been replaced by 'intermediaries' for the purpose of buying and selling shares in an electronic order facility. The effect of the amendment will allow intermediaries who are owned by financial institutions to deal in the securities of their parent company.

It should be noted that, where a subsidiary remains a member of its holding company, it will not be permitted to vote at general meetings or at separate class meetings of the holding company.

Accounting purposes

For auditing and accounting matters the definition of a group of companies is dealt with by s 258 of the Companies Act 1985 (introduced by s 21, CA 1989). The statutory requirement for a holding company to produce group financial statements has been in force since 1947. The requirement is necessary to produce a true and accurate financial overview of companies which, whilst independent entities, are nevertheless closely related and under the influence of a dominant company. Prior to the implementation of s 258, the legislature made no distinction between the definition of a holding company/subsidiary relationship for the purpose of group accounts and the definition of a group relationship for other purposes. A distinction was required as a result of the UK's need to comply with the EC Seventh Company Law Directive, which was adopted on 13 June 1983 and implemented into UK law by the Companies Act 1989. The distinction was thought necessary in order to widen the criteria by which companies could be made responsible for the preparation of group accounts in situations where a company exerted a dominant influence over another business enterprise.

In accordance with s 258, a group relationship is now defined as a parent/subsidiary relationship. While the parent business must be a corporate entity, the subsidiary may be any form of 'undertaking', corporate or otherwise. Section 258 is framed in similar terms to s 736 of the Companies Act 1985, save that it provides additional criteria by which a parent/subsidiary relationship is to be established. In addition to the definitions found in s 736, s 258 provides that a parent/subsidiary relationship exists where a company has the right to exercise a dominant influence over another company by virtue of provisions contained in the other company's memorandum or articles or by virtue of a control contract (s 258(2), CA 1985). The section also defines the existence of a parent/subsidiary relationship in circumstances where a company has a participating interest in another company and actually exercises a dominant influence over that other company, or where both companies are managed on a unified basis (s 258(4), CA 1985). A participating interest will ordinarily amount to a holding of at least 20 per cent of the shares of an undertaking (s 260(3), CA 1985).

Where a parent/subsidiary relationship exists, the group accounts must, as a result of s 227(2) of the Companies Act 1985, be in a consolidated form. The parent company is also obliged to produce its own individual accounts in addition to consolidated group accounts (see Sch 4A, CA 1985). It is to be noted that the statutory requirement for a parent company to prepare consolidated accounts ignores the individual characteristic of the subsidiary company as a distinct and separate legal entity. Therefore, for accounting purposes, a group of companies is treated as a single economic entity.

However, an exception in respect of preparing group accounts exists in relation to a subsidiary company which is part of a small or medium-sized group of private companies under the control of a holding company which is itself a small or medium-sized private company. Here, in accordance with s 248 of the Companies Act 1985, the group accounts are not required to be presented in the consolidated format. From January 2004, the Companies Act 1985 (Accounts of Small and Medium-Sized Enterprises and Audit Exemption) (Amendment) Regulations 2004 (SI 2004/16) provide that a group is to be classified as 'small or medium' dependent on the following conditions:

Small group (meeting any two of these requirements)

(1) aggregate turnover not exceeding £5.6 million net or £6.72 million gross;

(2) aggregate balance sheet total not exceeding £2.8 million net or £3.36 million gross; and

(3) aggregate number of employees (monthly average) not exceeding 50.

Medium size group (meeting any two of these requirements)

(1) aggregate turnover not exceeding £22.8 million net or £27.36 million gross;

(2) aggregate balance sheet total not exceeding £11.4 million net or £13.68 million gross; and

(3) aggregate number of employees (monthly average) not exceeding 250.

CHANGING THE STATUS OF A COMPANY

A registered company may at some time during the course of its existence wish or be obliged to change the status with which it was originally registered. For example, a rapidly expanding private company limited by shares, in a desire to secure further capital to finance future growth, may decide that it must, in order to expand, increase its share capital by offering securities to the general public. In order to legitimately offer its securities to the general public, the company must re-register itself as a public company. Conversely, where a public company's issued share capital falls below the minimum requirement of share capital permitted for a public company, the public company must re-register itself as a private company. The following statutory rules provide the framework by which a company may change its registered status.

Private limited company to a public limited company

A private limited company, other than a private company which is without a share capital, may change its status to become a public company by complying with the procedures laid down by ss 43–48 of the Companies Act 1985. The procedures require, *inter alia*, the general meeting of the company to pass a special resolution to effect the company's re-registration as a public company. The special resolution must alter, where necessary, the form of the company's memorandum and articles to comply with the statutory requirements for a public limited company. If the Registrar of Companies is satisfied that a private limited company has complied with all the necessary statutory requirements applicable for its re-registration, the company will be issued with a new certificate of incorporation confirming its status as a public limited company.

Public limited company to a private limited company

In accordance with ss 53–55 of the Companies Act 1985, a public company may alter its status to that of a private company limited by shares or guarantee. A public company may be re-registered as a private company where the members at a general meeting of the company pass a special resolution to that effect. The special resolution must, where necessary, alter the terms of the company's articles and memorandum to comply with the registration requirements for a private company.

A public limited company's application to re-register as a private company may be challenged within 28 days of the resolution approving the company's change of status (s 54(3), CA 1985). The ability to challenge the application provides a possible safeguard for shareholders who hold shares for investment or speculative reasons, because the loss of public limited status may severely weaken the shareholders' ability to realise their investment in the company; that is, the possible market in which shares can be sold will be greatly restricted. Another potential difficulty for this class of shareholder will be the loss of a tangible market value for the shares; the ascertainment of the market value of a share in a private company may prove an especially difficult task (discussed in Chapter 9).

An application made to the court to cancel the resolution to alter the status of a public company may be made by holders of not less than five per cent in nominal value of the company's issued share capital, or holders of five per cent of any specific class of share, or by not less than 50 of the company's members. A shareholder of the company has the right to challenge a proposed change to the company's status providing the shareholder in question did not consent or vote in favour of the resolution to amend the company's status (s 54(2), CA 1985). On hearing the application to challenge the resolution, the court may order that it should be confirmed or cancelled. The court may also make the order subject to specific terms: for example, it may compel the company to purchase the shares of the dissentient members (s 54(5), CA 1985). When the Registrar is satisfied that the requirements of the re-registration process have been complied with, the company will be issued with a certificate of incorporation confirming the company's new status as a private company (s 55, CA 1985).

Private limited company to an unlimited company

A private limited company may seek re-registration as an unlimited company in accordance with ss 49–50 of the Companies Act 1985. A public limited company cannot re-register as an unlimited company (s 49(3), CA 1985). For a private company limited by shares or guarantee to re-register as an unlimited company, the company must have had no previous existence as an unlimited company (s 49(2), CA 1985). To comply with the re-registration formalities, the company must make all the necessary amendments to its memorandum and articles. The entire membership of the company must assent to the change in status (s 49(8), CA 1985) because on becoming an unlimited company, should the company become insolvent, the membership will be exposed to the risk of having to make contributions to the company's debts. Following compliance with the requirements of s 49, the Registrar will issue the company with a certificate of incorporation confirming the company's new status as unlimited (s 50, CA 1985).

Unlimited company to a private limited company

Providing an unlimited company complies with the statutory requirements of s 51 of the Companies Act 1985, it is entitled to re-register as a private limited company. In order to change its status, s 51 requires the unlimited company to pass a special resolution to complete the change. The resolution must state whether the company is to be limited by shares or by guarantee; in either case the resolution must provide for the necessary alterations to be made to the company's articles and memorandum so as to comply with the registration requirements for a limited company.

A company which is re-registered as an unlimited company in accordance with s 49 of the CA 1985 cannot, by virtue of s 51 of the Companies Act 1985, be subsequently re-registered as a private limited company. It should be noted that where a company, previously registered as an unlimited company, is subsequently wound up within three years of its re-registration as a limited company, then both the present and past members of the company may be personally liable to contribute towards its debts (see s 77, IA 1986).

Unlimited company to a public limited company

Where an unlimited company wishes to re-register as a public limited company (s 43, CA 1985), it must comply with the change in status requirements applicable to a change in status from a private to a public limited company. Further, the unlimited company must include within the terms of the special resolution the fact that it is to be limited by shares (s 48(2), CA 1985). If an unlimited company was previously registered as a limited company, it cannot under the procedures contained in ss 43–48 of the Companies Act 1985 subsequently be re-registered as a public limited company.

DEREGULATION AND REFORM OF PRIVATE COMPANIES

Government policy has seen a radical departure from a call for the unification of the rules applicable to private and public companies that prevailed in the 1960s. The change of attitude has largely been due to the UK's need to encourage the growth of small private enterprises. The desire to expand the population of small private companies has met with a desire to remove certain formal requirements previously applicable to all limited liability companies, requirements that are generally apt to discourage and hamper the creation of the small corporate enterprise.

Despite the aforementioned change in government policy, at present the Companies Act 1985 is deemed to regulate both private and public companies with little reference or concern as to the actual size of the enterprise. However, while not radically altering the applicability of a common set of company law rules for both private and public companies the Companies Act 1989 did introduce a legislative programme which in future years is likely to be expanded, with the probability that a distinguishable split will be created between the legislature's treatment of private and public companies. The reforms implemented by the 1989 Act are generally to be welcomed in so far as they reduce the administrative burdens of a private company by, for example, dispensing with the statutory requirement to pass resolutions at general meetings of the company and more significantly by introducing a system of elective resolutions. (The elective regime is discussed further in Chapter 21.)

Future reform

The CLR and both of the government's White Papers (2002 and 2005) recognise the need to promote the interests of small companies. In Chapters 2 and 4 of the CLR Final Report (2001), it was acknowledged that the current companies legislation required simplification in the context of small private companies for it imposed on such concerns excessive and unnecessary burdens. Basically, the report (endorsed by the White Papers) considered that the companies legislation was directed at large companies and inept in its transparency, treatment and understanding of the needs of small companies. To remedy this position the CLR concentrated proposals for reform in the following four areas:

- the internal administration of private companies
- minority shareholders
- capital maintenance and accounting and audit
- drafting of legislation.

The internal administration of private companies

In seeking to improve the internal administration of small companies the CLR's objective was to improve the internal efficiency of small companies by removing the unnecessary regulatory hurdles that are often irrelevant to the proper governance and running of the company's affairs. Here, as a starting point, the CLR recommended the codification (and possible extension) of the common law unanimous consent rule so that members could unanimously agree on a particular course of action by the company without the need to pass a formal resolution. (However, both White Papers rejected this proposal, discussed further in Chapter 21.)

Where the unanimous consent of members could not be obtained, the CLR recommended that a resolution should still be capable of being passed without the need to call a formal meeting of the members and that the same could be achieved by reforming the current requirement that all written resolutions should require unanimity. Accordingly, it was proposed that a written resolution should be capable of being passed by the requisite majority as determined by the type of the resolution in question: that is, either a simple majority or a majority of 75 per cent in the case of a special resolution (although a company could, in the case of a written resolution, choose to increase the requisite majority required). This proposal was endorsed by the government: see clauses D3 and D7 of the White Paper (2005) (discussed further in Chapter 21).

In addition to the aforementioned proposals, the CLR also sought to:

- simplify the understanding of directors' duties (accepted by the White Paper (2005), discussed further in Chapter 17);

- abolish the need to appoint a company secretary (accepted by the White Paper (2005), discussed in Chapter 16);

- abolish the need for shareholder authorisation (via s 80, CA 1985) for the allotment of shares (accepted by the White Paper (2005), discussed in Chapter 9);

- remove the rule requiring a single director to declare a conflict of interest (accepted by the White Paper (2005), discussed further in Chapter 17);

- create a simpler model constitution (accepted by the White Paper (2005), discussed in Chapter 4).

Minority shareholders

The CLR, mindful that expensive minority actions may destroy small companies, proposed that such actions should be kept within proper well-defined boundaries and, as such, approved the conservative approach taken by the House of Lords in *O'Neill* v *Phillips* (discussed further in Chapter 24). Further, in seeking to reduce the potential for expensive litigation, and in line with the spirit of the Civil Procedure Rules, the CLR advanced the cause of alternative dispute resolution (ADR), suggesting that the government should increase awareness of and accessibility to ADR and work to establish an arbitration scheme designed specifically for shareholder disputes. It should be noted that the White Paper (2005) makes no mention of such schemes.

It is also to be noted that the CLR sought the introduction of a statutory derivative action to replace in total the existing derivative action based upon the exceptions to the rule in *Foss* v *Harbottle*. This proposal was accepted by the White Paper (2005) (discussed in Chapter 23).

Capital maintenance, accounting and audit

The proposals for the reform of the capital maintenance provisions in respect of small companies are dealt with in Chapter 10 of this book and reforms to general audit requirements are dealt with in Chapter 20. In relation to accounting matters, the CLR noted that small companies already had the benefit of a separate regime but opined that the said scheme could be improved upon to afford greater flexibility and accountability. In terms of transparency, the CLR and both government White Papers (see White Paper (2005), clauses G5–G28) recognised the importance of maintaining the following requirements for all types of companies, namely:

- to keep individual accounting records
- to prepare fair and accurate accounts (see below)
- to file accounts at Companies House
- to circulate accounts to shareholders. (However, the CLR recommended that there should be no specific requirement for a small private company to lay accounts annually in general meeting (currently s 241, CA 1985). This view was not adopted in the White Paper (2005): see clause G21.)

The existing regime for small companies

The existing scheme for small-sized private companies allows small (and medium-sized companies) an exemption in relation to preparing accounts in compliance with the requirements of the Accounting Standards Board. Further, for small and medium-sized companies, accounts delivered to the Registrar for public filing need only be in an abbreviated form and may be absent of a directors' report and, in the case of a small company, a profit and loss account.

In accordance with s 246 of and Sch 8 to the Companies Act 1985, the accounts of small private companies (but not a private company belonging to a group of companies which includes a public company: see s 247A, CA 1985) may be presented in a less formal format than otherwise prescribed by Sch 4 to the Companies Act 1985 (for the presentation of accounts for medium-sized companies, see s 246A).

Section 246 allows the small-sized private company to input far less information into its accounts (including the accounts presented to shareholders), reducing the time, difficulty and cost associated with the preparation of accounts. From January 2004, the Companies Act 1985 (Accounts of Small and Medium-Sized Enterprises and Audit Exemption) (Amendment) Regulations 2004 (SI 2004/16) provide that a company is to be classified as 'small' if two or more of the following requirements are met: (a) turnover is not more than £5.6 million; (b) the balance sheet total is not more than £2.8 million and the number of employees is not more than 50. A company is classed as a medium-sized company where two out of the three following conditions are met: (a) turnover is not more than £22.8 million; (b) the balance sheet total is not more than £11.4 million; and (c) the number of employees is not more than 250.

Reforming the existing regime

In seeking to improve the existing regime, the CLR recommended the following:

- Abolishing abbreviated accounts in so far as the information provided is often too imprecise and will often be absent of details relating to profit margins. This view was supported in the government's White Paper (2002), para 4.26 but not accepted by the White Paper (2005) at p 46 (see clause G11 *et seq*). The White Paper (2005) does, however, provide that both small and medium-sized companies should be required to disclose the amount of turnover for the relevant financial year.
- A small-sized company should only need to produce one set of accounts which would be distributed to members and filed at Companies House.

- With the objective of improving transparency in relation to achieving a more up-to-date picture of the financial standing of the company, reducing the filing of accounts time period for small-sized companies from ten months, from year-end, to seven months, and, in the case of public companies, reducing the said period from 7 months to 6 months. This view was supported in the government's White Paper (2002), para 4.24 and White Paper (2005) at p 46.

- Distributing accounts to members (but no compulsion to do so at the AGM) prior to or at the same time as they are filed at Companies House, to allow members sight of the accounts before they are generally available to public inspection.

- Raising the audit threshold for small companies (discussed in Chapter 20).

Finally, it should be observed that the procedures for the preparation of accounts is tied, in terms of compliance, with the EC Fourth Directive, originally adopted on 25 July 1978. The Fourth Directive (as amended) together with the Seventh Directive (as amended) prescribe standard (detailed) formats for the preparation and presentation of company accounts. In accordance with these Directives, companies have to prepare full accounts for their shareholders, although, as noted, certain exceptions to the accounting requirements are made in respect of small and medium-sized private companies.

Drafting of legislation

Given the complexity of some of the existing companies legislation, the CLR recommended that future legislative measures should, in so far as they applied to small companies, be clearer and more accessible (this was accepted by the government White Papers). The recommendation is clearly born of common sense but is equally applicable to all future companies legislation irrespective of whether it is directly applicable to small companies or not. However, the difficulty in putting this admirable objective into practice may prove extremely difficult.

A more practical and sustainable recommendation of the CLR concerned the need, wherever possible, to clearly distinguish between provisions applicable to private companies and those concerned with public companies. The CLR suggested that future companies legislation should, whenever possible, adopt a policy in drafting laws to clearly distinguish between private companies and public companies. However, the CLR stopped short of suggesting distinct legislation: that is, one Companies Act for private companies and another for public companies. The CLR's views were accepted by the government in both of its White Papers.

Inherent dangers in relaxing regulations for small companies

Although there may be an obvious need to encourage the expansion of small business enterprises, there is, however, an inherent danger in the apparent legislative desire to reduce the obligations and regulations applicable to the creation and running of small private limited companies. The inherent danger is that the incorporation of vastly unorganised and undercapitalised concerns may be encouraged to the detriment of the public interest. If the 'price' to be paid for encouraging undercapitalised concerns prejudices the interests of the small trade creditors and customers of such 'lame' companies, the UK economy will undoubtedly suffer. While the concept of limited liability is a valuable shield affording protection to the human constituents of a corporate enterprise against the imposition of personal liability, it is a shield which should not be transformed into a corporate sword; it must not have a capacity to slay and generally prejudice the interests of third parties who deal with small companies.

The relaxation and greater ease in an ability to incorporate and administer a limited liability company may also have the effect of devaluing the prestige attributed to the general standing of the concept of limited liability. The trust and confidence of the business community in small private limited companies has, from the time of *Salomon* v *A. Salomon Ltd*, been tinged with suspicion and further moves to relax its regulation may result in a more emphatic loss of confidence. While, as previously stated, the reforms which were incorporated into the 1989 Act are to be welcomed, the move towards an even greater relaxation and distinctive regime for private limited companies should be viewed with some caution. To safeguard the value of the concept of limited liability it may, for example, be beneficial to increase the registration fee for incorporation (which in October 1994 was in fact reduced from £50 to £20) and also to follow the majority of our European counterparts in specifying a minimum capital requirement for the incorporation of small limited liability companies. However, it is noted that if the UK established a minimum capital requirement for private companies this could (certainly in theory) have a negative economic impact on the UK given that the UK, in comparison to other EU states, is currently an attractive state for private companies within the EU to establish themselves, that is, to evade the minimum capital requirements set within other European jurisdictions. The ability for an individual or private company based in Europe to incorporate a private company in the UK to escape the minimum capital requirements of their home country was established in the case of *Centros Ltd* v *Erhverus-og Selskabsstyrelsen* [2000] 2 WLR 1048 (ECJ).

Another potential solution to safeguard the value attached to a limited-liability status could be found in the creation of a new type of incorporated company, a company especially designed and tailored to meet the needs of very small concerns, a type of private company which would trade without a limited-liability status, or one based more on the lines of the guarantee company. However, the creation of a new unlimited type of company was rejected by the CLR and had earlier been rejected by a feasibility study commissioned by the Law Commission into the reform of company law for private companies (published by the DTI, November 1994). Indeed, unless a minimum capital requirement was introduced for private companies (one which was closer to the present £50 000 requirement for public companies), it seems highly improbable whether the incorporation of a new unlimited type of company for very small concerns would ever be viewed by small businesses as an attractive proposition.

Suggested further reading

Corporate structures

Freeman (1994) 57 MLR 555

Hicks, Drury and Smallcombe [1995] ACCA Research Report 42

Hicks (1995) 16 Co Law 171

Riley (1995) 58 MLR 595

Lower (2003) 24 Co Law 166

Griffin (2004) 25 Co Law 99

Community interest companies

Cross (2003) 19 SLT 157

European corporate structures

O'Neill (2000) 21 Co Law 173

Lowry (2004) 63 CLJ 331

Group relationship

Schmitthoff [1978] JBL 218

Lower [2000] JBL 232

Partnership law and the limited liability partnership

Morris and Stevenson (1997) 60 MLR 538

Henning (2004) 25 Co Law 163

6

CORPORATE LIABILITY

INTRODUCTION

This chapter seeks to examine a company's liability for wrongful acts that have been carried out in the company's name name by its officers and corporate servants. The chapter concentrates its attention on analysing the conceptual difficulties involved in seeking to impose liability on a company for a wrong which requires proof of a requisite 'guilty mind'. A company's liability for manslaughter is considered in some depth together with the government's proposals to reform this area of the law.

THE NATURE OF THE LIABILITY

Civil liability – vicarious liability

A company, as with any other employer, may be vicariously liable for the tortious acts of one of its employees, be that an act connected with a fraud or one of negligence. A company may be held vicariously liable for the actions of its employees even where, during the course of employment, an employee acts contrary to the company's instructions, or where the employee carries out his/her duties in a dishonest manner. However, other than where the company adopts an unauthorised act, liability will cease where the employee acts beyond the scope of his/her authority without an express permission from the company, that is, where the employee acts other than in the capacity of an agent of the company: see, generally, *Cornfield* v *Carlton Bank Ltd* [1899] 1 QB 392, *Lloyd* v *Grace, Smith & Co* [1912] AC 716, *Credit Lyonnais Bank Nederland NV* v *Export Credits Guarantee Department* [1999] 2 WLR 540.

The directing mind – criminal liability

In the context of the commission of a legal wrong by an employee of a company (other than in tort where vicarious liability may apply) the extent of a company's responsibility for the wrongful act will be determined by ascertaining whether the human person responsible for the physical commission of the wrongful act can properly be identified as part of the company's directing mind (the identification principle). Where the person in question does command a position within the company's directing mind, the court will, where necessary (i.e. where the wrongful act requires the proof of a mental state (*mens rea*)), impute that person's mental state to the company. For example, in *Lennard's Carrying Co Ltd* v *Asiatic Petroleum Co Ltd* [1915] AC 705 a company ran a business that involved the management and maintenance of a ship; the ship was damaged due to a failure to correct a fault in its boiler system. The failure in question was directly attributable to the company's director.

Proceedings were commenced against the company, which sought to defend itself on the premise that the damage to the ship had occurred without the company's actual fault or privity; namely, the state of mind of the company's director was not attributable to the company. The company failed in its defence and the House of Lords held the company liable under s 502 of the Merchant Shipping Act 1894. In the oft-quoted words of Viscount Haldane LC:

> 'My Lords, a corporation is an abstraction, it has no mind of its own any more than it has a body of its own; its active and directing will must consequently be sought in the person of somebody who for some purposes may be called an agent, but who is really the directing mind and will of the corporation, the very *alter ego* and centre of the personality of the corporation.' (at p 713)

Although the directing mind of a corporation will often be found in a person who is regarded as the *alter ego* of a company (see e.g. the judgments of Lord Parker in *John Henshall (Quarries) Ltd* v *Harvey* [1965] 1 All ER 725 at p 729 and Denning LJ in *Bolton Engineering Co Ltd* v *T J Graham & Sons Ltd* [1957] 1 QB 159 at p 172), it must be stressed that whilst the *alter ego* of a company will normally be found in a dominant director(s), the directing mind of a company may be found in a different class of person. However, in the latter case, the problem of identifying whether a person was a part of the directing mind of a company is most problematic because the person in question will be devoid of any actual authority in relation to corporate decision making. Nevertheless, the acts of a company servant may have been undertaken as a result of implied or ostensible authority to the extent that the said authority may still be sufficient to attribute liability to the company.

For example, in the case of *El Ajou* v *Dollar Land Holdings plc* [1994] BCC 143 the Court of Appeal held a company liable under the terms of a constructive trust in circumstances where it was doubtful whether the company employee, in knowingly participating in that breach, was, in the strictest sense, a part of the company's directing mind. Culpability was established notwithstanding the need for a *mens rea* requirement (knowing receipt). The case involved a former director (F) of the company who had knowingly been a party to the fraudulent receipt of moneys acquired as a result of a massive share fraud. The plaintiff in this action sought to trace proceeds from that fraud which had been invested in a property project overseen by the defendant company. The defendant company was controlled by two US citizens but was managed by S, an appointed agent. However, S was not a member of the company's board of directors; the board was comprised of three nominees, one of which was F, who acted as the company's chairman.

F was asked by S to find an investor for a proposed building project. Having found a willing investor (C), F made the necessary arrangements between C and the company. After negotiations had been completed, F played no further part in the subsequent dealings between C and the company; shortly after he finalised the agreement, F ceased to be a director of the company. C's investment in the company's property project, of over £1 million, represented funds fraudulently obtained from the plaintiff; a fact known to F, but one not known by S or any of the company's other directors. Indeed, the company's board had never authorised negotiations between C and F.

At first instance, in determining the question of whether F could, for the purpose of the transaction with C, be regarded as the directing mind of the company so as to impute F's knowledge of the fraud to the company, Millett J ([1993] BCC 698) concluded that the directing mind of the company was S, or S and his American principals, in so far as F had exercised no independent judgement in the matter. F had been instructed by S to secure an investor. However, overturning the first instance decision, the Court of Appeal concluded that F had been given the sole responsibility by S to find and conduct dealings with an investor for the property project, a responsibility which F undertook on behalf of the company. The company was liable through its directing mind which, for the purposes of this transaction, was F.

To establish whether a person can be considered as a part of a company's directing mind, it is often necessary, if not essential, to pierce the corporate veil to examine the company's management structure and chain of command. Such an examination will aid the determination of whether an employee's wrongful act was directly attributable to the company, that is, whether the employee had or was delegated an authority to act as part of the directing mind or held a position in the corporate structure which could be construed as being a part of its directing mind. As such, the question of whether an employee was a part of a company's directing mind cannot be resolved by the application of a simple set of rules. The question can only be resolved on a case-by-case analysis of the nature of the employee's act and the position which that servant occupied in the corporate structure.

The leading authority on the judicial identification of a company's directing mind is the decision of the House of Lords in *Tesco Supermarkets Ltd* v *Nattrass* [1972] AC 153. Here, Tesco was charged with an offence under s 11(2) of the Trade Descriptions Act 1968 (TDA 1968), that is, for offering to supply goods (in this case a packet of washing powder) at a price higher than the one which had been indicated as applying to the goods in question. (Section 11, TDA 1968 has since been repealed, but a consumer retains protection against misleadingly priced goods by virtue of s 20 of the Consumer Protection Act 1987.) In seeking to defend the action, Tesco relied upon s 24(1) of the TDA 1968 which states that, subject to s 24(2) of the TDA 1968 (see below), a defence may be established where the accused can prove (a) that the commission of the offence was due to the fault of another person or some other cause beyond his control, and (b) that he took all reasonable precautions and exercised all due diligence to avoid the commission of the offence by himself or a person under his control. Section s 24(2) of the TDA 1968 requires notification to the prosecutor by the accused of the person who the accused believes was at fault. Tesco complied with s 24(2) of the TDA 1968 by notifying the prosecutor that the fault in question was attributable to the supermarket's manager. The question to be determined by the court was whether the supermarket manager's fault was directly attributable to Tesco.

At first instance, the magistrates took the view that the store manager was not 'another person' but rather a part of the company, so that Tesco's defence under s 24(1), TDA 1968 failed. The Divisional Court found that the magistrates had been incorrect in respect of their interpretation of the term 'another person'. Nevertheless, the court concluded that the company had delegated responsibility for the pricing of its goods to its managers and, as such, the store manager was a part of the company's directing mind; Tesco was therefore guilty of the offence charged.

However, on appeal, the decision was overturned by the House of Lords. On the crucial question of whether the company's directing mind could delegate authority, that is, whether the store manager could (as held in the Divisional Court) be construed as a part of Tesco's directing mind, the House was of the unanimous opinion that he could not. Lord Reid, in attempting to define the conceptual boundaries of a company's directing mind, disagreed with the notion that company servants engaged in the 'brain work' of a company could automatically be classed as part of a company's directing mind. Lord Reid opined that only a company's superior officers – those persons who ultimately controlled the overall corporate policy of an enterprise – could be regarded as a part of a company's directing mind. The store manager did not have the capacity to determine Tesco's corporate policy. Nevertheless, Lord Reid did recognise that a board of directors could:

'. . . delegate some part of their functions of management, giving to their delegate full discretion to act independently of instructions from them.' (at p 171)

The House, in concluding that Tesco was not guilty of the offence charged, construed s 24(1) of the TDA 1968 in a manner whereby it did not impose any form of vicarious liability. A store manager who acted in contravention of corporate policy could not be said to have acted as the company. Therefore, delegation of corporate tasks to a company's store manager could not be interpreted as the delegation of authority in respect of corporate policy so as to render the store manager to be a part of the company's directing mind. In finding that the store manager was not part of Tesco's directing mind, the House of Lords allowed Tesco's defence under s 24(1) of the TDA 1968. The identifiable directing mind of Tesco, the company's board of directors, had set up an effective system to avoid the commission of the offence charged under s 11(2) of the TDA 1968. The directing mind had not delegated any form of discretion to the store manager to act independently of its instructions. In the words of Lord Diplock:

'To treat the duty of an employer to exercise due diligence as unperformed unless due diligence was also exercised by all his servants to whom he had reasonably given all proper instructions and upon whom he could reasonably rely to carry them out, would be to render the defence of due diligence nugatory and so thwart the clear intention of Parliament in providing it.' (at p 203)

Nevertheless, a company acting through its directing mind may be convicted of a criminal offence irrespective of whether the offence is of a regulatory nature (often an offence of strict liability) or one which involves proof of a guilty mind (*mens rea*). As Lord Reid said in *Tesco Supermarkets Ltd* v *Nattrass* [1972] AC 153:

'If the guilty man was in law identifiable with the company then whether his offence was serious or venial his act was the act of the company.' (at p 164)

However, an ability to attribute the mental state of an individual to the directing mind of a company, to establish criminal liability, is marred by uncertainty in relation to the degree and extent by which a delegation of authority emanating from the 'directing mind' is sufficient to create the necessary level of proximity between the company and the individual responsible for the commission of the criminal act. How can a company be identified with the mental state of an employee when that mental state is attached to the performance of criminal activity that is outside the authority of the employee and contrary to corporate policy? But for corporate liability to ensue the act of the employee must be seen and identified as the act of the company.

Indeed, the difficulty in attributing a company with the necessary culpability to warrant the company's conviction for a criminal offence, involving proof of *mens rea*, is one which has caused much vexation and confusion and is one likely to depend upon the particular terms of the offence in question. Up until 1944, a company had never been successfully convicted of a criminal offence involving a *mens rea* requirement. Yet, in that year there were three convictions. The convictions were sustained in: *DPP v Kent & Sussex Contractors Ltd* [1944] KB 146 on a charge of deception; *R v ICR Haulage Ltd* [1944] KB 551, on a charge of conspiracy involving a company's transport officer; and *Moore v I Bresler Ltd* [1944] 2 All ER 515, on a charge of fraudulent evasion of tax related to a company's sales manager.

By contrast to the successful prosecutions outlined above, many cases have failed because of an inability to establish culpability through the directing mind of the company. For example, in *J Henshall Ltd v Harvey* [1965] 2 QB 233 (also see *Tesco Supermarkets Ltd* v *Nattrass*, discussed above), the wrongful act of a company employee was deemed not to be attributable to the company. Here, the company was deemed to have had no responsibility for its weighbridge man's unlawful act of allowing a lorry to be driven contrary to weight restriction regulations. The company escaped conviction because, although the weighbridge man was a company employee, he was not an officer of the company and therefore was deemed not to be a part of the company's directing mind (but note the contrasting decision of *National Coal Board* v *Gamble* [1959] 1 QB 11, where on similar facts the prosecution was sustained).

Possibly an alternative explanation for the decision in *Henshall Ltd v Harvey* may be found in the decision of the Divisional Court in *Richmond-on-Thames BC v Pinn* [1989] RTR 354, where it was held that a company could not be charged with an offence which involved driving a vehicle in so far as an artificial person was incapable of the physical act of 'driving'. However, while it is impossible for a company to drive a vehicle, the court's reasoning in *Richmond-on-Thames BC v Pinn* seems quite absurd and must in the light of subsequent cases (see below) be considered redundant. All crimes involve the performance of a human skill or act, of which driving is one; surely the crucial question to ask is whether that human skill or act was performed on behalf of the company during the course of the employee's employment? If the act was so performed then the company must, through its employee, be deemed responsible, via the identification principle, for committing the *actus reus* of the criminal offence.

General exceptions to criminal liability

Section 5 of and Sch 1 to the Interpretation Act 1978 provides that a corporate entity may, unless otherwise stated, be construed as a 'person' in terms of being considered culpable for an offence which requires the wrongful act of a person. Therefore, while a company may generally be regarded as an entity to which criminal liability may attach, a company cannot be convicted of a crime which is defined in a way whereby it **specifically** requires the commission of the physical act (*actus reus*) to have been committed by a human entity. Further, such offences are often of a type whereby it would be impossible to connect the wrongful act to the pursuit of any activity associated with the company's affairs. For example, an artificial person cannot be convicted of bigamy, rape or any other sexual offence. Neither may a company be convicted of the offence of conspiracy in circumstances where the persons charged are the company and an officer representing its directing mind. The offence of conspiracy involves at least two independent minds conspiring together, whereas a company and its directing mind are one and the same: see e.g. *R v McDonnell* [1966] 1 All ER 193. However, where a company and a person representing its directing mind are involved in a conspiracy with other persons, the company may be charged with conspiracy: see e.g. *R v IRC Holdings* [1944] 1 All ER 691. Finally, a company may not be convicted of an offence where the punishment for the crime charged is such that a sentence is incapable of being imposed on the artificial corporate entity: for example, life imprisonment following conviction for murder.

CORPORATE MANSLAUGHTER

Although there are obvious difficulties in establishing a company's culpability for a criminal act perpetrated by one of its employees, it is possible, in accordance with the identification principle, for a company to be charged and convicted (by way of fine) of the most serious crimes. For example, it is possible, following *R v Coroner for East Kent, ex parte Spooner* [1987] 3 BCC 636, for a company to be charged with involuntary manslaughter. Involuntary manslaughter is classed as either causing death by an unlawful act, gross negligence or subjective recklessness. In *R v Coroner for East Kent, ex parte Spooner*, the Divisional Court, in hearing an application for the judicial review of a coroner's decision into deaths resulting from the sinking of a passenger ship, 'The Herald of Free Enterprise', expressed the view that on appropriate facts a corporation could be convicted of manslaughter. However, in subsequent proceedings (*R v P & O Ferries (Dover) Ltd* (1990) 93 Cr App R 72) the case was withdrawn from the jury because of a lack of evidence to substantiate the finding that the directing mind of the company (the company's directors) had the necessary *mens rea* to warrant a conviction.

However, a conviction for manslaughter was subsequently recorded against a company: see the *Lyme Bay Canoe* case (noted in [1994] *The Times*, 9 December). Here, following the conviction of its managing director for manslaughter the company, OLL Ltd, was also convicted of manslaughter given that it was accepted that the company's managing director was the company's directing mind (the company was a small concern; the managing director was the alter ego of the company). The managing director was convicted of manslaughter on the premise that, despite being warned by former employees of failings in the safety standards of the business (the same eventually contributed to the deaths of the customers to which the manslaughter charge related), he had failed to correct the said safety standards. (Also see *Jackson Transport (Ossett) Ltd* (unreported, 1996). Here a company was convicted of manslaughter; again, the enterprise was a small private company with the managing director being regarded as the alter ego of the company.) It is to be noted that, since 1992, there have only been six corporate convictions for manslaughter, all involved small organisations.

In *Attorney General's Reference (No 2 of 1999)* [2000] 3 WLR 195, the Court of Appeal considered the circumstances in which a company could be convicted of involuntary manslaughter, with specific reference to the offence of manslaughter by gross negligence (i.e. the category of manslaughter associated with the prosecution of a company). The Court of Appeal's opinion was delivered at the request of the Attorney General and followed the Southall rail disaster of 1997, in which seven train passengers were killed. The court was asked to consider two questions.

- Can a defendant be convicted of manslaughter by gross negligence without the need to establish the defendant's state of mind?

- Can a non-human defendant be convicted of manslaughter by gross negligence in the absence of evidence establishing the guilt of an identified human being for the same crime?

In relation to the first question the court gave an affirmative answer because following the decision of the House of Lords in *R v Adomako* [1995] 1 AC 171, the definition of manslaughter, by gross negligence, is such that a defendant's guilt may, in an appropriate case, be established on the basis of the defendant having had an obvious and reckless disregard for human life, recklessness being construed in an objective sense with no prerequisite of having to prove *mens rea*. However, in respect of the second question the Court of Appeal answered this in the negative. The court held that in seeking to establish a company's guilt it was still necessary to show that, in causing death, the act of the employee (with the employee being liable for manslaughter) was an act attributable to the company, via its directing mind. In effect, the identification principle is as relevant to the *actus reus* as it is to the *mens rea* of a crime (see e.g. the comments of Bingham LJ in *R v Coroner for East Kent, ex parte Spooner* (1987) 88 Cr App R 10 (at p 16)).

Following the decision of the Court of Appeal in *Attorney General's Reference (No 2 of 1999)*, it may be stated that a company can have no **personal** or **direct** liability for the offence (discussed further below), and it is still necessary to identify the directing mind of the company and determine whether the culpable employee could be classed as a part of it. Clearly, if the employee is high up the ladder in terms of corporate responsibility then there will be a greater chance of establishing him as a part of the directing mind. However, in large corporations the ability to establish a mere employee (as, say, opposed to a director) as a part of the directing mind will be especially difficult unless there is a direct line in the delegation of authority from the directing mind to the employee. Corporate responsibility for an employee's act cannot be found by, for example, establishing an indirect link to the directing mind through, for example, an aggregation of individual failures, which leads to and eventually results in the commission of an offence.

Proposals for reform

Proposals to remove the identification principle in respect of establishing a charge of corporate manslaughter were given prominence in two Law Commission papers in the 1990s, namely the 1994 Law Commission's Consultation Paper No 135 and the second and final paper published in 1996, 'Legislating the Criminal Code: Involuntary

Manslaughter' (Consultation Paper No 237). In effect the Commission recommended a new statutory offence for companies, to be labelled 'corporate killing'.

For the new offence, a company would be convicted for causing the death of a person notwithstanding that the directing mind of the company was, via the identification principle, unconnected to the offence. The Commission contended that liability should ensue in circumstances where management failure by a company was the cause or contributed to the death of a person even if the immediate cause of death was the act or omission of an individual. Management failure was defined by the Commission to be present if there was a failure by the company in the way in which its activities were managed or organised to the extent that the company did not ensure the health and safety of persons employed in or affected by its activities. For liability to ensue, the Commission stated that the offending conduct would need to fall far below that standard which could reasonably be expected of the company in the circumstances of the case. Accordingly, for a company to be guilty of corporate killing, its management failures would, in the circumstances of a given case and in relation to the company's failure to identify and prevent a risk of death or injury, need to be significantly below a standard (akin to gross negligence), which might otherwise have been reasonably expected of the company.

In May 2000 the Home Office also published a consultation paper on involuntary manslaughter in which it broadly accepted the Law Commission's proposals in respect of a new offence of corporate killing. In addition, the Home Office report introduced the idea that liability for corporate killing should be extended to a parent or group of companies in circumstances where it could be shown that management failures of the parent or group contributed to the death of the victim. The Home Office also suggested that individuals involved in the management of a culpable company should be disqualified from acting in any future management role of a business. The report also raised the issue of whether an individual(s) who contributed to the management failures should also be potentially liable, following separate criminal proceedings, for the offence of corporate killing with, in their case, a penalty of imprisonment (this proposal had not been suggested in the Law Commission report).

For companies convicted of corporate killing, the Home Office proposed that the maximum penalty should be an unlimited fine and in appropriate cases a remedial order to correct the original failings of the company; failings which actually contributed to or resulted in the prosecution. In 2003, following on from the consultation exercise, the government announced that it would publish a Bill in which the offence of corporate killing would be proposed, albeit that it announced that it had abandoned its proposals to impose criminal liability against individual directors in circumstances where a director contributed to a management failure which ultimately resulted in the death of a person. The proposal to impose disqualification orders against directors involved in the management of a company found guilty of corporate killing was also abandoned. It is submitted that the removal of these proposals was regrettable and was most likely influenced by a large and powerful business lobby.

In November 2004, the Queen's Speech announced that a draft Bill to introduce a new offence of corporate killing (manslaughter) would be introduced into

Parliament. On 23 March 2005 a draft Corporate Manslaughter Bill was published. The draft Bill defines the new offence not as 'corporate killing' but as 'corporate manslaughter'. The draft Bill provides that an organisation (a company and some government departments listed in the Schedule to the draft Bill) will be guilty of the offence, if the way in which any of the organisation's activities are managed or organised by its senior managers:

(a) causes a person's death, and

(b) amounts to a gross breach of a relevant duty of care owed by the organisation to the deceased.

Liability will be by way of a fine. The Bill expressly provides that an individual cannot be guilty of aiding, abetting, counselling or procuring an offence of corporate manslaughter, albeit that an individual could in his/her own right still be convicted of a distinct offence: for example, an individual could (as now) still be found guilty of the manslaughter of an employee of the company.

Clause 2 of the draft Bill defines a senior manager as a person who plays a significant role in the decision-making and/or management process of the company. Clause 3 defines the ingredients of the offence as a gross breach of duty, the conduct of which falls far below what can reasonably be expected of the organisation in the circumstances. Whether conduct amounts to the said criteria will be a question for the jury to determine. The jury must determine the issue with reference to, *inter alia*, whether the organisation failed to comply with relevant health and safety legislation or guidance and, if so, how serious that failure was. The jury, in determining a company's culpability, must also consider whether:

(i) the senior managers of the organisation knew, or ought to have known, that the organisation was failing to comply with the relevant legislation or guidance;

(ii) the senior managers were aware, or ought to have been aware, of the risk of death or serious harm posed by the failure to comply; and, finally,

(iii) the senior managers sought to cause the organisation to profit from that failure.

Given the already lengthy and prolonged consultation exercise on this issue it is to be hoped that the Bill will produce some tangible conclusion which can be translated into legislation. However, it is suggested that there are a number of problems with the proposed offence of corporate manslaughter. For example, in defining a management failure, the draft Bill (in common with the Law Commission and Home Office report) states that conduct would have to fall 'far below' the standard which could reasonably be expected of the company in the circumstances. What is meant by the term 'far below' and the adoption of a reasonable standard to be expected of the company? The terms 'gross' and 'far below' connote a standard of care akin to an emphatic act of gross negligence, a standard that, in terms of identification, is very imprecise. Further, what is a reasonable standard to be expected of a company in the provision of health and safety matters? Will the standard be judged as a universal standard applicable to companies of a similar size or companies engaged in a particular industry, or a combination of these considerations? If a company has a history of complying with health and safety measures will it generally be judged competent in terms of its management policy, giving rise to a presumption that it does not fall 'far below' a reasonable standard? Conversely, if a company has a poor history in relation to health and safety issues will there be a presumption that a negligent act resulting in death would amount to conduct 'far below' a reasonable standard, that is, on the premise that the company's health and safety record is poor? Further, how can one define a standard giving rise to culpability which falls below a reasonable standard in circumstances where the so-called 'reasonable standard' may itself be driven by political and economical considerations and therefore already be set at too low a level? If a low or reasonable standard can be defined, then how much below a 'low level' standard does the company's standards have to fall to be classified as at a standard 'far below' those expected?

Finally, if the company's motive for pursuing the course of conduct which resulted in the death of an employee was driven by an admirable desire to, for example, improve the health and safety of the rest of the workforce rather than, say, to increase the company's profits, will the good and proper motive outweigh the actual gross negligence which was employed to achieve the non-profit-based motive? To what extent can a jury give weight to the motive behind the act of gross negligence; should not the motive be irrelevant? Possibly, the motive behind an act of gross negligence may be considered not as a means to determine liability but rather as a mitigating tool in relation to the extent of the fine to be imposed. However, if motive is to be used in terms of mitigating the extent of a fine, why should motive be a factor to be considered by the jury, for it is not the jury's place to determine the extent of a company's liability? Is it not for the court to determine the level of a fine?

EXTENDING CORPORATE LIABILITY

In some instances, a company may be deemed liable for an act of an employee where the language and interpretation of a statutory rule impliedly warrants the imposition of corporate liability. It should be stressed that this principle is similar in outcome but not the same as vicarious liability because, unlike vicarious liability, in this instance, liability is determined by a specific requirement of the statutory rule in question.

For example, in *Re Supply of Ready Mixed Concrete (No 2)* [1995] 1 AC 456, the House of Lords held that in defined circumstances the knowledge of a company's senior employees could be attributed to the company notwithstanding that such employees sought to bind the company in a manner outside the terms of its corporate policy. This case involved a company that had given an undertaking to the Restrictive Practices Court (in compliance with the Restrictive Trade Practices Act 1976) to refrain from entering into any restrictive arrangement which would amount to a breach of the undertaking. Notwithstanding the undertaking, senior employees of the company, acting within the scope of their employment, entered into a restrictive agreement. The employees acted without the consent of the company's board, which indeed had actively encouraged its employees to abide by the terms of the restrictive agreement. In finding that the actions of the employees could be attributed to the company (rendering the company to be in contempt of court) the House of

Lords concluded that an undertaking of this nature would have been worthless had the company been able to avoid liability for the acts of its employees by alleging (even if true) that its board of directors had been unaware of the actions of its employees.

In *Meridian Global Funds Management Asia Ltd* v *Securities Commission* [1995] BCC 942, the Privy Council also subscribed to the view that the knowledge of a company employee may, in specific circumstances, be attributed to the company, notwithstanding that the employee in seeking to bind the company acted in a manner which was contrary to corporate policy. In this case a company's senior investment manager entered into a security transaction in the name of the company. As a result of the acquisition, the company became a substantial security holder in another company. Contrary to the requirements of the relevant legislation (s 20, New Zealand Securities Act 1988), the company failed to give notice of the acquisition. The failure to give notice was as a result of the senior investment manager's desire to fraudulently attempt to purchase the securities with the objective of selling them on at a profit for himself. It was held that, although the company's board of directors had been unaware of the security dealings, the company was nevertheless imputed with the knowledge of its senior manager.

Lord Hoffmann, in giving the judgment of the Privy Council, sought to explain the Privy Council's decision by first setting out rules of primary and then general attribution. The primary rules governed the company in accordance with its constitution or were to be implied by the companies legislation; the general attribution rules were rules based upon principles of agency. Lord Hoffmann opined that, when the said rules were combined, they could normally be applied to determine a company's potential liability for a wrongful act of an employee. However, exceptionally, as in the case before the Privy Council, the rules of attribution would not always forge an answer to determine corporate liability. In such a case, Lord Hoffmann held that a company's liability, flowing from an act of an employee, could be determined by reference to the language and interpretation of the obligation or rule which the company's employee had contravened. Therefore, according to Lord Hoffmann, the decision in *Tesco Supermarkets Ltd* v *Nattrass* (discussed above) could be explained on the premise that the precautions taken by Tesco's board in seeking to eliminate the improper pricing of goods were sufficient to negate any corporate liability in so far as the company's actions were sufficient to satisfy s 24(1) of the TDA 1968. Similarly, according to Lord Hoffmann, the decision of the House of Lords in *Re Supply of Ready Mixed Concrete (No 2)* (discussed above) could be reconciled with *Tesco Supermarkets Ltd* v *Nattrass* because, if the company in *Re Supply of Ready Mixed Concrete* had not been in contempt, the statutory language of the Restrictive Trade Practices Act 1976 would have been worthless, a finding equally applicable in relation to the legislation relevant to the *Meridian* case.

Likewise, in *R* v *British Steel plc* [1995] 1 WLR 1356 (confirmed by the House of Lords in *R* v *Associated Octel Ltd* [1996] WLR 1543), where the defendant company was prosecuted under the Health and Safety at Work etc. Act 1974, following the death of a worker. The death resulted, in part, from the ineffective supervision of the worker by a more senior worker. The Court of Appeal held that there had been an obvious breach of the statutory duty imposed by the Health and Safety at Work etc. Act 1974, namely to ensure that persons were not exposed to risk, and the breach had been by the company. The company's defence, namely that its directing mind had sought to take reasonable care by implementing safety measures, was deemed irrelevant given the terms and nature of the statute. Lord Justice Steyn explained:

> 'If it be accepted that parliament considered it necessary for the protection of public health and safety to impose, subject to the defence of reasonable practicability, absolute criminal liability, it would drive a juggernaut through the legislative scheme if corporate employers could avoid criminal liability where the potentially harmful event is committed by someone who is not the directing mind of the company.' (at p 1362)

Following the death of an employee, it is thus evident that prosecution under the Health and Safety at Work etc. Act 1974 will be a far more common practice than a prosecution for manslaughter (see ss 2(1)–3(1) of the 1974 Act). The evidential requirements of the former are less daunting given that the identification principle is irrelevant in the prosecution of the corporate entity.

To return to and summarise Lord Hoffmann's analysis in *Meridian Global Funds Management Asia Ltd* v *Securities Commission*, Lord Hoffmann opined that if the primary rules of attribution failed to impose a liability on the company in a situation where the court considered this failure would defeat the very purpose of the legislation, then in such circumstances liability could still be attributed to the company to give effect to the intent of the legislation. The analysis advanced by Lord Hoffmann would appear to represent a commonsense approach to the determination of a company's liability, albeit that the very nature of what may be described as a 'flexible approach' may do little in reality, despite Lord Hoffmann's reassurance to the contrary (at p 950), to eradicate inconsistencies and difficulties in determining whether a servant's act can be attributed to the company. Naturally, the said difficulty will be particularly profound in cases where the construction of the relevant statutory provision or other obligation may provide a tentative inference as opposed to an overwhelming inference as to the imposition of corporate responsibility.

Suggested further reading

Burles (1991) 141 NLJ 609

Wells [1993] CLR 551

Clarkson (1996) 59 MLR 557

Gobert (2002) 118 LQR 72

Harris (2003) 8 AA&L 369

7

A COMPANY'S CONTRACTUAL CAPACITY

INTRODUCTION

The validity of a corporate transaction is dependent upon the contractual capacity of a company and issues relating to a directors' authority to bind the company. This chapter seeks to explain matters pertinent to the former; directors' authority is discussed in Chapter 8.

The law relating to contractual capacity has been the subject of substantial reform in the guise of the Companies Act 1989. Future reform of this area of corporate law is also proposed. The effect of the Companies Act 1989 and the potential future reform of this area will be discussed in detail; however, this chapter commences by considering the historical development of rules relevant to a company's contractual capacity. An understanding of the historical development of this area of the law is necessary in order to appreciate why issues relating to corporate capacity have, throughout the history of company law, been the source of much confusion and why, eventually, such vexation resulted in reforming legislation.

CORPORATE CAPACITY – THE *ULTRA VIRES* RULE

A company's capacity to enter into a contractual obligation was historically dominated by the *ultra vires* rule. The rule provided that where a contractual transaction exceeded a company's corporate capacity, so determined by the company's objects clause, the transaction would be deemed void. If void, not even the unanimous consent of the company's shareholders could validate the transaction.

The birth of the *ultra vires* rule in the context of limited liability companies may be traced back to cases involving statutory companies, many of these companies having been formed to construct public utilities (e.g. railways and canals). Statutory companies were restricted in the pursuit of legitimate business activities by the particular statute that granted them a corporate status. Any act by a statutory company which contravened a limitation placed upon its capacity would be deemed *ultra vires* and void: see e.g. the House of Lords' decision in *Eastern Counties Rlwy v Hawkes* (1855) 5 HLC 331.

In 1855, following the introduction of a limited-liability status for joint stock companies, the legislature considered it necessary to offer some means of protection for corporate creditors to curb the potential danger of them investing capital in enterprises which, as a consequence of their limited-liability status, offered investors minimal protection should the company fall into an insolvent state (i.e. the limited-liability status of companies precluded the personal resources of a company's membership from being used to repay corporate debts). Accordingly, the legislature introduced provisions into the Companies Act of 1856, whereby companies were obliged to register an objects clause; the said clause to be included in the company's memorandum. The objects clause specified a company's intended business purposes. Therefore, prior to entering into a credit agreement with a company, a creditor could inspect the company's objects clause to discover its business purposes, an inspection which could potentially influence the creditor's decision to advance loan funds.

In *Ashbury Railway Carriage and Iron Co v Riche* (1875) LR 7 HL 653, the House of Lords construed the 1862 Companies Act (which replaced the 1856 Act) in a restrictive manner, to hold that any matter not expressly or impliedly authorised by a company's objects clause would be one which was beyond the contractual capacity of the company. This strict interpretation of the 1862 Act was also subject to the *eiusdem generis* rule of construction. This rule limited the scope of any of the company's set objects to the extent that objects that were ancillary to the company's main object were to be construed in conjunction with the main object. Therefore, in *Ashbury*, an object which permitted the company to act as 'general contractors' could not be read as indicative of the company's ability to engage in a business as finance agents, although, arguably, the term 'general contractors' could have covered that activity. Applying the *eiusdem generis* rule, the object which permitted the company to act as general contractors was construed in relation to the company's main object, namely the company's principal business purpose of mechanical engineering. Thus, the company could only act as general contractors in connection with the business of mechanical engineering. By acting as general finance agents, the company had acted *ultra vires*; the transaction was deemed void.

The justification for the House of Lords' strict interpretation of the Companies Act 1862, and indeed the rationale for the *ultra vires* rule, was couched both in terms of shareholder and creditor protection. The *ultra vires* rule protected shareholders in so far as they could seek an injunction to restrain the company from entering into an *ultra vires* transaction, or, if a company's main object (substratum) had failed, they could petition the court for a winding up order: see e.g. *Re German Date Coffee* (1882) 20 ChD 169. Alternatively, where a company acted beyond its capacity the members of the company, by the passing of an ordinary resolution, could avoid the contract and seek the return of the subject matter of the contract, or, where that was not possible, seek compensation from the party (the constructive trustee) with whom the contract had been made.

Unsecured creditors, unlike shareholders, had no rights pertaining to the enforcement of the *ultra vires* rule, although a secured creditor, having taken a charge over the company's property, had the right to seek an injunction to restrain the company from entering into an *ultra vires* transaction: see e.g. *Cross v Imperial Continental Gas Association* [1923] 2 Ch 553.

The erosion of the ultra vires *rule*

While giving some form of protection to both shareholders and creditors, the *ultra vires* rule was not conducive to commercial business. Given that the objects clause was contained within the memorandum, a document available for public inspection, a person contracting with a company was deemed to have constructive notice of its contents, irrespective of whether any actual inspection of the document had actually taken place. Therefore, a person who dealt with a company could not subsequently complain if a transaction to which he was a party conflicted with the company's objects clause; the company could avoid the transaction. (It should be noted that at first instance in *Bell Houses Ltd* v *City Wall Properties* (1966) 1 QB 207 Mocatta J suggested that a third party could also invoke the *ultra vires* rule against a company. However, in subsequent cases this suggestion was never followed. On appeal, the decision of Mocatta J was overturned, but on different grounds.)

In an attempt to rectify the restrictive nature of the *ultra vires* rule, the courts in subsequent cases weakened the strict approach taken by the House of Lords in *Ashbury*. For example, in *A-G* v *The Great Eastern Railway Co Ltd* (1880) 5 App Cas 473, the House of Lords held that a company could pursue a course of business which was reasonably connected to its stated objects or, for that matter, could employ a power (e.g. the power to borrow money), where the power use was necessary to the fulfilment of the company's objects, irrespective of whether the particular power was absent from the company's objects clause. (The powers of a company, often contained within the objects clause, were tools to be employed to assist in the fulfilment of stated objects.)

In 1904 came one of the most significant decisions in connection with the weakening of the impeachable nature of the *ultra vires* rule, namely *Re David Payne & Co Ltd* [1904] 2 Ch 608. Here the Court of Appeal, in affirming the decision of Buckley J, inflicted what should have been a fatal blow to the *Ashbury* interpretation of the rule. Prior to *Re David Payne* it was considered that where a company employed a legitimate power but for a purpose not within its stated objects, then the exercise of the power would be *ultra vires* and void. In *Re David Payne* that view was discarded by restricting the question of whether a power use was *ultra vires*, to the issue of corporate capacity. Accordingly, the questions to ask were: (a) Was the power in question capable of being used to pursue the corporate objects? (b) Did the capacity to employ the power expressly or impliedly exist? Where a company was legitimately capable of exercising a corporate power, the use of that power would be valid (*intra vires*) even if ultimately the purpose for its use was for an activity outside the company's objects clause.

In *Cotman* v *Broughman* [1918] AC 514 the House of Lords, albeit reluctantly, struck another nail into the coffin of the *ultra vires* rule by refusing to invalidate an objects clause, the effect of which removed the main objects (or substratum) rule enunciated in the *Ashbury* case. In *Cotman* every stated object of the company was given an equal status thereby precluding the finding of a main object. The House of Lords, in giving its tacit approval to the *Cotman* objects clause, opined that once an objects clause had been approved by the Registrar, such approval was conclusive evidence that all the requirements of the Companies Act had been complied with (this is now governed by s 13, CA 1985).

In *Cotman*, although the House of Lords suggested that through the vigilance of the Registrar, similar clauses to the one found in *Cotman* should not be permitted, the House's suggestion was not followed. The *Cotman*-type clause became a regular feature in objects clauses. Due to the removal of the substratum rule (main objects rule) companies began to include a multitude of business objects within their objects clauses hopefully to expand their corporate capacity and preclude the fear of a transaction being challenged on the basis of the *ultra vires* rule. However, it should be noted that the power of a shareholder to petition for the winding up of a company on the basis that the company's main object had failed remained in respect of companies absent of a *Cotman*-type clause. (In *Re Kitson & Co Ltd* [1946] 1 All ER 435, the Court of Appeal diluted the substratum rule by providing that a company may not necessarily have one main object but may, in fact, have two.)

In *Bell Houses Ltd* v *City Wall Properties* [1966] 2 QB 656, the scope of a company's objects clause was further extended by the approval of a clause which authorised the company to carry on any business whatsoever which, in the opinion of the directors, could be advantageously carried out by the company in conjunction with or ancillary to any of the ventures specified in the objects clause.

The confusion between ultra vires and an abuse of powers

In relation to the issue of corporate capacity, a transaction, although not *ultra vires*, may have been entered into as a result of an abuse of the powers afforded to the company's directors. The legal consequences flowing from such a transaction were explained in *Re David Payne*: a transaction within the capacity of a company may nevertheless be voidable where the third party had actual notice of the transaction being used to pursue something which constituted an abuse of a director's power (the third party with actual notice would be liable as a constructive trustee; constructive trustees are discussed further in Chapter 17).

Unfortunately, the correct rationale of *Re David Payne* became confused with the concept of *ultra vires*. The confusion between *ultra vires* transactions and those which had taken place as a result of an abuse of directors' powers became commonplace. For example, in *Re Lee Behrens & Co Ltd* [1932] 2 Ch 46, a case concerned with an implied power to grant pension policies to employees and their spouses, Eve J, in considering whether the issue of a particular pension policy had been beyond the capacity of the company, declared that two questions had to be asked and answered in the affirmative before the transaction could escape the consequences of the *ultra vires* rule: first, was the transaction *bona fide*? Secondly, was the power used for the benefit and to promote the prosperity of the company?

In reality, the above questions had no relevance to the issue of capacity (*ultra vires*) but were instead concerned with whether directors of the company had abused their powers in allowing a particular transaction to proceed. Therefore, in declaring the pension policy in *Re Lee Behrens & Co Ltd* to be void on the premise that negative answers had been supplied to the two questions, Eve J clearly erred in his construction of the determination of a company's corporate capacity. The investigation into corporate capacity should not have been concerned with the state of mind of the officers of the company. In *Re Lee Behrens* the implied power was **capable** of being used to pursue the objects of the company and as such should not have been declared *ultra vires*.

Regrettably, the decision in *Re Lee Behrens* became widely accepted as an authority for determining whether a power use by a company incorporated an abuse of corporate capacity, thus rendering the power use *ultra vires*. The judgment of Eve J was applied in cases such as *Re Jon Beauforte Ltd* [1953] Ch 131, *Parke v Daily News Ltd* [1962] Ch 927, *Re Ward M Roith Ltd* [1967] 1 WLR 432 and *Introductions v National Provincial Bank* [1970] Ch 199.

The principles associated with *Re David Payne* were to remain clouded in confusion until the decision of Pennycuick J in *Charterbridge Corporation Ltd v Lloyds Bank* [1970] 1 Ch 62. Here, a company's (Castleford Ltd) ability to mortgage its property was called into question on the grounds of capacity. Castleford sought a mortgage from a bank to secure the indebtedness of a group of other companies to which Castleford belonged. Castleford, having taken a mortgage over its property, subsequently sold the property to the Charterbridge Corporation, but did so prior to repaying the mortgage owed to the bank. As the mortgage remained unpaid, the bank claimed the property in accordance with its mortgage terms. Charterbridge, which had been unaware of the existence of the mortgage, contended that notwithstanding that the power to mortgage property had been contained within Castleford's objects clause, the mortgage transaction should be viewed as *ultra vires* because it had not been entered into for the benefit of Castleford, but merely to support other companies in the group of companies to which Castleford belonged.

Pennycuick J had to determine whether the mortgage in relation to its benefit to Castleford was an issue of any relevance to the determination of an *ultra vires* transaction. Pennycuick J held that, as the power to mortgage was one which was capable of being used to pursue Castleford's objects, the use of the power could not be *ultra vires*. In other words, Eve J's benefit test had no application to the determination of whether or not the transaction was *ultra vires*. The confirmation of Pennycuick J's decision was provided in subsequent cases, namely *Re Halt Garages* [1982] 3 All ER 1016, *Re Horsley & Weight* [1982] Ch 442 and *Rolled Steel Products Ltd v British Steel Corporation* [1986] Ch 264. In this latter case, the Court of Appeal finally put to death any confusion that may have remained in relation to directors' powers and the *ultra vires* rule. The Court of Appeal killed off any suggestion that the doctrine of *ultra vires* was interwoven with issues relating to directors' powers. Accordingly, transactions which involved a dispute over the exercise of directors' powers, a director's authority to exercise delegated powers or a director's duty to exercise powers *bona fide* and for a proper purpose, had no place in the determination of a company's capacity to act.

STATUTORY REFORM OF THE *ULTRA VIRES* RULE

While the courts acted in a manner to curtail the severity of the *ultra vires* rule, albeit at times the judicial suppression of the rule being inconsistent and fraught with ambiguity, in contrast, the legislature had been slow to act to reform the rule. The first statutory intervention, following the recommendations of the Cohen Committee Report in 1945 (Cmnd 6659), was introduced into the Companies Act 1948, to permit a company to alter its objects clause by the passing of a special resolution (today this provision is contained within s 4, CA 1985). While this statutory reform allowed companies a greater degree of flexibility in the scope to alter the direction of their corporate purposes, it obviously failed to protect third parties in a situation where a company had entered into a prohibited type of business venture (prohibited by the existing objects clause) without having first altered its objects clause. If, however, the Cohen Committee recommendations had been enacted in full, the position would have been different; the committee had suggested that in relation to third party transactions, companies should have the powers of a natural person. Therefore, in effect, the *ultra vires* rule would have been abolished in respect of third party transactions.

In 1962, the Jenkins Committee (Cmnd 1749) proposed that the doctrine of constructive notice should be abolished. However, the committee's recommendations were not heeded. The statutory overhaul of the *ultra vires* rule was to remain sidelined until, as a result of the United Kingdom's entry into the European Community, the legislature was press-ganged into action. Section 9 of the European Communities Act 1972 was introduced to comply with the requirements of Art 9 of the EC First Company Law Directive. Article 9(1) provided that:

'Acts done by the organs of the company shall be binding upon it even if those acts are not within the objects of the company, unless such acts exceed the powers that the law confers or allows to be conferred on those organs.'

Section 9 of the European Communities Act 1972 later became s 35 of the Companies Act 1985. Section 35(1) (prior to its amendment by the Companies Act 1989) provided that:

'In favour of a person dealing with a company in good faith any transaction decided on by the directors is deemed to be one within the capacity of the company to enter into and the power of the directors to bind the company is deemed free of any limitation under the memorandum and articles.'

At first, many commentators considered that s 35(1) had achieved the desired effect of abolishing the *ultra vires* rule in relation to third party dealings; s 35(2) sought, in compliance with Art 9(2), to abrogate the constructive notice rule in circumstances where the conditions of s 35(1) had been satisfied. Certainly, in cases where the wording of s 35 was applicable, the removal of the *ultra vires* rule was achieved in relation to third party dealings. However, whilst the intention of s 35 had been to comply with Art 9 in its entirety, the language of the provision failed to achieve its objective: see e.g. *International Sales and Agencies Ltd* v *Marcus* [1982] 3 All ER 551, where the court questioned whether the words 'dealing' and 'transaction' covered gratuitous dealings, and *Barclays Bank Ltd* v *TOSG* [1984] BCLC 1, where Nourse J questioned the meaning of the term 'good faith'. (This latter case reached the House of Lords ([1984] AC 626), but no comments were made in respect of the analysis of the term 'good faith'.)

As a result of the problems associated with the wording of s 35, the ghost of the *ultra vires* rule remained. Whilst the threat of the *ultra vires* rule prevailed, companies, in drawing up object clauses, continued to create elaborate and well-defined clauses. Third parties who entered into contracts with companies were still advised to scrutinise and check the contents of object clauses. The *ultra vires* rule which had persistently hampered contractual freedom between companies and third parties, continued to be of a nuisance value.

The effect of the Companies Act 1989

In accordance with the proposals of the Prentice Report 1986 (a Department of Trade and Industry investigation into the legal and commercial implications of abolishing the *ultra vires* rule), s 110 of the Companies Act 1989 amended s 35 of the Companies Act 1985. The effect of the amendment was one which, in relation to a company's dealings with third parties, finally abolished the *ultra vires* rule. Section 35(1) (as amended) now provides as follows:

'The validity of an act done by a company shall not be called into question on the ground of lack of capacity by reason of anything in the company's memorandum.'

Although s 35 would have been more appropriately worded if it had stated, ' . . . an act would not be called into question by reason of anything excluded from a company's memorandum', it is clear that the statutory intention of the section is to abrogate the *ultra vires* rule in respect of third party interests in compliance with Art 9. While a company is not (contrary to the recommendations of the Prentice Report) theoretically possessed of the capacity of a natural person, capacity is nevertheless unrestricted by the contents of its memorandum. Note, however, that the authority of individual directors may be restricted by the company's articles or by the board of directors; a restriction which may potentially diminish the ultimate ability of a company to enter into a particular transaction (discussed further in Chapter 8).

While the Companies Act 1989 does not remove the need for an objects clause, it does seek to avoid the practice of prolonged clauses via the introduction of a standard type of objects clause (introduced by s 3A, CA 1985). The standard clause allows companies to pursue any activity within a commercial context. For existing companies, the option to adopt this new form of clause is exercised by the passing of a special resolution. By adopting an objects clause in line with s 3A, it should be noted that if a company wishes to place a limitation on a power to exercise the general commercial object (limitations on the exercise of objects were found in cases pre-1989 Act: see e.g. *Simmonds* v *Heffer* [1983] BCLC 298 and *Rosemary Simmons Memorial Housing Association Ltd* v *UDT Ltd* [1986] 1 WLR 1440), then such a limitation will need to be separately provided for in addition to the '3A type' objects clause. However, where limitations on the '3A type' objects are included, such limitations will not deflate the commercial capacity of a company in its dealings with third parties; s 35(1) prevents this from happening. Nevertheless, limitations contained in the objects clause will regulate the board of directors in relation to the board's own powers, and a transaction falling foul of a stipulated limitation, whilst not *ultra vires* a third party, will render any director acting contrary to the terms of the limitation (subject to a special resolution of the general meeting ratifying the director's act) liable to personally contribute to any loss sustained as a consequence of the transaction (see s 35(3), CA 1985, discussed below). In a like manner, corporate powers not covered by the s 3A definition but which the company wishes to include within its objects clause will need to be expressly provided for; such powers could possibly include the ability to make charitable or political donations. However, in respect of the latter it is to be noted that following the enactment, in February 2001, of the Political Parties, Elections and Referendum Act 2000, a company, if it is to make a political donation, will require the approval of the general meeting, by ordinary resolution. If this requirement is breached, the directors of the company are collectively liable to repay to the company the amount of the donation. The holders of not less than five per cent of the company's issued share capital may, with the leave of the court, enforce this right in the company's name against the directors (a type of statutory derivative action: see Chapter 23). (The relevant parts of the Political Parties, Elections and Referendum Act 2000 are inserted into the Companies Act 1985: see ss 347B–347K, CA 1985.)

Although the consequences of pursuing corporate purposes, other than those specified within the objects clause, will not, as a result of s 35(1), render the transaction void, it should be observed that the wording of s 35(3) does at first sight appear to provide a somewhat contradictory picture, in that it states:

'It remains the duty of the directors to observe any limitations on their powers flowing from the company's memorandum; and action by the directors which but for subsection (1) would be beyond the company's capacity may only be ratified by the company by special resolution. A resolution ratifying such action shall not affect any liability incurred by the directors or any other person; relief from any such liability must be agreed to separately by special resolution.'

In circumstances where a transaction exceeds a company's capacity as a consequence of an improper exercise of directors' powers, so defined within the memorandum, *prima facie*, s 35(3) would appear to suggest that the transaction would be unenforceable, save where the general meeting passed a special resolution to adopt it. Nevertheless, such an interpretation is flawed because s 35(3) expressly acknowledges that the transaction in question would have been unenforceable 'but for s 35(1)'. In other words, a transaction which falls outside a company's corporate capacity, having taken place as a result of an abuse of directors' powers (powers which are contained within the memorandum), will, in respect of third party interests, retain its validity because of the overriding s 35(1).

In terms of corporate capacity, the purpose of s 35(3) is restricted to a situation whereby the **company** itself seeks to enforce a transaction which goes beyond the directors' powers and is outside the scope of the company's capacity (i.e. as opposed to where a third party seeks to enforce a transaction under s 35(1)). Where a company does seek to enforce such a transaction, it must adopt the irregular transaction by a special resolution. A resolution ratifying such an action will not affect any liability incurred by the directors (for breach of powers) or any other person; relief from any such liability must be agreed to separately by an additional special resolution. The directors of a company will remain potentially liable (subject to the passing of a special resolution) for any transaction which exceeds any of their powers as contained within the memorandum even in a situation where the transaction is governed by s 35(1).

By retaining the concept of an objects clause, the 1989 Act maintains one of the initial justifications of the *ultra vires* rule, namely shareholder protection. Indeed, the ability of a shareholder to prevent the company from pursuing a transaction which falls outside its objects clause is expressly maintained by the 1989 Act (introduced as s 35(2), CA 1985). Section 35(2) provides that:

'A member of a company may bring proceedings to restrain the doing of an act which but for subsection (1) would be beyond the company's capacity; but no such proceedings shall lie in respect of an act done in fulfilment of a legal obligation arising from a previous act of the company.'

Nevertheless, s 35(2) incorporates a severe limitation on the ability of a shareholder to intervene in so far as it will not take effect where the company's act is in furtherance of an existing legal obligation. During the parliamentary passage of the Companies Act 1989, Lord Wedderburn of Charlton (speaking in the House of Lords) raised a salient observation in relation to the term 'legal obligation'. His lordship stated that a company would always need to enter into some form of legal obligation prior to the commencement of a commercial act. Therefore, a commercial transaction which is beyond a company's capacity, would, in so far as it was the subject of a contractual agreement prior to its actual performance, be outside the ambit of shareholder control because it is highly unlikely that a shareholder (other than shareholder/director) would have knowledge of the proposed transaction. Accordingly, as soon as the transaction is agreed upon, the legal obligation is created to negate the effect of s 35(2).

In the context of issues relating to corporate capacity, one specific shareholder right now lost following the implementation of s 35(1) is the shareholder derivative action (the derivative action is discussed further in Chapter 23). The concept of third parties holding property as constructive trustees in a situation where a company exceeds its corporate capacity no longer exists as a consequence of the newly formulated s 35(1). However, note that it may still be possible for a shareholder to pursue an action to recover corporate property in a situation where the breach of corporate capacity also involved a breach of a director's authority in the execution of the transaction (discussed further in Chapter 8).

Proposals for reform

In 2002, the government's White Paper, 'Modernising Company Law' (Cm 5553-1), followed the findings of the 2001 Final Report of the Company Law Review Steering Group (CLR), namely that the inclusion of an objects clause within a company's constitution served no useful purpose. However, the White Paper suggested that the objects clause should be allowed to be retained in the constitution by companies formed after the adoption of reforming legislation, albeit that its significance would be confined to matters of internal management. The findings of the White Paper (2002) were in part endorsed by the White Paper (2005). However, the latter still provides for the compulsory retention of an objects clause, to be maintained in the articles (the memorandum will cease to have any constitutional effect, see Chapter 4). Nevertheless, Clause A39 of the White Paper (2005) provides that, unless a company's articles provide otherwise, the objects of the company are to be unrestricted (in effect defeating any purpose of the objects clause in relation to a company's dealings with third parties). Where the objects of a company are in any way restricted, again the restriction will have no effect in relation to third party dealings. Therefore, in such a case the objects clause will only affect the relationship between the membership and its directors.

The practical effect of the 2005 White Paper's proposal will, in respect of a company's dealings with third parties, do no more than to clarify the present position (s 35, CA 1985) to ensure that all companies have an unlimited capacity in relation to third party dealings. The basis for the need for further clarification is a fear that the problem surrounding *ultra vires* transactions continues to exist. However, it is submitted that this fear is unwarranted in the context of corporate capacity. In truth, following the reforms of the 1989 Companies Act, a third party's inability to enforce a transaction with a company is not a matter which will involve questions relating to a lack of capacity but rather it will be concerned with whether an officer of the company, in authorising the transaction in question, had the requisite authority to bind the company (discussed in Chapter 8).

Historically, objects clauses have caused confusion and uncertainty in relation to commercial transactions between companies and third parties. However, objects clauses may, in some cases, provide safeguards for both shareholders and creditors of the company. Admittedly, such safeguards are largely toothless, but they nevertheless serve as a constraint on the powers of directors who will, as a matter of internal management, be obliged to abide by the terms of the objects clauses or suffer the possibility of being made personally liable under s 35(3). Accordingly, it is submitted that the 2005 White Paper's proposal to maintain the existence of an objects clause is to be preferred to the recommendation of the White Paper (2002) which in effect sought to eradicate the requirement for an objects clause. Indeed, at a time when issues of corporate governance are paramount, the objects clause should be retained as an obligatory part of a company's constitution, albeit having no effect in inhibiting a company's unlimited contractual capacity in relation to third party transactions. Further, to strengthen the significance of what may be termed the 'internal objects clause' (i.e. protection for shareholders and creditors) it is suggested (although admittedly this may be an extreme suggestion) that companies could, if adopting the present '3A type' clause, be required to list within that clause any business activities which a majority of the membership decided (by special resolution) that the company should not pursue (i.e. entrench the prohibited clauses). As with any clause within the new constitutional document, the said 'negative objects' could be removed or added to by means of a special resolution.

Suggested further reading

History and progression of the ultra vires *rule*
Griffin (1998) 2 MJLS 1

Confusion between powers and objects in relation to the ultra vires *rule*
Baxter [1970] CLJ 280

Article 9 of the EC Act 1972
Prentice (1973) LQR 518
Sealy and Collier [1973] CLJ 1

Reform of the ultra vires *rule pre-1989*
Pennington (1987) 8 Co Law 103

The effect of the 1989 Act
Poole (1991) 12 Co Law 43
Ferran (1992) 13 Co Law 124, 177

8

THE AUTHORITY OF DIRECTORS AND OTHER OFFICERS TO BIND THE COMPANY

INTRODUCTION

This chapter examines the rules relating to the authority of directors and other authorised persons in the context of their ability to enter into binding transactions on behalf of a company. It commences by explaining the agency rules applicable to the delegation of corporate authority and then considers the significant reforms which have been made to this area of company law by the Companies Act 1989. The reader should be warned that the aforementioned reforms are complex and at times vague. It is hoped that future law reform will resolve some of the difficulties associated with the interpretation of some of the reforming provisions of the 1989 Act. Future proposals for the reform of this area of law are dealt with at the end of the chapter.

THE AGENCY RELATIONSHIP

Whether an individual officer of a company has an authority to bind the company in a contractual relationship with a third party is dependent upon the rules of agency. Prior to s 9 of the European Communities Act 1972 (previously discussed in Chapter 7), the formation of an agency relationship was dependent upon the potential scope of an officer's authority to act as determined by the company's constitutional documents: that is, the contents of the memorandum and articles. Where a third party relied upon an officer's authority to bind a company, the third party's case would fail if the type of authority alleged was outside the ambit of the officer's authority as determined by the company's constitution.

A third party was deemed to have constructive notice of the contents of the memorandum and articles. However, as a consequence of the 1972 EC Act and subsequent legislation, culminating in the Companies Act 1989, the relevance of the memorandum and articles as the ultimate source of a company's capacity to delegate authority is no longer of crucial importance in relation to third party transactions. Providing a third party acts in good faith when entering into a contract with a company, the power of the board of directors to bind the company or authorise others to do so is, as a result of s 35A(1) of the Companies Act (introduced by the Companies Act 1989), deemed to be free of any limitation under the company's constitution.

However, although the validity of a corporate transaction cannot be called into question by anything contained in a company's memorandum (see s 35(1) of the Companies Act 1985, discussed in Chapter 7), it must be emphasised that, in order for any contractual agreement entered into by a company to be enforced against the company, the transaction must have been authorised by the board of directors or a company officer acting with the delegated authority of the board.

Types of authority

There are two principal forms of valid authority: actual authority – which may be express, implied, or usual (real); and, secondly, ostensible (apparent) authority.

Actual authority

The board of directors acting as a collective body is invested with the powers of the company; the company is the principal in the agency relationship. Subject to a contrary intention within a company's articles, the actual authority to exercise the powers of the board or part of those powers may be delegated to individual directors, a committee of directors or to directors occupying an executive position (e.g. a director appointed to the post of managing director): see Table A, art 72. Furthermore, the board of directors may give powers of attorney delegating the exercise of any of its powers to any person: see Table A, art 71.

The delegation of actual authority takes place as a result of a resolution passed by the board to appoint a director or committee of directors to take charge of specific corporate powers. A delegation of the board's actual authority in any matter is termed an express actual authority. The delegation of actual authority may also be implied. For example, where a director is expressly or impliedly appointed to a particular executive position, the director concerned will have an implied authority to bind the company in a manner consistent with the powers associated with that position, that is, a usual (real) authority. An executive position to which an implied actual authority is attached may be subject to express restrictions, imposed by either the board or the company's articles, in which case the implied authority granted may be more restrictive than the usual authority ordinarily associated with the position in question. Prior to the Companies Act 1989, a third party was deemed to have constructive notice of any restrictions placed on a director's authority by the company's constitution. However, in accordance with the rule advanced in *Royal British Bank* v *Turquand* (1856) 6 E & B 327 (discussed below), a third party, when dealing with a company, was not bound to ensure that all the internal regulations of the company had been complied with in respect to the exercise and delegation of authority. A third party was not deemed to have notice of matters of internal management which sought to impose restrictions upon a director's authority. Where the *Turquand* rule was operative, the third party was permitted to rely on the authority of the director as determined in accordance with his usual/real authority, namely the authority usually associated with the particular type of position occupied by the director in question.

An oft-quoted case example of the operation of implied actual authority is *Hely Hutchinson* v *Brayhead Ltd* [1968] 1 QB 549. This case concerned the extent and determination of an authority vested in a company chairman to bind a company to a contract in a situation where the chairman had not sought the prior approval of the company's board to so approve the terms of the contract. The Court of Appeal found that, as the chairman was accustomed, often without consultation with other board members, to committing the company to like contracts, his actions were akin to those of a *de facto* managing director. In common with the chairman's previous dealings, the remaining members of the board had not sought to curb the chairman's powers. As such, the court held that the chairman's authority to bind the company contractually could be implied from the executive position he was allowed to occupy: he acted as the company's *de facto* managing director.

Ostensible authority

Unlike actual authority, which operates on the basis of an express or implied delegation of authority from the company (the principal) to an officer of a company (the agent), ostensible authority operates as a result of a representation from the company (the principal) to a third party. The representation is to the effect that a particular person (the agent) possesses the necessary authority to bind the company. An officer of a company who possesses ostensible authority will have no actual authority to perform the act to which the ostensible authority relates.

In effect, ostensible authority will be established where there is a representation from the board of directors or duly authorised executive, which expressly, by implication or by conduct, acknowledges the right of the company's agent to bind the company in a particular transaction. From the judgment of Slade LJ in *Rolled Steel Products (Holdings) Ltd v British Steel Corp* [1986] Ch 246, a company will, by implication, hold out its directors as having ostensible authority to bind the company to any transaction which falls within the powers expressly or impliedly conferred on it by its memorandum. Where, however, a director purports to bind the company in a manner permitted by the company's constitution, but the director in question has no actual authority to do so – a fact which is known by the third party to the transaction – then in such circumstances the transaction may be avoided. In *Heinl v Jyske Bank (Gibraltar) Ltd* [1999] Lloyd's Rep 511, Nourse LJ summarised the position as follows:

> 'Where an agent is known by the other party to a purported contract to have no authority to bind his principal, no contract comes into existence. The agent does not purport to contract on his own behalf and the knowledge of the other party unclothes him of ostensible authority to contract on behalf of the principal.' (at p 519)

In all instances of alleged ostensible authority the third party must rely upon a representation of authority from the company and must have altered his position as a consequence of that reliance. It should be noted that, in establishing ostensible authority, where the representation of authority relied upon by a third party is contained within the company's constitutional documents, then reliance upon the contents of the documents must have been as a direct result of the third party's actual notice of them; the concept of constructive notice will not work to the advantage of a third party: see e.g. *Rama Corporation Ltd v Proved Tin & General Investments Ltd* [1952] 2 QB 147.

An oft-quoted case example of ostensible authority is *Freeman & Lockyer v Buckhurst Park Properties Ltd* [1964] 2 QB 480. Here, Kapoor (K), a director of the defendant company (C), entered into a contract with the plaintiffs (P), without first seeking the approval of the three other members of C's board. The board subsequently refused to honour the terms of the contract on the premise that K had no authority to enter into the contract. The Court of Appeal held that, whilst K had never been appointed to a position which carried an actual authority to bind the company in the contractual relationship with P, the board had nevertheless been aware of K's managerial activities: K had been left in charge of the day-to-day management of the company. As such, P was justified in relying on K's ability to bind the company. The company by its conduct (or by its acquiescence in allowing K to act) had represented to P that K had an authority to act, an authority which P had relied upon.

It will be observed that the cases of *Freeman & Lockyer* v *Buckhurst Park Properties Ltd* and *Hely Hutchinson* v *Brayhead Ltd* are, in many respects, similar. While the latter case was one concerned with implied authority, the distinction between implied authority and ostensible authority may, on occasions, be a very fine one. In seeking to attempt to distinguish the two cases (although this is a difficult task!), it is suggested that in *Freeman & Lockyer* the reason why the court was unwilling to find an implied authority was because K had never formally or impliedly been appointed to a management position consistent with that of a *de facto* managing director. The acquiescence of the individual members of the board to K's activities was perhaps insufficient to amount to a valid authority to permit the finding that K should manage the day-to-day business of the company in a position akin to that of a managing director. By contrast, in *Hely Hutchinson*, the company chairman was accustomed and was permitted to act in a manner consistent with the position of a managing director.

A case example which establishes the flexibility of the concept of ostensible authority is *First Energy Ltd* v *Hungarian International Bank Ltd* [1993] BCC 533. Here, the Court of Appeal held that a bank's senior manager had, from his position as a senior employee of the bank, an ostensible authority to communicate to the plaintiff the bank's apparent approval of the plaintiff's proposed transaction. The court so held, notwithstanding that the bank had not given its approval to the transaction in question and notwithstanding that the plaintiff was indeed aware that the manager did not have an actual authority to approve the transaction without first seeking the approval of the bank's head office. Although the Court of Appeal accepted that the bank manager would not ordinarily have had an ability to self-authorise transactions without the approval of his head office (by analogy, see e.g. *Armagas Ltd* v *Mundogas SA* [1986] 2 All ER 385), the court found that, in the instant case, the bank's head office (the principal) had clothed its agent (the bank manager) with the trappings of authority in a manner capable of inducing the plaintiff to rely on the existence of the agency relationship (i.e. ostensible authority had been given). The bank had done so by, for example, allowing the bank manager, in previous dealings between the bank and the plaintiff, to instigate negotiations for loans on behalf of the bank and to communicate the bank's acceptance of short-term credit facilities to the plaintiff. The plaintiff relied on the bank manager's ostensible authority in dealings with the bank; the bank manager having been held out as having an accepted power to bind the bank in respect of communicating the bank's acceptance of the type of transaction in question.

Indeed, it would have been nonsensical and contrary to commercial reality had the court reached a contrary judgment because, had it done so, it would have resulted in a bizarre conclusion: namely, the plaintiff would have been expected to seek the approval of the bank's head office whenever it sought to confirm a communication in relation to a proposed transaction, a communication which would have already been given to the plaintiff by the bank's manager. The bank manager was a person occupying a position of some responsibility and surely a person whom the plaintiff could reasonably be expected to rely upon in respect of the communication of a loan agreement.

The indoor management rule (the Turquand rule)

The indoor management rule, which is derived from the case of *Royal British Bank v Turquand* (1856) 6 E & B 327, provides that, when dealing with a company, a third party is not bound to ensure that all the internal regulations of the company have been complied with in respect of the exercise of an authority to bind the company. The operation of the rule is subject to a number of exceptions, namely:

- a third party with actual knowledge that a transaction is outside the authority conferred by the company's constitution cannot plead the rule (see e.g. *Howard Patent Ivory Manufacturing Co* (1833) 38 ChD 156);

- a third party cannot rely on the rule in circumstances where he is an insider, namely where he/she is an officer of the company (see e.g. *Morris v Kansen* [1946] AC 459);

- where there are suspicious circumstances surrounding the authorisation of a transaction and the third party should reasonably have been aware of such circumstances, the third party will not be able to rely on the rule (see e.g. *Underwood v Bank of Liverpool & Martins Ltd* [1924] 1 KB 755);

- the rule will not operate in circumstances where the contractual authorisation was a forgery (see e.g. *Ruben v Great Fingall Consolidated* [1906] AC 439);

- finally, where the necessary authorisation for a transaction requires the passing of a special resolution, a third party will be deemed to have notice of the outcome of the resolution, as a special resolution must be registered and therefore is open to public inspection (see e.g. *Irvine v Union Bank of Australia* (1877) 2 App Cas 366). However, the rule would apply in a situation where an ordinary resolution was required to validate an exercise of authority because an ordinary resolution does not require registration.

While the indoor management rule is operative (subject to the above exceptions) in relation to the company's internal procedures, that is, in respect of the company's ability to validate an exercise of authority, the rule, **taken on its own**, cannot extend to issues relating to the ability of a board of directors to confer ostensible authority. Thus, a third party is not entitled to rely on the indoor management rule for the purpose of assuming that an officer was given an authority by the board to act in excess of his actual or usual authority.

A case example which illustrates the relationship between the *Turquand* rule and ostensible authority is *Mahony v East Holyford Mining Company* (1875) LR 7 HL. This case involved a claim by a company to the effect that its bank had paid moneys from the company's account without due authorisation. The bank, in making payments from the company's account, had done so in the belief that it was following the conditions laid down in the company's articles; the articles prescribed that payments should only be made when cheques had been signed by two directors and then countersigned by the company secretary. The difficulty in this case was that no director or company secretary had actually been appointed by the company. However, the persons who purported to authorise the payments for the company had been allowed to do so by the company. The House of Lords held that the bank was allowed to assume (as it had no actual notice to the contrary) that the internal regulations of the company had been complied with, and that appointments to the positions of corporate responsibility had been made (operation of indoor management rule). The House found that the acquiescence of the company in its failure to deny that the persons acting for the company had an authority to act created a representation upon which the bank could rely (operation of ostensible authority).

THE EFFECT OF THE COMPANIES ACT 1989

Prior to its amendment by the Companies Act 1989, s 35(1) of the Companies Act 1985 was not exclusively confined to questions relating to the validity of a purported *ultra vires* transaction. Indeed, s 35(1) was of importance whenever the authority of a director was called into question. Section 35(1) provided that:

> **'In favour of a person dealing with a company in good faith any transaction decided on by the directors is deemed to be one within the capacity of the company to enter into and the power of the directors to bind the company is deemed free of any limitation under the memorandum and articles.'**

Where the section was applicable (note the problems created by the wording of the section: see Chapter 7) the board of directors' authority to bind the company was deemed free of any limitation placed upon it by the company's memorandum and articles. Accordingly, providing a third party acted in good faith, the third party could rely on the authority of the board of directors. Where s 35(1) was applicable, s 35(2) of the 1985 Act abolished the concept of constructive notice.

In addition to severely restricting the ambit of the *ultra vires* rule, the Companies Act 1989 (s 108(1)), in its attempt to produce a climate of contractual freedom, further seeks to limit the restrictions placed upon the authority of company directors. The reforms applicable to directors' authority are aimed at complementing those made in connection with matters relating to the overall scope of a company's capacity to enter into contractual relationships. The 1989 Act amends and introduces new sections into the relevant parts of the 1985 Act. A new s 35A(1) of the Companies Act 1985 provides:

> **'In favour of a person dealing with a company in good faith, the power of the board of directors to bind the company, or authorise others to do so, shall be deemed to be free of any limitation under the company's constitution.'**

In accordance with s 35A(1), the status of the board is that of guardian for its principal's (the company's) ability to delegate authority. In an attempt to overcome the difficulties associated with the interpretation of the wording used in the old s 35(1) (discussed in Chapter 7), a new s 35A(2)(a) of the Companies Act 1985 provides that a person will deal with a company if he is 'a party to any transaction or other act to which the company is a party'. As such, the section should be construed as not only being applicable to commercial acts, but to any act of the company. In addition, s 35A(2)(b) and (c) attempt (in a negative way) to clarify the meaning of 'good faith' by providing that a person is not to be regarded as having acted in bad faith solely as a result of knowing that a corporate act was beyond the powers of the directors under the company's constitution; indeed a person is presumed to have acted in good faith unless the contrary is proved (this extends the protection afforded by the *Turquand* rule in so far as it removes the first exception to the *Turquand* rule: see above). However, it is somewhat unfortunate that no guidance is given as to what actually constitutes bad faith. However, it is suggested that 'bad faith' may be found if in the circumstances of a particular case it would have been unconscionable for the third party to seek to enforce the contract; by analogy consider the case of *Bank of Credit and Commerce International (Overseas) Ltd* v *Akindele* [2001] Ch 437 (this case was concerned with 'knowing receipt': see Chapter 17).

It should also be observed that although s 35A(1) uses the term 'limitations under the company's constitution', the term 'constitution' is, in accordance with s 35A(3), given an extended meaning, because it includes limitations deriving from a resolution of the general meeting, a meeting of any class of shareholders and limitations derived from a membership agreement.

In the unlikely event of a third party being unable to rely on s 35A, a transaction involving a breach of director's authority may nevertheless be ratified by ordinary resolution. However, note that the ratification of a transaction which was entered into with an authority that exceeds a limitation on the board's powers, so specified within the memorandum, may only be achieved by means of a special resolution of the general meeting (s 35(3), CA 1985).

The legislature's decision not to confer individual directors with the authority to bind the company as of right was in sharp contrast to the recommendations of the Prentice Report (1986). However, in this respect, the legislature's decision in not adopting the Prentice Report's proposals was perhaps understandable. Following the proposals of the Prentice Report, there would have been a radical departure from the traditional position of ultimate authority as vested in the board of directors, to the extent that a director, responsible and with authority to bind the company in, say, contract type X, would have had an equal and independent right to bind the company in contract type Y. The director's ability to bind the company in contract type Y would have existed without any form of delegation of authority from the board and would have bound the company to the contract despite the fact that the director in question may not have had any expertise in business matters related to contract type Y.

Although the Companies Act 1989, in its retention of the board as the ultimate source of authority, denies individual directors an unfettered right to bind the company contractually, s 35A allows individual directors a right to bind the company where the director's act is the result of a delegation of authority from the board. The power to bind the company is deemed free of any limitation under the company's constitution (s 35A(3), CA 1985). Therefore, a company officer, with an authority delegated from the board to bind the company in contract type Y, for example, will be able to bind the company to that type of contract, irrespective of the fact that the individual director's position in the company conferred no usual authority to bind the company in respect of transaction Y and notwithstanding the fact that the company's constitution prohibited the company from entering into a type Y contract (but subject to s 35(3), CA 1985).

However, it must be stressed that, to bind a company, the director's authority must have been delegated to him/her from the board. Although s 35A states that a third party is not to be deprived of the benefit of a contract where the board exceeds limitations placed upon its authority by its constitution, such 'limitations' cannot extend to a situation where the authority to enter into the transaction occurs without the approval of the board. Accordingly, if a contract is entered into on behalf of the company by an individual director who, for example, mistakenly believes his authority so to act has been approved by the board, when in reality no such authority has been given, then in such circumstances the third party will be unable to rely on the director's authority.

Unlike the wording of the previous s 35 of the Companies Act 1985, the effect of the Companies Act 1989 abrogates the constructive notice rule without any form of restrictive limitations. Under the old s 35, the abolition of the constructive rule had no effect unless the contract in question was of a commercial nature and was one decided upon by all the directors (see Chapter 7). However, although a third party is not deemed to have constructive notice of an act which is beyond the company's constitution, he must nevertheless assure himself that the person with whom he dealt was authorised to act by the board. This is impliedly confirmed by the new s 35B, CA 1985, which states:

'A party to a transaction with a company is not bound to enquire as to whether it is permitted by the company's memorandum *or as to any limitation on the powers of the board of directors to bind the company or authorise others to do so.*' (emphasis added)

Although s 35B removes a third party's need to be concerned about the existence of a limitation on the board's authority, the section, by implication, nevertheless preserves the requirement for an authority to act: the transaction must still be sanctioned by the board or a duly authorised person.

The removal of the doctrine of constructive notice to all areas of company law, save for company charges, was proposed via s 142(1) of the Companies Act 1989, which sought to create a new s 711A of the Companies Act 1985. However, this provision was never enacted. Interestingly, s 711A(2) of the Companies Act 1985 provided that the abolition of the constructive notice rule would:

'. . . not affect the question as to whether a person is affected by notice of any matter by reason of a failure to make such enquiries as ought reasonably to be made.'

The wording of s 711A(2) was perhaps vaguely constructed and in conflict with s 35B of the Companies Act 1985. Nevertheless, in so far as the section was concerned with corporate capacity and directors' authority, it is suggested that it may have been construed as reinforcing the fact that it remains a third party's responsibility to ensure that an agent of a company had some form of authority to act on behalf of his/her principal.

The abolition of the constructive notice rule via s 35A and 35B, in so far as it affects the ability of an authorised person to bind the company, is, however, subject to one exception: where the board enters into a contract with an insider (i.e. a director or person connected to a director) and the board exceeds any limitations on its powers under the company's constitution, the transaction (or any other act) will become voidable at the company's option. As such, insiders are not protected by the abolition of the constructive notice rule and will not be able to seek the absolute protection of ss 35A and 35B. The insider, and any director of the company who authorised the contract, remains personally liable to account to the company for any gain made or loss incurred as a result of the transaction (s 322A, CA 1985). Where, however, an innocent *bona fide* third party acquires rights as a result of the insider transaction, the company will, in such a case, be unable to avoid it.

The interpretation of ss 35A and 322A was considered by the Court of Appeal in *Smith* v *Henniker-Major & Co* [2003] Ch 182. The somewhat unusual facts of the case concerned the validity of an agreement to assign a right of action vesting in a company to a director of the company (S). The agreement was entered into by an inquorate board, that is the transaction was agreed to at a board meeting but the meeting was inquorate because only one director (S) attended; the company's articles required a quorum of two directors. If the assignment was invalid then S had no standing to commence the action. S contended that, under s 35A(2)(b), knowing that an act is beyond the powers of the directors did not prevent a person (here, S himself) from seeking to rely on s 35A, and, further, that a person must be presumed to have acted in good faith unless the contrary was proved (s 35A(2)(c)). S argued that a quorum requirement should, in the context of s 35A, be treated as a 'limitation', thus extending the prescribed ambit of s 35A(3). At first instance, Rimer J ([2002] BCC 544) held that a director could not bind the company via s 35A where there had been no delegation of authority from the board to the director. Rimer J rightly pointed out that in this particular case the agreement in question had never, in accordance with s 35A, been authorised by the board. In effect, S sought to ignore the crucial requirement of s 35A: a director's authority to act must originate from a properly constituted board. Clearly a director who had entered into an agreement that was purportedly authorised by an inquorate board could not save the validity of the agreement by claiming that the quorum requirement was a limitation on the power of the directors, therefore bringing the transaction within the scope of s 35A.

On appeal, the decision of Rimer J was affirmed in relation to the s 35A point, although only by a majority of the court. Dissenting on the s 35A point, Robert Walker LJ accepted that s 35A would ordinarily be employed by an independent third party, but took the view that s 35A was also applicable where the 'person' involved (as, in effect, the third party) was a director of the company. Robert Walker LJ believed that a director of a company could rely on s 35A, although the validity of a transaction could still be trumped (yet, strangely, not in this case) and therefore avoided via s 322A of the Companies Act 1985.

The majority of the court, Carnwarth and Schiemann LJJ, disagreed with Robert Walker LJ. Schiemann and Carnwarth LJJ accepted the reasoning of Rimer J. Carnwarth LJ opined that, as the agreement was concluded at an inquorate board meeting, S had no more authority to take a decision in the name of the company than its office boy; the agreement was therefore a nullity. However, his lordship did qualify this view by adding that in appropriate circumstances an independent third party (i.e. not a director or connected party) may be able to rely on the apparent authority of a person who represented (albeit without actual authority) to the third party that a transaction had been authorised by the board (by analogy, consider, the case of *First Energy Ltd* v *Hungarian International Bank Ltd* [1993] BCC 533, discussed above).

Although Carnwarth and Schiemann LJJ accepted that in a technical sense a director could be classed as a 'person' for the purposes of s 35A, both lordships found that in the instant case, S could not rely on his own error to turn his own decision into a decision of the board. In effect, s 322A prevailed.

The decision of the Court of Appeal in *Smith* v *Henniker-Major & Co* conveys, in part, an understandable degree of confusion in the context of the interpretation to be afforded to s 35A and s 322A. However, it is respectfully submitted that the interpretation of s 35A, so provided by the trial judge and the majority of the Court of Appeal is, for the most part, to be accepted as correct. First, the statutory language of s 35A would appear clear as to the point that a validly constituted board of directors must confer authority; the said authority cannot run to an individual director who mistakenly believes he has an authority akin to that of the board. However, a director's authority to bind the company, even if absent of an actual authority from the board, could still be binding in a situation which establishes ostensible authority. Secondly, where a transaction or other act is an internal transaction (i.e. involving a director), the director will not, as of right, be able to rely on s 35A in so far as that provision is subject to s 322A. Where, in accordance with s 322A, the transaction in question is ratified by the company then, possibly, s 35A may be applicable – ratification would still be deemed ineffective if the director failed to satisfy the requirements of s 35A. However, it is submitted that this latter point must be considered with some caution because here the reasoning is inconclusive in relation to the construction of the relevant statutory provisions. Indeed, as Schiemann LJ observed, s 322A is distinct from s 35A and should therefore be confined to issues involving the internal relationship between the company and its directors. It is to be noted that this point would appear to have been lost in *Cottrell* v *King* [2004] BCC 307, where, in construing s 35A (s 322A should have been applied!), Kevin Garnett QC, sitting as a deputy judge, considered that the defendant, a director of the company, was not deemed to have had constructive knowledge of the company's articles.

Following on from *Smith* v *Henniker-Major & Co*, it is to be noted that the Court of Appeal in *EIC Services* v *Phipps* [2004] 2 BCLC 589 (see the judgment of Peter Gibson LJ at pp 559–661) has construed s 35A in a manner whereby a 'person dealing with a company' cannot be expected to be interpreted to include a member of the company. The court held that, in the context of a company, s 35A (in giving effect to Art 9(2) and the term 'third parties') naturally referred to persons other than the company and its members. (The case of *EIC Services* v *Phipps* is discussed further in Chapter 9.)

Shareholder rights

In respect of shareholders' rights, shareholders retain the power to prevent a transaction from taking place in circumstances where, if the transaction had been allowed to proceed, the board would have exceeded its authority (s 35A(4), CA 1985). However, where a contract is to be performed in fulfilment of a previous legal obligation, no shareholder intervention is possible. Accordingly, a transaction which exceeds the board's authority will (in so far as it is the subject of a contractual agreement, i.e. prior to its actual performance) be outside the ambit of shareholder intervention: it is highly unlikely that a shareholder (other than a shareholder/director) will have any knowledge of a proposed transaction, the effect of which will, when performed, exceed the board's authority.

It should be noted that the board or a person authorised by the board will remain personally liable to the company in respect of a transaction which was entered into outside the scope of the company's constitution (s 35A(5), CA 1985). However, it must be stressed that where a third party acts in good faith, no shareholder action (save for the limited right under s 35A(4)) will be able to prevent the enforcement of a contract with a company in circumstances where the contract was entered into by a duly authorised officer of the company, even in a situation where the contract type is not permitted by the company's constitution, or possibly where the enforcement of the contract may otherwise have been regarded as a fraud on minority interests. Indeed, the minority shareholders' position is weakened by the fact that a third party's actual knowledge of a limitation on a director's authority to enter into a contract will not necessarily preclude the third party from having acted in good faith (s 35A(2), CA 1985). As to the actual meaning of good faith, the 1989 Act fails to define the term, albeit that it is suggested that good faith would not be found where, for example, a third party committed a fraud or other illegal act in the procurement of the contract.

The position of the Turquand rule after the Companies Act 1989

In abolishing the doctrine of constructive notice, the Companies Act 1989 has, to a large extent, extinguished the need for the *Turquand* rule. However, the *Turquand* rule may still be of assistance in matters concerning a board's delegation of authority. For example, where the board delegates authority to a company agent, but in doing so places internal restrictions (other than restrictions contained in the constitution) on the ability of the agent to carry out his functions (a matter not covered by s 35A(3), CA 1985), then, in accordance with the *Turquand* rule, the third party will not, unless he is considered to have acted in bad faith, be deemed to have knowledge of such restrictions; he/she may assume that the director in question acts with a usual authority. The *Turquand* rule will also continue to be of assistance in those cases where there is no valid appointment of a company officer, notwithstanding that the company's constitution provides for such appointment: see e.g. *Mahony* v *East Holyford Mining Co* (1875) LR 7 HL (discussed above).

Proposals for reform

Although, as currently drafted, the nature of s 35A and related provisions may be viewed as confusing, the White Paper (2005) contains no recommendations in relation to the reform of the law governing directors' authority. However, the earlier White Paper 'Modernising Company Law – Draft Clauses' (July 2002, Cm 5553-II) (draft clause 17), while not attempting to change the spirit of the law in relation to directors' authority did make an attempt to spell out the meaning of the relevant provisions in a clearer format. Under the proposed draft clause 17, in relation to dealings with companies, a person (other than a director or connected person) would, as is the present case, be entitled to assume that the board of directors was entitled (without limitation from the constitution) to enter into a transaction or other act (or authorise others to do so) to bind the company. However, in dealing with a company, a person would still need to ensure that the transaction or act was authorised by the board of directors or that an individual director was authorised to act by the board of directors.

In effect, draft clause 17 sought to present s 322A of the Companies Act 1985 as an exception (draft clause 17(5) and (6)) to the main intent of draft clause 17(2) (clause 17(2) resembles the present s 35A). The integration of the present s 322A into an all-embracing provision (draft clause 17) would be welcomed. However, the effect of draft clause 17(5) and (6) would not change the present law. A director or connected party falling under s 322A cannot advance s 35A and neither would a director or connected party falling under draft clause 17(5) and (6) be able to take the benefit of draft clause 17(2). A transaction falling under draft clause 17(5) and (6) would be invalid, but as with any breach of director's authority, it could be ratified by the general meeting.

Suggested further reading

The effect of the 1989 Act

Griffin [1991] NILQ 38

Griffin (1991) 12 Co Law 98

Poole (1991) 12 Co Law 43

Ferran (1992) 13 Co Law 124, 177

Farrar (2003) 62 CLJ 45

9

THE LEGAL NATURE AND CHARACTERISTICS OF HOLDING SHARES IN A LIMITED COMPANY

INTRODUCTION

A company limited by shares is founded on an undertaking by its members to contribute capital in consideration for the issue of shares. The aim of this chapter is to explain the legal characteristics associated with the various types of share capital. In addition to identifying the legal characteristics attributed to the various types of shares, this chapter will briefly discuss the valuation of shares and the powers of both the court and the Secretary of State to impose restrictions on rights associated with share ownership. Share issues in public companies are specifically dealt with by Chapter 11. The maintenance of a company's share capital is dealt with in Chapter 10.

THE LEGAL CHARACTERISTICS OF A SHARE

The extent of a shareholder's undertaking to contribute capital to a company, the shareholder's right to participate in dividend distributions and the ability of a shareholder to vote at general meetings are all matters related to the number and class of shares held in the company. Once share capital is contributed it becomes the property of the company; the company is not to be regarded as a debtor in respect of its repayment or restoration.

An acknowledged definition relating to the legal nature of a company share is that advanced in the judgment of Farwell J, in *Borland's Trustee* v *Steel Bros & Co Ltd* [1901] 1 Ch 279. His lordship stated:

> 'A share is the interest of a shareholder in the company measured by a sum of money, for the purposes of liability in the first place and interest in the second, but also consisting of a mutual set of covenants entered into by all the shareholders *inter se.*' (at p 288)

In respect of the above quotation, 'the sum of money' is the price attached to a share. Following the advancement of the full purchase price, a person's liability to contribute capital ceases. The minimum amount by which the share may be purchased from the company is termed the nominal value (par value) of the share (see e.g. *Ooregum Gold Mining Co of India* v *Roper* [1892] AC 125). Where a company offers to sell shares at a price in excess of their nominal value, the monetary difference between the price paid for the shares and the nominal value is termed the 'share premium' and must be placed in a share premium account (see Chapter 10).

The extent of a shareholder's interest in the company is measured by the number and class of shares purchased. A shareholding interest is comprised of all the legal rights of membership contained within a mutual set of covenants: the company's memorandum and articles of association. However, the exact scope of a membership interest is likely to extend beyond strict legal rights; the extent of a membership interest will be dependent upon the nature of the shares and the type of company in which they are held. (The scope of a membership interest is discussed further in Chapter 24.)

Unless a company is unlimited or limited by guarantee, its memorandum must indicate the amount of share capital that the company is permitted to issue (authorised share capital clause), together with the way in which the capital is to be divided into shares of a fixed amount (s 2(5), CA 1985). The total nominal capital of a public company must not be less than £50 000. A company is not permitted to issue shares beyond its authorised share capital limit, although, where a company's articles permit, the authorised share capital may be altered in accordance with s 121(1) and (2) of the Companies Act 1985. Where a company adopts the standard Table A articles, Table A, art 32 provides that an alteration to the authorised share capital clause may be instigated by an ordinary resolution. However, if the company is a private company, the alteration powers contained within s 121 may be employed without the need to call a general meeting, that is, providing that the members of the company unanimously agree to the alteration in writing. It is to be noted that the Company Law Review (CLR) proposed that the authorised capital clause should be abolished as a compulsory requirement. This proposal was accepted by the White Paper, 'Modernising Company Law' (2002) and subsequently endorsed by the White Paper, 'Company Law Reform' (2005). Abolishing this measure of capital should have no significant effect in that it provides creditors with no accurate measure of a company's capital; it represents but a theoretical ceiling on a company's ability to issue capital (a ceiling that may be amended: see above) as opposed to a practical identification of actual capital contributed to the company.

Identifying a member of a company

A person may become a member of a company in one of four ways:

- by subscribing to the memorandum on the incorporation of the company;
- by making a successful application to the company for shares;
- by purchasing shares from an existing member of the company; or
- by acquiring shares as a result of a member's death or bankruptcy.

While the use of the terms 'member' and 'shareholder' are often synonymous, it is nevertheless possible for a person to be a member but not a shareholder of a company. For example, a company limited by guarantee has members, but not shareholders. Conversely, it is possible to be a shareholder but not a member of a company. For example, the holders of 'bearer shares' are classed as shareholders but, although shareholders, they may not necessarily be members of the company. A holder of bearer shares is entitled to specific shares identified in a share warrant. Subject to any contrary provision within the articles, the bearer of a share warrant is entitled to have his name entered in the register of members only upon the surrender of the share warrant (s 188, CA 1985).

The register of members

Section 352 of the Companies Act 1985 provides that every company must keep a register of its members, the same to provide details of their names, addresses and the extent of each member's shareholding in the company. The subscribers to a company's memorandum are deemed to have agreed to become members of the company and, following the company's registration, must be entered as members in the company's register of members (s 22(1), CA 1985). Section 22(2) of the Companies Act 1985 further provides that every other person who has otherwise assented to become a member, and whose name is entered in the register of members, is a member of the company. For a person to assent to become a member of a company it is unnecessary to establish a binding contract between that person and the company. Accordingly, a person's membership of a company will *prima facie* be conclusive where, irrespective of the absence of a binding contract, that person's name (if he/she has assented) is added to the register (see e.g. *Re Nuneaton Borough AFC Ltd* [1989] BCLC 454). However, it should be noted that in *POW Services Ltd* v *Clare* [1995] 2 BCLC 205, Jacob J held that although the conditions laid down in s 22 may be met, a person's membership of a company could nevertheless be denied, as of right, in circumstances where, for example, that person became a member of the company in contravention of a term (or terms) of the company's articles.

Following the implementation of the Uncertificated Securities Regulations 2001 (SI 2001/3755) it is now possible (but not obligatory) for public companies to keep a second register in computerised form (the CREST system). Although this new system may have a potential to confuse matters, its objective is in fact to speed up the share transfers. This system of registration is applicable only to shares held in electronic form (uncertified shares); it does not apply to shares held via the traditional form of share certificates. Admission to the system requires the prior consent of both the company issuing the securities and the company operating the computer system (at present only one operator exists, CrestCo). Further, it is not obligatory for a holder of the electronic form of shares to have his/her name entered on the CREST system. Shareholders who participate in the CREST system are offered some degree of protection in relation to unauthorised transactions (see regs 36 and 46). When entered on the CREST system, a member must also be entered in the register maintained by the company, although the specific details of his/her holding need only be maintained via the CREST system.

Rectification of the register

Where the details entered in a register of members are incorrect in some material respect, they may be challenged in accordance with s 359 of the Companies Act 1985. For a person to successfully challenge an entry, it is necessary to establish a legitimate interest in the shares to which the entry relates. A legitimate interest may be defined as one which is in the best interests of the company as a whole. For example, in *Re Piccadilly Radio plc* [1989] BCLC 683, the court refused to correct an entry in the register relating to the transfer of shares, notwithstanding that the shares had been transferred in breach of the company's articles (however, note the decision of Jacob J in *POW Services Ltd* v *Clare*, discussed above). The court refused to sanction a rectification of the register because those seeking to rely on s 359 did so to protect their own membership interests rather than the interests of the company. The members who sought to challenge the transfer of shares sought to prevent the transfer of shares to a party opposed to a takeover bid in which they, the objecting members, had a personal interest. As such the members who sought to rely on s 359 did so for a collateral and improper purpose.

In addition to establishing a legitimate interest for the purposes of s 359, it is also necessary to establish that the application was made without unreasonable delay or prejudice to innocent third parties. For example, in *Re ISIS Factors plc* [2004] BCC 359, Blackburne J held that a six-year delay and the undoubted prejudice to a third party who had acquired control of the company in ignorance of the claimant's interest, rendered the provision inapplicable.

The case of *Re Thundercrest Ltd* [1994] BCC 857 provides an example of a successful application under s 359. The case concerned a proposed allotment of a rights issue of shares. The company's three shareholders/directors had all expressed a willingness to participate in the issue. However, one of the shareholders, the plaintiff (P), failed to reply to the letter of provisional allotment. The letter had, in accordance with the terms of the company's articles, been sent by recorded delivery. As a result of P's failure to reply to the offer letter (although the letter was correctly addressed, P never received the offer letter), the two other shareholders (the defendants) wrongly assumed that P had decided to decline to participate in the rights issue. The shares, which had provisionally been earmarked for P, were therefore allotted between the defendants.

The share issue was declared invalid in accordance with s 359 because the period of notice allowed for the acceptance of the offer had, contrary to s 90(6) of the Companies Act 1985, been less than the prescribed 21 days. Although the offer letter had been properly posted in accordance with the terms of the company's articles, and despite the existence of a provision in the articles which allowed the notice for the acceptance period to expire after 'a set time period' (the time period for acceptance of this particular rights issue was set at 18 days), nevertheless, Paul Baker J observed that the company's articles provided that the relevant legislation (s 90(6)) would apply unless it was inconsistent with the articles. As the terms of the company's articles did not **specifically** make mention of a **definite** expiry period in relation to the acceptance of an allotment offer, Paul Baker J held that the expiry period should be governed by s 90(6). It was insufficient for the defendants' case that the company's articles had permitted the company to set an expiry period, other than the one specified by s 90(6). Further, the learned judge considered the defendants' case had been prejudiced in so far as P's offer letter had been returned by the post office to the company's office prior to the date for the allotment of the shares (i.e. the defendants should have been aware that P had never received the letter). Accordingly, the company's register was modified to cancel the said shares.

Share certificate

The articles of a company often provide for the form and content of the company's share certificate: see e.g. Table A, arts 6 and 7. A share certificate is not a document of title to shares but provides *prima facie* evidence of title. Share certificates must be issued by a company within two months of the allotment of shares (s 185, CA 1985).

Share transfers

A share may be transferred in accordance with the terms of a company's articles. The articles of a private company often include a clause which restricts a member's ability to transfer shares. The articles of a private company may even give the directors of the company a power, in defined circumstances, to compel a member to transfer shares: see e.g. *Sidebottom* v *Kershaw, Leese & Co Ltd* [1920] 1 Ch 154 (discussed in Chapter 4).

A more common type of restriction on the transfer of shares is one which provides a right of pre-emption, whereby a member who wishes to sell shares must first offer the shares to existing members of the company. Where a member wishing to sell shares is compelled to sell to an existing member of the company, the company's articles will normally contain a valuation procedure. The valuation of shares will normally be undertaken by the company's auditor. Other than where fraud is alleged, the auditor's valuation cannot ordinarily be challenged (see e.g. *Jones* v *Sherwood Computer Services plc* [1992] 1 WLR 277), albeit that an aggrieved member may, in an appropriate case, seek redress under s 459 of the Companies Act 1985 (discussed in Chapter 24) or a just and equitable winding up order against the company (see s 122(1)(g), IA 1986, discussed in Chapter 24). An example of an appropriate case may arise in a situation where a member's entitlement to a proportion of the company's realised assets amounts to a sum in excess of the valuation figure: see e.g. *Re Abbey Leisure* [1990] BCC 60, discussed further in Chapter 24. In addition, in an appropriate case, a member may be able to pursue an action in negligence against the person deemed responsible for the share valuation (see e.g. *Whiteoak* v *Walker* [1988] 4 BCC 122).

A company's articles may also provide that the directors of the company may, at their absolute discretion, refuse a transfer of shares or approve only one on specified grounds. Where this power of veto exists, the company will be required to give notice of any refusal to register shares within two months of the presentation of the transfer (s 183(5), CA 1985). Where such notice has not been given, as in *Re Swaledale Cleaners Ltd* [1968] 1 WLR 1710 and more recently in *Re Inverdeck Ltd* [1998] BCC 256, then, in accordance with s 359 of the Companies Act 1985, a person to whom the shares have been transferred will be entitled to an order requiring the company to register the transfer of shares. If, in accordance with a company's articles, a refusal to transfer shares may only take place in specified circumstances, then the specified circumstances must have been met, prior to the company's refusal to register a transfer: see e.g. *Re Bede Steam Shipping Co Ltd* [1917] 1 Ch 123.

Transfer procedure

The procedure for transferring shares is normally set out in a company's articles (see e.g. Table A, arts 23–28). However, in addition to any regulatory provision within the articles (e.g. in a private company compliance with pre-emption rights), the regulation of fully paid-up share transfers is provided for by the Stock Transfer Act 1963. The Act applies to transfers of all types of transferable securities. Transfers of partly paid shares are outside the ambit of the 1963 Act. It is unlawful for a company to register a transfer of shares unless a proper instrument of transfer has been delivered to the company: see e.g. *Nisbet* v *Shepherd* [1994] BCC 91. A company's power to refuse to register a transfer of shares is one which must be exercised *bona fide* for the benefit of the company: see e.g. *Tett* v *Phoenix & Investment Co Ltd* [1984] BCLC 599.

Prior to April 1997, the transfer of securities listed on the stock exchange operated via a computerised system called the Talisman system. This system was introduced following the Stock Exchange (Completion of Business) Act 1976. Under this system, transactions on the London Stock Exchange were based in part on computerised trading; however, the completion of the transfer of title to securities was effected manually. The implementation of a totally paperless system for the transfer of listed securities was proposed in 1981, a system to facilitate the Stock Exchange being brought into line with the major European markets. Section 207 of the Companies Act 1989 was passed to enable regulations to be made containing the necessary changes to the law governing the transfer of securities by a computerised system. An initial computerised system, which was to be known as the Taurus system, was abandoned in March 1993, after a meeting of the London Stock Exchange considered that its cost would be too expensive.

Nevertheless, a less onerous system, known as CREST, was developed and put into operation in July 1996; it replaced the Talisman system over a nine-month transition period. The CREST system is not compulsory and is only applicable to a company which has been approved as a 'participating issuer'. (See the Uncertificated Securities Regulations 2001 (SI 2001/3755).)

ISSUING SHARES

Shares are issued (allotted) by a company as a result of a resolution from the company's board of directors. The board must be vested with the power to issue shares; the said power is usually contained within the company's articles. An authority to allot shares will last for a maximum of five years whereupon it may, if so desired, be renewed by the general meeting (s 80, CA 1985). Alternatively, the power to issue shares may be authorised by an ordinary resolution in general meeting. However, it should be noted that a private company may, in accordance with s 80A of the Companies Act 1985, elect by ordinary resolution to authorise its directors to allot shares to a maximum specified amount over a fixed or indefinite period. This authority may be revoked by general meeting (discussed further in Chapter 21).

A director who knowingly and wilfully contravenes, permits or authorises a contravention of s 80 is liable to a fine. However, a person who purchases shares which have been issued without a proper authority (i.e. in shares issued contrary to s 80) will nevertheless obtain a good title in respect of the issued shares (s 80(10), CA 1985). It should be noted that a company cannot allot shares to itself: see e.g. *Trevor* v *Whitworth* (1887) 12 App Cas 409.

Where shares are issued with the appropriate authority, the issue may nevertheless be voidable in circumstances where the issue was deemed to have been for an improper purpose: for example, where the underlying purpose of the issue was to manipulate voting control as opposed to raising additional share capital (discussed further in Chapter 17). In appropriate circumstances, a share issue may also be avoided where it constitutes a fraud on minority interests (see Chapter 23), or alternatively where its effect was to unfairly prejudice the interests of the members generally or a part of the membership (i.e. contrary to s 459, CA 1985: see Chapter 24).

Nominee holdings

Shares may be registered in the name of a nominee; the nominee will hold the shares directly or indirectly for the true owner (beneficial owner). While shares may be registered in the name of a nominee for a legitimate reason, the use of a nominee may disguise a more sinister purpose. For example, nominee holdings may mask an attempt by the true owner of the shares secretly to purchase sufficient capital to instigate a takeover bid of the company. The Companies Act 1985 seeks to remedy any potential abuse of nominee holdings in public companies (Part VI, CA 1985, as amended by s 134, CA 1989): for example, under s 198 of the Companies Act 1985, notification of known interests in voting shares in a public company must be communicated to the company concerned within two days of the obligation arising. An 'interest' normally means a holding of three per cent in the shares of the company; the interest must be recorded in a register of interests in shares which must be kept by all public companies. The provisions contained within Part VI of the Companies Act 1985 are supplemented by the powers of investigation afforded to the Department of Trade and Industry (see Chapter 25).

Proposals for reform

The CLR's Final Report (2001) recommended that s 80 should no longer apply to private companies other than where the company has, or will after the share issue have, more than one class of share. It was considered that s 80 should be retained in respect of the latter exception with the objective of seeking to prevent any unauthorised change in the relative power of the different classes of shares. The said proposal is adopted in the government's White Paper (2005): see clause H5. Accordingly, it is proposed that where a private company has only one class of shares, the directors may exercise any power of the company to allot shares of that class. As a consequence of this suggested change, the White Paper (2005) proposes that the current s 80A of the Companies Act should cease to have effect (see clause 116).

The EC Second Directive deems that s 80 is obligatory in respect of public companies. The Second Directive was adopted on 13 December 1976 and contains provisions relating to the classification of companies, rules on the raising of share capital and its maintenance and rules relating to dividends. The provisions were implemented in the UK by the Companies Act 1980 and are specifically applicable to public limited companies.

Holding shares in a private company

Although a private company may seek offers for its shares from persons other than existing members (but not a general offer to the general public), it is a common feature of a private company's articles to find restrictions as to who may or who may not hold shares: for example, the ownership of shares may be restricted to the existing members of the company or their relatives.

It should be stressed that it is an offence for a private company to make an offer of its shares to the general public (s 81, CA 1985). The offence is punishable by a fine as against the company and any officer in default of the provision. An offer to the public includes an offer to any section of the public (s 742A(1), CA 1985), although there are exceptions (s 742A(2), CA 1985), namely an offer is not to be treated as made to the public if it is an offer of a domestic type (to family members, existing shareholders, employees: see s 742A(3)–(6), CA 1985) or if it is not calculated to result, directly or indirectly, in the shares (or debentures) becoming available for subscription or purchase by persons other than those specifically receiving the offer. The said definition is not aligned with the definition of an offer to the public as provided by the Financial Services and Markets Act 2000 (FSMA 2000) and the Public Offers of Securities Regulations 1995 (POSR 1995); the latter are specifically concerned with offers in respect of public companies. While the legislation in this area clearly distinguishes between offers made by private companies as opposed to offers made by public companies, it is somewhat odd to observe that it may still be possible for a private company to be in breach of the definition of an offer to the public in respect of the FSMA 2000 and the POSR 1995, notwithstanding that it may escape liability under s 742A of the 1985 Act. (These issues are considered in Chapter 11.)

THE PAYMENT FOR COMPANY SHARES

Except in a situation where a company allots bonus shares to its existing members (discussed below), or where it resolves to extinguish any amount owing on shares which, at that time, were not fully paid up, then, in accordance with s 99 of the Companies Act 1985, the acquisition of a company's shares and the payment of any premium on the shares must be by means of a monetary consideration; the shares must be paid for with cash or something to which a monetary value can be attached, to include goodwill and know how (see s 738(2), CA 1985).

While a private company may accept an undertaking for the future performance of services in consideration for the sale of shares, a public company may not do so (s 99(2), CA 1985). Further, a public company may not allot shares for a consideration which includes any other form of undertaking which is to be, or may be, performed more than five years after the allotment of shares (s 102, CA 1985).

Although the full purchase price of a share can be paid in instalments (partly paid shares), a public company may not issue a share unless at least 25 per cent of its nominal value and the whole of any premium payable on it has been made (s 101(1), CA 1985). An exception to this rule is provided for by s 101(2) of the Companies Act 1985, whereby shares may be allotted in pursuance of an employee's share scheme (discussed below).

Where the consideration to be provided for the purchase of shares in a private company is other than for a cash consideration, there is clearly the possibility of an abuse of the rule that shares should not be issued at a discount (see below). However, the court will not generally enquire into the adequacy of the consideration: see e.g. *Re Wragg* [1871] 1 Ch 796. Nevertheless, the court may intervene where the consideration is clearly inadequate, namely if it appears that some form of fraud or bad faith is involved: see e.g. *Hong Kong & China Gas Co* v *Glen* [1914] 1 Ch 527.

However, to enforce the ideal of protecting the public interest (and also to comply with the EC Second Directive), where a public company accepts payment in exchange for an allotment of shares, other than by a cash payment, the company must ordinarily obtain a valuation or validation of the value of the consideration in question (s 103, CA 1985). Section 103 of the Companies Act 1985 is applicable save in a situation where a company allots:

- bonus shares;
- shares to the shareholders of another company in exchange for the transfer or cancellation of shares in that other company; or
- shares to the shareholders of another company in exchange for the acquisition of the assets and liabilities of that other company.

Other than where one of the above exceptions applies, the valuation/validation must be undertaken by an independent person who must be qualified as an auditor (s 108(1), CA 1985). A copy of the independent report must be sent to the proposed purchaser of the shares. Where there is a contravention of the aforementioned provisions and shares are allotted, the allottee will be personally liable to pay an amount up to the nominal value of the shares, plus a part or whole of any premium on the shares. The allottee will be liable except in circumstances which indicate that he was unaware of any form of contravention. The court may exercise its discretion under s 113 of the Companies Act 1985, to exempt the allottee from the whole or any part of the liability.

It is to be noted that s 104 of the Companies Act 1985 duplicates the intent of the above procedure in relation to agreements for the transfer of non-cash assets, of a value equal to or in excess of 10 per cent of the company's nominal share capital, as between a public company and an original subscriber of the company (or a member of a private company which subsequently re-registers as a public company) in circumstances where the transfer is within a period of two years from the formation of the public company. However, in relation to s 104 there is an additional requirement, namely the company must, following receipt of the valuation report, sanction the transfer of assets by the passing of an ordinary resolution. The provision is not applicable to a situation where the transfer of assets is judged to have arisen in the ordinary course of the company's business or the transfer is pursuant to the supervision of the court.

An issue of shares at a discount

A company may not, subject to limited implied exceptions, issue shares for a consideration which is less than the nominal value of the shares (s 100(1), CA 1985). A person who purchases shares at a discount will be liable to pay to the company an amount equal to the discount, plus interest (s 100(2), CA 1985). The exceptions to s 100(1) are as follows:

- a debenture, which is subsequently converted into a share, may be issued at a discount, providing that the right to convert the debenture was not an immediate right; and

- property which is exchanged for shares in a private company may be of a lesser value than the nominal value of the shares issued.

An issue of shares at a premium

Shares may be issued at a premium, that is, the selling price of the share may exceed its nominal value. Where a company issues shares at a premium, a sum equal to the amount of the premium payment must be transferred into a special account: the account is called the share premium account (s 130, CA 1985). Where a company acquires the shares of another company in exchange for the issue of its own shares and the nominal value of the issue of its own shares is less than the value of the shares acquired, then the difference between the two values must be transferred to the share premium account.

Proposals for reform

The White Paper (2005) contains no proposals for law reform in relation to the purchase procedures for shares. However, following on from the recommendations of the CLR, the government's White Paper, 'Modernising Company Law' (2002) (clauses 25–47), sought the clarification and implementation of minor technical changes to the law in relation to the payment for shares, albeit that the intention of the existing law was to be retained. The proposed changes to the existing law, in so far as they were relevant, may be briefly summarised as follows:

- Clause 26(1) specifically provides that a company must not allot shares as fully or partly paid up by means of a person providing an undertaking to subscribe or procure subscriptions for any shares in the company. Accordingly, a company may not accept, as payment for shares, a future promise relating to their payment.

- The law in relation to issues of shares at a discount was intended to be given a greater statutory footing by clauses 26(2)–29. The said clauses basically prohibit (other than in cases of payment via commission sanctioned by the constitution) a company from making a payment or transfer of any non-cash assets (other than out of distributable profits) for the purpose of inducing a person to purchase shares: i.e. the shares must be paid for in full.

- Further provisions are recommended in the context of public companies. Most of the said provisions basically duplicate the intent of the existing law. However, it is to be noted that, in accordance with clause 30, when shares are issued to founding members of a public company, the company will be permitted to accept only a cash payment. (Founders' shares are discussed below.)

TYPES OF SHARES

A company may create different types of shares, that is the legal rights of a particular type of share (class rights) may vary from those of other types of shares issued by the company. The legal rights attached to shares may be seen as comprising:

- rights as to dividend payments;
- voting rights; and
- rights to the return of capital on an authorised reduction of capital or on the winding up of a company.

The legal rights of any given type of share are determined either by the terms of the company's constitution (i.e. the memorandum or articles) or by the terms of the particular share issue.

Ordinary shares

Where a company's shares are issued without any special rights being attached to distinct classes of shares, then the shares will be ordinary (equity) shares. If a company issues shares that have specific class rights (discussed below), any remaining shares to which the specific rights are not attached will be construed as ordinary shares. The greatest part of a company's share capital will usually consist of ordinary shares. An ordinary share is usually the only type of share to carry votes at general meetings of the company's shareholding body. Where a company declares a dividend payment, the dividend payable on ordinary shares will usually be determined in accordance with the performance of the company and therefore will vary according to the fortunes of the company. Dividends payable on ordinary shares are paid after dividends have been paid to preference shareholders (discussed below).

It is permissible for a company, if authorised by its constitution, to issue different types of ordinary shares. Ordinary shares may be created as non-voting shares, shares with limited voting rights, or shares with enhanced voting rights. For example, a company's ordinary shares may be divided into a class A ordinary share and a class B ordinary share. Although both class A and class B shares may carry the same rights in respect to dividend payments, the class A share may carry 100 votes per share, whereas the class B share may carry only one vote per share: see e.g. *Holt* v *Holt* [1990] 1 WLR 1250.

As stated, a company may create ordinary shares which, in specific circumstances, carry enhanced voting rights. For example, the voting rights attached to the shares held by a director of a company may, in accordance with the terms of the company's articles, be increased in circumstances where the general meeting proposes to remove the said director from office: see e.g. *Bushell* v *Faith* [1970] AC 1099 (discussed in Chapter 4).

Preference shares

A preference share is a share to which certain preferential rights are attached, rights which would not be attached to an ordinary share. Although there is no statutory definition to expose the specific nature of this type of share, the most common distinctive attribute attached to a preference share is the preferential payment of dividends in priority to other types of shares. However, as noted below, this may not be the only preferential type of right to be attached to the preference share. A company may also issue convertible preference shares; this type of preference share may, subject to the terms of the issue, be converted into ordinary shares at the option of the shareholder.

The extent of the legal rights attached to a preference share will be dependent upon construing that part of a company's constitution (or terms of the specific share issue) which governs the particular share issue. The terms of the relevant regulations (or terms of the share issue) exclusively define the rights attached to a class of shares: see e.g. *Scottish Insurance Corporation Ltd* v *Wilsons & Clyde* [1949] AC 462. It must be observed that in the absence of specific regulations to determine the rights attached to a particular type of share, the rights of the holders of all classes of shares (ordinary and preference shareholders) are deemed to be the same: see e.g. *Birch* v *Cropper* (1889) 14 App Cas 525.

The voting rights attached to preference shares are normally defined whereby preference shareholders are entitled to a right to vote only in circumstances where their dividend payments are in arrears, or in a situation where a proposed variation of the rights attached to the preference share is advanced: see e.g. *Willow International Investments Ltd* v *Smiths of Smithfield Ltd* [2003] BCC 769. Where the voting rights of preference shareholders are not so defined, the principle in *Birch* v *Cropper* will apply: preference shareholders will be accorded the same voting rights as the holders of ordinary shares.

Preferential right to dividend payments

The holder of a preference share will usually be entitled to a fixed rate of return (fixed dividend). This dividend is paid before any dividend payments are made to the company's ordinary shareholders. Alternatively, the rate of return may be fixed with an additional payment to represent a share in the company's profits. This latter type of preference share is called a participating preference share. The right of participation is limited to an entitlement to share in any surplus profits (i.e. to be paid after a dividend has been paid to the company's ordinary shareholders). For a preference share to have been created as a participating preference share, the company's constitution (or share issue) must specify that the preference share was so created: see e.g. *Will* v *United Lankart Plantations Co Ltd* [1914] AC 11.

A preference shareholder's entitlement to a fixed payment will be dependent, in any given year, on the company's ability to declare a dividend. The entitlement to a fixed payment may be either cumulative or non-cumulative. Where the payment is of a cumulative nature and the company is unable to pay a fixed payment in any one year, it must make up the difference at some future date, namely when it is able to declare a dividend. Unless the terms of a preference share issue state otherwise, there is a presumption that a preference share is cumulative: see e.g. *Webb* v *Earle* (1875) LR 20 Eq 556. Where a company is in liquidation, the entitlement of the company's preferential shareholders to any outstanding amount owed in respect of a cumulative dividend payment will be dependent upon whether the company's constitution (or share issue) made provision for such payments. Where a company's constitution does specifically provide for such payments, any arrears owing to preference shareholders will, following prior payment of the company's debts, be paid out of the company's remaining surplus assets. If a company's constitution contains no specific provision of entitlement, it will be assumed that preference shareholders are unable to claim arrears of dividend: see e.g. *Re Crichton's Oil Co* [1902] 2 Ch 86.

Preferential rights to capital assets

On the winding up of a company (discussed in Chapter 15) or upon a reduction of capital (discussed in Chapter 10), a company's preference shareholders may, by the terms of the company's constitution (or share issue), be given a preferential right to the return of their capital investment and/or a right to participate in the distribution of a company's surplus assets. Whether a specific right exists in relation to the return of capital, or an ability to participate in surplus assets, is a matter determined by the construction of the company's constitution (or terms of the share issue). Where the company's regulations make it clear that preference shareholders have no pre-ferential right to the return of capital or the right to participate in the distribution of surplus assets then effect will be given to such a term. Where the company's regulations simply afford a preferential return of capital, the company's regulations will be exhaustive of that right; the preference shareholders will take a preference in the return of their capital investment but will not be entitled to participate in a division of any surplus capital (i.e. assets that remain after the company's creditors have been paid and after all shareholders have had their initial capital investment in the company returned to them: see e.g. *Scottish Insurance Corporation* v *Wilsons & Clyde Coal Co Ltd* [1949] AC 462). Where no provision is made within the regulations for the distribution of capital or surplus assets, all shareholders of all classes will participate equally: see e.g. *Birch v Cropper* (1889) 14 App Cas 525. Here, Lord Macnaughten, expressing the unanimous view of the House of Lords, stated:

> 'Every person who becomes a member of a company limited by shares of equal amount becomes entitled to a proportionate part in the capital of the company, and, unless it be otherwise provided by the regulations of the company is entitled as a necessary con-sequence, to the same proportionate part in all the property of the company, including its uncalled capital.' (at p 543)

However, difficulties in respect of the entitlement of preference shareholders to participate in the surplus assets of a company have arisen in circumstances where a company's surplus assets include accumulated income; income which prior to the company's liquidation could, by the terms of the company's constitution, have only been distributed to the company's ordinary shareholders. As dividend payments cease to be made to ordinary shareholders when a company is in liquidation any accumulated income should, following liquidation, be considered as part of the company's surplus assets. However, in *Re Bridgewater* [1891] 2 Ch 317, the Court of Appeal took a contrary view. The court's decision in *Re Bridgewater* was founded upon the premise that, irrespective of a company's liquidation, certain non-capital assets of the company could retain their character as income and as such the income could only be converted into capital if an intention to that effect had been made clear by the company's constitution. While the decision in *Re Bridgewater* avoided the anomaly of income which was exclusively earmarked for ordinary shareholders being distributed to both ordinary and preference shareholders, it is suggested that the decision impugns the logical assumption that in liquidation the rights of the company's shareholders should no longer be governed by regulations specifically formulated to regulate the company whilst a going concern. Indeed, subsequent cases – see e.g. *Re Isle of Thanet Electricity Supply Co Ltd* [1950] Ch 161 and *Dimbula Valley (Ceylon) Tea Co Ltd* v *Laurie* [1961] Ch 353 – would appear to confirm the view that, unless specifically provided for by the company's constitution, the rights of shareholders, following the liquidation of a company, cannot be calculated according to shareholder rights pre-liquidation.

Deferred/management/founders' shares

This type of share may be issued to the founders of a company. The right to a dividend payment is deferred on a founder's share, namely the dividend payment is held back until a dividend payment has been made to the company's other shareholders; the holders of founder shares are then entitled to the remainder of whatever amount the company has reserved for dividend payments. Founders' shares are now rare to extinct, especially in public companies, where strict Stock Exchange listing requirements curtail their existence. These stricter rules were introduced to curb promoters of public companies from exploiting their positions (i.e. promoters were often able to take founders' shares to a value in excess of the value of their services to the company).

Employee shares

Many companies operate schemes whereby company employees are encouraged to take up shares. Employee share schemes allow the workers in a company to participate in the profits they help create. In addition to allowing the employees a right to a share of the company's profits, employee share schemes may be seen as a means of motivating the workforce to attain higher profit levels. Section 743 of the Companies Act 1985 defines an employees' share scheme as one for the benefit of the *bona fide* employees or former employees of the company, the company's subsidiary or holding company, or a subsidiary of the company's holding company, or the wives, husbands, widows, widowers or children or step-children under the age of 18 of such employees or former employees.

Where shares are offered to the employees of a company, the general pre-emption rules contained within s 89 of the Companies Act 1985 (discussed below) are not applicable (i.e. a company is not required first to offer the shares designated for the employees, to existing members of the company). However, where a general allotment of shares is proposed, the pre-emption rules operate in favour of the employee share scheme so that a portion of the general issue of shares must first be offered to holders of existing employee shares.

CLASS RIGHTS ATTACHED TO SHARES

The rights attached to a particular type of share are termed class rights. Class rights may be ascertained by examining the contents of a company's constitution (see e.g. Table A, art 2), the terms of a particular share issue or the terms of a special resolution related to a particular class of shares (see *Re Old Silkstone Collieries Ltd* [1954] Ch 169, discussed below).

Further, in accordance with the decision in *Harman* v *BML Group Ltd* [1994] 2 BCLC 674, class rights may be created by the terms of a shareholders' agreement. In *Harman* v *BML Group Ltd*, the Court of Appeal (overturning a decision of Paul Baker QC sitting as a deputy High Court judge) upheld the validity of a quorum provision contained in a shareholders' agreement to which all the members of the company were party. The facts of this case are quite bizarre and the conclusion reached by the Court of Appeal may be considered equally puzzling. The shareholder agreement provided that the holder of B shares (Z or his proxy) had an absolute right to be present at all shareholder meetings. The capital of the company was divided between the holders of 'A' ordinary shares of which C and D held a majority (X and Y held a minority of the 'A' shares), and the holder of the 'B' ordinary shares (Z held all of this class). The class A and B shares carried equal rights. In terms of voting rights C and D held an overall majority. A dispute arose between C and Z, whereby Z alleged that C and D had perpetrated a fraud against the company. As a consequence of this dispute, an extraordinary meeting was convened by Z; the meeting was convened with the intention of passing a motion to dismiss C and D from their directorships. The meeting (lasting for only one minute) resulted in C and D being dismissed from their directorships; the vote was taken by a show of hands. Z, X and Y voted in favour of the motion; the meeting was closed before C and D could seek the right to a poll vote, a vote which they would have won given that they held the majority of the voting shares.

As a result of their dismissal, C and D sought to convene a meeting of the shareholders to reverse the decision taken at the extraordinary meeting. Z refused to attend the meeting which, in accordance with the shareholder agreement, would have been rendered invalid had it proceeded. C and D therefore sought to hold a meeting pursuant to s 371 of the Companies Act 1985 (discussed further in Chapter 21) which would have allowed them to convene the meeting irrespective of the terms of the shareholder agreement. The Court of Appeal concluded that an order under s 371 would have overridden Z's class rights and was therefore inappropriate. While the decision may be viewed as a technical victory for the procedural requirements of the shareholder agreement, the facts of the case would appear indicative of a breach of C and D's right to cast their votes in accordance with s 14 of the Companies Act 1985 (discussed in Chapter 4).

In addition to a shareholder agreement, class rights may also be created where, by the terms of a company's constitution, rights have been conferred on a particular member of the company in that member's capacity as a shareholder. Here, the class rights exist notwithstanding that they are not specifically attached to the shares held by the member. For example, in *Cumbrian Newspapers Group Ltd* v *Cumberland & Westmorland Herald Newspaper & Printing Co Ltd* [1987] Ch 1, the plaintiff acquired a 10.67 per cent holding in the defendant company (Cumberland). As a condition of the acquisition, Cumberland's articles were altered to confer on the plaintiff specific rights designed to prevent an outside party from acquiring control of the company. Irrespective of the fact that the rights were not attached to the shares acquired by the plaintiff, Scott J held that such rights were class rights. As such, the rights could only be altered pursuant to the statutory procedure laid down by s 125 of the Companies Act 1985 (see below).

It should be noted that shares which are *prima facie* issued on the same terms may also be impliedly subdivided by the court into separate classes, even in circumstances where no specific rights or benefits were conferred on a particular shareholder. The implied creation of class rights is rare and will only take place in very well-defined circumstances. An example of the implied subdivision of shares into separate classes is to be found in *Re Hellenic & General Trust Ltd* [1976] 1 WLR 123.

The variation of class rights

A company may wish to vary the rights attached to a particular class of its issued shares. The complex procedure which governs a company's ability to vary class rights is regulated by s 125 of the Companies Act 1985. Prior to an analysis of s 125, it is first necessary to determine whether an alteration to the terms of a particular share issue does in fact amount to a variation of class rights.

What amounts to a variation in class rights?

The Companies Act 1985 provides little guidance as to the definition of factors which establish a variation of class rights, save that s 125(7) provides that an alteration of a provision contained in a company's articles to vary the rights of a class of shareholders, or the insertion of such a provision into the articles, is to be construed as a variation of class rights. Section 125(8) further provides that references to a variation of class rights are to be read to include an abrogation of such rights. However, it does not always follow that a cancellation of class rights will have the effect of varying those rights.

For example, in *Re Saltdean Estate Co Ltd* [1968] 1 WLR 1844 a company resolved to reduce its capital by paying off the company's preference shareholders, that is by returning the preference shareholders' capital investments in the company. The company was profitable and the preference shareholders had been accorded a right of participation in the company's profits. As a consequence of returning the preference shareholders' capital, the preference shares were cancelled. The preference shareholders alleged that the company's action amounted to a variation of class rights. The court held that the return of capital to preference shareholders, thereby ending their right to participate in the company, could not be regarded as a variation of the preference holders' class rights. On the contrary, the reduction of the company's capital and the subsequent return of capital was in accordance with the class rights of the preference shareholders as defined by the company's articles. Although the company's articles provided that the consent of a class meeting was required for a proposal which would affect, modify, deal with or abrogate in any manner the rights and privileges of that class of preference shareholders, the articles also provided that holders of preference shares should be the first class of share-holders to have capital returned in the event of the company being wound up. However, in *Re Saltdean*, the preference shareholders' right to a return of capital was expressed to be on the winding up of the company and not upon a reduction of cap-ital. Nevertheless, it would appear that the ability of a company to reduce its capital and pay off preference shareholders is *prima facie* an implied consequence of the preference shareholder's preferential right to the return of capital in the event of the company being wound up. This view was impliedly confirmed by the House of Lords in *House of Fraser plc* v *ACGE Investments Ltd* [1987] AC 387.

In determining whether preference shareholders have a right to a return of capital, it is essential to construe the company's constitution or the terms of the share issue, a point illustrated by the Court of Appeal's decision in *Re Northern Engineering Industries plc* [1994] 2 BCLC 704 (affirming the first instance decision of Ferris J [1993] BCLC 1151). This case involved a proposed reduction of a com-pany's capital by paying off preference shares and cancelling that class of shares. The company's articles provided that the rights of any class of shares would be varied by a reduction of the capital paid up on the shares. The company contended that its articles did not apply to the proposed cancellation of preference shares because the articles only had effect where there was a reduction of capital as opposed to a can-cellation of the shares. It was held that a cancellation of shares necessarily implied a reduction of share capital. As the variation of the preference shareholders' rights had not been put to a separate meeting of the preference shareholders in accordance with s 125 of the Companies Act 1985 (see below), the court refused to confirm the reduction in capital.

In considering whether a variation of class rights has taken place the courts have drawn a distinction between the rights of a class of shareholders and the enjoyment of those rights. Therefore, to establish a variation of class rights, the rights of a class of shareholders must be fundamentally and specifically altered. Where a company acts merely to affect the rights of a class of shareholders without expressly altering such rights, that act will not be construed as a variation but merely as an act which changes the enjoyment of those rights. For example, in *Greenhalgh* v *Arderne Cinemas Ltd* [1946] 1 All ER 512, the company's share capital was divided between two classes of shares: one class of 2s (10p) shares and the other of 10s (50p) shares. Both classes carried one vote for each share. An ordinary resolution was passed which had the effect of subdividing the shares valued at 10s each (50p) into shares of 2s each (10p); each new share was to carry one vote. The resolution increased the voting power (5x) of shareholders who had previously held the 10s (50p) shares. The plaintiff, Greenhalgh (G), objected to the subdivision of the 10s (50p) shares on the ground that its effect was to vary his class rights because prior to the resolution, G, who held the bulk of the 2s (10p) shares, had control of over 40 per cent of the membership votes, whereas after the resolution, his voting powers were reduced to less than 10 per cent of the votes. The court held that no variation of the rights, appertaining to G's 2s (10p) shares, had taken place, as the resolution subdividing the 10s (50p) shares had not specifically altered G's rights. G still had the same quantity of 2s (10p) shares; each share still carried one vote. Although the effect of the resolution resulted in G's loss of control of over 40 per cent of the membership votes, the resolution had not altered the specific nature of the rights attached to the 2s (10p) shares. (See also *White v Bristol Aeroplane Co Ltd* [1953] Ch 65 and *Re John Smith's Tadcaster Brewery Co Ltd* [1953] 1 All ER 518.)

Case examples to illustrate an actual variation of class rights are quite rare. However, one such example is *Re Old Silkstone Collieries Ltd* [1954] Ch 169. This case involved a colliery which had been nationalised (i.e. the colliery had been taken over from private ownership by the National Coal Board). The company which operated the colliery remained in existence to collect compensation payable as a result of nationalisation. Although the company reduced its capital, by returning a part of the preference shareholders' capital investment, the company resolved that all its shareholders should participate in the forthcoming compensation award. Despite such assurances, a further reduction in capital was proposed, the effect of which would have been to cancel the class of preference shares. The court held that such a proposal would, if implemented, amount to a variation of class rights in that the preference shareholders had been promised a right to participate in the compensation payments. The proposed variation was declared unfair and as such the court refused to sanction the further reduction of capital.

Other examples of a variation of class rights would include the following:

- a proposal whereby one type of share was to be converted into another type of share – for example, where a company sought to convert ordinary shares into preference shares and vice versa;
- where a company sought to alter the voting rights, dividend rights or capital rights attached to a particular class of share;
- as in the recent case of *Willow International Investments Ltd* v *Smiths of Smithfield Ltd* [2003] BCC 769, where a company sought to alter the pre-emption rights of the class of ordinary shareholders by attempting to pass a special resolution to alter the articles with the purpose of distinguishing between shareholders as to the application of those rights.

Section 125 of the Companies Act 1985

Where a company proposes to vary the rights of a given class of share, it must, prior to implementing the variation, comply with the procedures contained within s 125 of the Companies Act 1985. A company cannot simply alter its articles whereby the effect of that alteration would be to vary class rights. Section 125(6) provides that a meeting held to consider a variation of class rights must consist of a quorum of the holders of (or representing by proxy) at least one-third of the nominal value of the class of share concerned; the meeting must be attended by at least two members of that class (other than an adjourned meeting, where the attendance requirement is one member (or proxy) of the class concerned). The precise procedure for a variation of class rights is determined in accordance with the following requirements.

Class rights contained in the memorandum

Where the rights of a particular class of share are contained within a company's memorandum, such rights may be varied in accordance with the following procedures.

1 If the procedure for the variation of class rights is also contained within the memorandum, the rights may be varied in accordance with that procedure providing the variation is not concerned with the giving, variation, revocation or renewal of an authority for an allotment of shares under s 80 of the Companies Act 1985, or with a reduction of the company's share capital under s 135 of the Companies Act 1985 (see s 125(3), CA 1985). Where the variation of rights is connected with the above matters, the procedure for the variation must be carried out in accordance with s 125(2) of the Companies Act 1985. Section 125(2) provides that the holders of three-quarters in nominal value of the issued shares of the class to be varied must consent to the variation in writing. Alternatively, an extraordinary resolution passed at a separate meeting of the holders of the class may sanction the variation; by s 125(6)(b) a member of the class may demand a poll vote. In addition to the requirements provided by s 125(2), the company must comply with any further requirement of its variation procedure within the memorandum.

2 Where class rights are contained in the memorandum but the variation procedure for the particular class rights is contained within the articles, the procedure within the articles must be followed providing that the variation procedures contained therein were in existence as of the date of the company's original incorporation. Where the procedure was not in existence as of the date of incorporation, s 125(5) will apply (see below). Nevertheless, even if the alteration procedures were contained within the articles as of the date of the company's original incorporation, the procedure for the variation of class rights will not be adhered to where the class rights which are to be varied accord with those contained in s 125(3)(c) (see above). Class rights concerned with those matters may only be varied in accordance with the procedure laid down by s 125(2) (see above).

3 If the rights of a particular class of share are contained within the memorandum but neither the memorandum nor the articles of the company provide a procedure whereby those rights may be varied, then, in accordance with s 125(5), the class rights may be varied only by the unanimous agreement of all members of the company.

Class rights contained otherwise than in the memorandum

Where rights are attached to a class of shares otherwise than by the memorandum, then the variation procedure will be as follows.

1 If the variation procedure for the class rights is contained within the articles or memorandum, such rights will, subject to s 125(3)(c) (see above), be varied in accordance with the terms of the articles or memorandum.

2 Where the class rights are contained otherwise than in a company's memorandum and no variation procedure exists within the memorandum or articles, the rights of the class may be varied in accordance with s 125(2), CA 1985 (see above).

Proposals for reform

The complexities associated with the wording of s 125 were considered during the CLR. Given that the CLR recommended that the present articles and memorandum of a company should be merged into one constitutional document (see Chapter 4), the simplification of the statutory procedure for an alteration of class rights was, naturally, advanced. The CLR proposed (see 'The Final Report' (2001), para 7.28) that in all cases a variation of class rights should, if it was to be approved, require at least a 75 per cent majority vote of the class affected. The 75 per cent requirement could be greater in circumstances where a company's constitution so provided (see 'The Final Report', para 16.68). The said recommendation was endorsed in the government's White Paper (2002), although, surprisingly, it is not mentioned in any detail in the subsequent White Paper (2005).

The minority's right to object to a variation of class rights

Where a decision is taken by a separate meeting of the class of shareholders to sanction a proposed variation of class rights (s 125(2), CA 1985), and a minority of the class objects to the terms of the variation, the minority shareholders may, provided that they hold at least 15 per cent of the shares concerned and did not consent to or vote in favour of the variation, apply to the court to have the variation cancelled (s 127, CA 1985). An application to the court under s 127 has the effect of suspending the variation of class rights until such a date as the court decides whether to confirm the variation. The objecting minority must apply to court within 21 days of the decision affirming the terms of the variation. In deciding whether to affirm the variation, the court must consider the extent to which the variation would affect the class. Where the effect of the variation would cause unfair prejudice to the class as a whole, the variation will be refused. (The meaning of unfair prejudice for the purpose of determining an application to cancel a variation of class rights may, by analogy, be compared to the definition afforded to 'unfairly prejudicial conduct' found within s 459 of the Companies Act 1985 (see Chapter 24).)

In affirming a variation of the rights of a specified class of shares, the members of the class must exercise their power to vote *bona fide* for the purpose of benefiting the class as a whole. As such, a conflict of interest may arise in a situation where a member (X) holds, for example, both class A and class B shares and where a proposed variation of class A shares, whilst detrimental to the general interests of holders of A shares, would nevertheless benefit the holders of B shares and, as a result of the extent of X's holding of B shares, that said benefit would outweigh the detriment X suffered in respect of the variation of the A shares. In such a situation would X be expected to vote for the greater good of the class (class A) or to benefit his own personal interests?

The above problem arose in *Re Holders Investment Trust Ltd* [1971] 1 WLR 583. The case involved a proposed reduction of capital, whereby the company proposed to replace the company's existing preference shares with unsecured loan stock. The cancellation of the preference shares would have benefited the holders of the company's ordinary shares in so far as their dividend payments would no longer have been diminished by the prior payment of interest to preference shareholders. The majority holders of the preference shares also held a majority holding of the company's ordinary shares and voted in favour of the proposal. The minority holders of the preference shares opposed the variation. The court, in refusing to sanction the variation, held that the principal consideration for a member of a class of shares when deciding to affirm a variation of class rights was the overall benefit of the class and not his/her own personal interests.

THE CLASSIFICATION OF SHARE ISSUES

Rights issue (pre-emption rights)

When a company issues shares, the issue may be subject to a pre-emption right that the shares must, in the first instance, be offered to existing members of the company (a rights issue), that is, prior to being offered to non-members of the company (note that the pre-emption right will not apply to employee share schemes, discussed above). The rules which currently govern such pre-emption rights owe much to the implementation of the EC Second Company Law Directive. The Directive was implemented by the Companies Act 1980. Although the Directive was concerned with the regulation of rights issues in public companies, the rules enacted in the Companies Act 1980 were applied equally to private companies. The rules have since been incorporated into the Companies Act 1985 (ss 89–96, CA 1985). In accordance with s 89(1) of the Companies Act 1985, where a company offers an issue of equity securities (ordinary shares) for cash, it must, in the first instance, make the offer to its existing ordinary shareholders. A 'rights issue' must be made in direct proportion to the number of shares held by each ordinary shareholder. A private company may exclude s 89(1) by a provision contained within its memorandum or articles (s 91, CA 1985).

Company directors (of both public and private companies), if authorised to allot shares in accordance with s 80 of the Companies Act 1985, may be empowered to disapply or modify the effect of s 89(1) either generally or in relation to a particular allotment (s 95, CA 1985). To disapply or modify such rights generally, the directors must have been given an authority within the company's articles or alternatively must have been authorised to do so by a special resolution. In relation to a specific allotment of shares the general meeting may, by special resolution, decide that s 89(1) should not be applied to the specific allotment. Alternatively, the general meeting may decide that s 89(1) should apply only in some modified form.

A contravention of s 89(1) (subject to the above exceptions) will render every officer of the company who knowingly authorised or permitted the contravention to take place, jointly and severally liable to compensate any member of the company to whom an offer of shares should have been made (s 92, CA 1985).

A bonus issue

A bonus issue of shares is facilitated by a company using reserve funds from the company's reserve accounts to pay up unissued shares (see Table A, art 110). In accordance with art 110, an ordinary resolution is required to authorise the bonus issue. The bonus shares are distributed to the existing members of the company. Article 110 provides that the number of bonus shares issued will be in proportion to a member's existing entitlement to dividend payments. However, Table A, art 104 further provides that 'all dividends shall be declared and paid according to the amounts paid up on shares on which the dividend is paid'. As such, in issuing bonus shares, the issue must be in proportion to the actual amount paid up on the shares. A resolution to issue bonus shares as fully paid up to all shareholders will be rendered void for mistake where the shares held by a part of the membership are not fully paid up: see the decision of the Court of Appeal in *EIC Services* v *Phipps* [2004] 2 BCLC 589. In this case it was also contended that s 35A(1) of the Companies Act 1985 (discussed in Chapter 8) could be applied to save the validity of the bonus issue. The Court of Appeal rejected this argument on the basis that the shareholders in receiving the bonus issue were not **persons dealing** with the company in good faith, that is, in accordance with the true meaning of the provision, which was directed at a 'bilateral transaction between the company and a person dealing with the company' (per Peter Gibson LJ at p 660).

Redeemable shares

A redeemable share is a share which the company may, at its option, buy back from the shareholder at some specified date in the future (redemption date). The reason a company may wish to issue this type of share may be connected to the company's desire to raise short-term capital. A company which is so authorised by its articles, is permitted by s 159 of the Companies Act 1985 to issue redeemable shares, providing that the issue does not represent the totality of the company's share capital. Section 159A (introduced by s 133, CA 1989) provides that the date (or dates) on which the shares may be redeemed must be specified in the company's articles or, if the articles so provide, fixed by the directors; in the latter case the date(s) must be fixed before the shares are issued. Any other circumstances in which the shares are to be or may be redeemed must also be specified in the company's articles. The repayment of the redeemable shares cannot be deferred beyond the redemption date, although, subject to the shares having been fully paid up, the shares may be redeemed at the option of the company or shareholder at a date prior to the one specified by the terms of redemption.

Section 160 of the Companies Act 1985 provides that the company must redeem the shares out of its distributable profits or out of the proceeds of a new share issue. However, it should be noted that a private company may, in certain circumstances, redeem shares out of its own capital (discussed in Chapter 10). Where shares are redeemed out of a company's distributable profits, an amount equal to the amount by which the company's issued share capital is diminished on the cancellation of the shares must be transferred to a reserve fund known as the capital redemption reserve (s 170, CA 1985).

THE VALUATION OF SHARES

On occasions, it may be necessary for a court to determine the valuation of a company's shares; for example, a valuation of shares may be required to assess a person's liability to capital gains tax or inheritance tax. Whether it is necessary for the valuation of shares to be determined by the court may depend upon the inclusion and adequacy of any valuation procedures, contained, for example, in the company's articles: see e.g. *Gillatt* v *Sky Television Ltd* [2000] 1 All ER 461. Where the particular shares to be valued are listed shares, their value will often be calculated according to their current quoted market price. However, as the vast majority of companies are not listed, it will often be necessary for the court itself to undertake a valuation of the company's shares.

Shares that are the subject matter of a court's valuation must be valued in an objective manner. Unless the articles provide for a contrary procedure, an objective test will be employed on the basis of a sale as between a willing but not anxious vendor and a willing but not anxious purchaser. The crucial factors which determine any share valuation are the size of the shareholding and the expected dividend and asset realisation of the shares in question. In relation to private companies, an important consideration will be whether the company's articles purport to restrict the potential market for the sale of the shares: see e.g. *Holt* v *IRC* [1953] 1 WLR 1488. While the valuation of shares can never be an exact science (see e.g. *Holt* v *Holt* [1990] 1 WLR 1250) the courts ordinarily employ the following guidelines.

- Where the block of shares to be valued carry enough votes to enforce a winding up of the company (i.e. 75 per cent or more votes), the most likely method of valuation will be by reference to the value of the company's assets. This method of valuation incorporates a valuation of the net corporate assets of the company. The number of shares to be valued is then represented as a percentage of the value of the total net assets to give the pre-liquidation valuation figure. For example, if 80 out of an issued share capital of 100 shares are to be valued and the company in question has net assets to the value of £10 000, the valuation figure would be £8000 divided by 80, which would equate to £100 per share. Where the company is to be wound up, a deduction in the valuation figure will be made to take account of the liquidation costs: see e.g. *McConnel's Trustees* v *IRC* 1927 SLT 14.

- The asset valuation method may still be employed where the block of shares to be valued falls below 75 per cent. In such cases, a discount on the asset valuation will be made in accordance with the size of the holding. A majority holding of 50 per cent or more will warrant a discount in the region of 5 per cent, whereas a minority holding of, for example, 10 per cent may warrant a reduction of up to 20 to 30 per cent.

- An alternative method for the valuation of shares is one calculated according to the earning capacity of the shares to be valued (i.e. the calculation of the potential dividend entitlement of the shares). In assessing the value of dividends it will be necessary for a court to forecast expected profits. In so determining the potential dividend yield of a share, it is seldom practicable to look more than two to three years ahead. For private companies the court will normally estimate the dividend yield for the last three to five years prior to the date of valuation: see e.g. *Re Lynall* [1972] AC 680. Forecasts that the future profits of a company will be markedly different from recently recorded profits will be treated with caution. Where the expected future profits of a company are minimal or perhaps non-existent, the share valuation will normally be reduced to take account of the relative lack of marketability of the shares. As with the asset valuation method, the smaller the shareholding interest, then the greater the reduction in the final valuation figure of the shares.

It should be noted that, in determining the value of shares in cases brought under s 459 of the Companies Act 1985, the court may consider matters other than those outlined above (discussed in Chapter 24).

INVESTIGATIONS INTO SHARE OWNERSHIP

Section 442 of the Companies Act 1985 (as amended by s 62, CA 1989), permits the Secretary of State to appoint inspectors to investigate the share ownership of a company. Members of a company may apply to the Secretary of State to instigate such an investigation. If an application is made by 200 or more members, or by members holding 10 per cent or more of the company's issued shares, then, unless the Secretary of State considers the application to be vexatious or considers that an alternative type of action under s 444(1) of the Companies Act 1985 is more appropriate, he must appoint inspectors. The type of action governed by s 444(1) is one whereby the Secretary of State may require, of any person, information appertaining to the ownership of shares. As a result of action taken under ss 442 or 444, the Secretary of State may impose a freezing order on the relevant shares (s 445, CA 1985) (discussed below).

Where the company is a public limited company, the company itself may seek information as to whether at any time within the last three years a person had (or still has) an interest in its voting shares (s 212, CA 1985): see e.g. *Re Lonrho plc (No 3)* [1989] BCLC 480. Shareholders holding 10 per cent or more of the voting shares in a public limited company may call for the board to exercise these powers. The information obtained must be recorded on the company's register of interest in shares.

Freezing orders

The court or the Secretary of State may order that restrictions be placed upon the ownership rights attached to specified shares. Where an order is made, it is referred to as a freezing order. A breach of a freezing order constitutes a criminal offence (s 455, CA 1985).

The Secretary of State's powers to make a freezing order are determined in accordance with s 445 of the Companies Act 1985. This section may be used in accordance with the Secretary of State's powers of investigation into the ownership of specified shares (see above) or under s 210(5) of the Companies Act 1985, i.e. where a person has been convicted of failing to disclose a substantial interest in the shares of a company. Further, the courts may impose a freezing order on specific shares in circumstances where a public company has failed to receive an adequate response to a request for information under s 212 of the Companies Act 1985.

The effect of a freezing order (ss 454–457, CA 1985) is to:

- prevent the shares from being transferred;
- restrain the votes attached to the affected shares from being exercised;
- suspend rights of pre-emption attached to the affected shares; and

- prevent dividends from being paid and capital (except where the company is in liquidation) from being returned to the holders of the shares.

As a consequence of s 445(1A) of the Companies Act 1985, the court may modify the extent of the effect of a freezing order in circumstances where it considers that the consequences of a full order would unfairly affect the rights of third parties.

A person who holds shares in breach of the restrictions may be liable to a fine. Where shares are issued in contravention of the restrictions the company and every officer in default may be liable.

Any person who objects to the imposed restrictions may apply to the court for an order reversing their effect. The success of that application will depend upon satisfying the court or the Secretary of State that all relevant facts about the shares have subsequently been disclosed to the company and that, as a result of the earlier failure to disclose, no unfair advantage was caused to any person (s 456(3)(a), CA 1985), or that the shares are to be transferred for value (s 456(3)(b) and s 456(4), CA 1985). Any order made by the court or Secretary of State may be couched in terms whereby the restrictions continue but in a limited form (s 456(6), CA 1985).

Suggested further reading

General

Pickering (1963) 26 MLR 499

Pennington (1989) 10 Co Law 140

Pre-emption rights

MacNeil [2002] JBL 78

Myers *Pre-emption Rights: Final Report* DTI Publications (2005) (available at DTI website)

Share freezing orders

Milman and Singh (1992) 13 Co Law 15

Class rights/variation

Reynolds [1996] JBL 554

10

THE CLASSIFICATION AND MAINTENANCE OF SHARE CAPITAL

INTRODUCTION

This chapter seeks to explain how the Companies Act 1985 regulates the maintenance of a company's share capital. Share capital equates to that part of a company's assets which are made up of members' contributions for the company's shares. While a company is likely to have other capital assets – e.g. property, realised profits, etc. – the law does not classify this 'other capital' as capital for capital maintenance purposes. The capital contributed by shareholders is in effect a sum which is to be maintained and regulated with the ultimate objective of offering some degree of a protective buffer for creditors should the company fail. Prior to an exposition of the capital maintenance rules and the proposed reforms in this area, a classification of share capital will be undertaken. Finally, the chapter also provides a brief examination of the rules pertinent to the regulation of dividend payments.

MAINTENANCE OF SHARE CAPITAL

A company's share capital represents the shareholders' investment in the company; it comprises sums received from the issue of shares, together with any sums held in the company's share premium account or other statutory capital reserves such as the capital redemption reserve. In relation to accounting procedures, the company's share capital represents a notional liability: namely, in theory, on the winding up of the company it would, following the payment of creditor debts, be returned to shareholders. However, in practice the capital maintenance rules are designed to safeguard the interests of creditors, to ensure that capital is maintained as a secure fund, one which cannot (other than following a winding up) be distributed to shareholders.

A company's net assets must be maintained in conjunction with the company's notional liability. A company's share capital represents a measure by which asset values should correspond. However, unlike share capital, a company's net assets are prone to economic fluctuations in value: for example, the values attached to a factory or piece of land are likely to be dependent upon external factors. As such, the values attached to a company's share capital and the company's capital assets are in reality unlikely to be the same. Where the sum representing a company's share capital is in excess of the company's net assets, there may be a presumption of insolvency; however, this presumption may be false because the value of a company's real assets may still exceed its real liabilities (discarding the notional liability to shareholders). Nevertheless, in the case of a public company, s 142 of the Companies Act 1985 deems that if the company's net assets fall to an amount which is equal to or below half of its called-up share capital, the company must, within 28 days of that fact becoming known to one of the company's directors, convene an extraordinary general meeting for not later than 56 days thereafter. The meeting must consider the steps, if any, which should be taken to correct the situation.

While a company is a going concern, its capital cannot be returned to shareholders in the form of dividend payments. A company's capital assets are used to generate future wealth and profit; such profit may be distributed to shareholders in the form of dividend payments. A company's capital assets represent security upon which loan funds may be raised. The formulation of rules which regulate the maintenance of a company's share capital (especially in the context of public companies) owe much to the implementation of the EC Second Company Law Directive. In respect of rules relating to share capital, the Second Directive adopts provisions which are designed to ensure the preservation of capital by prohibiting reductions through improper distribution to shareholders, and by setting limits on a company's right to acquire its own shares. The Directive also affords protection to shareholders and creditors in relation to an increase or reduction in share capital and further specifies conditions in respect of a company's ability to acquire its own shares.

THE CLASSIFICATION OF SHARE CAPITAL

A company's share capital is measured in monetary terms and represents an amount which when contributed becomes part of the company's overall capital assets. However, this rather simplistic definition ignores the different ways in which the term 'share capital' is classified and employed.

Authorised share capital

A company's authorised share capital represents the total nominal value of shares which may be issued by the company. The sum which represents the authorised share capital is fixed by the company's memorandum (the capital clause). A public company must have an authorised capital of at least £50 000 (s 118, CA 1985).

It is to be noted that the White Paper (2005) proposes that an authorised share capital clause should no longer be considered as an obligatory requirement for companies. This recommendation follows the lead of the CLR's Final Report (2001) and is in accordance with earlier proposals advanced by the CLR (see e.g. the CLR reports: 'Company Formation and Capital Maintenance' (1999) and 'Capital Maintenance' (2000)). The recommendation was also included in the White Paper (2002). This proposal is designed to remove the arduous procedure for alterations to share capital (see s 121, CA 1985, discussed below). However, public companies will still have to maintain a minimum authorised share capital (currently £50 000).

Issued capital

The part of a company's authorised share capital that has been issued to its shareholders is referred to as the company's issued share capital. A public company must have an issued share capital of £50 000 (i.e. if a public company has an authorised share capital of £50 000, then all of its share capital must be issued).

Unissued share capital

The difference between the nominal value of a company's authorised share capital and the nominal value of its issued share capital, minus any amount of issued capital which has not been called up by the company, represents the sum of the company's unissued share capital.

Called-up share capital

Called-up share capital is the total amount of consideration that those who hold company's shares have been required to pay to the company in return for the issue of the company's shares.

Uncalled share capital

The difference between the nominal value of a company's issued share capital and the value of the company's called-up share capital represents the amount of the company's uncalled capital. Any amount outstanding on the issue of partly paid-up shares will form a part of the company's uncalled share capital. Although the majority of companies issue fully paid-up shares, a partly paid issue may on occasions prove to be a more attractive proposition to a potential investor in so far as the payment for the shares will be spread over a period of time as opposed to a demand from the company for one initial payment.

Paid-up share capital

The total amount of consideration actually contributed for a company's shares is termed its paid-up share capital.

Reserve capital

In accordance with s 120 of the Companies Act 1985, the members of a company may, by special resolution, decide to set aside a part of the company's uncalled share capital as a fund for the payment of unsecured creditors should the company be wound up. This reserve fund of capital cannot be reconverted back into uncalled capital or be used by the company as security for a loan. The reserve capital fund can, however, be reduced with the consent of the court (see s 135, CA 1985, discussed below).

Capital reserve accounts

The most common forms of capital reserve accounts are (a) the share premium account, (b) the capital redemption reserve, and (c) the revaluation reserve. Sums in a capital reserve fund cannot be used to pay dividends, although they may be used to finance an issue of bonus shares. A company's capital reserves should be contrasted with its revenue reserves; the latter represent a company's retained profits. Retained profits, unlike reserve capital, may be used to pay dividends.

(a) The share premium account

A company share has a nominal value; a share cannot be issued at a discounted value below that of its nominal value. However, a share may be issued for a consideration in excess of its nominal value (i.e. the share may be issued at a premium). The difference in value between a share's nominal value and any premium paid on the share must be transferred to the company's share premium account (s 130, CA 1985).

(b) The capital redemption reserve

Sections 160 and 162 of the Companies Act 1985 provide that a company may, in certain circumstances, redeem or purchase its own shares out of its distributable profits. As a result of such a purchase or redemption, the company's capital will be reduced by the extent of the loss in the value of the shares purchased or redeemed. Therefore, in order to maintain its capital balance, the company must place in its capital redemption reserve an amount equal to the reduction in share capital (s 170, CA 1985).

(c) Revaluation reserve

A revaluation reserve represents an amount by which the value of a company's assets has increased. An amount equal to an increase in the value of a corporate asset should be transferred to the company's revaluation reserve.

INCREASING OR REDUCING SHARE CAPITAL

Increasing share capital

A company, where permitted by the terms of its articles, may alter the conditions of its memorandum (capital clause) to effect an alteration in share capital (s 121, CA 1985). Table A, art 32 provides that an alteration in accordance with s 121 may take place by the passing of an ordinary resolution. Where, in effecting an alteration, a company increases share capital, it must, within 15 days of passing the resolution to authorise the increase, give notice to the Registrar. The notice must include details of any conditions attached to the new shares.

Reduction of share capital (s 143, CA 1985)

A company may wish to reduce its share capital for a number of legitimate reasons; for example, the company's net assets may have fallen to a value below that of its share capital. A reduction of share capital may not necessarily be detrimental to the interests of the company's shareholders; one of the objectives of writing off share capital may be to enable the company to resume paying dividends or to allow it to continue to pay dividends at a higher rate. However, in so far as the reduction of share capital may have an adverse affect on the saleable value of the share, the reduction may cause prejudice to the interests of shareholders.

Section 143 of the Companies Act 1985 provides statutory confirmation of a long-established principle of company law in the context of a company's capacity to reduce and/or expend its capital. The principle was expressed by Lord Herschell in *Trevor* v *Whitworth* (1887) 12 App Cas 409:

> 'The capital may, no doubt, be diminished by expenditure upon and reasonably incidental to all the objects specified. A part of it may be lost in carrying on the business operations authorised. Of this all persons trusting the company are aware, and take the risk. But I think they are right to rely, and were intended by the Legislature to have a right to rely, on the capital remaining undiminished by any expenditure outside these limits, or by the return of any part of it to the shareholders.' (at p 415)

The purpose behind s 143 is to prevent a return of capital to shareholders and hence the general depletion of capital funds. Nevertheless, the Companies Act 1985 (discussed below) contains exceptions to permit companies to purchase or redeem their own fully paid-up shares, thus returning capital to shareholders. A company may also acquire its own fully paid-up shares otherwise than for valuable consideration – for example, by way of gift; however, a public company which acquires shares in this manner must dispose of them or sell them within three years of their acquisition (s 146, CA 1985).

In *Acatos & Hutcheson plc* v *Watson* [1995] BCC 450, it was necessary for the court to consider whether a company (A) in purchasing the entire issued share capital of another company (B) had infringed s 143. B's sole asset comprised a holding of 29.4 per cent of the issued share capital in A. In purchasing the entire issued share capital of B, A would, albeit indirectly, purchase an overriding interest in its own shares (i.e. B's 29.4 per cent stake in A). The background to this case was as follows. B had been used by members of A (including H, A's chairman and chief executive) as a vehicle to acquire shares in A, with the intention that H and other members of B would eventually make a takeover bid for A. However, although this objective was abandoned, B's holding in A created an adverse effect on the level of trading in A's shares. The most obvious solution would have been to put B into liquidation with its holding in A returned to B's shareholders (B had no outstanding creditors). However, such a scheme would have attracted a substantial tax burden.

Accordingly, an alternative method was advanced, whereby A proposed to purchase the entire share capital of B's members in exchange for an issue of its own shares. Therefore, B would retain its shares in A, but the independent status of B would be removed, as it would become a wholly owned subsidiary of A. In addition, A proposed to alter the rights attached to the shares which B held in A, to the extent that the shares would carry no votes or rights to dividend payments. Basically, while B would technically continue to exist, it would do so in a lifeless state with no power or future capacity in terms of voting rights to influence the affairs of its newly adopted holding company.

In sanctioning the validity of the proposed agreement, Lightman J opined that the share purchase did not infringe s 143 because A did not intend to purchase its own shares but rather it sought to purchase shares in B, as held by the existing members of B. Although the purchase impliedly meant that A would purchase an outright interest (as B Ltd's holding company) in its own shares, Lightman J considered that this was not the same as an express purchase of its own shares. The learned judge also found that the transaction, in so far as B, as a subsidiary of A, would hold shares in its holding company, did not transgress s 23 of the Companies Act 1985 because the shares held in A, by B, had been rendered devoid of voting rights. Finally, Lightman J concluded that A's proposed purchase of shares in B would have no adverse effect on the creditors or shareholders of A; Lightman J construed the purchase as being in the best interests of all the concerned parties.

Although the decision taken by Lightman J in *Acatos & Hutcheson plc* v *Watson* appears to have served the interests of all the parties concerned (with the exception of the Inland Revenue), it must be viewed with some caution in terms of future precedent. In reality, the practical, if not the theoretical, result of the transaction was one whereby A acquired its own shares, albeit that the acquisition was a result of an indirect procurement of the shares.

Procedure for reducing capital

A company, if it wishes to reduce its issued share capital, must first be authorised to do so by its articles (authorisation is contained within the Table A articles by art 34). Secondly, the company in general meeting must pass a special resolution to sanction the reduction. Finally, the company must obtain the court's approval (s 135, CA 1985). The group of persons most likely to be concerned by a reduction in a company's share capital is the company's creditors because the effect of a reduction in capital depletes the company's recognised measure of capital. Should the company fall into liquidation, the pool of assets from which creditors may be paid would, in theory, be reduced.

In accordance with s 135(2) of the Companies Act 1985, a company will normally be permitted to reduce its share capital in one of three ways.

- First, it may extinguish or reduce liability on its partly paid shares.
- Secondly, it may cancel paid-up share capital which has been lost in relation to available assets (i.e. by reducing the nominal value of its shares).
- Thirdly, a company may, either with or without extinguishing or reducing liability on any of its shares, pay off any of the paid-up share capital which is in excess of its needs. For example, a company may choose to return to its ordinary shareholders 10p for every fully paid-up £1 share; instead of repaying the specified amount in cash, the company may allot debenture stock to its shareholders.

In relation to the second described method (i.e. by cancelling paid-up share capital to correspond with a loss in the value of corporate assets), this method avoids having to retain profits to replace lost capital: see e.g. *Carruth* v *Imperial Chemical Industries Ltd* [1937] AC 703. In *Re Jupiter House Investments Ltd* [1985] 1 WLR 975 Harman J held that to prove a loss of capital, the loss should be construed as permanent and not a temporary loss in the value of a capital asset. Nevertheless, Harman J took the view that where the loss could not be proved as permanent, the company could, albeit in exceptional circumstances, attain court approval for a reduction in circumstances where it had set aside a non-distributable reserve to ensure that, if the loss of capital was subsequently recovered, the same would not be distributed in the form of dividend payments. However, it should be noted that in *Re Grosvenor Press plc* [1985] 1 WLR 980, Nourse J took a contrary view by declaring that although a fall in the value of a capital asset may only be temporary, there remained no compelling reason, except in exceptional circumstances, for the court to require a reserve to be set aside.

Indeed, the primary concern of the court, in deciding whether to affirm a company's reduction of share capital, will be to consider the effect of the reduction in respect of the company's ability to repay its debts (s 136, CA 1985): see *Poole* v *National Bank of China* [1907] AC 229. Where a proposed reduction of share capital has the effect of reducing liability in respect of unpaid share capital or where the reduction would result in the payment of paid-up share capital to shareholders, creditors of the company will be more likely to object to the reduction and may do so under s 136(3)–(6) of the Companies Act 1985. However, under s 137 of the Companies Act 1985, where the court is satisfied that the effect of the reduction in capital would not leave the company's creditors in a perilous position, it may confirm the reduction or may impose upon it such terms and conditions as it sees fit. In seeking to satisfy the court that the reduction would not leave the creditors in a perilous position, it may be advisable for the company to set aside a reserve fund to meet the potential claims of creditors.

In addition to considering the effect of a reduction of capital on the company's creditors, the court must, in appropriate cases, consider the effect of the reduction upon the various classes of company shareholder: see e.g. *Re Ratners Group plc* [1988] 4 BCC 293. The court must determine whether the reduction of capital would vary the rights of a class of shareholder. For example, where preference shareholders are given the right to a repayment of capital in preference to ordinary shareholders, upon a reduction of a company's paid-up capital, the preference shareholders should be paid in full, prior to any payment to the ordinary shareholders. The consent of a class of shareholders must be obtained where a proposed reduction of capital would result in a variation of class rights (see s 125, CA 1985, discussed in Chapter 9).

Proposals for reform

In October 1999, the company law review steering group (CLR) issued a consultation document entitled 'Modern Company Law for a Competitive Economy – Company Formation and Capital Maintenance', which proposed a relaxation in the rules governing the reduction of share capital. The rationale for the reform of this area of company law is obvious in the sense that the present rules are both complex and onerous, especially in the context of small private companies. The CLR proposed that a reduction in capital should be permissible providing a company passed a special resolution to authorise the reduction and in addition supported that authority with a solvency statement. Accordingly, if this proposal was implemented it would no longer be necessary for the company to seek the approval of the court before instigating a reduction in share capital, although in the case of a public company it would, in accordance with the EC Second Directive, still be possible for the company's creditors to apply to court to seek an annulment of the resolution.

In 2001, the CLR issued its Final Report (2001). In the report, the proposals of its earlier 1999 report (see above) and subsequent reports entitled 'Capital

Maintenance: Other Issues' (2000) and 'Completing the Structure' (2000), were considered. As a result of the Final Report, the spirit of the CLR's earlier recommendations remained intact, although the Final Report considered that such recommendations should be introduced as an alternative, as opposed to an outright replacement for the current procedure which deems that court approval must be obtained prior to a capital reduction. The justification advanced for maintaining a means of obtaining court approval for a reduction in capital was that for some companies it would provide a greater degree of certainty so that, once approved by the court, the reduction would be difficult to challenge. These recommendations were accepted by the government in its White Paper, 'Modernising Company Law' (2002) and, in part, by the subsequent White Paper (2005) 'Company Law Reform'. The 2005 White Paper's draft clauses contain the following proposals:

- Draft clause H14: This provides what would be expected to become the usual procedure for a reduction in capital. Here, a private company may reduce its capital in any way providing it passes a special resolution to authorise the same; the resolution must meet the solvency statement requirements. The latter requirements (draft clause H15) provide that the directors must be sure, as of the date of the statement, that the company can pay its debts and that if the company is wound up within a year of the date of the statement that the company will be able to pay its debts in full within 12 months commencing from the date of the winding up. It is proposed that a director who makes a solvency statement without having reasonable grounds for the opinions expressed therein will be liable to imprisonment for a maximum of two years or a fine, or both. On passing the special resolution, a copy of the resolution containing details of the reduction in share capital and the solvency statement (including statements from the directors accepting the accuracy of the same) must be delivered to the Registrar within 15 days of the passing of the resolution.

It is to be noted that the White Paper (2005) does provide that the new procedure will be an **alternative** to the current court approval procedure (discussed above). In the White Paper (2002), (draft clauses 59–61), the current court procedure was also reviewed. Here, it was provided that a company (both a private and a public company) should be allowed to reduce its capital in any way providing the reduction was approved by a special resolution which was then approved by the court. The court would be able to approve the reduction unconditionally or on such terms as it thought fit. Although under this procedure a solvency statement would not be required, qualifying creditors would be protected where the company proposed to reduce liability in respect of unpaid share capital, or where there was a payment to a shareholder of any paid-up share capital, and further, in any other case, where the court so directed. A qualifying creditor was generally defined as a creditor of the company who, at the date fixed by the court, was entitled to any debt or claim which, if that date had been the commencement of the winding up of the company, would be admissible in proof against the company. The court would be obliged to direct the company to settle the claims of the qualifying creditors, although the court would have a discretion to direct that any class or classes of creditors should not, in respect of a particular reduction, be classed as qualifying creditors.

The White Paper (2005) failed to provide the detail as outlined above and further restricted any change in the capital reduction mechanism to private companies. Indeed, the White Paper (2005) stopped short of recommending any changes in the law in respect of public companies. The recommendations of the CLR and the White Paper (2002) were (as outlined below) more extensive in the following respects:

- White Paper (2002), draft clauses 52–58: These were to apply to public companies to provide a similar solvency statement procedure to that detailed for private companies (described above). However, in addition to the requirements for private companies, public companies would have been obliged to meet publicity requirements (i.e. advertising the proposed reduction in the *Gazette* and a national newspaper). The public company would also have needed to inform all its current creditors (where an address was available) of the terms of the reduction. An accidental omission to inform a creditor would not render the resolution void, although every office holder deemed responsible for the omission would be liable to a fine. Any creditor within a period of six weeks from the date on which the special resolution was passed would have been allowed to apply to court for the resolution to be cancelled.

Exceptions to section 143 of the Companies Act 1985

At present, the law permits a number of deviations to the basic rule represented by s 143 of the Companies Act 1985. The said deviations are detailed below. However, as a consequence of the government's proposed reforms (detailed above) it is anticipated that the current procedures in respect of the redemption or re-purchase of shares in private companies may be significantly altered. However, it is to be noted that, save where a company is permitted to purchase its shares from capital, the present purchase procedures already seek to safeguard any unauthorised reduction in capital. Other than in a situation where shares are purchased from capital, any purchase of shares by the company must be complemented with measures to maintain the current level of the company's overall capital requirements (i.e. so as to avoid a reduction in capital).

Redemption and purchase procedures

Notwithstanding s 143, a company may in specified circumstances purchase its own shares whether or not the shares are issued as redeemable shares. A company may redeem its own shares if authorised to do so by its articles – the articles must also detail the procedure for redemption (1985 Table A, art 35 so authorises). However, the shares may be redeemed only if they have been fully paid up. On the redemption of shares, the company's issued share capital will be reduced by the nominal value of the redeemed shares.

Where a company is permitted by its articles to purchase its own shares (redeemable or not) the procedure for purchase is governed by ss 159–161 of the Companies Act 1985 (on the application of these provisions, see generally *BDG Roof Bond Ltd* v *Douglas* [2000] 1 BCLC 401). The funds for the purchase must be taken from the company's profits or, alternatively, from the proceeds of a new issue of shares; the new issue having been specifically created for the purpose of purchasing the company's existing shares (see ss 161(a) and 162(2), CA 1985). Additionally, a private company, **but not** a public company, may, in an off-market purchase (see below), purchase its own shares from capital.

Where shares are purchased (or redeemed) wholly or partly out of profits, then a transfer of funds, equal to the par value of the shares, must be made to the capital redemption reserve. Any premium payable on the shares must normally be paid out of profits. However, where a company's shares were initially issued at a premium, any premium attached to the shares on the date of purchase by the company may be paid out of the proceeds of an issue of new shares up to an amount not exceeding the lesser of:

(a) the total amount of premium obtained from the shares when they were first issued; and

(b) the amount standing to the credit of the share premium account at the time of issue. This amount includes any premium obtained on the new issue.

Other than in the case of treasury shares (discussed below), following a company's purchase of its shares, the shares must be cancelled (see s 162(2), CA 1985). Accordingly, the shares cannot be kept in reserve and resold at some later date, the latter rule affording a degree of investor protection – if the shares were reissued this would increase the number of shares then available (increased supply), which may produce a general fall in the share value. Further, if the shares were capable of being reissued they could possibly be issued for the purpose of manipulating voting control. Section 162 has some merit, especially in the context of public companies, but its universal application, without any form of exception, would appear unduly cautious, especially as there is little to prevent a company creating a new issue of shares in the future. (Note also in this context the White Paper's proposal to abolish 'authorised share capital'.)

Market purchase of a company's shares

A market purchase of shares affects public companies and is a purchase made on a recognised UK investment exchange (a public company may also make an off-market purchase under s 163(b) of the Companies Act 1985 (discussed below)). A public company may authorise a market purchase if it is given authority to do so by the general meeting; the general meeting may authorise the transaction by ordinary resolution. In addition, the company must comply with the statutory procedures contained within s 166 of the Companies Act 1985, namely the resolution granting the authority to purchase must specify a maximum number of shares to be acquired and the maximum and minimum prices to be paid for the shares. The resolution must also specify a date when the authority will expire; the maximum duration for the authority is 18 months. A copy of the resolution which authorises the share purchase must be sent to the Registrar within 15 days of the resolution having been passed. (Note that s 166 provides an exception to the general rule concerning the notification of resolutions to the Registrar; normally only special resolutions must be filed with the Registrar.)

In accordance with Stock Exchange requirements, a market purchase of five per cent or more of a company's share capital within a period of 12 months must be made either by way of tender or a partial offer to all the company's existing share-holders. Purchases below this limit may be made through the market if the price paid is not more than five per cent above the average of the middle market quotations taken from the Official List for the ten business days prior to the date of purchase.

Off-market purchase of a company's shares

An off-market purchase comprises a purchase of shares otherwise than on a recog-nised UK investment exchange or, if the shares were purchased on a recognised investment exchange, in a situation where the shares purchased had not been the subject of a marketing arrangement (see s 163(1), CA 1985). An off-market transac-tion is normally executed by means of a private contract between a company and one of its existing shareholders.

An off-market purchase must be approved by a special resolution of the general meeting (s 164(1) and (2), CA 1985); a copy of the proposed purchase contract should be made available for inspection by the company's membership 15 days prior to the meeting at which the motion to approve the contract is to be considered. The member of the company with whom the contract is made is not permitted to vote on the motion. Where the company is a public company, the authority contained in the resolution will last no longer than a period of 18 months (s 164(4), CA 1985). It should be noted, following the decision of Lindsay J in *Re R W Peak* (*King's Lynn*) *Ltd* [1998] BCC 596, that an informal resolution cannot be used to validate a pur-chase by a company of its own shares. However, by contrast, in *BDG Roof Bond Ltd* v *Douglas* [2000] 1 BCLC 401, a case concerned with an off-market purchase of shares but also involving other issues, Park J opined that, following the principle applied in *Re Duomatic Ltd* [1969] 2 Ch 365, formal shareholder procedures could be discarded providing that there was unanimous shareholder support. (The *Re Duomatic* principle is discussed further in Chapter 21.)

A contract of purchase may be contingent upon giving either the company or member, or both, an option to purchase. If a company provides consideration for an option to purchase, the consideration must be taken from its distributable profits (see ss 165 and 168, CA 1985, and see *BDG Roof Bond Ltd* v *Douglas* [2000] 1 BCLC 401, where the validity of the share purchase was defeated on the ground that it con-travened ss 165 and 168). The company in making an off-market purchase must deliver a return to the Registrar. The return must notify the Registrar of the details of the transaction and be delivered no later than 28 days from the date of purchase. A copy of the purchase contract must be kept at the company's registered office for a period of ten years (s 169(4) and (5), CA 1985). In relation to a public company, the Registrar must be informed of the aggregate amount paid for the shares, together with details of the maximum and minimum prices paid for each class of share pur-chased (s 169(2), CA 1985).

Treasury shares

In accordance with the Companies (Acquisition of Own Shares) (Treasury Shares) Regulations 2003 (No 1) and (No 2), public companies now have the option to purchase their own shares (providing the shares satisfy the qualifying conditions) without the need to cancel them; the company then has an ability to subsequently reissue the shares at a later date. This allows greater flexibility and is a less arduous procedure than seeking a new issue of shares. Shares held in this manner are known as treasury shares. The ability to deal with shares in this way is impliedly permitted by Articles 19(1)(b) and 22 of the EC Second Directive. The new Regulations do not change the content of existing provisions (which must still be complied with) that deal with a company's acquisition of its own shares; they add to the said provisions (see ss 162A–162D).

For shares to 'qualify' under the new regulations, the shares must be listed or traded on the Alternative Investment Market and the purchase of the shares must be made out of distributable profits and not capital. The Regulations provide a limit as to how many shares may be held as treasury shares, namely ten per cent of the nominal value of issued shares or ten per cent of a particular class of issued shares. Treasury shares must be recorded in the company's register of members although obviously the shares whilst held by the company do not retain their voting rights. However, bonus shares may be allotted to treasury shares (in the same way as other types of qualifying share) and, if so, such bonus shares will also be held as treasury shares. Where treasury shares cease to be qualifying shares, the shares must be cancelled.

Any subsequent sale of the treasury shares must be for cash and the shares must not be sold at a discount (below par value). However, the treasury shares may be used in the context of an employees' share scheme or cancelled under the existing rules. Where the proceeds of sale are equal to or less than the purchase price, the proceeds are treated as distributable profits of the company. Where the proceeds exceed the original purchase price an amount equal to the excess must be transferred to the share premium account.

An obvious danger with the concept of treasury shares is a company's ability to sell the shares not for the purpose of injecting more capital into the company but rather to manipulate the market. To correct any potential for such abuse, the Listing Rules have been amended with the objective of restricting the ease with which treasury shares may be sold (see the Listing Rules, r 15.19(b)) and have also provided detailed disclosure requirements to monitor the holdings and disposals of treasury shares.

PAYMENT FOR A COMPANY'S OWN SHARES OUT OF CAPITAL (PRIVATE COMPANIES ONLY)

Providing a private company is authorised to do so by its articles (note that no such authority is contained within the Table A articles), it will, in accordance with s 171 of the Companies Act 1985, have a capacity to use capital as a means of redeeming or purchasing its own shares. However, a private company may expend capital only if the company's distributable profits are of an insufficient value to facilitate the redemption or purchase. A private company that expends capital for the purpose of purchasing its own shares does not require any court authorisation, notwithstanding that the purchase represents a reduction in capital. However, the company will require authority in the form of a special resolution (s 164(2), CA 1985). A member who holds shares on which the motion to purchase applies is not permitted to vote on the resolution. A company's purchase or redemption of shares from capital will be unlawful unless the company complies with the prerequisite statutory procedures (see ss 173–175, CA 1985).

Any expenditure for the purchase or redemption of shares that is to be taken from capital is referred to as 'the permissible capital payment' (s 171(3), CA 1985). The calculation of the permissible capital payment will, in accordance with s 171(6), be the sum of capital which, in addition to any sum representing the proceeds of a new issue of shares, is the amount required for the purpose of the redemption or purchase of the company's own shares. Where the permissible capital payment for the shares to be redeemed or purchased is of a sum lower in value than the shares' nominal value, the amount of the difference must be transferred to the company's capital redemption reserve (s 171(4), CA 1985). If, however, the permissible capital payment is greater in value than the nominal amount of the shares to be acquired, then, either the capital redemption reserves, share premium account or fully paid share capital of the company, and any amount representing unrealised profits standing to the credit of any revaluation reserve (or a combination of the aforementioned), may be reduced by a sum not exceeding the amount by which the permissible capital payment exceeds the nominal amount of the shares (s 171(5), CA 1985).

If a company uses capital to purchase its own shares, the directors of the company are required to make a statutory declaration to the effect that, despite the company's expenditure from capital, the company is still capable of meeting its debts throughout the year immediately following the purchase (s 173(3), CA 1985). The declaration, which must be made within the week before the special resolution to authorise the payment from capital, must be accompanied by an auditor's report to support the terms of the declaration. Any member who did not vote in favour of the resolution, or any creditor of the company, may within five weeks of the date of the special resolution authorising payment from capital, apply to the court for an order to prohibit the payment (s 176(1) and (2), CA 1985). Under s 177, the court may, on the hearing of an application under s 176, adjourn the proceedings so that an arrangement may be made for the company to compensate the dissentient members or the claims of the dissentient creditors (s 177(1)) and/or, the court may make an order under s 177(2) either confirming or cancelling the resolution which sought to give effect to the purchase or redemption of the company's own shares. In addition, under s 177(3), the court may order that the company purchase the shares of any dissentient member.

Where a company redeems or purchases its shares out of capital, but within a year immediately following the capital expenditure, falls into liquidation and cannot pay its debts, the directors of the company who were responsible for the declaration of solvency, together with the person from whom the shares were redeemed or purchased, will be liable to contribute towards the assets of the company. A director may escape liability if it is shown that he had reasonable grounds to believe in the accuracy of the declaration (s 76, IA 1986). However, where a director made a declaration without grounds to believe in its accuracy, the director concerned may be liable to a fine or imprisonment, or both (s 173(6), CA 1985).

Court orders for the purchase of shares

In addition to a voluntary purchase by a company of its own shares, a company may be ordered by the court to purchase shares from one of its members (see ss 54(6) and 461, CA 1985).

FINANCIAL ASSISTANCE GIVEN TO A THIRD PARTY FOR THE PURCHASE OF A COMPANY'S SHARES

The general rule

Section 151 of the Companies Act 1985 prohibits (but with exceptions) both private and public companies from giving financial assistance (whether directly or indirectly: see s 152, CA 1985) for the purpose of aiding a person's acquisition of shares in the company or the company's subsidiary. Section 151 seeks to protect creditors and shareholders of companies from potential financial abuses in respect of the acquisition of company shares. Frequently, a breach of the financial assistance rules will also give rise to a breach of fiduciary duty (discussed further in Chapter 17). However, it should be stressed that liability under s 151 is not in any way dependent upon establishing a breach of fiduciary duty and a director may be held liable under the provision notwithstanding the absence of any such breach: see e.g. the decision of the Court of Appeal in *Chaston v SWP Group plc* [2003] BCLC 675 (discussed further below).

Section 151 is drafted to cover a wide range of categories of financial assistance and the definition of financial assistance should not, for example, be restricted to the obvious (i.e. loans granted to aid a bidder). For s 151, the crucial question to ask is simply whether any form of assistance of a financial nature was given to assist in a share acquisition? As Aldous LJ explained in *Barclays Bank plc v British & Commonwealth Holdings plc* [1996] 1 BCLC 1:

> '. . . there should be assistance or help for the purpose of acquiring the shares and that assistance should be financial.' (at p 39)

For the purposes of s 151, the assistance may be given at a date well in advance of the share acquisition, providing that, when given, the share acquisition had been in the contemplation of the company. Section 152(1) provides that financial assistance may be by way of gift, guarantee, security or loan, or any other type of financial assistance given by a company, the effect of which is to reduce the company's net assets by a material extent: see e.g. *Belmont Finance Corporation v Williams Furniture Ltd (No 2)* [1980] 1 All ER 393, *Charterhouse Investment Trust Ltd v Tempest Diesels Ltd* [1985] 1 BCC 99, 544 and *MacPherson and Anor v European Strategic Bureau Ltd* [2002] BCC 39.

Section 151(1) will not be applicable where the alleged financial assistance was unrelated to the share acquisition. For example, in *Dyment v Boyden and Ors* [2005] BCC 79, property owned by A and B was leased to company X, after A and B ceased to be members of X. The Court of Appeal held that the said leasing agreement did not incorporate the giving of any financial assistance in respect of the acquisition of the shares of A and B notwithstanding that the rent was in excess of its apparent market value. The court held that, on the facts of the case, the share acquisition had taken place at a time prior to the company's decision to commit itself to the lease agreement.

However, under s 151(2), the prohibition is extended to cover those cases in which shares have already been acquired. Here, a company cannot give financial assistance to a third party for the purpose of reducing or discharging liabilities incurred as a result of the acquisition. In *Dyment* v *Boyden & Ors* [2005] BCC 79 (see above) it was argued that s 151(2) should be applicable. Here the court was required to focus on two purposes.

● First, the acquisition of shares. Here a relevant liability had to be incurred for that purpose. It was contended that Z (the controlling shareholder of X) had entered into the lease for the purpose of acquiring the shares with the objective of discharging an obligation (liability) to the local authority, namely the local authority had demanded that A and B should cease to be members of the company.

● Secondly, it had to be shown that the company gave financial assistance directly or indirectly for the purpose of reducing or discharging the liability.

The Court of Appeal held that the transfer of the shares was necessary in order to comply with the local authority's demands. However, while entering into the lease (the source of the potential financial assistance) was an event which could clearly be connected with the share purchase, it was not the **purpose** of the share acquisition. The company had entered the lease to obtain the premises. The company had paid an excessive rent because the owners of the premises were in a 'market' position to demand that high rent. In effect, according to the Court of Appeal, the prevailing circumstances and market conditions of this case were such that there was no form of financial assistance given by the company. The rent could not be viewed to be unduly excessive and therefore could not have amounted to the giving of financial assistance.

Exceptions to the general rule (s 153, CA 1985)

Section 151 is, however, subject to exceptions (provided by ss 153–158, CA 1985). Where applicable, the exceptions allow the giving of financial assistance for share acquisitions (discussed below). The exceptions apart, the giving of financial assistance is not merely prohibited, but it is also punishable as a criminal offence. The company itself may be fined, and any director or officer in default may be fined and/or imprisoned for a maximum of two years (s 153(3) and Sch 24, CA 1985). Under s 8 of the Accessories and Abettors Act 1861, any other person who knowingly took part in such a transaction (including the recipient of the assistance) may be liable as an accessory to the offence. Furthermore, since the giving of financial assistance is unlawful, any security or guarantee offered by or to the company as part of such an arrangement will be void: see e.g. *Heald* v *O'Connor* [1971] 1 WLR 497.

Section 153(1) allows a company to give financial assistance for the purchase of its shares (or shares in its holding company) if the company's principal purpose in giving the assistance is not given for the purpose of any such acquisition, or the giving of assistance for the share acquisition is but an incidental part of some larger purpose, the assistance being given in good faith in the interests of the company. In effect the purpose of the assistance must not in itself have been driven by a desire to facilitate the acquisition of the shares.

Section 153(2) provides a further, like exception, where the company's principal purpose in giving assistance is not to reduce or discharge any liability incurred by a person for the purpose of acquiring shares in the company or its holding company, or the reduction or discharge of any such liability was but an incidental part of some larger purpose of the company. In respect of qualifying under s 153(1) *and* (2), the assistance must have been given in good faith and must have been in the best interests of the company.

Section 153(3)–(5) provide additional exceptions to s 151. Section 153(3)(b) states that s 151 is to have no application in respect of an allotment of bonus shares. Section 153(4) permits certain companies to give financial assistance in the form of loans where the lending of money is a part of the company's usual business activities. Section 153(4)(b) as amended (by s 132, CA 1989) also provides that a company may offer financial assistance for the purchase of its shares in respect of an employee share scheme, providing the assistance is given in good faith and in the interests of the company. In respect of public companies, s 153(4) is only applicable where the company's net assets are not reduced as a result of assistance being given, or, to the extent that those assets are reduced, the assistance provided is taken from distributable profits (s 154, CA 1985).

Additional exception for private companies

In relation to private companies, s 155 of the Companies Act 1985 creates a further and far-ranging exception by providing that a private company has a general authority, by the passing of a special resolution in general meeting, to authorise financial assistance for the purchase of its own shares or shares in its holding company. The holding company must also be a private company and the group of companies, controlled by the holding company, must have no public company within its ranks. In accordance with s 155, financial assistance may be given providing the company's net assets are not, as a result of the assistance, reduced, or, to the extent that they are reduced, assistance is provided out of distributable profits. The special resolution authorising financial assistance must be passed within a week of the date on which the directors of the company made a statutory declaration as to the company's immediate solvency (see below).

In accordance with s 157(2), where a special resolution is passed to effect the grant of financial assistance, an application may be made to the court by the holder(s) of not less than ten per cent in nominal value of the company's issued share capital, or any class of it, for the cancellation of the resolution. However, a member who consented to or voted in favour of the resolution must not make the application. In addition, the application must be made within four weeks of the passing of the resolution (s 158, CA 1985).

Where, by s 156, a private company gives financial assistance for the purchase of its own shares, the directors of the company must make a statutory declaration that they are of the opinion that the company will remain solvent for a period of 12 months from the date on which the financial assistance was given (s 156(1)–(3)): see *Re In a Flap Envelope Co Ltd (in liq)* [2003] BCC 487. The directors' declaration must be supported by a report from the company's auditors which must confirm the directors' assessment of the company's financial state as reasonable (s 156(4), CA 1985): see, generally, *Harlow v Loveday* [2004] EWHC 1261 (Ch) (*The Times*, 11 June 2004).

Judicial interpretation of the exception rules

In *Brady v Brady* [1988] BCLC 579, the House of Lords was called upon to determine a number of issues pertinent to the interpretation of the financial assistance rules and their exceptions. The case involved a family business which was carried on by two brothers (J and B). The business had operated successfully as a private limited company (Brady) since 1959; it was also comprised of a number of subsidiary companies. J and B were the sole directors of Brady; the company's issued share capital was split between B, who held 46.68 per cent, and J, who held 46.66 per cent; the remaining 6.66 per cent of the issued share capital was held by X Ltd, a private company. Up until 1982, the Brady group flourished, but in that year the group encountered trading difficulties. The group's difficulties were largely expounded by a management deadlock between J and B.

In an attempt to resolve the management deadlock, an agreement was reached whereby the assets of the group were to be split between the two brothers. It was decided that the assets would be split without liquidating Brady. In order to facilitate the reorganisation, the business interests of the group were to be merged and eventually split in equal proportions between two new companies, M Ltd, which was to be controlled by J, and A Ltd, controlled by B. The reorganisation was planned to take place via the transfer of the Brady assets to M Ltd; M Ltd would then issue loan stock to A Ltd, i.e. representing an equal share of the group's assets. The loan stock was to be redeemed by the subsequent transfer of assets from M Ltd to A Ltd.

However, before the scheme was completed, B became dissatisfied with the proposed division of assets and as a result refused to abide by the terms of the agreement. As a consequence of B's refusal to honour the agreement, J sought an order for specific performance. In his defence, B claimed (amongst other matters) that the transfer of assets from Brady to M Ltd, assets that would eventually be used to discharge M Ltd's debt to A Ltd (the redemption of its loan stock), constituted an illegal transaction.

B's assertion that the transaction was illegal rested in part on the premise that the transaction was contrary to s 151(2), namely Brady would have given financial assistance to M Ltd to reduce M Ltd's liability in respect of its acquisition of Brady shares. J contended that the transaction was within the ambit of the exception to s 151 as provided for by s 153(2). At first instance, the court found in favour of J and ordered specific performance. However, the Court of Appeal disagreed ([1988] BCLC 20) (Croom-Johnson LJ dissenting) on the applicability of the s 153(2)(b) exception. The majority of the Court of Appeal concluded that any assistance to M Ltd would not be in good faith nor for the benefit of Brady, in so far as it comprised a gratuitous disposition and was therefore contrary to the company's objects and thus *ultra vires*.

On appeal to the House of Lords, the House disagreed with the Court of Appeal's findings in relation to the interpretation of good faith and corporate benefit. Lord Oliver, expressing the unanimous opinion of the House, explained the reasons why Brady's decision to give financial assistance was one which could be couched in terms of having been taken in good faith and in the best interests of the company. His lordship opined:

> 'In the circumstances of this case, where failure to implement the final stage of the scheme for the division of the two sides of Brady's business is likely to lead back to the very management deadlock that it was designed to avoid and the probable liquidation of Brady as a result, the proposed transfer is not only something which is properly capable of being perceived by Brady's directors as calculated to advance Brady's corporate and commercial interests and the interests of its employees but is indeed, viewed objectively, in the company's interest.' (at p 597)

Nevertheless, somewhat surprisingly, the House of Lords (contrary to the findings of both the High Court and Court of Appeal) took the view that Brady's principal purpose in giving financial assistance to M Ltd was not an incidental part of some larger purpose and as such s 153(2)(a) was not satisfied. Lord Oliver feared that the term 'larger purpose', if construed liberally, could be viewed as a 'blank cheque' for the purpose of avoiding s 151. In interpreting the term 'larger purpose' in the context of the *Brady* case, Lord Oliver stated as follows:

> 'The purpose and the only purpose of the financial assistance is and remains that of enabling the shares to be acquired, and the financial or commercial advantages flowing from the acquisition, whilst they may form the reason for forming the purpose of providing assistance, are a by-product of it rather than an independent purpose of which the assistance can properly be considered to be an incident.' (at p 599)

Accordingly, Lord Oliver viewed the assistance given to M Ltd by Brady for the purchase of Brady shares as devoid of a larger purpose.

Lord Oliver's narrow construction of the term 'larger purpose' restricts the ease by which s 153(2) may be used to avoid s 151; as a consequence of his lordship's comments it is somewhat difficult to imagine a situation in which s 153(2) would be applicable. It is suggested that Lord Oliver's restrictive interpretation went too far in its desire to protect the s 151 provision. Surely, in *Brady* the purpose of the assistance was ultimately to facilitate the reorganisation of the group; it is suggested that the financial assistance would be devoid of any meaningful purpose had this not been the case (see the comments of Croom-Johnson LJ: [1988] BCLC 20 at p 32).

Nevertheless, despite the House of Lords' findings in respect of the larger purpose point, J's appeal was allowed. As Brady was able to provide the assistance out of distributable profits, or the effect of the proposed transaction would not have reduced Brady's assets, the exception to s 151 represented by s 155(2) was applied.

In *Chaston v SWP Group plc* [2003] BCLC 675, the Court of Appeal was called upon to revisit some of the controversial points considered in *Brady*. The *Chaston* case highlights the technical and arbitrary nature and construction of s 151. Here, shares in company X were purchased by A; however, fees incurred by A as a consequence of instructing accountants to prepare a report into the affairs of X were paid for by B. B was the director of a subsidiary of X. Overturning the first instance decision of Davis J, the Court of Appeal held that although B's assistance was given in good faith and was given for the ultimate benefit of X, causing the company no detriment, it nevertheless constituted financial assistance within the meaning of s 151, the instructions to the accountants having been directly connected with the negotiations for the sale of X's shares. Further, the breach of s 151 could not be saved on the basis that the assistance was given in advance of and not in the actual course of the share acquisition or that the payment of the fees had no impact on the share price. Adopting a 'commercial realities of the transaction' approach, expounded by Hoffmann J in *Charterhouse Investment Trust Ltd* v *Tempest Diesels Ltd* [1986] BCLC 1 (at pp 10–11), Arden LJ opined:

'As a matter of commercial reality, the fees in question smoothed the path to the acquisition of shares.' (at p 688)

The assistance clearly facilitated the share purchase and there was no 'larger purpose' within the meaning of s 153 to save the transaction. The approach taken by Lord Oliver in *Brady*, namely distinguishing between 'reason' and 'purpose', was applied. Here, the reason for the financial assistance may have been to benefit X, but the purpose of the transaction was the acquisition of X's shares. There was, in respect of the transaction, no other larger purpose.

In contrast to the Court of Appeal's findings in *Chaston*, in the case of *M T Realisations Ltd (in liq.)* v *Digital Equipment Co Ltd* [2003] 2 BCLC 117, a differently constituted Court of Appeal could find no breach of s 151. Here, the claimant company, M, was insolvent and owed £8 million to its holding company (D). T agreed to purchase M for £1 and pay £6.5 million for an assignment of the sum owed by M to D. A loan agreement between T and D was entered into in relation to the repayment of the £6.5 million. T had difficulty in meeting the payments and thus a further agreement (the second agreement) was entered into whereby, until the sum of £6.5 million was re-paid, any moneys owing to M from business transactions between M and D and any of D's subsidiaries was to be retained by D; the said sums to be set off against the debt of £6.5 million. In total, under this agreement, approximately £2 million was retained by D and set off against the sum of £6.5 million. The outstanding amount of the loan was subsequently re-paid by T, one year after the second agreement between T and D (in respect of the loan there is no mention in the law report of any interest charges having been imposed). M subsequently went into liquidation; the liquidator claimed that the set-off agreement between T and D was, in effect, a breach by M of s 151 (i.e. the set off agreement equated to financial assistance in respect of T's acquisition of M).

The Court of Appeal held that, having regard to the commercial realities of the agreement, there was no breach of the provision because there was never any financial assistance; nothing was given by M to T which it had not already acquired as its own (i.e. **prior** to entering into the set-off agreement with D, T had acquired the right to M's assets, to enforce debts owing to M, which could in turn be used to re-pay D). T's agreement with D had nothing to do with the purchase of M's shares. Yet, despite the apparent logic of the decision, the outcome of this case appears somewhat questionable if one applies the stricter analysis found in *Chaston*. It seems strange (albeit this is perhaps too cynical a view) that in terms of commercial realities, the set off agreement between D and T had never been contemplated, other than after the purchase of M's shares. Further, in accordance with s 151(2), T incurred a liability (the debt of £6.5 million) as a direct result of the share acquisition in the knowledge that the repayment of this liability was a condition attached to the share purchase. The liability was incurred as part and parcel of and related to the purpose of the acquisition. Therefore, in relation to this liability was there not financial assistance via the terms of the second agreement, that is, an extended repayment period, one possibly devoid of any interest charges?

Proposals for reform

In October 1993, the Department of Trade and Industry (DTI) issued a consultative document in relation to a proposed relaxation of the statutory rules relating to compliance with ss 151–158 of the Companies Act 1985. The consultative document, while recognising the need for protective measures to prevent the abuse of the financial assistance rules, took the view that the current prohibitions were too restrictive and inflexible.

In order to inject more flexibility into the exception to the rule represented by s 151, the consultative document recommended the replacement of the 'principal purpose' exception contained in s 153. The consultative document considered that this exception should be replaced with one which allowed financial assistance to be permitted where it was given in good faith and the predominant reason for assistance was one undertaken in the best interests of the company. The consultative document also favoured a second type of exception, namely to allow financial assistance providing there was no material reduction in the net assets of the company.

In November 1996, the DTI commenced a further consultation exercise. The result of that exercise was published in April 1997. The DTI, in confirming the findings of the October 1993 consultation document, concluded that the 'larger purpose' test expounded in *Brady* v *Brady* should be abolished and replaced by the 'predominant reason' test, thereby avoiding a narrow construction of the 'larger purpose' test as applied in *Brady*. The 1997 DTI recommendations also sought to amend or reform other aspects of the financial assistance rules and exceptions. For example, the DTI suggested that companies which gave financial assistance should not be subject to criminal sanctions and that a defence should be made available to company officers who were subject to prosecution. Further, the DTI recommended that a transaction should not be rendered void solely on the grounds that it constituted unlawful financial assistance.

In October 1999, the CLR issued a consultation document, 'Company Formation and Capital Maintenance', which hinted at (although it did not accept) a more radical reform, namely, in following the example of the USA, a total removal of the rules which prohibit financial assistance by a private company for the acquisition of its own shares. Indeed, the removal of private companies from the financial assistance rules was adopted by the CLR report, 'Developing the Framework' (2000). This proposal was subsequently endorsed by the CLR report, 'Completing the Structure' (2000). As such, if the proposals were adopted by the legislature, the present rules contained in ss 151–158 would not be applicable to private companies. Indeed, the proposals have been adopted by the White Paper (2005) albeit that financial assistance will remain prohibited in circumstances where the assistance is provided by a public company (or any subsidiary of the public company) and the acquisition of shares relates to the shares of a subsidiary (private company) of that public company (see clause H18 of the White Paper).

In respect of public companies, the CLR endorsed earlier recommendations of the DTI by concluding that the 'predominant reason' test should replace the existing 'principal purpose' test. This was approved in the White Paper (2002) (albeit that no draft clauses were provided in respect of proposed future legislation). However, in the White Paper (2005), it would appear (as there is no mention of the matter) that the government has decided not to proceed with any change to the present 'principal purpose' test.

Summary

The giving of financial assistance for the purchase of a company's shares is a complex and at times confusing area of company law. It is made more confusing because of the incompleteness of the meaning of the term 'financial assistance'. The commercial reality test appears a logical way to determine assistance, albeit that it is not a solution because its application is as a 'jury question' and, as such, attitudes to what is within or what is outside the test may be apt to change with the wind, thus resulting in uncertainty.

In so far as it is necessary to comply with the EC Second Directive, it is contended that, for public companies, a move to relax the cumbersome 'principal purpose' test expounded in *Brady* v *Brady* [1988] BCLC 579 is to be welcomed. The application of the proposed test of predominant reason, linked to the best interests of the company, is an improvement on the present position although the term 'predominant reason/purpose' may require some degree of statutory clarification to prevent its interpretation being subject to the constraints associated with the 'principal purpose' test.

However, contrary to the recommendation of the White Paper (2005), it is suggested that private companies should not be afforded an absolute freedom to offer financial assistance for the purchase of their shares; indeed, the potential for an abuse in the giving of financial assistance may be more apt in private companies, which are generally devoid of public scrutiny. Therefore, it is suggested that the present rules contained in ss 155–158 should be retained in modified form (possibly just the retention of the requirement to pass a special resolution would suffice).

DISTRIBUTION OF PROFITS – THE PROVISION FOR DIVIDEND PAYMENTS

A dividend payment may be seen as the return on a shareholder's investment for the purchase of shares in a company, that is, dividend payments represent a share in company profits. A dividend is usually payable to a shareholder in proportion to the nominal value of the shares held in the company although, in accordance with s 281 of the Companies Act 1985, the memorandum or articles of a company may place restrictions on the payment of dividends.

Provision for the regulation of a company's payment of dividends is usually made within the company's articles. For example, Table A, art 102 specifies that a company may by ordinary resolution declare a dividend, but that no dividend shall exceed an amount recommended by the company's directors: see *Scott* v *Scott* [1943] 1 All ER 582. In deciding whether to recommend the payment of a dividend, the directors must act in the best interests of the company.

When a dividend is declared, it represents a debt due from the company to its shareholders. Although a company is not bound to declare a dividend, it should be noted that, if the company is capable of doing so, a failure to declare a dividend may unfairly prejudice the interests of its members, thus giving rise to the possibility of an action under s 459 of the Companies Act 1985: see e.g. *Re Sam Weller & Sons Ltd* [1990] BCLC 80 (discussed in Chapter 24).

In order to protect the interests of creditors, a dividend cannot be paid from a company's capital assets and may only be paid out of the profits that are available for distribution to shareholders (s 263, CA 1985). Profits available for distribution are defined by s 263(3) as accumulated realised profits which have not been previously utilised by distribution or capitalisation, minus any accumulated realised losses which have not been previously written off in a reduction or reorganisation of capital. Therefore, a company may not pay a dividend on the premise of one good year's trading if its overall (present and past) profits (accumulated profits) are of a lesser value than its accumulated losses. Further, a dividend cannot be declared unless the profits are realised, although bonus shares may still be paid for out of unrealised profits (s 263(2)(a), CA 1985).

Public companies are subject to additional and more stringent restrictions imposed by the EC Second Directive. Section 264 provides that a public company may only make a distribution out of its profits if the amount of its net assets is not less than the aggregate of its called-up share capital, plus any undistributable reserves. Further, the distribution must not reduce the amount of those assets to less than the aggregate of its called-up share capital plus undistributable reserves. Undistributable reserves are defined by s 264(4) as:

(a) the share premium account,

(b) the capital redemption reserve,

(c) the amount by which the company's accumulated, unrealised profits (not previously utilised by a capitalisation detailed in s 264(4)) exceed its accumulated, unrealised losses (not previously written off in a reduction or reorganisation of capital), and

(d) any other reserve which the company is prohibited from distributing by any enactment or by a provision in its memorandum or articles.

Where the directors of a company decide that a dividend should not be declared (or decide to declare a reduced dividend), the company may retain its profits in the business; indeed, most companies retain at least a proportion of their profits to inject back into future business projects. The directors of a company may create reserves (taken from what would have been distributable profits) and such reserves may be capitalised and used to allocate bonus shares (see Table A, art 110). Dividend payments must, unless the contrary is specifically provided for in the company articles, be paid in cash, although it should be noted that Table A, art 105 allows a company to pay dividends other than in cash.

If a dividend is declared in contravention of s 263 or, in the case of a public company, in contravention of s 264, then, in accordance with s 277, any member who was aware or had reasonable grounds for believing that there had been a contravention of the statutory procedures will be liable to repay the dividend payment to the company: see e.g. *Precisions Dippings Ltd* v *Precious Dippings Marketing Ltd* [1986] Ch 447. Further, in such a case, the directors of the company having declared the dividend, will have acted in breach of their duties and in abuse of their powers and, as such, will *prima facie* be liable to make good any loss incurred by the company.

Suggested further reading

Capital maintenance
Armour (2000) 63 MLR 355

Leyte (2004) 25 Bus LR 84

Financial assistance
Sykes (2000) 21 Co Law 65

Cabrelli [2002] JBL 272

Armour (2003) 62 CLJ 266

Shutkever (2004) 25 Co Law 34

Treasury shares
Morse [2004] JBL 303

11

THE ACQUISITION OF SHARES IN A PUBLIC COMPANY

INTRODUCTION

The purpose of this chapter is to explain the rules applicable to the regulation of an offer of shares in both listed and unlisted public companies. The said rules are at times complex and confusing given that, pre-implementation of the new EC Prospectus Directive, alternative legislative mechanisms regulate, on the one hand, public offers of listed securities and, on the other, public offers of unlisted securities. However, despite the alternative regulatory systems, there is, in reality, little difference in their content, a situation that naturally justifies the merger of the two sets of regulations, a merger which will take place as a consequence of the implementation of the new EC Prospectus Directive. Finally, this chapter will also consider the available remedies for loss or damage following on from a non-contractual representation of a false or misleading nature in respect of the purchase of shares in a public limited company.

PURCHASING SECURITIES

Other than a purchase of shares on the Stock Exchange, the most likely method of acquiring shares in a public company will be to apply to a company's advertisement (contained within a prospectus or listing particulars) for the sale of its shares. Acceptance of the offer takes place when the company gives notice to the applicant that an allotment of shares has been made. Securities include shares and debentures and certificates which represent property rights or contractual rights in shares and debentures. At the time of writing (but see the proposed reform of this area, discussed below), Part VI of the Financial Services and Markets Act 2000 (FSMA 2000), in conjunction with Listing Rules formulated by the Financial Services Authority (FSA), regulate public offers of securities which are to be listed on the Official List of the Stock Exchange. The Public Offers of Securities Regulations 1995 (SI 1995/1537) (the 1995 Regulations) deal with public offers of securities which are not to be listed (the 1995 Regulations will cease to have effect following the UK's implementation of the Prospectus Directive, discussed below). The Financial Services Act 1986 aimed to consolidate the regulation of listed and unlisted securities in one Act; Part IV of the 1986 Act dealt with listed securities and Part V related to unlisted securities. However, Part V was never brought into force, the principal reason being the UK's need to comply with a former EC Prospectus Directive (89/298).

Listed securities

Listed securities are securities which have been admitted to listing on the London Stock Exchange, the principal UK market for security transactions. Prior to 1984, listing on the Stock Exchange was almost exclusively regulated by the Stock Exchange's own Listing Rules. In 1984, in addition to the Exchange's Listing Rules, three EC Directives – the Admissions Directive (No 79/279), the Listing Particulars Directive (No 80/390) and the Interim Reports Directive (No 82/121) – were implemented in the form of the Stock Exchange (Listing) Regulations 1984. The aforementioned Directives were superseded by a further EC Directive (No 2001/34) which required a statutory framework for listing rules but permitted national governments to appoint a competent authority to undertake the task. In the UK, the appointed authority was initially the Stock Exchange, but it is now under the guardianship of the Financial Services Authority (FSA).

The Listing Rules and admission to the Official List

For admission on to the Official List of the Stock Exchange, a company must first comply with the admission and disclosure requirements of the Stock Exchange. Thereafter, the listing rules of the FSA regulate the listing of securities, although if, as is the common practice, a company applies for listing and wishes to make a public offer of (listed) securities at the same time, then the Listing Rules will also regulate the offer of the securities. The Listing Rules comprise a comprehensive set of require-ments which are too extensive to be reproduced in this text. However, a summary of the main requirements of the rules (in relation to an issue of shares) include:

- details of the applicant's registered name, registered office, directors, auditors, solicitors and other persons involved in the preparation of the issue together with the responsibilities undertaken by those so involved in the issue of the securities;
- details of the share issue together with information related to the company's issued and paid-up share capital and the classes of shares into which it is divided. This information must include the names of any persons who hold three per cent or more of the issued share capital;
- the company's trading record, which must be for a period of at least three years and for which audited accounts must be available. In addition, a company must include within its annual report and accounts a statement by the directors to the effect that the business is a going concern; and
- a detailed record of the company's management team and their business interests. If the company has been in existence for less than five years, details of the com-pany's promoters must also be included.

Further, the company's directors must make a declaration to the effect that, to the best of their knowledge and belief, the information which they have provided for the purpose of the issue is correct.

As a result of the 1995 Regulations, the offer document which must comply with the Listing Rules is, for a first-time offer of listed securities, referred to as a prospectus and not, as was previously the case, listing particulars (the document is still referred to as listing particulars for offers other than a first-time offer). Unless an issue falls within the exemptions provided by Sch 3 to the 1995 Regulations/Sch 11 to the FSMA 2000 (the exceptions are discussed below, in the context of unlisted securities), the production of a prospectus is mandatory where the issue of securities is being offered to the general public for the first time. An advertisement to sell securities to the general public is deemed an offer to sell such securities albeit that in contract law an advertisement for sale is normally regarded as an invitation to treat. Although there is no precise definition of what constitutes an offer to the public, it is to be noted that the 1995 Regulations (reg 6) (also see Sch 11, FSMA 2000) provide that:

> 'an offer which is made to any section of the public, whether selected as members or debenture holders of a body corporate, or as clients of the person making the offer, or in any other manner, is to be regarded as made to the public.'

Section 80 of the FSMA 2000 imposes an overriding duty on the applicant to disclose all the information which investors and their professional advisers would reasonably require and reasonably expect to find for the purpose of making an informed assessment of the creditability of an issue. Where a significant change in the circumstances of any matter relevant to the determination of information contained in the prospectus or listing particulars occurs before dealings in the securities commence, the publication of a supplementary prospectus is required to explain such changes (s 81, FSMA 2000).

The FSA is responsible, in the case of an offer for listed securities, for vetting applications for the publication of a prospectus or listing particulars. The prospectus or listing particulars must, prior to being published, be submitted in draft to the FSA for their formal approval. In circumstances where the FSA views the application to be detrimental to the interests of investors, the application may be refused; albeit that such a decision may be subject to judicial review.

UNLISTED SECURITIES

History

In 1980, the London Stock Exchange created the Unlisted Securities Market (USM) in an attempt to encourage the trading in securities of public companies which were not sufficiently established, or willing to offer securities on the listed market. Initially, acceptance onto the unlisted market was more relaxed, in terms of its procedural requirements, than entry onto the listed market. However, as a consequence of less stringent standards of admission into the principal markets of other EU countries (following the passing of two EC Directives (89/298 and 87/345)), the lowering of standards for admission onto the listed market became an inevitable consequence of the London Stock Exchange's desire to remain competitive with other EU markets. As a result, the regulatory distinction between the listed and unlisted markets was significantly reduced. A new market was created in place of the USM, namely the 'Alternative Investment Market' (AIM). This new market officially opened in June 1995 and basically performs the same function as that which had originally been perceived for the USM. The vast majority of public companies which trade their securities do so on the AIM.

Admission to the Alternative Investment Market

The principal requirements for admission are as follows:

- the company must be incorporated in accordance with the national laws of the country in which it was registered and must be allowed to offer securities to the public;

- the securities to be traded on the market must be freely transferable;

- the company must appoint and retain a nominated adviser and a nominated broker;

- the company must accept continuing obligations with regard to such matters as preparation of accounts, completion of transfers of securities and dealings in securities by directors and employees.

Regulating public offers of unlisted securities

Public offers of unlisted securities are regulated by the Public Offers of Securities Regulations 1995. The 1995 Regulations demand the publication of a prospectus whenever convertible securities are to be offered to the general public for the first time (convertible securities are defined by reg 3(1)(b), and naturally include shares and debentures). To comply with the 1995 Regulations, the company issuing the securities must publish a prospectus which, during the duration of the offer, must be made available to the general public at a UK address; no charge must be levied for the prospectus (reg 4(1)).

Prior to its publication, the prospectus must be delivered to the Registrar of Companies for registration (reg 4(2)). In addition to including detailed disclosures about the issuer and the securities to be offered in the issue (1995 Regulations, Sch 1), the 1995 Regulations (reg 9(1)) provide, with the exception of pre-emptive issues falling within reg 8(4) and issues previously made within the preceding 12 months (reg 8(6)), that the issuer must include within the prospectus all information which would enable investors to make an informed assessment of the issuer's assets and liabilities, its profits and losses, the financial state and immediate prospects of the issuer and the specific rights to be attached to the securities subject to the offer (unless the publication of certain information is considered to be detrimental to the issuer (reg 11(3)).

An offer of securities 'for the first time' includes securities that are of the same class as securities which have previously been offered by the offeror to the public in the UK. However, where the number or value of the securities to be offered is less than ten per cent of the number or value of the securities already offered, and detailed and up-to-date information about that class of securities is available, namely information which would otherwise have complied with Sch 1 to the 1995 Regulations, then, in accordance with reg 8(5), the need to issue a prospectus in respect of such securities is dispensed with.

The 1995 Regulations apply if the offer is for a cash or non-cash consideration and are also applicable to a situation where the offer is made other than in writing. The scope of the 1995 Regulations extends to a situation where the shares are being offered other than by the issuing company (i.e. they will apply to a shareholder or underwriter of an issue), albeit that the necessary disclosure requirements in relation to the issuing company will, in such a situation and as one might expect, be less severe than if the company itself was purporting to make the offer of the securities (see reg 11(2)).

Exceptions to the 1995 Regulations/FSMA 2000

Offers of securities which are not within the ambit of the 1995 Regulations are described and listed in reg 7. These exceptions are in fact applicable to both listed and unlisted securities and, where relevant, deem that the exempted offer may be instigated without the production of a prospectus. The list of exceptions is extensive and includes the following types of offers:

- where the securities are offered to persons acting in the course of a business which is involved or may reasonably be expected to be involved in the acquisition, holding, managing or disposing of investments: for example, commercial banks and listed investment trusts;

- where the securities are offered to persons in the context of their trades, professions or occupations;

- if the securities are offered to no more than 50 persons. The possibility of exploiting this exception by subdividing the issue so that, for example, a first issue of securities to 50 persons could immediately be followed by a second, third, etc., issue to 50 persons is dealt with by reg 7(6). This regulation precludes such exploitation by prohibiting an offer of a class of securities which would otherwise have fallen within this exception where, during the previous 12 months, another offer of the same class of securities either had been open to the general public or had been made in accordance with this exception. It is also to be noted that offers of securities made to trustees of a trust or members of a partnership are deemed to be offers to a single entity (person);

- where the securities are offered to members of a club or association (whether or not incorporated) in circumstances where it can reasonably be ascertained that the members share a common interest in the club or association and the purpose to which the proceeds of the offer will be put;

- where the securities are offered in connection with a *bona fide* invitation to enter into an underwriting agreement in respect of them;

- if the securities are those of a private company and are offered to existing members or their families, existing employees or their families or holders of debt securities;

- where the securities are offered to a restricted circle of persons, who would, to the knowledge of the offeror, be reasonably aware of the risks involved in taking up the offer. (This exception may apply where there is an issue of securities by a private company if the issue is other than to family members, etc.);

- where the securities of a private company are offered in accordance with pre-emption requirements in the company's articles or an agreement between holders of securities in the company;

- if the offer comprises a bonus issue (i.e. shares issued on a fully paid-up basis to a company's shareholders). For the purpose of this exception, 'shareholders' include any person who held shares in the company up to 60 days prior to the date of the offer;

- where the securities are offered by an incorporated company (or employee trust) to its employees or former employees, or the spouse or children (under the age of 18) of the company's employees or former employees. In addition, the exemption will apply where employees are made offers of securities in a company which is a member of the group of companies to which the employer belongs;

- if the securities are offered to the UK government, a local authority or public authority;

- where the total consideration to be paid for the issue does not exceed ECU 40 000 (approximately £30 000 at current rates). Regulation 7(6) prohibits an offer of a class of securities which would otherwise fall within this exception where, during the previous 12 months, another offer of the same class of securities either had been open to the general public or had been made in accordance with this exception;

- if the securities are offered in connection with a takeover offer or a merger as defined by the 'Merger Directive' (78/855). In relation to takeovers involving offers for UK companies, the definition of a takeover is provided by Part XIIIA of the Companies Act 1985, namely a takeover offer means 'an offer to acquire all the shares, or all the shares of any class or classes, in a company (other than shares which at the date of the offer are already held by the offeror), being an offer on terms which are the same in relation to all the shares to which the offer relates or, where those shares include shares of different classes, in relation to all the shares of each class'. The definition of a takeover for takeover offers of companies outside the UK extends the definition in Part XIIIA of the Companies Act 1985 and applies to offers to acquire substantially all or a specified proportion of the shares (or class of shares) of the target company.

Mutual recognition of prospectuses

The 1995 Regulations give effect to the mutual recognition of prospectuses or listing particulars across the EU. Therefore, provided that a prospectus or listing particulars has been vetted in the course of satisfying a member state's regulations, the securities which form the subject matter of the prospectus or listing particulars may be offered or admitted to listing in other member states. Although there is no obligation under the 1995 Regulations to submit a prospectus relating to unlisted securities to the FSA for its approval, the 1995 Regulations allow for the submission of the prospectus to the FSA in compliance with the mutual recognition provisions. In such a case the information contained in such a prospectus will, for vetting purposes, be governed by the Listing Rules and not the 1995 Regulations.

Proposals for reform/the new Prospectus Directive

On 29 April 2004, the European Commission implemented the new Prospectus Directive 2003/71/EC. The Prospectus Directive deals with the initial disclosure requirements when securities are offered to the public or admitted to trading on a regulated market. The Directive is part of other EC initiatives on accounting standards and transparency requirements which together are aimed at producing a strategy to improve the quality of information provided to investors (see Chapter 12).

The Directive is expected to take effect from July 2005 and is concerned with securities that are to be offered to the public or admitted to trading on a regulated market in the EU. The purpose of the Directive is one which seeks to set a uniform level of minimum information requirements for the contents of a prospectus and will be applicable to an issue of securities, other than where the issue falls below a prescribed sum. As with the majority of EC legislation, the Directive is, to say the least, comprehensive in terms of detail and the number of regulatory provisions. The Directive provides that a prospectus to which it relates shall contain obligatory information, the nature of which will depend on the type of issuer and securities involved; the said information is similar but more comprehensive than under the 1995 Regulations (set out in Annexes I to XVII of the Directive).

The Prospectus Directive is aimed at unifying the regulatory regimes to promote cross-border offers. Nevertheless, when implemented it will have an instant effect on the UK system. As the Directive covers all issues of securities which are made to the public, the fragmented UK regulations will be unified into a single set of disclosure rules (other than where the issue is less than the prescribed sum). In compliance with the EC Directive, Part VI of the FSMA 2000 will require amendment to incorporate offers of non-listed securities and admissions of securities to trading on a regulated market. Although the 1995 Regulations will cease to have effect, much of the substance of the Regulations is mirrored by the Prospectus Directive.

COMPENSATION FOR A FALSE OR MISLEADING STATEMENT CONTAINED WITHIN A PROSPECTUS OR LISTING PARTICULARS

Any person who subscribes to a public offer of listed or unlisted securities may have the right to pursue a claim for compensation if he/she suffers loss or damage when acquiring the securities to which the offer document relates. Compensation will be payable where the damage or loss occurs as a result of any untrue or misleading statement, or any omission in the offer document which should, in accordance with the relevant statutory provisions (see s 90, FSMA 2000 and reg 14, 1995 Regulations) have been included within the prospectus or listing particulars. Liability is not dependent upon whether the subscriber placed reliance on the misstatement or had knowledge of any omission. Liability also extends to supplementary listing particulars and prospectuses.

Compensation is payable to any person who suffered damage or loss as a result of acquiring securities which were **advertised** in the prospectus. Accordingly, the class of persons to whom compensation is payable is wider than under the previous regulatory provision (s 67, CA 1985) where the class of persons capable of claiming compensation was restricted to the subscribers of the share issue, namely persons who purchased the securities directly from the issuing company. Under the existing law, a claim for compensation will *prima facie* exist whenever the purchaser of the securities can establish that the advertised securities had been subject to a misrepresentation that was contained in the prospectus. Therefore, there is no longer a specific requirement for the purchaser of the securities to establish that he/she was a subscriber to the issue (i.e. in a contractual relationship with the issuing company). This extends the scope of the remedy beyond other legislative measures which are designed to provide a remedy for false and misleading statements: see, for example, the Misrepresentation Act 1967.

Any compensation payable under the 1995 Regulations (and Part VI, FSMA 2000) will be calculated on tort principles, namely by attempting to put the plaintiff back in the position he was in prior to the untrue or false statement, the tort measure of damages having been historically applied to the term 'compensation': see e.g. *Clark* v *Urquhart* [1930] AC 28. For example, if shares are purchased at £1000 but as a consequence of a false or misleading statement within the prospectus, were, at the time of their sale, in reality only worth £500, the damages recoverable would amount to £500. The value of the shares purchased must be determined, as of the date of their acquisition (i.e. in the above example, the value would be £500: see *Davidson* v *Tulloch* (1860) 3 Macq 783).

Accordingly, although a false and misleading statement in a prospectus or listing particulars may result in a gradual but continuous fall in the value of shares, in the above example, the shares may after six months of their purchase fall to a value of, say, £100, the court will not, in its assessment of compensation, ordinarily take account of the slide in share value from the date of their acquisition. In relation to the above example, damages would still only be calculated at £500 (and not £900). Prior to the House of Lords' decision in *Smith New Court Securities* v *Scrimgeour*, the above rule operated in relation to the valuation of shares, notwithstanding that the misrepresentation was of a fraudulent nature and despite the fact that, in assessing damages for the tort of deceit, it is possible for the court, subject to the remoteness of the loss, to award damages for consequential losses flowing from an untrue statement: see e.g. *Doyle* v *Olby* (*Ironmongers*) *Ltd* [1969] 2 All ER 119. Indeed, by analogy, contractual misrepresentations of both a fraudulent and negligent character which have invoked the implementation of the Misrepresentation Act 1967, have led the courts to award damages for loss which occurred after the date of the plaintiff's reliance on the offending misrepresentation: see e.g. *Naughton* v *O'Callaghan* [1990] 3 All ER 191 and *Royscot Trust Ltd* v *Rogerson* [1991] 3 All ER 294.

However, following the decision of the House of Lords in *Smith New Court Securities Ltd* v *Scrimgeour Vickers* (*Asset Management*) *Ltd* [1996] 4 All ER 769, it would now appear permissible for the court, when valuing shares purchased as a consequence of a fraudulent misrepresentation, to consider events which actually occurred prior to the acquisition of the shares, where such events would have been relevant to determining the valuation of the shares prior to their acquisition. The facts of the case were as follows. The plaintiff (SNCS) purchased shares in Ferranti International Signal plc. The plaintiff purchased the shares through the defendant (SV), who sold the shares as an agent for Citibank NA (C). Shortly after the sale, the price of Ferranti shares fell dramatically. SNCS subsequently sold the shares, but lost over £11 million on the sale. SNCS claimed damages from SV and C on the premise that it had been induced to purchase the shares as a consequence of a fraudulent misrepresentation, namely SNCS was induced to purchase the shares because it had been falsely informed by a director of SV (acting for C) that two other reputable bidders were willing to make bids for the shares.

At first instance ([1992] BCLC 1104), Chadwick J held that the fraudulent misrepresentation had the effect of creating a false market in the shares. In determining the true market value of the shares, the learned judge considered events prior to the acquisition as relevant to the calculation of the value of the shares, the significant event in question being that the price of Ferranti shares (at the time of SNCS's acquisition) had itself been inflated by a fraudulently misleading preliminary announcement as to Ferranti's end of year profits. The eventual effect of the fraudulent announcement, a reduction of the price of a Ferranti share, only became apparent after SNCS's acquisition of the Ferranti shares.

Chadwick J found that the shares, which had been purchased by SNCS at a price of 82.25p per share, had an apparent market value of 78p at the date of their acquisition. However, in taking account of the fraudulent announcement of Ferranti's end of year profits, the true market value of the shares had been only 44p per share (a figure based on the price of the shares prior to the fraudulent announcement relating to the end of year profits). As such SNCS received damages of 38.25p per share.

Although the Court of Appeal ([1994] BCLC 212) agreed that SNCS's claim for damages should be upheld as a result of the fraudulent misrepresentation relating to the additional bidders for the shares, the court strongly disapproved of the valuation method employed by Chadwick J. The Court of Appeal refused to accept that when valuing shares it was correct to take account of events unknown to both parties at the time of the transaction. Accordingly, the Court of Appeal valued the shares in accordance with the ascertainable market value of the shares at the time of the sale. As a result, the amount of damages payable to SNCS was reduced from 38.25p per share to 4.25p per share. The Court of Appeal's reasoning was based on the fact that if the valuation was to take account of the fraudulent announcement of Ferranti's end of year profits, the defendants would, in effect, have been deemed accountable for a diminution in the value of the shares, notwithstanding that they had no knowledge of the operative deception.

The House of Lords, in reversing the decision of the Court of Appeal, concluded that damages in the tort of deceit, in respect of the valuation of shares, could be calculated on the basis of an assessment of any consequential loss suffered by SNCS as a result of acquiring the Ferranti shares. Accordingly, the valuation could take account of the value of the Ferranti shares prior to the inflationary effect on that value by the fraudulent announcement of Ferranti's end of year profits. In effect, the House concluded that it was possible to assess the loss flowing directly from the transaction without any reference to the date of the actual transaction. The House so concluded, despite the fact that in cases such as *Doyle* v *Olby (Ironmongers) Ltd* the assessment of damages had been calculated on the basis of damage **directly** flowing from the fraudulent inducement. In *Smith New Court*, the House of Lords extended the calculation of damages to cover events **prior to** the fraudulent inducement. Accordingly, the level of damages awarded in favour of SNCS was restored to the level provided at first instance.

Persons deemed responsible for a prospectus or listing particulars

The entity/persons deemed responsible for the publication and contents of an offer document and any supplementary prospectus or listing particulars are listed by the FSMA 2000 (Official Listing of Securities) Regulations 2001 (SI 2001/2956) in respect of listed securities, and, in relation to unlisted securities, by reg 13 of the 1995 Regulations. The said persons are the same for both listed and unlisted securities, namely:

- the issuer of the securities to which the offer document relates or the offeror of the securities where they are issued other than by the issuer. However, where securities are issued other than by the issuer, the offeror will not be deemed responsible where the prospectus was primarily drawn up by the issuer or where the offeror is making the offer in association with the issuer;

- where the offeror of the securities is not the issuer of those securities but the offeror is an incorporated company, any person who is a director of that company at the time when the prospectus is published;

- any director of an issuer which is an incorporated company at the time when the listing particulars (or prospectus for listed securities) are submitted to the Stock Exchange or, in the case of unlisted securities, when the prospectus is published. An exception is provided where the issuer had not made or authorised the offer contained in the offer document. Further, a director of an issuer is exempted where the offer document was published without his knowledge or consent and on becoming aware of its publication he gave public notice of the fact that it was published without his knowledge or consent. It would appear from the terms of the 1995 Regulations that this latter exception would not apply where the securities were offered other than by the issuer (i.e. where a person is the director of the offeror of securities in a situation where the offeror is not the issuer);

- any person who accepts, and is so stated as accepting in the listing particulars or prospectus, responsibility for, or for any part of, the particulars or prospectus;

- any person who does not fall within any of the above definitions is nevertheless responsible for authorising the contents of, or any part of, the particulars or prospectus.

Defences

Various defences are available to a person or persons who may otherwise be liable for a false or misleading statement or omission in the offer document or any supplementary document. The defences are applicable irrespective of whether the securities to be offered are listed or unlisted securities. The defences are contained in reg 15 of the 1995 Regulations (Sch 10, FSMA 2000). The defences are as follows.

- The person or persons responsible for the offer document may escape liability where it is established that the subscriber was aware on subscribing that the offending statement was indeed untrue or misleading or had knowledge that a matter which should have been included in the offer document had in fact been omitted.

• The person or persons responsible for a false or misleading statement or omission may also escape liability where the statement or omission was of an innocent nature (i.e. the person or persons responsible for the misrepresentation or omission, having made such enquiries as were reasonable to make in the circumstances, reasonably believed at the time when the statement was delivered for registration that it was true or, in the case of an omission, that the offending omission would have been unnecessary had it been included within the offer document). The belief in the accuracy of the offer document must continue up until the time when the securities were acquired.

• There will be no liability where loss resulted from a statement (included in the offer document), which was made by an official person or taken from a public document, provided that the statement was proved to have been accurately, and fairly, produced.

• Liability may be evaded for not producing a supplementary offer document where it is established by a person responsible for the original offer document that the alteration of an inaccuracy contained therein, did not, as a result of a reasonably held belief, merit the production of the supplementary document. It should nevertheless be noted that an error as contained in the original offer document may of itself still give rise to a primary liability.

• Liability may be evaded even where the person(s) responsible for the offer document had knowledge of an innocent but nevertheless misleading statement or omission prior to the purchase of securities, provided that:

(a) the securities were acquired before it was reasonably practicable to have brought the correction to the attention of persons who were likely to acquire the securities; or

(b) a reasonable, albeit unsuccessful, attempt (for example, publishing the fact of the error in the national press) had been made to bring the correction to the attention of persons likely to acquire the securities; or

(c) the securities to which the misstatement or omission was applied were acquired after a reasonable lapse of time and, if the securities were dealt in on an approved exchange, the person or persons responsible for the offer document were unaware of the misstatement or omission until after the commencement of those dealings.

It is to be observed that the part (c) defence begs the question as to the period of time deemed necessary to substantiate a reasonable time lapse and also, if applicable, the point in time at which the person or persons responsible for the misstatement or omission, having discovered the error after the commencement of dealings in the securities, should have disclosed that fact. Where, for example, the relevant misstatement or omission was discovered by the person responsible for the offer document shortly after the commencement of dealings but, despite such a discovery, no attempt was made to publicise or correct the error at that time and, subsequently, a reasonable period of time elapsed before the error was generally made public, it would appear that the defence, if read literally, would still apply, that is, where the shares were purchased after a reasonable period of time but prior to the publication of the error. This must surely be a flaw in the legislation, as it could encourage non-disclosure of errors in the offer document.

● Further, a person responsible for an offer document containing an untrue or misleading statement may escape liability where such a person proves reasonable reliance on the accuracy of a statement made by and with the consent of an expert; the skill and knowledge of whom could not have been reasonably doubted by the person responsible for the offer document. The belief must continue up until the time the securities were acquired. However, liability may still be evaded in circumstances where:

(a) the securities were acquired before it was reasonably practicable to have brought the expert's incompetence (as it turned out) to the attention of persons who were likely to acquire the securities; or

(b) a reasonable, albeit unsuccessful, attempt (for example, by publishing the error in the national press) had been made to bring the mistake to the attention of persons likely to acquire the securities; or

(c) the securities to which the expert's statement had been applied were acquired after a reasonable lapse of time and, where the securities were dealt in on an approved exchange, the person or persons responsible for the offer document continued to believe in the accuracy of the expert's statement and the expert's consent to the statement appearing in that document until after the commencement of those dealings.

Again, it is regrettable in relation to (c) that the legislation fails to make any mention of the period of time deemed necessary to substantiate a reasonable time lapse and also, if applicable, the point in time at which the person or persons responsible for the offer document should disclose the fact that the expert's statement/omission was inaccurate.

SHARES PURCHASED FOLLOWING A NON-CONTRACTUAL REPRESENTATION

Where, following a misleading statement made by a company, a purchaser is induced to acquire securities in that company, **other than** securities which are or have been actually offered in a prospectus or listing particulars, the purchaser will be unable to claim a statutory remedy against the company or its directors. However, a purchaser of such securities may be able to obtain a remedy for the misstatement in two distinct situations. First, where it is possible to establish an action in deceit; it would be necessary for the purchaser to prove that, as a direct result of a fraudulent misstatement, he/she had been induced to purchase the shares. Alternatively, the purchaser may be able to commence an action based upon negligent misstatement, where it is established that the company owed the purchaser a duty of care.

In *Hedley Byrne Ltd* v *Heller Ltd* [1964] AC 465 the House of Lords established that a duty of care would arise in a situation where there was a 'special relationship' between the parties: a relationship establishing a sufficient degree of proximity, the ability to establish the relationship being dependent upon evidence indicative of the representee's reasonable reliance upon the misstatement. The potential scope of the proximity test was subsequently reviewed by the House of Lords in *Caparo Industries plc* v *Dickman* [1990] 2 AC 605, where Lord Oliver expressed its definition in the following manner:

> 'What can be deduced from the *Hedley Byrne* case, therefore, is that the necessary relationship between the maker of a statement or giver of advice ("the adviser") and the recipient who acts in reliance upon it ("the advisee") may typically be held to exist where (1) the advice is required for a purpose, whether particularly specified or generally described, which is made known, either actually or inferentially, to the adviser at the time when the advice is given; (2) the adviser knows, either actually or inferentially, that his advice will be communicated to the advisee, either specifically or as a member of an ascertainable class, in order that it should be used by the advisee for that purpose; (3) it is known, either actually or inferentially, that the advice so communicated is likely to be acted upon by the advisee for that purpose without independent inquiry, and (4) it is so acted upon by the advisee to his detriment. That is not, of course, to suggest that these conditions are either conclusive or exclusive.' (at p 637)

In accordance with the above statement it may be observed that the proximity test is, in respect of a representee's detrimental reliance on a misstatement, only satisfied where the representee relies upon the misstatement for a purpose which must have been ascertainable and within the representor's reasonable contemplation at the time the misstatement was made. Further, the representor must have been aware that the misstatement would be relied upon by the representee in a manner in which it was actually relied upon. The defendant must assume responsibility for the task, albeit that the assumption need not be an assumption of legal responsibility for the statement: see e.g. the comments of Lord Browne-Wilkinson in *White* v *Jones* [1995] 2 AC 207 at p 273. The effect of the above analysis generally places an onerous burden on the representee in terms of establishing a negligent misstatement. For example, in *Al Nakib Investments (Jersey) Ltd* v *Longcroft* [1990] 3 All ER 330, it was held that while the directors of a company owed a duty of care to persons who subscribed for shares in reliance on a prospectus, no such duty was owed to a person who purchased shares in the company on the open market, albeit that the purchase was made in reliance upon the contents of the said prospectus. In applying the test advanced in *Caparo Industries plc* v *Dickman* to the facts of the *Al Nakib* case, Mervyn Davies J concluded that a duty of care was not to be attached to a situation where a statement had been made for a particular purpose but was used for another purpose. Accordingly, the purpose of the prospectus was to invite offers for shares subject to the prospectus issue and not a subsequent purchase of shares on the open market (see also *Galoo Ltd and Ors* v *Bright Grahame Murray* [1994] BCC 319, *Bank of Credit and Commerce International (Overseas) Ltd (in liq) and Ors* v *Price Waterhouse and Anor* [1997] BCC 584).

A more liberal interpretation of the principles derived from *Caparo Industries plc* v *Dickman* may be implied in the judgment of Lightman J in *Possfund Custodian Trustee* v *Diamond* [1996] 2 All ER 774. Here, the claim was based on a market acquisition of shares. Lightman J opined that the plaintiff's contention that a prospectus had an implied purpose of seeking to encourage the purchase of shares in the market (in addition to its principal purpose of inviting shares in accordance with the terms of the prospectus), could, if that claim was sustainable, be of a sufficient character to establish a duty of care.

Rescission

Where a person acquires securities in a company in reliance on a fraudulent, negligent or innocent misrepresentation in relation to an offer of those securities (an omission may also be classed as a misrepresentation) proceedings may, if the offeree so desires, be taken to rescind the contract. A person may only exercise a right of rescission against the company issuing the securities where the company allotted the securities in question. In other cases the right to rescind may be exercised against the offeror of the securities. Following rescission, the purchase price of the securities plus any interest will be returned to the offeree. A person's right to rescind the contract may be lost where the offeree, after becoming aware of the misrepresentation, acted in a manner to affirm the contract, or where there was an unreasonable delay in seeking to rescind the contract, or where the issuing company went into liquidation.

It should be noted that the rule of law established in the case of *Houldsworth* v *City of Glasgow Bank* (1880) 5 App Cas 317, namely that any claim for damages against a company may only be sustained if the contract relating to the security issue is rescinded, was expressly overturned by s 111A of the Companies Act 1985 (introduced by s 131(1), CA 1989).

Suggested further reading

Pre-1995 Regulations
Welch (1985) 6 Co Law 247

Griffin (1991) 12 Co Law 209

Post-1995 Regulations
Alcock (1996) 17 Co Law 262

Leighton [1998] Comm LJ 19

The new Prospectus Directive
Pretorius and Ferreira (2005) 20 JIBLR 56

Offering shares for sale – duty of care
Grier (1998) 19 Co Law 311

12

INSIDER DEALING, MARKET ABUSE AND RELATED MATTERS

INTRODUCTION

This chapter examines the concepts of insider dealing, market rigging and market abuse in the context of the acquisition, trading and disposal of shares and securities in registered companies. The issues dealt with under these headings, although primarily matters of criminal and financial services law, are nevertheless important in the context of company law because they govern the processes by which most company securities are bought and sold. Brief consideration is also given to the rules governing the disclosure and investigation of share dealings.

THE BASIC CONCEPTS

Insider dealing can be defined for most purposes as the misuse of unpublished 'inside information' relating to a company for the purpose of gaining an unfair advantage in transactions involving company shares or other company securities. It will typically involve the sale of securities by a company officer, employee or professional adviser who knows, on the basis of such information, that the price of those securities is about to fall, or the purchase of securities by an insider who knows that they are about to rise. It is most frequently associated with Stock Exchange transactions and it is in relation to such transactions that most of the relevant legislation is directed.

Insider dealing is in certain circumstances punishable as a statutory offence, as are various forms of market rigging and fraud, but prosecutions for such offences are infrequent, and when brought are often difficult to prove. In recent years increasing reliance has been placed on alternative civil procedures and sanctions. The Financial Services and Markets Act 2000, Pt VIII, introduced the concept of 'market abuse', which includes both insider dealing and certain other forms of misconduct that are likely to mislead or distort securities markets. The Act empowers the Financial Services Authority ('FSA') to investigate suspected cases of market abuse, and provides for individuals or corporations who are adjudged guilty of such abuse to be fined or shamed, but such proceedings are deemed to be civil rather than criminal and liability need only be established on a balance of probabilities.

Before examining the law in more detail, it may be helpful to look briefly at some of the factors that may influence share prices, because it will be to such matters that inside information and market abuse will generally relate.

INFLUENCES ON SHARE PRICES

Although company shares or debentures are issued with specific nominal values, their actual market value (i.e. the price at which they are bought or sold) may vary from day to day, and will be influenced by a range of market forces. It would be wrong to assume that if a company has net assets of (say) £100 million and has issued 100 million shares, the shares must necessarily be valued at £1 each. Investors will be interested in prospects for future growth and (to a lesser extent) in dividends, but will not usually be keen to buy shares in a company which has been trading or performing poorly, even if it has ample capital assets. Conversely, expectations of strong future growth may propel the price of a company's shares to a level well above that suggested by asset values alone. The winning or losing of a major contract may therefore have an immediate influence on the company's share prices, as may the announcement of better or worse than expected trading results. Much depends here on what kind of result the markets were expecting. Thus, the announcement of a £10 million trading loss can actually precipitate a *rise* in that company's share prices, if dealers had previously marked down their prices in anticipation of much worse results, and a £10 million profit may cause a fall in prices if they had expected profits in the order of £50 million.

Prices may also be influenced by national or international events that lie beyond the company's own control: currency or interest-rate fluctuations, wars, disasters, recessions and changes of governments may all play their part in the rise or fall of a company's share price. This can most easily be seen in relation to those public companies whose shares are traded on investment exchanges such as the London Stock Exchange (LSE). Dealers on such exchanges continually adjust their prices to take account of all relevant factors. In private companies (or in unquoted public ones), there will be no publicly quoted price for shares, but market forces may still influence the price that a vendor might hope to obtain from a sale. It should, for example, be possible to get a good price for a substantial block of shares in a well-run company where business is good and future prospects encouraging, but, in times of recession especially, it may be impossible to find a buyer for a minority stake in a badly managed and loss-making private company.

Paradoxically, a decline in share values to a level well below the value of a company's assets may make it an attractive target for a potential takeover bidder, who may be willing to offer existing shareholders a better price for their shares than they could hope to obtain under normal trading conditions. It is for this reason that the announcement or mere expectation of a takeover bid almost invariably precipitates a surge in the price of the target company's shares, and 'insiders' who know of an as yet unpublicised takeover proposal may be tempted to take advantage of that knowledge, before this price surge occurs.

The unfair advantage of inside knowledge

Investing in company securities can be a risky business. They can appreciate in value much more quickly than money placed in a savings account, but their value can also fall. The more knowledge that investors have concerning the companies in which they intend to invest, the better their chances become of making profits. It is for this reason that strict rules govern the publication and contents of listing particulars or prospectuses when shares are to be issued to the public (see Chapter 11). Disclosure of information is seen as being vital to the cause of investor protection, and thus to the maintenance of investor and market confidence. This cause is not helped, however, if some buyers or sellers (the insiders) possess advance knowledge of matters which will seriously affect future prices, but which for the time being remain undisclosed and therefore unknown to other investors.

It is not always easy to identify specific 'victims' in cases of insider dealing, particularly where shares are traded on an investment exchange. Such transactions do not ordinarily take place between individual investors, and nobody is likely to be tricked into buying or selling shares which he or she would not otherwise have bought or sold to or from someone else. Investors deal with firms that are members of the exchange, and these firms also deal with each other. If, for example, investor X decides to sell his 5000 shares in Megacorp plc, he may instruct his stockbroker or bank to make the sale on his behalf. A broker must sell at the best price he can obtain on the market, but X may specify a minimum price below which shares must not be sold. Similarly, if investor Y is seeking to buy Megacorp shares, he will buy them through his own broker or bank, and not directly from X. On the LSE, the shares of listed companies are bought and sold from dealers (or 'market makers') who will at any given time offer a lower price for shares they are prepared to buy (their bid price) than for identical shares they are prepared to sell (their offer price). Dealers, who may also act as brokers, compete to quote the best prices. These prices are continuously updated in response to news and demand and are displayed on numerous computer screens under the SEAQ (Stock Exchange Automated Quotation) and SETS systems, so uncompetitive quotes will attract no custom.

If a company is one of the UK's largest companies (one of those which make up the FTSE 350 index), bid and offer orders can be matched automatically under what is known as SETS, or the electronic order book system. Slightly different systems are used for shares in smaller companies traded on the LSE's Alternative Investment Market (AIM) or on the OFEX exchange, which is independent of the LSE but provides a market for the trading of unlisted and unquoted securities (such as shares in football clubs) in the UK.

Whichever system is used, however, shares sold to an 'insider' prior to a dramatic rise in their value are likely to be shares which would in any case have been sold at a similar price to other investors, and shares sold by such an insider may in any case have been resold to a third party prior to any slump in their market value.

This spurs some lawyers and economists to argue that insider dealing should not be a crime at all. Such arguments were first advanced by the law and economics movement in the United States, where insider dealing has been legally controlled since the 1930s. In *The Economics of Legal Relationships*, for example, Manne argued that if directors or other insiders were allowed to trade on the basis of their inside knowledge, this would produce gradual adjustments in share prices as markets react to increased buying or selling (which pushes prices up or down) and as the inside information gradually becomes general knowledge. In contrast, a public announcement of price-sensitive information that has hitherto been kept as a carefully guarded secret may trigger a sudden and possibly damaging surge or drop in the market price. Insider dealing would, in other words, produce a 'more efficient market'.

The opinions expressed by writers such as Manne arguably overlook or neglect the fact that the real victims of uncontrolled insider dealing are likely to be the reputations of the markets and the confidence of potential investors, who may come to feel that investing on such markets is akin to playing poker with opponents who know the markings on the backs of the cards as well as the fronts. Insider dealing on regulated markets therefore appears to be prohibited for the sake of maintaining public confidence in those markets, rather than for the sake of protecting individual investors. Significantly, the position in relation to private transactions that do not go through regulated markets and do not use or involve professional intermediaries is largely untouched by the current legislation, and the position there is still governed only by general equitable principles (discussed below).

RIGGING OR MISLEADING THE MARKETS

Compared to insider dealing, 'market rigging' is a more obvious fraudulent activity, and one that has been outlawed for much longer. In contrast to the insider who exploits natural market movements by keeping one step ahead of them, the 'rigger' attempts to precipitate, or in some cases prevent, price movements, either by circulating false information or by creating a misleading and artificial demand for shares or other marketable securities.

This can, in some cases, involve explicit lies and deception. In the notorious case of *R* v *de Berenger and Others* (1814) 105 ER 536, false rumours were circulated concerning the supposed death of Napoleon Bonaparte, in order to boost the value of government securities (then known as 'consuls') held by the defendants. Those alleged to be responsible (including the famous naval hero, Lord Cochrane, who was later pardoned) were convicted of a conspiracy to effect a public mischief. This form of conspiracy no longer exists (s 5, Criminal Law Act 1977), but a charge of conspiracy to defraud would still be possible on such facts, as would a charge under s 397(3) of the Financial Services and Markets Act 2000 (below).

Conspiracy to defraud is a common law offence, the essence of which consists of an agreement by two or more persons dishonestly to cause or risk loss to another, or dishonestly to deprive another of some right or advantage to which he might be entitled (see *Scott* v *Metropolitan Police Commissioner* [1975] AC 819 and *Adams* v *R* [1995] BCLC 17). The offence now contained in s 397(3) of the Financial Services and Markets Act 2000 is more specific and requires no conspiracy. It provides as follows:

'Any person who does an act or engages in any course of conduct which creates a false or misleading impression as to the market in or the price or value of any investments is guilty of an offence if he does so for the purpose of creating that impression and of thereby inducing another person to acquire, dispose of, subscribe for or underwrite those investments or to refrain from doing so or to exercise, or refrain from exercising, any rights conferred by those investments.'

There have been many subsequent attempts to 'rig' the price of shares in specific companies, and such schemes may perhaps be facilitated by the ever increasing reliance on computers and electronic information systems, which may be vulnerable to abuse.

In the prosecutions that followed the takeover of the Distillers Group by Guinness plc, it was alleged that directors of Guinness had used their company's very considerable resources to support the market price of its own shares (e.g. by paying other persons to buy and/or retain those shares). This, it was alleged, stimulated artificial demand and forced up the market price for the purpose of making the Guinness takeover bid more tempting to the Distillers shareholders, who were being offered Guinness shares in exchange for their old ones. Such conduct, if proved, would also have contravened s 151, Companies Act 1985 (discussed in Chapter 10), which makes it unlawful for a company to give financial assistance to persons who are acquiring its own shares; but it should be noted that, in relation to major new issues, a limited form of manipulation for the purpose of 'price stabilisation' or 'control of information' may be permitted in accordance with s 397(5) of the Financial Services and Markets Act 2000.

OPTION DEALING BY DIRECTORS ETC.

Section 323 of the Companies Act 1985 prohibits directors or shadow directors from buying either 'put' or 'call' options relating to the shares of their own company, its subsidiary or holding company, or subsidiaries of the same holding company, if those shares are listed on any stock exchange in Britain or elsewhere. Under s 327, the s 323 prohibitions are extended to the spouses, civil partners and infant (i.e. minor) children or step-children of such directors. Breach of the prohibitions is punishable by a fine and/or up to two years' imprisonment, but it is a defence for someone charged by virtue of s 327 to prove that he had no reason to know of his spouse's or parent's status as a director of the company in question.

Put and call options entitle their holders to require other parties to buy or sell relevant shares at a specified price and within a specified time. Option dealing is therefore a form of speculation, rather than a form of investment. It is akin to a gamble on the future price of the shares concerned. The purchaser of an option to acquire, say, 100 000 Megacorp shares at £2.25 each will clearly not exercise his option if the market price falls to £2.20, but may make a handsome profit by so doing if the price rises within the specified period to, say, £2.50 per share.

Clearly, directors of companies are likely to have inside knowledge as to the probability of future price movements, and would therefore be in a position to exploit such knowledge unfairly through option dealing. This risk is so obvious that the prohibition against dealing in options is made absolute in their case. Here, the prosecution would not have to prove that a defendant actually had inside knowledge of any likely future price movement, and the offence is, to that extent, distinct from that of insider dealing. The rationale behind it is, however, largely the same, and it should be noted that suspicious instances of option dealing by persons who fall outside the scope of ss 323 and 327 may sometimes be prosecuted for insider dealing contrary to the Criminal Justice Act 1993 (see below).

The above rules control the buying and selling of options, but do not preclude companies from providing their directors or other executives with share options as part of a salary and remuneration package. If the company prospers and its share price rises, the options rights may well prove to be more valuable than the director's basic salary. In recent years, the excessive value of some directors' option rights has called into question the whole issue of directors' remuneration.

INSIDER DEALING AS A CRIMINAL OFFENCE

Historical background

Insider dealing was first made an offence by the Companies Act 1980, and the relevant provisions were largely re-enacted in the Company Securities (Insider Dealing) Act 1985. This original legislation, which was repealed and superseded by provisions contained within Part V of the Criminal Justice Act 1993, created an unnecessarily complicated series of offences, which were spread between several lengthy sections of the legislation. There were really only two or three different kinds of criminal behaviour, but different provisions would apply depending on what type of insider was involved.

The repeal and replacement of this legislation was eventually dictated by the need to comply (albeit belatedly) with a European Community Directive on Co-ordination of Insider Dealing Regulations (89/592/EEC). This required the extension of insider dealing controls to cover dealings in a wider range of securities, including government stock (gilts), local authority debt securities, 'futures' and contracts for differences (these last being effectively bets on future fluctuations in share or stock indices). The DTI took the view that, if major changes were in any event necessary, the opportunity should be taken to reform the insider dealing laws as a whole. This was achieved in Part V of the Criminal Justice Act 1993.

The basic offence

In contrast to the legislation it replaced, the Criminal Justice Act 1993 uses just one short section (s 52) to state the offence. Section 52(1) and (3) provide that an *individual* (not a company) who has information as an insider commits the offence of insider dealing if he/she deals in securities that are price-affected in relation to that information and does so on a regulated market or acts as or in reliance on a professional intermediary. Section 52(2) adds that offences of insider dealing can also be committed (a) by encouraging another person so to deal (whether or not that other person is aware of the situation) or (b) by improperly disclosing insider information. It follows that there are in fact three legally distinct offences: insider dealing by virtue of dealing in securities; insider dealing by virtue of encouraging another person to deal in securities; and insider dealing by virtue of a disclosure of information.

The remaining 12 sections and two schedules define the relevant terms, provide defences and state the penalties applicable. The resulting structure (which is similar in many ways to that adopted in ss 1–7 of the Theft Act 1968) is manifestly more logical than that which existed under the Insider Dealing Act, but it could further have been improved by placing all the applicable defences in the main body of the Act (as is normal in criminal legislation), rather than spreading them confusingly between the main body and the schedules.

Definitions for the purpose of section 52(1)

The prosecution must be able to prove in any case of alleged insider dealing under s 52(1):

(a) that relevant securities were involved;

(b) that the accused dealt in them;

(c) that he did so whilst in possession of information as an insider;

(d) that the securities were price-affected in relation to that information; and

(e) that the dealing concerned took place either on a regulated market or with the involvement of a professional intermediary.

In the absence of defence concessions, the prosecution must prove each of these elements beyond reasonable doubt. Only then might it become necessary for the defence to seek to establish one of the statutory defences set out in s 53 and Sch 1.

(a) Securities

Securities are defined in Schedule 2 to the Act. This complies with the EC Co-ordination Directive (above) by extending to government and local authority debt securities, financial futures, depository receipts, traded options and contracts for differences, as well as to shares, warrants and debt securities or debentures issued by companies. As to options, see also ss 324 and 327 of the Companies Act 1985.

(b) Dealing

Dealing is defined in s 55 of the Criminal Justice Act to mean the acquisition or disposal of securities, or the direct or indirect procuring of such acquisition or disposal by another person.

Acquisition and disposal are then defined in turn to include agreements to acquire or dispose of securities, or contracts which create such securities. This definition covers cases in which the insider arranges for his nominee or agent to do the dealing, even if the nominee or agent is a company. The principal offender must be an individual, but the person whose acts are procured need not be, nor need that person be party to the offence.

(c) Information as an insider

This is dealt with in s 57, which provides that a person has information as an insider if and only if he knows it to be inside information and knows that he has acquired or obtained it from an inside source.

These terms are then defined in turn by other provisions of the Act. To find the definition of 'inside information' one must refer back to s 56, which provides that it means information which: (a) relates to particular securities or to a particular issuer (e.g. a company) rather than to securities or issuers generally, (b) is specific or precise, (c) has not been made public, and (d) would significantly affect prices, if it were published.

To have this information from an 'inside source', the accused must be a director, employee or shareholder of a company (but not necessarily of the same company) or of another issuer of securities, or must alternatively have access to that information by virtue of his employment, office or profession (s 57(2)(a)), or knowingly obtain his information from a person in one of those categories (s 57(2)(b)). This scope of the definition is wide enough to cover 'tippees' (i.e. persons who obtain confidential price-sensitive information directly or indirectly from insiders) and also covers, for example, insiders in company X who know that X is going to bid for company Y and buy shares in Y in anticipation of the price rise that will inevitably follow the announcement of the bid. There is therefore no need, as there was under the Insider Dealing Act, for separate offence-creating provisions dealing specifically with such conduct. It does not matter whether the insider or tippee deliberately sought to obtain such information or whether it was unsolicited (see *Attorney-General's Reference (No 1 of 1988)* [1989] BCLC 193).

Breach of confidentiality, an essential ingredient in the old insider dealing offences, is not mentioned anywhere in the Criminal Justice Act. What then of the position of market analysts or other experts, who might possess price-sensitive information derived from their own researches, rather than from any tip-offs or leaks, but nevertheless obtained by virtue of their professions? Are such persons barred from dealing or from passing on their knowledge to their clients? And what of market makers or dealers who may become aware through their work of major market transactions that may influence subsequent prices?

Part of the answer would seem to lie in s 58, which provides, *inter alia*, that information may be regarded as having been made public, even if it can be acquired only by observation, or by persons exercising diligence or expertise. Section 58 also provides that information is made public if it is derived from information that has been made public. Analysts whose work is based on the study of published information should remain able to trade freely on that basis. Analysts who work on the basis of leaks from insiders may of course be in a very different position.

Market makers or dealers who become aware through their work of unpublished price-sensitive 'market information' (typically relating to major acquisitions or disposals of securities) may be left in a more uncertain position, and their subsequent actions may need to be judged against imprecise concepts of reasonableness or good faith, under special defences contained in Sch 1 to the Act (as to which, see under 'defences' below).

(d) Price affected

Securities are 'price affected' by inside information if that information would be likely, on publication, to have a significant effect on prices or values (s 56(2)–(3)). This is a question of fact, not one of law, and the facts of each case must be assessed on their own merits.

(e) Regulated markets/professional intermediaries

Regulated markets are defined by the Insider Dealing (Securities and Regulated Markets) Order 1994 and currently include not only those markets established by the LSE but also NASDAQ and markets established under investment exchanges throughout the European Community and the European Economic Area. Exchanges dealing in financial futures and derivatives (such as LIFFE and OMLX) are also covered. Professional intermediaries are defined in s 59. The involvement of a professional intermediary is relevant to liability only in the case of off-market transactions, and the definition is wide enough to include professional market makers in OTC (over-the-counter) transactions, usually involving shares in small public companies which do not have a proper market quotation or listing. Face-to-face transactions involving no such intermediaries (such as a privately negotiated sale of shares within a private family company) remain wholly outside the scope of the legislation, but it should be remembered that any false reasons given for sales or purchases (e.g. 'I'm only selling because I need the money for my sick mother . . .') could give rise to prosecutions for offences under the Theft Act 1968.

Encouraging others to deal: section 52(2)(a)

Under s 52(2)(a), an individual who has unpublished price-sensitive information as an insider will be guilty of insider dealing if he encourages another person to deal in the affected securities in a way that he himself would be forbidden to do. This is not the same as procuring acquisition or disposal under s 52(1) because, for the purpose of s 52(2), no actual dealing need occur. Encouragement is enough in itself, even if the other person flatly refuses to act. Nor need any inside information be disclosed. It would be enough for an insider to say to a friend, 'Megacorp shares look a good buy at the moment; why don't you get some?' It would be a defence, however, for the accused to prove that he honestly believed the inside information had already been published or that no illicit profit would be made (s 53(2)).

Unlawful disclosure of inside information

Under s 52(2)(b), the improper disclosure of inside information to someone who has no right to receive it (e.g. disclosure to one's spouse or golfing partner) is deemed to amount to insider dealing. It need not be coupled with any encouragement to deal, nor need any such dealing ever occur. This apparently draconian provision is, however, subject to possible defences under s 53(3), under which the accused may, for example, escape conviction by proving that he did not expect any insider dealing to result from his indiscretion.

Jurisdictional limitations

One more issue must be considered before turning to special defences under the Act, namely that of territorial extent. This is dealt with in the Criminal Justice Act 1993, s 62, the gist of which is that there must be some territorial link with the United Kingdom. *Either* the dealing itself must take place on a UK regulated market (defined as the LSE markets together with LIFFE, OMLX virt-x, COREDEALMTS and OFEX) *or* (in cases of encouraging dealing or disclosing information) some other crucial element of the offence must take place within the UK. Thus, it would suffice if D in London discloses inside information to E in New York, who then deals on a regulated market in Frankfurt or Paris.

Defences

Defences to prosecutions for insider dealing are set out in s 53 and in Sch 1 to the Act. Schedule 1 does not interpret or qualify s 53 (as one might expect such a schedule to do). Instead, it adds further defences that, it seems, could not be accommodated in the main body of the Act. Nevertheless, both provisions represent an improvement on the old law, under which it was far from clear where the burden of proof actually lay. (See e.g. *R v Cross* (1990) 91 Cr App R 115.) It is clear that the burden of proving the new defences lies on the accused. This burden may (as with all such defence burdens) be satisfied on the balance of probabilities: the court must be satisfied that the defence is probably true, but it need not be entirely convinced by that defence.

It must be remembered that the ability to prove a s 53 or Sch 1 defence will not be relevant unless the basic definitional elements of the offence itself can be proved by the prosecution. Where, for example, D is alleged to have been guilty of insider dealing as a tippee, it is for the prosecution to prove, not only that D held inside information when he dealt, but also that he knew it to be inside information. If this cannot be proved, then he cannot be regarded as an insider under s 57 and cannot be guilty under s 52, whatever the position under s 53.

In essence, the defences deal with situations in which the accused was not seeking to profit or avoid loss by means of his inside information, was not seeking to help anyone else to profit by it, or was otherwise doing his job in good faith. If, for example, a new company director buys shares in his company merely in order to satisfy a minimum shareholding requirement stipulated by the company's articles of association, he will not be guilty of insider dealing, even if he holds inside information at the time. His innocence will be all the more obvious if the inside information points to a likely *fall* in the price of shares he buys. Acts done in accordance with price stabilisation rules (e.g. in relation to Euro-security issues) are also expressly exempted from liability under the new legislation.

Prosecutions and penalties

The maximum penalty for insider dealing is imprisonment for up to seven years, and/or a fine at the discretion of the court. Prosecutions require the consent of the Director of Public Prosecutions or the Secretary of State for Trade and Industry, but may also be brought by the FSA if the relevant consent can be obtained. Disqualification from involvement in company management may be added to these penalties under the Company Directors Disqualification Act 1986 (*R v Goodman* [1993] 2 All ER 789). The conviction of an individual who is authorised to conduct investment business may also lead to the revocation of that authorisation, and the consequent loss of his livelihood.

MARKET ABUSE UNDER THE FINANCIAL SERVICES AND MARKETS ACT 2000

Prosecutions for the offences of insider dealing or market rigging have proved infrequent and often unsuccessful. There are typically no more than one or two successful prosecutions a year, and in some years there may be none at all; yet it is clear that insider dealing is far more widespread than these figures might suggest.

Accordingly, s 118 of the FSMA 2000 introduced an alternative 'civil' procedure for addressing insider dealing and other (more widely defined) forms of market abuse. Its purpose was to create a quicker, more flexible and more effective mechanism to punish unacceptable forms of share dealing or other market misconduct, even where such conduct does not strictly speaking amount to insider dealing. Although technically a civil procedure, which does not involve the criminal courts or criminal convictions, actions brought by the FSA in order to enforce the relevant laws are both coercive and punitive. Fines may be imposed and the role of the FSA is similar in many respects to that of a prosecuting authority. Because of this 'quasi-criminal' character, it seems clear that any infringement of the defendant's right to a fair trial in such cases would give rise to remedies under Art 6 of the European Convention on Human Rights.

EC Directive on Insider Dealing and Market Manipulation

Section 118 was redrafted in 2005 to take account of a European Union Directive on Insider Dealing and Market Manipulation (Directive 2003/6/EC). The new version of s 118 (as substituted by the Financial Services and Markets Act 2000 (Market Abuse) Regulations 2005 (SI 2005/381)) redefines market abuse as behaviour by one person acting alone or two or more persons acting jointly or in concert, which relates to 'qualifying investments' (or in some cases 'related investments') that have been admitted to trading on a prescribed market or in respect of which a request for admission to trading on such a market has been made, and which:

- involves insider dealing in a qualifying investment or related investment or an attempt so to deal;

- involves the disclosure of inside information to another person otherwise than in the proper course of employment, profession or duty;

- involves the use of information not generally available to those using the market but which would be likely to be regarded by a regular user of the market as relevant when deciding the terms on which transactions should be effected, where such use is likely to be regarded by a regular user of the market as a failure on the part of the person concerned to observe the standard of behaviour reasonably expected of a person in his position;

- consists of effecting transactions or orders to trade (otherwise than for legitimate reasons and in conformity with accepted market practices) which give, or are likely to give, a false or misleading impression as to the supply of, or demand for, or as to the price of, one or more qualifying investments, or secure the price of one or more such investments at an abnormal or artificial level;

- consists of effecting transactions or orders to trade which employ fictitious devices or any other form of deception or contrivance;

- consists of the dissemination of information by any means which gives, or is likely to give, a false or misleading impression as to a qualifying investment by a person who knew or could reasonably be expected to have known that the information was false or misleading; or

- is likely to give a regular user of the market a false or misleading impression as to the supply of, demand for, or price or value of, qualifying investments, or would be, or would be likely to be, regarded by a regular user of the market as behaviour that would be likely to distort the market in such an investment; and such behaviour is likely to be regarded by a regular user of the market as a failure on the part of the person concerned to observe the standard of behaviour reasonably expected of a person in his position.

Section 118A requires a territorial connection between the alleged misconduct and the United Kingdom or its markets before any prohibitions or sanctions under the Act may bite. It also exempts things done in conformity with the Commission Regulation (EC) No 2273 of 2003 as regards exemptions for buy-back programmes and stabilisation of financial instruments.

Sections 118B and 118C define who are insiders and what constitutes inside information for the purposes of the Act. The definitions for this purpose are broader than those provided by s 57 of the Criminal Justice Act in respect of the criminal offence of insider dealing.

By s 119 the FSA is required to publish a code containing guidance on whether or not behaviour amounts to market abuse. In determining what are and what are not accepted market practices, the FSA must have regard to the procedures laid down in Articles 2 and 3 of Commission Directive 2004/72/EC.

Enforcement

The FSA may take enforcement action if it considers that market abuse has been committed. In serious cases it may seek to prosecute individuals for insider dealing, as explained above, but in other cases it is more likely to proceed under the FSMA 2000. It must first warn the alleged offender of what it proposes to do. This may either involve a financial penalty (effectively a fine) of such amount as it considers appropriate (s 123(1), FSMA 2000) or it may propose instead to 'name and shame' the transgressor by publishing a statement to the effect that he has engaged in market abuse (s 123(3)). The warning gives the alleged offender an opportunity to satisfy the FSA that he reasonably believed his behaviour did not amount to an abuse, or that he took all reasonable precautions to avoid any such abuse. If, however, the FSA is unconvinced by his defence, and decides to impose a penalty or to name and shame him, it will serve a 'decision notice' to that effect: he then has 28 days within which he may demand a full hearing before the Financial Services and Markets Tribunal (s 127), which will rule on the merits of the case and if necessary direct the FSA to take appropriate action. The standard of proof required here is the civil standard: market abuse must be proved, but only on a balance of probabilities.

OTHER FORMS OF LIABILITY FOR INSIDER DEALING OR MARKET ABUSE

In *Percival* v *Wright* [1902] 2 Ch 421, the directors of a coal mining company were offered some shares in the company, which they purchased from the plaintiffs at an agreed price of £12.10s (£12.50) each. The shares were not listed on any Stock Exchange, and so the price was determined by an independent valuation, but neither the valuer nor the plaintiffs were aware that the directors were negotiating a possible sale of the colliery itself, at a price far higher than that indicated by the £12.10s per share valuation. When the plaintiffs eventually became aware of the negotiations, they sought rescission of the share transfer, but it was held that the directors had been under no duty to disclose any information concerning the negotiations, and the action failed.

Percival v *Wright* is sometimes taken as authority for the proposition that directors owe no fiduciary duties to shareholders, and sometimes as authority for the proposition that insider dealing involves no risk of civil liability, but it would be dangerous to rely on the validity of either proposition. Directors and other company officers are in a fiduciary position as against the company itself, and in certain circumstances (although perhaps not in all) they may come to owe duties to members of the company as well (see Chapter 17). It is also possible for a client of a person who is authorised to conduct investment business under the FSMA 2000 to bring an action for damages against that authorised person, if it can be proved that the latter's breach of the insider dealing legislation has caused the client loss.

Liability to the company

It is unusual for the company itself to suffer anything more than embarrassment as a result of insider dealing on the part of its directors or officers, and there does not seem to be any reported case under English law in which a company has even attempted to sue one of its officers for insider dealing; but it is nevertheless possible that an insider dealer's company could sue him, on the basis of the equitable rules governing the fiduciary relationship between them. As explained in Chapter 17, it is a well-established rule of equity that a fiduciary, such as a company director, may only profit from his position to the extent that is expressly authorised by the person to whom his fiduciary duty is owed (in this case, the company). Any unauthorised profit derived from his position must be deemed to belong, in equity, to that person, and it was held by the House of Lords in *Boardman* v *Phipps* [1967] 2 AC 46 that this rule extends to profits derived from the use of valuable information acquired in a fiduciary capacity. It does not matter whether the company (or other person to whom the duty was owed) was ever in a position to exploit the information, nor does it matter that its exploitation was incapable of causing it any harm. It is, in effect, the same doctrine as that applied in *Regal Hastings Ltd* v *Gulliver* [1967] AC 134 (see Chapter 17), and it might be thought that its application in insider dealing cases would be rather less controversial or unjust than was its application in *Regal Hastings* itself.

The lack of reported cases is not, however, surprising. Where insider dealing by directors or other corporate officers is revealed, the company may well be keen to secure the resignation of those responsible and, in the case of listed companies, the regulatory bodies may insist upon it. A criminal prosecution may result in a disqualification order lasting several years, but, if the company's main loss is to its reputation or image, it will probably prefer to ensure that the case is forgotten as soon as possible. A prolonged civil action in the courts is not the way to achieve this.

There is nevertheless at least one American case in which a company forced directors to disgorge their ill-gotten insider gains: *Diamond* v *Oreamuno* (1969) 248 NE 2d 910, a decision of the New York Court of Appeals. The directors of a company sold their shares on the market at US $28 per share, shortly before publication of disastrous trading figures precipitated a collapse of the price to $11, and were held liable to account to the company for the difference. The lesson here is perhaps that civil action by the company becomes more likely when the shares concerned are off-loaded just before a collapse. Such off-loading may leave the company with a number of bitter and angry shareholders, whilst at the same time weakening the position within the company of the insider dealers themselves.

Liability for breach of duty to shareholders

An individual with inside information does not necessarily owe any civil duty to shareholders or potential future shareholders whose investments might be affected, but some insiders might find themselves in a position where such duties arise. Thus, in *Allen* v *Hyatt* (1914) 30 TLR 444, the directors of a company offered to assist the other shareholders by procuring the sale of their shares to an outside buyer. They obtained and exercised options to purchase the shares, but then made a substantial profit for themselves by reselling them at a much higher price. Distinguishing *Percival* v *Wright* [1902] 2 Ch 421, the Privy Council held that the directors had held themselves out as agents for the shareholders, and were accountable to the shareholders on the basis of that agency relationship.

Allen v *Hyatt* might be seen as a case turning on its own rather unusual facts, but a somewhat wider principle appears to be behind the decision of the New Zealand Court of Appeal in *Coleman* v *Myers* [1977] 2 NZLR 225 and that of Browne-Wilkinson V-C in *Re Chez Nico (Restaurants) Ltd* [1991] BCC 736. In *Coleman* v *Myers* it was held that directors of a private family company owed fiduciary duties to its shareholders, as a result of the shareholders' high degree of dependence upon their information and advice, and of the role of the directors in procuring the transactions in question. Approving of this decision and doubting *Percival* v *Wright*, Browne-Wilkinson V-C in *Chez Nico (Restaurants)* agreed that,

> '. . . fiduciary duties, carrying with them a duty of disclosure, can arise, which place directors in a fiduciary capacity vis-à-vis the shareholders.' (at p 750)

Rescission or avoidance of contracts

Section 63(2) of the Criminal Justice Act 1993 provides that 'no contract shall be void or *unenforceable* by reason only of s 52'. This contrasts with the wording of the repealed Insider Dealing Act, which provided only that contracts would not be rendered void or *voidable*. In *Chase Manhattan Equities Ltd* v *Goodman* [1991] BCLC 897, Knox J held that the earlier provision was intended to do nothing more than prevent the unscrambling of completed Stock Exchange transactions, and that uncompleted contracts tainted with insider dealing would not be enforceable by the guilty party, by virtue of the principle, *ex turpi causa non oritur actio* (a legal action cannot be based on a wrongful cause). It seems that the re-wording of the replacement provision can only have been intended to overcome and reverse the effect of that precedent. In other words, an insider might be able to enforce an executory contract for which he could be jailed! On the other hand, such a contract may still be unenforceable if some other kind of illegality or fraud can be proved to taint it.

DISCLOSURE AND INVESTIGATION OF SHAREHOLDINGS AND DEALINGS

The control of insider dealing and related evils depends to a significant effect on the keeping of accurate records relating to potentially significant share transactions. These include dealings transacted by company directors and certain dealings transacted by other major investors, including those whose own dealings may be modest, but who are acting in concert with others for the purpose of obtaining or consolidating control over the company.

Disclosure by directors

Section 324 of the Companies Act 1985, together with Sch 13 to that Act, lays down rules requiring directors or shadow directors to notify their companies in writing of any relevant shares or debentures held on taking office and of subsequent transactions affecting those holdings. Relevant shares include those in related companies, such as holding or subsidiary companies. Section 328 extends the disclosure requirement to cover the holdings of spouses, civil partners and minor children of directors, and it is clear from Sch 13 that the disclosure requirement extends even to the price paid or received for the shares. This is obviously not the kind of disclosure that a director would wish to make if he were engaging in insider dealing, but non-compliance with these requirements is itself a criminal offence, punishable by a fine and/or up to two years' imprisonment, and may sometimes be easier to prove than insider dealing. In some cases, disclosure will also be required, in a different form, on the basis that the director is also a substantial shareholder or is acting in concert with others.

The information supplied to the company must then be kept on a register, as provided by ss 325 and 326 of the Companies Act 1985 and, where the shares or debentures are listed on a UK investment exchange, the exchange must itself be notified in accordance with s 329. The obligation to notify the exchange is the company's, and, when notified, the exchange may publish it in whatever manner it deems appropriate.

Disclosure by substantial shareholders and concert parties

Part VI of the Companies Act 1985 sets out detailed provisions relating to the disclosure of substantial interests in the relevant (i.e. voting) share capital of public companies. Disclosure of such interests (including the combined interests of persons acting in concert with a view to acquiring or tightening control of the company) helps to ensure fair dealing in relation to takeover bids, and it is in relation to takeover bids that cases of insider dealing most frequently occur.

The basic rule is that acquisition by one person of an interest in three per cent or more of a public company's voting shares (or three per cent of any one class of voting shares) gives rise to a duty of disclosure (ss 198–199). The duty of disclosure extends to subsequent transactions, whether the percentage of shares held is increased or decreased, and ceases only after the company has been notified that it has fallen below the three per cent limit. Three per cent of the voting shares of a major listed company may in fact be an enormous block of shares, worth millions of pounds, and the effect of disclosure clearly becomes more significant the larger the disclosed holdings become. Non-compliance with disclosure requirements is, once again, punishable by a fine and/or imprisonment (s 210). For investment and unit trusts or collective investment schemes holding shares in listed companies, the applicable limit was raised to ten per cent by the Disclosure of Interests in Shares (Amendment) Regulations 1993.

A person will be taken to be interested in shares held by his spouse, civil partner or minor children, or by another company effectively controlled by him (s 203), and, where a number of persons agree to act in concert with a view to acquiring shares in a given company (the target company), they may be deemed to form a 'concert party', in which case each would be deemed to have an interest in the holdings of the others (ss 204–205). In other words, disclosure would become mandatory once the total shareholding of the different party members reaches three per cent. Effective compliance with the disclosure requirement would also require full identification of the concert party and its members, thus making it impossible for control of a company to be achieved by stealth, before other shareholders or the market can react to it.

There are detailed and complex (some would say impenetrable) rules governing the quantification of relevant interests and the exact definition of a concert party, but the real problem in such cases is that an undisclosed concert party may be very hard to detect or to prove once its existence is suspected, particularly where its membership is based abroad and where the shares are registered in the names of nominees for the true, beneficial, owners. To this end, a public company may launch an investigation into the ownership of its shares (s 212), under which it may (*inter alia*) write to certain shareholders, requiring them to state whether any other person has an interest in the shares, and whether that person is a member of a notifiable concert party. Failing a satisfactory answer to such enquiries, the company may seek the appointment of inspectors by the DTI, for the specific purpose of enquiring into the ownership of the company (ss 442–443, CA 1985: discussed in Chapter 25).

If in either case the investigation is blocked or frustrated by the non-compliance of shareholders to whom enquiries are directed, a powerful sanction is available in the form of a 'freezing order', which may be imposed by the court under s 216 or by the Secretary of State under s 445 (discussed in Chapter 9). This prevents the exercise of transfer, voting, pre-emption or dividend rights in respect of the shares concerned (ss 454–457). A similar order may be imposed by the Secretary of State following a s 210 conviction for non-disclosure of a requisite interest in shares.

Where the rights of innocent third parties are unfairly affected by the imposition of such sanctions, their application may be modified or rescinded in so far as those parties are concerned (s 456(1A), inserted following the unsatisfactory position previously revealed in *Re Lonrho plc* [1988] BCLC 53).

Investigations into suspected insider dealing or market abuse

The most significant investigation provisions in this context are those contained in s 168 of the Financial Services and Markets Act 2000. These empower the FSA or the Secretary of State to appoint inspectors where it appears that there are circumstances suggesting possible breaches of the insider dealing legislation. Refusal to cooperate with the appointed inspectors may be referred by them to the High Court, and, if the court is satisfied that there was no reasonable excuse for the refusal, it may fine or imprison the persons concerned, as if they had been guilty of contempt of court.

The scope of these provisions was illustrated in *Re an Enquiry under the Insider Dealing Act* [1988] AC 660, where a financial journalist was held to be in contempt of court through his refusal to disclose the sources of an article he had published, concerning leaks of insider information from the Monopolies and Mergers Commission, Office of Fair Trading and DTI. He had argued that he was justified in protecting his sources under s 10 of the Contempt of Court Act 1981, but the House of Lords held that this provision could not justify or excuse his non-cooperation once it had been proved that disclosure was necessary for the prevention of future crime.

The use in criminal trials of self-incriminating admissions made to inspectors during DTI investigations was held to be inconsistent with the UK's obligations under Art 6 of the European Convention on Human Rights (see *Saunders* v *United Kingdom* [1998] 1 BCLC 362). This was because (in contrast to police interviews) persons interviewed by DTI inspectors may be legally obliged to answer incriminating questions. The ruling in *Saunders* led to amendments made under the Youth Justice and Criminal Evidence Act 1999, s 59 and Sch 3, as a result of which statements made to DTI inspectors can no longer be used in evidence in criminal trials. This limits the value of a DTI inspection as a mechanism to gather evidence in anticipation of a criminal prosecution, but, even where statements are not admissible, incriminating evidence subsequently unearthed as a result of such statements may be admissible. Furthermore, disqualification proceedings brought in the civil courts under the CDDA 1986 are not criminal trials, and statements made to DTI inspectors may still be used as evidence in such proceedings: see *R* v *Secretary of State for Trade, ex parte McCormick* [1998] BCC 379 (discussed in Chapter 19).

Suggested further reading

McKee (2001) 3 JIFM 137

Filby (2003) 24 Co Law 334

13

LOAN CAPITAL

INTRODUCTION

The availability of credit facilities is an integral part of the commercial world in which limited companies operate. Banks and other institutions that operate credit facilities often demand security to counter the potential risk of default; security normally takes the form of a charge on the assets of the debtor company. The law in relation to the enforcement of security interests has undergone radical reforms following the enactment of the Enterprise Act 2002 and amendments to the Insolvency Act 1986 by subsequent secondary legislation. Much of the discussion in relation to the Enterprise Act 2002 will be reserved for Chapters 14 and 15. The former deals with priority issues and the registration of charges and the latter is concerned with insolvency law regimes. The basic premise of this chapter is to explain the various types of credit facilities available to companies and the nature and effect of security interests.

THE DEBENTURE

A document, which purports to acknowledge a credit arrangement between a company and a creditor, is commonly referred to as a debenture. There is no precise legal definition of a debenture: see e.g. the judgment of Bowen LJ in *English & Scottish Mercantile Investment Trust* v *Brunton* [1892] 2 QB 700. The Companies Act 1985 makes no attempt to define a debenture, although s 744 provides that a debenture includes debenture stock, bonds and any other securities of a company, whether constituting a charge on the assets of a company or not. A debenture holder is entitled to obtain payment of the sums due to him, whether they be principal or interest; the prescribed rate of interest, which is stipulated in the debenture, must be paid to the debenture holder irrespective of whether or not the debtor company is in profit.

Many of the statutory rules which regulate the issue of shares (discussed in Chapter 9) apply equally to an issue of debentures (see Part IV, CA 1985). For example, it is an offence for a private company to offer debentures to the public (s 81, CA 1985). However, unlike an issue of shares and always providing that debentures do not confer an immediate right of conversion into shares (see e.g. *Campbell's case* (1876) 4 Ch D 470), a company may offer debentures at a discounted price (see e.g. *Moseley* v *Koffyfontein Mines Ltd* [1904] 2 Ch 108).

Where debentures are offered on the basis that at some future date they may be converted into shares, the directors of the issuing company must be authorised by the general meeting, or by its articles, to make such an issue (s 80, CA 1985). Convertible debentures must first be offered to existing shareholders or debenture holders before being offered to the general public (ss 89 and 94, CA 1985).

Debentures are normally redeemable within a specified time period. However, although equity generally prevents the clogging of the right to redeem, debentures may be perpetual or only redeemable on the occurrence of a very remote event (s 193, CA 1985): see e.g. *Knightsbridge Estates Trust Ltd* v *Byrne* [1940] AC 613. Unless there is a provision within a company's articles to the contrary, a company may reissue debentures which have been redeemed (s 194, CA 1985).

The ability of a company to issue debentures will end on the appointment of a receiver or on the winding up of the company. A company may continue to issue debentures up until the appointment of a receiver, even in a situation where the application for a receiver's appointment has been made: see e.g. *Re Hubbard & Co Ltd* (1898) 79 LT 665.

Debenture stock

As with a company share, a debenture is transferable; it may be sold on by its original holder. Nevertheless, a debenture may only be transferred in its original form (i.e. a debenture for £100 cannot be sold off in units of £10). However, an issue of debentures can be made in the form of debenture stock; the company may create a loan fund out of which a holder of the stock obtains a certificate for, say, £1000-worth of the loan fund (debenture stock). The holder of the loan stock is then able to transfer units of whatever minimum denomination is attached to the particular debenture stock issue. Where debenture stock is issued, holders of the stock will, in terms of priority of repayment of the funds invested in the stock, take equally (i.e. *pari passu*). Where a company issues loan stock, it is usual for it to enter into a trust deed with a trustee company. The purpose of this trust relationship is to confer on the trustee the power to enforce the conditions laid down in the debenture in favour of the holders of the stock, namely the beneficiaries of the trust agreement.

SECURITY INTERESTS

When a company wishes to raise finance, especially long-term finance, it will almost inevitably be obliged to give security for the amount it wishes to borrow. An action by a secured creditor to realise a security interest will normally be impossible until the debtor company fails to meet its obligations under the terms of the debenture contract. However, where a company borrows money by way of an overdraft facility, the overdraft may be expressed to be repayable on demand.

The mortgage/legal charge

The essential characteristic of any mortgage, be it of a legal or equitable nature, is that it is a conveyance of an interest in property with a provision for redemption. A legal mortgage may be created over personal or real property. In the case of a legal mortgage taken over land, the mortgage may only be created in one of two ways. First, it may be created by a transfer of the property for a term of years absolute (i.e. a lease, which is subject to a provision providing that the lease will terminate when the mortgagor (debtor) repays the debt owed to the mortgagee (creditor)). Secondly, and more commonly, a mortgage may be created by a charge by deed expressed to be by way of legal mortgage; this is often referred to as a legal charge. With the second method, the mortgagee (chargee) obtains no estate in the land secured by the mortgage, but, by s 87(1) of the Law of Property Act 1925, should the mortgagor fail to make the repayment of sums due under the mortgage, the chargee may take possession of the mortgaged property.

A mortgage may also be of an equitable character: for example, where a mortgage of land is created in writing other than by deed, or if the mortgage is not evidenced by any form of document but the party seeking to enforce the mortgage can establish some form of part performance such as the deposit of title deeds. A mortgage will also be of an equitable nature where the interest which forms the subject matter of the mortgage is itself of an equitable as opposed to a legal nature: for example, a beneficial interest under a trust. Under s 53(1) of the Law of Property Act 1925, a transfer of an equitable interest in property must be in writing and signed by the transferor or his duly authorised agent. The remedies for enforcing a legal or equitable mortgage are: foreclosure, sale, possession or the appointment of a receiver.

The fixed/specific charge

A fixed charge (alternatively referred to as a specific charge) is generally regarded as a type of mortgage and is equitable in its character. However, unlike a mortgage, a fixed charge does not involve a conveyance of any interest in the assets that form the subject matter of the security, but merely gives the chargee certain rights over the charged property.

In order to create a fixed charge over a corporate asset, the asset in question must be identifiable, although it need not be in existence at the time the charge was created: see e.g. *Re Yorkshire Woolcombers Association Ltd* [1903] 2 Ch 284 (i.e. a fixed charge may attach to future property). The holder of a fixed charge obtains certain rights in relation to the secured assets, rights that may be pursued in the event of default by the chargor (company creating the charge). As with any charge, the precise rights of the chargee are to be found within the document (debenture) creating the charge.

Subject to the requirements of registration (discussed in Chapter 14), a fixed charge confers an immediate security over the charged property. A company, having created a fixed charge over its property, cannot sell or deal with the charged asset without first obtaining the permission of the fixed charge holder. In *Re Yorkshire Woolcombers* [1903] 2 Ch 284, Vaughan Williams LJ stressed that it was quite inconsistent with the nature of a specific charge for the chargor to be at liberty to deal with the relevant property as he pleased. His lordship stated:

> 'I do not think that for a "specific security" you need have a security of a subject matter which is then in existence. I mean by "then" at the time of the execution of the security; but what you do require to make a specific security is that the security whenever it has once come into existence, and been identified or appropriated as a security, shall never thereafter at the will of the mortgagor cease to be a security. If at the will of the mortgagor he can dispose of it and prevent its being any longer a security, although something else may be substituted more or less for it, that is not a specific security.' (at p 294)

Property which is subject to a fixed charge and which is sold on to a third party without the chargee's consent will remain subject to the charge unless the third party is a *bona fide* purchaser without notice of the existence of the charge. However, providing the charge is registered, the third party will be deemed to have notice of its existence.

The floating charge

Although it may be advisable for a person when loaning funds to a company to secure the advancement of funds by means of a fixed charge or mortgage, a company may have already created a fixed charge or mortgage over the particular asset with which the subsequent creditor wishes to secure his loan. In such circumstances, priority issues may deem that it is not in the subsequent creditor's interests to secure his loan by a second fixed charge or mortgage (priority issues are discussed in Chapter 14). Indeed, the merits of taking a second mortgage/fixed charge will depend upon the value of the asset in relation to the amount of credit that the first fixed charge or mortgage purports to secure. Where circumstances are such as to render the creation of a subsequent fixed charge or mortgage ineffectual, a creditor may secure his loan by means of a floating charge (note there are other advantages in taking a floating charge, discussed below).

The floating charge is a device which can only be given as security for a debt incurred by a limited company, a device created by the Court of Chancery. The origins of the floating charge may be traced back to the *Panama* case (1870) 5 Ch App 318. The nature of a floating charge is such that the charge does not attach itself to a specific corporate asset until an event, 'crystallisation', occurs. The floating charge is created over a class of assets which by their very nature are deemed to lack a degree of permanence, thus preventing them being readily identified (i.e. the assets are of a constantly changing nature), the impractical implication of trying to create a fixed charge over such assets being that the holder of the fixed charge would need to be continually renewing the terms of his charge so as to keep pace with the changing nature of the assets. In addition, if such assets were the subject of a fixed charge, the company would be put under the most difficult condition of having to notify and seek the permission of the holder of the fixed charge whenever it wished to dispose of an asset forming part of the chargee's security.

Property to which a floating charge is likely to be attached will include stock, plant, tools and other transient assets of a company. While the companies legislation provides no exhaustive definition of the term 'property', this term should, in accordance with the decision of the House of Lords in *Sharp* v *Woolwich Building Society* [1998] BCC 115, be construed as comprising property in which, at the least, a beneficial interest was held. It is common for a floating charge to be expressed to encompass the whole of the company's undertaking (i.e. the charge will, following its crystallisation, be intended to take priority over all corporate assets other than those which are subject to a fixed charge or mortgage). Where a company's assets are of a variable nature, a charge on the company's undertaking is normally expressed to be by way of floating charge. However, a company with assets comprised of only one major fixed asset (e.g. an office block) may create a fixed charge on this property; this, in effect, will constitute a fixed charge on the company's undertaking.

Therefore, the floating charge is created over assets of a shifting nature; the sale of such assets is one of the means by which the company will earn income from which it can meet its obligations under the terms of the debenture under which the floating charge was created. In *Illingworth* v *Houldsworth* (*Re Yorkshire Woolcombers Association Ltd*) [1903] 2 Ch 284, Romer LJ tentatively identified the floating charge as possessing the following characteristics:

- a charge on all of a class of assets of the company present and future;
- a class of assets which in the ordinary course of a company's business would be changing from time to time;
- a charge which would allow the company to carry on its business in the ordinary way (i.e. the company would have the ability to trade in the assets which were subject to the floating charge).

Characteristics of the floating charge

It is normal practice in a contract of floating charge to include within its terms express clauses which stipulate (a) that the company will not deal with its assets otherwise than in the normal course of its business, and (b) that the company will not grant a further charge over the charged asset which would rank, in terms of priority, ahead of the floating charge (the negative pledge clause). This latter clause may be seen as somewhat contradictory to the first clause in that it restricts a company from dealing with its assets in the ordinary course of business; namely, it precludes the company from creating further charges ranking above the floating charge. Nevertheless, the validity of the negative pledge clause has remained unchallenged and is now regarded as a standard and unexceptional term of most floating charge contracts. Indeed, a threatened breach of either clause would entitle a chargee to obtain an injunction to prevent the breach or, where the actual security interest was threatened by a potential breach, it may entitle the chargee to apply to the court for the appointment of a receiver: see e.g. *Re London Pressed Hinge Ltd* [1905] 1 Ch 576.

Crystallisation of the floating charge

A company may continue to deal with assets which are the subject of a floating charge up until the time the charge crystallises: see e.g. *Re Borax* [1901] Ch 326. A floating charge will crystallise when a creditor takes action to realise the security following the happening of a specified event (i.e. the event will be specified within the debenture document – for example, non-payment of interest). Prior to the bringing into force of the relevant provisions of the Enterprise Act 2002 (in force from 15 September 2003) the crystallisation of a floating charge normally occurred: (a) from the date of the appointment of an administrative receiver; (b) if the charge was deemed to crystallise automatically (see below); or (c) where crystallisation was triggered by an event implied by law (see below). A floating charge created after 15 September 2003, under the regime established by the Enterprise Act 2002, would now appear to be subject to crystallisation following the appointment of an administrator or by operation of law.

Crystallisation by operation of law

Crystallisation may be triggered by an event implied by law in circumstances where the company is subject to the appointment of a liquidator, the appointment of a receiver (by another secured creditor) and the cessation of the company's business: see *Re Woodroffes (Musical Instruments) Ltd* [1985] BCLC 227 and *Re The Real Meat Co Ltd* [1996] BCC 254. For floating charges created after 15 September 2003, the appointment of an administrator will also be a specified event. Following crystallisation, the class of assets subject to the floating charge will become identifiable; the floating charge will crystallise into an equitable fixed charge: see e.g. *Re Griffin Hotel* [1941] Ch 129.

Automatic crystallisation

A clause in a debenture contract that provides for a floating charge to crystallise into an equitable fixed charge on the happening of a specified event without the need for the creditor to make claim to the assets subject to the charge (by, for example, appointing an administrative receiver) is termed an automatic crystallisation clause. The legal effectiveness of such a clause was once doubted but the judicial acceptance of the automatic crystallisation clause is now well established on the premise that the court should seek to give effect to the contractual intention of the parties subject to the charge.

The principal criticism levied against the concept of automatic crystallisation is based upon public policy issues. (See, in particular, the Report of the Review Committee on Insolvency Law and Practice (Cmnd 8558 (1982)), paras 1570–1582.) The criticism bites on the fact that no registration procedure is in place for the crystallisation of automatic crystallisation clauses: see the comments of Berger J in *R v Consolidated Churchill Cooper Corporation Ltd* [1978] 5 WWR 652 (the problem of automatic crystallisation in relation to priority issues is discussed further in Chapter 14).

The judicial acceptance of automatic crystallisation clauses was a gradual one. In *Re Brightlife Ltd* [1986] BCLC 418, Hoffmann J opined that automatic crystallisation clauses would be effective in circumstances where very clear language had been used to create a term of the debenture giving effect to the process of automatic crystallisation. Hoffmann J interpreted the decision of the House of Lords in *Government Stock & Other Securities Investment Co Ltd v Manila Rlwy Co Ltd* [1897] AC 81 as indicative of the view that the potential validity of an automatic crystallisation clause should be sought by the construction of the term purporting to create it. He supported the decision of the New Zealand court in *Re Manurewa Transport Ltd* [1971] NZLR 909, which gave effect to the contracting party's freedom to include a term within a debenture, which permitted the automatic crystallisation of the floating charge. Hoffmann J stated:

'It seems to me fallacious to argue that once the parties have agreed on some terms which are thought sufficient to identify the transaction as a floating charge, they are then precluded from agreeing to any other terms which are not present in the standard case.' (at p 427)

The acceptance of the validity of an automatic crystallisation clause was again confirmed by Hoffmann J in *Re Permanent Housing Holdings Ltd* [1988] BCLC

563. For a more recent case example confirming the judicial acceptance of automatic crystallisation clauses, see *Griffiths* v *Yorkshire Bank plc* [1994] 1 WLR 1427 (discussed further in Chapter 14).

However, following the Enterprise Act 2002, the effectiveness of an automatic crystallisation clause may be doubted in relation to charges created post-15 September 2003 in that para 15(2) of Sch B1 to the Insolvency Act 1986 now provides that a qualifying floating charge takes prior to another floating charge if it is either prior in time or if it is to be treated as having priority in accordance with an inter-creditor agreement. In other words, given a literal construction of the term 'prior in time' it would appear that a floating charge which is subject to an automatic crystallisation clause may no longer, in terms of priority, trump a floating charge which was created prior to the floating charge to which the automatic crystallisation clause was attached.

The advantages and disadvantages of the floating charge

The principal advantage of the floating charge is that it allows a company to offer a secured form of loan without seriously restricting the company's ability to carry on its business. Further, the company's ability to offer this type of security interest attracts creditors who might otherwise have been reluctant to offer finance. Although a creditor, having taken a floating charge, will not have his loan secured to the same degree as if secured by a fixed charge or mortgage, the floating charge security interest is better than none at all and indeed, after the Enterprise Act 2002, the floating charge security is, in terms of priority interests, far stronger than was previously the case (discussed further in Chapter 14). However, a theoretical if not practical disadvantage of the floating charge is that the security interest is dependent upon a class of assets which, in terms of their volume and therefore value, may depreciate, even to a level which falls below the amount of the loan secured by the charge.

As yet, the negative pledge clause, commonly inserted into a floating charge, offers little practical advantage to a creditor who inserts such a clause into the debenture document (i.e. for priority purposes, a subsequent chargee is not deemed to have constructive notice of the clause). Nevertheless, if s 95 of the Companies Act 1989 **had been** implemented (as s 399, CA 1985), the prescribed particulars to be delivered to the Registrar (of which a subsequent chargee is deemed to have constructive notice) may have included a negative pledge clause. However, it is to be observed that, while such a change would be welcomed in respect of the chargee who takes a first floating charge over a class of assets, registration of a negative pledge clause would restrict the ability of a company to create subsequent charges over a particular class of assets already subject to a charge containing a negative pledge clause; thus restricting a company's ability to raise finance.

Another important advantage of a floating charge, where the charge was created pre-15 September 2003, is that the charge holder will be able to appoint an administrative receiver (defined by s 29(2) of the Insolvency Act 1986) to realise the security interest. An administrative receiver, although subject to priority rules, acts as an agent to protect the interests of the charge holder; the position carries extensive powers (see Sch 1 to the Insolvency Act 1986). However, with the coming into force of the Enterprise Act 2002, a floating charge holder, having taken a floating charge security after 15 September 2003, will, save in very exceptional and well-defined circumstances, be unable to appoint an administrative receiver but must now appoint an administrator to realise the security. The said exceptional circumstances relate to larger corporate lending agreements, such as capital market investments of a minimum of £50 million.

The objective of the new administration system is one geared to corporate rescue and, in accordance with a new Sch B1(c), para 3(2) to the Insolvency Act 1986, the administrator must perform his functions for the interests of the company's creditors as a whole. While an express objective of the new administration regime is the realisation of property for the purpose of making a distribution to one or more secured creditors, the administrator's first duty, if practicable, is to achieve a rescue of the company and also to achieve an equitable outcome for all of the company's creditors.

Appointment of an administrator

Following the implementation of the Enterprise Act 2002, a holder of one or more qualifying floating charge(s) may appoint an administrator. Paragraph 14 of Sch B1 to the Insolvency Act 1986 (introduced by the Enterprise Act 2002) provides that a qualifying floating charge holder may appoint an administrator of a company. A qualifying charge is one created by an instrument which states that para 14 is to apply or, where it seeks to empower the holder to appoint an administrator and on its own or taken with other securities, extends to the whole or substantially the whole of the company's property.

Where there is more than one qualifying floating charge holder, para 15(1) provides that an administrator may not be appointed:

- without giving at least two business days' written notice to the holder of any prior floating charge; or unless the holder of any prior floating charge has consented in writing to the appointment. Paragraph 15(2) provides that a floating charge is defined as being prior to another if it is either prior in time or if it is to be treated as having priority in accordance with an inter-creditor agreement.

Therefore, providing a charge holder has given notice to the holder(s) of any prior floating charge(s), the charge holder may appoint an administrator by simply filing a notice of appointment at court, without requiring a court application or hearing, or without demonstrating that the company is or is likely to become unable to pay its debts. Where a floating charge was created before 15 September 2003, it will, in relation to the appointment of a receiver, be unnecessary to seek the court's approval. In addition, the appointment of an administrative receiver will prevent the subsequent appointment of an administrator (i.e. without the receiver consenting to such an appointment).

Avoidance of floating charges

In accordance with s 245 of the Insolvency Act 1986, a floating charge may be invalidated where it was created in the 12 months prior to the onset of the chargor's insolvency, unless the charge was created in consideration for money paid at the same time as or after its creation. The charge may be invalidated where at the time of its creation the company was unable to pay its debts or, as a result of the transaction creating the charge, the chargor company became unable to pay its debts. In the case of a charge created in favour of a person who is connected with the company, the charge will be deemed invalid where it was created two years prior to the company's insolvency, unless it was created in consideration for money paid at the same time as or after its creation.

Distinguishing the floating and fixed charge

First, it is important to note that it would be most incorrect to seek to distinguish a floating charge from that of a fixed charge solely in terms of the fact that the asset over which the floating charge operates may be used in the company's ordinary course of business. An asset subject to a fixed charge will also be used in the pursuit of a company's business activities. In reality, the distinguishing factor between a floating and fixed charge is the capacity of the company that created the charge to dispose or deal with the charged asset. A floating charge will allow the chargor to dispose or deal with the assets made subject to the charge without any form of substantive restriction, that is until the charge crystallises: see e.g. *Re G E Tunbridge Ltd* [1994] BCC 563. In *Evans v Rival Granite Quarries Ltd* [1910] 2 KB 979, Buckley LJ explained that:

> 'A floating security is not a specific mortgage of the assets, plus a license to the mortgagor to dispose of them in the course of his business, but it is a floating mortgage applying to every item composed in the security, but not specifically affecting any item until some event occurs or some act on the part of the mortgagee is done which causes it to crystallise into a fixed security.' (at p 999)

Accordingly, a fixed charge will exist where the assets over which the charge is taken cannot readily be disposed of or dealt with by the chargor without the chargee's permission. However, it may be feasible (albeit difficult in theory) for a fixed charge to exist in circumstances where there is a well-defined, but nevertheless limited, right on the part of the chargor to dispose or deal with assets subject to the charge, although in such a case the consent of the chargee will still be required before the chargor is permitted to dispose of or deal with the assets in question: see e.g. *Re Cimex Tissues Ltd* [1995] 1 BCLC 409.

In relation to a floating charge, such a charge may still be construed as floating in character despite the fact that it contains some form of restriction (albeit that the restriction must be very limited) on the chargor's ability freely to dispose of the assets charged in the ordinary course of the company's business. For example, a floating charge may well contain a negative pledge clause, the intended effect of which is to restrict the chargor from creating future charges over the charged assets that would rank ahead of or *pari passu* with the floating charge. It should be noted that in *Re Cosslett (Contractors) Ltd* [1997] BCC 724, the Court of Appeal held that, in considering the nature of a floating charge, it was essential to determine whether the chargor retained control over the charged assets and not necessarily whether he had an **absolute freedom** to employ the charged assets in the ordinary course of its business. Millett LJ observed:

'The essence of a floating charge is that it is a charge, not on any particular asset, but on a fluctuating body of assets which remain under the management and control of the chargor, and which the chargor has the right to withdraw from the security despite the existence of the charge. The essence of a fixed charge is that the charge is on a particular asset or class of assets that the chargor cannot deal with free from the charge without the consent of the chargee. The question is not whether the chargor has complete freedom to carry on his business as he chooses, but whether the chargee is in control of the charged assets.' (at p 734)

A fixed or floating charge? The problem cases – book debts

The general priority position of floating charges (discussed further in Chapter 14) deems it more advantageous for a creditor to take security in the form of a fixed charge as opposed to a floating charge. As such, the floating charge may be regarded as a 'second class' type of security interest, albeit that following the enactment of provisions contained in the Enterprise Act 2002 (brought into force as of 15 September 2003), a floating charge created after the said commencement date will now have priority over a substantial class of preferential creditors; a priority previously denied prior to the 2002 Act. (Also note the impact of *Buchler* v *Talbot* [2004] 2 WLR 582, discussed in Chapter 14.)

Although the priority position of a fixed charge is superior to that of a floating charge, creditors in purporting to secure a loan by way of a fixed charge have often fallen short of achieving their purpose, even where the debenture specifies, in terms of language, that the security interest is a fixed charge. Irrespective of how the charge is identified, the courts will construe a debenture contract to detect the true nature of the charge. Where a charge is described as fixed but in reality its characteristics are more akin to those of a floating charge, the debenture will be construed as but a floating charge; indeed, if there is any doubt as to whether the charge is fixed or floating, the charge will be construed as a floating charge. Therefore, a debenture which attempts to create a fixed charge and which may expressly refer to the charge as being fixed, may in reality be construed as only a floating charge: see e.g. *Royal Trust Bank* v *National Westminster Bank plc* [1996] 2 BCLC 682.

Book debts

In relation to a charge taken over a company's book debts, the charge represents a security interest in both the uncollected debts owed to the company and the realised proceeds of such debts. Although a charge over book debts cannot attach itself to the proceeds part of the secured assets until such a time as the debts are realised, a security interest in acquired property operates as a present interest where it is intended to take immediate effect, subject only to its acquisition by the debtor. Therefore, as from the date of its creation, a charge over book debts is of a continuous nature and will apply to both the unrealised debt and the realised proceeds of the debt. Once book debts have been realised, the asset over which the charge was originally taken will be substituted by the proceeds of the book debt.

The decision of Hoffmann J in *Re Brightlife* [1987] Ch 200 provides a classic example of a charge taken over a company's book debts being construed as a floating charge, notwithstanding that the terms of the charge purported to create a fixed charge. The case involved a security interest expressed to be by way of a first specific charge over the present and future book debts of a company named Brightlife Ltd. In accordance with the terms of the charge, Brightlife Ltd was prohibited from selling, factoring or discounting its book debts and from dealing with the same otherwise than in the ordinary course of getting in and realising the debts. Accordingly, as the chargor was fundamentally prohibited from dealing with the unrealised debts, the effect of the charge over the uncollected book debts appeared to be that of a fixed charge.

However, in so far as the terms of the charge failed to restrict Brightlife Ltd from disposing of the proceeds of its book debts in the ordinary course of its business, then clearly the nature of the charge over the proceeds part of the debts was the natural subject of a floating charge. Indeed, irrespective of restrictions placed upon the chargor's ability to sell, factor or discount the unrealised debts and, given the ability of the chargor freely to dispose of the realised assets, the overall charge was held to be floating in nature. Hoffmann J further sought to explain his finding, namely that the overall security interest should be construed as a floating charge on the basis that the nature of a floating charge allowed some form of restriction to be placed on the company's ability to deal with the charged assets; albeit that the usual form of restriction was a negative pledge clause: see also *Re Armagh Shoes Ltd* [1982] NI 59 and *Norgard* v *DFCT* (1987) ACLR 527.

A somewhat contradictory decision to the one arrived at in *Re Brightlife* is to be found in the earlier decision of Slade J in *Siebe Gorman & Co Ltd* v *Barclays Bank* [1979] 2 Lloyds Rep 142. This case concerned the interpretation of a debenture contract, which purported to create a specific charge over the present and future book debts of a company named R H McDonald Ltd, the charge having been created in favour of Barclays Bank. The debenture contract provided that during the continuance of the security interest the company was obliged to pay the proceeds received from all present and future book debts into its account held at Barclays Bank and that, subject to the prior consent of the bank in writing, the company would not charge or assign the 'same' in favour of any other person.

The charge was construed as a specific charge, notwithstanding that the proceeds of the book debts were to be paid into the company's current account, an account normally associated with current day-to-day business expenditure. However, notwithstanding that once paid into the account the proceeds of the book debts could be used in the ordinary course of the company's business, Slade J considered that the bank's general lien and rights over the funds in the current account (in operation until the charge had been extinguished) enabled it to control and restrict the account, even if in credit, thus disabling any contention that the company had a freedom to draw on the account at its absolute will.

In *Siebe Gorman*, the correctness of construing the security interest as one of a fixed charge was, to say the least, controversial. In theory, a degree of control over the assets subject to the charge was in the hands of the chargee. However, doubt must be attached to the practical consequences of the decision in *Siebe Gorman*; doubt in the sense that the parties to the charge must have contemplated that, whilst in credit to the bank, the company would be at liberty to draw on its current account (which it did without having to obtain the permission of the chargee) to satisfy its everyday commercial commitments. Indeed following the decision of the Privy Council in *Agnew* v *Commissioner of Inland Revenue (Re Brumark)* [2001] 2 AC 710, the case of *Siebe Gorman* was a most dubious authority, and following the decision of the House of Lords in *National Westminster* v *Spectrum Plus Ltd* [2005] UKHL 41, the decision in *Siebe Gorman* has been overruled. (However, note the conflicting decision of the Court of Appeal in *Spectrum Plus Ltd*, (discussed below) which sought to affirm the correctness of *Siebe Gorman*.)

Notwithstanding the practical doubts associated with the decision in *Siebe Gorman*, it had, as an authority, been followed (although sometimes regarded with suspicion) for over twenty-five years. Indeed, in subsequent cases, it may be argued that the courts have exhibited an even more liberal approach to the acceptance of a charge as a specific charge notwithstanding that it exhibited the characteristics of a floating charge, see e.g. the Court of Appeal's decision in *Re Atlantic Computer Systems plc* [1990] BCC 859 and the decision of Vinelott J in *Re Atlantic Medical* [1992] BCC 653.

A more satisfactory way to create a charge that has the effect of establishing a specific charge over book debts may be found within the debenture considered by the Supreme Court of Ireland in *Re Keenan Bros Ltd* [1986] 2 BCC 98, 970 (so approved by the House of Lords in the *Spectrum* case). In *Re Keenan*, the terms of a debenture sought to create a specific charge over the book debts of Keenan Bros Ltd in favour of Allied Irish Banks Ltd (AIB). The terms of the charge specified that the company could not, without the prior consent of AIB, purport to waive, assign or otherwise deal with the book debts in favour of any other person. The charge also obliged the company to pay all moneys received, in respect of realised book debts, into a designated account held with AIB; an account that had been opened for the sole purpose of collecting the proceeds of book debts. Once realised, the proceeds of the book debts were to be paid into a special account and as such were isolated and identifiable as separate funds; if necessary the specific funds could have been monitored to ensure they were not withdrawn to satisfy the company's ordinary commercial requirements (see also *Re CCG International Enterprises* [1993] BCLC 1428).

In the cases hitherto examined, it was a common feature of the judicial construction of a charge over book debts, that the charge should be construed as indivisible (i.e. the charge was either fixed or floating in its application to both the unrealised and realised book debts). However, the decision of the Court of Appeal in *Re New Bullas Trading Ltd* [1994] 1 BCLC 485 altered the perception of a charge over book debts as always having to be construed as indivisible. The case concerned an application by administrative receivers in relation to the order of priority by which payments should be made to a company's secured creditors. The sums available for distribution comprised the realised proceeds of the company's book debts, the debts having been uncollected prior to the appointment of the administrative receivers.

A secured creditor of the company claimed priority in respect of moneys which had been loaned to the company, a loan partially secured by a charge over the company's book debts. The terms of the charge prohibited the company from selling, factoring or discounting the book debts and provided that all outstanding book debts were to be the subject of a specific charge, the proceeds of which were to be paid into a nominated account. The charge further provided that, on the realisation of the debts, the proceeds were to be dealt with in accordance with the chargee's instructions.

However, in the absence of any such instructions, sums paid into the account were to be released from the specific charge to become subject to a floating charge.

At first instance, Knox J construed the charge over the book debts in accordance with the accepted judicial interpretation of such charges: namely the charge was indivisible and, in so far as the charge allowed the company a capacity to deal with the proceeds of the debts in the ordinary course of its business, it was floating in its nature. In reversing the decision of Knox J, the Court of Appeal held that the security interest had intended to operate as a specific charge in relation to the unrealised book debts and a floating charge in respect of the proceeds of the debts. The court's acceptance of the divisible nature of the charge in its application to the uncollected debts (fixed charge) and the proceeds of the debts (floating charge) necessitated the recognition of a procedure by which the assets secured by the specific charge could be transferred to the floating charge and to this end the court gave weight to the parties' own intentions as to how the transfer of assets would be achieved.

It should be stressed that the decision in *Re New Bullas* was arrived at on the basis that the express terms of the charge sought to create a specific charge over uncollected debts and a floating charge over the proceeds of the debts. The wording of the charge in *Re New Bullas* accorded with the natural division of a charge over book debts, thereby creating two distinct characteristics of a single charge in relation to its application to the two distinct characteristics of book debts (i.e. the unrealised debts and the collected debts). Accordingly, a single charge which purported to split itself to create a fixed charge over uncollected debts and a floating charge over the proceeds of the debts had to specifically spell out such an intention within the terms of the debenture, otherwise it would fail to create the divisible charge: see e.g. *Re Westmaze Ltd* [1999] BCC 441.

Although the decision in *Re New Bullas* portrays a degree of commercial logic in identifying the distinct and split characteristics of book debt assets and also by championing the principle of freedom of contract, the decision was subsequently declared to have been wrongly decided by the Privy Council, in *Agnew v Commissioner of Inland Revenue (Re Brumark)* [2001] 2 AC 710 (a New Zealand case). The Privy Council's criticism of *Re New Bullas* was directed at the methodology applied by the Court of Appeal in the construction of the charge as divisible (i.e. fixed over uncollected debts and floating over the proceeds of the realised debts).

In *Agnew* the charge was drafted in almost identical terms to the charge in *Re New Bullas*. Indeed, the only difference between the two charges (which the Privy Council considered to be immaterial) was that in *Re New Bullas* the proceeds of the book debts were not released from the fixed charge until they were actually paid into the company's bank account, whereas in *Agnew* the book debts were released from the fixed charge as soon as they were received by the company. Therefore, in *Agnew* the parties' intention was that, other than if the chargee intervened to the contrary, the chargor should be able to collect the proceeds of the book debts, whereupon the proceeds would become subject to a floating charge. As such, the proceeds of the book debts would be used in the ordinary course of the company's business unless there was a contrary direction from the chargee to direct that the proceeds or a part of the proceeds be paid into a nominated account and therefore remain subject to the fixed charge.

In *Re New Bullas* the Court of Appeal had accepted the validity of the divisible charge on the premise that a fixed charge over uncollected book debts and a floating charge over the proceeds of the debts appeared to equate to a natural and logical division of the distinct elements of a book debt. Further, the Court of Appeal accepted that the parties to the debenture had a contractual freedom to agree the precise moment in time when the fixed charge would convert into a floating charge. In *Agnew*, Lord Millett, in delivering the judgment of the Privy Council, opposed both of these propositions. Lord Millett explained that there was a two-stage process to determine whether a charge was fixed or floating. The first stage was to construe the debenture to gather the intentions of the parties (albeit that the said construction could not be considered as the key to determining the nature of the charge). The second and crucial stage was to categorise the construction in terms of the legal consequences that could be attached to the parties' intentions. Accordingly, if the interpretation afforded to the parties' intentions was to grant certain rights over the charge which, irrespective of any natural division between the unrealised book debts and the proceeds of the debts, were inconsistent with the identification of a fixed charge, then the charge would be construed as floating in nature. In *Agnew*, as in *Re New Bullas*, the intention of the parties was to create a fixed charge over the uncollected book debts, which would convert to a floating charge in respect of the realised debts. However, according to Lord Millett, the said intention could not equate with its desired effect. Lord Millett held that the freedom afforded to the chargor in respect of an ability to convert assets away from the fixed charge was in essence destructive of the nature of a fixed charge in that the objective of a fixed charge was to vest absolute control of the assets over which the charge attached into the hands of the chargee and not into the hands of the chargor. The express power on the part of the chargee to intervene, at will, to prevent the disposal of the realised debts in the ordinary course of the company's business was considered to be an inadequate method of control for the purpose of confirming the charge as specific in nature.

Although Lord Millett accepted that book debts comprised two different assets, his lordship concluded that a receivable (uncollected debts) which did not carry the right of receipt could have no value. Therefore, in effect, following Lord Millett's judgment post-*Agnew*, it will not be commercially feasible for the same creditor to attempt to create a fixed charge over the unrealised debts and a floating charge over the proceeds part of the debt. Lord Millett explained that a fixed charge security over uncollected debts would be worthless where the chargee permitted the debts to be collected by the company, to be used by the company for the purposes of its own business.

However, to doubt in part Lord Millett's assertions, surely an uncollected debt may carry a value prior to realisation. For example, a company may be placed into liquidation and its assets may in part be comprised of uncollected book debts. Such assets, having not been realised prior to liquidation, will not have been disposed of by the company in the ordinary course of its business and therefore cannot attach to a floating charge security. In effect, such assets will be realised by the liquidator but they will not be deployed for use in the ordinary course of the company's business; rather, they will, in all likelihood, be used to discharge the debts of secured creditors. As such, why should it not be possible for a company to create a divisible charge for the benefit of a single creditor; a fixed charge over its uncollected book debts and a floating charge over realised debts where the terms of the charge specifically provide that the fixed charge will only operate over book debts which remain uncollected at the point in time when an administrator, receiver or liquidator is appointed to the company?

To return to the judgment and significance of the *Agnew* case, clearly a general implied authority to allow a chargor to dispose of assets in the ordinary course of its business (as in *Agnew* and *Re New Bullas*) is now to be viewed as inconsistent with the existence of a fixed charge, notwithstanding that the charge allows the possibility of notice being given by the chargee to direct that the proceeds of the book debts be paid into a nominated account, so converting the charge over the assets back to a fixed charge (confirmed by the decision of the House of Lords in *National Westminster Bank plc* v *Spectrum Plus* – discussed below). Further, if the unrealised debts and proceeds of the book debts are both construed as subject to a fixed charge, the chargee's control of the charged assets must be absolute. (With a fixed charge over both the unrealised book debts and the proceeds of the book debts – see the correct approach taken in *Re Keenan Bros Ltd* – it should be pointed out that it is not inconsistent with the nature of a fixed charge for the chargee to appoint the company (the chargor) as its agent to collect the book debts for its account and on its behalf.)

The decision in *Agnew* marks a victory for a technical and arbitrary construction of charges. Given the judicially accepted interpretation of the characteristics of both a fixed and floating charge, the decision of the Privy Council affords no flexibility in its rigid adherence to a mechanical-like definition of charges. Indeed, the flexibility shown in, for example, *Re Cimex Tissues Ltd* [1995] 1 BCLC 409 (noted above), must now also be doubted.

The decision in *Agnew* eliminates the freedom of the parties to decide for themselves the manner by which a chargee is to exercise control over the security. While it may be possible to grant a hybrid form of a combination of a fixed and floating charge whereby the chargee is given a fixed charge over unrealised debts coupled with a floating charge over the proceeds of the debts, but only in a situation where the chargor has no right to dispose of the realised assets without an express authority from the chargor and under the control of the chargee (as opposed to a contractual discretion on the part of the chargee to intervene to prevent the disposal of the assets), the likelihood of such a charge is most improbable.

However, more importantly, it is most unlikely that the uncollected proceeds part of a charge over book debts will ever be construed as being subject to a fixed charge in circumstances where the chargee allows the chargor a general discretion to use and deal with the proceeds in the course of the company's business. Following *Agnew*, a general discretionary authority which permits a fixed charge to revert into a floating charge in accordance with the intentions of the contracting parties, but subject to a contractual proviso that the said authority may at any time be revoked, will be unacceptable to a finding that the chargee had sufficient control over the assets, thereby defeating its existence as a fixed charge at any stage.

While the decision in *Agnew* has generally been accepted as one which corrects a radical departure from the norm (i.e. *Re New Bullas*), the Privy Council's decision also eroded any confidence in the decision of Slade J in *Siebe Gorman*. The said erosion was, in a theoretical sense, perhaps welcome and indeed was confirmed by the decision of Morritt V-C in *Re Spectrum Plus Ltd* [2004] 2 WLR 783. Here, Morritt V-C fully supported the decision of the Privy Council in *Agnew*. However, with a sting in the tail, the V-C's decision was subsequently overruled by the Court of Appeal in *National Westminster Bank* v *Spectrum Plus Ltd* [2004] 3 WLR 503, albeit on appeal, the sting was reversed. The House of Lords affirmed the decision of Morritt V-C in respect of accepting that Slade J had erred in construing the nature of the charge in *Siebe Gorman*.

The facts of *National Westminster Bank* v *Spectrum Plus Ltd* gave rise to issues which were almost identical to those found in the *Siebe Gorman* case. The bank (NW) had purported to create a fixed charge over the book debts of Spectrum (S) with the charge in question providing, *inter alia*, that the company had to pay proceeds arising from its realised book debts into its bank account, which was held with NW. The charge contained *Siebe Gorman*-type restrictions in respect of the disposal of the unrealised debts but, in respect of the realised proceeds, these were to be paid into a trading account that S could (subject to NW's contractual right to decline to release funds) employ in the ordinary course of its business.

At first instance, Morritt V-C had held that the debenture created a floating charge. Following the principles applied in *Agnew*, and attacking the principles expounded in *Re New Bullas*, the V-C found that the charge could not be classed as fixed because the debenture, in allowing S (unless NW intervened) to use the proceeds of the realised book debts in the ordinary course of its business, rendered the charge inconsistent with the characteristics of a fixed charge. Morritt V-C, applying the Privy Council's decision in *Agnew*, considered that the case of *Siebe Gorman* had been impliedly overruled.

In overturning the decision of Morritt V-C, the Court of Appeal opined that the V-C's preference for adopting the reasoning of *Agnew* over a binding Court of Appeal decision, namely *Re New Bullas*, was contrary to the requirements of precedent: see *Young* v *Bristol Aeroplane Co Ltd* [1944] KB 718. Although the Court of Appeal considered that the decision in *Re New Bullas* was most dubious, a Privy Council decision (*Agnew*) could not usurp the binding precedent of *Re New Bullas*, albeit that in reality it was highly unlikely that the House of Lords would indeed wish to follow *Re New Bullas*. However, while the attack on Morritt V-C in respect of the rules of precedent was, in a technical sense, quite valid, it must be observed that *Re New Bullas* was a decision which, in terms of precedent, must be confined to a very specialist type of charge, the nature of which was not akin to the *Siebe Gorman*-type charge found in *National Westminster Bank* v *Spectrum Plus Ltd*. Unfortunately, there was little or no discussion of the case of *Siebe Gorman* in *Re New Bullas*. However, it is most evident that in *Agnew* the Privy Council could find no favour with *Siebe Gorman*.

However, in reversing the decision of Morritt V-C in respect of the standing of the *Siebe Gorman*-type charge, the Court of Appeal, in effect, sought indirectly to challenge the Privy Council's reasoning in *Agnew*. Lord Phillips MR, in delivering the judgment of the Court of Appeal, accepted that the proceeds of the book debts could, subject to the bank's intervention, be used in the ordinary course of S's business but found that any funds drawn against the account into which the book debt proceeds had been paid were funds which were devoid of any regulation by the charge.

However, such funds were regulated by the contractual relationship between banker and client. Nevertheless, the fact that the funds had to be paid into a bank account which was controlled by the chargee was sufficient to establish the necessary degree of control over the proceeds of book debts, thus establishing the fixed charge over the book debts. Lord Phillips MR stated:

> 'I consider that the fact that the debenture required the proceeds of book debts to be paid into an account at the chargee bank was of critical importance in *Siebe Gorman* and is of critical importance in the present case.' (at p 529)

Lord Phillips MR explained (relying on the banking case of *Foley* v *Hill* (1848) 2 HLC 28) that, once the proceeds of book debts had been paid into the bank, the said funds became the property of the bank, to the extent that the bank could employ such funds as it saw fit. While the bank had a contractual duty to repay, on demand, an amount equivalent to the deposit (providing the account of the depositor was in credit to the said amount) the said contractual duty did not impugn the standing of the charge as one created as a fixed charge. Lord Phillips MR stated that:

> '. . . It seems to me that it is at least arguable that a debenture which prohibits a chargor from disposing of book debts before they are collected and requires him to pay them, beneficially, to the chargee as and when they are collected properly falls within the definition of a fixed charge, regardless of the extent of his contractual right to draw out sums equivalent to the amount paid in. Strictly speaking the chargor is neither entitled to dispose of the book debts before they fall due for payment, nor dispose of the proceeds. What he does enjoy are contractual rights to payments, whether as a lender or as a borrower, from the bank. The extent to which, at any moment in time, a bank is contractually bound to permit a customer who has charged his book debts to make withdrawals which are back to back with the amounts of book debts collected will depend upon the terms of the contract between banker and customer and possibly on the financial consequences of mutual dealings. It is not satisfactory that the categorisation of a charge created by a debenture should turn upon the precise details of a bank's relationship with its customer.' (at p 531)

On appeal to the House of Lords [2005] UKHL 41, the House reversed the decision of the Court of Appeal. While accepting that the Court of Appeal had been correct in refuting the authority of Morritt V-C in seeking to sidestep the binding precedent of the decision of the Court of Appeal in *Re New Bullas*, the House could find no favour with the Court of Appeal's acceptance of a *Siebe Gorman*-type charge giving rise to the finding of a specific as opposed to a floating charge. In this respect the House of Lords favoured the analysis and approach taken by the Privy Council in *Agnew* to the extent that the House of Lords overruled *Siebe Gorman* with immediate effect. The House also favoured the approach of the Privy Council in respect of its criticism of *Re New Bullas*. While the House of Lords criticism of *New Bullas* may be considered in the context of obiter comments, it is patently evident that the case would not be followed by the House if a *New Bullas* type charge came before it. Indeed, given that the House favoured the strict and arbitrary definition of the nature of a charge as advanced in *Agnew*, which it applied in the construction of the charge in *Spectrum*, it is virtually certain that even a court of first instance could, in applying the said construction, validly discount any requirement to follow *New Bullas*.

Summary

The validity of the decision of Slade J, in *Siebe Gorman*, is no more. Accordingly where a chargee is a bank or other financial body holding an account into which the proceeds of the chargor's book debts are paid, then in such circumstances, a fixed charge over books debts will be defeated on the premise that the chargor has an ability to use such funds in the ordinary course of its business. The decision in *Re New Bullas* is now a most dubious, if not extinct authority, notwithstanding that *Re New Bullas* provides a common sense approach and natural division of unrealised (fixed charge) and realised book debts (floating charge). As a precedent, *Re Brightlife* is now in the ascendancy and any technical distinction (so found in *National Westminster Bank* v *Spectrum Plus Ltd*) between whether the chargee is, or is not a bank, has rightly disappeared. Confused and perplexed, the law was in quite a mess before the judgment of the House of Lords in *Spectrum*. Following the judgment of the House, the picture is now much clearer, albeit the conclusion is somewhat less flexible.

Suggested further reading

The nature of a charge

Pennington (1960) 23 MLR 630

Boyle (1985) Co Law 277

Ferran [1988] CLJ 213

Naser (1994) 15 Co Law 12

Worthington [1994] CLJ 81

Goode (1994) 110 LQR 592

Griffin (1995) 46 NILQ 163

Gregory and Walton [2001] LMCLQ 123

Capper (2003) 24 Co Law 325

Atherton and Mokal (2005) 26 Co Law 10

14

THE PRIORITY RIGHTS OF CREDITORS AND THE REGISTRATION OF CHARGES

INTRODUCTION

The purpose of this chapter is to discuss the priority rights of competing corporate creditors. The position in relation to priority has undergone radical reform following the introduction of the Enterprise Act 2002 (the Act received Royal Assent on 7 November 2002). Following the implementation of the Enterprise Act 2002 (implemented on 15 September 2003 by the Commencement No 4 and Transitional Provisions and Savings Order 2003) together with an exhaustive list of secondary legislation, the position in respect of priority interests is now complex in the sense that the Enterprise Act, in effect, creates a two-tier system of priority rights. In addition to priority issues, this chapter will also undertake an examination of the registration procedure for charges and will consider proposals for the future reform of the existing procedure.

PRIORITY RIGHTS

Where a receiver, administrator (under the rules post-15 September 2003) or liquidator of a company is entrusted with the responsibility of selling a corporate asset(s) for the purpose of discharging the debts of a company, the realisation of such an asset(s) may be insufficient to discharge the amount of debt owed to individual creditors. To determine whether a particular creditor is entitled to be paid in priority to other creditors it is necessary to examine the rules that govern the priority interests of competing charge holders.

Priority between fixed charges

A duly registered legal or equitable fixed charge, acquired *bona fide* for value without notice, will take in priority to a subsequently created and registered legal or equitable fixed charge. Where, in accordance with the registration procedures (discussed below), a charge is registered over corporate assets, any subsequent chargee, having taken security over the same assets, is deemed to have constructive notice of the earlier charge. However, if the prior created legal or equitable fixed charge is not duly registered in accordance with the registration procedures, the holder of the subsequently created and registered legal or equitable fixed charge will take priority over the first created charge. It should be noted that, although there is no means by which crystallised floating charges can be registered, a company cannot subsequently create a fixed charge ranking in priority to a crystallised floating charge.

Where a company creates a legal fixed charge over its property but subsequently sells the property to a third party, the property will remain charged in the hands of the new owner, even if the third party did not have notice of the existence of the fixed charge. Where a company creates an equitable fixed charge over its property, but later sells the property, the property will remain charged if, at the time the property was purchased, the new owner had notice of the chargee's interest.

Priority between fixed and floating charges

By its very nature, a floating charge will not attach itself to a particular asset until the date of its crystallisation. As such, a fixed charge which is created over a particular asset (an asset to which the floating charge may later become attached on the date of its crystallisation) will, if it is duly registered, take in priority to the floating charge (see e.g. *Re Hamilton Windsor Ironworks Co Ltd* (1879) 12 ChD 707 and see s 464(4), CA 1985).

A subsequently created fixed charge will take priority over an earlier created floating charge, even if the floating charge expressly includes a covenant on the part of the company not to create a charge ranking in priority or *pari passu* with the floating charge (i.e. provided that the subsequent fixed charge was created without **actual** notice of the covenant: see e.g. *English & Scottish Mercantile Investment Trust* v *Brunton* (1892) 12 ChD 707). While the subsequent charge holder will be deemed to have constructive notice of the earlier created floating charge, he will not be deemed to have constructive notice of the covenant (negative pledge clause): see e.g. *Wilson* v *Kellard* [1910] 2 Ch 306.

Priority in relation to competing floating charges

Where a company creates more than one floating charge over a class of assets, the floating charge that was the first in time (if it is duly registered), will take priority. This priority rule applies even where the first floating charge did not include a negative pledge clause: see e.g. *Re Benjamin Cope & Sons Ltd* [1914] Ch 800. However, in the case of two competing floating charges and from the decision of Morritt J, in *Griffiths* v *Yorkshire Bank plc* [1994] 1 WLR 1427, it would appear that if a later registered floating charge crystallises prior to the crystallisation of the first registered floating charge, then it (the later charge) will take priority in so far as it will have been converted into an equitable fixed charge before the first charge was so converted via crystallisation. This position certainly appeared to be the case prior to the implementation of the Enterprise Act 2002. However, following the implementation of the Enterprise Act 2002, floating charges created after 15 September 2003 will, in terms of any dispute concerning automatic crystallisation, have their priority determined solely in accordance with the date on which they were created to the extent that, in effect, automatic crystallisation clauses will be nullified. Following the Enterprise Act 2002, secondary legislation amends the Insolvency Act 1986 to create a new para 15(2) of Sch B1 to the Insolvency Act 1986, which provides that a qualifying floating charge is deemed to have priority over a competing floating charge if it is either prior in time or if it is to be treated as having priority in accordance with an inter-creditor agreement. *Prima facie*, automatic crystallisation is not covered by para 15(2) of Sch B1 to the Insolvency Act 1986 (also discussed in Chapter 13).

It should also be noted that where a company creates a first floating charge and that charge contains a negative pledge clause which is expressed to govern a specific and defined class of assets, then a subsequent floating charge with actual notice of the terms of that negative pledge clause may take priority over the first floating charge in respect of the class of assets that are **not** covered by the negative pledge clause contained in the first floating charge: see e.g. *Re Automatic Bottle Markers Ltd* [1926] Ch 412.

The payment of preferential creditors – the position prior to the Enterprise Act 2002

The preferential debts of a company are listed in Sch 6 to the Insolvency Act 1986. Preferential debts rank equally amongst themselves. Prior to the Enterprise Act 2002, preferential creditors were categorised as: debts due to the Inland Revenue, debts due to Customs and Excise, social security contributions, contributions to occupational pension schemes, remuneration of employees, and, finally, levies on coal and steel production.

In relation to priority issues before the implementation of the Enterprise Act 2002 (i.e. 15 September 2003), s 196 of the Companies Act 1985 (as amended by Sch 13, IA 1986) and s 40 of the Insolvency Act 1986 provided for the priority position of preferential creditors in a situation where a company was not in the course of being wound up. Section 40 of the Insolvency Act 1986 applied in the case of a company where an administrative receiver was appointed on behalf of the holders of any debentures of the company secured by a charge which, as created, was a floating charge. Here, preferential debts were to be paid out of the assets coming into the hands of the receiver in priority to any claims for principal or interest in respect of the debentures.

Therefore, in accordance with s 40, where a debenture was created by a company as a floating charge, a receiver appointed before a winding up order had been made, first had to discharge the debts of the company's preferential creditors in priority to the claims of the floating charge holder, irrespective of whether or not the floating charge had crystallised prior to the appointment of the receiver. Where possession of the assets were taken by or on behalf of the debenture holder without the appointment of a receiver, the position was also as above, namely preferential debts had to be paid in priority to the claims of a holder of a floating charge (s 196(1), CA 1985, amended by Sch 13, IA 1986).

Accordingly, the company's preferential creditors were paid out of the assets coming into the hands of the receiver in priority to any claims in respect of the holder of a debenture secured by means of floating charge. Prior to the implementation of s 40, it had been thought that a floating charge could still take in priority to the claims of preferential creditors in a situation where the floating charge had crystallised into a fixed equitable charge before the appointment of a receiver (i.e. a fixed charge takes in priority to preferential creditors: see e.g. *Re Permanent House Holdings Ltd* [1988] BCLC 563). However, following the implementation of s 40, it seemed highly unlikely that a crystallised floating charge could take such a priority. Yet, the decision of Morritt J in *Griffiths v Yorkshire Bank plc* [1994] 1 WLR 1427 appeared to paint a contradictory picture. Here, Morritt J was of the opinion that s 40 was only applicable to a crystallised charge where the holder of that charge had appointed the receiver (i.e. s 40 was not applicable where a receiver had been appointed by another charge holder).

Notwithstanding that the literal interpretation afforded to s 40 by Morritt J had some force, clearly the effect of such an interpretation was one which created a loophole in the section's application, a loophole which was unlikely to have been intended by the legislature. Indeed, in *Re H & K (Medway) Ltd* [1997] 2 All ER 321, Neuberger J came to the conclusion that s 40 should and indeed could be interpreted in a manner which allowed for its application in a situation where the holder of a crystallised floating charge was not responsible for the appointment of the receiver. The learned judge held that on its true construction, the expression 'the debentures' in s 40(2) was a reference to any debentures of the company secured by a charge which, as created, was a floating charge, and not merely a reference to debentures under which a receiver had been appointed. Indeed, this latter interpretation made much sense in so far as it prevented the potential abuse of the provision in a situation where the holders of two competing floating charges (the charges having automatically crystallised) reached an agreement whereby one of the charge holders appointed a receiver so that the other charge holder escaped the consequences of s 40 by taking in priority to the company's preferential creditors.

In a situation where a company created a composite charge (i.e. a fixed charge over specified identifiable assets and a floating charge over the remainder of the company's undertaking), a receiver had only to apply the assets subject to the floating charge to meet the priority demands of the preferential creditors and not the totality of the assets over which the composite charge was expressed. The assets over which the fixed charge was created would be free from the claims of the preferential creditors: see e.g. *Re Lewis Merthyr Consolidated Collieries Ltd* [1929] 1 Ch 498.

Section 175, IA 1986 concerned the priority position (pre-15 September 2003) of preferential debts when a company was in the process of being wound up. Where a company was in the course of being wound up, the preferential debts had also to be paid in priority to debts expressed to be secured by means of a floating charge. However, the payment of the preferential debts, out of funds realised from the sale of assets subject to a floating charge, was subject to the prior claim of the winding up expenses.

Prior to the recent decision of the House of Lords in *Buchler v Talbot* [2004] 2 WLR 582, s 175 was interpreted in a manner whereby liquidation expenses were paid in priority, out of the realised assets of the company, over the claims of both preferential creditors and the holder of a charge which had been created as a floating charge: see *Re Barleycorn Enterprises Ltd* [1970] Ch 465. However, following the *Buchler* case (overruling *Barleycorn*), the House of Lords provided that liquidation expenses could not be taken ahead of the claims for principal and interest owing to the holder of a floating charge. Accordingly, the realisation/priority position after *Buchler* in respect of the winding up of a company is as follows:

- The first call on the company's realised assets is to repay any amount (principal and interest) secured by any fixed charge.

- The liquidation expenses would then be met, but only from funds (classed as the company's free funds) which were not subject to the claims of a holder of a floating charge.

- The claims of any preferential creditors would then be met. Any funds out of which a floating charge holder was to be paid would be subject to the prior claims of the preferential creditors (position prior to 15 September 2003 but not after that date, discussed below).

- A holder of a floating charge would therefore be paid out of the assets which were subject to the charge, in priority to the payment of liquidation expenses (other than for expenses incurred in realising the floating charge security). However, the floating charge holder would only be entitled to the sum of those assets, minus the sum of assets which were required to discharge the payment of preferential creditors (position prior to 15 September 2003 but not after that date, discussed below).

- If there were any free funds left after the payment of liquidation expenses, these would be applied to the payment of unsecured creditors unless the company still owed moneys to its preferential creditors (position prior to 15 September 2003 but not after that date, discussed below).

(In cases involving a receivership (i.e. s 40 cases) the position in relation to priority will be as above, save that issues relating to liquidation expenses will not enter into the equation.)

The above position (i.e. post-*Buchler*) represents a dramatic change in the application of the law and is one which may have serious consequences for a liquidator in determining expenditure in the realisation of the company's assets: e.g. whether the liquidator should expend funds in the pursuit of actions to recover corporate assets, say, wrongful trading claims (discussed in Chapter 18). For floating charges created after 15 September 2003, the impact of *Buchler* will be to give a windfall in cases where a company is being wound up (i.e. a holder of a floating charge will take payment in priority over both Crown preferential creditors and liquidation expenses) (discussed below).

Unsecured creditors – the position prior to the Enterprise Act 2002

Prior to 15 September 2003, an unsecured creditor of a company was in a very weak position when it came to the settlement of debts. An unsecured creditor's claim for the recovery of moneys advanced to a company would, in terms of priority rights, rank at the bottom of the payment list, albeit that the unsecured creditor could (and still can) advance a claim based upon the contractual rights attached to the agreement between the parties, namely the unsecured creditor may sue for the principal and interest and obtain judgment from the court. Failure on the company's part to meet the judgment will then allow the judgment creditor to obtain a court order for the sale of the company's property. Where a judgment creditor obtains judgment against the company and the goods are seized and sold by the appointed sheriff, a creditor with a floating charge secured over the assets made subject to the judgment order will lose priority in favour of the unsecured creditor. Pending judgment, an unsecured creditor will have no claim to a debtor's property. However, where judgment is obtained in favour of the unsecured creditor, the debtor's property cannot be sold to realise the amount of the debt unless a court order has been obtained to sanction the sale.

An unsecured creditor may also petition the court to have the company wound up in accordance with s 122(1)(f) of the Insolvency Act 1986, on the ground that the company is unable to pay its debts (see s 123, IA 1986). However, in such a case the creditor will receive payment only in accordance with the general priority position (see below).

The payment of preferential creditors and unsecured creditors – the position after the Enterprise Act 2002

The rationale for changes to the priority position of creditors, introduced by the Enterprise Act 2002 (see the Transitional Provisions (Insolvency) Order 2003 (SI 2003/2332), is one that seeks to improve the position of unsecured creditors in respect of their share of the distribution of assets following a company's insolvency. (As noted below, the position of floating charge holders is also greatly enhanced.)

To effect a more equitable distribution of assets with the objective of benefiting unsecured creditors, the Enterprise Act 2002 abolishes the Crown's preferential rights by removing paras 1 and 2 (debts due to Inland Revenue), paras 3–5C (debts due to Customs and Excise) and paras 6 and 7 (social security contributions) from Schedule 6 to the Insolvency Act 1986. The preferential status of other contributions in Schedule 6 is retained.

To ensure that the funds (which other than for the passing of the 2002 Act would have been distributed to Crown preferences) are made available for unsecured creditors, the Enterprise Act 2002 provides for a prescribed portion (reserve fund) of the net property (i.e. after fixed charge holders and liquidation/administration fees have been paid) to be set aside specifically for unsecured creditors (see below). Other than where the administration of the reserve fund would be uneconomic to administer (the cost in terms of the administration of the fund is in excess of the size of the fund) unsecured creditors will take the prescribed portion of the available assets in priority to the holders of floating charges. In exceptional cases, a floating charge holder may be able to participate in the reserve fund but only in circumstances where funds are still available after the unsecured creditors have been paid. However, save for the prescribed portion, floating charge holders gain in terms of climbing the priority tree and do so at the expense of the Crown's preferential rights, which are now relegated to the position of unsecured debts (i.e. the Crown is now treated as an unsecured creditor; note, however, the possibility of the Crown securing its debts by means of a fixed charge).

The calculation of prescribed portion

The prescribed part of the company's net property available for the repayment of the company's unsecured debts will be calculated in accordance with a new s 176A of the Insolvency Act 1986 Act, namely:

- Where the company's net property is no more than £10 000 in value, then 50 per cent of that property is reserved to the prescribed part.

- Where the company's net property exceeds £10 000 in value, then:

  50 per cent of the first £10 000 in value will be set aside for the prescribed part; and

  20 per cent of any sum in excess of £10 000 will be set aside for the prescribed part.

- However, the value of the prescribed part to be made available for the satisfaction of unsecured debts of the company cannot exceed £600 000.

The revised priority position (ranking position in ascending order)

The revised priority position (ranking in ascending order) is as follows:

- fixed charge holders;
- liquidation/administration expenses (but applying the principle in *Butcher*, liquidation expenses may not be taken from the funds available from realised assets secured by means of a floating charge);
- preferential creditors (but **not** Crown debts);
- floating charge holders (minus the cost of realising the security and a sum representing the prescribed part, i.e. the reserve fund for unsecured creditors);
- unsecured creditors (this group will now include preferential creditors, i.e. comprised of Crown debts).

It should be stressed that holders of floating charges created prior to and up until 15 September 2003 receive a triple bonus in terms of priority. These floating charge holders will rank ahead of preferential creditors (Crown debts) but will not be affected by the 'prescribed portion' system. Floating charge holders will also benefit from the ruling in *Buchler*. Holders of floating charges created after 15 September 2003 will gain a double bonus in terms of priority (i.e. as above, but absent of exemption from the 'prescribed portion' scheme).

An agreement to alter priority rights

While at first sight it may be difficult to appreciate why a creditor with a charge over corporate property (the first chargee) should wish to transfer his priority interest in favour of another creditor, the other creditor having an inferior priority ranking charge over the same property as the first chargee, in practice, a contractual agreement between the first and second chargees to effect such an alteration in the priority position may afford some advantage to the first chargee. The first chargee's priority rights may be transferred without the need to seek the approval of the company having created the charge: see *Cheah Theam Swee* v *Equiticorp Finance Group Ltd* [1992] BCC 98 (Privy Council).

A further example of the workings (and possible difficulties) of a priority agreement is seen in *Re Portbase (Clothing) Ltd* [1993] BCC 96. Here the holder of a fixed charge entered into a contract with the holder of a floating charge with the effect that the fixed charge would be postponed to rank in priority immediately after the floating charge. Chadwick J held that the effect of so transferring the priority interest did not transfer the fixed charge holder's priority in respect of payment ahead of preferential creditors to the floating charge holder. Therefore, the holder of the fixed charge took payment after the floating charge holder, who took payment after the preferential creditors. However, it is to be noted that if this particular priority agreement had been determined after 15 September 2003, its intention would have succeeded – namely the floating charge would have ranked ahead of the fixed charge and the claims of preferential creditors, comprising Crown debts – albeit that a percentage of the funds received by the floating charge holder would have been reserved to the claims of the company's unsecured creditors, claims which would have included the company's preferential creditors.

THE REGISTRATION OF CHARGES

A company, in charging property, will not normally give up physical possession of the secured property. Accordingly, future creditors may be duped into believing that the property remains unencumbered, with the result that a creditor may advance funds to a company on the strength of its apparent but nevertheless illusionary wealth. Therefore, in order to prevent the potential for such an abuse, government-administered registers have been devised for the purpose of recording non-possessory charges. In addition to the government registration requirements, a non-possessory charge on almost any kind of property belonging to a registered company will require further registration with the Registrar of Companies, under the Companies Act 1985.

The registration system

At present, Part XII of the Companies Act 1985 governs the registration system for company charges. Part IV of the Companies Act 1989 contained a significant number of recommendations in relation to the reform of the present registration system, many of the proposals for reform apparently having been based upon suggestions put forward by the Diamond Report, 'A Review of Security Interests in Property' (1989). However, the proposed introduction of Part IV of the Companies Act 1989 was subject to much criticism and doubt and will now not take place. The Part IV proposals were regarded as a cost-cutting exercise without any real and lasting benefits. Many commentators considered that they failed to do justice to the full recommendations of the Diamond Report. The criticism and doubts focused, in part, on the fact that the new legislation would not have had a retrospective effect, therefore its implementation would have created two registration systems operating side by side, an obvious recipe for confusion. Although Part IV of the Companies Act 1989 will never be implemented in its entirety, certain changes to the present registration system, based on aspects of Part IV of the 1989 Act and other proposed reforms (discussed below), are likely to be enacted at some future date.

Registration

Section 395 of the Companies Act 1985, places a company under an obligation to register a charge with the Registrar within 21 days after the date of its creation. The term 'charge' is not defined, although it is unlikely whether any type of non-monetary obligation would create a registrable charge: see e.g. *Stoneleigh Finance* v *Phillips* [1965] 2 QB 537. It is to be noted that s 93 of the Companies Act 1989 sought to define a charge as any form of security interest (fixed or floating) over property (including future property) other than an interest arising by operation of law; for example, a lien over goods arises by operation of law. However, Part IV of the 1989 Act did not define the specific nature of a security interest.

Charges that require registration

Charges that require registration are listed in s 396(1) (CA 1985), namely:

(a) a charge for the purpose of securing an issue of debentures;

(b) a charge on uncalled share capital of the company;

(c) a charge created or evidenced by an instrument, which, if executed by an individual, would require registration as a bill of sale;

(d) a charge on land or any interest in land other than a charge for rent or any other periodical payment;

(e) a charge on book debts of the company;

(f) a floating charge on the company's undertaking or property;

(g) a charge on calls made but not paid;

(h) a charge on a ship or aircraft, or any share in a ship;

(i) a charge on goodwill, trademarks, patent, copyright, etc.

In registering a charge, s 401 requires specific information to be registered: for example, the date of the creation of the charge, the amount secured by the charge, short particulars of the property charged and the persons entitled to the charge.

Book debts

The term 'book debt' is not defined by the Companies Act 1985. It is to be noted that the Diamond Report had suggested that a book debt should be defined as 'debts due or to become due to the company in respect of goods to be supplied or services rendered or to be rendered by the company in the course of the company's business' (see Diamond Report, para 23.9.22). A charge on an insurance policy is not to be treated as a charge on book debts, in so far as the debt on the insurance policy is a contingent debt: see e.g. *Paul & Frank Ltd* v *Discount Bank (Overseas) Ltd* [1967] Ch 348. Further, a negotiable instrument given to secure the payment of any book debts of a company, that is used by way of security for an advance to the company, is not regarded as a charge on the book debts of the company (s 396(2), CA 1985).

While it has become common practice for the Registrar to accept, for registration purposes, floating charges taken over a company's bank account, there is no statutory provision which indicates that a company's bank account should be regarded as a book debt owed to the company so as to render it the subject matter of a charge. Indeed, the judicial view would seem to indicate that a company's bank account (while in credit) should not be regarded as a book debt: see e.g. Hoffmann J in *Re Brightlife* [1987] Ch 200.

The registration certificate

The registration certificate is deemed to be conclusive evidence that, in terms of registration, the requirements of the Companies Act have been satisfied. The Registrar has the ultimate responsibility for checking the contents of particulars sent to him. It is for the Registrar to decide what charges have been created; where the Registrar makes a mistake as to the contents of the particulars he/she may be liable for any loss suffered as a consequence of the mistake. The actual instrument creating the charge must be delivered to the Registrar within 21 days of the charge's creation.

Failure to register the charge

A company and any officer of the company in default in failing to register a charge will be punishable by fine. The failure to register may be taken into account in any disqualification proceedings instigated against a director. A charge which has not been registered within the requisite period, but which should have been, will be void against the liquidator and any creditor of the company, although the obligation to repay the money secured by the charge is not invalidated by a failure to register; indeed, it becomes immediately repayable upon demand.

Rectification

The certificate of registration is conclusive; errors in the filed particulars of a charge do not prevent enforcement of the rights contained therein: see e.g. *Re Nye* [1971] Ch 1052. However, s 404 of the Companies Act 1985 permits rectification of the register in circumstances where the court is satisfied that:

- an omission or misstatement of any particular was accidental;
- an omission or misstatement was due to inadvertence or to some other sufficient cause;
- the omission or misstatement was of a nature to prejudice the position of creditors or shareholders of the company; and
- it is just and equitable to grant relief on other grounds.

Rectification will not be permitted where, for example, the matter subject to a claim for rectification is not concerned with the particulars which the Registrar is required to enter on the register of charges in accordance with s 401 of the Companies Act 1985: see e.g. *igroupLtd* v *Owen* [2004] BCLC 61.

Late delivery

The only method by which particulars may be registered after the elapse of the 21-day period is by a court order via an application under s 404: see e.g. *R* v *Registrar of Companies, ex parte Central Bank of India* [1986] 2 QB 1114. In considering an application under s 404, there must be evidence which justifies the court to allow registration out of time; the court must consider whether it is equitable to grant relief and in doing so must consider the effect of allowing late registration in respect of the interests of other creditors: see e.g. *Re Telomatic Ltd* [1993] BCC 404.

The company register

In accordance with ss 406 and 407 of the Companies Act 1985, a company must keep, at its registered office, a copy of every instrument creating a charge, irrespective of whether the charge requires to be registered in accordance with the Companies Act 1985. The register is open to public inspection. A failure to enter a charge on the register will not invalidate the charge but the company and any officer of the company in default will be liable to a fine.

FUTURE REFORM

Principal recommendations of the Companies Act 1989

- If the amending provisions of Part IV of the Companies Act 1989 had ever been introduced a security interest would not have been excluded from the registration procedure merely because it allowed the chargee to take possession of the goods on default of payment (see s 93, CA 1989). This provision may have required retention of title clauses, hire purchase contracts, conditional sale agreements or finance leases to be registered (this was the intention of Part II of the Diamond Report: see paras 23.6 and 23.7).

- In accordance with Part IV of the 1989 Act, the Registrar would have been relieved of the responsibility and any potential liability for certifying the registration of particulars. The registration certificate would only have been considered to be conclusive evidence of the fact that the specified particulars had been delivered to the Registrar no later than the date stated in the certificate; it was to be presumed, unless it was established to the contrary, that the specified particulars were not delivered earlier than that date. Under the 1989 Act, any person would have been able to require the Registrar to provide a certificate stating the date on which any specified particulars of, or other information relating to, a charge had been delivered to him. The registration certificate would only have been considered to be conclusive evidence of the fact that the specified particulars had been delivered to the Registrar no later than the date stated in the certificate; it was to be presumed, unless it was established to the contrary, that the specified particulars were not delivered earlier than that date.

- It would have been the duty of a company creating the charge, or acquiring property subject to a charge, to deliver the prescribed particulars of the charge in the prescribed form to the Registrar for registration within 21 days of the charge's creation or, in the case of acquiring property subject to a charge, the date of acquisition.

- A prior created charge (unregistered) would not have been void as against a later charge for want of registering relevant particulars unless some or all of the relevant particulars of the later charge were delivered for registration within 21 days of that charge's creation, or before complete and accurate relevant particulars of the earlier charge were delivered for registration.

Current proposals for reform

Following criticism of the proposals to reform the registration system in accordance with the 1989 Act, further and far more radical suggestions concerning the future reform of this area of the law have been made by the CLR and the Law Commission. In the CLR Final Report (2001) a new 'notice filing' system was favoured in preference to amending the existing system. This recommendation was echoed by the findings of two Law Commission Reports ((2002) and (2004)). The major proposals in respect of a new notice filing system are intended to ease and simplify the registration procedure. All in all, the major changes may be summarised as follows:

- The replacement of the present system for the registration of company charges by a notice-filing system – the security interest to be filed by the party taking the security interest but **only** with the debtor's consent (the debtor company would no longer be responsible for registering the charge). (This notice-filing system would be similar to the one which has operated in the USA for over fifty years: see art 9 of the US Uniform Commercial Code.) Under this new proposed system there would be no need for the full details of a security interest to be registered but instead a notice would be filed to the effect that a security interest had been taken (or was intended to be taken in the future) in relation to the identified asset(s). The proposal that a provisional notice, with a set time limit for its expiry, could be filed in advance of the conclusion of an agreement to take a security interest (i.e. 'or was intended to be taken in the future') is, it is suggested, a controversial move. For example, if creditor A agrees to take a provisional security interest over asset Y and files a notice to that effect, creditor B, on discovering the filed notice, may pull out of a proposed transaction with the company concerned because B specifically sought security over asset Y. The company may subsequently face difficulties if A decides not to confirm the security interest over asset Y.

- It is expected that the notice-filing system will operate via an online system with the intention that the new system will replace the paper-based registration system.

- Priority will be determined as between competing security interests according to the point in time when the security interest was filed. This had been a principal recommendation of the Diamond Report and will remove the 21-day registration period and the need for the current rules in relation to the late registration of charges. As stated, priority will therefore be determined on a first come first served basis via notice filing. However, interests granted over newly acquired assets, which secure funds loaned for the purchase of the said assets, will ordinarily take priority over pre-existing security interests: for example, this type of interest will take priority over a pre-existing interest which was expressed to cover the company's undertaking (i.e. the new assets would otherwise be a part of the company's undertaking).

- The notice-filing system will extend and operate beyond the list of security interests which are currently required to be registered, with the possibility of extending the new filing system to, for example, a retention of title clause, hire purchase agreements and conditional sale agreements (these interests are discussed below).

- Security interests which require registration in more than one register (i.e. government registers – e.g. interests in land, ships, etc. – will need to be registered only once; in such a case registration in the companies register would be unnecessary.

- It is proposed that the present classification of a charge as either a fixed or floating charge will be replaced by a new and unified classification of charge (i.e. introduction of an all-embracing security interest). This is probably the most controversial proposal for reform and the one which is most likely not to be adopted. Although there would appear to be an obvious conflict in having two distinct types of security coupled with a system which attempts to afford priority to the first interest registered, it is suggested that it would still be possible for the notice-filing system to operate as between the two categories of charge, albeit that this would entail a greater depth and clarity in the registration of the particulars in an attempt conclusively to identify the character and identity of the charge. At present, it is sometimes necessary to obtain judicial clarification of the nature of a charge (see Chapter 13 – especially the discussion on book debt charges), a fact which would clearly detract from the ease and speed attached to the proposed new system of notice registration (if the present classification of charges was maintained). However, it is suggested that cases illustrating ambiguity in the characteristics of a charge as between fixed and floating will become far less common in the light of the decision of the House of Lords in the case of *Spectrum Plus Ltd* (see Chapter 13). The proposal for the removal of the two distinct types of charge would surely remove the choice and flexibility attached to an ability to create a security interest, a choice which is likely to be influenced by the circumstances surrounding the creation of the security interest and the nature and type of asset over which the security interest is taken (see Chapter 13). In addition, such a change would create serious and costly administrative and re-drafting problems in terms of replacing the existing law and rules relating to the present format of security interests.

EXAMPLES OF INTERESTS THAT DO NOT CREATE REGISTRABLE CHARGES

Hire purchase agreements

Where a company has acquired goods on hire purchase terms (HP), ownership in those goods will not pass to the company until it has fulfilled all of its obligations under the HP agreement. A company cannot create a charge over goods subject to an HP agreement in so far as, while the HP agreement is in force, the company is not the legal owner of the goods. Nevertheless, the position is not quite so straightforward where goods acquired under an HP agreement are affixed to land over which the company has created a mortgage or charge. In circumstances where the goods subject to the HP agreement were affixed to the land before the security interest was created, then ordinarily the HP firm may repossess the goods where there is a breach of the hire purchase agreement. However, this general rule will not apply where the security interest is in the form of a legal mortgage, for here, if the holder of the mortgage had no notice of the HP agreement when the mortgage was created, he/she will be allowed to treat the affixed goods as part of the land over which the security was created: see e.g. *Hobson* v *Gorringe* [1897] 1 Ch 182.

Where goods subject to an HP agreement are attached to land over which a specific mortgage of land of a legal or equitable nature had previously been created, the mortgagee will be entitled to count the goods as part of his security interest: see e.g. *Longbottom* v *Berry* (1869) LR 5 QB 123.

The retention of title clause

A retention/reservation of title clause, also sometimes referred to as a *Romalpa* clause, is a contractual provision inserted into a contract of sale which purports to allow the seller to retain title in the goods he/she sells. The seller reserves title in the goods until such a time as the buyer has fulfilled certain conditions contained within the contract of sale. In terms of priority interests, a supplier of goods with a valid retention of title clause, will, in the event of a company going into receivership or liquidation, be paid moneys owing to him in priority to a creditor secured by means of a registrable charge. Where a seller successfully reserves the right of ownership in goods, the buyer will be unable to create a charge over the goods (i.e. it is impossible for the buyer to create a charge over something that he does not legally own). The legal effect of a valid retention of title clause is therefore similar to a hire purchase (HP) contract, save that under an HP contract the prospective buyer of the property has no legal right to pass title in the goods. By contrast, a term will be implied into a contract containing a valid retention of title clause to the effect that the prospective buyer of the goods will have the legal right to pass title in the goods.

The ability of a seller to retain title in goods is given legal effect by the Sale of Goods Act 1979. Section 17 of the Act states:

> 'Where there is a contract for the sale of specific or unascertained goods the property in them is to be transferred to the buyer at such time as the parties to the contract intend it to be transferred.'

Section 19 of the Sale of Goods Act 1979 provides:

> 'Where there is a contract for the sale of specific goods or where goods are subsequently appropriated to the contract, the seller may, by the terms of the contract or appropriation, reserve the right of disposal of the goods until certain conditions are fulfilled; and in such a case, notwithstanding the delivery of the goods to the buyer, or to a carrier or other bailee or custodier for the purposes of transmission to the buyer, the property in the goods does not pass to the buyer until the conditions imposed by the seller are fulfilled.'

While the practice of a seller retaining title in goods can be traced back to the nineteenth century, the scope of this contractual device has been extended in more recent times. The development and subsequent debate over the ambit of the retention of title clause can be directly attributed to the decision of the Court of Appeal in *Aluminium Industrie Vaasen BV* v *Romalpa Aluminium Ltd* [1976] 2 All ER 552. The facts of the case were as follows. A Dutch company (AIV) supplied aluminium foil to the defendant company (R). The sales contract was subject to a retention of title clause, which included:

(a) an all moneys restriction; no property in the goods was to pass until all the goods supplied had been paid for;

(b) a condition that foil supplied by AIV should, until it was used in the manufacturing process, be stored separately;

(c) a stipulation which provided that objects made from the foil as supplied by AIV would become the property of AIV as security for the payment of moneys owing to AIV;

(d) a restriction which stated that, until all debts owing to AIV had been paid, R would hold the unused foil and products made from the foil supplied, in the capacity of a fiduciary owner; and

(e) a condition that if R sold the foil, or goods manufactured from the foil, to a sub-buyer, AIV would have a claim on the proceeds of such sales or, alternatively, the right to take over any claim that R might have against such sub-buyers for debts arising from the sale of foil or products manufactured out of the foil.

R went into receivership owing AIV £122 000. R's receiver certified that R held £50 000-worth of unused foil which had been supplied by AIV and that a further £35 000 had been received from the sale of such foil; these funds had been placed in a separate bank account. On the basis of clauses (a), (b) and (d) (see above), AIV claimed the right to recover the unused foil from R's premises. In reliance upon clause (e), AIV also claimed the right to the £35 000 held in the bank account. As R had not used the foil to manufacture other goods, clause (c) did not come into play.

The Court of Appeal held that AIV was entitled to claim both the unused foil and the proceeds of the sub-sales of the foil. In respect of AIV's right to claim the proceeds of the sub-sales of foil it was necessary for AIV to establish that the retention of title clause created a fiduciary relationship between the contracting parties, thereby enabling AIV to contend that they were entitled to an equitable tracing order in respect of the £35 000 (i.e. that R held the £35 000 in a form of trust for the benefit of AIV (see e.g. *Re Hallets Estate* (1880) 13 Ch D 696 and, more recently, *Re Fleet Disposal Services Ltd* [1995] BCC 605). In deeming that there was a fiduciary relationship between the contracting parties on the basis of an agency relationship, Roskill LJ stated:

'If an agent lawfully sells his principal's goods he stands in a fiduciary relationship to his principal and remains accountable to his principal for those goods and their proceeds.'
(at p 563)

However, it is surprising to note that R conceded that it had acted as a bailee for the foil, thus confirming the notion that property in the foil had not passed and hence strengthening the argument that AIV and R had, indeed, intended to create a fiduciary relationship. A fiduciary relationship was found despite the fact that AIV had extended a 75-day credit period to R, a fact which suggested that R would not immediately have been liable to account for the proceeds of sale, a consideration which in itself appeared contrary to the establishment of a fiduciary type of relationship. Another controversial facet of the case was that the establishment of a fiduciary relationship implied that R would have had to account for all moneys received from the sub-sales of the foil (i.e. any profit received from the sub-sales would have been held for the benefit of AIV). Such a notion would appear quite peculiar in a commercial-type relationship in the sense that, would R have entered into a contractual relationship that forbade it from dealing with profits obtained from the sale of the foil? Surely AIV was entitled to the proceeds of sale only in so far as necessary to discharge the amount of moneys owed to it by R?

Is a clause seeking to reserve title a valid retention of title clause?

There seems little doubt, but note the case of *Re Andrabell* [1984] 2 All ER 407, that if a contract of sale contains a retention of title clause which does no more than to retain the legal ownership in goods until such a time as the full purchase price of the goods has been paid, such a clause will, in accordance with s 19 of the Sale of Goods Act 1979, be upheld as reserving title in the property: see e.g. *Clough Mill v Martin* [1984] 3 All ER 982. However, it should be noted that a clause which purports to retain equitable and beneficial ownership will not reserve title in the property: see e.g. *Re Bond Worth* [1980] Ch 228 and *Stroud Architectural Systems Ltd v John Laing Construction Ltd* [1994] BCC 18. Difficulties in respect of the effect and validity of a purported retention of title clause have occurred in the situations described below.

The all moneys restriction

A retention of title clause may purport to retain ownership in goods which have already been paid for by the buyer. For example, a contract for the sale of goods may consist of the consignment of goods: A, B, C and D. The buyer may have paid in full for goods A and B but not for goods C and D. In this given example, the effect of an 'all moneys restriction' contained within a retention of title clause would, if upheld, be that the seller would retain ownership in goods A, B, C and D until payment for all four goods had been met. Thus, even though the buyer had paid for goods A and B he would not have acquired the legal title in those goods until the amount owing in respect of goods C and D had been discharged.

Although it is arguable that a seller's claim to retain title in goods that have already been paid for by the buyer would render the contract of sale void as a result of a total failure of consideration (note that the Cork Committee Report 1982 (Cmnd 8558) proposed that an all moneys clause should not be given effect and accordingly treated as creating a registrable charge), the validity of an 'all moneys clause' was supported by the House of Lords in *Armour and Anor v Thyssen Edelstahlwerke AG* [1990] BCC 929. In supporting the potential validity of such a clause, the House of Lords placed a strong emphasis on the correctness of giving effect to the intention of the parties as taken from the actual terms of the contractual agreement. Lord Keith, expressing the unanimous opinion of the House of Lords observed:

> 'In the present case the parties to the contract of sale clearly expressed their intention that the property . . . should not pass . . . until all debts due . . . had been paid. In my opinion there are no grounds for refusing to give effect to that intention . . . Counsel . . . argued that the word "conditions" in s 19(1) must be read as excluding any condition which had the effect of creating a right of security over the goods. I am, however, unable to regard a provision reserving title to the seller until payment of all debts due to him by the buyer as amounting to the creation by the buyer of a right of security in favour of the seller. Such

a provision does in a sense give the seller security for the unpaid debts of the buyer. But it does so by way of a legitimate retention of title, not by virtue of any right over his property conferred by the buyer.' (at pp 928–929)

A manufactured goods restriction

A restriction, whereby the seller purports to retain title in goods manufactured from those supplied under the contract of sale, has fallen to be considered by the courts on a number of occasions. As yet, there is no reported case in which the validity of such a restriction has been upheld. The principal justification for not giving effect to the validity of such a clause is that goods which have been supplied by the seller and which have been through the manufacturing process inevitably lose their original identity. Accordingly, the resulting manufactured goods can no longer be identified as those over which the retention of title clause was placed: see e.g. *Borden UK v Scottish Timber Products Ltd* [1981] Ch 25, *Re Peachdart Ltd* [1984] Ch 131, *Hendy Lennox Ltd v Grahame Puttick Ltd* [1984] 1 WLR 485, *Clough Mill v Martin* [1984] 3 All ER 982, *Modelboard Ltd v Outer Box Ltd* [1992] BCC 945, *Ian Chisholm Textiles Ltd v Griffiths* [1994] BCC 96 and *Chaigley Farms Ltd v Crawford, Kaye & Grayshire Ltd* [1996] BCC 957. In this latter case, a farmer sought to incorporate a retention of title clause in a contract for the sale of livestock. The clause provided that until the animals had been paid for in full, the farmer would retain title in the livestock. The purchaser sent the livestock for slaughter. Garland J held that the retention of title clause could have no effect in so far as the livestock were not of the same character following their slaughter (i.e. carcasses of animals were not the same 'goods' as animals in a living state).

A proceeds of sale restriction

A proceeds of sale restriction within a retention of title clause is one which purports to restrict the buyer's ability to deal with the proceeds of sale; a clause which allows the seller to trace the proceeds of sale. Such clauses may afford the seller a right to the proceeds of sale of the original goods or may be extended to allow the seller a right to the proceeds of a sale of goods manufactured from the goods supplied under the original sales contract. Save for the decision in *Aluminium Industrie Vaasen BV v Romalpa Ltd* [1976] 1 WLR 676, there is no other authority in which a restriction of this nature has been accepted, otherwise than by creating a charge on the goods: see e.g. *Re Bond Worth* [1979] 3 All ER 919, *Pfieffer Weinkellerei Weineinkauf GmbH & Co v Arbuthnot Factors Ltd* [1988] 1 WLR 150, *Compaq Computers Ltd v Abercorn Group Ltd and Ors* [1991] BCC 484 and *Modelboard Ltd v Outer Box Ltd* [1992] BCC 945.

In *Modelboard Ltd v Outer Box Ltd,* Michael Hart QC, sitting as a deputy High Court judge, was called upon to determine the nature of an agreement between a seller (S) and purchaser (P) in respect of a term of a sale contract which provided that P would sell finished goods manufactured from goods supplied by S, as agents and bailees for S, and that the entire proceeds of sale would be held on trust for S and kept separate from P's other moneys. Despite the clear intention of the language of the term (i.e. the creation of an agency/bailee relationship), Michael Hart QC construed this term in the light of commercial reality and as such found that its intention could not have been to vest the total purchase price paid for the finished goods (which would include the profit made by P, over and above the contract price paid to S) in the hands of S. Accordingly, the purported existence of a fiduciary relationship, between P and S in respect of the entire proceeds of sale, was denied. S's interest in the proceeds of sale was found to be an interest by way of charge that was rendered void as a consequence of its non-registration.

Criticism of the potential effect of a retention of title clause

The principal criticism of the concept of the retention of title clause is that at present there is no requirement to register such a clause. Accordingly, a creditor wishing to take a charge over corporate assets will find it difficult to establish whether the assets, which are to be the subject of the charge, are already the subject of a retention of title clause. As such, the very nature of a retention of title clause may be considered unfair, that is, charge holders are relegated, in terms of priority rights, by the prior claims of the holder of a retention of title clause.

In cases after *Romalpa*, the courts, in construing retention of title clauses, have concentrated their attention on the substance and commercial reality of the clause (this is akin to the manner in which charges are construed) with the result that in the overwhelming majority of cases retention of title clauses have been construed as failing to create a fiduciary relationship between the parties. Indeed, many retention of title clauses have been construed to be unregistered charges. For example, in *Compaq Computers Ltd* v *Abercorn Group Ltd* [1991] BCC 484, Mummery J opined that:

> 'In determining whether any given agreement creates a charge, equity looks to the substance and reality of the transaction. What on the face of it may appear to be . . . an out-and-out disposition of a beneficial interest in property by way of trust, may in fact be by way of security only, with a right of redemption and therefore, in the nature of a charge . . .' (at p 493)

The trust device

As a general rule, a creditor who invests funds into a company will not be deemed to have become the beneficiary of any trust relationship with the company. Nevertheless, in exceptional circumstances the courts have recognised the possibility of a creditor inserting a trust device into a contract, the effect of which is to create a trustee–beneficiary relationship between the contracting parties. The validity of a trust device will afford a creditor a priority in the funds governed by the trust, ahead of other creditors who may seek to lay claim to the funds.

A trust device may operate in circumstances where funds are delivered to a company for a specified purpose; the funds are held on trust by the company until the specified purpose is achieved. A case example, which illustrates the potential validity of a trust device, is *Re Kayford* [1975] 1 WLR 279. Here a mail order company took the commendable step of attempting to protect customers' funds by establishing a special trust fund into which advance payment for goods was to be deposited. The mail order company went into liquidation. The question which the court had to decide was whether this purported trust fund had the effect of protecting the company's customers' interests or whether such funds should be included as part of the assets available for distribution to the general body of the company's creditors. Megarry J found in favour of upholding the validity of the trust device. The learned judge stated that:

> 'Different considerations may perhaps arise in relation to trade creditors but here I am concerned with members of the public, some of whom can ill afford to exchange their money for a claim to a dividend in the liquidation.' (at p 282)

Suggested further reading

The effect of the Enterprise Act 2002

Finch [2003] JBL 527

The Leyland Daf *case*

Mokal [2004] LMCLQ 387

Reforming the registration system

McCormack [2003] Insol Law 2

Glister [2004] LMCLQ 460

15

INSOLVENCY LAW PROCEDURES

INTRODUCTION

With an increase in the availability of credit and the increased perception of companies large and small becoming unable to pay all their debts, the law of insolvency has, in the past twenty years, moved from being a niche specialist area into the mainstream. Insolvency law was completely overhauled in the mid-1980s with a new emphasis on the so-called 'rescue culture' and has been the subject of several Parliamentary interventions since that time. In particular, the Enterprise Act 2002 has introduced major changes in relation to the regulation of insolvency law. The purpose of this chapter is to provide an outline of the main insolvency procedures and to explain how they have developed and how they operate. What may be termed 'non-terminal' procedures such as receivership, administration and company voluntary arrangement will be considered, together with the 'terminal' procedure of liquidation or winding up (these two terms may be used synonymously). It should be noted that this chapter does not extend to cover the EC Regulation on Insolvency Proceedings 2000 (operative as from 31 May 2002). The scope of the Regulation covers personal and corporate insolvency where the affairs of an insolvent are conducted in one or more member state of the EU.

HISTORICAL SKETCH OF CORPORATE INSOLVENCY LAW

The need for corporate insolvency law obviously began with the introduction of registered companies in 1844 (by the Joint Stock Companies Act 1844). The Winding Up Act 1844 was passed to regulate the winding up of such companies. Insolvency is not the only reason for a company to be wound up but it is by far the most common ground. The Winding Up Act 1844 limited the rights of a company's creditors to look to the assets of the company only, and in general prevented them from seeking repayment of corporate debts directly from the members of the company.

At times, the rules regulating the operation of companies generally and the rules for winding up such companies were incorporated into a single Act of Parliament, such as the Companies Act 1862. In more modern times, the rules for dealing with the insolvency of companies have been separated into distinct Acts, so that today we have the Companies Act 1985 (covering the general regulation of companies) and for winding up and other insolvency procedures we have the Insolvency Act 1986.

The progression of insolvency law

In the latter half of the nineteenth century companies registered under the Companies Acts became progressively more popular; not only large undertakings were being incorporated. By way of example there is the classic case of *Salomon v A Salomon &*

Co Ltd [1897] AC 22. By the end of the nineteenth century, the practice of the incorporation of small sole trader businesses became extremely common. Along with the benefits of limited liability, companies were able to borrow on the strength of executing a floating charge (something individuals and partnerships were legally prevented from doing by the Bills of Sale Act 1882). In the latter part of the nineteenth century, the floating charge became a very common form of secured lending.

Together with the power to borrow on the security of a floating charge came powers taken by the charge holder to enforce the charge when the company defaulted under the loan agreement. Although it was possible for the charge holder to take possession of the charged assets and realise those assets as a mortgagee in possession, it became common practice for such debenture holders to appoint a receiver instead, to realise the charged assets. The main reason for this seems to have been a fear that debenture holders could incur serious personal liability under the potentially onerous duties owed by mortgagees in possession. At first, debenture holders who wished to enforce their security would ask the court to appoint a receiver, who would then realise the assets in order to pay off the lender. As time went by, it became common practice to include in standard form debentures the power to appoint a receiver out of court, which led to cheaper and swifter realisations of companies' charged assets. Court appointed receivers are extremely rare nowadays and are only sought where a particularly difficult legal or other problem has arisen.

This system of debenture holders appointing receivers out of court remained largely undisturbed for about a hundred years. Insolvent companies that had secured borrowing would often find themselves plunged into receivership and, when the receiver had finished realising the charged assets to pay off the debenture holder, a liquidator would be appointed to finish off and dissolve the company. This scenario is still very commonly encountered today. Receivers are appointed by debenture holders to realise assets to pay off the secured loan. Often during the receivership the company will enter liquidation and the liquidator will wait in the wings for the receiver to complete the receivership, before moving in as a sort of corporate executioner finally to dispatch the company.

The corporate insolvency landscape became a little more crowded in the mid-1980s with the introduction of administration and company voluntary arrangements. These procedures were hailed as bringing a new 'rescue culture' to insolvent companies. At this time, the most common form of receivership (where the receiver is appointed over the whole or substantially the whole of the company's undertaking) was re-christened administrative receivership. The report of the Insolvency Law Review Committee, 'Insolvency Law and Practice' (Cmnd 8558, 1982) (known as the 'Cork Report'), marked the beginning of modern insolvency law. The Cork Report is a highly regarded document and critically evaluated a number of shortcomings of the then system of insolvency law. The Cork Report's recommendations were, in the main, given effect to by the Insolvency Act 1986. Importantly, this resulted in an attempted change of emphasis away from merely debt enforcement by creditors, to a new system where businesses would be rescued, whenever possible.

Since 1986, only licensed insolvency practitioners have been able to act as administrative receivers, administrators, nominees and supervisors of company voluntary arrangements and liquidators (see s 390, IA 1986). This has also influenced other areas such as directors' disqualification, where the reports of insolvency practitioners are crucial in proving directors are unfit to be directors of companies. From 1986, there have also been substantial amendments in the form of the Insolvency Act 1994, the Insolvency Act 2000 and, most importantly, the Enterprise Act 2002. As will be observed, although administration was only introduced in 1986, its ability to initiate widespread company rescue was limited to the extent that it was substantially re-invented in 2002. The Enterprise Act has also spelt the prospective end to debenture holders being able to enforce their debentures by the appointment of administrative receivers.

RECEIVERSHIP

As the name suggests, a receiver is a person who receives or takes control of property belonging to another. Receivers are encountered in situations other than corporate insolvency. For example, a receiver may be appointed under the Partnership Act 1890 where a partnership is being dissolved, or to take control of a charity where there have been irregularities in the charity's administration. Receivers perform different tasks in different contexts. When a company is placed into receivership, the reason is usually that the company has defaulted under its secured loan agreement with a debenture holder.

Strictly speaking, a receiver appointed under a debenture can only take control of assets subject to the debenture and receive income from those assets: e.g. rent from a block of flats charged. In addition to any express powers given to the receiver under the terms of the debenture, for example, a power to sell the charged assets, the receiver will also benefit from powers implied by the Law of Property Act 1925. A receiver appointed under a debenture containing only a fixed charge is referred to as a fixed charge or Law of Property Act receiver. A fixed charge receiver will rarely have the power to manage the company's business.

As noted in Chapter 13, when a company borrows money it is usual for it to execute security over all its assets both present and future, not just fixed assets. A common form debenture will create fixed charges over certain specified assets present and future and also a floating charge over the company's 'undertaking'. The important thing to note here is that 'undertaking' includes all the other assets of the company (e.g. stock in trade) present and future and the right to carry on the company's business. The consequence of this is that when a receiver is appointed over the company's undertaking, the receiver has the power to run the business of the company and, in realising the charged assets, will have the ability to sell all of the company's assets including the business as a going concern. This is important, because a sale of a company's business as a going concern will invariably realise a greater sale price than would be achieved by a 'fire sale' of all the company's assets piecemeal. This type of receiver is referred to as a 'receiver and manager' due to the management powers associated with his/her position. He or she will usually have powers to take control of the charged assets, manage the business of the company to the exclusion of the directors and to sell assets either individually or as a going concern: see e.g. Jessel MR in *Re Manchester & Milford Ry Co* (1880) 14 ChD 645 at 653. Receivers exercising these powers owe certain duties to interested parties. The most commonly encountered type of receiver in an insolvency context is a receiver and manager appointed under a debenture, which includes a floating charge, over the whole or substantially the whole of a company's undertaking. Following the Cork Report's recommendations, s 29(2) of the Insolvency Act 1986 re-classified this type of receiver as an 'administrative receiver'.

The 1986 Act contains a number of provisions that regulate receivers generally, as well as other provisions which only cover administrative receivers. Administrative receivers may now be viewed as an endangered species given that the Enterprise Act 2002 has abolished the power to appoint administrative receivers under debentures created after 15 September 2003. However, they will still be encountered routinely for many years to come as, for debentures entered into prior to 15 September 2003, debenture holders retain the power to appoint an administrative receiver.

The appointment of a receiver

A debenture holder who decides to appoint a receiver must ensure that the appointment is made consistently with the wording of the debenture. It is usual to list in a debenture a number of default events: for example, failure to pay interest owing to the debenture holder within a specified period of it becoming due. If one or more of the specified events has occurred, the debenture will normally state that the default will cause all moneys owing to the debenture holder to become payable on demand. The debenture holder will then serve a formal demand on the company for immediate payment of all moneys: both capital and interest. If the company fails to pay (as is likely, otherwise it would not have defaulted), the debenture holder can then appoint the receiver. As the money will usually be expressed as being payable on demand, the company is afforded no time to allow it to attempt to renegotiate its finances. The company is only given sufficient time to put the 'mechanics of payment' into effect. Accordingly, the company is only given the time to pay as it would take the company to go to a convenient place to collect the funds owed; that is, the company will have no more than an hour or so to pay the money over otherwise the receiver will be appointed to take control of the company's assets: see e.g. *Cripps (Pharmaceuticals) Ltd* v *Wickenden* [1973] 1 WLR 944 and *Bank of Baroda Ltd* v *Panessar* [1987] Ch 335.

The appointment of a receiver will usually be in writing (prepared ahead of time) but may need to be by deed if so required by the debenture's terms. There is no statutory form of appointment which needs to be satisfied. The appointment will take effect when it is given to the prospective receiver and the receiver has accepted the appointment. The appointment of an administrative receiver is only effective if it is accepted before the end of the business day after that on which the instrument of appointment is received. The date of the appointment is backdated to the date of receipt of the instrument of appointment (s 33, IA 1986). All invoices for goods and other business letters of the company must disclose the fact that a receiver has been appointed (s 39, IA 1986).

It should be noted that it is commonly reported in the media that a company has called in the receivers. This is not the case, as it is the debenture holder who will appoint the receiver, although it should be appreciated that frequently companies will inform their bank, the debenture holder, that the company cannot continue and will invite the bank to appoint a receiver. Not all appointments are therefore hostile.

The appointment of an administrative receiver will crystallise any floating charge (if this has not already occurred), and it will generally prevent the company from entering administration (see paras 15–17, 25 and 39 of Sch B1 to the IA 1986). The appointment will not generally terminate contracts of employment because the company as a separate legal entity continues as before, just under the new management of the receiver. The appointment of a receiver will not, in itself, affect contracts between the company and third parties, although many such contracts specify that by entering administrative receivership the contract will be brought to an end.

Powers of receivers

A receiver is appointed to realise the charged assets and pay off, as best he/she can, the debt of the appointing debenture holder. Although clearly acting on behalf of the debenture holder, a receiver will act as agent of the company. Administrative receivers are deemed to be agents of the company under s 44(1)(a) of the Insolvency Act 1986. Fixed charge receivers are deemed to be agents of the company under s 109(2) of the Law of Property Act 1925. Other types of receiver will be expressly stated by the debenture to be appointed as agents of the company.

The agency relationship is unusual as the receiver cannot be dismissed by the principal (the company) and the agent's primary duty is owed to the appointing debenture holder and not the company. It is also an unusual type of agency relationship because a receiver may become personally liable on contracts entered into by the company.

Any well-drafted debenture will list extensive powers which the receiver may exercise: e.g. to get in and sell company assets. In addition, an administrative receiver has statutory powers implied by ss 42 and 43 of and Sch 1 to the Insolvency Act 1986. Once appointed, an administrative receiver takes control of the company, usurping the management powers of the directors: see *Re Emmadart* [1979] Ch 540. When selling company assets, the receiver may sell as agent of the company but, without an appropriate deed of release from the debenture holder, cannot transfer assets free from the debenture under which the appointment was made: see *Re Real Meat Co* [1996] BCC 254. The alternative to this is for the debenture holder to appoint the receiver as its agent for that particular purpose only (i.e. to give an unencumbered title to the buyer).

Statutory duties of receivers

Administrative receivers owe a duty under s 47 of the Insolvency Act 1986 to obtain a statement of affairs from company officers, detailing the company's assets and liabilities. A report must be prepared by the administrative receiver and made available to creditors. The report will explain how the company came to be in receivership and what the receiver is planning to do with the assets. It will also give an indication of how much each secured and preferential creditor is likely to receive (an administrative receiver will not make distributions to unsecured creditors).

An administrative receiver's function is to realise enough of the charged assets to pay off the appointing debenture holder. Even where the business can be sold on as a going concern, there is frequently insufficient money to pay off the debenture holder. Once the assets have been realised the administrative receiver must distribute the proceeds in a set order, namely:

1 any secured creditor with priority over the debenture under which the administrative receiver is appointed;

2 the administrative receiver's own costs, expenses and remuneration;

3 fixed charges contained within the debenture under which the administrative receiver is appointed;

4 debts due to preferential creditors under s 40 of the Act. Following the abolition of the Crown's preferential status in insolvency by the Enterprise Act 2002, preferential creditors are now essentially limited to certain claims by employees. The maximum amount of remuneration that an employee may claim for the period prior to the receivership is four months' pay with an aggregate maximum of £800. This rather modest right is extended slightly by a right to a redundancy payment from the National Insurance Fund under s 184 of the Employment Rights Act 1996, where up to eight weeks' pay (maximum £250 per week) may be claimed;

5 debts secured by a floating charge (the top slicing of floating charge assets in favour of unsecured creditors introduced following the Enterprise Act 2002 by the new s 176A of the Insolvency Act 1986 Act, will not usually be deducted in an administrative receivership because the receivership will generally have been commenced under a debenture entered into prior to 15 September 2003, and one consequence of this is that the debenture will not be subject to the top slice (s 176A is discussed further in Chapter 14));

6 if any money remains, it will be handed back to the company. If, as is commonly the case, the company is by this time in liquidation, the money will be handed over to the liquidator.

Duties owed by receivers at common law or in equity

Although acting as agent of the company, nevertheless a receiver owes a primary duty to the appointing debenture holder. Secondary duties are owed to others who have an interest in the equity of redemption of the charged assets such as the company itself, any guarantors and any prior or subsequent charge holders. The reason for this is that if the receiver manages the business negligently or conducts the sale of the business in an incompetent fashion, this may cause the secured assets not to be realised in the most beneficial way. If the sale price is low, for example, the appointing debenture holder and other secured creditors may not be paid. The debenture holder may have to call in personal guarantees given by third parties. No duty is owed to directors, shareholders or unsecured creditors as they are seen as having no direct interest in the charged assets: see e.g. *Burgess* v *Auger* [1998] 2 BCLC 478 and *Medforth* v *Blake* [1999] BCC 771.

In considering the exact duties owed by receivers, a number of preliminary points need to be made. First, due to the similarity of function between a receiver and a mortgagee in possession, it is common for the case law examining the duties owed by both mortgagees and receivers to use the authorities in one area as authoritative in the other. Secondly, the case law is somewhat contradictory. Thirdly, there is a debate as to whether receivers owe duties of care at common law in the form of normal negligence principles or whether they are only subject to equitable rules. The better view seems to be that the duties are owed only in equity but arguably the distinction is of little, if any, practical importance.

In the nineteenth century, two lines of case law developed. In one, the courts held that as long as a receiver (or mortgagee in possession) acted within his/her powers and exercised those powers in a *bona fide* manner, the court would not look to impose any liability even where the sale price achieved was low: see e.g. *Warner* v *Jacob* (1882) 20 ChD 220 and *Kennedy* v *de Trafford* [1897] AC 180. During the same period, a conflicting line of cases held that a receiver (or mortgagee in possession) could be held personally liable if a sale was conducted negligently resulting in the sale price being too low (see e.g. *Robertson* v *Norris* (1859) 1 Giff 421 and *Tomlin* v *Luce* (1889) 43 ChD 191), or where charged assets were allowed to deteriorate due to negligence and therefore needlessly reduced in value (see e.g. *McHugh* v *Union Bank of Canada* [1913] AC 299). In the words of Sir George Jessel MR in *Nash* v *Eads* (1880) SJ 95 a mortgagee, when exercising a power of sale:

'. . . **"must conduct the sale properly, and must sell at a fair value."** ' (at p 95)

Until recently, modern case law conveyed a similar polarisation of views. The Court of Appeal in *Re B Johnson & Co (Builders) Ltd* [1955] 1 Ch 634, limited the duty owed by receivers to a duty to act in good faith and within their powers. It was explained that there could be no duty to carry on the company's business nor to preserve its goodwill. The receiver is given powers of management not for the benefit of the company but to realise the assets for the debenture holder. By the 1970s, the courts had decided to extend common law negligence principles to a mortgagee in possession. In *Cuckmere Brick Co Ltd* v *Mutual Finance Ltd* [1971] Ch 949, the duty to act in good faith was extended to include a duty to act with reasonable care to obtain what the members of the court variously described as the 'proper market value' or 'best price' or 'proper price'. There is no duty to choose the best possible time to sell but, once the decision to sell is made, the sale needs to be carried out with reasonable care. The Court of Appeal couched the test in terms of the 'neighbour' principle and discussed the concept of 'proximity'. This extension of common law negligence principles to a previously exclusively equitable domain caused subsequent problems. It became possible, from this extension, to argue that a duty should even be owed to unsecured creditors, although in reality this argument has never seriously been considered by any court. The common law formulation of duties was followed in *Standard Chartered Bank* v *Walker* [1982] 3 All ER 938. In *Palk* v *Mortgage Services Funding plc* [1993] 2 All ER 481, the court considered the duties owed by a mortgagee to exist both at common law and in equity. Reasonable care was required in managing the property and in conducting a sale of it.

In what appears to be a bid to turn back the relentless expansion of common law negligence, the Privy Council, in *Downsview Nominees* v *First City Corporation* [1993] AC 295, explained that receivers owed a duty in equity only and not at common law. The Privy Council attempted to limit the case of *Cuckmere* and ended up with a somewhat unsatisfactory compromise between different viewpoints. Their lordships effectively held that the duty owed by a receiver was to act within his/her powers and to act *bona fide* in exercising those powers. This is fairly straight *Re B Johnson* fare. However, the rather strange effect of the Privy Council's decision was to graft onto this restrictive traditional view, a limited view of *Cuckmere*. The ratio of the case is therefore that receivers must act generally within their powers and *bona fide*, but when they exercise their power of sale they have the additional specific duty to take reasonable care to ensure a proper price is achieved.

Happily, the law has now been largely rationalised by the Court of Appeal in *Medforth* v *Blake* [1999] BCC 771. The court rejected the rather restrictive view of *Downsview* but did not go headlong into a restatement of the law in terms of common law negligence. The case concerned the receivership of a pig farm. The main issue was whether or not the receiver owed a duty of care to the mortgagor in conducting the farming business. The Court of Appeal assessed some of the previous case law and concluded that it was inconsistent in places because equity was by its nature a flexible thing. The court also concluded that whether the matter was viewed as being governed by equity or the common law, the result would be the same and the distinction was not important. Seven propositions were laid down:

- a receiver owes duties to anyone interested in the equity of redemption of the charged assets;
- the duties include, but are not necessarily limited to, a duty of good faith;
- any additional duty will depend on the facts of a particular case;
- in exercising powers of management, the receiver's primary duty is to pay off the secured debt;
- subject to the primary duty, the receiver owes a duty to manage the property with due diligence;
- due diligence does not require the receiver to continue to carry on the business;
- if the receiver does carry on the business, due diligence requires that reasonable steps be taken to try to do so profitably.

Therefore, *Medforth* brings some welcome clarification to the area and suggests that the duty owed to persons with an interest in the equity of redemption is one whereby the receiver should act with due diligence. It would appear that this duty extends to both managing the business and, once a sale has been decided upon, conducting the sale process. The decision as to when to sell assets is one for the receiver and no duty of care is owed as to the timing of any sale: see *Silven Properties Limited* v *Royal Bank of Scotland plc* [2004] 4 All ER 484. In assessing what price should reasonably be obtained, the court will assess the market value to see whether the price realised falls within an acceptable margin of error: see *Michael* v *Miller* [2004] EWCA Civ 282.

Contractual liability of administrative receivers

Section 44 of the Insolvency Act 1986 governs the personal liability of an administrative receiver under contracts entered into by the company. As an agent of the company the administrative receiver may enter into contracts on behalf of the company and will frequently need to do so to keep the business ticking over. The administrative receiver will be personally liable on any contracts entered into by the company during the receivership unless (as is common) the contract provides otherwise. If personally liable, the administrative receiver has the benefit of an indemnity from the company's assets (under s 44(1)(c), IA 1986).

As the administrative receiver acts as agent of the company, normal agency rules apply to contracts entered into by the company prior to the receivership, that is, the company (as principal) remains liable under the contract and the receiver incurs no personal liability: see e.g. *Hay* v *Swedish and Norwegian Ry Co* (1892) 8 TLR 775. As agents, receivers incur no personal liability if they cause the company to breach existing contracts. Although the company may be liable for the breach, the receiver is free from any liability: see e.g. *Airline Airspares* v *Handley-Page* [1970] Ch 193.

Accordingly, in deciding how best to continue the business of a company, the receiver is given a relatively free hand (i.e. he/she may decide not to pay certain creditors or may, for example, decide to change suppliers). Although generally free to ignore a third party's contractual rights, a receiver cannot ignore proprietary rights which have already passed under a contract: for example, under a specifically enforceable contract where the equitable interest has already passed to the contracting party (see e.g. *Freevale* v *Metrostore Holdings* [1984] Ch 199).

An important decision, which faces an administrative receiver on taking office, is whether to keep on or dismiss employees. If a sale of the business as a going concern is to be considered, some employees will need to be retained. If an administrative receiver causes an employment contract to remain in force by not acting to terminate it within 14 days of taking office, the administrative receiver will be deemed to have adopted the contract. The receiver will be personally liable to pay out under the contract for services rendered after the contract is deemed to be adopted, that is, for services rendered after the 14 days have elapsed (s 44, IA 1986). Again, the receiver has an indemnity from the company assets for this liability. Any liability incurred to employees under s 44 is in addition to any payment which the employee may be entitled to as a preferential creditor or under s 184 of the Employment Rights Act 1996.

Termination of receivership

A receivership will normally cease when the receiver completes the task of realising enough of the charged assets to pay off the debenture holder and other creditors who are required to be paid in priority to the debenture holder. Once the money has been handed over, the receiver informs the Registrar of Companies that he/she is vacating office. The receivership is then over. As the company itself may, by this point, be an empty shell, due to the sale of all or most of its business and assets, the company will usually be placed into liquidation if it is not already being wound up.

Abolition of administrative receivership

As previously mentioned, the Enterprise Act 2002 has signalled a slow and lingering death for administrative receivership (s 72A, IA 1986). With the exception of certain specific types of company charges – for example, charges given by public private partnerships (see ss 72B–72F of the IA 1986 for the full list of six) – debentures which constitute a 'qualifying floating charge' (defined under para 14 of Sch B1, IA 1986 as a floating charge over the whole or substantially the whole of the company's property) entered into after 15 September 2003 can no longer be enforced by the appointment of an administrative receiver. Instead, the debenture holder is able to appoint an administrator out of court. The main reason for this change is the perception that the interests of unsecured creditors of companies are inadequately protected in administrative receivership, that is, the receiver owes no duties to unsecured creditors. In contrast, an administrator owes a duty to all the company's creditors. The collective nature of administration has therefore been preferred over the regime of administrative receivership where the primary duty is owed to the appointing debenture holder. However, it is to be noted that fixed charge receivers may still be appointed as their operation is not affected by the Enterprise Act. For the many thousands of debentures which came into existence prior to 15 September 2003, the holders of these debentures now have a choice whether to enforce by appointing an administrative receiver or an administrator.

ADMINISTRATION

The administration procedure was introduced following the Cork Report's recommendations. Together with company voluntary arrangements, it was heralded in the 1980s as the start of the 'rescue culture'. This original administration regime (hereafter referred to as the 'old regime') was brought into effect by Part II of the Insolvency Act 1986. The old regime remains in force for certain types of companies: for example, water companies, railway companies and building societies (see s 249 of the Enterprise Act 2002). For other companies, indeed the vast majority of companies registered under the Companies Act, the old regime is replaced, following the Enterprise Act 2002, by a new Sch B1 to the Insolvency Act 1986 (hereafter referred to as the 'new regime'). It is the new regime which is set to replace administrative receivership as the most common remedy for debenture holders.

Initially, the reason why the Cork Report recommended the introduction of administration was to fill a gap. It was recognised that a company's business could be saved by the company entering administrative receivership. Even if the company was eventually wound up, the advantage of the receiver being appointed often led to the business being restructured and sold on as a going concern. The gap that was identified was that it is not always the case that a company borrows from only one secured lender. In such circumstances, there will be no single debenture holder with the power to appoint an administrative receiver. The Cork Report recommended that such companies should still be able to take advantage of the appointment of a specialist insolvency practitioner, who could work either to save the company or its business or to ensure the company's assets were realised in the most beneficial manner. This was essentially the purpose of the old regime (see s 8, IA 1986 for the purposes for which an administration order may be made under the old regime). The primary purpose under the new regime is to attempt to rescue the company.

The really innovative characteristic of administration under both regimes is that it creates a moratorium on actions against the company. During administration, creditors' rights are frozen. Creditors cannot enforce their legal rights against the company without leave of the court. This temporary freedom from creditor harassment is designed to allow the administrator some breathing space within which he/she can put a proposal to the creditors to attempt to rescue the company or achieve some other beneficial realisation of the company assets.

Under the old regime, the administrator is appointed by the court. This process is expensive and time consuming. Under the new regime, although court appointment is still possible, nearly all administrators are appointed out of court. Administration has taken over from administrative receivership as the only option open to a debenture holder whose debenture was created after 15 September 2003.

The main changes made to administration by the new regime cover the appointment of the administrator, the purpose of the administration and the termination of the administration. Much of the old regime remains largely intact in the new regime. Such matters as the moratorium on actions and the duties owed by administrators remain largely as before. A reader with an interest in the old regime is directed to Part II of the Insolvency Act 1986. The text now concentrates on the new regime.

Appointment of administrators

A company enters administration when an administrator is appointed. A company cannot usually enter administration if it is already in administration, is in liquidation or is subject to an effective administrative receivership. An administrator may be appointed in one of three ways:

(1) By the holder of a 'qualifying floating charge'

Under para 14 of Sch B1 to the Insolvency Act 1986, the holder of a qualifying floating charge may appoint an administrator without the involvement of the court. A floating charge is qualifying for these purposes if, either on its own or together with other securities, it relates to the whole or substantially the whole of the company's property (a standard form floating charge). The power to appoint an administrator therefore covers debentures executed both before and after 15 September 2003. A debenture holder may appoint the administrator out of court once the charge has become enforceable under its own terms. If there is another floating charge holder whose debenture was executed first in time (or has priority due to some agreement between the parties), the second floating charge holder must give the prior charge holder at least two business days' notice of an intention to appoint an administrator. The prior floating charge holder may decide to appoint its own administrator instead.

A person who appoints an administrator under para 14 must file, *inter alia*, a notice of appointment at the court. The notice will contain the consent of the administrator to act and a statement that the floating charge has become enforceable. The appointment takes effect from the date of the filing of the notice of appointment: see *Fliptex Ltd* v *Hogg* [2004] EWHC 1280.

(2) By the company or its directors

Under para 22 of Sch B1, either the company (by members' resolution in general meeting) or the directors (including an appointment by a majority of directors) may appoint an administrator without the involvement of the court. However, restrictions are placed upon this power to appoint. For example, no appointment is possible if the company had been in administration during the past 12 months before the intended (new) appointment where the (previous) appointment of the administrator had been made by the company or its directors.

At least five business days' notice of any proposed appointment must be given to any debenture holder who may be entitled to appoint an administrative receiver or administrator. The debenture holder may decide to appoint its own administrative receiver or administrator during this period. Such an appointment has the effect of vetoing the proposed appointment by the company or its directors. Primacy is given to the interests of the secured creditor. Once the five days' notice has expired the appointment may be made. The appointor must file notice of appointment at the court. The appointment takes effect when all the paperwork has been filed at court.

(3) By the court

It is unlikely that many applications for administration orders will be made under the new regime. The parties who can apply for such an order are essentially the company, its directors or any of its creditors (see Sch B1, para 12). Attempts by unsecured creditors to obtain an administration order are unlikely to meet with any great success as they are unlikely to know enough about the company's business to be able to draft an extensive and full application (see e.g. *Re Colt Telecom Group plc (No 2)* [2003] BPIR 324, a case decided under the old regime; and *Re Simco Digital UK Ltd* [2004] 1 BCLC 541, decided under the new regime). Notice of any application has to be served on any person with the power to appoint an administrator or administrative receiver. A debenture holder with security over the whole of the company's undertaking can effectively veto the application by appointing its own administrator or administrative receiver.

Effect of appointment

As soon as an administrator is appointed, he/she must notify the company, its creditors and the Registrar of Companies of the appointment and publish a notice of appointment in the prescribed manner. Whilst in administration, any business document of the company must state the name of the administrator and that the affairs of the company are being managed by the administrator. The administrator must request a statement of affairs from the company's officers.

Purpose of administration

Once an administrator is appointed he/she must act with the purpose of:

- rescuing the company as a going concern; or
- achieving a better result for the company's creditors as a whole than would be likely if the company were wound up (without first being in administration); or

- realising enough property in order to make a distribution to one or more secured or preferential creditors.

The aforementioned purposes are listed in order of primacy. Only if the administrator thinks that the first purpose is not reasonably practicable can he/she move to consider the second purpose and so on to the final purpose. As practice develops under the new regime, it is probable that the first purpose will rarely be achieved and that a sale of the business as a going concern under the second purpose becomes the most commonly adopted purpose.

Moratorium on actions

In order to assist the administrator in achieving the purpose of the administration, a company in administration is effectively protected by a moratorium against the enforcement of actions by creditors. This moratorium was present under the old regime and has survived into the new regime with only a very slight rewording. It is submitted that the substance of the moratorium has not changed and therefore case law under the old regime will still be relevant under the new regime. Without the benefit of the moratorium, the whole purpose of the administration may be frustrated. For example, without the moratorium, suppliers of goods could repossess under valid retention of title clauses. Judgment creditors could enforce their judgments by writs of fifa. Landlords could distrain for unpaid rent (seize goods on the tenanted premises without the need for a court order and sell the assets to pay the rent). If these things occurred whilst the administrator was trying to rescue the company or straighten out its business, it could clearly prevent the administration being effective.

Once in administration, the moratorium prevents any resolution to wind up the company from being passed and no winding up order may be made. In addition, the following actions are precluded without either leave of the court or the permission of the administrator:

- No step may be taken to enforce any security over the company's property. The term 'security' is defined widely to mean 'any mortgage, charge, lien or other security' (s 248, IA 1986). Section 436 of the Insolvency Act 1986 defines 'property' to include 'money, goods, things in action, land and every description of property wherever situated and also obligations and every description of interest, whether present or future, vested or contingent, arising out of, or incidental to, property'. However, for an unusual case where the court gave leave for the appointment of a receiver notwithstanding administration, see *Sinai Securities Ltd v Hooper* [2004] 2 BCLC 575.

- No step may be taken to repossess goods in the company's possession under a hire purchase agreement. For these purposes, 'hire purchase agreement' includes conditional sale agreements, chattel leasing agreements and retention of title agreements. For an example of how this operated in attempts to repossess computers held under hire purchase and leasing agreements, see the leading case of *Re Atlantic Computer Systems plc* [1992] Ch 505.

- A landlord may not exercise a right of forfeiture by peaceable re-entry in relation to tenanted premises.

- No legal process may be instituted or continued against the company. This includes any legal proceedings, execution (by judgment creditors) and distress (landlords' self-help remedy). This part of the moratorium has, for example, been held to prevent employees bringing actions in the employment tribunal (see *Re Divine Solutions (UK) Ltd* [2004] BCC 325).

Any creditor who wishes to enforce his/her rights during the administration must either persuade the administrator to permit enforcement (unlikely in most circumstances; however, by example, repossession of hire purchase machinery may be permitted where the administrator has no use for it) or obtain leave of the court. In deciding whether to allow a creditor to enforce rights against the company in administration the Court of Appeal in *Re Atlantic Computer Systems plc* [1992] Ch 505 laid down a number of guidelines, namely:

- If the enforcement of rights is unlikely to impede the purpose of the administration, the court would normally grant leave. In other cases, the court must undertake a balancing exercise.

- The interests of the applicant creditor must be balanced with the interests of other creditors. Due weight must be given to the applicant creditor's proprietary rights. If the owners of property have their property used to finance the administration but are not being paid, the court will usually give leave.

- If significant loss would be occasioned by the applicant creditor if leave was refused, this would tend to sway the balance in favour of granting leave.

In making any decision, the court will consider the company's financial state, its ability to make payments to creditors, the administrator's proposals, the likely effect of giving leave on those proposals, the duration of the administration and the conduct of the parties.

Administrators' proposals

An administrator's job is to put together a proposal in an attempt to satisfy one of the three statutory purposes of the administration. The administrator has eight weeks from appointment to prepare the proposal (this period may be extended by the court). A meeting of the company's unsecured creditors is called to consider the proposal within ten weeks of appointment (again this time period may be extended by the court). The proposal cannot affect the priority rights of secured or preferential creditors without their consent. If the administrator is proposing a rescue package for the company this may take the form of a company voluntary arrangement (discussed below).

Duties of administrators

An administrator is subject to various statutory duties. He/she must take control of the company's property and must manage the company in accordance with any proposal approved by the creditors. An administrator must act in the interests of the company's creditors as a whole.

A creditor or member of the company may bring an action against an administrator if it can be shown that the administrator is acting in a way which unfairly harms the interests of the creditor or member (either alone or in common with other creditors or members). This right is largely untested in the courts but appears to bear some resemblance to s 459 of the Companies Act 1985 (discussed in Chapter 24). In the case of *Re Charnley Davies Ltd* [1990] BCC 605, the court held that administrators owed a company the same duties owed by all professionals, namely to exhibit the standard of care one would expect from an ordinary skilled practitioner. If it can be shown that the administrator acted in breach of duty to the company by, for example, misapplying company property, an application may be brought against the administrator by, amongst others, a creditor of the company (see paras 74 and 75 of Sch B1 to the IA 1986).

In *Oldham* v *Kyrris* [2004] BCC 111, the Court of Appeal concluded that administrators owe no general duty of care to individual creditors. They do owe a duty to act in the best interests of creditors generally and this duty is similar to the duty that directors of a solvent company owe to its shareholders. If breached, a creditor may bring a form of representative action on behalf of all creditors.

Powers of administrators

An administrator acts as an agent of the company. The administrator has the power to do 'anything necessary or expedient for the management of the affairs, business and property of the company' (para 59, Sch B1, IA 1986). In addition to this very wide power, administrators have the same specific powers as administrative receivers as listed in Sch 1 to the Insolvency Act 1986. Additional powers are littered throughout Sch B1, such as the power to remove or appoint directors, call meetings of creditors or members and the power to apply to court for directions in connection with the administration. An administrator has the same powers as a liquidator to apply to the court to upset transactions at an undervalue (s 238, IA 1986), preferences (s 239, IA 1986), extortionate credit bargains (s 244, IA 1986) and floating charges (s 245, IA 1986) (ss 238 and 239 are discussed below; s 245 is discussed in Chapter 14). An administrator may dispose of assets subject to a floating charge and, with the consent of the court, dispose of assets subject to fixed charges or even hire purchase goods.

Frequently, the only realistic option for an administrator will be to attempt to sell the company's business quickly. Rescue may be out of the question. There may be a buyer present who will not wait. The nature of the business may be that its goods are perishable and continuing to trade for any length of time may be financially out of the question. If a quick sale is the best way forward, the administrator has a problem in that, if the sale goes ahead, it makes the drafting of proposals and calling of meetings of creditors rather redundant. After some judicial wavering, it is now possible for an administrator in this position to exercise professional judgment and to opt for a quick sale. In order to prevent allegations of negligence or breach of statutory duty an administrator should consider taking the following steps to protect himself/herself from personal liability (taken from Neuberger J's judgment in *Re T & D Industries plc* [2000] BCC 956 and approved under the new regime in *Re Transbus International Ltd* [2004] BCC 401):

- In normal circumstances a creditors' meeting should be held.

- Administrators may have to make urgent and important decisions; this is their job. Administrators cannot come to the court for guidance every time a difficult decision needs to be made. The court cannot be used as a 'sort of bomb shelter'.

- Administrators should not take unfair advantage of creditors. Some consultation with major creditors should be possible even where time is short.

- An application to the court may still be necessary, where, for example, the administrator is convinced the sale is essential but the creditors are not in agreement.

- If a court hearing is needed, it will usually need to be an *inter partes* hearing.

- If of sufficient importance and there is time, the court may be asked to call a creditors' meeting on short notice.

- In making a decision to sell the whole of the company's undertaking, the administrator must bear in mind that such a sale effectively renders a subsequent creditors' meeting meaningless.

Contractual liability of administrators

Similar rules apply to administration contracts as apply to those in administrative receivership, with one major difference, namely that an administrator is not made personally liable on any contractual liability of the company (see para 99 of Sch B1, IA 1986).

The administrator acts as agent of the company. This agency cannot be terminated by the company. The appointment does not, in itself, terminate any contracts with third parties although, as with receivership, some contracts will specify that a company entering administration will bring the contract to an end. An administrator may decide to continue existing contracts. If creditors are not paid out under such contracts, the creditors are prevented by the moratorium from enforcing their rights against the company without leave of the court. Having stated this, it is usual for an administrator to pay such creditors, at least for liabilities arising during the administration.

If new contracts are entered into by the company in administration, the administrator incurs no personal liability. Only the company is liable. However, creditors owed money under such contracts are entitled to what is sometimes called 'super priority' in that such debts are paid ahead even of the administrator's own remuneration and expenses.

In respect of employment contracts, as with administrative receiverships, much turns upon whether the contracts have been adopted by the administrator. If an employee is kept on for more than 14 days after the commencement of the administration, the contract of employment is deemed to be adopted. The employee is then entitled to be paid 'wages or salary' for the period worked after the contract has been adopted. The administrator is not personally liable to pay this amount but the employee is entitled to 'super priority', that is the employee will be paid this amount before the administrator can claim his/her fees and expenses. Employees may also be entitled to payment for work carried out prior to the administration, in part anyway, due to their claim as preferential creditors in the administration and may also have a statutory claim for redundancy under the Employment Rights Act 1996.

Ending administration

Under the new regime an administrator has the power to make distributions to secured and preferential creditors. An administrator can only make distributions to unsecured creditors with leave of the court or if the administrator thinks it is likely to assist in the achievement of the purpose of the administration. Such distributions must be made in order of priority under s 175 of the Insolvency Act 1986 (discussed in Chapter 14). The administrator's remuneration and expenses are charged upon and payable out of any property he/she had control over at the end of the administration and are to be paid out in priority to any floating charge holder.

An innovation of the new regime is that, following the completion of administration, the administrator may, by notice, convert the administration into a creditors' voluntary liquidation or by notice merely dissolve the company. This leads to a saving of fees and expenses. If, for example, distributions have been made by the administrator to secured and preferential creditors and no money is left, there is no point in going through the procedure to put the company into liquidation. It is more sensible for the administrator to send a notice to the Registrar of Companies informing him to dissolve the company. If there is money left to be distributed to unsecured creditors, the alternative under the new regime is to convert the administration into a creditors' voluntary liquidation with the administrator usually acting as liquidator. This saves time and money and the liquidator will not have to familiarise himself/herself with the company's background as he/she will have previously conducted the administration.

If the company has survived administration and has been successfully rescued, the administrator merely notifies the Registrar of Companies that the administration has finished and hands back control of the company to the directors (for details of termination of administration, see paras 76–86 of Sch B1, IA 1986).

COMPANY VOLUNTARY ARRANGEMENTS

When a company finds itself in financial difficulty its directors may attempt to re-finance its obligations or come to some other arrangement with the company's creditors. The arrangement may be formal or informal. The company may be forced into receivership, administration or liquidation. It may wish to go into a formal insolvency procedure. If there is time and the company is looking to restructure itself, a scheme of arrangement under s 425 of the Companies Act 1985 may be considered (for a recent discussion of this type of arrangement see *Re Waste Recycling Group plc* [2004] BCC 328). Depending on how dire its financial problems are, the company may also consider a company voluntary arrangement (hereafter 'CVA') under Part I of the Insolvency Act 1986.

The problem with negotiating with creditors in an informal way is that any deal agreed will not bind all the creditors. If one creditor decides to break ranks and take action against the company, the whole arrangement may come tumbling down. Getting all the company's creditors to agree to a deal will also be no mean feat. The Cork Report recognised that there was a need for the introduction of a simple procedure whereby the will of the majority of the creditors could be given effect, even where some creditors disagreed. This became, in 1986, the CVA (a similar form of procedure was introduced for individual debtors, called an individual voluntary arrangement ('IVA'); the case law decided in relation to CVAs is authoritative in the area of IVAs and vice versa).

Back in 1986, it was part of the plan that administration and CVAs would operate together. A company would have the benefit of the moratorium on actions and, during this period of protection, the administrator could draft a proposal for a CVA. It did not quite work out that way, as the old regime of administration became very expensive and time consuming. It was only really available to large companies with substantial assets; small and medium-sized companies were priced out of administration. This problem was recognised belatedly. The Insolvency Act 2000 created a procedure specifically for small companies considering a CVA to obtain a 28-day moratorium on creditor action to facilitate the CVA (introduced as Sch A1, IA 1986). Unfortunately, events rather overtook this initiative, as the 2000 Act's provisions only came into force shortly before the Enterprise Act 2002's new regime for administration. The consequence of this is that it is far easier and cheaper for a company considering a CVA to go first into administration (with the concomitant moratorium) than it would be to consider using the 2000 Act moratorium procedure. The 2000 Act procedure is dead in the water and will rarely, if ever, be used. It will not be mentioned further in this chapter.

A company in distress may put forward a proposal for a CVA itself or first go into administration and put forward the CVA from that protected environment. A CVA can take a variety of forms. It may be a composition of debts where the company promises to pay only a percentage of the debt owed: this is frequently referred to as a promise to pay, for example, 10p in the pound. The CVA may be in the form of a scheme of arrangement, which in this context means that the creditors will be paid in full but they will have to wait a certain period of time. A CVA may take the form of a debt equity swap where the creditor agrees to swap some or all of the debt owed for a shareholding in the company. The CVA may be a mixture of the above.

The exact legal nature of a CVA is not entirely clear. It is usually viewed as a form of statutory contract. It binds all the company's members and unsecured creditors and is supervised by a supervisor who usually holds CVA assets or money on trust for the creditors bound by the CVA. The courts tend to call it a contract, a statutory binding or a trust depending on the context (see e.g. *Johnson* v *Davies* [1998] 2 BCLC 252, *Re Arthur Rathbone Kitchens Ltd* [1998] BCC 450 and *Re Bradley-Hole* [1995] BCC 418). There would appear to be few practical consequences to this divergence in terminology.

The CVA may last for a short period of time or go on for years. It may be funded by the sale of company assets, by benevolent third party funders, or be based on monthly payments by the company from its trading profits. An insolvency practitioner will act as supervisor of the CVA to ensure adherence to its terms.

Procedure to approve a CVA

The procedure may be initiated either by the company's directors or, if the company is in administration (or liquidation), by the administrator (or liquidator – although it is possible for a company to enter a CVA from liquidation, this is a rare event). If the directors commence the procedure, they must approach an insolvency practitioner to act as 'nominee'. The Insolvency Act 1986 states that the directors will approach the nominee with a proposal for a CVA, but in practice the nominee will usually assist in the drafting of the proposal. The nominee will then report to the court whether the proposal has a reasonable prospect of being approved and implemented. The report to the court is a matter of record. There is no hearing. If the nominee's report is positive, the nominee will proceed to call meetings of members and creditors to consider the proposal. If the company is in administration or liquidation, the administrator or liquidator acts as nominee. No report to the court is made. The administrator or liquidator proceeds directly to calling meetings of members and creditors.

Approval of the CVA

The CVA becomes effective when it is approved. The proposal cannot affect the rights of secured or preferential creditors without their consent. Until the Crown lost its preferential creditor status under the Enterprise Act 2002, the Crown's preference and insistence on full payment was seen as a determinative factor in some proposed CVAs never being approved.

At the members' meeting, an ordinary resolution is needed to approve the CVA. Votes at the creditors' meeting are calculated according to the value of the creditors' unsecured debt. A creditor owed a debt for an unliquidated amount, such as a contingent creditor, may vote and will have the value of £1 placed upon the debt unless the nominee agrees to put a higher figure on the debt. The creditors' meeting must approve the proposal by a majority of more than 75 per cent. Providing the creditors approve the proposal, it binds the company even if the members have voted against it. The CVA is implemented with the nominee usually continuing to act as supervisor of the CVA. If the company was in administration, the administration will usually be terminated at this point, as the terms of the CVA will usually contain a provision continuing the block on creditors enforcing their rights. If the company was in liquidation, the winding up will usually be stayed by the court.

Once approved, the CVA takes effect as if made by the company at the creditors' meeting and binds every person who was entitled to vote at either meeting (whether or not present or represented at the meeting), or would have been entitled if he or she had received notice of the meeting, as if he or she were a party to the CVA. If approved, the CVA will therefore bind creditors with no notice of the meeting or creditors who were in fact unknown to exist at the time of the meeting. A disgruntled creditor or member has the right to apply to the court on the grounds that the CVA unfairly prejudices the interests of a creditor, member or contributory of the company or that there has been some irregularity at the meeting.

Duties owed by nominees/supervisors

Nominees and supervisors owe various statutory duties to appraise the initial proposal, call and hold meetings and supervise the CVA in accordance with the Insolvency Act 1986 and the terms of the CVA. Any breach of these statutory duties gives creditors a right to apply to the court. The court has wide powers, for example, to remove and replace a supervisor, to overturn a decision of the meetings and to regulate the supervision of the CVA generally (see ss 6 and 7, IA 1986). There is a general duty to exercise independent professional judgment (see e.g. *Re a Debtor (No 222 of 1990)* [1993] BCLC 233). Although the supervisor may be characterised as holding assets on trust for the creditors, the supervisor holds no private law duties to the creditors. No action for breach of trust, duty or contract is available against a supervisor. A supervisor cannot be sued for negligence because the courts view the nominee/supervisor as being under the control of the courts and, as the courts have ample power to control their respective activities, no private law action is needed (see *King* v *Anthony* [1998] 2 BCLC 517). This would seem a little strange, especially when receivers, administrators and liquidators may be sued in private law actions.

The nominee/supervisor does need to be careful though. Frequently, the nominee/supervisor may also be advising the client company, as well as acting in an official capacity. If negligent advice is given to the client in the capacity of adviser rather than as nominee/supervisor, a private law action will be available (see *Prosser* v *Castle Sanderson Solicitors* [2003] BCC 440).

Variation of a CVA

Commonly it is the case that, as circumstances change, the terms of a CVA may require some amendment. The company may need more time to pay, or less money than expected may have been realised by the sale of an asset. As a CVA is usually viewed as a form of contract, its terms cannot be changed unilaterally. Any attempt to vary its terms must either be under a specific variation clause contained within the CVA or be agreed to by all the persons bound: see e.g. *Raja* v *Rubin* [1999] BCC 579. In practice, a variation clause is invariably contained within a CVA stating that its terms may be changed if over 75 per cent of the unsecured creditors agree. Such a clause will be valid: see e.g. *Horrocks* v *Broome* [1999] BPIR 66.

Termination of a CVA

A CVA may be a success or a failure. It may run its course and the company may pay off all its debts and thereafter return to profitable trading. This is the intention of the legislation, albeit that there is not always such a happy ending. A company may run up substantial post-CVA debts with new creditors who may petition for the company's winding up. The company may not make the profits it expected. The supervisor or a creditor may petition for the company's winding up on the basis that the CVA has been breached. Frequently, a company in CVA enters liquidation. If this occurs, one important issue is what happens to assets being held by the supervisor. Are they held on trust for the CVA creditors or must they be handed over to the liquidator for the benefit of all the company's creditors? The answers to such questions may be taken from the decision of the Court of Appeal in *Re N T Gallagher & Sons Ltd* [2002] BCLC 133, namely:

- Where a CVA provides for moneys or assets to be paid to CVA creditors, this will create a trust of those moneys or assets for those creditors.
- The effect of the liquidation of the company on a trust created by the CVA will depend upon the terms of the CVA.
- If the CVA provides what is to happen on liquidation, or other failure of the CVA, effect must be given to it.
- If the CVA does not so provide, the trust will continue notwithstanding the liquidation or failure.
- The CVA creditors can prove in the liquidation for so much of their debt as remains after payment of what has been recovered under the trust.

Once the final distributions are made by the supervisor, the CVA comes to an end. The supervisor gives notice to the Registrar of Companies, the court, the creditors and the members that it has either been fully implemented or that it has terminated prematurely (whichever is the case).

LIQUIDATION

Liquidation is the process by which a company ceases to exist. If a company is insolvent either in the 'balance sheet' sense, that is, its liabilities outweigh its assets (see s 123(2), IA 1986), or in the 'cash flow' sense, that is, where the company is unable to pay its debts as they fall due (see s 123(1), IA 1986), liquidation may result. Although a company may have entered receivership or administration and these procedures were deemed a success, the endplay may be that the company is still put into liquidation. The fall-back position for all insolvent companies is to kill the company off, by winding up its assets and then formally having the company dissolved.

The main purposes of the liquidation of an insolvent company are:

- to provide for the equitable and fair distribution of the assets of the company amongst its creditors;
- to put an end to the continued existence of hopelessly insolvent companies;
- to allow for the investigation of the company's affairs, with particular regard being paid to the events leading to the company's failure. Such investigation may lead to civil liability of the company's directors (e.g. for breach of fiduciary duty or wrongful trading) or to criminal liability (e.g. fraudulent trading) or to quasi-criminal proceedings under the Company Directors Disqualification Act 1986.

There are two types of winding up, namely voluntary and compulsory. Although the vast majority of liquidations occur following a company's insolvency, voluntary and compulsory windings up are equally applicable to solvent companies. The procedure for placing a company into compulsory winding up (or winding up by the court: see generally ss 122–130, IA 1986) is essentially the same whether the company is solvent or insolvent. It will begin with a winding up petition to the court.

With voluntary windings up (which occur without any court involvement), there is a marked difference in the procedure for the winding up of a solvent company (referred to as a 'members' voluntary winding up': see generally ss 90–96 and ss 107–116, IA 1986) and an insolvent winding up (referred to as a 'creditors' voluntary winding up': see generally ss 97–116, IA 1986).

The main differences between the various types of liquidation relate to the procedure up to and including the appointment of the liquidator. The duties owed by the liquidator and the process of liquidation after appointment are broadly the same for both types of liquidation. All liquidators are required to be licensed insolvency practitioners.

Voluntary winding up

As the name suggests, voluntary liquidation is where the company voluntarily decides to wind itself up. It is usually a quicker and cheaper process than compulsory winding up, as the court and the Official Receiver are not involved. The procedure begins with the company in general meeting passing a resolution (a special or extraordinary resolution, i.e. 75 per cent majority of the members) to wind up the company (see s 84, IA 1986). If the company is insolvent the liquidation will be called a 'creditors' voluntary liquidation'. In a creditors' voluntary liquidation, the policy of the Insolvency Act 1986 is to permit the creditors' interests to be treated as paramount. In effect, the creditors exercise a degree of control over the progress of the liquidation. As there will be no money left in the company and therefore there will be no capital to return to members, the members will have no financial interest in the liquidation. The creditors have a clear interest in how the liquidation progresses. Depending on how it proceeds, they may see more or less of the money owed to them. Following the members' meeting where the resolution to wind up is passed, a creditors' meeting will be held. Although a liquidator may have been appointed at the members' meeting (by an ordinary resolution), the creditors' meeting has the power to overrule that appointment; that is, the creditors may choose their own liquidator (voting at the creditors' meeting is based upon the amount of unsecured debt owed to each creditor). The creditors may also decide to form a liquidation committee which has various powers including fixing the remuneration of the liquidator and the right to inspect financial records kept by the liquidator (see s 101, IA 1986).

If, on the other hand, the company is solvent, the liquidation will be a 'members' voluntary liquidation'. Here the members effectively control the winding up process. The creditors have no say in how the winding up progresses as they will in any case be paid in full. The interests of the members are paramount because, depending upon how efficiently the company's assets are realised, they stand to receive a larger return on their capital investment. Accordingly, there is no meeting of creditors in a members' voluntary winding up (unless the liquidator becomes aware that the company is in fact insolvent, in which case the liquidator will call a meeting of creditors and the liquidation will thereafter progress as a creditors' voluntary liquidation).

In the period of five weeks prior to the general meeting that is held to pass the resolution in a members' voluntary liquidation, the directors of the company are required to make a statutory declaration of solvency (see s 89, IA 1986). This declaration must state that the directors have made a full enquiry into the affairs of the company and, having done so, have formed the opinion that the company will be able to pay its debts in full within a stated period of time of not more than 12 months from the date of the resolution. The directors will commit a criminal offence if, having made the statutory declaration of solvency, the company is unable to pay its debts within the specified period of time. Negligence will suffice to establish the directors' culpability and the commission of this offence may only be averted if the directors can overturn a statutory presumption of culpability, that is, the burden of proof is on the directors to establish that they were not negligent in the making of the statement.

Compulsory winding up

Section 122 of the Insolvency Act 1986 lists the grounds upon which a winding up petition may be made. Section 124 lists the persons eligible to present a petition. The most common type of petition is one brought by a creditor on the ground that the company is unable to pay its debts. Under s 123 this may be proved by a creditor in a number of ways:

- if a creditor who is owed a debt exceeding £750 and has served a statutory demand on the company requiring payment within three weeks, has not received payment or some other form of reasonable satisfaction within that time;
- if the creditor is a judgment creditor and has issued execution on the judgment but has had the execution returned wholly or partly unsatisfied;
- if it is proved to the satisfaction of the court either that the company is unable to pay its debts as they fall due or that the value of the company's assets is less than the amount of its liabilities, taking into account its contingent and prospective liabilities.

The statutory demand procedure is most commonly used in practice and, if the demand is correctly served and the company has no genuine grounds to dispute the debt (the leading case on which is *Mann* v *Goldstein* [1968] 1 WLR 1091), the court will usually make the winding up order.

Once a winding up order is made, the Official Receiver (an employee of the Department of Trade and Industry) will take control of the company's assets. The Official Receiver will investigate the reasons for the company's liquidation. If there are sufficient assets, the Official Receiver will call meetings of members and creditors to appoint a private sector liquidator (if there is any dispute the creditors' candidate is appointed). If the company is effectively an empty shell with few, if any, assets, there will be no meetings and the Official Receiver will continue to act as liquidator.

General effect of a winding up

Initially, the corporate personality of the company remains unaffected by its being placed in liquidation. The affairs of the company are wound up by the liquidator who takes over the powers of management of the company. The liquidator acts as agent of the company. One consequence of entering liquidation is that the company's business may no longer be carried on except for the limited purpose of the winding up: see e.g. s 87, IA 1986; *Re Great Eastern Electric Co Ltd* [1941] 1 Ch 241; and Sch 4, IA 1986. To safeguard the company's goodwill, it may prove necessary to continue the business for a short period, in the hope that the business may be purchased as a going concern. Once in liquidation, all business letters, invoices and orders for goods issued by the company must contain a statement that the company is in winding up.

Winding up severely affects the company's powers to deal with its assets. Under s 127 of the Insolvency Act 1986 (s 88, IA 1986, a more limited provision, applies to voluntary windings up) any disposition of property of a company in compulsory winding up, made after the commencement of the winding up, will be void (unless the court orders otherwise). This effectively avoids any transfer of money or property made by the company after the presentation of the petition. The purpose of the section is to prevent the improper disposal of companies' assets by the directors once a petition has been served. Section 127 has been the subject of a significant amount of case law, especially in the area of payments out of a company's bank account (see e.g. *Re Gray's Inn Construction Co Ltd* [1980] 1 WLR 711 and *Bank of Ireland* v *Hollicourt (Contracts) Ltd (in liq)* [2000] 1 WLR 895).

Although winding up does not, in itself, terminate contracts with outsiders, it will usually result in the contract being frustrated or terminated by the company's inability to continue its terms. The contract may specifically deal with what is to happen upon the company's winding up. Any party who suffers loss due to the termination of the contract will be able to prove in the liquidation, usually as an unsecured creditor (see e.g. *Ogdens Ltd* v *Nelson* [1905] AC 109).

Winding up will usually terminate all contracts of employment. In a compulsory winding up, the publication of the winding up order operates as a notice to dismiss all employees: see e.g. *Re General Rolling Stock Co* (1866) 1 Eq 346. The position is not so clear cut in voluntary liquidations: see e.g. *Midland Counties Bank* v *Attwood* [1905] 1 Ch 357 and *Fowler* v *Commercial Timber Co Ltd* [1930] 2 KB 1.

When a winding up order is made, all proceedings and actions against the company are automatically stayed (s 130, IA 1986). In a voluntary winding up, the liquidator may apply to the court to exercise its power to stay actions and proceedings (s 112, IA 1986). The purpose of these provisions is to ensure a fair distribution of the company's assets amongst its creditors and to prevent some creditors jumping the queue.

Duties of liquidators

As with the agencies of receivers and administrators, the agency of the liquidator is not a normal type of agency. The liquidator controls the principal's assets and cannot usually be dismissed by the principal. The liquidator's fiduciary duties to the company (principal) are limited by overriding statutory duties to get in the company's assets, realise them and to pay the proceeds out to the company's creditors. The liquidator is not usually liable on any contracts entered into as agent of the company: see e.g. *Stead Hazel & Co* v *Cooper* [1933] 1 KB 840.

As a fiduciary officer, the liquidator must act honestly and exercise his/her powers *bona fide* for the purpose for which they are conferred: see e.g. *Ayerst* v *C & K*

(Construction) Ltd [1976] AC 167. The liquidator's personal interest must not conflict with his/her duty to the company: see e.g. *Silkstone Coal Co v Edey* [1900] 1 Ch 167. A liquidator must act in a totally impartial way as between the persons interested in the company's property and those interested in the company's liabilities: see e.g. *Re Lubin, Rosen & Associates Ltd* [1975] 1 WLR 122.

A liquidator owes a duty of skill and care and must display a level of competence reasonably expected of a well-paid professional: see e.g. *Re Windsor Steam Coal Co* [1929] Ch 151. An action in negligence may lead to the liquidator being liable in damages and he/she may lose all or part of his/her claim to be remunerated: see e.g. *Re Silver Valley Mines* (1882) 21 ChD 381.

A number of more specific duties are owed under the Insolvency Act 1986. Notice of a liquidator's appointment must be filed with, amongst others, the Registrar of Companies. A liquidator must settle a list of contributories. This refers to a list of company members who are liable to contribute in the winding up, e.g. if they have only partly paid-up shares. In a compulsory liquidation, the Official Receiver must provide creditors and contributories with a statement of affairs of the company and a report on the statement. Importantly, a liquidator must take custody or control of all company property (s 144, IA 1986) and ensure it is protected or preserved. If assets are missing, an investigation will need to be carried out. To realise certain assets or to maximise the assets available to the company's creditors, the liquidator may have to commence legal proceedings. An investigation of how and why the company failed must be carried out to assist the liquidator in locating assets of the company and identifying any action available to the liquidator. The investigation may also lead to a report being prepared which may be used in subsequent disqualification proceedings against unfit directors.

Crucially, the liquidator is under a duty to realise the assets. The liquidator has a power to sell or otherwise dispose of all or any part of the company's property (para 6 of Sch 4, IA 1986). There is also a general obligation to pay all liabilities (as far as is possible). Frequently, assets subject to fixed charges will have been enforced prior to the liquidator taking office. Any distribution to creditors will be subject to the statutory priority order (discussed in Chapter 14).

Powers of liquidators

The powers enjoyed by liquidators in compulsory and creditors' voluntary liquidations are essentially the same, although different provisions apply to each form of winding up. Most powers can be found in Sch 4 to the Insolvency Act 1986. Some of these powers can only be exercised with the approval of the court or the liquidation committee. Liquidators are given powers to effect compromises, to defend or commence proceedings, to sell company assets, to appoint agents (but not to delegate the exercise of any discretion), to call meetings of members or creditors, to apply to the court for directions and to do all such things as are necessary for winding up the affairs of the company and distributing its property.

The liquidator may take action against directors for breach of duty under s 212 of the Insolvency Act 1986 (discussed in Chapter 14). Importantly, the following proceedings under the Insolvency Act 1986, cannot, *inter alia*, be commenced by the liquidator without the sanction of the court or liquidation committee:

- s 213 action for fraudulent trading (discussed in Chapter 8);
- s 214 action for wrongful trading (discussed in Chapter 18);
- s 238 action to attack a transaction at an undervalue;
- s 239 action to avoid a preference.

(Reference could also usefully be made to liquidators' powers under s 178 (to disclaim onerous property), s 244 (to attack extortionate credit bargains), s 245 (avoidance of floating charges: see Chapter 14) and s 423 (to avoid transactions designed to defraud creditors).)

Transactions at an undervalue

Under s 238 of the Insolvency Act 1986, a court may make any order adjusting a transaction at an undervalue. A liquidator or an administrator has the power to apply to the court for an order. The office holder must establish that the transaction in question was entered into during the two years preceding the onset of insolvency (i.e. the date the company entered liquidation or administration). At the time the transaction was entered into, the company must have been unable to pay its debts or became unable to pay its debts as a result of entering into the transaction. If the transaction is in favour of a person connected to the company, there is a rebuttable presumption that the company was unable to pay its debts at the time. The meaning of 'connected person' is defined in s 249 and includes, for example, directors and their spouses.

A transaction is at an undervalue where the company makes a gift or enters into a transaction where the value of the consideration provided by the company, in money or money's worth, is significantly less than the value of the consideration received by the company. In *Re MC Bacon* [1990] BCLC 324, it is explained that, for a claim to be successful, the liquidator must establish in monetary terms what the value of the consideration was, passing to and from the company. If it can be shown, for example, that the company has paid £20,000 for an asset, worth at the time only £10,000, this would appear to satisfy the test that the company has received significantly less consideration than it provided.

Transactions may take many forms, and the more complex the details the more difficult it may be to establish the value of the consideration in monetary terms. If the value of a transaction is speculative, then the party who relies upon the consideration must establish the value: see the decision of the House of Lords in *Phillips* v *Brewin Dolphin Bell Lawrie Ltd* [2001] 1 WLR 143. In assessing whether the consideration received is significantly less than that provided, the court must form a view as to what the value of the consideration would have been in the open market. This gives the 'correct valuation' (see *National Westminster Bank plc* v *Jones* [2001] 1 BCLC 98 – a case decided under s 423, IA 1986 but the reasoning of which applies equally to s 238). Following the valuation of the consideration, the court will assess, in percentage or proportionate terms, how much less is the value of the consideration transferred than that received. As yet, the courts have not given any clear indication of how much the discrepancy has to be to constitute 'significantly less'.

The substantive law under s 238 has proven difficult. The liquidator may have difficulty in establishing the open market value of the assets involved. It may be difficult to prove that the company was insolvent at the time of the transaction. The presumption of insolvency against a connected person is useful in this context but does inhibit actions against company outsiders. It is a defence to a s 238 action to show that the company entered into the transaction in good faith, for the purpose of carrying on its business, and that when entering into the transaction there were reasonable grounds to believe that the transaction would benefit the company. If the company is experiencing extreme cash flow problems, it is perhaps arguable that a sale of assets, even if at a very low price, would indeed benefit the company.

If the court decides that a transaction falls within s 238, it may make such order as it deems fit to restore the position to what it would have been if the transaction had not been entered into. Although the court has a wide discretion, it will usually order that the transaction be, in effect, rescinded. Any order made by the court must not prejudice any interest in property acquired by a third party from a person who is not the company, providing the third party acquires the interest in good faith and for value.

Preferences

To ensure that creditors are all treated equally in the distribution of a company's assets, s 239 allows an administrator or liquidator to apply to the court to avoid a preference. A preference is some action by the company which, in the event of the company entering insolvent liquidation or administration, has the effect of putting a creditor of the company into a better position than he or she would otherwise be in. As with s 238, where the court establishes a preference it may make any order to restore the position to what it would have been if no preference had been given. Any security which constitutes a preference under s 239 will usually be avoided by the court.

Liquidation and administration are designed to be collective procedures, whereby duties are owed to all creditors to ensure an equal distribution of the company's assets. It would offend this basic *pari passu* principle if, for example, one creditor was given the benefit of a floating charge just prior to the company entering insolvent liquidation. The office holder must prove that the transaction in question was entered into by the company, within the period of six months prior to the onset of insolvency (date of the administration or liquidation) or, if the transaction is in favour of a person connected to the company, the period is extended to two years prior to the insolvency. The other party to the transaction (the person being preferred) must be one of the company's creditors or a surety or guarantor of the company's debts.

It must be shown that the company was 'influenced by a desire' to prefer the other party. It must also be established that the company was unable to pay its debts, at the time of, or as a result of, the transaction. The office holder does not have the benefit of a presumption of insolvency if the preference is in favour of a person connected to the company. Instead, there is a presumption, if the transaction is in favour of a connected person, that the company was influenced by the requisite desire to prefer. It must be noted that it is not always straightforward to establish that a company was insolvent at the time of the preference because companies that are struggling do not always keep complete and accurate financial records of their dealings.

In order to establish whether a creditor has been preferred, the court will need to compare the position the creditor would have been in, if the alleged preference had not taken place, with the creditor's ultimate position. If the preference has the effect of disturbing the statutory order of priorities as regards payments in an insolvency, then, *prima facie*, the creditor will have been preferred. One of the main problems faced by office holders under s 239 is proving that the company was influenced by a desire to prefer the creditor. The leading case on this issue is *Re MC Bacon* [1990] BCLC 324. It is clear from this case that the word 'desire' is to be construed subjectively, so that it must be shown that the company positively wished to prefer the creditor in question. Establishing what the mind of an artificial creation such as a company is thinking is notoriously difficult: see e.g. *Re Transworld Trading Ltd* [1999] BPIR 628. Although the requisite desire may be inferred from the facts of the case, the desire must have influenced the decision to prefer. There must be a connection between the desire and entering into the transaction. The desire need not be the only or main motivation for the decision but it must have been influential. The desire may have been only one of several factors. If a company is put under pressure by a lender to provide, for example, some security for existing indebtedness, the decision to provide the security will not usually satisfy the requirement of desire. If the desire is to keep the company's business going, and a necessary by-product of that desire is to put the lender in a preferred position, that is not a preference because such a decision is not influenced by a desire to prefer the lender; rather, it is influenced by a desire to keep the company going. Such commercial pressure will therefore prevent any claim by an office holder that the company's actions constitute a preference (by analogy, see the bankruptcy case of *Rooney v Das* [1999] BPIR 404).

Therefore, proving that a transaction falls within s 239 is a difficult proposition. Proving the company was insolvent at the time of the transaction and establishing what a company is thinking is far from straightforward. Further, in the absence of express admissions by the company's directors, proving the requisite subjective motive of the company will be particularly difficult. Indeed, unless the preference is in favour of a person connected to the company – see e.g. *Re DKG Contractors Ltd* [1990] BCC 903 and *Wills v Corfe Joinery Ltd* [1997] BCC 511 – there is little chance of proving a preference. If the preferred creditor can point to some commercial pressure placed upon the company forcing it to enter the transaction in question, the s 239 action will usually fail (for rare exceptions see *Re Living Images Ltd* [1996] BCC 112 and *Re Agriplant Services Ltd* [1997] BCC 842).

Problems facing liquidators in funding litigation

Until recently, a liquidator considering taking any action – for example, to attack a transaction at an undervalue or a preference – had to take a significant personal risk.

Due to the decision of *Re MC Bacon Ltd (No 2)* [1991] Ch 127, it was until recently the case that the costs of any failed office holder actions (such as under s 214, s 238 or s 239) taken by a liquidator could not be claimed as an expense of the liquidation. The case turned upon an interpretation of Insolvency Rule 4.218(1)(a). The consequence of this was that, if the liquidator brought an office holder action (i.e. actions which vest in the liquidator personally as opposed to the company itself such as for breach of fiduciary duty) and lost, the liquidator would have to bear his/her own costs and the costs of the other party out of his/her own money. Without the benefit of an indemnity from the company's creditors or some other form of funding in place, it is no surprise that liquidators have been reluctant to bring office holder actions. The costs implications have been a significant factor in few such actions reaching the courts. This position has now been remedied by a new Insolvency Rule 4.218(1)(a) (in force 1 January 2003), which permits the costs of even failed litigation to be claimed as a legitimate expense of the liquidation. However, there still remains the problem that the company may not have any assets from which the liquidator may claim the costs of the action: see *Buchler* v *Talbot (Re Leyland Daf)* [2004] 2 AC 298 (discussed further in Chapter 14).

Dissolution

A company continues in liquidation until it is dissolved. Dissolution is the final act in the life of the company and will constitute the final act to complete the liquidation. In a compulsory liquidation, dissolution occurs automatically at the end of a three-month period following the registration by the Registrar of Companies of a receipt to the effect that a private liquidator has held a final meeting of creditors or, in the case of the Official Receiver, that the winding up is complete. In a creditors' voluntary liquidation, dissolution takes place automatically three months after the Registrar of Companies registers the fact that he/she has received the liquidator's final account and return stating that a final meeting has been held.

INTERACTION BETWEEN THE DIFFERENT INSOLVENCY PROCEDURES

Administrative receivership and administration

These two procedures are mutually exclusive. A company can be in either administrative receivership or administration; it cannot enter both at the same time, and it would be almost impossible to conceive of a scenario whereby a company may enter these two procedures sequentially.

Administrative receivership to liquidation

It is very common for a company to enter administrative receivership and at the same time, or shortly thereafter, to enter liquidation. It is also possible, but less common, for a company to enter into liquidation and for an administrative receiver to be appointed during the liquidation. One of the main problems that has occurred in recent times is how the fees and expenses of the respective office holders and the respective preferential creditors are to be paid. For many years following *Re Barleycorn Enterprises* [1970] Ch 465, it was assumed that, if an administrative receiver was appointed and the company entered liquidation during the same period, prior to the floating charge holder being paid out in the receivership, the fees and expenses of the liquidator and the liquidation preferential creditors would be paid out first. This is no longer the case following the House of Lords' decision in *Buchler* v *Talbot (Re Leyland Daf)* [2004] 2 AC 298. As the law now stands, the liquidator and his/her preferential creditors will not get paid from the realised assets, ahead of a floating charge holder. This has enormous implications for dealing with the effective winding up of a company crippled by an administrative receivership which has limited if no assets left to finance a liquidation. It is a matter which may require legislative intervention.

Administration to liquidation

A company cannot be in administration and liquidation at the same time. This is largely the reason why the *Buchler* case has no impact outside the scenario where companies go into administrative receivership and liquidation. The costs and fees of the administration are paid out ahead of any floating charge. When the administration ends, the company may have been successfully rehabilitated. If the company cannot continue to trade, if it has sufficient assets to finance payments to unsecured creditors, the administration may be converted into a creditors' voluntary liquidation and the liquidator's costs will be paid. If there is no money left to pay out to unsecured creditors, the administration may proceed straight to dissolution.

Administration to CVA

It would be most strange for a company to go from administrative receivership into a CVA. It is possible but also rare for a company to go from liquidation into a CVA. The Insolvency Act 1986 is designed to encourage a distressed company to enter administration and to take advantage of the subsequent moratorium on actions to allow it to go into a CVA, usually with the former administrator acting as supervisor of the CVA.

The future

The Enterprise Act 2002 has had and will continue to have a major impact on how insolvent companies are dealt with in the future. Administrative receivership is gradually being phased out and is set to be replaced by administration. Problems created by decisions such as *Buchler* look set to accelerate the adoption by major institutional lenders of the administration procedure. The benefits of, *inter alia*, the administration moratorium, the collective nature of administration and the likely costs savings of companies going from administration to liquidation or dissolution may lead to administration becoming a single gateway for most financially distressed companies.

Suggested further reading

Bailey *Voluntary Arrangements* (LexisNexis/Butterworths, 2003)

Finch *Corporate Insolvency Law: Perspectives and Principles* (Cambridge, 2002)

Fletcher *The Law of Insolvency* (3rd edn) (Sweet & Maxwell, 2002)

Goode *Principles of Corporate Insolvency Law* (2nd edn) (Sweet & Maxwell, 1997)

Keay *McPherson's Law of Company Liquidation* (Sweet & Maxwell, 2001)

Keay and Walton *Insolvency Law: Corporate and Personal* (Pearson, 2003)

Lightman and Moss *The Law of Receivers and Administrators of Companies* (3rd edn) (Sweet & Maxwell, 2000)

Sealy and Milman *Annotated Guide to the Insolvency Legislation* (7th edn, 2nd Rev) (Sweet & Maxwell, 2004)

16

DIRECTORS AND THE MANAGEMENT
OF A COMPANY

INTRODUCTION

This chapter is the first of seven chapters to examine the legal characteristics, powers and responsibilities associated with the management of a company. The management functions of a company are predominantly conferred on company directors and other officers, although shareholders are afforded some limited powers. This chapter incorporates an analysis of the different types of company officer, the constitution and characteristics of a company's board of directors, issues relating to directors' remuneration, directors' service contracts and the methods by which directors may be removed from office.

COMPANY DIRECTORS

The Companies Act 1985 provides little guidance in relation to identifying the managerial characteristics associated with the office of a director. Section 741(1) of the Companies Act 1985 provides the only reference, albeit negligible, to the identity of the office. The section states that the term 'director' includes:

'Any person occupying the position of director, by whatever name called.'

This rather scant definition permits a person to be classified as a director in circumstances where that person is formally appointed to hold office (a *de jure* director) or in a situation where a person absent of any formal appointment to hold office performs tasks and duties ordinarily associated with the office of a director (a *de facto* director).

The appointment of a de jure *director*

In accordance with the terms of a company's articles, shareholders, entitled to attend and vote at general meetings, are ultimately responsible for sanctioning the appointment of a company's *de jure* directors. A *de jure* director may in effect be appointed as an executive director, or a non-executive director. Unless a company's articles provide otherwise, a director's appointment will be approved by the passing of an ordinary resolution. Section 282 of the Companies Act 1985 provides that a public company registered on or after 1 November 1929 must have at least two directors, whereas a private company, whenever registered, need only have one director. A director is not required to be a natural person, therefore any legal entity – for example, a local authority, a limited liability partnership or a company – may be the director of another company.

However, it should be noted that, in accordance with the Government's White Paper, 'Modernising Company Law' (2002), it is proposed that future legislation will provide a prohibition against the appointment of corporate directors (and one would assume the appointment of any other non-human entity). Indeed, in the subsequent White Paper, 'Company Law Reform' (2005), it is provided (clause B57) that a company must have at least one director who is a natural person. This measure, which is commonplace in most other countries, is to be welcomed in so far as the imposition of duties, responsibilities and regulations attached to the office of a director cannot be performed other than through individuals. Although at present it may be possible to classify individuals who control the functions of the corporate director as either *de facto* or shadow directors (discussed below), this may not always be the case. A corporate director may mask and hide those individuals who are impliedly responsible for implementing the functions associated with holding office to the extent that such persons may evade responsibility and potential liability by contending that any duty or obligation is solely vested in the corporate director.

Following a director's appointment, details of the director's name, nationality, occupation and address, together with details of any other directorships held or directorships held within the preceding five years, must be entered into a register which is kept at the company's registered office; the register is open to public inspection. A previously held directorship does not have to be declared in a situation where the company in which the director held office no longer exists, or where it was part of the group of companies in which the director now holds office (ss 288–289, CA 1985). The Registrar of Companies must also be notified of the details of persons appointed to directorships; such details are entered in a register, which is also open to public inspection (s 288(2), CA 1985).

Qualifications

Unlike a company secretary (discussed below), a person appointed to a directorship does not require any formal qualifications to hold office; in theory it is even possible for an infant to be appointed to a directorship – see e.g. *Marquis of Bute's case* [1892] 2 Ch 100 – although it should be noted that a minor cannot legally bind a company. (The White Paper (2005) intends to alter this position: it stipulates that there should be a minimum age requirement for a director, namely a director must be at least 16 years old (see clause B58).)

In some companies the articles may require a person to hold a specified number of shares (share qualification) before taking up a directorship. Where the articles of a company do require a share qualification, s 291 of the Companies Act 1985 states that, unless the articles provide otherwise, the share qualification must be taken up within two months of the director's appointment.

Retirement

Once appointed, a director will hold office for a period to be determined by the company's articles or by an independent service contract. Where a company adopts articles prescribed by Table A of the Companies (Table A–F) Regulations 1985 ('Table A articles'), art 73 states that a company's first director(s) must retire at the first annual general meeting of the company or seek re-election. At subsequent annual general meetings one-third of the directors must retire or seek re-election. The one-third requirement is determined by a director's length of service, namely the one-third of directors to retire at any given annual general meeting will, at the time of the meeting, be those directors who held their directorship for the longest period of time. Article 73 is, however, subject to art 84, which provides that a managing director and any other director who holds an executive office will not be subject to retirement by rotation. Accordingly, art 73 will have no application where directors are appointed under service contracts.

Except in a situation where a director holds office in a public company or in a company that is a subsidiary of a public company, there is no compulsory retirement age for a director. Where the compulsory age requirement is applicable, a director must retire at the age of 70, unless he continues to hold office with the approval of the company's general meeting (s 293(1), CA 1985). It is to be noted that the White Paper (2005) has proposed to abolish the compulsory age requirement.

The executive director

An executive director will normally be a full-time officer of the company, who will be employed by the company to perform specific tasks. A company which adopts Table A articles may, subject to the provisions of the Companies Act 1985, appoint one or more of their number to the office of managing director or to any other executive office (Table A, art 84). An obvious example of holding an executive office will be where a person has been appointed to the post of managing director/chief executive. A managing director is normally appointed to oversee the day-to-day running of a company. The terms of an executive director's service contract (discussed below), and the specific powers delegated to the office held, are determined by the collective board of directors.

The non-executive director

Historically, the position of non-executive director has been one which carries no contractual managerial responsibilities, to the extent that a non-executive director is not a salaried employee of the company and as such may not be expected to play a significant or demanding role in the management of a company's affairs. However, in public companies, following the trend of recent corporate governance initiatives (discussed further in Chapter 20), the role of a non-executive director has now taken on a far more important position in management structures.

The role of non-executive directors has been elevated to a position akin to that of independent guardians and monitors of the interests of shareholders and the general public interest (see Chapter 20 and the terms of the revised Combined Code). Non-executive directors in public companies will be expected to contribute to the development of corporate strategy by, for example, scrutinising the performance of executive directors and by satisfying themselves that financial controls and systems of risk management are robust and defensible. Non-executive directors of public companies should not only be independent of mind but also be seen to be independent and divorced from the interests of persons with large financial or shareholding stakes in the company in which they hold office. What is particularly striking about the revised Combined Code is the increased momentum in the non-executive director's assumption of greater responsibility in the internal structures of the public company. The Combined Code now provides that the composition of the board of a UK public company should be made up of at least 50 per cent independent non-executive directors and that non-executive directors should play a significant role on board committees (discussed further in Chapter 20).

However, given the greater responsibility of non-executive directors it is likely that persons occupying these posts will face a greater threat of potential liability for lapses and breaches of responsibility and duty in so far as a non-executive director may be held personally liable for a breach of corporate duty or other statutory obligation in a like manner to an executive director. A non-executive director, once appointed, will hold office for a period determined by the company's articles (see Table A, art 73), although, in accordance with the terms of the revised Combined Code, a non-executive director of a public company should not ordinarily serve beyond a period of six years and may not serve for a period in excess of nine years.

The company chairman

The company chairman is an appointed director of the company with responsibilities of a supervisory nature. The chairman presides over meetings of the board of directors. Table A, arts 42–43 also provide that the chairman of the board, or in his absence some other director, is to preside over general meetings of the company. Although a company chairman will normally have no special powers, where a vote at a meeting of the board or general meeting is tied, he may be entitled to a second or casting vote (Table A, art 88 so provides).

The alternate director

Where a director is to be absent from board meetings, he may appoint a person to act in his place; the said person is termed an alternate director. The authority to appoint an alternate director must be provided for in a company's articles. Companies which adopt Table A, arts 65–69 provide such an authority. The said articles of Table A provide that an alternate director may attend and vote at all the board meetings or committee meetings at which the duly appointed director would have been eligible to attend and vote. The person appointed to act as an alternate director may be an existing director of the company or any other person. The board of directors must approve the appointment of an alternate director. Although an alternate director acts as a director's replacement, he/she is not an agent for the absent director; accordingly, the alternate director may act and vote according to his own conscience. As such, an alternate director is responsible for his own acts.

THE BOARD OF DIRECTORS

A company's board of directors is comprised of the individually appointed *de jure* directors of the company. The board is the ultimate decision-making body and determines the delegation of powers throughout the company; it is considered to be the

primary organ of the company. The company's articles determine the scope of a
board's management powers. Subject to specific powers conferred on the general
meeting, articles akin to the format of Table A, art 70 will confer the general management powers of a company to the company's board. Table A, art 70 provides:

> 'Subject to the provisions of the Act, the memorandum and the articles and to any direc-
> tions given by special resolution, the business of the company shall be managed by the
> directors who may exercise all the powers of the company. No alteration of the memor-
> andum or articles and no such direction shall invalidate any prior act of the directors
> which would have been valid if that alteration had not been made or that direction had not
> been given. The powers given by this regulation shall not be limited by any special power
> given to the directors by the articles and a meeting of directors at which a quorum is pre-
> sent may exercise all powers exercisable by the directors.'

Although the power structure of a company is now firmly rooted in the board of
directors, at the time of the birth of the registered company, a company's board
of directors was viewed as subservient to the general meeting. The gradual decline
in the influence of the general meeting (discussed further in Chapter 21) may be
attributed to a number of factors. In the case of larger companies, apathy and dis-
interest in shareholder meetings has resulted in a fall in the influence of shareholders
and, in respect of smaller companies, directors of the company are often the company's majority shareholders, therefore rendering the independence and significance
of the general meeting somewhat illusory.

While the collective board may be regarded as an organ of the company, it should
be stressed that, save in a situation where the board delegates all of its powers to an
individual director or where the board is comprised of just one director, an individual
director cannot in any way be considered as a distinct organ of the company. The
terms of a director's management functions are delegated to the extent that an individual director cannot *prima facie* bind the company in situations outside the limits
imposed upon the director's individual authority, by the board. Nevertheless, the
board can, as an organ of the company, pursue and authorise any corporate act.
Indeed, as a result of the Companies Act 1989, the board may even bind the company
in a situation where the corporate act is outside the company's own contractual
capacity (i.e. as determined by the company's constitution: see Chapter 8).

Board meetings

The company's articles determine the regulation of board meetings. Where Table A,
arts 88–89 are adopted, the ability to call and regulate board meetings will be
decided upon by the directors. Table A, arts 88–89 provide that any director may call
a board meeting. Ordinarily, a board meeting must have a quorum of two directors
unless the directors decide otherwise or unless the company is comprised of but one
director. Resolutions of the directors should, unless otherwise provided for by the
articles, be passed at properly convened board meetings. In terms of voting on motions
put before the board, each member of the board is entitled to one vote. A resolution
is passed by a simple majority of directors. However, in accordance with Table A,
art 94, a director is generally prohibited from voting on a matter in which he has an
interest or duty which is material and which conflicts or may conflict with the interests

of the company (discussed further in Chapter 17). Where, in relation to a resolution put before the board, there is an equality of votes, the resolution will be lost: see e.g. *Re Hackney Pavilion Ltd* [1924] 1 Ch 276. To avoid the possibility of a deadlock situation it is quite common for a company's articles to provide for the company's chairman to have a casting vote in the case of a tied vote (Table A, art 88).

Where all the directors of a company informally agree on the outcome of a motion, it would appear that the informal agreement of the board will be valid without the need to formally pass a resolution at a board meeting: see e.g. *Re Bonelli's Telegraph Co* (1871) LR 12 Eq 246. Table A, art 93 provides that the informal agreement must be in writing and signed by all the company's directors. (By analogy, for the discussion on informal resolutions of the general meeting, see Chapter 21.)

Table A, art 88 seeks to regulate the notice requirements for board meetings. Except for directors who are absent from the UK, notice of board meetings must be given to all the members of the board. It should be noted, following the decision of Carnwarth J in *Hood Sailmakers Ltd* v *Axford* [1997] 1 BCLC 721, that a resolution passed by a single director in the absence of a co-director will be invalid where it impugns the quorum requirement provided by Table A, art 99, notwithstanding that, as in the *Hood Sailmakers* case, the co-director in question was abroad and therefore not entitled to notice of the meeting at which the resolution was passed (see also *Globalink Telecommunications Ltd* v *Wilmbury Ltd & Ors* [2002] BCC 958). The decision in *Hood Sailmakers* would appear logical in so far as it would be unjust to allow a director an ability to evade the quorum requirements by simply waiting for his fellow director(s) to be absent from the UK. However, as in the *Hood Sailmakers* case, a company may be estopped from denying the validity of the resolution in a situation where it acted on the terms of the resolution and where it would have been unconscionable subsequently to deny its validity.

Although art 88 fails to specify what amounts to an appropriate period of notice, in determining this matter, the court will be influenced by whether it was reasonable to expect a director to attend a particular meeting, given the period of notice and the individual circumstances surrounding the calling of the meeting. For example, in *Bentley-Stevens* v *Jones* [1974] 1 WLR 638, Plowman J opined that there was inadequate notice in a situation where a letter was sent to a director on a Sunday, convening a meeting of the board for the morning of the next day (Monday). The director in question had been away on a weekend holiday and did not discover the letter until the Monday evening by which time the board meeting had taken place. However, despite the fact that the notice was inadequate, Plowman J concluded that the director's absence would not have altered the outcome of the board meeting and therefore the resolution passed at the meeting was not overturned. Accordingly, the learned judge refused to invalidate the meeting. Plowman J quoted with approval from the judgment of Lindley LJ in *Browne* v *La Trinidad* (1887) 37 ChD 1. Lindley LJ stated:

'I think it is most important that the court should hold fast to the rule upon which it has always acted, not to interfere for the purpose of forcing companies to conduct their business according to the strictest rules, where the irregularity complained of can be set right at a moment.' (at p 17)

Where a board meeting is called and a director's non-attendance would not affect the outcome of any vote taken at the meeting, it would appear logical that the court should not set aside the meeting on the basis that it was called at short notice. However, in some situations this apparent logic may be misplaced, especially where, for example, an individual director, had he attended the meeting, may have been able to influence other members of the board to vote in a manner which would have in fact reversed the outcome of the final vote.

Delegation of the board's powers to individual directors

It is commonplace for a company's articles to empower its board of directors to appoint committees of one or more of the directors to exercise powers normally reserved to the board. For example, Table A, art 72 states:

> 'The directors may delegate any of their powers to any committee consisting of one or more directors. They may also delegate to any managing director or any director holding any other executive office such of their powers as they consider desirable to be exercised by him. Any such delegation may be made subject to any conditions the directors may impose, and either collaterally with or to the exclusion of their own powers, and may be revoked or altered. Subject to any such conditions, the proceedings of a committee with two or more members shall be governed by the articles regulating the proceedings of directors so far as they are capable of applying.'

The necessity for a board to delegate its powers arises from the practical difficulties which occur in the day-to-day management of a corporate enterprise. A company would cease to function if all senior managerial decisions could only be justified on the basis of a resolution of the company's board.

SERVICE CONTRACTS AND DIRECTORS' REMUNERATION

A director's remuneration is a payment received by a director for services provided to the company in which he holds office. The method of remuneration may be in cash or other financial type incentives such as share options. It should be noted that a director is not entitled, as of right, to any remuneration other than in a situation where the director holds a service contract under which remuneration representing an annual salary package is included as a contractual term of the director's employment. The majority of company directors appointed to executive posts hold service contracts. The salary package for the services of such directors may often be negotiable on an annual basis. The terms of a director's service contract will be determined in accordance with the company's articles. Where a company adopts articles in the form of Table A, art 84, the salary package for the services of executive directors will be determined by the board of directors. In accordance with Table A, art 94, a director is prohibited from voting on the terms of his own service contract. Table A, art 95 further provides that a director cannot be counted as part of the quorum for the meeting at which his service contract is to be considered. Other than where s 319 of the Companies Act 1985 is applicable (discussed below), the terms of a director's service contract do not ordinarily require the approval of the general meeting, although s 318 of the Companies Act 1985 states that a director's service contract must be made available for inspection by the general meeting. However, following the introduction of the Directors' Remuneration Report Regulations 2002, SI 2002/1986, for financial years ending on or after 31 December 2002, quoted companies are now required to publish a directors' remuneration report as part of their annual reporting cycle and to file a copy at Companies House. The regulations amend the Companies Act 1985, inserting a new Sch 7A which incorporates the disclosure requirements. The remuneration report must disclose details of individual directors' pay packages, details of the board's consideration of directors' pay, the membership of the remuneration committee, the names of any remuneration consultants used, a statement of the company's policy on directors' remuneration, an explanation of how the remuneration packages relate to performance, together with details and an explanation of policy on contract and notice periods, and a performance graph providing information on the company's performance in comparison with an appropriate share market index. A shareholder vote must be held on the report at the company's annual general meeting, although the vote may be considered in somewhat negative terms, given that the company is not obliged in law to adhere to the wishes of the general meeting in a situation where the report is not approved. (The remuneration of directors in public companies is discussed further in Chapter 20.)

Although the terms of a director's service contract are normally decided upon at a formal board meeting, in *Runciman* v *Walter Runciman plc* [1992] BCLC 1084 it was held that, providing the members of a company's board unanimously agree to the terms of a service contract, an informal agreement will suffice to effect a valid service contract without the need to call a board meeting. (The *Runciman* case is discussed further in Chapter 18, in relation to s 317, CA 1985.)

In accordance with s 318 of the Companies Act 1985, the terms of a director's service contract must be made available for inspection by the company's membership. However, where a director's service contract or director's contract for services or consultancy is for a period in excess of five years and contains a term under which the company cannot terminate the director's employment by notice, or can only do so in specified circumstances, the contract must be approved by general meeting (s 319, CA 1985). It is to be noted that the CLR (Final Report) recommended that this period should be reduced to three years. It is also to be noted that, following the decision of the Court of Appeal in *Atlas Wright (Europe) Ltd* v *Wright* [1999] BCC 163, the formal approval of the general meeting may be waived in a situation where there was an implied approval of the service contract by the entire body of shareholders.

Section 319(2) further provides that where there is more than six months of a director's service period to run and the company enters into a new service agreement with the director, then the period of the former service contract which is yet to expire should be added to the new period of the service contract for the purpose of calculating whether the new service contract is one which should be approved by the general meeting. For example, if a director has a service contract for a period of four years and after three years the company decides to renew the service agreement for a further period of five years, the new service contract would require the approval of the general meeting (i.e. the one year left on the original service contract would be added to the new service contract to give a total of six years). However, a contract of services, supplied by a parent company to its subsidiary, does not have to be approved in accordance with s 319 if the only reason for treating the parent company as the subsidiary's shadow director is based on the fact that the subsidiary's directors are accustomed to act in accordance with the holding company's directions.

Other than in the case of service contracts, where a company adopts Table A, art 83, directors are entitled to receive such remuneration as the company by ordinary resolution determines. A remuneration award may be paid to a director in addition to his/her annual salary specified in a service contract. As the power to grant remuneration is vested in the general meeting, the board has no authority to delegate this power to individual directors or a committee of directors. However, where a company has not elected to adopt Table A, art 83, its articles may provide that the board should determine remuneration awards. For example, in *Guinness v Saunders* [1990] 2 AC 663 Guinness' (G) articles provided that G's board could determine directors' remuneration up to £100 000; anything in excess of that amount was to be determined by the general meeting. G's articles further provided that the board was responsible for fixing any special remuneration payable to a director who served on a committee. A committee of three directors with full authority from the Guinness board was appointed to facilitate a takeover bid. Mr Ward (W), a member of the committee, undertook successful negotiations which resulted in the takeover of the target company. W was paid, in accordance with the committee's instructions, remuneration to the sum of 0.2 per cent of the estimated value of the takeover; he was paid a total of £5.2 million! The validity of this payment was later challenged by G on the ground that the committee had no authority to authorise the remuneration award. (The payment was also challenged in that it infringed s 317 of the Companies Act 1985 (non-declaration of a director's interest in a contract (discussed in Chapter 17)).

In addition to the relevant articles of G (noted above) G's articles also contained a regulation similar in format to Table A, art 72 (see above) so that the board was defined as, 'The directors of the company for the time being . . . or any committee authorised to act on its behalf.' In determining the case, the House of Lords found in G's favour. Lord Templeman considered the company's articles to be incompatible with a finding that a committee could be regarded as 'the board'. His lordship found that the intention behind the wording of the article which provided that the board was responsible for fixing the remuneration of a director who served on a special committee would have been meaningless if a committee itself had the capacity to award remuneration to its own members (i.e. a committee of directors could not be regarded as the board). His lordship remarked:

> 'It cannot have been intended that any committee should be able to grant special remuneration to any director . . . The board must compare the work of an individual director with ordinary duties of a director. The board must decide whether special remuneration shall be paid in addition to or in substitution for the annual remuneration determined by the board . . . These decisions could only be made by the board surveying the work and remuneration of each and every director.' (at p 687)

Nevertheless, despite the commonsense wisdom of Lord Templeman's words, it is submitted that a literal construction of G's articles inferred that the committee of three directors were indeed capable of awarding one of their number special remuneration.

The articles clearly permitted a duly appointed committee to undertake the functions of the board, functions which included the power to award remuneration. Indeed, although the interpretation afforded to the relevant articles by Lord Templeman may appear to be one born of a practical logic, the interpretation may be criticised on the premise that it was based on an assumed interpretation of the company's articles rather than the actual literal wording and meaning of those articles.

THE REMOVAL OF DIRECTORS

It is commonplace for a company's articles to contain conditions which govern the circumstances whereby directors may be removed from office. For example, Table A, art 81 provides that a director will cease to hold office if he resigns, is prohibited by law from holding office, becomes bankrupt, is committed to a mental hospital or is absent from board meetings without due excuse for a period of six months. While outside the ambit of Table A, it is also commonplace to find that the articles of public companies often provide that a director may be removed by a simple resolution of the board.

In accordance with s 303(1) of the Companies Act 1985, and notwithstanding any contrary provision in a company's articles or an agreement between a company and any director, a director may be removed from office by the passing of an ordinary resolution (but note the possibility of a weighted voting clause (see below) or a clause prohibiting dismissal within a membership agreement, discussed in Chapter 4). However, s 303(5) of the Companies Act 1985 provides that the power of the general meeting to dismiss a director will not deprive the director of a claim to compensation or damages for a breach of service contract: see e.g. *Southern Foundries Ltd* v *Shirlaw* [1940] AC 701 (discussed in Chapter 4). Special notice (28 days) must be given to the company of the intention to introduce a motion calling for the dismissal of a director (s 303(2), CA 1985). A director must be given a copy of the form of motion together with the opportunity to present a defence, a copy of which may, if required, be distributed to members (s 304, CA 1985). One exception to a director's right to present a defence is in a situation where the court finds that the rights conferred by s 304 are being abused to secure needless publicity for a defamatory matter.

Although a company's articles are not permitted to preclude the implementation of s 303, it is nevertheless possible to include within the articles a device commonly known as a 'weighted voting clause'. This device seeks to confer weighted voting rights on a director in a situation where a motion for his removal is proposed. The weighted voting clause affects voting rights and does not theoretically operate to fetter s 303. Nevertheless, where a director is able to take the benefit of a weighted voting clause, the practical effect of increased voting rights clearly frustrates the intention behind s 303. The concept of the weighted voting clause was approved by the House of Lords in *Bushell* v *Faith* [1970] 1 All ER 53 (the facts of this case are discussed in Chapter 4). In giving its approval to the weighted voting clause, the House of Lords emphasised that the clause was concerned with the allocation of a company's voting rights and, because Parliament had never sought to fetter the right of a company to issue a share with special rights or restrictions, it was, in the opinion of their lordships, certainly not a matter in which the judiciary should interfere.

Although a weighted voting clause is concerned with voting rights as opposed to the creation of a direct assault on the ability of a company to exercise its statutory power pursuant to s 303, the practical effect of a weighted voting clause is one which fetters the power of removal embodied in s 303. If a director with the benefit of a weighted voting clause does not wish to be dismissed there seems little the company's membership can do to execute his removal, other than to offer to purchase the director's shares, a purchase which could result in an inflated price tag being attached to the shares. Lord Morris of Borth-y-Gest, in a dissenting judgment in the *Bushell* case, opined that the acceptance of a weighted voting clause made a mockery of the law in that it nullified the exercise of the statutory power to remove a director. It is difficult to disagree with such logic. It is interesting to note that the decision in *Bushell* v *Faith* would have been reversed by legislation had the Companies Bill of 1973 been passed and not lost as a result of the political instability of that time. In today's corporate world weighted voting clauses are commonly used by private companies although they are prohibited, in the case of listed companies, by Stock Exchange rules. The continued acceptance and validity of weighted voting clauses is indicative of the view that statutory powers, whilst workable in theory, can, in specified circumstances, be manipulated to such an extent whereby they are of little practical worth.

THE *DE FACTO* AND SHADOW DIRECTOR

The de facto *director*

In addition to a formally appointed director (a *de jure* director), a person may also, in accordance with s 741 of the Companies Act 1985, be deemed to act as a *de facto* director, in so far as the identification of a company director is not necessarily dependent upon a formal appointment to office. Therefore, a person may be deemed a *de facto* director where that person performs managerial tasks properly associated with the office of a director. The tasks performed by that person must exceed those of a mere employee; they must extend to an authority in matters related to the management and administration of the company's affairs.

Although the courts have attempted to expose the nature and degree of control which is necessary to identify a person as a *de facto* director, formal guidelines have not always been of a uniform nature. Historically, two tests emerged to determine the character of a *de facto* director, namely the 'equal footing test' and 'the holding out test'. The former test, first advanced by Lloyd J in *Re Richborough Furniture* [1996] 1 BCLC 507, considered a *de facto* director to be identifiable, where there was

'. . . clear evidence that he had been either the sole person directing the affairs of the company (or acting with others all equally lacking in a valid appointment . . .) or, if there were others who were true directors, that he was acting on an equal footing with the others in directing the affairs of the company.' (at p 524)

The characteristics of the equal footing test were revised following the decisions of Judge Cooke in *Secretary of State for Trade and Industry* v *Elms* (16 January 1997, unreported) and Jacob J in *Secretary of State* v *Tjolle* [1998] BCLC 333. In *Secretary of State* v *Tjolle*, Jacob J quoted with approval the following passage taken from the judgment of Judge Cooke in *Secretary of State for Trade and Industry* v *Elms*:

'At the forefront of the test I think I have to go on to consider by way of further analysis what Lloyd J meant by "on an equal footing". As to one, it seems to me clear that this cannot be limited simply to statutory functions and to my mind it would mean and include any one or more of the following: directing others, putting it very compendiously, committing the company to major obligations, and thirdly, (really I think what we are concerned with here) taking part in an equally based collective decision process at board level, i.e. at the level of a director in effect with a foot in the board room. As to Lloyd J's test, I think it is very much on the lines of that third test to which I have just referred. It is not I think in any way a question of equality of power but equality of ability to participate in the notional boardroom. Is he somebody who is simply advising and, as it were, withdrawing having advised, or somebody who joins the other directors, *de facto* or *de jure*, in decisions which affect the future of the company?'

By contrast, in *Re Hydrodam (Corby) Ltd* [1994] 2 BCLC 180, Millett J defined a *de facto* director in the following way ('the holding out test'):

'A *de facto* director is a person who assumes to act as a director. He is held out as a director by the company, and claims and purports to be a director, although never actually or validly appointed as such. To establish that a person was a *de facto* director of a company it is necessary to plead and prove that he undertook functions in relation to the company which could properly be discharged only by a director. It is not sufficient to show that he was concerned in the management of the company's affairs or undertook tasks in relation to its business which can properly be performed by a manager below board level.' (at p 183)

However, irrespective of any given formula or test, the decision as to whether a person acted as a *de facto* director will ultimately be a question of fact to be determined from the circumstances of each individual case. Indeed, in *Re Kaytech International plc, Portier* v *Secretary of State for Trade and Industry* [1999] BCC 390, the first ever case to reach the Court of Appeal on the question of the interpretation of a '*de facto*' director, the court approved a statement (at p 402) taken from the judgment of Jacob J in *Secretary of State* v *Tjolle*, namely:

'. . . it may be difficult to postulate any one decisive test. I think what is involved is very much a question of degree. The court takes into account all the relevant factors. Those factors include at least whether or not there was a holding out by the company of the individual as a director, whether the individual used the title, whether the individual had proper information (e.g. management accounts) on which to base decisions, and whether the individual has to make major decisions and so on. Taking all these factors into account, one asks "was this individual part of the corporate governing structure?", answering it as a kind of jury question.'

Accordingly, to determine whether a person acts as a *de facto* director, one cannot apply a single decisive test. Matters pertinent to the equal footing test and the holding out test will be relevant, but such matters cannot be decisive in any prescribed formula. However, there will be a strong presumption that a person acts as a *de facto* director where that person contributes skills and knowledge to the internal management of a company and, being concerned with its affairs, portrays to the outside world an obvious understanding and relationship with functions ordinarily exercised by a director of the company.

The shadow director

Section 741(2) of the Companies Act 1985 defines a shadow director as:

'A person in accordance with whose directions or instructions the directors of a company are accustomed to act . . . a person is not deemed a shadow director by reason only that the directors act on advice given by him in a professional capacity.'

In contrast to a *de facto* director, a shadow director will never be held out as a director of the company: see the judgment of Millett J in *Re Hydrodam (Corby) Ltd* [1994] BCC 161 (especially at p 162). Attaching responsibility to a person who directs and influences corporate activity through a formally appointed board of directors is necessary to prevent such a person from evading duties that are designed to prevent the mismanagement of corporate affairs. Equity also recognises the potential liability of a shadow director in that persons who are knowingly party to a breach of a fiduciary duty may be liable to the company as constructive trustees: see e.g. *Selangor United Rubber Estates Ltd* v *Cradock (No 3)* [1968] 1 WLR 1555 (discussed further in Chapter 17).

Although s 741(2) of the Companies Act 1985 would appear expressly to exempt a person from being construed as a shadow director when acting in a professional capacity, the exemption is limited and will not cover a situation where, for example, a professional offers advice beyond the reasonable scope of advice one would normally expect from a person occupying a similar professional status. For example, in *Re Tasbian Ltd (No 3)* [1992] BCC 358 an accountant, Mr Nixon (N), was employed by a finance company, Castle Finance Ltd (C), to act as financial consultant to C's subsidiary and client, Tasbian Ltd (T). The Court of Appeal, in upholding the first instance decision of Vinelott J, held that in order to justify a finding that N acted as a shadow director of T, it was necessary to establish that N exercised a degree of control over the company's affairs which went beyond the influence one would expect from an accountant offering financial advice to a company. In concluding that there was sufficient evidence to establish a finding that N had acted as a shadow director of T, Balcombe LJ stated:

'Mr Nixon decided which cheques drawn by the company could and which could not be submitted to the bank. This meant that he was concerned with which of the company's creditors were paid and in which order, and to that extent it would appear – I say no more than that, that he was able to control the company's affairs.' (at p 364)

The court's finding was strengthened by the fact that N had manipulated the management functions of the company's appointed directors. (See also *Re a Company (No 005009 of 1987)* (1988) 4 BCC 424 in which Knox J refused to hold, on a preliminary point of law, that a company's bank was incapable of acting as the company's shadow director.)

As a shadow director is defined as a person in accordance with whose directions or instructions the directors of a company are accustomed to act, it may be expected that a person occupying such a position will exert influence over the company's board of directors in such a way that his/her directions and instructions will ordinarily be followed. Consequently, at first sight it would appear a logical assumption to conclude that a shadow director will be identified as any person who exerts a dominant and controlling influence over the company's affairs, that is a person who is responsible for engineering and directing corporate activity through what may be described as a 'puppet' board of directors. Further, the term 'shadow' would appear to imply that a person acting in such a capacity will operate in a hidden capacity, directing and controlling the activities of a company through persons who are expressly or impliedly held out by the company as its *de jure* or *de facto* directors. The aforementioned characteristics expound a position of superiority and control over the company's affairs. Indeed, prior to 2000, the said characteristics dominated the courts' identification of a shadow director.

However, following the decision of the Court of Appeal in *Secretary of State* v *Deverell* [2001] Ch 340, a controlling and dominant, but hidden influence in the affairs of a company must now be viewed as an exaggeration of the level and degree of involvement deemed necessary to identify a shadow director. In *Deverell* the Secretary of State sought a disqualification order against D and H in accordance with s 6 of the Company Directors Disqualification Act 1986 (the disqualification of directors is dealt with in Chapter 19). It was contended that both had acted as shadow directors of E Ltd. In defending the proceedings, D and H argued that their involvement in the affairs of E Ltd had been as management consultants and not as directors.

In relation to D, although never formally appointed as a director of E Ltd, he had been involved in the management of the company from the time of its incorporation. As one of the signatories to the company's bank account, D was an active player and influence in the accounting and financial structures of the company and was its principal negotiator in business dealings. D's involvement and attachment to the company was substantial to the extent that he personally guaranteed a loan entered into by and on behalf of the company.

In contrast to D's transparent involvement in the internal management structures of E Ltd, H's involvement in the company's affairs was more illusive. Having been made subject to a bankruptcy order, H was precluded from any involvement in the company's formal management structures. Nevertheless, irrespective of H's inability to expressly involve himself in the internal affairs of the company, his informal participation and influence in management issues was considerable, especially in the context of advising the company on its future direction. For example, notwithstanding the company's insolvent position and concerns expressed by the company's board of directors in respect of the company's financial state, H had instructed the company's *de jure* directors to continue to trade, an instruction which was obeyed.

At first instance, Judge Cooke held that neither D nor H could properly be construed as shadow directors. The Court of Appeal was to overturn this decision. Morritt LJ, delivering the leading judgment of the court, rejected Judge Cooke's interpretation of a shadow director as a person who would always be in a position to cast the board in a subservient role. Morritt LJ considered that it was unnecessary to establish a subservient relationship between a person and the board of directors to conclude that the said person had acted as a shadow director. His lordship reached this conclusion on the premise that s 741(2) in the use of the term 'accustomed to act' should not be interpreted as conclusive of establishing that the board must always be compelled to obey the guidance of a shadow director. Accordingly, a person was capable of acting as a shadow director even if the board had a capacity to exercise independent judgment.

In respect of finding that H had acted in the capacity of a shadow director and, more specifically, the issue of whether the giving of advice could be equated with a 'direction or instruction', Morritt LJ opined that if advice was given on a regular and consistent basis it could be considered in the same vein as a direction or instruction because a direction, instruction, or the giving of advice all shared the common characteristic of an act of guidance. Therefore, according to his lordship, once it was established that there was a sufficient degree of guidance, the court would be in a position to ascertain objectively whether the direction, instruction or advice so relied and acted upon by the board of directors carried real influence in relation to the business activities of the company. In so deciding, it would be immaterial that there was any expectation that the guidance would be followed. Further, according to Morritt LJ, it was unnecessary to establish that the 'real influence' extended over the whole of the company's business operations.

Following the judgment of the Court of Appeal in *Deverell*, a shadow director may therefore be identified in the following manner, namely as a person who customarily tenders advice, instructions or directions to the company's board of a type which, as an act of guidance, carries real influence in relation to a part or the whole of the company's business affairs. While the company's board will normally follow the guidance tendered by a shadow director, it is not essential that it is habitually followed or that there is any expectation that it will be followed. A shadow director may be independent from or form a part of the internal management structures of the company.

This reformulated definition now casts a wide net into which a person may be caught and labelled as having acted as a shadow director. Nevertheless, the evidence to substantiate a finding that a person acted as a shadow director must, following the judgment of Rattee J in *Secretary of State v Becker* [2003] 1 BCLC 555, portray a pattern of conduct as opposed to an isolated act of guidance; in *Becker* the single isolated act of guidance related to the period of the company's insolvency. (See also *Lord (Liquidator of Rosshill Properties Ltd) v Sinai Securities Ltd* [2005] 1 BCLC 295.)

Although the new (*Deverell*) definition may be applauded in the sense that it increases the pool of persons who, as shadow directors, may be held personally accountable following a company's demise, affording greater protection to the interests of creditors and the general public, the credibility of the reformulated definition may be doubted. First, can mere advice be equated with a direction or instruction? While a direction, instruction or the giving of advice may all share the common characteristic of an act of guidance, a direction or instruction, as an act of guidance, implicitly carries an expectation of obedience. In contrast, 'advice' is, as an act of guidance, couched more in the form of a suggested course of action and therefore is deficient of any expectation that it must ordinarily be followed.

Secondly, in *Deverell*, Morritt LJ interpreted the term 'accustomed to act' in a passive sense by indicating that it was unnecessary to establish that a shadow director dominated the company's *de jure* directors, thereby casting the board of directors in a subservient role. However, with respect, although the term 'accustomed to act' may be interpreted in a manner whereby a company's board need not *always* act in accordance with a direction or instruction, the term nevertheless implies that it would be unusual for a direction or instruction to be ignored. Surely the question of whether a board of directors is 'accustomed to act' will rest upon a case by case analysis of whether a person in directing or instructing the board of directors was obeyed on a regular basis, and, more specifically, whether that person's directions or instructions were ordinarily obeyed in relation to decisions crucial to the governance, direction and pursuit of the company's internal, external and financial affairs.

Finally, following *Deverell*, a shadow director may be identified as a person involved either in the internal management structure of the company or as an external contributor to a company's affairs, despite the fact that the expression 'shadow' suggests that a person so classified will exert influence over corporate affairs from outside formal management structures. Indeed, would not a person exerting influence from inside management structures be more aptly described as a *de facto* director? In *Deverell*, although D exerted considerable influence in the management of the company's affairs, would he not have been more aptly described as a *de facto* director or, perhaps more correctly, a *de facto* managing director?

The distinction between a de facto and a shadow director

Although in a practical sense, the ability to distinguish between a person's activities as either a *de facto* director or shadow director may be irrelevant in calculating a person's potential liability as a director, the existence of two distinct labels of director would suggest that as separate classifications the characteristics of each type of directorship are different.

Although both a *de facto* director and shadow director share common characteristics in having a capacity to exert real influence in the management of a company's affairs, there is, surprisingly, little judicial consideration of a distinction between the two types of directorship. Moreover, on occasions, the distinction has been portrayed as unnecessary and irrelevant. For example, in *Re Tasbian (No 3)* [1993] BCLC 297, the Court of Appeal, affirming the decision of Vinelott J ([1991] BCLC 792), made no attempt in analysing the facts of the case to distinguish between a person's involvement in the management of a company as a *de facto* or shadow director. Instead, the court was quite satisfied to conclude that the evidence of the case was sufficient to establish that the person acted as either a *de facto* director or a shadow director.

However, post *Deverell*, the hallmarks of a shadow director have been modified to such an extent that any previous distinction between a shadow and a *de facto* director is now significantly blurred. For example, prior to *Deverell*, evidence to justify a person being labelled as a shadow director required the exertion of a dominant and controlling influence over the company's affairs; following *Deverell*, a person's classification as a shadow director may, in common with that of a *de facto* director, be established without proof of a controlling influence. Secondly, prior to *Deverell*, a shadow director would have been defined as a person detached from the company's internal management, operating in a hidden capacity; post *Deverell*, a person may now be classed as a shadow director where he wields influence over a company's affairs irrespective of whether that influence is as a part of the company's internal management structure. Finally, prior to *Deverell*, a shadow director would have been expected to be in a position to give directions or instructions that would ordinarily be obeyed by the company's board. Following *Deverell*, the giving of advice is now equated with directions or instructions to the extent that a shadow director is in effect on an 'equal footing' with the company's *de jure* directors in a sense previously construed as relevant only to the identification of a *de facto* director. Indeed, after *Deverell*, it will be remarkable if the courts attempt to distinguish between the characteristics of a *de facto* and shadow director; it may become commonplace for the courts to declare that a person acted as either a *de facto* or shadow director: see e.g. *MCA Records Inc* v *Charly Records Ltd* [2002] EMCR 1 and *The Official Receiver* v *Zwirin* [2001] WL 825078.

THE COMPANY SECRETARY

At present, in accordance with s 283(1) of the Companies Act 1985, every company must have a company secretary. However, it should be noted that if the terms of the White Paper (2005) are to be adopted in a future legislative reform of company law, then, in the case of private companies, the obligatory requirement to have a company secretary will be abandoned.

As the law stands, Table A, art 99 provides that the company secretary is to be appointed by the company's directors on such terms as they may decide and that the power to remove the secretary is to be vested in the directors. A company must keep details at its registered office (similar to those kept for directors) of its company secretary (s 290, CA 1985). It must also send the relevant details of its secretary to the Registrar of Companies, who must be notified of any change in the person appointed to the post of company secretary (s 288(2), CA 1985).

A sole director of a company is not permitted to act as the company's secretary (s 283(2), CA 1985). However, in companies where there is more than one director, a director may be authorised by the board to act in the place of a formally appointed secretary; the director may so act providing a task which requires the act of both the secretary and director is not performed by one person acting as both the director and secretary (s 284, CA 1985). A company may itself act as the secretary of another company providing that in doing so it does not side-step the requirements of s 283(4). The rather confusingly drafted requirements of s 283(4) may be summarised by the following example:

> Company A cannot appoint company B as its secretary where the sole director of both A and B is the same person. In addition, A cannot appoint a person as its secretary where that person is the sole director of B in a situation where B is also the sole director of A (s 283(4), CA 1985).

In relation to a public company, the secretary must be a suitably qualified person, that is, the directors of the company must consider the secretary to have the necessary experience to perform the secretary's functions and/or the secretary must have a professionally recognised qualification (s 286, CA 1985).

Although a secretary's responsibilities are primarily of an administrative, as opposed to a managerial, nature, the role of a company secretary is nevertheless vital to the proper functioning of the corporate entity. The specific responsibilities of a company's secretary will depend upon the size and nature of the company in which the office is held. However, tasks common to all secretaries will include maintaining the company's registers, sending relevant details to the Registrar of Companies, preparing share certificates, making arrangements for board meetings, drafting the minutes of such meetings, keeping the company's documentation in order, and keeping abreast of the relevant companies legislation in so far as it affects the running and administration of the company.

As a company secretary's responsibilities are geared to the administration of the company's affairs, the post may carry with it an authority to bind the company in contracts which are specifically concerned with functions within the ambit of a particular secretary's actual or ostensible authority: see e.g. *Panorama Developments Ltd v Fidelis Furnishing Fabrics Ltd* [1971] 2 QB 711. It is to be noted that the role and authority of the company secretary is, in today's corporate world, of marked contrast to the nineteenth and early part of the twentieth century, at which time the company secretary was regarded as a 'somewhat humble character'. Indeed, in *Barnett Hoares v South London Tramways* (1877) 18 QB 815, a company's secretary was described as 'a mere servant', a person who was supposed to do what he/she was told and who had no authority to represent the company and upon whom third parties should not rely.

Suggested further reading

Identifying and classifying a director

Griffin [2003] Insol Law 127

Griffin (2003) 54 NILQ 43

17

THE DUTIES OF THE MANAGEMENT OF A COMPANY

INTRODUCTION

The board of directors, together with persons expressly or impliedly authorised to act on the board's behalf, represent the brain – the nerve centre – of the corporate body. Against this backcloth of corporate power, fiduciary, common law and statutory duties have evolved in an attempt to eradicate abuses of power. The purpose of this chapter is to iden-tify and analyse the scope of such duties. The penalties, which arise as a consequence of a director's breach of duty, will also be examined. Proposals to reform the law relating to the duties and responsibilities of directors are discussed at the end of the chapter.

FIDUCIARY DUTIES

Directors and other company officers owe fiduciary duties to the company in which they hold office. In practical terms, the exact scope of an individual director's duties will often depend upon the responsibility he or she is afforded in the corporate struc-ture and the manner in which the company's business is organised. The most com-mon analogy of the fiduciary duties owed by a director to a company is that of a trust or agency relationship. In relation to a trust relationship, in *Re Lands Allotment Co* [1884] 1 Ch 616, Lindley LJ opined:

> 'Although directors are not properly speaking trustees, yet they have always been con-sidered and treated as trustees of money which comes to their hands or which is actually under their control; and ever since joint stock companies were invented, directors have been held liable to make good moneys which they have misapplied upon the same foot-ings as if they were trustees'. (at p 631)

The basis for a comparison between directors' duties and the duties arising from a trustee–beneficiary relationship can be traced back to the early part of the nine-teenth century. Prior to the passing of the Joint Stock Companies Act of 1844, un-incorporated companies vested the property of the company in trustee directors (see Chapter 1). However, in today's corporate world the analogy between trustees and directors seems less likely. Although directors may be regarded as occupying the status of a trustee in situations where they are responsible for the management of corporate funds and property, a more apt analogy of the general relationship between a director and company is that of agency. As agents, the directors stand in a fiduciary relationship to the principal (the company). In *Bristol & West Building Society v Mothew* [1998] Ch 1, Millett LJ defined a fiduciary in the following terms:

> 'A fiduciary is someone who has undertaken to act for or on behalf of another in a par-ticular matter in circumstances which give rise to a relationship of trust and confidence.

The distinguishing obligation of a fiduciary is the obligation of loyalty. The principal is entitled to the single-minded loyalty of his fiduciary. This core liability has several facets. A fiduciary must act in good faith; he must not make a profit out of his trust; he must not place himself in a position where his duty and his interest may conflict; he may not act for his own benefit or the benefit of a third person without the informed consent of his principal . . .' (at p 18)

The duty to act *bona fide* in the interests of the company

A director must conduct the business affairs of a company for the benefit of the company as a whole and not for some other collateral purpose: see e.g. *Re Smith & Fawcett Ltd* [1942] Ch 304. The test to determine whether a director acted in breach of the *bona fide* duty is a subjective one, that is, the court must consider whether the director considered that he/she was acting for the benefit of the company as a whole: see e.g. *Extrasure Travel Insurances Ltd* v *Scattergood* [2003] 1 BCLC 598. The test is subjective and may even be passed where the court considers the actions of a director to have been unreasonable, that is, providing the court is of the opinion that the director honestly believed that he was acting in the company's best interests. The issue is therefore one that is concerned with the director's state of mind. Accordingly, in the majority of cases, the subjective nature of this test will favour the director and it will be difficult to establish a breach of the duty: see e.g. *Regentcrest plc* v *Cohen* [2001] BCC 494 (discussed below).

However, there may be cases in which it is patently obvious that the director's intention could not have been to benefit the company as a whole. The case of *Re W & M Roith Ltd* [1967] 1 WLR 432 provides an excellent example of a factual situation which gave rise to a breach of the *bona fide* duty. Here, a director, who was in very poor health, entered into a new service agreement with the company, an agreement which included within its terms a provision for a generous pension to be paid to his widow in the event of his death. The director, who failed to disclose his poor health, died shortly after entering into the agreement. His widow claimed the benefit of the pension. As the deceased director's service agreement had been entered into with the object of enabling his wife to make a claim upon the company's assets (in the form of the pension payments) in excess of an amount that might otherwise have been considered appropriate by the company had it been aware of the seriousness of the undisclosed illness, the court held that the director had acted contrary to the interests of the company as a whole. The director's sole intention was to benefit his wife, without consideration for the interests of the company.

The duty to act for a proper purpose

Although a director may honestly believe that in entering into a transaction he/she is acting in the best interests of the company as a whole, he/she will nevertheless be held to be in breach of his/her fiduciary duty if, objectively, it is viewed that the purpose of the transaction was outside or an abuse of the director's allocated powers, notwithstanding that the transaction may not have been outside the contractual capacity of the company: see e.g. *Hogg* v *Cramphorn* [1967] Ch 254. The duty to act for a proper purpose applies to the exercise of any of a director's powers. In

Bishopsgate Investment Management Ltd [1993] BCC 140, Hoffmann LJ described the duty thus:

'If a director chooses to participate in the management of a company and exercises powers on its behalf, he owes a duty to act bona fide in the interests of the company. He must exercise the power solely for the purpose for which it was conferred. To exercise the power for another purpose is a breach of his fiduciary duty.' (at p 140)

A leading case on the application and interpretation of the proper purpose duty is the Privy Council's decision in *Howard Smith Ltd* v *Ampol Petroleum Ltd* [1974] AC 821. The facts of this case were as follows. Ampol (A) controlled 54 per cent of the issued share capital in a company (X) and unsuccessfully submitted a bid for X's remaining shares. Howard Smith Ltd (H) then submitted a rival bid for the remaining shares but that bid was also rejected (Ampol, X's majority shareholder, rejected the bid). X's board of directors favoured H's offer and, to overcome the problem of A's majority control in X, the board allotted unissued shares to H. The purpose of the allotment was to provide needy capital as well as relegating A to the position of a minority shareholder (i.e. following the allotment, A's shareholding in X would have fallen below the 50 per cent mark).

A objected to the allotment of the new share issue on the ground that it had not been for a proper purpose. X's directors argued that the allotment had been in the best interests of the company as a whole (i.e. that they had not been motivated by self interest but had genuinely believed that the company's best interests would be served if H was in a position to secure majority control in X). The Privy Council, in giving judgment in favour of A, held that X's power to allot shares had not been used for a proper purpose. Lord Wilberforce opined that, in order to decide whether the allotment was for a proper purpose, the court should first consider the *bona fide* intentions of the directors. However, even if the directors honestly believed that they acted for the benefit of the company, the *bona fide* test could not be viewed in isolation. The court then had to consider, in an objective sense, whether the underlying reason for the allotment had been made for a proper purpose.

In applying the objective test, the Privy Council concluded that although X would have benefited from the capital raised from the sale of shares to H, the dominant purpose behind the share allotment had been an improper one, namely the allotment had, as its primary purpose, the aim of manipulating voting control in favour of H. Lord Wilberforce stated:

'Just as it is established that directors, within their management powers, may take decisions against the wishes of the majority shareholders, and indeed that the majority of shareholders cannot control them in the exercise of these powers while they remain in office, . . . so it must be unconstitutional for directors to use their fiduciary powers over the shares in the company purely for the purpose of destroying an existing majority, or creating a new majority which did not previously exist. To do so is to interfere with that element of the company's constitution which is separate from and set against their powers.' (at p 837)

The reasoning of the Privy Council – namely the court must seek out the dominant purpose behind a power use to determine whether the proper purpose duty has been infringed – is one which has been universally applied by the courts. For example, in *Mutual Life Insurance Co* v *The Rank Organisation Ltd* [1985] BCLC 11, a company decided to issue further shares, a proportion of which were to be made available to its existing shareholders. However, the company resolved not to make the offer of the issue available to shareholders situated in the USA and Canada. Although the company's decision may *prima facie* have suggested some form of discrimination, Goulding J held that the dominant purpose behind this share allocation did not purport to discriminate against the shareholders situated in the USA and Canada. The learned judge held that the company's decision was based upon the practical commercial reality of avoiding the considerable expense involved in complying with the share issue procedures in the USA and Canada. The decision not to offer shares to members in those countries was a legitimate exercise of the board of directors' discretion to consider the best interests of the company as a whole.

A more recent decision of the Court of Appeal which is emphatic as to the dominance of the proper purpose test is the case of *Lee Panavision Ltd* v *Lee Lighting Ltd* [1992] BCLC 22. Here, Panavision Ltd (P) was given an option to purchase the share capital of Lee Lighting Ltd (L). During the period of time in which the option had to run, P had been given a proxy over the voting shares of L and had been given the right to appoint the directors of L. P decided not to exercise the option to purchase the share capital but a majority of the directors of L (appointees of P), acting under the instructions of P, and aware of the fact they would soon be removed from office when the option period came to an end, voted in favour of extending the management agreement with P. Such a vote was against the wishes of L's majority shareholder. A dominant reason why P wished to carry on managing L was to ensure L paid sums due under a loan agreement made in favour of one of P's associated companies.

Although the Court of Appeal considered that it was for the directors of L to decide if it was in the company's best interests to continue the management agreement with P, the court considered that, in determining that issue, the directors should have taken into account the views of the general body of shareholders as opposed to the artificial interests of the company as a commercial entity. The Court of Appeal held that it was unconstitutional for the directors, knowing that the general body of shareholders were proposing to end the management agreement with L, to commit the management powers of L to P, thus removing the powers of L's future board of directors. The purpose behind the vote – to retain P's domination over the management functions of L – was clearly one which had been taken for an improper purpose, namely to secure L's payment of a debt to P's associated company.

Although the Privy Council's reasoning in the *Ampol* case is now firmly established as dictating the policy of deciding between any potential conflict as to the priority to be afforded between the *bona fide* duty and the proper purpose duty – namely the latter will, if relevant to the facts of a particular case, always prevail – the outcome of subsequent cases involving the allotment of shares and takeover bids may appear to stretch and challenge the conceptual boundaries of the *Ampol* perception and interpretation of the duty to act for a proper purpose. For example, in *Re a Company (No 005136 of 1986)* [1987] BCLC 82, Hoffmann J expressed the view that a company as a separate legal entity was unconcerned with the identity of its shareholders. However, in the context of potential takeover bids, it is respectfully contended that this opinion must be doubted given that it suggests that the directors of a company have no duty to consider the consequences of issuing shares in circumstances where the issue, albeit raising capital, results in a change in the identity of a company's majority shareholder. By contrast, in the Scottish case of *Dawson International plc v Coats Paton plc* 1988 SLT 854, Lord Cullen took the view that, in cases involving a takeover bid, the directors of a company could be justified in considering the identity of the majority shareholder in deciding whether or not it was in the best interests of a company to permit the takeover to go ahead (see also the Commonwealth decisions (pre-*Ampol*) of *Savoy Corp Ltd v Development Underwriting Ltd* (1963) NSWR 138, *Harlowe's Nominees Ltd v Woodside Oil Co* [1968] 121 CLR 483 and *Teck Corporation Ltd v Millar* [1973] 2 WWR 385). Indeed (post-*Ampol*) in *Cayne v Global Natural Resources plc* [1984] 1 All ER 225, Sir Robert Megarry V-C gave support to the proposition that directors may use their powers to issue shares with a view to resisting a takeover bid in circumstances where they considered that the exercise of such powers would be in the company's interests. Having referred to *Howard Smith Ltd* (at pp 834–836), Sir Robert Megarry V-C gave the following example of a legitimate use of directors' powers in seeking to defeat a takeover bid:

'If Company A and Company B are in business competition, and Company A acquires a large holding of shares in Company B with the object of running Company B down so as to lessen its competition, I would have thought that the directors of Company B might well come to the honest conclusion that it was contrary to the best interests of Company B to allow Company A to effect its purpose, and that in fact this would be so. If, then, the directors issue further shares in Company B in order to maintain their control of Company B for the purpose of defeating Company A's plans and continuing Company B in competition with Company A, I cannot see why that should not be a perfectly proper exercise of the fiduciary powers of the directors of Company B. The object is not to retain control as such, but to prevent Company B from being reduced to impotence and beggary, and the only means available to the directors for achieving this purpose is to retain control. This is quite different from directors seeking to retain control because they think that they are better directors than their rivals would be.'

Therefore, it may be concluded that the proper purpose rule will defeat an allotment of shares **other than** where the dominant purpose for the issue is for raising capital (*Ampol*) or, in exceptional circumstances, where the dominant purpose for the issue was to safeguard the very existence of the company; as opposed to a dominant motive which merely sought to manipulate a company's management structure and/or status of its controlling shareholder. This conclusion draws significant strength from the Court of Appeal's application of the proper purpose rule to the facts found in *Criterion Properties plc v Stratford UK Properties* [2003] BCC 50. However, it must be **stressed** that here, the actual application of the proper purpose rule constituted an incorrect application of the law and as such was the subject of much criticism in the subsequent appeal of the case to the House of Lords [2004] 1 WLR 1846 (discussed further below).

In the *Criterion* case, an American company (O) and a UK plc (C) were parties to a joint venture. The terms of the venture were governed by an investment and shareholders' agreement. Subsequently, a second supplementary agreement (the 'SSA') was entered into on behalf of C by one of its directors (X) (but without the approval of the full board of directors) by way of a variation of the first agreement. The purpose of the SSA was to protect C against a possible takeover and change of management (departure of the current directors) by what was described as a 'poison pill arrangement'. The effect of the SSA was that C would be made subject to heavy financial penalties if the terms of the SSA were breached. Therefore, it was anticipated that a potential takeover bidder would be put off from trying to seize control of C.

C subsequently sought to rescind the SSA, contending that in entering the agreement X had acted for an improper purpose (to the knowledge of O; alleging that O should therefore be denied the benefit of the agreement – see constructive trustees, discussed below). At first instance, Hart J found that the SSA agreement was entered into for an improper purpose in so far as the exercise of the power, while seeking to deter potential takeover bids, also exposed the company to the possibility of economic damage to the extent that, if the SSA agreement was breached, its effect on C may have been more damaging than if C had been acquired by an unwanted predator. The Court of Appeal accepted that Hart J had been correct to hold that the agreement was outside the powers of C's directors because the SSA went beyond anything which could be justified for the purpose of deterring an unwelcome predator. A breach of the agreement could be triggered by any takeover, not only a hostile one, and further it could be triggered by the departure of the 'named' directors even in circumstances which had nothing to do with a change of control: for example, the death or dismissal of a 'named' director due to misconduct. However, the Court of Appeal observed that the validity of the agreement may have been upheld if it had been drafted in a manner which **confined** its purpose to seeing off a particular predator in circumstances where the motive of that action was to protect and further the survival and interests of the company. (See also *CAS (Nominees) Ltd* v *Nottingham Forest FC* [2002] 1 BCLC 613, discussed further in Chapter 24.)

The case was appealed to the House of Lords. The House discarded the relevance of the 'proper purpose rule' issue. The House considered that the crucial legal point, and one that had failed to find relevance in the lower courts, was the issue of directors' authority (directors' authority is discussed in Chapter 8). If X had a valid authority to conclude the SSA (actual or ostensible authority) then there was no reason (other than the question of 'bad faith' on the part of O) why the SSA should not have been enforceable (see ss 35A and 35B, CA 1985, discussed in Chapter 8). If X did not have a valid authority, then the transaction would be set aside; the issue of O's knowledge of the improper purpose would be quite irrelevant. In effect, the question as to whether X had the requisite authority was the crux of the matter. As the 'authority issue' had not been addressed or discussed in the lower courts and because counsel had not had the opportunity to advance arguments on the 'authority issue', the House recommended that such issues be resolved at a separate trial.

While not relevant to the issue of a potential takeover bid, the decision of Jonathan Parker J in *Regentcrest plc* v *Cohen* [2001] BCC 494 may also be of particular interest in the context of the proper purpose rule (or rather its non-application – but here, unlike the *Criterion* case, it should most probably have been applied). In *Regentcrest*, a company (R), through its liquidators, contended that one of its directors (A) had acted in breach of his fiduciary duty in voting to waive the clawback of sums due to the company. R had acquired all the issued shares in a company (G), the sole asset of which comprised development land. The consideration for the purchase of G's shares had been an allotment of shares in R. The vendors of the G shares included two directors of R (Y & Z). The sale agreement contained, *inter alia*, a clause providing that, if the value of the development land fell, the vendors (Y & Z) would be liable to repay any shortfall to R (the clawback agreement).

R subsequently encountered serious financial difficulties notwithstanding that two of its directors, A and B (who were not directors in G), injected some £5 million of their own money into the company. The value of the development site fell, giving rise to a shortfall of £1.5 million, an amount the vendors were liable to pay under the clawback agreement. However, R agreed to waive any claim under the agreement in return for Y & Z's future free services as directors of R. Less than a year later, R was compulsorily wound up. R's liquidators claimed damages against A for breach of fiduciary duty, alleging that in voting in favour of the resolution to waive the claim he had acted other than in the best interests of the company.

In dismissing the claim, Jonathan Parker J considered that a subjective test had to be applied to determine whether A was in breach of his fiduciary duty. R was insolvent when the clawback claim was waived but A and B remained willing to support the company, as evidenced by the injection of £5 million of their own funds in an attempt to ensure its survival. The learned judge concluded that A and B had genuinely believed that there was a real chance of rescuing the company. Further, there were viable commercial reasons for releasing the claim against Y & Z who were also directors of R: that is, to retain their services and enable the board to present a united front. R's chances of survival would have been impaired if it had commenced contested proceedings against two of its own directors. A and B knew that it was doubtful whether Y & Z could meet any judgment against them. In all the circumstances, the learned judge came to the conclusion that A honestly believed that waiving the clawback claim was in the best interests of R.

Therefore, according to Jonathan Parker J, A passed the *bona fide* test; he performed his duties in the best interests of the company. But what about the 'proper purpose' duty? Objectively, did A act for a proper purpose in exercising his vote to release R's claim against Y & Z? R was in serious financial difficulty at the time of the vote, with perhaps only an optimistic chance of survival; Y & Z appeared to be on friendly terms with A, as well as being fellow directors of R. If Y & Z's obligation to R had not been cast away, the resulting moneys may, in any case, have ended up in the pockets of R's creditors and not have benefited the living (but then dying) company. However, was the purpose for discarding Y & Z's liability a proper purpose in an objective sense: namely was the dominant purpose one which sought to safeguard the stability and future of R? Surprisingly, as the learned judge pointed out (at p 514), a breach of the proper purpose duty was never even (although it surely should have been) contended in argument.

THE CONFLICT OF INTEREST RULE

The conflict of interest rule, as a rule of equity, is closely related to the fiduciary duties owed by a director of a company. However, it should be noted that, although in many reported cases a breach of the conflict of interest rule will also result and be considered as a breach of a fiduciary duty, this may not always be the case: see e.g. *Regal*

(*Hastings*) *Ltd* v *Gulliver* [1942] 1 All ER 378, [1967] 2 AC 134 (discussed below). The conflict of interest rule may be stated as a rule which prohibits a company director from using a corporate opportunity or potential opportuntity for his own personal use. This principle of equity, equally applicable to a trustee–beneficiary relationship, is often referred to as the 'fair dealing rule'. A director assumes the duties of a trustee in relation to dealings in the company's property: see e.g. *JJ Harrison Properties Ltd* v *Harrison* [2002] 1 BCLC 162. Frequently, the conflict of interest rule may be said to incorporate duties of loyalty and fidelity but technically, as stated, the rule is not strictly a duty: see *Movitex Ltd* v *Bulfield and Ors* [1986] 2 BCC 99, 40 (discussed below).

Except in circumstances where a company's articles provide for a relaxation of this equitable principle (discussed below), a transaction which involves a conflict of interest will, unlike a breach of a fiduciary duty, be set aside without enquiry as to whether any harm was inflicted on the company; there will be no consideration of whether the act in question was performed *bona fide* in the interests of the company as a whole. In *Aberdeen Railway Co* v *Blaikie Bros* (1854) 1 Macq 461, Lord Cranworth proposed that this rule involved:

> '. . . a rule of universal application that no one, having . . . duties to discharge, shall be allowed to enter into engagements in which he has, or can have, a personal interest conflicting, or which may possibly conflict, with the interests of those whom he is bound to protect.' (at p 471)

In *Boardman and Anor* v *Phipps* [1967] AC 46, Lord Upjohn suggested that Lord Cranworth's remarks relating to the 'possibility of conflict' should be construed to mean:

> '. . . the reasonable man looking at the relevant facts and circumstances of the particular case would think that there was a real sensible possibility of conflict.' (at p 124)

Accordingly, while the effect of the conflict of interest rule is strict, the nature of the conflict giving rise to its application must involve more than a trivial interest: that is there must be a real and viable possibility of conflict. Prior to *Boardman and Anor* v *Phipps*, in *Boulting* v *ACTAT* [1963] 2 QB 606, Lord Upjohn remarked that the conflict of interest rule should be applied in the following manner:

> '. . . a broad rule like this must be applied with common sense and with an appreciation of the sort of circumstances in which over the last 200 years and more it has been applied and thrived. It must be applied realistically to a state of affairs which discloses a real conflict of duty and interest and not some theoretical or rhetorical contract.' (at p 637)

Application of the conflict of interest rule

Corporate opportunity/secret profits

A director of a company will be in breach of the conflict of interest rule where, by virtue of his fiduciary position, he uses, to his own advantage, information which came into his hands whilst holding office (information of which the company had (or potentially had) an interest); see the judgments of Malins V-C in *Imperial Mercantile Credit Association* v *Coleman* (1871) LR 6 Ch App 558 at p 563, Lord Blanesburgh in *Bell* v *Lever Bros Ltd* [1932] AC 161 at p 194, and the more recent Court of Appeal judgment in *Bhullar* v *Bhullar* [2003] 2 BCLC 241. A director will be in breach of the conflict of interest rule even in circumstances where the company in which he holds/held office could not itself have benefited from the opportunity in question. The prohibition against a director benefiting from a corporate opportunity is operative for the duration of a director's term of office but may also be enforced against the director following his departure from the company, albeit that an ex-director will not be precluded from using his general fund of skill and knowledge, or his personal connections, to compete with his former company.

In relation to the potential liability of an ex-director, liability will arise in circumstances where he/she exploited information which was directed towards the company in which he/she held office and which came to his/her attention during the period in which he/she held office. If a director exploits the corporate opportunity for the benefit of another company which then takes advantage of the opportunity, then both the director and the new company will be liable to account as they will have jointly participated in a breach of trust: see e.g. *CMS Dolphin Ltd* v *Simonet* [2002] BCC 600 and *Quarter Master UK* v *Pyke* [2005] 1 BCLC 245. It should be stressed that an ex-director of a company will not be deemed to have misused a corporate opportunity where he merely obtains an advantage by reason of a past association with the company. In order to abuse a corporate opportunity the director must exploit an opportunity which came into his possession whilst holding office: see e.g. *Cranleigh Precision Engineering Ltd* v *Bryant* [1964] 3 All ER 289 and *Island Export Finance Ltd* v *Umunna* [1986] BCLC 460.

An oft-quoted example of the operation of the conflict of interest rule is the case of *Industrial Development Consultants Ltd* v *Cooley* [1972] 1 WLR 443. Here, a director was approached by a third party who wished to employ him in a personal capacity (i.e. without involving the director's company). As a result of this offer, the director retired from the company on the grounds of ill health. Shortly after his retirement the ex-director took up the offer from the third party. The court found that the director had improperly taken advantage of the third party's employment offer, in that the opportunity was one which came to his notice in his capacity as a director of the company. As such, the director was made liable to account for the profit made as a consequence of entering into the contract. (Also see *CMS Dolphin Ltd* v *Simonet* (above), where a director of *CMS Dolphin* (C) breached the conflict of interest rule by resigning from C to divert a maturing business opportunity of C to a new business venture which he had formed.)

By contrast to the *Cooley* case, it is interesting to note the decision of Blackburne J in *Framlington Group plc* v *Anderson* [1995] BCC 611. Here the conflict of interest rule was deemed inapplicable in a situation which *prima facie* appeared similar to the one found in *Cooley*. The facts of the *Framlington* case were as follows. Two directors (A & B) of a holding company (F) were appointed to the board of F's wholly owned subsidiary (S). S was subsequently sold by F to another company (R). The directors of S (i.e. A, B and a third director (C)) were subsequently employed by R to continue the management of S's business. During the negotiations for the sale of S to P, it had been understood by all parties that A, B and C would be employed by P to manage S's business. However, unknown to F, in consideration of A, B and C's continued employment with S, R had paid the three directors a considerable sum (in the form of shares in R), a sum which was related to the value of the business transferred from F to R. It was alleged by F that the three directors had obtained a secret profit as a result of the sale of S.

Here, the *Cooley* case was distinguished on the basis that in *Framlington* the directors who were accused of acting in breach of the conflict of interest rule had never sought to divert to themselves a business opportunity which had belonged to the company. The said business opportunity was made available to the company (i.e. the sale of S) and indeed was exploited by the company. Although the directors impliedly benefited from the opportunity, they did so without prejudice to the company's own interests.

The conflict of interest rule is strict in the sense that it fails to distinguish between, on the one hand, directors who have purposely set out to exploit a corporate opportunity for their own benefit (an intentional/reckless abuse of the rule and an obvious breach of fiduciary duty), and, on the other hand, directors who personally profit from a corporate opportunity in a situation where the company was, at the time of the opportunity, unable or unwilling to act upon the opportunity (a technical but often unintentional abuse of the rule which may not invoke a breach of a fiduciary duty). An example of an intentional exploitation of a corporate opportunity is to be found in *Cook v Deeks* [1916] 1 AC 554. In this case, directors of a company were aware that a lucrative contract was to be made available to the company. They resigned their directorships and formed another company. The newly formed company was awarded the lucrative contract. In such circumstances it was patently obvious that the directors had resigned from office with the intention of exploiting the corporate opportunity obtained from their former company.

A case example of an unintentional exploitation of a corporate opportunity is to be found in *Regal (Hastings) Ltd v Gulliver* [1942] 1 All ER 378, [1967] 2 AC 134. The case involved a company (R) which was the owner of a cinema. The directors of R wished to obtain two more cinemas with a view to eventually selling the company as a going concern. R formed a subsidiary company (A) for the purpose of obtaining a leasing agreement for the two other cinemas in question. In order to secure the leasing agreement the subsidiary company was required to raise £5000. However, R was unable to meet this requirement, as a result of which R's directors injected their own personal funds (£3000) to finance the balance between R's contribution and the total amount required. The directors subsequently sold their shares in both A and R, making a substantial profit in the process. The new controllers of R sought to recover the profit which the directors had made from the sale of the shares in A in so far as it was alleged that the directors had made that profit as a result of an exploitation of a corporate opportunity.

The House of Lords unanimously held that the directors were liable to account for the profits made from the sale of the shares. Lord Russell, commenting on the conflict of interest rule, declared that:

'The rule of equity which insists on those, who by use of a fiduciary position make a profit, being liable to account for that profit, in no way depends on fraud or absence of bona fides; or upon such questions or considerations as whether the profit would or should otherwise have gone to the plaintiff, or whether the profiteer was under a duty to obtain the source of the profit for the plaintiff, or whether he took a risk or acted as he did for the benefit of the plaintiff, or whether the plaintiff has in fact been damaged or benefited by his action. The liability arises from the mere fact of a profit having, in the stated circumstances, been made. The profiteer, however honest and well intentioned, cannot escape the risk of being called to account.' (at pp 144–45)

The strict application of the conflict of interest rule is most probably derived from the judiciary's fear that a relaxation in its severity would result in a director being more inclined to disregard the company's interests in favour of the consideration of personal interests. Nevertheless, it is to be noted that a more liberal and just interpretation of the rule would seem to be indicated by its interpretation in some Commonwealth jurisdictions. For example, in Canada the construction of the rule is such as to only impose liability in circumstances which suggest that the director in question acted in bad faith. For example, in *Peso Silver Mines Ltd* v *Cropper* (1966) 58 DLR (2d) 1, a company's (P) board of directors failed to act upon the advice of the company's geologist in respect of the purchase of certain prospecting claims. The geologist left the employment of the company and formed his own company (X) which purchased the said prospecting claims. One of P's directors became a shareholder in X and made substantial profits following the success of the prospecting claims. P brought an action against the said director claiming that he should account to P for the profits made as a result of information relating to the claims which he had initially received as a director of P. P's action failed. The court held that the relevant information relating to the potential success of the claims had never been withheld from P; the director had acted in good faith and had not attempted to exploit his position as a director of P.

Competing directorships

Although there is no specific statutory provision or common law principle which prohibits a person from holding a directorship in two or more companies – see e.g. *London & Mashonaland Exploration Co Ltd* v *New Mashonaland Exploration Co Ltd* [1891] WN 165 – the test to determine the existence of a conflict of interest could, in theory, be indicative of a positive finding of conflict in such cases; especially in circumstances (as, for example, in the *Mashonaland* case) where the director holds office in two distinct companies which by virtue of their business purposes may be viewed to be in direct competition with each other. The potential conflict is clearly implied: how can a director who, for example, holds office in company A, black out information, projects, dealings, potential contracts in relation to that company when, in also acting as a director of company B, he/she is considering business matters, projects, dealings and potential contracts of a type which are equally relevant to company A? How in such circumstances can a director act in the best interests of both companies? (Note that a brief discussion of the problems associated with competing directorships may be found in the *obiter* comments of Sedley LJ: *In Plus Group Ltd and Ors* v *Pyke* [2003] BCC 332.)

Another potential situation where a conflict of interest may arise is where a director is appointed with the support of a holding company to the board of the holding company's subsidiary. In such circumstances the loyalty of the director in respect of the subsidiary company's interests may be called into question and, despite owing his/her duties to the subsidiary company, it is not inconceivable that the director may be influenced by the holding company to pursue policies which, while beneficial to the holding company, are detrimental to its subsidiary: see e.g. *Scottish Co-Op Wholesale Society Ltd* v *Meyer* [1959] AC 324 (discussed in Chapter 2).

Disclosure in relation to contracts in which a director has an interest

Unless otherwise provided for by the terms of a company's articles – for example, where Table A, art 85 is adopted (see below) – a contract to which the company is a party and in which a director has a conflicting interest may be avoided by the company: see e.g. *Hely Hutchinson* v *Brayhead Ltd* [1968] 1 QB 549. In such circumstances, the director must reimburse the company for any benefit gained or loss sustained as a result of entering into the contract. A dishonest agreement between a company's directors to impede the exercise of the company's right to recover any benefit gained as a result of a director entering into a transaction involving a conflict of interest will constitute a conspiracy to defraud: see *Adams* v *R* [1995] BCC 376 (Privy Council).

Where a director has an interest in a contract to which the company is a party, s 317 of the Companies Act 1985 requires the director to disclose the interest to a meeting of the full board of directors; disclosure to a committee of directors will not suffice. To comply with s 317, a director is not required to provide specific details of the nature of his interest; all he/she is required to do is provide a general notice of the interest. A director who fails to notify a meeting of the board of directors of such an interest is liable to be fined in accordance with s 317(7). As a breach of s 317 constitutes a criminal and not a civil wrong, the non-disclosure of an interest in contravention of the provision will not, in itself, invalidate the contract in which the director has an interest: see e.g. *Coleman Taymar Ltd* v *Oakes* [2001] 2 BCLC 749. However, the contract will become voidable on the basis of the actual conflict of interest, that is its ultimate validity will depend upon a resolution of the general meeting: see the comments of Lord Goff in *Guinness plc* v *Saunders* [1990] 2 AC 663 and Knox J in *Cowan de Groot Properties Ltd* v *Eagle Trust plc* [1991] BCLC 1045.

However, from the Court of Appeal decision in *Lee Panavision Ltd* v *Lee Lighting Ltd* [1992] BCLC 22, it would appear that, for the purpose of complying with s 317, disclosure may be given informally. Here, the Court of Appeal held that there was no breach of s 317 in circumstances where the interest in question had been informally made known to the members of the board, albeit that the said interest had never been declared at a formal board meeting.

The Court of Appeal's decision in *Lee Panavision* was subsequently applied and possibly extended by the decision of Simon Brown J in *Runciman* v *Walter Runciman plc* [1992] BCLC 1084. Here, Simon Brown J held that disclosure may be implied from circumstances which **suggest** that all the directors of the company were aware of the interest. The facts of the *Runciman* case were as follows. The plaintiff (P), the former chairman of the defendant company (R), was dismissed from office following a hostile takeover of R. P claimed damages for unfair dismissal. R conceded that P had been unfairly dismissed but sought to reduce the damages payable to P. R sought to reduce the damages payable on the basis that P's service contract had, as with the other service contracts of executive directors of the company, been invalidly extended (i.e. there had been no board approval of the extensions).

Secondly, R contended that P had failed to disclose his personal interest in respect of the extension of his own service contract and as such the contract was voidable as a breach of s 317. Thirdly, R contended that the decision to extend the service contract had not been made in the interests of the company.

In relation to R's first contention, P argued that, as a matter of practice, he had the executive authority (albeit ostensible in nature) to formulate the nature of salary increases for the company's executive directors, providing that such increases were approved by two non-executive directors of the company. R contended that P's authority was inappropriate, in so far as it conflicted with the company's articles which provided that the office of an executive director was held on such terms as the company's directors determined at a meeting of the directors. Although the directors had not been involved in the decision-making process in relation to both the level of salary to be paid to executive directors and the length of service contracts, Simon Brown J held that, because all of the executive directors had impliedly agreed to the decisions taken by P in the exercise of the alleged authority, it was immaterial that such an agreement had not been approved at a formal board meeting.

In relation to the second argument, R contended that for P to have complied with the company's articles in relation to disclosure of an interest (the relevant article was similar to Table A, art 85), P would have been required to disclose, at a board meeting, the nature of his interest in respect of the variations to his own service contract. Compliance with the relevant article would have also meant compliance with s 317. R argued that P's failure to disclose the interest rendered the variations in his own service contract invalid, unless ratified by the general meeting. On this point, Simon Brown J accepted that there had been a technical breach of s 317, but held that the circumstances of the case were such as to deem the breach ineffectual in so far as it would be a nonsense if a director had to declare an interest in his own service contract in circumstances where it was blatantly obvious to anyone involved in the management of the company that such an interest existed.

Finally, R's third contention was rejected on the basis that the purpose of extending the executive service contracts had been to prevent the executive directors from being 'head hunted', a purpose which the court regarded as beneficial to the interests of the company.

In accordance with the liberal but justifiable decisions in *Lee Panavision Ltd* v *Lee Lighting Ltd* and *Runciman* v *Walter Runciman plc*, it is difficult to justify the logic of the decision in *Neptune (Vehicle Washing Equipment) Ltd* v *Fitzgerald* [1995] BCC 474. Here, Lightman J, in giving summary judgment, ruled, amongst other matters, that a sole director of a company was subject to the disclosure requirements of s 317. This decision is surprising because it seems improbable that a sole director would ever seek to consider declaring an interest to a meeting of the board where he is in effect the only board member. Indeed, how is it possible for a sole director to have a board meeting with himself as the only board member? However, Lightman J thought otherwise and explained his decision in the following manner:

'The sole director may hold a meeting attended by himself alone or he may hold a meeting attended by someone else, normally the company secretary. When holding the meeting on his own, he must still make the declaration to himself and have the statutory pause for thought, though it may be that the declaration does not have to be out loud, and he must record that he made the declaration in the minutes. The court may well find it difficult to accept that the declaration has been made if it is not recorded. If the meeting is attended by anyone else, the declaration must be made out loud and in the hearing of those attending, and again should be recorded. In this case, if it is proved that the declaration was made, the fact that the minutes do not record the making of the declaration will not preclude proof of its making. In either situation the language of the section must be given full effect: there must be a declaration of interest.' (at p 481)

It is respectfully suggested that the learned judge's strained explanation was one born of a technical desire to apply the wording of s 317 to a situation which, in all reality, should not fall within the ambit of the provision. It is interesting to note that at the trial of the proceedings (following the preliminary hearing), A G Steinfield QC, sitting as a deputy judge of the Chancery Division [1995] BCC 1000, concluded that, as there was no appeal against the judgment of Lightman J in respect of the s 317 issue, he was bound to follow that judgment. Nevertheless, commenting on the interpretation afforded to s 317 by Lightman J, A G Steinfield QC stated:

'Accordingly it is a ruling which I am bound to follow and apply even if I had doubts as to its correctness.' (at p 1003)

The waiver of the conflict of interest rule

A company may waive the conflict of interest rule by including within its articles a provision which corresponds to the form adopted by Table A, art 85. Article 85 is drafted in the following manner:

'Subject to the provisions of the Companies Act, and provided that he has disclosed to the directors the nature and extent of any material interest, a director notwithstanding his office –

(a) may be a party to, or otherwise interested in, any transaction or arrangement with the company or in which the company is otherwise interested;

(b) may be a director or other officer of, or employed by, or party to any transaction or arrangement with, or otherwise interested in, any body corporate promoted by the company or in which the company is otherwise interested; and

(c) shall not, by reason of his office, be accountable to the company for any benefit which he derives from any such office or employment or from any such transaction or arrangement or from any interest in any such body corporate and no such transaction or arrangement shall be liable to be avoided on the ground of any such interest or benefit.'

The relationship between article 85 and section 317 of the Companies Act 1985

Although both s 317 and Table A, art 85 are concerned with disclosure requirements, it is important to observe that the extent of the disclosure required to comply with s 317 is not as extensive as under Table A, art 85; disclosure under art 85 must be of a specific nature, whereas disclosure under s 317 may be of only a general nature. It is unclear whether an informal type of disclosure to the board will, as under s 317, suffice for the purpose of complying with art 85; see e.g. *Gwembe Valley Development* v *Koshy* [1998] 2 BCLC 613.

While the company's ability to rescind a contract because of non-compliance with s 317 may (as with any conflict of interest) be waived by an ordinary resolution of the general meeting, it is almost certain that the provision would be complied with in a situation where a director followed the disclosure provisions in respect of Table A, art 85. However, it should be noted that, in accordance with s 317(9), nothing contained within s 317 prejudices the operation of any rule of law restricting directors from having an interest in contracts with the company: that is, compliance with s 317 will not in itself waive the conflict of interest rule unless compliance with s 317 satisfies the requirements of art 85.

Where a director fails to disclose an interest in a particular contract, but the failure to disclose does not result in a breach of duty to the company, the company cannot waive its right to rescind the contract and at the same time compel the director to account for any profit obtained under the contract: see e.g. *Burland* v *Earle* [1902] AC 83.

The relationship between article 85 and section 310 of the Companies Act 1985 (s 309A, CA 1985)

At first sight, Table A, art 85 may appear to conflict with s 310 of the Companies Act 1985 (s 310 is now embodied in a new s 309A, CA 1985, discussed below) because s 310 precludes a company from including a provision within its articles or in any contract with a director, the effect of which purports to exempt a director from liability in respect of a breach of duty. The potential discrepancy between s 310 (s 309A) and Table A, art 85 was considered by Vinelott J in *Movitex Ltd* v *Bulfield and Ors* [1986] 2 BCC 99, 403. Vinelott J concluded that the conflict of interest rule was an overriding rule of equity, a distinct rule of equity, a breach of which would not necessarily cause harm to a company or result in a breach of duty. Therefore, according to Vinelott J, a company's articles could relax the application of the equitable rule without necessarily bringing itself into conflict with s 310. Vinelott J stated:

> 'The true principle is that if a director places himself in a position in which his duty to the company conflicts with his personal interest or duty to another, the court will intervene to set aside the transaction without inquiring whether there was any breach of the director's duty to the company. That is an overriding principle of equity. The shareholders in formulating the articles can exclude or modify the application of the principle. In doing so they do not exempt the director from the consequences of a breach of duty owed to the company.' (at pp 99, 423)

It should be noted that, as a result of an amendment made to s 310 (inserted by s 137(1), CA 1989), a new s 310(3)(a) of the Companies Act 1985 permits a company to purchase and maintain insurance for company directors in respect of a liability which may arise as a result of a breach of duty.

THE COMMON LAW DUTY OF CARE

A director of a company will, by the very nature of business and commercial reality, occasionally be called upon to enter into business transactions the nature of which carry a potential element of risk. A commercial gamble may be necessary to secure economic stability and/or growth. Accordingly, although a director will be expected to exhibit a reasonable degree of care in the performance of his duties, it is clear that the standard and extent of care will be far less onerous than, for example, a trustee.

The standard of care required of a director is not measured in terms of a professional standard applicable to directors as a class, but is in part dependent upon the abilities and qualifications of the particular director in question. Mere errors of judgment or acts of imprudence will not necessarily constitute a breach of duty, although directors qualified in a particular business-related area will be expected to exhibit a reasonable standard of skill appropriate to that area of expertise.

To comply with the duty of care, a director must pay diligent attention to the business affairs of the company in which he holds office. Clearly the duty of a director to participate in the management of a company will depend on the manner in which the particular company's business is organised and the part the director is reasonably expected to play. A director's non-performance of an act which it is his duty to perform may result in a breach of his duty of care. For example, in *Re Duomatic* [1969] 2 Ch 365, a director who failed to seek specialist help or guidance (in this case from the general body of shareholders), when it was reasonable in the circumstances for him to do so, was found to be in breach of his duty of care.

Historically, the judicial interpretation of the nature of the duty of care expected of a director was based upon the judgment of Romer J in *Re City Equitable Fire Insurance Co Ltd* [1925] Ch 407. Romer J identified the characteristics of the duty in the following way:

- a director need not exhibit in the performance of his duties a greater skill than may be expected from a person with a knowledge and experience akin to that of the director;

- a director is not bound to give continuous attention to the affairs of a company. A director's duties are of an intermittent nature to be formed at periodical board meetings. A director is not bound to attend all board meetings although he should do so whenever possible (see e.g. *Re Cardiff Savings Bank* (*Marquis of Bute's case*) [1892] 2 Ch 100);

- in respect of duties which are left to some other official in the company, a director is, in the absence of suspicious circumstances, justified in trusting that official to perform the delegated responsibilities in an honest manner. For example, in *Dovey v Cory* [1901] AC 477, a director was deemed not to have been negligent in approving irregular accounting records which had been drawn up by the company's chairman and general manager.

However, the characteristics put forward by Romer J have been subjected to a significant shift towards a stricter approach to the construction of the duty. In the light of cases such as *Lister v Romford Ice & Cold Storage Ltd* [1957] AC 555, *Norman v Theodore Goddard* [1991] BCLC 1028 and *Re D'Jan of London Ltd* [1993] BCC 646, the first characteristic of the duty of care advanced by Romer J has been modified to extend the objective nature of the duty. The characteristic may now be said to comprise a standard whereby a director need not exhibit in the performance of his duties any greater degree of skill than could be expected from **a reasonable diligent person**; the diligent person is imputed with the general knowledge, skill and experience that may reasonably be expected of the holder of the position in question. In accordance with this test, where, for example, the knowledge, skill and experience of a director falls below the standard expected from a reasonable diligent person, the director cannot rely on his/her poor standards in an attempt to argue that he/she did not breach the duty of care. The test is therefore comparable to the one used to determine wrongful trading under s 214 of the Insolvency Act 1986 (for a discussion of this test, see Chapter 18).

In relation to the second characteristic put forward by Romer J, this is no longer applicable in the case of executive directors and indeed it is also questionable whether it is applicable to non-executive directors. The third characteristic is still probably applicable, although a director who relies upon another official in the company to perform delegated tasks may be negligent in circumstances where he/she allows the official to assume exclusive control over such tasks without any form of supervision. Indeed, in *Equitable Life Assurance Society* v *Bowley* [2003] BCC 829, Langley J held that a non-executive director could not delegate his/her responsibilities to some other official, if delegation meant an unquestioning reliance upon others to do his/her job.

Although one may ordinarily presume that the standard of care expected from executive directors would be of a higher standard than for non-executive directors, the presumption may be displaced where, for example, non-executive directors are entrusted with specific business matters or deal with matters in which they have a personal expertise. For example, in *Dorchester Finance Co Ltd* v *Stebbing* [1989] BCLC 498, a company successfully commenced an action against two non-executive directors for a breach of their duty of care. One of the said directors was a chartered accountant while the other had considerable accounting experience. The company commenced the action because the two directors had been in the practice of signing blank cheques relating to the company's bank account. As experienced accountants, the directors should have known better; their actions amounted to a breach of their duty of care to the company.

DIRECTORS' LIABILITY – THE EFFECT OF THE COMPANIES (AUDIT, INVESTIGATIONS AND COMMUNITY ENTERPRISE) ACT 2004

The Companies (Audit, Investigations and Community Enterprise) Act 2004 received its Royal Assent on 28 October 2004. Provisions of the 2004 Act (see ss 19 and 20, in force from 6 April 2005) inserting ss 309A, 309B and 309C into the Companies Act 1985, are directly relevant to a company's ability to indemnify (but not exempt) its directors against liability. Basically, and in accordance with the 2004 Act, a company will be able to provide an indemnity to directors in cases where proceedings are instigated by a third party (subject to exceptions, discussed below), to include a shareholder action against a director. In the case of any other officer of the company (but not an auditor) – for example, a company secretary – the 2004 Act removes any prohibition on exception from, or indemnification against liability.

Section 19(2) of the 2004 Act amends s 310 of the Companies Act 1985 to the extent that the latter provision is no longer applicable in relation to the directors of a company (the provisions of the 2004 Act do not apply to auditors, although note that the White Paper (2005) seeks to provide auditors with indemnity rights akin to those now in operation for directors). Although s 310 of the Companies Act 1985 is no longer applicable to directors, in effect, its purpose remains intact in respect of a director's liability for breaches of duty to the company. Section 309A of the Companies Act 1985 now provides that where a company seeks to exempt a director from liability (or provide an indemnity) in relation to a breach of duty to the company, then this will be void. What is new is the fact that a company may now provide an indemnity (but not to exempt a director) in relation to a 'qualifying third party indemnity provision'. Third party indemnity provisions must be made available for inspection by the company's shareholders.

Section 309B defines a 'qualifying third party indemnity provision' to include an indemnity, other than (a) where the director's liability is incurred directly to the company or an associated company, (b) where liability is in the form of a fine imposed in criminal proceedings or a sum payable to a regulatory authority (e.g. the FSA) by way of a penalty, (c) where a director incurs liability in defending criminal proceedings in which he is convicted, or civil proceedings brought by the company or an associated company in which judgment is made against him, and (d) where the the court refuses a director relief in an application under ss 144(3) and 727 of the Companies Act 1985.

TO WHOM ARE DUTIES OWED?

A company director owes duties to the company in which he holds office and accordingly will not ordinarily owe duties to individual shareholders or creditors of the company: see e.g. *Percival* v *Wright* [1902] 2 Ch 421 (discussed further in Chapter 12). However, it would be very misleading to consider that in this context 'the company' should be interpreted solely in terms of a commercial entity. A corporate entity, while possessing a legal identity of its own, is in reality a lifeless figurehead. Typically, corporate activity will be determined by the concerns and constraints of human self-interest. Directors of companies will aim to maximise the profit potential of a company; a director's inability to do so may often result in his dismissal. The general body of shareholders will, for the most part, seek a return on their investment. Likewise, creditors will inject capital into a company with the belief and objective of making a profit. Company employees will seek to protect and better their salaries and conditions of employment.

Accordingly, a company may be viewed as a collection of individuals whose participation in the corporate entity is most typically inspired by a desire to promote their own individual self-interests. The view that a company can have a separate and distinct interest in a given project, an interest which is independent of the interests of its human constituents and players, is in reality, somewhat of a myth. As such, management duties may, in appropriate cases, be owed specifically to the general body of shareholders, company creditors and company employees. Indeed, in interpreting the term 'the company', the company may be properly viewed as comprising the interests of the company as a whole, that is, the interests of all of its human constituents and persons who have a financial stake in its well being.

The interests of the shareholding body

Where a company is solvent, the term 'the interests of the company as a whole' is quite frequently interpreted by the courts as equating to 'the interests of the general body of shareholders'. For example, in *Gething* v *Kilner* [1972] 1 WLR 337, it was held that in the course of competing takeover bids, the directors of a company would be in breach of a fiduciary duty where they failed to inform the shareholding body of the nature of the relevant bids; the directors in giving such details were obliged to provide information which was not of a misleading nature. Indeed, in the case of *Heron International* v *Lord Grade* [1983] BCLC 244, the Court of Appeal went one step further by suggesting that, when considering competing bids, the directors of a company were under a duty to ensure that they did not exercise their powers to prevent shareholders obtaining the best possible price available for their shares.

However, following the decision of the Court of Appeal in *Peskin* v *Anderson* [2001] BCC 874, a member of a company will be unable to contend that the company's directors acted in breach of their fiduciary duties in circumstances where the directors failed to disclose that they were considering plans to invite offers for the sale of the business. In this particular case, the RAC, through its holding company, negotiated to sell the club's motoring services business; the business was sold in 1999 and members of the club, as of July 1998, each received payments of about £34 000 in respect of the sale. The claimants had ceased to be members between 1995 and 1998 by retiring or allowing their membership to lapse but contended that the directors of RAC's holding company and committee members of the club had breached their fiduciary duties by failing to disclose the plans for the de-mutualisation of the club. In effect, the claimants were unhappy that they had lost out in terms of receiving a share of the sale proceeds; clearly they would not have ceased to be members of the club if they had been aware of the directors' plans to sell the business.

The Court of Appeal dismissed the former members' appeal. Mummery LJ stated that whether or not fiduciary duties were owed by the directors to shareholders was dependent on establishing a special factual relationship between the directors and the shareholders in the particular case. Here the factors were insufficient to found a claim for the existence and breach of a fiduciary duty to disclose to the claimants the proposals and plans for de-mutualisation. In particular, there had never been any relevant dealings, negotiations, communications or other contact directly between the directors and the members. The actions of the directors had not caused the members to retire and, more importantly, prior to March 1998 there had been nothing sufficiently concrete and specific, either in existence or in contemplation, for the directors to disclose to the members. There was no wrongdoing and no duty to disclose the contemplated proposals that eventually led to the 1998 sale.

Although directors do not owe fiduciary duties to individual shareholders, it is conceivable that where a single shareholder dominates a company, say, with 90 per cent voting control, the collective body of shareholders may well be interpreted as the majority shareholder's interest. By way of an analogy, in the New Zealand case of *Coleman* v *Myers* [1977] 2 NZLR 225, it was held that in a domestic type company, fiduciary duties could be owed by the directors of a company to those shareholders (or shareholder) who had been responsible for their appointment.

A creditor's interest

While a director may owe duties to the general body of shareholders, the scope of a director's duty does not ordinarily extend to a consideration of the interests of a company's creditors: see e.g. *Multinational Gas & Petrochemical Co v Multinational Gas & Petrochemical Services Ltd* [1983] Ch 258. This view can be supported on the basis that a company's objective is normally to maximise profits in order to pay dividends to its shareholders. Therefore, the interests of the shareholding body outweigh considerations relating to the payment of company creditors.

Nevertheless, in a situation where a company continues trading, having reached a state of insolvency (a state of insolvency is defined by s 123 of the IA 1986 as applicable to a situation where a company's liabilities exceed its assets), it is apparent that the interests of creditors will begin to outweigh those of the general body of shareholders. This is apparent in the sense that once a company becomes insolvent there is a substantial risk that it may be unable to discharge its debts. Accordingly, following a company's slide into an insolvent state it is logical to surmise that the interests of creditors will become paramount, to the extent that the company's directors will owe a duty to creditors in respect of the maintenance of corporate assets. Indeed, the interests of creditors may take hold prior to a 'technical insolvency', that is, in circumstances where the company's dire financial position places the creditors at imminent risk: see e.g. *Whalley (Liquidator of MDA Investment Management Ltd) v Doney* [2004] BPIR 75 (at p 102).

The so-called 'insolvency qualification' in respect of the determination of directors' duties owes a great deal of its development to the Australian High Court's decision in *Walker v Wimbourne* [1976] 137 CLR 1. The English courts' acceptance of the insolvency qualification is a much more recent phenomenon. One of the earliest cases to discuss the possibility of the company's interest being construed in terms of creditor interests was the Court of Appeal's decision in *Re Horsley & Weight Ltd* [1982] Ch 442. Subsequent case law has confirmed that creditor interests may displace those of the general body of shareholders in circumstances where a company has declined into a state of insolvency. For example, in *Brady v Brady* [1988] BCLC 20 Nourse LJ expressed the following opinion:

> **'Where the company is insolvent, or doubly solvent the interests of the company are in reality the interests of the existing creditors alone.'** (at p 40)

(While the House of Lords overturned the Court of Appeal's decision in *Brady* [1989] AC 755, the above comments of Nourse LJ were not criticised or disapproved of.)

The Court of Appeal's decision in *West Mercia Safetywear Ltd v Dodd* [1988] BCLC 250, reaffirmed Nourse LJ's reasoning in the *Brady* case. In *West Mercia Safetywear* a holding company was owed some £30 000 by its subsidiary company. Both the holding company and its subsidiary were in an insolvent state. D, a director of both the holding company and its subsidiary, personally guaranteed the repayment of debts owed to the parent company's bank. D was responsible for authorising the payment of £4000 from the account of the subsidiary in order to pay part of the subsidiary's debt to the holding company. Upon the subsidiary company's liquidation, the liquidator sought to recover the £4000 from D on the ground that the payment constituted a breach of duty to the subsidiary company. The Court of Appeal, in reversing the first instance judgment of Ward J, held that because the subsidiary company was insolvent the interests of the company's creditors should have been considered as paramount. Accordingly, D acted in breach of his fiduciary duties in not considering the interests of the creditors of the subsidiary company. D was made personally liable to account for the £4000. (See also *Gwyer & Associates Ltd* v *London Wharf (Limehouse) Ltd* [2002] EWHC 2748 (Ch).)

In respect of the judicial acceptance of the insolvency qualification, the interests of the company as a whole will therefore comprise the interests of creditors. The director's duty to consider the interests of creditors should not, however, be viewed as an independent duty; the creditor's interests are but a constituent part of a specific group of interests which are captured under the general corporate umbrella, albeit that they will take centre stage when a company trades in an insolvent state.

The interests of company employees

As a result of s 309(1) of the Companies Act 1985, the matters to which the directors of a company should have regard include the interests of their employees. This duty is not directly enforceable by employees, in the sense that the enforcement of this duty would be dependent upon a resolution supported by a majority of the company's shareholders, or, most probably, if the company becomes insolvent, the support of company creditors. Accordingly, the duty can properly be considered to be of a negative character. Whilst the enforceability of this duty is dependent upon the support of the other constituent parts of the 'company as a whole', it is nevertheless an improvement on the position prior to the implementation of s 309(1). Prior to s 309(1), the majority shareholders of a company had an ability to prevent the interests of employees being taken into account, in that a consideration of employee interests would ordinarily have been *ultra vires* (i.e. a matter outside the objects of a company: see e.g. *Parke* v *Daily News Ltd* [1962] Ch 927).

THE CONSEQUENCES OF A BREACH OF DUTY/CONFLICT OF INTEREST

Where a director is discovered to be contemplating the pursuit of a transaction, which, if completed, would amount to a breach of duty or a breach of the conflict of interest rule, the company may apply for an injunction to restrain the commission of the breach. In circumstances where a breach of duty or a breach of the conflict of interest rule has actually occurred, the director in breach may be liable to account for any profit made or loss sustained as a result of his transgression. However, save in a situation where a breach of duty or a breach of the conflict of interest rule results in a fraud on the minority (discussed in Chapter 23), the company may legitimately excuse the breach by the passing of an ordinary resolution. However, somewhat perversely, a director in breach of duty or in breach of the conflict of interest rule will be permitted to vote at the general meeting at which the motion to excuse the breach is to be considered.

Relief available from the court

In accordance with s 727 of the Companies Act 1985, the court may partly or wholly relieve from liability any director for a breach of duty or breach of trust on such terms as it thinks fit: see e.g. *Selangor United Rubber Estates Ltd* v *Cradock and Ors (No 3)* [1968] 1 WLR 1555. Section 727 may only be relied upon where proceedings are brought by a company against one of its directors: see e.g. *Commissioners of Customs & Excise* v *Hedon Alpha Ltd* [1981] QB 818. A director may apply for relief in the course of proceedings – see e.g. *Re Kirby's Coaches Ltd* [1991] BCC 130 – or he may make an anticipatory application under s 727(2).

The court's jurisdiction to make an order under s 727 arises if the court considers that the applicant acted honestly and reasonably. Section 727 enables judges to take into account the economic realities of a case in seeking to do justice between a variety of interests, including the interests of creditors: see e.g. *Re Loquitur Ltd* [2003] 2 BCLC 442. The burden of satisfying the court on the merits of the s 727 defence lies upon the applicant: see e.g. *Bairstow* v *Queen's Moat Houses plc* [2002] BCC 91 at p 106. The applicant must convince the court that in instigating a course of conduct he/she did not intend to cause prejudice to the interests of the company as a whole. The director must establish that the conduct was not undertaken with a view to benefiting his/her own interests or the interests of some other third party. Although a director may have held a genuine belief that his/her actions were in the best interests of the company as a whole, he/she will not succeed in establishing the s 727 defence where, in relation to all the circumstances of a case, the court views his/her conduct as unreasonable. Indeed, even if the court is satisfied that a defendant acted honestly and reasonably, the court, under its general discretion, may still decide to decline relief: see e.g. *Coleman Taymar Ltd* v *Oakes* [2001] 2 BCLC 749. The court must consider all the circumstances of the case in determining whether the defendant ought fairly to be excused.

Following the decision of Hoffmann LJ in *Re D'Jan of London* [1993] BCC 646, s 727 may prove itself an appropriate defence in circumstances where a negligent breach of duty is alleged. In *Re D'Jan of London Ltd*, a director (D) held 99 per cent of the company's issued share capital; the remaining one per cent of share capital was held by his wife. D was negligent in authorising the contents of an insurance form because he allowed his insurance agent to complete the form to include a misrepresentation relating to D's past experience as a director of another company. D signed the completed insurance form without checking its contents. Following a fire at the company's premises, in which stock to the value of £174 000 was destroyed, the insurance company refused (as a result of the misrepresentation) to indemnify the company's losses.

In the course of the company's liquidation, the liquidator commenced proceedings on the basis that D's negligent conduct had prevented the company from recovering a loss that it may otherwise have been entitled to recover. Hoffmann LJ observed that, in relation to D's conduct:

'People often take risks in circumstances in which it was not necessary or reasonable to do so. If the risk materialises, they may have to pay a penalty. I do not say that a director must always read the whole of every document which he signs. If he signs an agreement

running to 60 pages of turgid legal prose on the assurance of his solicitor that it accurately reflects the board's instructions, he may well be excused from reading it himself.
But this was an extremely simple document asking a few questions which D was the best
person to answer. By signing the form he accepted that he was the person who should
take responsibility for its contents.' (at p 648)

In *Re D'Jan of London*, although in an objective sense the respondent's conduct
was unreasonable, thereby justifying liability for the negligent breach of duty,
Hoffmann LJ held that such conduct could, for the purposes of s 727, still be viewed
as both honest and reasonable. This decision was taken on the basis that s 727 lent
itself to a subjective consideration of the director's conduct and, although the director's
negligent conduct could not be ignored, the director's error of judgment was, in this
particular case, of a type which could happen to any busy man.

However, it is suggested that the ability to apply the s 727 defence to a case involving a negligent breach of duty must be viewed with some caution, in so far as the
defence should not be construed with an emphasis on a subjective standard; that is,
it should only apply in circumstances where the director acted in both an honest
(subjective standard) **and reasonable way** (objective standard). Indeed Hoffmann LJ,
conceded that:

'It may seem odd that a person found to have been guilty of negligence which involves failing to take reasonable care, can ever satisfy a court that he acted reasonably.' (at p 649)

FETTERING THE FUTURE EXERCISE OF A DIRECTOR'S DISCRETION

A director will exercise corporate powers in a fiduciary capacity and as such it may
be assumed that he may not, by a contractual agreement or otherwise, fetter the
future exercise of such powers. However, commercial reality dictates that on occasions it may be necessary for a director to bind the company to a certain course of
future conduct. The Australian High Court recognised this need in *Thornby* v
Goldberg [1964] 112 CLR 597, where Kitto J stated:

'There are many kinds of transactions in which the proper time for the exercise of the
directors' discretion is the time of the negotiation of a contract and not the time at which
the contract is to be performed . . . If at the former time they are bona fide of opinion that
it is in the interests of the company that the transaction should be entered into and carried
into effect I see no reason in law why they should not bind themselves.' (at pp 605–06)

Prior to the Court of Appeal's consideration of the matter in *Fulham Football
Club Ltd* v *Cabra Estates plc* [1992] BCC 863, the extent by which the rule against
the fetter on a future exercise of a director's discretion would be enforced was somewhat unclear. However, support for the view that a director was unable to bind a
company to a future course of conduct, where subsequently it became apparent that
the conduct in question was contrary to the company's interests, may be found in
the High Court decisions of *Rackham* v *Peek Foods Ltd* [1990] BCLC 895 and
John Crowther Group plc v *Carpets International plc* [1990] BCLC 460. Both of
the aforementioned cases were concerned with agreements which sought to bind
company directors to recommend share acquisition agreements to the shareholders
of their respective companies. In both cases the share acquisition agreements were

subsequently found to be contrary to the interests of the shareholding body and as such were not enforced.

The case of *Fulham Football Club Ltd* v *Cabra Estates plc* involved an undertaking by the plaintiffs, four directors of Fulham Football Club (F), to the effect that they would support, in preference to a plan proposed by the local authority, a planning application by the ground's owners (Cabra Estates plc (C)) for the future development of 'Craven Cottage' (the football club's ground). At the time of giving the undertaking, given in return for substantial financial support by C to the football club, the directors believed that their decision had been taken in the best interests of the company. In accordance with the terms of the agreement, F supported C's proposals at a public inquiry.

However, subsequent events resulted in the directors and shareholders of F changing their minds in relation to the terms of the agreement on the pretext that it could no longer be construed as beneficial to F. The plaintiffs sought a declaration from the court that they were not bound by the agreement in that to honour the undertakings would have been inconsistent with their fiduciary duties to F. At first instance, Chadwick J found in favour of the plaintiffs on the basis that, whilst it was permissible for F's directors to bind F to a future course of conduct, the terms of the agreement extended only to the first public inquiry (i.e. F had fulfilled its obligation at that inquiry). However, the Court of Appeal, showing complete agreement with the principles enunciated in *Thornby* v *Goldberg* (1964) 112 CLR 597, allowed C's appeal. Therefore, F was bound by the terms of its agreement with C, an agreement which had not been restricted to the first public inquiry. In so far as F had obtained a substantial benefit at the time of entering into the agreement, it was permissible for the directors to have acted to bind the company to the agreed future course of conduct.

It is submitted that the decision of the Court of Appeal in *Fulham*, in respect of allowing company directors to bind the company to some future course of conduct, irrespective of whether that conduct was subsequently found to be detrimental to the company's interests, must be viewed with some caution; it should not be seen as setting an absolute and irreversible precedent. However, in considering the particular facts of the *Fulham* case – that is, the length of time the agreement was in force before it was challenged (over two years), the substantial financial consideration which F received on entering into the agreement, and the fact that the agreement was, at the time of its conception, supported by the company's directors and shareholding body – the decision of the Court of Appeal may, in the light of such circumstances, be regarded as just.

THE CONSTRUCTIVE TRUSTEE

Where corporate property is transferred to a director or other party as a result of a breach of fiduciary duty, the company may be able to recover the property or the value of the same from its recipient in circumstances where the recipient of the property acted as a constructive trustee. However it must be noted that, irrespective of any breach of duty on the part of a company director, if property is transferred by the company to a third party pursuant to a contractual agreement or other act, the company will not ordinarily be able to recover the said property on the basis that the third party's capacity was that of a constructive trustee. Here the issue must be dealt with by s 35A and 35B of the Companies Act 1985 (discussed in Chapter 8; see the House of Lords' decision in *Criterion Properties plc* v *Stratford UK Properties* [2004] 1 WLR 1846 (discussed above)).

A person (or, of course, a corporate entity) may become a constructive trustee where the person 'received and became charged with some part of the trust property' (knowing receipt) or, secondly, where the person 'assisted with knowledge in a dishonest and fraudulent design' (knowing assistance). Under the first head (knowing receipt) the recipient's state of knowledge must be such as to make it unconscionable for him to retain the benefit of the receipt: see the decision of the Court of Appeal in *Bank of Credit and Commerce International (Overseas) Ltd* v *Akindele* [2001] Ch 437. Here the test may be satisfied without the necessity of establishing fraud/ dishonesty; it is a flexible test and is not dependent upon categorising the extent of a recipient's knowledge, but rather whether the knowledge in question makes it unconscionable for him to retain the benefit of the receipt. (However, note *Brown* v *Bennett* [1999] BCC 525.)

Under the second head (knowing assistance), it is possible for a third party who is a stranger to the trust, having never had possession of the trust property, to be made liable as a constructive trustee; in the sense of being an accessory to the breach of trust. Here, the criteria to establish a third party's responsibility and liability as a constructive trustee takes its roots from the *dictum* of Lord Selborne LC in *Barnes* v *Addy* (1874) LR 9 Ch App 244. Lord Selborne opined that the liability of third parties may exist:

> '. . . if they are found . . . actually participating in any fraudulent conduct of the trustee to the injury of the *cestui que trust*. But . . . strangers are not to be made constructive trustees merely because they act as the agents of trustees in transactions within their legal powers, transactions, perhaps of which a Court of Equity may disapprove, unless those agents receive and become chargeable with some part of the trust property, or unless they assist with knowledge in a dishonest and fraudulent design on the part of trustees.'

Nevertheless, the nature of the conduct and state of mind necessary to establish a person's liability as a constructive trustee has been marred by a degree of uncertainty in terms of the judicial terminology applied to the manner in which a person's knowledge may be sufficient to establish that person's conduct as a constructive trustee. According to the decision of Ungoed-Thomas J in *Selangor United Rubber Estates Ltd* v *Cradock and Ors (No 3)* [1968] 1 WLR 1555, knowing assistance may be established where the circumstances of a case indicate that a person who had no actual or obvious knowledge of the illegality of the transaction was nevertheless in a position to have been reasonably suspicious of the situation and, as such, should have acted upon those suspicions. Therefore, this decision would seem to suggest that a person's recklessness or perhaps negligence in not acting upon suspicious circumstances surrounding a transaction may suffice to satisfy the requirement of 'knowing assistance'. This interpretation was followed, in part, in *Lipkin Gorman* v *Karpnale Ltd* [1989] 1 WLR 402 and *Baden Delvaux & Lecuit* v *Société Générale pour Favoriser le Développement du Commerce et de l'Industrie en France SA* [1983] BCLC 325, affirmed by the Court of Appeal [1985] BCLC 258.

Subsequent cases which have been concerned with the interpretation of 'knowing assistance' have sought to adopt a reformulated test with an emphasis upon a need to prove the dishonesty of a third party's assistance re the breach of trust: see e.g. *Re Montague's Settlement Trusts* [1987] Ch 264 and *Polly Peck International* v *Nadir (No 2)* [1992] 4 All ER 769. Indeed, the decision of the Privy Council in *Royal Brunei Airlines Sdn Bhd* v *Tan Kok Ming* [1995] BCC 899, echoes the importance to be placed upon the dishonesty element in relation to establishing a third party's participation as a constructive trustee. However, in *Royal Brunei Airlines Sdn Bhd*, the Privy Council stressed that dishonesty should not be interpreted as indicative of a person's subjective understanding of a situation. Accordingly, dishonesty is to be measured against the standard of honesty one would reasonably expect a person to display in the circumstances of a given case, taking into account the personal attributes of that person, such as his experience and intelligence. As such, conduct may be perceived as dishonest where the conduct is objectively perceived to be of a commercially unacceptable nature: see e.g. *Cowan de Groot Properties Ltd* v *Eagle Trust plc* [1992] 4 All ER 700.

While the two tests to establish 'knowledge' – that is 'the reasonable suspicion test' so advanced in *Selangor* and the 'dishonesty test' championed by the Privy Council in *Royal Brunei Airlines* – may appear somewhat contradictory, in reality, the distinction between the two tests is a very fine one. As both tests adopt an objective standard to determine a person's potential liability as a constructive trustee, conduct which is construed to be of a suspicious nature in a commercial setting may, it is suggested, usually give rise to a finding that the conduct should, in an objective sense, be classed as dishonest.

OTHER STATUTORY DUTIES AND OBLIGATIONS

The companies legislation has made considerable inroads into regulating the activities of directors. In addition to the statutory provisions dealt with in an earlier part of this chapter, the companies legislation purports to regulate the activities of directors in a number of other ways.

Substantial property transactions

In accordance with s 320 of the Companies Act 1985, a company is prohibited from entering into an arrangement whereby a director or connected person acquires, or is to acquire, one or more non-cash assets of the requisite value from the company (the requisite value is currently set at £100 000 or 10 per cent of the company's net assets; transactions of less than £2000 are not included). In addition, the section prohibits an arrangement whereby the company acquires or is to acquire one or more non-cash assets of the requisite value from a director or connected person. A connected person includes, amongst others, the director's spouse, child or step-child and a company with which the director is associated: that is, if the director and the persons connected with him/her, hold at least one-fifth of the associated company's share capital, or are entitled to exercise or control the exercise of more than one-fifth of the voting power at any general meeting of that body (s 346(2), CA 1985). (Note clause

B24 of the government's White Paper, 'Company Law Reform' (2005) which seeks to restrict a situation in which a director of an insolvent company acquires a requisite non-cash asset – discussed further in Chapter 18.)

In *Re Duckwari plc* [1997] 2 BCLC 713, the Court of Appeal was called upon to determine whether s 320 was applicable in respect of the following facts. C was a director and shareholder of a company (O). O agreed to purchase freehold property for £495 000 and paid a ten per cent deposit. However, on completion, the property was conveyed to another company (D), of which C was also a director. D paid the balance of the purchase price and reimbursed O for the deposit. However, as a result of a decline in the market value of the property, D sought to avoid the transaction on the premise that it contravened s 320. O was connected with C for the purposes of s 320(1)(b). The contravention was alleged in the sense that D acquired from O the benefit of the contract to purchase the property. At first instance, the contravention was established.

On appeal, O and C argued that the transaction did not incorporate the acquisition of an asset by D from O, but, rather, there had been a novation of the purchase contract. The Court of Appeal dismissed the appeal, finding that there had been no novation; the asset acquired by D was a single asset which could be described as either the benefit of the purchase contract or O's beneficial interest in the property. They were both non-cash assets within the meaning of s 739 of the Companies Act 1985, worth at least £495 000. (See also *Lander v Premier Pict Petroleum Ltd and Anor* [1998] BCC 248.)

An arrangement of the type covered by s 320 may nevertheless be made where it is disclosed to the general meeting and to the board of directors in accordance with s 317. The general meeting must approve the arrangement although the interested director is entitled to vote on the matter. It should be noted that a shareholder agreement (as opposed to a resolution of the general meeting) which seeks to validate an arrangement will not ordinarily amount to shareholder approval under s 320, save perhaps in a situation where the agreement represents the unanimous consent of the membership and where it specifically includes all the necessary details of the terms of the proposed arrangement: see e.g. *Demite Ltd v Protec Health Ltd and Ors* [1998] BCC 638.

Where an arrangement involving a substantial property transaction with a director or connected person is not approved by the general meeting, the transaction will become voidable at the company's option (s 322, CA 1985). A company will lose its right to avoid the transaction where restitution of the subject matter is no longer possible or where the company is indemnified by any other person for the loss or damage which it has suffered, or where rights to the property have been acquired by a *bona fide* third party for value without actual notice of the contravention of s 320. Regardless of whether the transaction is or can be avoided, the director or connected person in breach of s 320 and any other director who authorised the transaction will be liable to account to the company for any profit or loss sustained as a result of the breach of the provision (the loss sustained may be measured in relation to any depreciation in value of the asset(s) acquired in contravention of s 320: see *Re Duckwari plc (No 2)* [1998] 2 BCLC 315 and *Re Duckwari plc (No 3)* [1999] 1 BCLC 168). However, where the breach of s 320 was committed by a connected person, the director with whom the person is connected will not be liable if he/she can prove that all reasonable steps had been taken to secure the company's compliance with s 320. The connected person and any authorising director may also escape liability if they can establish that at the time of the transaction they were unaware that they were acting in contravention of s 320.

Exceptions to section 320

The following are exceptions to s 320:

(1) Group transactions

An exception to s 320 is provided by s 321(2) of the Companies Act 1985 which allows holding companies to acquire or transfer assets from or to their wholly owned subsidiaries, or wholly owned subsidiaries within a group of companies to acquire or transfer assets from or to other wholly owned subsidiaries within the same group.

(2) Winding up

Section 321(2)(b) provides an exception to s 320 where a company, in the course of being wound up, enters into an arrangement for the acquisition of a non-cash asset (the provision does not apply to a members' voluntary winding up petition because here the members will retain an interest in the disposal of the company's assets (discussed in Chapter 15)). It should be noted that the operation of s 320 will not be excluded in relation to a sale made by a company through a receiver (acting as the company's agent): see e.g. *Demite Ltd* v *Protec Health Ltd and Ors* [1998] BCC 638.

(3) Members

Section 321(3) provides a further exception to s 320, namely a person may acquire an asset from the company in which he is a member providing the arrangement is made with that person in his character as a member and not in some other capacity.

Contracts for loans and guarantees

In an attempt to curb any potential abuse of the use of corporate funds by directors, statutory rules (see s 330–342, CA 1985) seek to regulate a company's ability to enter into loans with its directors and connected persons (connected persons are defined in s 346(2): see above). The statutory rules are at times complex, a point recognised in the government's White Paper (2005) (see clauses B33 et seq: these attempt to clarify the position). The general prohibition in relation to loans and guarantees under s 330 of the Companies Act 1985 applies where a company makes a loan to a director, shadow director, or a director of its holding company, or where it enters into any guarantee or provides any security in connection with a loan made by any person to a director, shadow director, or director of its holding company, in circumstances where the loan is in excess of £5000 (s 334, CA 1985). (Note that the government's White Paper, 'Modern Company Law' (2005), proposes to lift the general prohibition in circumstances where the members of the company approve the transaction in question by means of an ordinary resolution – see clause B33.)

It should be noted that a payment to a director in the form of remuneration cannot ordinarily be considered to be a loan, although a loan could possibly be dressed up as remuneration in an attempt to avoid s 330. The test to determine whether moneys paid to a director can properly be regarded as an award of remuneration is one not concerned with the ability of a company to make the level of the remuneration award in question; rather it is solely concerned with the actual purpose of the payment. The test was advanced by Mummery LJ in *Currencies Direct Ltd* v *Ellis* [2002] 2 BCLC 482. His lordship opined that a payment is one of remuneration if it is consideration for work done or to be done, albeit that the nature of the consideration can take different forms and does not necessarily have to take the form of a conventional salary payment; nor does there have to be a specific agreement fixing or defining the level and date on which the remuneration award is to be made.

In addition to the general prohibition in respect of loans etc., certain other prohibitive rules apply to 'relevant companies' (see s 330(3)–(4), CA 1985). A 'relevant' company is defined as a public company but can include a private company in a situation where the private company is part of a group of companies to which a public company belongs. The additional prohibitions made against relevant companies are as follows:

- **Quasi-loans**
  A quasi-loan is defined by s 331(3) as an arrangement under which a company meets some financial obligation of a director, a connected person, or its holding company: e.g. the payment of a credit card. Quasi-loans are prohibited in the case of a relevant company unless the quasi-loan is a short-term loan (see s 332, CA 1985) and is to be reimbursed within two months and the total amount outstanding on all quasi-loans made by the company does not exceed £5000. The prohibition in relation to quasi-loans also applies to guarantees entered into by a company in respect of a quasi-loan made by a third party for the benefit of a director, connected person or holding company.

- **Credit transactions**
  Any credit transaction entered into by a relevant company for the benefit of a director, connected person or holding company is prohibited, as is a guarantee given by the company in respect of a credit transaction between a director, connected person or holding company, and a third party. The only exception to this prohibition is in respect of a credit transaction which does not exceed £10 000, that is, providing the credit transaction is entered into in the ordinary course of a company's business upon terms which the company would have been prepared to extend to any unconnected person of the same financial standing (s 335(2), CA 1985).

Although the general theme of the legislation seeks to prohibit all forms of loans (and also guarantees of directors' debts), certain exceptions to the general prohibitions are allowed. The following statutory provisions provide exceptions to s 330.

- **Section 333, CA 1985**
  A loan or quasi-loan made by a relevant company to another member of the group of companies to which it belongs, or the provision by the relevant company of a guarantee or security in connection with a loan or quasi-loan made by any person to a member of the group is permissible. A quasi-loan is defined by

s 331(3) as an arrangement under which a company meets some financial obligation of a director, a connected person, or its holding company. The obligation is met on the understanding that it will be reimbursed at some later date.

- **Section 336, CA 1985**
  A loan made by a subsidiary to its holding company or the provision of a guarantee or of security in connection with a loan or quasi-loan made to the subsidiary's holding company by any person, is permitted; as is a credit transaction by a company, whereby the company acts as a creditor for its holding company or where it enters into a guarantee or provides security in connection with a credit transaction made by any person for the benefit of the holding company.

- **Section 337, CA 1985**
  It is permissible for a company to make funds available (maximum amount of £20 000) to a director for the purpose of company business to facilitate the performance of the director's duties. The general meeting must first approve the purpose and amount of expenditure incurred; full disclosure of the purpose for the required funding must be made known to the general meeting.

- **Section 338, CA 1985**
  Money lending companies enjoy wide exceptions. Any loan, quasi-loan or guarantee made by a money lending company is permissible providing it is made within the ordinary course of business on terms which the company might reasonably have afforded to an unconnected person of the same financial standing. A loan made to one of the company's directors or a director of the company's holding company enabling the director to purchase or improve his main residence is permissible, providing the loan is made on such terms as would normally be made available to an employee of the company. A money lending company which is a relevant company (unless it is a banking company) may not enter into any loan, quasi-loan or guarantee if the aggregate of the relevant amount exceeds £100 000 (s 338(4), CA 1985).

Civil and criminal penalties for a breach of section 330

A breach of s 330 will render the transaction in question voidable: see e.g. *Re Ciro Citterio Menswear plc* v *Thakrar* [2002] 1 BCLC 672. The company may (although it is not obliged to) avoid the transaction (by ordinary resolution), in which case a director and/or connected person to whom the payments were made (and any director who authorised such payments) will be liable to account for any loss incurred by the company as a consequence of the breach. However, an authorising director or a director to whom a person was connected may escape liability where it is proved that at the time of the transaction he was not aware of the relevant circumstances constituting the contravention of s 330 (s 341, CA 1985).

Criminal sanctions apply only in the case of relevant companies. The company and any director who, with knowledge or reasonable cause to be aware of a breach of s 330, authorised or permitted the breach to occur, and any other person who, with knowledge or with reasonable cause to know of the contravention, procured the transaction or arrangement, will be guilty of an offence and as such will be liable on conviction to be imprisoned, fined, or both. A relevant company may escape liability if it can prove that, at the time the transaction or arrangement was entered into, it did not know (i.e. the company's directing mind did not know of the relevant circumstances which gave rise to the contravention (s 342, CA 1985)).

PROPOSALS FOR REFORMING DIRECTORS' DUTIES AND REGULATING CONFLICTS OF INTEREST

Statutory list of duties

In 1998, the Law Commission issued a consultation paper (No 153) entitled 'Company Directors: Regulating Conflicts of Interest and Formulating a Statement of Duties'. (The responses to that consultation are contained in the Commission's 1999 consultation paper (No 173) of the same name.) The consultation paper considered (amongst other matters) the possibility of a statutory codification of directors' duties and considered whether codification should comprise a comprehensive codification, a partial codification, a statutory statement for guidance purposes only, or a non-binding statement on the principal duties in the general law to be used in certain prescribed forms. In considering the said recommendations, the CLR proposed a codification of directors' common law duties with the objective of seeking to provide greater clarity in their determination and a more accessible means of information in respect of the duties. In the main, the White Paper, 'Modernising Company Law' (2002) accepted the CLR proposals, agreeing the need for a statutory code of duties. However, contrary to the suggestion made by the CLR, the White Paper (2002) considered it unnecessary for directors to sign a statement to the effect that they had read and understood the statutory statement. The White Paper (2002) discarded this proposal on the ground that the statement would not necessarily include all of a director's responsibilities: for example, it would not cover directors' obligations to make returns to Companies House. Further, signing the statement would have no legal effect, as the duties would be binding irrespective of whether or not a director signed the statement. In the subsequent White Paper (2005) the proposals advanced in the earlier White Paper (2002) were agreed.

The 2005 White Paper's suggested statutory list of directors' duties is outlined below (the list is also applicable to regulate former directors). The list is similar in content to that contained in the earlier White Paper (2002), although in parts it is not as detailed. It is written in a 'plain English'-type style, no doubt in an **attempt** to clarify and simplify some complex issues. However, in some respects, the absence of detail may cause confusion rather than produce clarity.

> *Clause B2*: A director of a company must (a) act in accordance with the company's constitution (b) only exercise powers for the purposes for which they were conferred [the proper purpose rule].

> *Clause B3* (1): A director must act in good faith, in a manner most likely to promote the success of the company for the benefit of its members as a whole.

> (3) In determining what is most likely to promote the success of the company the director must take into account:
> (a) the consequences of the act both in the short and long term;

(b) the company's need to foster (i) & (ii) its business relationships including those with its employees and suppliers and the customers for its products and services, (iii) the impact of its actions on affected communities and the environment and (iv) the need to maintain a reputation for high standards of business conduct;

(c) the need to act fairly as between members of the company who have different interests.

Clause B4 (1): A director must exercise independent judgment in relation to the exercise of his powers.

(2) The above duty is not infringed by:

(a) A director acting in accordance with an agreement entered into by the company, which restricts his/her future exercise of discretion.

(b) A director acting in accordance with the company's constitution.

Clause B5 (1): A director must exercise reasonable care, skill and diligence.

(2) The care, skill and diligence is that which would be exercised by a reasonably diligent person with both:

(a) the knowledge, skill and experience which may reasonably be expected of a director in his position, and

(b) any additional knowledge, skill and experience that the director may have.

Clause B6: (1) A director is not permitted to have a direct or indirect interest that conflicts or may possibly conflict with the interests of the company.

(2) The interest applies in particular to the exploitation of any property, information or opportunity (and it is immaterial whether the company could take advantage of the interest in question).

(3) The duty is not infringed:

(a) if there was no real possibility of a conflict of interest;

(b) if the conflict arises in relation to a proposed transaction or arrangement with the company (subject to clause B8 (below));

(c) if the conflict arises in relation to a transaction or arrangement duly entered into by the company;

(d) if authorisation has been given by the company in accordance with (4) (below).

(4) Authorisation may be given:

(a) if the matter is approved by the members of the company (ordinary resolution); or

(b) if the company is a private company and the matter is authorised by the board of directors (providing the constitution of the company does not invalidate such an authorisation);

(c) if the company is a public company and the matter is authorised by the board of directors in accordance with the constitution (providing the constitution permits the board to authorise such matters).

(5) Any director who is interested in a matter governed by clause B6 is not permitted to take part in proceedings to authorise the same and, where an interested director acts in a contrary manner, the authorisation will only be valid where it would have been agreed without the participation of the interested director.

Clause B7: (1) A director must not accept any benefit from a third party that is conferred by reason of:

(a) & (b) being a director or exercising the powers of a director.

(4) The duty is not infringed if clause B6 (3(a)) or B6 (4(a)) applies (see above).

Clause B8: (1)–(5) A director must declare the nature and extent of any potential conflict of interest (direct or indirect) to the company. The declaration may be made to the board of directors or to the members of the company. The declaration must be made before the company enters into the transaction to which the potential conflict of interest relates. A director cannot escape the consequences of not making a declaration (or the full extent of the declaration) in circumstances where he ought reasonably to have been aware that a declaration should have been made. A subsequent declaration of interest must be made where the terms of an original declaration have altered.

With some confusion clause B8 (disclosure of a conflict of interest) is also subject to clause B12. The latter clause reiterates the intent and purpose of clause B8 (there is no substantive difference save that in clause B12 it is specified that the disclosure of the interest must be to the directors; B8 states directors **OR** members). However, clause B12 further specifies that a director will also be deemed to have a potential conflict of interest in circumstances where a person connected to the director, has an 'interest'. For example, where the connected person has an interest in a transaction in which the company is also interested, then the director to whom the connected person is connected will also be deemed to have that same interest. A breach of clause B12 (and therefore by implication clause B8) is also a criminal offence punishable by fine or, in the case of a dishonest act, a fine and/or a term of imprisonment up to a maximum of seven years (see clause B14). (The intent of this provision is similar to the current s 317 of the Companies Act 1985 but, unlike s 317, requires a full disclosure of the interest.) In respect of the type of interest which should be disclosed to the company, clause B16 provides that the interest does not need to be disclosed if it cannot reasonably be regarded as giving rise to a real possibility of a conflict of interest, or where the other directors of the company are already aware of the interest or, in the circumstances, should ought reasonably to have been aware of the interest.

Summary

All in all, the draft clauses reiterate the present position in respect of a director's common law and equitable duties and responsibilities, save that clause B6 specifically deems the conflict of interest rule to be a duty as opposed to an equitable rule (discussed below). Clause B7 may be viewed as a newly formulated duty (an extension of the conflict of interest duty) given that it specifically provides that directors should not, unless the interest in question does not amount to a real conflict or where the conflict of interest is approved by the general meeting, accept, for example, payments/rewards (other than from the company itself) in consideration of occupying the position of a company director. It is suggested that this 'newly formulated duty' is aimed at a situation where a director is perhaps 'wined and dined' and given other perks by outsiders in, for example, an attempt on the part of the third party to secure a contract with the company. This duty may be particularly difficult to enforce.

The draft clauses are similar in content (although not necessarily in the style of wording) to those recommended by the CLR, save that the CLR sought the inclusion of two further clauses, namely:

(A) At a time when a director knows or should know that it is more likely than not that the company will at some point be unable to pay its debts as they fall due then duty (2) (above) will not apply and instead he/she must in the exercise of his powers take such steps (excluding any breach of duty 1–5) as he/she believes will achieve a reasonable balance between –

    (i) reducing the risk that the company will be unable to pay its debts as they fall due; and

    (ii) promoting the success of the company for the benefit of its members as a whole.

What is a reasonable balance is to be decided on the basis of good faith by the director but it must take into account the degree of risk involved.

(B) At a time when a director of a company knows or would know but for a failure on his part to exercise due skill and care that there is no reasonable prospect of the company avoiding going into insolvent liquidation then neither duty 2 (above), or A (above) applies. The director must, in the exercise of his powers, take every step with a view to minimising the potential loss to the company's creditors (excluding anything which would breach his duty under duty 1 to 5, above) and due care and skill here means the care, skill and diligence required by duty 4 (above).

The White Paper (2002) rejected proposal A on the premise that it may serve to encourage excessive caution on the part of directors in exercising a decision at a time when the company is experiencing financial difficulties (i.e. between actively pursuing its business activities or, on the other hand, reducing entrepreneurial risk by pursuing a more cautious business policy). It is suggested that the White Paper's rejection of proposal A was misguided in the sense that proposal A serves as a timely warning to directors of companies approaching a possible state of insolvency, that they should start to consider seriously the interests of creditors in addition to the interests of shareholders. In effect, proposal A may, by implication, have given a statutory reminder of the common law position represented by cases such as *Whalley (Liquidator of MDA Investment Management Ltd)* v *Doney* [2004] BPIR 75. The inclusion of proposal A into the statutory list would therefore have been a useful addition expounding the duty to consider the interests of creditors at a time when the company was moving closer to the edge of a possible collapse. Indeed, cautious business policy at such a time should surely be encouraged.

In rejecting proposal B, the White Paper (2002) considered it unnecessary to duplicate the law: that is, proposal B is a near duplicate of s 214 of the Insolvency Act 1986. This is clearly the case, but it is submitted that the inclusion of proposal B into the statutory list would have served as a strong reminder to directors of the existence and significance of s 214 (albeit that the significance of the provision in terms of its practical application may be overstated – discussed further in Chapter 18).

Conflicts of interest

In relation to the conflict of interest rule, the statutory list incorporates the rule as a specific duty: see clause B6. The said duty sets out the basic premise of the conflict of interest rule. The company may, in any given instance, waive the application of the rule. Here, the board of directors of a private company (providing members of the board are independent of the conflict) may waive any potential conflict of interest without any requirement to incorporate specifically the waiver provisions of current Table A, art 85. However, for public companies, the conflict may only be waived (by independent board members) if the company's constitution permits waiver; in effect, this duplicates the present need for Table A, art 85. However, the conflict of interest (for both public and private companies) may also be waived by the general meeting.

It should be noted that in labelling the conflict of interest rule as a duty, a potential problem could arise in respect of the operation of s 310 of the Companies Act 1985 (now s 309A, CA 1985) in respect of the ability of a company to waive a duty (i.e. the conflict of interest rule). However, the White Paper (2005) provides (clause 12(6), adopting in part the recommendations of the CLR – Final Report, para 6.3) that the general duties have effect notwithstanding any other enactment or rule of law or anything in a company's constitution (i.e. s 309A will not defeat any waiver).

Clause B16 provides that the interest does not need to be disclosed if it cannot reasonably be regarded as giving rise to a real possibility of a conflict of interest. One must therefore assume that the interest would need to be 'material' (see CLR, 'Completing the Structure' (2000), para 4.11). The test to determine what is or is not a discloseable interest (i.e. material) is not specifically alluded to. However, if the CLR proposal was adopted, the 'material interest' would be determined by an alarmingly vague objective test, namely whether the board would have considered the interest to be material.

It would appear that the intent of s 317 will *prima facie* remain intact, albeit in a reformed version (implicit in clauses B8 and B12). Support for the recommendation of both the CLR and the White Paper (2002) in respect of exempting companies with a single director from disclosure in the context of the conflict of interest duties (currently s 317) – that is, seeking to overturn the decision in *Neptune Ltd* v *Fitzgerald* [1995] BCC 474 – is implicit within clause B19 of the White Paper (2005).

Suggested further reading

Fiduciary duties/conflict of interest

Sealy [1967] CLJ 83

Xeuberg [1988] MLR 156

Grantham [1991] JBL 1

Lowry (1997) 48 NILQ 211

Walters (1999) 20 Co Law 138

Worthington (2000) 116 LQR 638

Berg [2000] JBL 472

Worthington (2001) 64 MLR 439

Koh (2003) 66 MLR 894

Edmunds and Lowry (2003) 66 MLR 195

Insolvency – directors' responsibilities

Keay [2002] JBL 379

Milman [2004] JBL 493

Management duties/problems in respect of corporate groups

Yeung [1997] LMCLQ 209

Duty of care

Finch [1992] MLR 179

18

A DIRECTOR'S PERSONAL LIABILITY TO CONTRIBUTE TOWARDS THE DEBTS AND LIABILITIES OF THE COMPANY

INTRODUCTION

Although the separate legal identity of a limited liability company (discussed in Chapters 1 and 2) ordinarily divorces the company's interests and responsibilities from its membership and management, the corporate veil may be disturbed by statute to penalise directors for corporate malpractice. Where a statutory provision disturbs the corporate veil in this way, a director may be made personally liable to discharge a particular liability of the company or, alternatively, be made liable to contribute towards the company's assets. It is the purpose of this chapter to discuss the aforementioned issues. However, the chapter opens with a brief account of the circumstances in which a member/director of a company may be deemed responsible for the repayment of a corporate debt in circumstances where he/she gave a personal undertaking to repay the debt.

THE LIABILITY OF A DIRECTOR FOR PERSONAL UNDERTAKINGS

Where a director acts in accordance with his designated authority, the corporate veil will usually shield the director from the incursion of personal liability. However, a director's immunity from the imposition of personal liability will not be safeguarded where he/she undertook a collateral and personal obligation on behalf of the company, notwithstanding that the undertaking was instigated to benefit the company. For example, in circumstances where the assets of a company are insufficient to secure corporate liabilities, a director may be obliged to enter into a contractual obligation personally to guarantee the repayment of the company's debts.

A binding contractual agreement to guarantee a corporate debt may also be found in the guise of a letter of comfort. A letter of comfort may take the form of a personal assurance from a director of a company whereby he/she personally promises that a corporate debt will be met. Where, in reliance on the terms of the letter, its recipient alters his/her position in respect of a right to enforce the debt, that reliance may amount to consideration, thereby in law substantiating the creditor's right to enforce the director's promise that the debt will be met: see e.g. *Edwards* v *Skyways* [1964] 1 All ER 494.

A director of a company will also be personally liable on any contract which he entered into on behalf of the company at a time prior to the company's incorporation (discussed in Chapter 3). Although a pre-incorporation contract may be for the future benefit of a company, until the company is incorporated it can have no legal existence; therefore, a company that is incorporated at a date subsequent to the pre-incorporation contract cannot be bound by contracts made in its name or on its behalf. Even after its incorporation, a company cannot expressly or by conduct retrospectively ratify or adopt a contract made in its name or on its behalf.

A DIRECTOR'S LIABILITY UNDER SPECIFIC PROVISIONS OF THE COMPANIES ACT 1985

Section 117 of the CA 1985

When applicable, this provision disturbs the corporate veil by imposing a liability on the directors of a public company. The section provides that if the directors of a public company enter into a transaction prior to receiving a trading certificate from the Companies Registrar (the certificate confirms that the Registrar is satisfied that the nominal value of the company's allotted share capital is not less than the author-ised minimum of £50 000), the directors concerned may be held personally liable for the transaction if the company fails to meet its liability within 21 days from being called to do so.

Section 349(4) of the CA 1985

An officer of a company or other authorised person acting on behalf of a company may incur personal liability in accordance with s 349(4) of the Companies Act 1985. Section 349(4) of the Companies Act 1985 provides:

> 'If an officer of a company or a person on its behalf signs or authorises to be signed on behalf of the company any bill of exchange, promissory note, endorsement, cheque or order for money or goods in which the company's name is not mentioned as required by subsection (1) he is liable to a fine; and he is further personally liable to the holder of the bill of exchange, promissory note, cheque or order for money or goods for the amount of it (unless it is duly paid by the company).'

Although the section is rarely invoked, it is of some practical importance and is not restricted to public companies. The section applies where an officer of a company or a person acting on the company's behalf signs any bill of exchange, promissory note, endorsement, cheque or order for money or goods without reference on the docu-ment concerned to the company's correct and full name. The only exceptions to the 'full and correct use of a company's name' are that 'limited' may be abbreviated to 'Ltd' (and 'plc' in the case of a public company), the word 'company' may be replaced by the abbreviation 'Co' and, further, the word 'and' may be replaced by '&'. Other than for the aforementioned exceptions, an officer in breach of s 349(4) may be made personally liable for the amount specified on the document. In addi-tion, personal liability may be attached to any officer of a company who knowingly authorised the endorsement of an instrument containing a misdescribed form of the company's name unless, in applying a reasonable man test, that officer was unaware that the instrument in question contained a misdescription of the company's name: see e.g. *Civil Service Co-operative Society* v *Chapman* [1914] WN 369 and *Wilkes Ltd* v *Lee (Footwear) Ltd* [1985] BCLC 444.

The section also imposes criminal liability in the form of a fine. In respect of an officer who signs a relevant instrument, s 349(4) imposes a strict form of liability. Although the provision deems that the company may discharge the director's liability, in reality, other than where a company retains a financial viability, an individual in breach of s 349(4) will be most unlikely to be offered an indemnity by the company even where, in endorsing the instrument, the individual acted on behalf of the company and acted with valid authority and in accordance with his duties. In circumstances where the company in question is insolvent, clearly the company will be unable to protect the director's position.

The historical roots of s 349(4) may be traced back to s 31 of the Joint Stock Companies Act 1856, a provision which sought to counter a potential danger which flowed from the birth of the registered company and the benefits of limited liability. With the creation of the limited liability company, it became increasingly important for third parties, in advancing credit to a business, to be able to identify the business as a limited liability company, in so far as any monetary obligation owed by the enterprise to the third party would be put at risk if the company fell into a state of insolvency.

However, the protection afforded by s 349(4) is far more extensive than merely imposing personal liability against a director for omitting to include the limited-liability status of the company, in so far as the provision is drafted in such a way that any error in the representation of the linguistical characteristics of a company's name may give rise to the implementation of the provision: see e.g. *Atkin & Co v Wardle* (1889) 61 LT 23. Indeed, s 349(4) and its previous statutory reincarnations have been exposed to a strict and arbitrary application. Accordingly, even small variations in the representation of a company's name have proved fatal to an officer of a company in his attempt to escape the rigours of the provision; even a minor spelling mistake or error in the order in which a company's name is represented may invoke the implementation of the provision. For example, in *Hendon v Adelman* (1973) 117 SJ 631, Mackenna J held that a cheque endorsed in the name 'L.R. Agencies Ltd' was, in so far as the correct name of the company should have been represented as 'L & R Agencies Ltd', contrary to the terms of the provision; see also *Barber & Nicholls Ltd v R&G Associates (London) Ltd* (1981) 132 NLJ 1076.

The judicial obedience to an austere construction of the statutory provision is such that an officer of a company, having incorrectly represented the company's name, may not seek, in an attempt to avoid the liability imposed by the provision, reliance on the fact that the instrument in which the error in name occurred did not in any way cause its recipient any confusion in respect of the company's true identity. The provision, in its requirement for the 'name' of a company to be properly mentioned on an instrument, is also construed to prohibit a trading name of the company being used on an instrument instead of the company's registered corporate name, notwithstanding that the recipient of the instrument may be fully aware of the company's trading name and aware that it was being used to represent the company's true corporate identity see e.g. *Maxform v Mariani & Goodville Ltd* [1981] 2 Lloyd's Rep 54.

Judicial support for a more flexible and less onerous interpretation of s 349(4) has found little favour, albeit that the provision has given way to some imaginative attempts to curtail its application. For example, in *Durham Fancy Goods Ltd* v *Michael Jackson (Fancy Goods) Ltd* [1968] 2 QB 839, Donaldson J avoided applying the section by advancing the equitable remedies of promissory estoppel and rectification to case facts which, with respect, did not justify the attention of either of the equitable doctrines. A more recent example of a flexible approach to the construction of the section is to be found in *Jenice Ltd* v *Dan* [1993] BCLC 1349. Here, the plaintiffs commenced actions under s 349(4) in respect of five cheques which had been signed by a director of a company named 'Primekeen Ltd'. The cheques incorrectly represented the company's name as **Primkeen** Ltd, i.e. the representation of the company's name omitted the letter 'E' so that the first part of the company's name read 'PRIM' instead of 'PRIME'.

According to Titheridge QC (sitting as a deputy High Court judge), common sense dictated that the spelling error's effect caused no confusion in relation to the identity of the company, thus precluding a finding that the company's name had been identified other than in accordance with s 349(4). Somewhat surprisingly, the learned deputy judge opined that his commonsense approach was not inconsistent or overshadowed by any binding precedent which obliged him to find in favour of the plaintiffs. Although Titheridge QC accepted that s 349(4) should, in accordance with accepted judicial practice, be construed strictly, he nevertheless found that the degree and extent of the error in the case before him did not prevent the company's name, as identified in the cheque, from meeting the primary requirement of s 349(4), namely that the company's name was properly mentioned on the cheque.

Despite the obvious commonsense logic which flows from the conclusions drawn by Titheridge QC, the belief that an omission of one letter or the misplacing of two letters in the name of a company should not give rise to a successful action under s 349(4), even in circumstances where the error was incapable of causing confusion, is clearly inconsistent with the accepted judicial interpretation of the provision. Indeed, the most recent decisions of the Court of Appeal that have been concerned with the interpretation of the section – *Blum* v *OCP Reparation* [1988] BCLC 170 and *Lindholst & Co* v *Fowler* [1988] BCLC 166 – indicate that it is extraneous to consider whether an error in the company's name was liable to cause confusion.

A DIRECTOR'S LIABILITY UNDER SPECIFIC PROVISIONS OF THE INSOLVENCY ACT 1986

One of the most serious attempts to safeguard the interests of corporate creditors is provided by the statutory obligations placed upon directors and officers of a company in respect of their potential personal liability for the debts and liabilities of the company, following the company's slide into a state of insolvency. In accordance with the statutory provisions discussed below, a company may be viewed to be insolvent in a situation where its liabilities exceed its assets (see s 123(2), IA 1986). In calculating liabilities, contingent and prospective liabilities are taken into account. Directors and other officers of the company may be made personally liable to contribute towards the company's liabilities and debts under the following statutory provisions.

Section 212 of the Insolvency Act 1986 (misfeasance proceedings)

Where a company is in liquidation, s 212 of the Insolvency Act 1986 allows the court, on the application of the Official Receiver, liquidator or any creditor or contributory (member), to examine the conduct of any promoter, officer of the company, liquidator, administrator or administrative receiver of the company, in respect of an alleged misfeasance. In law, the term 'misfeasance' is employed in a generic sense to describe conduct which results in any breach of duty, conflict of interest or breach of trust, where the consequences of the wrongful act results in an improper application of the company's assets or property.

Section 212 is a procedural device and provides a summary remedy whereby persons who were involved in the management of a company may be held accountable for any breach of duty or other act of misfeasance. Accordingly, proceedings under s 212 may only be pursued where, prior to a company's liquidation, the misconduct that forms the subject matter of the misfeasance claim was capable of being made the subject of an action by the company. Therefore, the wrong which forms the basis of the proceedings must have been perpetrated against the company and not in violation of the interests of an individual shareholder or individual corporate creditor. Further, as a prerequisite to successfully pursuing a misfeasance claim, the applicant must establish that the breach of duty or other act of misfeasance resulted in a pecuniary loss to the company.

However, pecuniary loss is defined in wide terms so that an action under s 212 may still be sustained even in a situation where the company suffered no accountable financial loss: for example, in a situation where a director exploited his position to obtain a secret profit (see e.g. *Regal (Hastings) Ltd* v *Gulliver* [1942] 1 All ER 378, [1967] 2 AC 134 (discussed further in Chapter 17)). However, the decision of the Court of Appeal in *Re Derek Randall Enterprises Ltd* [1990] BCC 749 should be noted. Here, a director of a company made secret profits (retention of commissions), yet the said profits were subsequently used to guarantee the company's overdraft. Following a decline in the company's fortunes, the company's bankers demanded the repayment of the overdraft and called in the sum guaranteed. Although the retention of the commissions amounted to an abuse of the director's fiduciary position, the Court of Appeal held that the director was not liable to compensate the company in so far as the company had benefited from the funds represented by the guarantee. In effect, the director's potential liability to the company under s 212 was set off against the sum representing the guarantee.

Under s 212, misfeasance proceedings may be commenced in circumstances where a director is in breach of any of his corporate duties. In accordance with the decision of Hoffmann LJ in *Re D'Jan of London Ltd* [1993] BCC 646, the term 'any duty' is indicative of the provision's applicability to both a breach of fiduciary duty (and conflict of interest) and a breach of a director's duty of care (directors' duties are discussed in Chapter 17).

A potential difficulty in implementing s 212 may arise in circumstances where, prior to a company's liquidation, a breach of duty or other act of misfeasance was ratified by the company's general meeting. Other than where the director's wrongful act results in a fraud on the company (discussed in Chapter 23), ratification will ordinarily excuse the delinquent director from the incursion of any personal liability incurred as a consequence of the wrongful act. However, in circumstances where the ratification of the breach of duty or other act of misfeasance occurred at a time when the company was insolvent – that is, at a time when creditor interests were paramount – the effectiveness of ratification may be questioned. Where a company is insolvent, the interests of the company's creditors will effectively override the interests of its shareholders in so far as the latter's financial interest in the company will be superseded by the former's expectation of participating in the liquidation of the company's assets. As Street CJ observed in *Kinsela* v *Russell Kinsela Pty Ltd (in liq)* (1986) 4 NSWLR 722:

> 'In a solvent company the proprietary interests of the shareholders entitle them as a general body to be regarded as the company when questions of the duty of directors arise. If, as a general body, they authorise or ratify a particular action of the directors, there can be no challenge to the validity of what the directors have done. But where a company is insolvent the interests of the creditors intrude. They become prospectively entitled, through the mechanism of liquidation, to displace the power of the shareholders and directors to deal with the company's assets. It is in a practical sense their assets and not the shareholders assets that, through the medium of the company, are under the management of the directors pending either liquidation, return to solvency, or the imposition of some alternative administration.' (at p 730)

The effectiveness of ratification will be particularly dubious in a situation where the alleged wrong occurred at a time when the company's liquidation was an inescapable certainty: see *West Mercia Safetywear Ltd* v *Dodd* [1988] BCLC 250.

In accordance with s 212(3) any person responsible for any misapplication of corporate funds may be compelled to:

(a) repay, restore or account for the money or property or any part of it with interest, at such rate as the court thinks just; or

(b) contribute such a sum to the company's assets by way of compensation in respect of the misfeasance or breach of fiduciary or other duty as the court thinks just.

Where there are mitigating factors, the extent of a director's liability (if deemed by the court to be any) may be less than the actual loss sustained by the company. For example, where a director's potential liability for misfeasance is of a greater monetary value than the company's debt to its creditors, then the s 212(3) order may reflect this fact – see e.g. *Re VGM Holdings Ltd* [1942] Ch 235 – to the extent that the director's liability may be of a lesser sum than the loss sustained by the company. See also *Re Home & Colonial Insurance Co Ltd* [1930] 1 Ch 102 and *Re Loquitur Ltd* [2003] 2 BCLC 442.

As the purpose for pursuing proceedings under s 212 is to enforce a pre-existing right of the company, it follows that the ability to pursue misfeasance proceedings is a property right of the company and that any proceeds obtained as a consequence of the proceedings will form part of the company's general assets. Accordingly, the ability of the company's unsecured creditors to participate in the fruits of the s 212 proceedings will be subject to the prior claims of the holder of any floating charge (i.e. where the charge on crystallisation is capable of attaching itself to the company's general assets).

Section 213 of the Insolvency Act 1986 (fraudulent trading)

Section 213 of the Insolvency Act 1986 purports to impose a civil liability for fraudulent trading. Section 213 of the Insolvency Act provides:

'(1) If in the course of the winding up of a company it appears that any business of the company has been carried on with intent to defraud creditors of the company or creditors of any other person, or for any fraudulent purpose, the following has effect.

(2) The court, on the application of the liquidator, may declare that any persons who were knowingly parties to the carrying on of the business in the manner above-mentioned are to be liable to make such contributions (if any) to the company's assets as the court thinks proper.'

Fraudulent trading is also a criminal offence, which is governed by s 458 of the Companies Act 1985. The constituent elements of both provisions are virtually identical; indeed the distinction between the civil law and criminal law provisions are primarily of a procedural nature. The procedural differences are as follows:

- The burden of proof in civil proceedings should, as with any other civil provision, be established on a balance of probabilities.

- A criminal prosecution, unlike a civil action, may be commenced irrespective of whether a company has been put into liquidation.

- In a civil action, the only party allowed to make an application to commence proceedings is the company's liquidator. In criminal proceedings, the applicant will be the Crown.

Fraudulent trading will *prima facie* be established in a situation where a person allowed the company's business to be carried on when he/she was fully aware that the company had no realistic prospect of being able to discharge a debt or debts. In determining whether a company was privy to an act of fraudulent trading, the court will assess the nature and degree of the alleged fraudulent conduct in respect of the company's present and potential capacity to repay its debts. In civil cases, the most obvious example of allowing a company to trade fraudulently will be where the company continues to trade and incur liabilities when, in a state of insolvency, it has little or no prospect of avoiding liquidation. In *Re William C Leitch Bros Ltd* [1932] 2 Ch 71, Maugham J observed that:

'If a company continues to carry on business and to incur debts at a time when there is to the knowledge of the directors no reasonable prospect of the creditors ever receiving payment of those debts, it is, in general, a proper inference that the company is carrying on business with intent to defraud.' (at p 77)

In determining whether a director(s) had knowledge of the fact that there was no reasonable prospect of the company's creditor(s) ever being paid, knowledge may be assumed in circumstances where a director(s) deliberately ignored the obvious: that is, deliberately shutting one's eyes to the obvious (it is suggested that a matter, as obvious, should be determined in the sense of whether a reasonable diligent person would consider the matter to be obvious given all the circumstances of the case). However, in order to impute the director with the requisite knowledge, it must be stressed that the knowledge, although obvious in the sense described above, would need to have been intentionally ignored, that is, it would not be possible to impute a director with the requisite knowledge in circumstances where he had, for example, been negligent in not appreciating the relevance of the matter in question: see e.g. *Re Bank of Credit and Commerce International SA (in liq) (No 14)* [2004] 2 BCLC 236. In *Manifest Shipping Co Ltd* v *Uni-Polaris Insurance Co Ltd* [2003] 1 AC 469, a decision of the House of Lords, Lord Scott sought to identify the essential constituents of the 'blind-eye' knowledge test. His lordship opined:

> '. . . blind-eye knowledge requires . . . a suspicion that the relevant facts do exist and a deliberate decision to avoid confirming that they exist. But a warning should be sounded. Suspicion is a word that can be used to describe a state of mind that may, at one extreme, be no more than a vague feeling of unease and, at the other extreme, reflect a firm belief in the existence of the relevant facts. In my opinion, in order for there to be blind-eye knowledge the suspicion must be firmly grounded and targeted on specific facts. The deliberate decision must be a decision to avoid obtaining confirmation of facts in whose existence the individual has good reason to believe. To allow blind-eye knowledge to be constituted by a decision not to inquire into an untargeted or speculative suspicion would be to allow negligence, albeit gross, to be the basis of a finding of privity.' (at para 116)

Although fraudulent trading may be committed by any person who was actively involved in the commission of the fraud – see e.g. *Re Gerald Cooper Chemicals Ltd* [1978] Ch 262 – in practice, liability will ordinarily fall on a person who is construed to have been a part of a company's directing mind – see e.g. *R* v *Miles* [1992] Cr LR 657. It must then be established that the person knowingly participated in the carrying on of a company's business with an intention to defraud creditors of the company or creditors of any other person, or for any fraudulent purpose. In addition to the non-payment of trade creditors, a company's evasion of Crown debts – for example, the non-payment of corporation tax, value added tax and national insurance contributions – may evoke a presumption of fraudulent trading: see e.g. *Re L Todd (Swanscombe) Ltd* [1990] BCLC 454 and *Re Cyona Distributors Ltd* [1967] Ch 889.

Unfortunately, the judicial interpretation afforded to 'carrying on business', coupled with a requirement to establish the respondent's intent to participate in fraudulent trading, relegates the applicability of s 213 to a minority of possible instances. As s 213 provides that it is sufficient to establish that 'any business' of the company was carried on, then 'any business' would appear to include a single transaction designed to defraud a single creditor: see e.g. *Re Gerald Cooper Chemicals Ltd* [1978] Ch 262. However, following the recent decision of the Court of Appeal in *Morphitis* v *Bernasconi* [2003] 2 WLR 1521, overturning the decision of the High Court [2001] 2 BCLC 1, s 213 will not be employed in every case where a transaction was designed to defraud a creditor or creditors.

In *Morphitis*, the alleged fraudulent trading involved a company's failure to discharge a debt to X in relation to a lease that it had taken over commercial property. The business of the company (TMC) was that of road haulage. TMC had, over a 12-month period, delayed paying the full amount of rent owed to X as part of a complex but ingenious scheme engineered in favour of the former directors of the company. In accordance with that scheme, the directors of TMC had resigned at the start of the said 12-month period and formed another company incorporated with a name, the initials of which could be abbreviated to TMC (hereafter referred to as TMC2). TMC carried on its usual business until company TMC2 was ready to trade, at which point company TMC ceased to trade as a road haulier and instead re-invented itself as a lessor of trailers. The trailers were leased to TMC2. In effect, in the course of the 12-month period, TMC was, save for its business with TMC2, trading as something of a shell.

Indeed, the ultimate objective of company TMC's continued existence was to avoid the full payment of the lease debt for a period of 12 months (the 12-month period being crucial to permit the directors to avoid liability under s 216 of the Insolvency Act 1986 (discussed below)). Once the 12-month period was at an end, the objective of the scheme was to put TMC into liquidation (i.e. abandon ship, having sold on TMC's shares and assets to associated companies and leaving X's lease debt unpaid).

In *Morphitis*, the Court of Appeal declined to invoke s 213, concluding that the provision only applied where any **business activity of the company** (one may assume, the commercial objectives which define the business) was **carried on** with an intent to defraud creditors. Therefore, not every fraudulent act or misrepresentation per-petrated by a company (for example, in *Morphitis*, delaying tactics incorporating a false representation as to the payment of rent) may be classified as carrying on trade in satisfaction of the company's business (i.e. the company's commercial objectives). Accordingly, the Court of Appeal's interpretation is such that a company is permitted to act as a vehicle or catalyst for the 'odd fraud or two', providing the sum of the fraud cannot be said to involve carrying on trade in relation to the business of the company. To establish liability in relation to the carrying on of the business, it must appear to the court 'that any **business of the company** had been carried on with an intent to defraud creditors of the company' – it would appear irrelevant if any creditor of the company had been defrauded in the course of the creditor carrying on business with the company. The fraud must be related to the pursuit, probably over a period of time, of the company's business activities, and the intention behind the pursuit of that specific business activity must have been to defraud creditors.

However, with respect, and notwithstanding the linguistical wizardry advanced by the Court of Appeal, the resulting logic of the court's interpretation is quite bizarre and, worse still, it offers far too much protection to the delinquent director. Surely, if a company is involved in any transaction with a third party and in the course of that transaction the company acts in a fraudulent manner, then the com-pany commits a fraud in the pursuit of its business (a company by entering into any transaction is, by definition, carrying on its business) to the extent that the fraud is one to which s 213 should apply. It is submitted that the term 'carry on business' in the context of incurring liability under s 213, should not be so restrictively defined. Surely and quite simply, a company may be said to 'carry on business' in circum-stances where, as a consequence of its very existence as a registered company, it engages in any trade or commercial activity, notwithstanding that the activity in question is just a 'one off' act or transaction.

In seeking to prove that a person intended to commit a fraudulent act, it is unnecessary to establish that, as a consequence of the fraud, any person touched by the fraudulent trading suffered any actual economic loss. The essential requirement of the provision is, quite simply, to establish that there was an intention to perpetrate the fraudulent act, an intention which must be established by proving that the accused was dishonest. Dishonesty is an essential constituent of establishing any type of fraudulent conduct: see e.g. the comments of the House of Lords in *Welham* v *DPP* [1961] AC 103.

In accordance with s 213 of the Insolvency Act 1986, a person's dishonesty will be ascertained on the basis of whether, at the time of the incursion of a corporate debt, he/she was aware that the debt would not be met on the date it was due or shortly after that date: see e.g. *Re Patrick Lyon Ltd* [1933] 1 Ch 786. The courts employ a subjective test to determine the state of mind of the respondent at the time of the alleged fraudulent trading. Although a person's culpability for fraudulent trading will be dependent upon whether he/she formed an intention to commit the fraudulent act, the definition of an intention to defraud has been stretched to the point whereby, in reality, it resembles a test based upon a very high degree of recklessness. In effect, the test may be satisfied providing the respondent was aware that it was virtually certain that the debt would not be met on the date it was due or shortly after that date: see *Dansk Skibsfinansiering* v *Brothers* [2001] 2 BCLC 324 and *Morris* v *State Bank of India* [2004] 2 BCLC 236. However, it should be noted that recklessness is measured in a subjective as opposed to an objective sense: see e.g. *R* v *Grantham* [1984] QB 675.

Nevertheless, although the court's perception of a whether a person intended to defraud will be measured by a subjective test, it would be misleading to suggest that objective considerations are completely ignored. Realistically, the subjective perceptions of a respondent must be viewed in the light of the factual circumstances surrounding an alleged act of fraudulent trading. For example, although the respondent may genuinely believe that the company, in which he was involved, would soon escape from its insolvent state, that belief may be without any reasonable foundation. Accordingly, to escape liability the respondent must honestly and reasonably believe that he was not participating in the fraudulent conduct: see *Re Augustus Barnett & Son Ltd* [1996] BCLC 170.

Extent of liability

Where a person is found liable for fraudulent trading under s 213, that person may be compelled to make such contributions (if any) to the company's assets as the court thinks proper. Notwithstanding that the fraudulent trading activities of a company may have predominantly caused damage to an individual creditor, any contribution which the court orders to be paid will be allocated to discharge the collective debts of the company's unsecured creditors (unlike s 212, IA 1986, any contribution ordered would not be classed as 'the property of the company' at the time of liquidation and therefore the contribution would not be subject to the claims of secured creditors: see s 115, IA 1986). The fairness of this approach may be doubted but is rooted in the fact that, under s 213, only a liquidator may commence proceedings for fraudulent trading.

Previously, under s 332 of the Companies Act 1948, an individual creditor could apply to the court and on such an application the creditor could be paid in priority to the company's other creditors. The reasoning for excluding applications from individual creditors is to prevent the possibility of multiple actions in individual cases. However, in practice, this reasoning is difficult to understand, especially in those cases where the fraudulent trading activities of a company are concentrated around a single or small group of creditors. Further, the cost of commencing proceedings under s 213 would clearly discourage a swarm of individual applications under the provision.

Section 214 of the Insolvency Act 1986 (wrongful trading)

The difficulties encountered in seeking to establish 'an intent to defraud' (i.e. to establish a case of fraudulent trading) led the Cork Committee 1982 (Cmnd 8558) to recommend the introduction of a new provision under which civil liability would arise in a much broader context. The recommendations of the Cork Committee were enacted, in part, in the form of s 214 of the Insolvency Act 1986.

As with the fraudulent trading provision, s 214 applies only where a company is in liquidation. However, unlike s 213, s 214 purports to impose liability on company directors (or shadow directors) only. In accordance with s 214, a director of a company in insolvent liquidation may incur a personal responsibility for the repayment of corporate debts in circumstances where the director allowed the company to continue to trade, at a date up to the commencement of the company's winding up, when he knew or ought to have concluded that there was no reasonable prospect of the company being able to avoid insolvent liquidation. Section 214 therefore seeks to prevent an abuse of the corporate form and also aims to protect the interests of unsecured creditors. The width of the provision is such that it will be applicable to any type of conduct that had the effect of depleting a company's distributable assets. Examples of such conduct would, during a period in which a company was insolvent, include over-generous dividend payments, the sale of corporate assets at an undervalue, and excessive payments of directors' remuneration.

In determining whether a director ought to have been aware that there was no reasonable prospect of the company avoiding liquidation, s 214(4) provides that:

'. . . the facts which a director of a company ought to know or ascertain, the conclusions which he ought to reach and the steps which he ought to take are those which would be known or ascertained, or reached or taken, by a reasonably diligent person having both –

(a) the general knowledge, skill and experience that may reasonably be expected of a person carrying out the same functions as those which were carried out by that director in relation to the company, and

(b) the general knowledge, skill and experience of the director.'

For a court to reach the conclusion that a director ought to have been aware that there was no reasonable prospect of the company avoiding liquidation, the liquidator must establish that the director's expectation of the company's ability to halt its decline into liquidation was unreasonable. Accordingly, a director's expectation of the company's future survival, based solely upon business instinct and which is speculative in its nature, will be viewed with much caution, whereas an expectation based upon factual evidence, indicative of a possible reversal in the company's fortunes, will be more apt in convincing the court that the company had a reasonable prospect of avoiding liquidation. The calculation of the state of a company's financial health will be gauged by, for example, examining the company's profit and loss accounts, its purchase and sales figures, its order books and its banking accounts.

A director's judgment, in allowing a company to continue to trade while in an insolvent state, must be assessed in relation to the circumstances prevailing at the time that decision was made: see *Re Sherbourne Associates Ltd* [1995] BCC 40. Although a company's insolvency may not have been in doubt, a director may still have concluded that there was a reasonable prospect of the company avoiding liquidation. The court must be mindful of evidence that portrays a creditable and realistic attempt to reverse the fortunes of the company.

For example, if a company is in serious financial difficulty but attracts a potential investor who is perceived as reliable and willing to inject funds into the company, the expectation that the company will be able to avoid liquidation may be sufficiently realistic (although in reality the investor proves unreliable in the sense of not injecting funds into the company) to warrant the conclusion on the part of a reasonable diligent person that there was a reasonable prospect that the company would avoid liquidation. However, the said expectation will be tainted and rendered redundant where, for example, over a period of time it became apparent (to any reasonable diligent person) that the investor was not going to make good his promise to inject funds into the company: see e.g. *Re The Rod Gunner Organisation Ltd* [2004] 2 BCLC 110.

In the first reported case in which s 214 was considered, namely *Re Produce Marketing Consortium Ltd* [1989] 5 BCC 569, Knox J construed s 214(4) in the following manner:

> 'The facts which the [directors] ought to have known or ascertained and the conclusions that they ought to have reached are not limited to those which they themselves, showing reasonable diligence and having the general knowledge, skill and experience which they respectfully had, would have known, ascertained or reached, but also those that a person with the general knowledge, skill and experience of someone carrying out their functions would have known, ascertained or reached.' (at p 593)

This interpretation confirms the importance of considering both the subjective and objective elements of the section. However, although s 214(4)(b) creates a flexible standard against which a director's awareness of a company's pending liquidation should be measured, it does not permit a purely subjective consideration of whether an individual director (at whatever level of skill or experience) was himself justified in believing (albeit mistakenly) that the company would have a reasonable prospect of avoiding liquidation. The particular level of skill, knowledge and experience attributable to any given director must, in effect, always be viewed through the eyes of and in accordance with the expectations of the reasonably diligent person: see e.g. *Rubin* v *Gunner* [2004] 2 BCLC 110.

However, in some circumstances, the subjective nature of s 214(4)(b) may be permissive of different levels of competency against which the standards of company directors may be gauged. For example, in *Re Produce Marketing Consortium Ltd*, Knox J, commenting on the effect of s 214(4)(b), stated that:

> '. . . the general knowledge, skill and experience postulated will be much less extensive in a small company in a modest way of business, with simple accounting procedures and equipment, than it will be in a large company with sophisticated procedures.' (at pp 594–95)

Liability under s 214 may be avoided in circumstances where the s 214(3) defence is satisfied. The defence will be established where the court is convinced that the director, on first becoming aware that there was no reasonable prospect of the company avoiding liquidation, took **every step** with a view to minimising the potential loss to the company's creditors. In pleading the defence, a director will be assessed by applying the reasonable diligent person test provided by s 214(4). Therefore, to satisfy the s 214(3) defence, the court must be persuaded that a reasonable diligent person, imputed with the director's own skill, experience and knowledge, would have been unable to have taken any further steps in seeking to minimise the loss to corporate creditors other than those actually taken by the respondent director (i.e. following the director's realisation that there was no reasonable prospect of the company avoiding liquidation). In the absence of any detailed judicial pronouncements on the scope and the requirements for establishing the s 214(3) defence, its potential application remains uncertain. However, for a director to establish the defence he/she must clearly establish that his/her participation in the company's affairs was, as from the date upon which he/she realised that there was no reasonable prospect of the company avoiding liquidation, both active and geared to the protection and interests of corporate creditors. For example, the taking of all possible steps may include seeking professional legal and accounting advice, attending/organising meetings with creditors to rearrange payment facilities, and regular attendance at board meetings and proof, via the minutes of such meetings, establishing his/her influence in seeking to minimise losses to creditors.

Although evidence which supports a director's claim to have taken every step to safeguard creditors' interests will be more readily found from the director's continued and active participation in the affairs of the company, in exceptional cases it may be possible to establish that a director's resignation from office was the final and only step available for the director to take: for example, in circumstances where the resignation followed a prolonged but unsuccessful attempt on the part of the director to convince the board of its folly in pursuing a particular course of action.

Where the court finds that a director was a party to wrongful trading, the court may order the director to contribute towards the assets of the company (as under s 213). The extent of a director's liability under s 214 will be calculated according to the effect that the director's conduct had on the company's losses as from the date that the director should have reasonably concluded that the company had no reasonable prospect of avoiding an insolvent state: see e.g. *Re Purpoint Ltd* [1990] BCC 121.

While the objective of introducing s 214 was to produce a stricter regime, in terms of policing and correcting abuses of managerial malpractice, the reality of the matter is that s 214 has not lived up to such expectations: see, generally, *Re Continental*

Assurance Co of London plc [2001] BPIR 733. One of the main reasons for the relative failure of the provision has been in relation to the ability to finance the action. Prior to 1 January 2003, the cost of pursuing a s 214 action (and also a s 213 action) was not regarded as a liquidation expense and therefore, in accordance with s 115 of the Insolvency Act 1986, could not be financed in priority to the claims of a company's preferential creditors and holders of floating charges (in accordance with priority rules: see Chapter 14).

Section 115 of the Insolvency Act 1986 provides that all the expenses incurred in the winding up of a company are payable out of the company's assets in priority to all other claims; the expenses in question relate to the realising or getting in of any of the assets of the company. However, in respect of proceedings under s 214, such an action was not regarded as an attempt to realise or get in an asset of the company. Although a successful s 214 action would result in a contribution being made to the company's assets, the said contribution had no existence at the time when the action was commenced (r 4.218(1) of the Insolvency Rules 1996): see e.g. *Re M C Bacon Ltd (No 2)* [1991] Ch 127, confirmed by Knox J in *Re Ayala Holdings (No 2)* [1996] 1 BCLC 467 and, more recently, by the Court of Appeal in *Re Oasis Merchandising Services Ltd* [1997] BCC 282.

However, as from 1 January 2003, r 4.218(1) was amended (by the Insolvency (Amendment) (No 2) Rules 2002, SI 2002/2712) so that litigation costs, and therefore the financing of a s 214 action (and s 213 action), may now be included as winding up expenses. (The sum of any contribution order is still made available to unsecured creditors.) Nevertheless, the apparent improvement in the ability to finance s 214 proceedings has itself been seriously prejudiced by the decision of the House of Lords in *Butcher* v *Talbot* [2004] 2 WLR 582 (see Chapter 14). Following the *Butcher* case, liquidation expenses may not be paid out of the company's assets in priority over the claims for principal and interest owing to the holder of a floating charge.

A further reason for the relative failure of the s 214 provision is that it is only operative at a time when a company is in liquidation. Accordingly, the liquidator, in seeking to commence an action under s 214, has the sometimes problematic task of having to establish that, prior to the liquidation of the company, the offending director(s) was aware or should have been aware that there was no reasonable prospect of the company avoiding liquidation. In some cases the liquidator's task may be straightforward in the light of overwhelming evidence indicative of a director's folly in permitting the company to continue to trade, but in other cases the evidence may be only marginal and less obvious because the liquidator's assessment of the situation necessarily requires the retrospective consideration of commercial decisions taken prior to the company's liquidation; decisions that, when taken, may have been speculative but driven by a perceived realistic possibility of preventing the company from entering liquidation.

An additional problem, and one associated with the time lapse of conduct giving rise to the s 214 action, is that the liquidator in seeking to commence proceedings under s 214 is required to assess the relevant dates as to when the wrongful trading was alleged to have occurred. The liquidator must select the relevant dates in his pleadings and a failure to select the correct dates when the wrongful trading could be established will be detrimental to the liquidator's cause. For example, in *Re Sherbourne Associates Ltd* [1995] BCC 40, his Honour Jack QC, sitting as a High Court judge, dismissed an action under s 214 on the basis that, although it was probable that the dates chosen by the liquidator were dates indicative of a period of the company's insolvent state, it was, however, by no means conclusive that by such dates the liquidation of the company had become inevitable. As such, there was a reasonable prospect, to which the directors had addressed their minds, that the company could still be saved at the time of the dates pleaded by the liquidator. The judge concluded that it was not until three months after the dates chosen by the liquidator that a reasonable assumption could have been made as to the inevitability of the company's liquidation. In so concluding, the learned judge refused to allow the liquidator to substitute new dates for the ones pleaded on the premise that this would have prejudiced the preparation of the respondent's defence.

It should be noted that the limitation period for a s 214 claim is six years under s 9(1) of the Limitation Act 1980; the period begins to run as from the date the company enters into liquidation. Once a liquidator commences an action under s 214, it must be prosecuted without inexcusable delay: see e.g. *Re Farmizer (Products) Ltd* [1995] BCC 926. Finally, it should be observed that the court, upon establishing a director's liability under ss 213 or 214 of the Insolvency Act 1986, may, in accordance with s 10 of the Company Directors Disqualification Act 1986, impose a disqualification order against the director for a period up to a maximum of 15 years: see e.g. *Re Brian D Pierson (Contractors) Ltd* [1999] BCC 26. (Disqualification orders are discussed in Chapter 19.)

Sections 216 and 217 of the Insolvency Act 1986 (the phoenix syndrome)

Sections 216 and 217 of the Insolvency Act 1986, follow, in part, the recommendations of the Cork Committee (Cmnd 8558) and seek to limit the ease with which a person, trading through the medium of a company, may liquidate the company, form a new company and then carry on trading much as before. Such a scenario is commonly referred to as the 'phoenix syndrome'. In law, the phoenix company will be treated as an independent entity and as such will be absent of any responsibility or accountability in respect of the debts of the liquidated company from which it was created. The potentially prejudicial effect of a phoenix company is most apparent where, prior to liquidation, the controllers of the failed company purchase the company's assets at a significant undervalue and then employ the assets for the benefit of the phoenix company or/and where the phoenix company adopts a name which is the same as or closely associated with the name of the liquidated company, in an attempt to benefit from any goodwill which that company may have built up.

It should be noted that ss 216 and 217 may even extend beyond the mischief which they seek to curb. For example, where a director of a company which has been placed into liquidation is also a director of another existing company and the names of the liquidated company and the other existing company are sufficiently similar, then the director's continued association with the other company may render him liable under ss 216 and 217, notwithstanding that the director never set out to exploit any similarity in corporate names (i.e. in a manner associated with the phoenix syndrome: see e.g. *Ricketts* v *Ad Valorem Factors Ltd* [2004] BCC 164).

Sections 216 and 217 do not completely attempt to eradicate the phoenix syndrome because the provisions are applicable only in a situation where the successor company adopts a name which is the same as or very similar to the liquidated company. In relation to the prohibition of the name of a successor company, this is not confined to the first company's registered name but will also apply where the first company's business was pursued via a trade name. The court, in determining whether the name of the successor company is sufficiently similar to that of the liquidated company, employs an objective test to ascertain whether the name of the successor company was so similar to the name of the first company as to indicate an association with the first company.

To establish liability there must be an obvious and definite linguistical link between the name of the successor company and the original (liquidated) company. Section 216(2)(b) provides, in relation to the similarity of name as between the liquidated company and the successor company that: '. . . it is a name which is **so similar** . . . as to suggest an association with that company'.

In *Archer Structures Ltd* v *Griffiths* [2004] BCC 156, Kirkham J found that it was patently obvious that the name of the successor company, 'MPJ Contractors Ltd', was so similar to that of the liquidated company, 'MPJ Construction Ltd', as to suggest an association between the two enterprises. Further, following the decision of the Court of Appeal in *Ricketts* v *Ad Valorem Factors Ltd* [2004] BCC 164, a consideration as to the similarity of the corporate names of the liquidated company and the successor company may be aided by an examination of the similarity of the products dealt in, the locations of the business, the types of customers dealing with the respective companies and those involved in the management of the two companies. Here, after considering the aforementioned factors, it was held that the name of the liquidated company, 'Air Component Co Ltd', was sufficiently similar to 'Air Equipment Co Ltd', thereby justifying the application of s 216.

However, strictly speaking, it must be pointed out that reliance on, for example, similar business activities as between the liquidated and successor company should not in itself justify the court in imposing liability; there must, in the first instance, be a strong and connectable similarity between the respective corporate names of the companies. Indeed, a literal interpretation of s 216 would seem to suggest that the conclusions reached in the cases of *Archer Structures Ltd* and, especially, *Ricketts* may, in respect of a similarity in corporate names, be open to doubt because clearly the word 'contractors' (*Archer Structures Ltd*) does not necessarily carry a similar identity or meaning as 'construction' and likewise the word 'component' (*Ricketts*) may have a meaning or identity which is not in accord with that afforded to the word 'equipment' (i.e. in both examples (especially in the *Ricketts* case) the names used to represent the successor company do not compel a clear similarity and association with the names used by the liquidated companies).

Section 216 prohibits a director or shadow director of a company which is in liquidation (the section applies to a director who had held office up to 12 months before the company's liquidation – note the case of *Morphitis* v *Bernasconi* [2003] EWCA Civ 289, discussed above in the context of s 213, IA 1986) from being involved, for the next five years as from the date of the company's liquidation, in the management of another company which adopts the name or a name closely associated with the insolvent company. A breach of the provision is a criminal offence (s 216(4), IA 1986). It is to be observed that it is not essential, in terms of establishing liability, for the director of the liquidated company to be formally appointed as a director of the successor company, albeit that involvement in the successor company must be at a managerial level. For example, in *Inland Revenue Commissioners* v *Nash* [2004] BCC 150, although the defendant (D) was not a registered director of the successor company (the registered director was D's son), D had been the director of the first liquidated company and, being impliedly involved in the management of the successor company, was the only person who had the requisite expertise and experience to make decisions on that company's behalf.

Although s 216 may be viewed as a strict liability offence (see *R* v *Cole, Lees & Birch* [1998] BCC 87), it must be observed that there are important exceptions that preclude the provision's operation. The said exceptions are contained in s 216(3). Potentially, the most far-reaching exception is the courts' discretionary power to grant leave to a person to be associated with the management of a company which has adopted a prohibited name: see e.g. *Re Bonus Breaks Ltd* [1991] BCC 546, *Penrose* v *Official Receiver* [1996] 1 BCLC 389 and *Re Lightning Electrical Contractors* [1996] BCC 950.

In accordance with s 217 of the Insolvency Act 1986, a person who is found guilty of an offence under s 216 is also personally liable for the debts of the company. However, it should be noted that liability under s 217 is not dependent upon an actual conviction under s 216, albeit that the constituent elements of s 216 must first be met before liability can be invoked under s 217.

Following a contravention of s 216, any creditor of the successor company may seek to recover a debt or other outstanding liability from any person who, in accordance with s 217, is deemed to be personally responsible for the relevant debts of the company. In circumstances where a person is deemed liable under s 217, the said person will be jointly and severally liable with the company and any other person who may be also deemed liable (i.e. liability will be in respect of the debts of the successor company which adopted the name of the insolvent company). A person will be personally liable to discharge the debts of a corporate creditor under s 217, irrespective of the fact that the creditor was aware and possibly aided and abetted the commission of the criminal offence under s 216: see the decision of the Court of Appeal in *Thorne* v *Silverleaf* [1994] BCC 109.

Although s 216 regulates the use of corporate names in relation to the successor company, it does not govern the practice whereby the controllers of an insolvent company purchase that company's assets at a significant undervalue for the ultimate benefit of a successor company. However, in an attempt to curb the prejudice suffered by corporate creditors as a consequence of the phoenix syndrome, specific provisions of the Insolvency Act 1986 (ss 98, 99, 114, 166 and 388) restrict the ease by which those in control of a company during the process of its liquidation are allowed to purchase its assets at an undervalue; a practice known as 'centrebinding', so called after the case of *Re Centrebind Ltd* [1967] 1 WLR 377. In addition, s 320 of the Companies Act 1985 prohibits a company from entering into an arrangement whereby a director or connected person acquires, or is to acquire, one or more non-cash assets of the requisite value from the company, unless the transaction is approved by the general meeting (s 320, CA 1985 is discussed in Chapter 17). However, as a party with an interest in the transaction is presently allowed to vote on the issue at the general meeting, the provision may be of little worth.

Future reform

In the Final Report of the CLR (2001) (paras 15.55–15.77) it was acknowledged that the present regulation of the phoenix syndrome is inept. However, as an alternative to reforming s 216 of the Insolvency Act 1986, the CLR suggested reform by means of extending the scope of s 320 of the Companies Act 1985. The CLR recommended that where a company is insolvent or becomes insolvent as a consequence of a transaction to which s 320(1) applies, and goes into liquidation within 12 months of a motion to approve the transaction, a resolution to approve the transaction should be declared invalid in circumstances where it involved a transfer of assets to a successor company which is a connected person of any of the directors of the liquidated company and where the resolution would not have been passed without the votes of the director in question or any person connected to that director. Alternatively, the CLR recommended that the resolution should be declared invalid where, notwithstanding unanimous shareholder approval for the transaction, the director in question, or together with any of his connected persons, held over 50 per cent of the company's voting rights in relation to a vote on the motion to approve the transaction. However, the CLR concluded that in all cases a transaction should retain its validity where the assets were sold for a value that corresponded to the terms of an independent valuation of the assets.

Where, in accordance with the aforementioned recommendations, a resolution was declared invalid, the CLR suggested that the company should have a capacity to avoid the transaction and sue the directors in question for an account of their profit or an indemnity against the company's loss. To prevent shareholders from subsequently approving the otherwise invalid transaction, the CLR contended that the votes of the director in question or any of his connected persons should be disallowed in respect of a motion to affirm the transaction. It is to be noted that the CLR's proposal was not included in the government's White Paper (2002) but that it has now been incorporated into the subsequent White Paper, 'Company Law Reform' (2005): see clause B24.

Suggested further reading

General

Griffin *Personal Liability and Disqualification of Directors* (Hart Publishing, 1999)

Sealy and Milman *Annotated Guide to the Insolvency Legislation* (7th edn, revised) (Sweet & Maxwell, 2004)

Section 349, CA 1985

Griffin [1997] JBL 438

Section 212, IA 1986

Oditah [1992] LMCLQ 207

Section 214, IA 1986

Oditah [1990] LMCLQ 205

Prentice (1990) 10 OJLS 265

Doyle (1992) 13 Co Law 96

Griffin (1999) 4 SLPQ 193

Section 216, IA 1986

Wilson (1996) 47 NILQ 344

Griffin (2002) 55 CLP 376

19

THE DISQUALIFICATION OF
COMPANY DIRECTORS

INTRODUCTION

The disqualification process is governed by the Company Directors Disqualification Act 1986 (CDDA 1986) and comprises the imposition of what may tentatively be described as a quasi-penal provision. Following a director's disqualification and with an ultimate objective of protecting the public interest, the CDDA 1986 temporarily removes the liberty attached to an individual's capacity to participate in the management activities of a limited company. The purpose of this chapter is to analyse the circumstances which give rise to the imposition of a disqualification order and the consequences which attach to the order. Much of this chapter is concerned with the disqualification of delinquent directors under s 6 of the CDDA 1986 and as such incorporates a discussion of the statutory undertaking procedure as introduced by the Insolvency Act 2000. The undertaking procedure was introduced with the intention of providing a more effective and efficient mechanism for imposing disqualifying orders under s 6 of the CDDA 1986.

AN OVERVIEW OF THE DISQUALIFICATION PROCESS

The disqualification process, regulated by the Company Directors Disqualification Act 1986 (CDDA 1986) seeks to weed out company directors who have abused their positions to the detriment of the public interest. The reported cases confirm that examples of corporate mismanagement giving rise to the imposition of a disqualification order will be most evident following the collapse of a corporate enterprise. While corporate failure may be attributed to factors unrelated to managerial abuse or incompetence, it is often caused or at least compounded by managerial error or wrongdoing.

Accordingly, although provisions of the CDDA 1986 may be implemented against a person involved in the management of a solvent company, the majority of disqualification proceedings will be commenced against persons who have been involved in the management of insolvent companies. In all but a minority of cases, a person who is subject to a disqualification order will have acted as a company director, although, other than for ss 6 and 8 of the CDDA 1986, a disqualification order may be imposed against a person whose management activities are not necessarily defined as those of a company director. During the period in which a director is subject to a disqualification order, the public interest will be protected by the removal of a director's capacity to repeat his past misconduct in respect of the future management of another company.

Section 1(1) of the CDDA 1986 provides that in accordance with the circumstances specified in the Act, a court may, and under s 6 shall, make a disqualification order against a person with the effect that the person shall not without the leave of the court:

(a) be a director of a company; or

(b) be a liquidator or administrator of a company; or

(c) be a receiver or manager of a company's property; or

(d) in any way, whether directly or indirectly, be concerned or take part in the promotion, formation or management of a company.

A disqualification period takes effect from the date of the order and, while the period of disqualification is operative, s 1(1) will, as confirmed by the judgment of the Court of Appeal in *Re Cannonquest, Official Receiver* v *Hannan* [1997] BCC 644, have the effect of disqualifying a person from acting in all the capacities indicated by s 1(1)(a)–(d). The effect of a disqualification order prevents a person from being a director, liquidator, administrator, receiver or manager of a company's property or in any other way from being involved, whether directly or indirectly, in the promotion, formation or management of a company. Under s 33 of the CDDA 1986, a breach of a disqualification order carries a maximum penalty of two years' imprisonment and a fine. A director in breach of the order will also be made jointly and severally liable (with the company and any other person) for the debts of the company incurred during the period in which the director acted in breach of the order (s 15, CDDA 1986). It is to be noted that the definition of a director for the purposes of the CDDA 1986 is, as in the Companies Act 1985, scantily alluded to. Section 22(4), CDDA 1986 states that a director is any person occupying the position of director, by whatever name called (an exact copy of s 741, CA 1985). (For a discussion relating to the definition of a director, see Chapter 16.)

Disqualification orders which may be imposed at the courts' discretion

Under ss 2 to 5 of the CDDA 1986, the courts have a discretion whether or not to impose a disqualification order.

Section 2

Section 2 provides that a court may make a disqualification order in circumstances where a person has been convicted of an indictable offence connected with the promotion, formation, management or liquidation of a company, or with the receivership or management of a company's property. The maximum period of disqualification is five years where the order is made by a court of summary jurisdiction and 15 years in any other case.

Section 3

In accordance with s 3, a disqualification order may be imposed where a director is in persistent breach of provisions of the companies legislation which require any return, account or other document to be filed with, delivered, or sent, or notice of any matter to be given to the Registrar of Companies: see e.g. *Re Civica Investments*

Ltd and Ors [1983] BCLC 456. In disqualifying a person under s 3, the relevant court may make an order for a maximum period of five years.

Section 4

The imposition of a disqualification order under s 4 will occur where, during the winding up of a company, evidence is placed before the court which establishes that a person involved in the management activities of the company acted in a fraudulent manner in the conduct of the company's affairs. For the purpose of a s 4 order, a person will be adjudged to have acted in a fraudulent manner where he appears to have been guilty of:

(a) fraudulent trading, under s 458 of the Companies Act 1985, irrespective of whether that person has been convicted of that offence; or

(b) where he has otherwise been guilty while an officer, liquidator, receiver of the company, or manager of the company's property – of any fraud connected with the management of the company or any breach of duty to the company.

Section 4 provides that a person may be disqualified up to a maximum period of 15 years.

Section 5

The circumstances giving rise to a court's ability to impose a disqualification order under s 5 of the CDDA 1986 are identical to those which give rise to disqualification under s 3 of the CDDA 1986: a disqualification order may be made against a person who has persistently breached those provisions of the companies legislation which require any return, account or other document to be filed with, delivered or sent, or notice of any matter to be given to the Registrar of Companies. As with s 3, the maximum period of disqualification under s 5 is five years. The difference between ss 3 and 5 is that, under the former provision, the imposition of a disqualification order may be made by a court which has a jurisdiction to wind up a company, whereas under s 5, the ability to impose a disqualification order is restricted to the court of summary conviction at which a person was found guilty of an offence which went to establish a finding of a persistent breach of companies legislation (i.e. in relation to the return, filing, etc. of relevant documents).

Disqualification following a DTI investigation

Section 8 of the CDDA 1986 provides that a person may be disqualified as a director following a DTI investigation (see Chapter 25) on the ground that the person is unfit to be concerned in the management of a company and that the disqualification order is in the public interest: see e.g. *Re Samuel Sherman plc* [1991] BCC 699. The maximum period of disqualification under s 8 is 15 years.

Disqualification for fraudulent/wrongful trading

Where a court finds a person liable under s 213 of the Insolvency Act 1986 (fraudulent trading) or under s 214 of the Insolvency Act 1986 (wrongful trading) (ss 213 and 214, IA 1986 are discussed further in Chapter 18), the court, under s 10 of the CDDA 1986, may, of its own volition, make a disqualification order against that person. For example, in *Re Brian D Pierson (Contractors) Ltd* [1999] BCC 26, Hazel Williamson QC, sitting as a deputy judge, disqualified two directors (a husband and wife) under s 10 for a period of five and two years respectively. The company in which the couple held office had an estimated deficiency for creditors in the sum of £1.18 million. In addition to being found liable for wrongful trading, the husband and wife were also held liable for contributions to preferences (under s 239 of the IA 1986) and for damages in respect of misfeasance/breach of fiduciary duties.

The maximum period for an order under s 10 is 15 years. While s 10 provides no guidance as to when a disqualification order should be imposed, it may be assumed that the fraudulent or wrongful trading would need to exhibit the hallmarks of conduct which is of an unfit nature, akin to that which is required for the purposes of establishing culpability under s 6 of the CDDA 1986 (discussed below). If the position was otherwise, a disqualification order could be imposed under s 10 in circumstances where a director's conduct fell below the 'unfit' standard represented by s 6. If that was the case, and notwithstanding the fact that both ss 10 and 6 of the CDDA 1986 carry the same maximum penalty of 15 years, two classes of culpability would be created in respect of determining the imposition of a disqualification order in circumstances indicative of managerial misconduct.

MANDATORY DISQUALIFICATION UNDER SECTION 6 OF THE CDDA 1986

Section 6(1) of the CDDA 1986 provides that it is the duty of the court to make a disqualification order against any person in a case where:

(a) that person is or has been a director of a company which has at any time become insolvent (whether while the person was a director or subsequently); and

(b) that person's conduct as a director of the company (either taken alone or taken together with the person's conduct as a director of another company or companies) makes the person unfit to be concerned in the management of a company.

Under s 6(4) of the CDDA 1986, the minimum period of disqualification, following a contravention of s 6(1), is two years. The maximum period for disqualification under s 6 is 15 years.

An insolvent company

An insolvent company is defined in broad terms by s 6(2) of the CDDA 1986 as either:

(a) a company which goes into liquidation at a time when its assets are insufficient for the payment of its debts and other liabilities and the expenses of the winding up;

(b) where an administration order is made in relation to a company; or

(c) where an administrative receiver is appointed to the company.

Commencement of proceedings

Section 7(1) of the CDDA 1986 specifies that if it appears to the Secretary of State to be expedient in the public interest that a disqualification order under s 6 should be made against any person, an application for the making of such an order against that person may be made:

(a) by the Secretary of State; or

(b) if the Secretary of State so directs in the case of a person who is or has been a director of a company, where the company is being wound up by the court in England and Wales, by the Official Receiver.

Accordingly, in respect of s 7(1)(b), where a director is subject to disqualification proceedings and the company in which he held office has already been wound up, the application should be made by the Secretary of State.

The standard of proof/right to a fair trial

As a contravention of s 6 invokes no form of criminal liability, the assessment of whether a director's conduct is of an unfit nature will be determined by the civil standard of proof, that is, by the balance of probabilities test. Given the civil nature of the proceedings, it follows that hearsay evidence and findings of primary and secondary fact will be more readily admissible than had the proceedings been dealt with under the criminal law. Further, as s 6 proceedings are of a regulatory as opposed to criminal nature, it is probable that Art 6 of the European Convention on Human Rights (ECHR) will have limited application. The Human Rights Act 1998 gives effect to the rights and freedoms guaranteed under the ECHR. According to the ECHR, Art 6(1) provides:

> 'In the determination of his civil rights and obligations or of any criminal charge against him, everyone is entitled to a fair and public hearing within a reasonable time by an independent and impartial tribunal established by law.'

Disqualification cases have not been found to be within the ambit of Art 6(1), because both the domestic courts and the European Court of Human Rights regard disqualification as a civil regulatory matter, and not a criminal charge: see e.g. *R v Secretary of State for Trade and Industry, ex parte McCormick* [1998] BCC 379, DC, *HS and AD v United Kingdom* [2000] BCC 710 and *Re Westminster Property Management Ltd* [2001] BCC 121. However, as observed in *WGS and MSLS v United Kingdom* [2000] BCC 719, the fact that disqualification proceedings are not criminal proceedings for the purposes of Art 6(1) will not remove the applicant's right to a fair hearing. Following *EDC v United Kingdom* [1998] BCC 370, delays in the prosecution of civil proceedings against a director under the CDDA 1986 may constitute a violation of Art 6(1); see also *Re Abermeadow Ltd (No 2)* [2001] BCC 724. However, a prolonged delay in the prosecution of s 6 proceedings will not necessarily constitute a violation of Art 6(1); much will depend on the individual circumstances of the case. For example, in *Re Blackspur Group plc (No 3); Secretary of State for Trade and Industry v Eastaway* [2003] BCC 520, Morritt V-C concluded that there had been no breach of the applicant's right to a fair trial within a reasonable time, notwithstanding that eight-and-a-half years had elapsed since disqualification proceedings had initially been commenced. On the evidence, the Vice Chancellor concluded that the time lapse was attributable to explainable factors: for example, the conclusion of criminal proceedings, and the subsequent but unsuccessful attempts by the applicant to have the proceedings stayed or struck out or disposed of under the *Carecraft* procedure (discussed below).

Notwithstanding that disqualification proceedings are regarded as a matter of civil law, allegations made in the course of disqualification proceedings may involve very serious insinuations of misconduct and as such the courts have on occasions been reluctant to apply a standard of proof based upon evidence which is indicative but not sufficiently conclusive of a director's culpability. Indeed, some case examples have specifically alluded to the standard of proof applicable to s 6 in language compatible to and, on occasions, positively affirmative of a standard more appropriate to criminal proceedings (i.e. proof beyond a reasonable doubt). For example, in *Re Swift 736 Ltd* [1993] BCLC 1, Hoffmann J construed s 6 as a penal provision and as such found that a court, in assessing the evidence of a case, should afford a director the benefit of any reasonable doubt in its perception of the evidence of the case. However, it must be noted that more recent judgments have reiterated the necessity for the application of the civil standard of proof as opposed to a criminal or some form of quasi-criminal standard: see e.g. the judgment of the Court of Appeal in *Secretary of State* v *Deverell* [2000] 2 All ER 365 at p 377.

Protecting the public interest

In accordance with s 7(1) of the CDDA 1986, the justification for commencing disqualification proceedings under s 6 is to protect the public interest from the unfit conduct of delinquent directors. To establish a director's culpability in respect of s 6, it is necessary to prove that the director's conduct in the management of a company (or of companies) makes him/her unfit to be concerned in the future management of a company. At first sight, s 6 suggests that a director's capacity to act in the future management of a company is the essential yardstick by which a court should determine whether or not to impose a disqualification order.

Yet, following a positive finding of a director's unfit conduct, the imposition of a disqualification order is mandatory and accordingly s 6 would appear to restrict the court's consideration of whether a director possessed a potential to reform his past misconduct. Indeed, the Court of Appeal in *Secretary of State* v *Gray* [1995] 1 BCLC 276 made it clear that under s 6 the court was obliged to make a disqualification order in circumstances where it was established that a director's past conduct was of an unfit nature, a conclusion which could not be disturbed by considering a director's potential to reform his past indiscretions. Although it was conceded in the *Gray* case that extenuating circumstances may affect the court's determination of whether a director's past conduct had reached an appropriate standard of unfitness, thereby justifying disqualification, it was stressed that any decision to impose a disqualification order should not be influenced by considering a director's capacity to reform his past activities.

Nevertheless, it should be noted that a director's potential to reform past misconduct, portrayed, for example, by his conduct in relation to the management of another company, is likely to be a significant mitigating factor in determining the length of a disqualification order: see e.g. *Re Pamstock Ltd* [1994] 1 BCLC 716. By contrast, a director who exhibits, by his/her conduct at the disqualification proceedings, an obvious indication of a failure to reform his/her past misconduct may be penalised with a disqualification period of a greater duration than had his/her conduct at the proceedings been of an acceptable standard (i.e. portraying a willingness to reform): see e.g. the comments of the Court of Appeal in *Reynard v Secretary of State for Trade & Industry* [2002] 2 BCLC 625.

Conduct of an unfit nature

Under s 6, the court, in assessing whether a director is unfit to act in the management of a company, should, in accordance with s 9 of the CDDA 1986, have particular regard to the matters set out in both Part 1 and Part 2 of Sch 1 to the CDDA 1986. However, as s 9 directs the court to have *particular regard* to the matters contained in Sch 1, as opposed to confining the court to the matters mentioned in Sch 1, conduct giving rise to a finding of unfitness may still be found in circumstances which are not directly governed by the Schedule.

The matters mentioned in Part 1 of Sch 1 require the court to consider whether a director, against which a disqualification order is sought, was responsible for:

1 any misfeasance or breach of any fiduciary or other duty in relation to the company;

2 any misapplication or retention by the director of, or any conduct by the director giving rise to an obligation to account for, any money or property of the company;

3 the extent of a director's responsibility for the company entering into any transaction liable to be set aside under Part XVI of the Insolvency Act (provisions against debt avoidance);

4 the extent of a director's responsibility for any failure by the company to comply with any of the following provisions of the CA 1985, namely:

   (a) s 221 (companies to keep accounting records);

   (b) s 222 (where and for how long records are to be kept);

   (c) s 228 (register of directors and secretaries);

   (d) s 352 (obligation to keep and enter up register of members);

   (e) s 353 (location of register of members);

   (f) s 363 (duty of company to make annual returns); and

   (h) ss 399 and 415 (company's duty to register charges which it creates);

   [It should be noted that former sub-paragraph (g) – time for completion of annual returns (s 365) – was removed from the above headings of relevant matters by s 139(4), CA 1989.]

5 the extent of the director's responsibility for any failure by the directors of the company to comply with:

(a) s 226 or s 227 (duty to prepare annual accounts); or

(b) s 233 (approval and signature of accounts).

The matters mentioned in Part 2 of Sch 1 (where a company has become insolvent) are as follows:

6 the extent of the director's responsibility for the causes of the company becoming insolvent;

7 the extent of the director's responsibility for any failure by the company to supply any goods or services which have been paid for (in whole or in part);

8 the extent of the director's responsibility for the company entering into any transaction or giving any preference, being a transaction or preference:

(a) liable to be set aside under s 127 or ss 238–240 of the Insolvency Act 1986; or

(b) open to challenge under s 242 or s 243 of the Insolvency Act 1986 (or any rule of law in Scotland);

9 the extent of the director's responsibility for any failure by the directors of the company to comply with s 98 of the Insolvency Act 1986 (duty to call creditors' meeting in creditors' voluntary winding up);

10 any failure by the director to comply with any obligation imposed on him by or under any of the following provisions of the Insolvency Act 1986:

(a) s 22 (company's statement of affairs in administration);

(b) s 47 (statement of affairs to administrative receiver);

(c) s 66 (statement of affairs in Scottish receivership);

(d) s 99 (directors' duty to attend meeting, statement of affairs in creditors' voluntary winding up);

(e) s 131 (statement of affairs in winding up by the court);

(f) s 234 (duty of anyone with company property to deliver it up);

(g) s 235 (duty to cooperate with liquidator, etc.).

In considering the matters mentioned in Sch 1, the court must, on a balance of probabilities, be satisfied that the nature of a director's conduct was sufficiently serious to justify his/her disqualification. The need to establish that a director's conduct was of a type which constituted a serious failure to have regard to a matter or matters mentioned in Sch 1 or other matters related to a director's involvement in the managerial activities of a company may be explained on the premise that the effect of a disqualification order may dramatically infringe upon the commercial liberty of a director in relation to his/her future ability to pursue employment in the management of a company.

The courts have expressed an unwillingness to impose disqualification orders in situations whereby the fault element attached to a director's act or omission was attributable to business practices of an improper but nevertheless naive and imprudent standard. Indeed, in the majority of cases, the courts have emphasised that, in order to justify the imposition of a disqualification order, a director's misconduct will need to be established at a level which is harmful to the public interest, whereby it conveys a clear exploitation of the privileges attributable to the limited-liability status of a company. In the majority, if not all cases, such exploitation will be exhibited by evidence of a wanton disregard and abuse of creditor interests, a director's recklessness or gross negligence in the management of a company or an obvious and serious (if not persistent) failure to comply with provisions of companies legislation.

In *Re Sevenoaks Stationers (Retail) Ltd* [1991] Ch 164, the first case in which the Court of Appeal was asked to consider the appropriateness of a disqualification order under s 6, the court emphasised that a disqualification order should be made only where there was conclusive proof of conduct which established that a director's actions amounted to commercially culpable behaviour of a type constituting a threat to the commercial community. The ability of a court to label a particular course of business malpractice as conduct constituting commercially culpable behaviour will obviously depend upon the individual circumstances and facts of a given case. Indeed, in *Re Sevenoaks Stationers (Retail) Ltd*, the Court of Appeal observed that the true question to be tried in s 6 proceedings was a question of fact. Cases in which a s 6 order have been imposed include the following examples of unfit conduct:

- a persistent failure to comply with a statutory provision(s) (see e.g. *Secretary of State* v *Arif* [1996] BCC 586);

- a serious breach of duty. In relation to disqualification proceedings, the courts will be particularly concerned with the effect of a breach of a director's duty. A director's breach of fiduciary duty may be equated with unfit conduct where its effect is to prevent the repayment of corporate debts (i.e. the breach of duty causes a company to fall into an insolvent state or where the breach exacerbates a company's already insolvent position: see e.g. *Secretary of State* v *Lubrani* [1997] 2 BCLC 115);

- reckless/negligent conduct (breach of duty of care) which exceeds mere business folly. Although conduct which is attributable to an act of mere commercial misjudgement or business folly will normally be discarded and regarded as conduct which does not equate to unfit conduct, such folly may be considered particularly relevant in circumstances where the commercial misjudgement was of a reckless as opposed to naive nature or where it exhibited the hallmarks of gross commercial incompetence: see e.g. *Re GSAR Realisations Ltd* [1993] BCLC 409, *Re Continental Assurance Co Ltd* [1997] BCLC 48, *Re Barings plc* [1999] 1 BCLC 433 (especially at pp 482–95) and *Re Queens Moat Houses plc (No 2)* [2005] 1 BCLC 136.

Conduct falling outside the ambit of section 6

Where a court perceives a director's imprudent conduct to have been undertaken without any form of malice, recklessness or serious neglect, then such conduct will not justify the application of s 6. At present, a director may escape being labelled unfit, even in circumstances where his conduct is considered to be of an unacceptable nature: see e.g. *Re Bath Glass Ltd* [1988] BCLC 329, *Re Austinsuite Furniture Ltd* [1992] BCLC 1047 and *Re Wimbledon Village Restaurant Ltd* [1994] BCC 753. However, other than where a director of an insolvent company honestly and reasonably believed that the company was capable of trading itself out of its financial difficulties, a director's continued involvement in the affairs of the insolvent company will provide *prima facie* evidence of his/her unfit conduct. However, it is to be observed, following the decision of Chadwick J in *Secretary of State* v *Gash* [1997] 1 BCLC 341, that a director of an insolvent company who continues to hold office, despite realising the folly of an existing corporate policy, may escape any charge of having acted in an unfit manner if it can be established that he objected to and took no part in, or had no responsibility for the deployment of, the ill-fated policy.

Determining the length of a disqualification order

Where, under s 6, the court finds a director to be unfit to be concerned in the future management of a company, it is obliged to impose a disqualification order. In accordance with s 6(4) of the CDDA 1986, the length of a disqualification order must be for a minimum of two years, the maximum period of disqualification being 15 years. In determining the length of a disqualification period, the court must be mindful of the seriousness and extent of a director's misconduct and will also take into account the director's position within the company's management structure. For example, where a director holds a senior executive position, or otherwise has a capacity to dictate a company's operations, it may ordinarily be presumed, in accordance with his position of responsibility, that the extent of his culpability (and the duration of any disqualification order) will be more pronounced than for, say, officers of the company who exerted less influence in the management of the company's affairs. Where a director's misconduct involves dishonest conduct, it is more logical to assume that the disqualification period will be of a greater duration than had the misconduct been of a reckless or negligent manner.

In *Re Sevenoaks Stationers (Retail) Ltd*, the Court of Appeal, in an attempt to alleviate the potential for inconsistency in setting disqualification periods, gave the following guidelines:

1 the top bracket of disqualification for periods of over ten years should be reserved for particularly serious cases. Disqualification in this bracket could include those cases where a director who had previously been disqualified was the subject of a further disqualification order;

2 the middle bracket of disqualification for a period between six and ten years should apply in serious cases which did not merit the attention of the top bracket of disqualification;

3 the minimum bracket of two to five years should be applied in cases where a director was found to be unfit to be concerned in the management of a company, but it was nevertheless established that the misconduct was not of a particularly serious nature.

However, notwithstanding that some form of guidance in relation to appropriate disqualification periods would be beneficial to the lower courts, in reality, the Court of Appeal's guidelines are of little assistance. In effect, they amount to no more than commonsense generalisations. Indeed, at best they may be regarded as but a reminder to the lower courts for the need to adopt a greater degree of consistency in the imposition of disqualification periods.

An application for leave to act (s 17 of the CDDA 1986)

Although a court is obliged to make a disqualification order under s 6 where a director's conduct in the management of a company was of an unfit nature, in some circumstances the court may be reluctant to fetter the future management activities of the director, especially where the director is successfully involved in the management of another company. In such a case the imposition of a disqualification order may adversely affect the interests of the successful company, causing prejudice to the company's employees and creditors. Accordingly, in such cases, the imposition of a disqualification order may, in terms of the public interest consideration, cause more harm than good.

A possible solution to the otherwise mandatory effect of a disqualification order is to be found in s 17 of the CDDA 1986. Section 17(1) provides:

As regards the court to which application must be made for leave under a disqualification order, the following applies –

(a) where the application is for leave to promote or form a company, it is any court with jurisdiction to wind up companies, and

(b) where the application is for leave to be a liquidator, administrator or director of, or otherwise to take part in the management of a company, or to be a receiver or manager of a company's property, it is any court having jurisdiction to wind up that company.

The practical effect of a grant of leave is the creation of a modified type of disqualification order, whereby a director is disqualified in a general sense but is nevertheless allowed to continue in the management of another company (or companies), as specified by the terms of the order: see e.g. *Secretary of State for Trade and Industry* v *Rosenfield* [1999] BCC 413. The director is in effect given a 'second chance' in respect of the specified company on the premise that his/her involvement in the management of that enterprise is considered to be beneficial to the public interest. While the adoption of a modified order may be considered justifiable in the sense that it protects the interests of the employees and creditors of the specified company, in reality, the nature of the order would appear to permit a director, with a dubious past history in the management of a company or companies, to, in part, escape the consequences of his past indiscretions.

Accordingly, the adoption of the modified order must be applied with caution and, when considering whether to grant leave, the court must ponder the likelihood of a director re-offending: see e.g. the comments of Hoffmann LJ in *Re Grayan* [1995] BCC 554 at p 574.

The prosecution of section 6 actions

In accordance with s 7(3) of the CDDA 1986, insolvency practitioners are under a statutory obligation to report to the Department of Trade and Industry (DTI) any director who is suspected of conducting the affairs of a company in an unfit manner. In submitting a report, the office holder must investigate conduct by reference to guidelines set out in Sch 1 to the CDDA 1986. The insolvency practitioner is required to consider matters of conduct on the basis of information acquired in the course of his normal duties and by reference to the books and records available to him. An insolvency practitioner is not obliged to undertake an investigation that he would not otherwise have considered necessary for the purposes of his administration. The Insolvency Service, a department of the DTI, is, through its Disqualification Unit, responsible for determining whether to commence proceedings.

REFORMING THE PROSECUTION OF ACTIONS UNDER SECTION 6 OF THE CDDA 1986

By the late 1990s, it was evident that the growing number of prosecutions under s 6 was such that there was a danger that an overburdened court system would soon be close to breaking point. For example, during the period 1997–2001, as an annual average, in excess of 1000 cases were pending prosecution under s 6. Further, for the period 2000–01, 58 per cent of s 6 cases had not been concluded within two years from the commencement of proceedings and, as such, exceeded the two-year limit specified by s 7(2) of the CDDA 1986. Indeed, had it not been for the courts' willingness to adopt a summary form of procedure – the *Carecraft* procedure (taking its name from *Re Carecraft Construction Co Ltd* [1994] 1 WLR 172, the first case in which the procedure was adopted) – the strain on the disqualification system would have been even more transparent. In 2000–01 the said summary procedure accounted for approximately 30 per cent of all s 6 cases and was applied in circumstances where the facts relating to a director's misconduct were not disputed and where both the Secretary of State and the respondent were willing to allow the case to be dealt with on the understanding that a disqualification order would be made for a period falling within one of the brackets specified in *Re Sevenoaks Stationers (Retail) Ltd*.

The Insolvency Act 2000 – the undertaking procedure

Following the Insolvency Act 2000, a new statutory undertaking procedure has been introduced in respect of the imposition of disqualification orders. The new procedure intends to effect a more efficient means of speeding up the disqualification process under s 6 (applicable also to s 8) of the CDDA 1986. Provisions relevant to the undertaking procedure were brought into force on 20 April 2001 by the Insolvency Act 2000 (Commencement No 1 and Transitional Provisions) Order 2001, SI 2001/ 766. The relevant provisions of the Insolvency Act 2000 add to the provisions of the CDDA 1986.

Section 1A of the CDDA 1986 now permits the Secretary of State to accept an undertaking as an alternative to pursuing disqualification proceedings through the courts. There is no compulsion on the part of a director to proceed via the undertaking procedure and clearly any contested case will continue to be heard by way of a court action. The Secretary of State may accept an undertaking if it appears expedient in the public interest to do so (s 2A, CDDA 1986). Under the undertaking procedure a defendant will agree to refrain from acting as a director or in any other capacity so specified by s 1A(1)(a) and (b) of the CDDA 1986, for a predetermined period (i.e. a minimum duration of two years and a maximum duration of 15 years).

A person who agrees to an undertaking may still seek leave to act under s 17 of the CDDA 1986.

The statutory undertaking procedure advances the *Carecraft* procedure in a most logical way. The efficiency of the undertaking procedure will permit the Insolvency Service to prosecute disqualification cases with greater speed, and possibly in greater numbers, although the fact that only very serious instances of corporate malpractice will justify disqualification under s 6 may inhibit any substantial increase in prosecutions. Nevertheless, the merits of the undertaking procedure will extinguish any future need for disqualification proceedings to be determined by way of the *Carecraft* procedure.

However, notwithstanding the advantages of the statutory undertaking procedure, it must be observed that as delinquent directors will largely be dealt with in the absence of judicial and public scrutiny, the disqualification process will lose its transparency (evidenced by, for example, a dramatic fall in the number of reported s 6 cases since the introduction of the undertaking procedure). Following a defendant's acceptance of the undertaking procedure, the courts will be called upon to consider the merits or otherwise of a disqualification order only in a situation where a defendant applies to have the duration of the order reduced or cancelled. The power of the court to vary the duration of an undertaking is provided for by s 8A of the CDDA 1986.

Although the adoption of the statutory undertaking procedure represents an essential reform in maintaining the efficiency of the disqualification system, the procedure, given its availability in all uncontested disqualification cases, may be viewed with a degree of caution. Given that the Disqualification Unit will encounter additional burdens in respect of managing and administering the procedure, such caution may be particularly justified in the more serious instances of commercially culpable conduct where, in an attempt to save time and reduce costs, the duration of a disqualification undertaking may be subject to an implied system of plea bargaining, the effect of which may be to reduce the duration of disqualification periods and thus deplete the deterrent effect of s 6.

Competition disqualification orders (CDOs)

Following the implementation of s 204 of the Enterprise Act 2002, amending the CDDA 1986 (s 204 of the Enterprise Act inserts ss 9A–9E into the CDDA 1986), the courts are obliged to impose a disqualification order against a director of a company, following a breach by the company of competition law and where the said breach illustrates that the director is unfit to be concerned in the future management of a company. A breach of competition law is described thus:

- the breach of a Chapter 1 (Competition Act 1998) prohibition (prohibition on agreements, etc. preventing, restricting or distorting competition);
- the breach of a Chapter 2 (Competition Act 1998) prohibition (prohibition on abuse of a dominant position);
- a breach of Art 81 of the EC Treaty (prohibition on agreements, etc. preventing, restricting or distorting competition);
- a breach of Art 82 of the EC Treaty (prohibition on abuse of a dominant position).

An application for a CDO may be made by the Office of Fair Trading (OFT) and specified regulators (the Director General of Telecommunications, the Gas and Electricity Markets Authority, the Director General of Water Services, the Rail Regulator and the Civil Aviation Authority). As under ss 6 and 8 of the CDDA 1986, a statutory disqualification undertaking (competition disqualification undertakings) may be accepted under s 9B of the CDDA 1986 by the OFT or a specified regulator. The maximum disqualification period is 15 years.

Decision to pursue CDOs

Prior to prosecuting an action, breaches of competition law will have to be established in decisions or judgments by the OFT or regulator, the European Commission, the Competition Appeal Tribunal or the European Court of Justice. Further, the breach must have an effect or at least a perceived effect on trade in the UK. The OFT or regulator will not consider CDO applications unless a financial penalty has been imposed. The grounds for pursuing a CDO are clearly distinguished from pursuing an order under s 6 of the CDDA 1986 in so far as s 9A(6) of the CDDA 1986 specifies that matters mentioned in Sch 1 to the CDDA 1986 are not relevant to determining a CDO.

The register of disqualification orders

Under s 18(2) of the CDDA 1986, the Secretary of State is obliged to maintain a register of disqualification orders which is open to public inspection on the payment of a small fee. The register contains the names of persons subject to a disqualification order. Where the duration of a disqualification order has expired, the Secretary of State must, in accordance with s 18(3) of the CDDA 1986, remove the entry from the register and all particulars relating to the order.

Suggested further reading

Finch (1990) 53 MLR 385

Dine (1991) Co Law 6

Milman (1992) 43 NILQ 1

Dine [1994] JBL 325

Hicks (1998) ACCA Research Report 59

Walters (2000) 21 Co Law 110

Hicks [2001] JBL 433

Griffin (2002) 53 NILQ 207

20

CORPORATE GOVERNANCE ISSUES

INTRODUCTION

This chapter aims to deal with specific issues relevant to the governance of companies. Debate, discussion and government intervention into issues of corporate governance are a natural consequence of the economic and social impact which companies effect in the generation and maintenance of personal and national wealth and prosperity. Corporate governance issues are concerned with the formal and informal regulation of both the internal and external mechanisms under which companies operate. Given this wide definition, all aspects of the regulation of company law fall to be defined by the term 'corporate governance.' The specific purpose of this chapter is to consider corporate governance issues with reference to a government's objective of regulating corporate law to stabilise and protect markets and the economic and social framework in which companies operate.

REGULATING TO ACHIEVE CORPORATE EFFICIENCY

Legislation and other regulatory powers are, in the context of companies, deemed essential instruments in seeking to protect the wellbeing and stability of both the economy and the general public interest. Regulation aims to promote corporate efficiency and a company's ability to generate profits. However, efficiency must also be determined in the context of the hidden costs of production: for example, the effect of a company's business on the natural environment and issues relating to social geography and the deployment of resources.

The desire to regulate companies is particularly apt in relation to large corporations. Although large public companies comprise only a very small proportion of registered companies, they generate the greatest part of a nation's economic wealth, employing millions of workers and generating business opportunities for many small businesses and individuals. With large public companies, and in a desire to protect the public interest, there is a need for external government influence because here shareholdings will rarely be concentrated, to the extent that a person(s) is unable to use his/her voting powers to exert influence over the company's affairs. Accordingly, in such companies the shareholders will generally function as investors as opposed to an active 'watchdog' in respect of the regulation of the company's affairs. The protection of the public interest is also paramount in the sense that many ordinary people will invest in large public companies to become shareholders or have an indirect interest in the wellbeing of a company as members of pension schemes (in which employees' contributions are invested in corporate shares and other corporate securities). In terms of the public interest, the interests of all stakeholders must be protected; and the champion for this protection is the regulatory system.

Corporate failure and scandal

Regulation and government interference into the corporate law field is often sparked by a serious corporate failure or scandal. The interference is driven by both an economic and political desire to rid the corporate infrastructure of systems and practices which may give rise to a potential for like or future failures and scandals. In seeking to clear up a 'corporate mess' a government's objective will be to calm and reassure investors, corporate players and markets, thereby protecting economic stability and the general public interest. Corporate law history is indicative of the introduction of governance measures following major corporate failures and scandals. Probably the earliest example of a corporate scandal giving rise to government intervention is the South Sea 'bubble' episode of the eighteenth century (discussed in Chapter 1). More recent examples have included the Robert Maxwell scandals of the early 1990s – intervention here resulted in improved mechanisms for controlling corporate reporting and accountability via the publication of the Cadbury Committee Report (discussed below) – and, in the mid–late 1990s, scandals relating to 'excessive director remuneration packages'. Here, in addition to the Greenbury Report (discussed below), government intervention eventually resulted in a move to achieve greater transparency. Following the introduction of the Directors' Remuneration Report Regulations 2002, SI 2002/1986, quoted companies are now required to publish a directors' remuneration report as part of their annual reporting cycle and to put decisions as to the award of remuneration packages to a meeting of the company's shareholders (discussed further in Chapter 5).

CORPORATE GOVERNANCE IN ACTION

The Cadbury Committee Report

In 1991, the Cadbury Committee was set up by the Financial Reporting Council, the London Stock Exchange and the accountancy professions to report on financial aspects of corporate governance. The report, issued in December 1992, recommended a code of best practice, to be complied with by the boards of listed companies as a condition of continued listing. The code was monitored by the Stock Exchange and a monitoring sub-committee of the Cadbury Committee (set up in May 1991). The code, which came into force for accounting periods ending after June 1993, recognised the importance of the following practices:

- The appointment of independent non-executive directors to the boards of listed companies.
- Appointments to the post of executive director to be vetted by a nomination committee, the appointees of which were to be taken principally from the ranks of a company's non-executive directors.
- The roles of chief executive and chairman should, where possible, not be held by the same person so as to promote the independent nature of the board.
- Service contracts in excess of three years should not be made to executive directors unless approved by the general meeting.

- Executive directors' salaries should be determined by means of a remuneration committee to be made up wholly, or principally, from non-executive directors.

- The creation of an audit committee to oversee the company's financial matters, the constitution of which should have a majority of non-executive directors.

The code required all listed companies to include a statement in its annual report acknowledging compliance with its terms or justifying instances of non-compliance. Although the code had no statutory force and compliance with its terms could not be regarded as an absolute prerequisite for listing, it was generally followed.

The Greenbury Committee Report

The Greenbury Report related to an investigation into directors' remuneration and was published in July 1995. The report followed the highly publicised criticism of the levels of remuneration awarded to directors of public limited companies and, more especially, the remuneration awarded to directors of the previously nationalised utility industries. The criticism appeared justified, given that the UK's economic policy in the 1990s had, in its desire to eliminate inflation, been geared to the promotion of a policy of minimal salary increases within both public and private sectors. Indeed, the massive salary awards and other incentives such as the issue of discounted share options, pensionable annual bonuses and compensation payments to departing directors, proved something of a political embarrassment.

The Greenbury Report contained a new code of best practice for directors of plcs and was specifically targeted at directors of listed companies. The report recommended that all listed companies should comply with its terms and that the nature and extent of that compliance should be reported annually to shareholders. The report's findings echoed many of the principles for reform as advanced in the Cadbury Report. In addition to the proposals contained in the Cadbury Report, the Greenbury Report recommended the following:

- The compilation (by a remuneration committee) of an annual report which should form part of the annual accounts and which should be put before the company's shareholders. The annual report would include a statement that full consideration had been given to the best practice provisions of the Greenbury Report (see below). Where there was non-compliance with such provisions, the report had to explain why that had been the case.

Examples of the best practice provisions

- The interests of both shareholders and directors should be considered by the remuneration committee in their determination of the levels of directors' remuneration.

- Share options should never be issued to directors at a discount and annual bonuses should not be pensionable.

- The notice periods for service contracts of executive directors should be no more than one year.

- Shareholders should approve long-term incentive schemes.

As from October 1995, the recommendations of the Greenbury Report, other than those concerned with rules relating to long-term incentive schemes, options and pension entitlements, were incorporated into the Stock Exchange's listing rules, taking effect from 31 December 1995. As such, compliance with many of the recommendations of the report was regarded as a prerequisite for a company's listing on the Stock Exchange.

The Hampel Committee Report

The Hampel Committee Report on Corporate Governance was published on 28 January 1998. The Hampel Report sought to progress and, where necessary, add to the recommendations of the reports of both the Cadbury Committee and Greenbury Committee. The remit of the Hampel Committee was to review the role of both executive and non-executive directors, to consider matters relating to directors' remuneration and to consider the role of both shareholders and auditors in corporate governance issues. As with the reports of the Cadbury and Greenbury committees, the Hampel Report was primarily, although not exclusively, concerned with public companies. The conclusions of the Hampel Report, in respect of management structures, were as follows:

- Both executive and non-executive directors should be subject to the same corporate duties. However, directors should be provided with more information and instruction in relation to such duties.
- Although the report fell short of recommending that executive directors should have some form of recognised qualification, the report considered that persons who held an executive directorship should have the necessary experience to be capable of understanding the nature and extent of the interests of the company in which they held office.
- The majority of non-executive directors in companies of all sizes should be independent and make up at least one-third of the board.
- An individual should not ordinarily occupy the role of both chairman and chief executive.
- All companies should have nomination committees for the purpose of recommending new board appointments. At least every three years directors should be obliged to seek re-election.
- Executive directors' remuneration should not be excessive and should be based upon recommendations from remuneration committees which should be comprised of non-executive directors. Remuneration should be related to performance and a general statement on remuneration policy should be included in the annual report.
- Directors' contracts should not exceed one year.

The Hampel Report also sought to generate a set of principles and a general code of good practice for public companies, embracing Cadbury, Greenbury and its own work, with the ultimate purpose of incorporation into the Listing Rules. Indeed, on 25 June 1998, the London Stock Exchange published a Code of Best Practice, 'The Combined Code', which was in effect based upon the Hampel Report. The said code became mandatory for all listed companies for financial years ending on or after 31 December 1998. However, it must be noted that the Combined Code, as with the Cadbury and Greenbury Reports, did not have the force of law: that is, it remained a code of best practice. However, the consequence of non-compliance with the code was that a company could be subject to a fine and in an extreme case could be refused listing.

The Turnbull Report

The Turnbull Report was published in 1999 and its objective was to ensure that the board of directors of a listed company had or put in place a system of risk management for identifying and managing key business risks. In accordance with the Turnbull Report, the board of directors had, amongst other matters, to consider the following:

- board evaluation of the likelihood of risk and the categories of risk facing the company;
- effective safeguards and internal controls to prevent or reduce risk;
- transparency of internal controls, incorporating an annual assessment of risk.

THE REVISED COMBINED CODE ON CORPORATE GOVERNANCE 2003

The revised code supersedes and replaces the Combined Code issued by the Hampel Committee in June 1998. The revised code, published in July 2003, had effect for reporting years beginning on or after 1 November 2003. With some minor modifications, the revised code embraces the recommendations contained in a report by Derek Higgs entitled 'Review of the role and effectiveness of non-executive directors' (DTI, Jan 2003). The revised code builds and adds to the previous Combined Code and the recommendations of the Turnbull Report. The spark which ignited the Higgs Report and the introduction of the revised code had its origins in the infamous American corporate disaster centred on the Enron Corporation.

The collapse and impact of Enron

In 2001/02, the collapse of Enron, a giant American corporation, served as the principal catalyst in a large-scale revamping of global corporate governance rules. The fundamental cause of Enron's demise was its rapid but unsustainable growth and the incursion of substantial debt to finance capital expenditure. As Enron's debt increased, the company sought an alternative method by which it could continue to finance its operations but one whereby it could avoid the declaration of any acceleration in debt, thereby maintaining investor confidence in the company's stock, so easing the pressure on its creditor ratings.

An apparent solution was the creation of investment partnerships, a form of limited liability partnership. As distinct legal entities, albeit in effect subsidiaries of Enron, the partnerships had their own legal capacity to borrow funds from the lending institutions. Many of the partnerships were structured in the form of 'Special Purpose Entities' (SPE), which, for accounting purposes, entitled any debts of the SPE to be kept off Enron's balance sheet.

However, many transactions involving the SPEs were not designed for the purpose of accomplishing *bona fide* economic objectives but rather to achieve favourable financial statement results for Enron. While, in theory, losses could be set off against the SPEs, in reality the losses remained as debt because the SPEs were but mirror images of the Enron corporation. However, despite Enron's use of the SPEs, by the end of 2001 the company was in debt to the sum of approximately £3 billion. Market confidence in the company was destroyed and, in December 2001, Enron filed for relief under Chapter 11 of the United States Bankruptcy Code.

In relation to the responsibility for Enron's demise, the greater part of any culpability was attached to the internal watchdogs, namely the company's directors, executives and auditors. In respect of Enron's auditors, their independence was compromised given that they also acted as financial consultants to the company. This was indeed a common practice across the USA. In Enron's case, the company's accounting principles were determined with extensive participation from the company's auditors, who helped structure many of the transactions which Enron used to improve the appearance of its financial statements.

In the USA, the ultimate responsibility for the internal governance of a public company rests on the shoulders of its board of directors. The board is comprised of a majority of directors who are devoid of day-to-day managerial responsibilities. Both State and Federal law regulate the directors of a public company. Directors are subject to duties of loyalty and care although, in accordance with the business judgement rule, directors operate under the favourable presumption that in making business decisions they will have acted on an informed basis, in good faith and in the honest belief that the decision was in the best interests of the company. Further, a director's personal liability for a breach of duty may be eliminated or limited by the company's constitution other than where the act or omission giving rise to the breach was instigated in bad faith or where it involved intentional misconduct, a knowing violation of the law, or where it involved a transaction whereby a director gained an improper personal benefit at the expense of the company. Basically, the US promotion of corporations is centred on an enterprise culture where risk taking is encouraged to the extent that company directors will escape the imposition of any form of liability other than where they acted in a fraudulent and dishonest manner.

Although, in the USA, the board is viewed as independent guardian of shareholder interests, the independence of external directors may often be more a theoretical objective than a practical reality as corporate interests may be compromised by the payment of consulting fees, sales contracts and other assorted benefits such as stock options. The financial incentives for directors may put them in a position whereby they are beholden to management and devoid of any real autonomy. In the Enron case, the board failed to act with sufficient diligence in its approval of the partnership transactions. Although the board put various controls and reviews in place, the rules and practices which were invoked were inadequate. The executive of the company misled the board, albeit, had it taken the opportunity properly to scrutinise the material available to it, the board should have been able to detect many of the company's problems. However, although the non-management directors of Enron may have been negligent in the performance of their corporate duties, the conduct of the company's executive directors was reckless and, in some instances, fraudulent. Further, in addition to breaches of duty and fraudulent practices, the management (and directors) of Enron engaged in insider dealing.

On 30 July 2002, the Sarbanes-Oxley Act was passed. The Act seeks to protect investors by improving corporate transparency via the accuracy and reliability of corporate disclosure and reporting procedures. The rationale for such regulation may be explained as a necessary prerequisite in regulating the consequences attached to the concept of the limited liability company and a separation between the investors' ownership of a company and the board of directors' power to manage the entity. Problems emanating from the division of ownership and control were identified as early as the eighteenth century by Adam Smith and, more recently, in the 1930s by Berle and Means – the latter thesis observed that the separation and fragmentation of ownership from management resulted in the reduction of effective shareholder intervention in the management and regulation of companies.

The UK's response

Although in recent times the UK has not witnessed the large-scale corporate collapses of the USA – and despite differences in balance sheet, accounting and auditing practices in the UK – the recent UK reforms have been strongly influenced by the corporate scandals witnessed in the USA. The UK reforms may be explained as an attempt to maintain a competitive edge in the retention of global confidence in the UK markets so as to avert any fear of an Enron type scandal.

The proposed UK reforms emanate from the Higgs Report, which was concerned with boardroom structures and the role of non-executive directors and the 2003 report of the Coordinating Group on Audit and Accounting Issues (CGAA) under the chairmanship of Sir Robert Smith (discussed further below). In common with the USA reforms, the UK reforms concentrate on boardroom structures of public companies and, in respect of accounting and auditing practices, have the objective of achieving higher standards of transparency, accountability and greater independent representation within the boardroom. However, in contrast to the US, the UK and other European states have not sought reform by way of a legislative approach. In the UK, the governance reforms are intended to build on the 'comply or explain' approach of the Combined Code.

The Higgs Report and the revised code

The central theme of the Higgs Report was to ensure that UK boards have an overriding responsibility in setting the company's values, standards and obligations. The report stressed a collective board responsibility in terms of the entrepreneurial leadership within a framework of prudent and effective controls. In relation to boardroom structure, Higgs preferred the existing unitary nature of the board structure adopted in the UK and rejected any form of substantial reform based on the European system, which typically separates managerial responsibility between a management and supervisory board, or the US system, whereby the board is composed largely of outside directors, with a small minority of management executives. By implication Higgs therefore rejected the EC Fifth Draft Directive, the effect of which would provide a radical reformation of the board structure for UK companies. Taking its model from the German system, the draft Directive makes provision for employee participation in management functions within certain public companies, that is those which alone or with subsidiaries employ one thousand or more persons. The participation envisaged by the draft Directive would be by way of directors appointed from the workforce, a works council, or a system established by collective agreement.

The core proposal of the Higgs Report related to the significance and role of non-executive directors of public companies, a theme which also played a dominant role in the Sarbanes-Oxley Act. Higgs considered that, as independent guardians of the interests of investors, non-executive directors should challenge and contribute to the development of corporate strategy by scrutinising the performance of executive directors and management and by satisfying themselves that financial controls and systems of risk management were robust and defensible. Higgs considered that non-executive directors should be viewed as independent and divorced from the interests of persons with large financial or shareholding stakes in the company. In common with new listing requirements in the US, France and emerging commercial nations such as China, Higgs considered that a majority of the board should be comprised of independent directors and recommended that in a UK public company at least 50 per cent of the board's composition should be comprised of independent non-executive directors. Higgs sought to define an independent non-executive director as a person who sits on the board free of any potential conflict of interest.

Despite not wishing to adopt the US or European systems, it is arguable that, through the promotion and reform of the role of independent non-executive directors, Higgs may have impliedly encouraged a more direct comparison between the US/European and UK systems. What is particularly striking about the Higgs proposals is the shift in influence and regulatory control, away from executive directors, to non-executive directors. Building on the recommendations of the then existing Combined Code, it is apparent that Higgs proposed an increased momentum in the non-executive director's assumption of greater responsibility in the internal structures of the public company.

As Higgs sought to increase the level of responsibility for a non-executive director, the report also considered it essential for persons appointed to non-executive posts to have the necessary skills and expertise to act; accordingly, it was recommended that the pool of potential non-executive directors should be broadened to include, for example, more executive directors and senior executives from other public companies, directors of private companies, lawyers and accountants, and a greater representation from the public sector.

With regard to the chairman of the board, the Higgs Report considered that a chairman should lead the company in terms of its organisation and efficiency, ensuring effective communication with shareholders, evaluating the board's performance and that of its committees, and facilitating the effective contribution of non-executive directors and general relations between executive and non-executive directors. The report considered that the role of chairman and managing director should be separate and that a division of their responsibilities should be set out in writing. Further, a person retiring from his position as managing director should be discouraged from becoming the company's chairman because of the potential conflict between the two roles.

The Higgs Report highlighted the importance of the role of board committees and, in wishing to promote the theme of independence, provided that independent non-executive directors should dominate in the composition and influence of the committees. In accordance with the terms of the final report of the CGAA, the Higgs Report sought to amend the Combined Code in respect of audit committees by strengthening the influence and role of the committee in relation to issues of financial accountability. For example, Higgs proposed that the committee should also make recommendations to the board in relation to the appointment and remuneration of the external auditor and have responsibility for reviewing the external auditor's independence and effectiveness. Higgs recommended that the audit committee be comprised of at least three directors, all of whom should be independent non-executive directors, with at least one member of the committee having had significant recent and relevant financial experience. The report further suggested that the directors' annual report should be obliged to include a separate section describing the role of the committee and the activities and action that it has taken.

In respect of the nomination committee, Higgs considered its role to be somewhat undeveloped. Higgs recommended that all listed companies should be obliged to have a nomination committee consisting of a majority of independent non-executive directors and be chaired by an independent non-executive director. The procedures and activities of the committee should be included in the company's annual report.

In relation to the composition of the remuneration committee, Higgs recommended that it should be exclusively made up of non-executive directors who were independent of management and who met the test of independence so prescribed by the report. The report stipulated that the committee should have at least three members. As a minimum responsibility, the report provided that the committee should have responsibility for setting the remuneration levels of all executive directors and the chairman, although it also recommended that the committee might also set remuneration levels for senior executives.

Key features and additions to management structures introduced by the revised code

- The existing unitary nature of the board structure is to be maintained.
- Recruitment of non-executive directors should be broadened to include, for example, more executive directors and senior executives from other public companies, directors of private companies, lawyers and accountants, and a greater representation from the public sector.
- At least 50 per cent of the board of directors of a public listed company should be comprised of independent non-executive directors. However, where, throughout the year prior to reporting, a company has been listed below the FTSE 350, then

the board of such a company is exempted from the requirement. However, in such a company there must be at least two independent non-executive directors.

- In relation to the test of independence for a non-executive director, a person who has served on the company's board for more than nine years (the Higgs Report had suggested a ten-year period) will not be classed as independent.

- Non-executive directors may serve, subject to re-election every three years, for a period in excess of nine years, albeit after nine years they will cease to be classed as independent. However, the decision to allow a person to serve a term beyond six years should be subject to a rigorous review.

- The importance and role of board committees should be given greater significance, with the committees being comprised of a majority of independent non-executive directors (the remuneration committee to be comprised solely of non-executive directors). Contrary to the recommendations of the Higgs Report, the nomination committee may be chaired by the chairman **or** an independent non-executive director.

- The role of chairman and managing director should be separate and a division of their responsibilities should be set out in writing. Ordinarily, a managing director of a company should not subsequently be appointed as the company's chairman; however, unlike the Higgs Report recommendation, the prohibition is not absolute. A board may, following consultation with the company's shareholders, appoint a former managing director as its chairman.

European response

Irrespective of the level of compliance with the revised code, it is probable that some governance measures will, in a need to comply with future EC Directives, take the form of legislation. On 21 May 2003, the European Commission announced that while, in accordance with the final report of the High Level Group of company law experts, it did not consider it necessary to compile a European governance code, nevertheless, it did consider it necessary for the EU to develop, via future Directives, a common approach to a selected range of core governance issues. In addition to promoting a modernisation of board structures by the appointment of more independent directors, the Commission identified the fundamental issues to include: annual corporate governance statements incorporating disclosure of the structure and practice relating to general issues of governance, boards, committees and shareholder meetings; information relating to the composition, participation and aspirations of institutional shareholders; and, for all shareholders, greater access to corporate information, including matters related to the remuneration of directors.

CORPORATE GOVERNANCE AND THE ROLE OF THE AUDITOR

All limited companies are required to prepare and file accounts with Companies House. A company, unless dormant, or exempted by the Companies Act 1985 (Audit Exemption) Regulations 1994 (SI 1994/1935), is obliged by the companies legislation to appoint an auditor to undertake certain statutory prescribed tasks. The purpose of the statutory audit is to provide an independent, external professional opinion that the company's accounts reflect a true and fair view of the company's financial returns. The role of the auditor, in terms of corporate governance, is as part of a framework that supports company reporting generally, so providing a level of transparency to investors. The 1994 Regulations (as amended in March 2004) exempt the statutory audit requirement for small private companies with a turnover below £5.6 million and a balance sheet total of £2.8 million. The exemption is justified on the basis that the potential costs involved in the audit procedure could, in comparison to a small company's turnover, be substantial and therefore unjustified in an economic sense.

An auditor, once appointed, holds office (s 384, CA 1985), but the nature of an auditor's office cannot be equated with the office held by a director or company secretary. An auditor is not part of a company's general management team; the auditor is an independent contractor who is responsible for verifying the company's accounts. In accordance with the Eighth EC Company Law Directive, the Companies Act 1989 provides stringent requirements for the appointment of auditors. (Note that ss 24–54, CA 1989 – provisions dealing with an auditor's appointment – are unique in that they do not amend or introduce new provisions into the CA 1985.) The 1989 Act requires that for a person to be appointed as an auditor he/she must be a suitably qualified member of a supervisory body, eligible for appointment under the rules of that body. The body must be recognised by the Secretary of State. The Secretary of State, in accordance with s 35 of the Companies Act 1989, is obliged to establish a register of individuals and firms eligible for appointment.

As previously noted, an auditor is an independent contractor and, as such, s 27 of the Companies Act 1989 expressly prohibits officers and employees of a company from being appointed as the company's auditor. Somewhat surprisingly, there is, however, no statutory prohibition against a member of a company being appointed as the company's auditor (other than where the member is an officer or employee), even in a situation where the member holds a substantial number of shares and therefore wields great influence over the affairs of the company.

Subject to a private company's ability to elect otherwise (discussed in Chapter 21), a company must appoint its auditor at its Annual General Meeting (AGM) (s 384(1), CA 1985). Once appointed, an auditor's task is primarily to advise the shareholding body in respect of the financial affairs of the company. Section 390A(1) of the Companies Act 1985 provides that an auditor's remuneration is to be determined by the shareholders in general meeting or in such a manner as the company in general meeting shall determine. In theory, s 390A, by removing the board of directors' influence over the monetary consideration payable to the company's auditor, dispels any charge that a company's board may influence the auditor in terms of dissuading him or her from pursuing a thorough investigation of the company's financial affairs. However, in practice, it is permissible, by the terms of s 390A(1), for the general meeting to delegate, by ordinary resolution, the determination of the auditor's remuneration award to the company's board.

In the USA, the Enron scandal highlighted inadequacies in the relationship between the role of an auditor and the management of a corporation, especially in the context of a most crucial characteristic of the auditor's role, namely the fact that an auditor should remain independent and distinct from management influences in the verification of the company's accounts and financial structures. Clearly, in Enron's case, the auditor was not independent; the accountancy firm that acted as the company's auditor was also paid substantial sums for non-audit work to advise the company's management in financial matters. For example, in 2000, the accountancy firm earned $52 million in fees from Enron, more than half of which was made up of consultancy fees. In effect, the link with Enron's management, and the financial dependency of that link, destroyed the auditor's objectivity to the extent that financial indiscretions and irregular corporate structures were hidden by the auditor in an attempt to preserve and protect the accountancy firm's relationship with the company.

In the USA, in an attempt to strengthen and tighten the regulation of auditors, Title I of the Sarbanes-Oxley Act 2002 created the Public Company Accounting Oversight Board, the duty of which is to police the auditing of public companies. Every public accounting firm must be registered with the board, which is required to establish auditing, quality control, ethics and independence standards for the use of registered public accounting firms in their preparation of audit reports. The Sarbanes-Oxley Act 2002 also contains a list of non-audit and audit services which are forbidden. The forbidden services include financial information systems design and implementation, internal audit, appraisal or valuation services, and legal services. Further, the USA disclosure requirements require separate disclosure of audit fees; audit-related fees; tax fees and all other fees.

In May 2002 the European Commission produced a recommendation on auditor independence (this is to be incorporated into the Commission's proposal for a revised Eighth Company Law Directive) which, whilst not advocating a complete ban on non-audit services by auditors, recommended the mandatory disclosure of audit and non-audit fees paid by companies to auditors; these recommendations are similar to the requirements of the USA Securities and Exchange Commission (SEC). The European Commission concluded that the total fee income of auditors should be broken down into categories of statutory audit services, assurance services, tax advisory services and other non-audit services.

In the UK, concern over the independence of auditors and the role of audit committees led to the publication of the Smith Report (2003) and the more recent enactment of the Companies (Audit, Investigations and Community Enterprise) Act 2004 (discussed below). The Smith Report included the following recommendations in respect of the role of audit committees; the same have been incorporated into the revised Combined Code:

- The audit committee should monitor and review the effectiveness of the company's internal audit function.
- The committee should make recommendations to the board in relation to the appointment of the external auditor and approve the remuneration and terms of engagement of the external auditor.
- The audit committee should monitor and review the external auditor's independence, objectivity and effectiveness, taking into consideration relevant UK professional and regulatory requirements.

- The committee should develop and implement policy on the engagement of the external auditor to supply non-audit services, taking into account relevant ethical guidance regarding the provision of non-audit services by the external audit firm.

Removal of the auditor

Notwithstanding any agreement between a company and its auditor, he/she may be removed by an ordinary resolution (s 391(1), CA 1985). Nevertheless, dismissal will not preclude the auditor from seeking recompense for a breach of any service contract. Special notice (those proposing the motion to dismiss must give at least 28 days' notice to the company before the meeting at which the motion to remove is to be heard) is required for a resolution to remove an auditor where the removal would take place prior to the expiration of the auditor's term of office. Before calling the meeting to consider an auditor's removal, the auditor may make written representations to the company for distribution to the company's members (s 391A, CA 1985).

Where an auditor resigns from office, he/she is entitled to require the company to convene an extraordinary general meeting for the purpose of receiving and considering an explanation of the circumstances which the auditor considers relevant to his decision to resign (s 392, CA 1985).

The Companies (Audit, Investigations and Community Enterprise) Act 2004

The UK government, in seeking to protect and improve the standards and competency of business practices, considers that robust regulation is the key to achieving its objectives. Clearly the recent major corporate failures in the USA have shocked and perhaps caused some degree of panic in respect of the UK government's desire to reform the regulatory framework of corporate and financial markets. To strengthen the existing regulatory regime may help to maintain the confidence of investors but, on the other hand, a thirst for excessive regulation may, in increasing the costs and limiting the time efficiency of companies, hamper the growth of corporate enterprise and as such deter market investment. The Companies (Audit, Investigations and Community Enterprise) Act 2004 seeks to hit the middle ground. While, in this respect, the 2004 Act introduces a more stringent regulatory system, the new system is not unduly unnecessary or unwarranted. The Companies (Audit, Investigations and Community Enterprise) Act 2004 received Royal Assent on 28 October 2004, and the majority of the provisions related to auditors came into force on 6 April 2005, with further regulations to follow during the course of 2005; it is expected that all provisions will be in force by 1 October 2005.

Auditing procedures

The Act seeks to strengthen and extend the regulation and independence of auditors and, in doing so, follows many of the recommendations of the report of the Coordinating Group on Audit and Accounting Issues (January 2003). In seeking to strengthen the independence, transparency and regulation of auditing procedures, ss 1–2 of the 2004 Act (in force from 6 April 2005, amending Sch 11, CA 1989) require specific regulatory activities, relating to the audits of listed companies and companies in which matters are raised which concern the public interest, to be conducted by the Professional Oversight Board for Accountancy (POBA), a body attached to the Financial Reporting Council (FRC). The specific regulatory activities are:

- the setting of technical audit standards and standards relating to the integrity and independence of auditors;
- the monitoring of audits of public interest companies; and
- the investigation and discipline of public interest cases involving auditors.

The FRC is an independent body that sets, monitors, regulates and enforces the accounting and auditing standards of the professional accountancy bodies. The specific activities will therefore be carried out independently of the professional accountancy bodies. Although the Recognised Supervisory Bodies (RSBs) (of which an auditor must be a member) will not be directly involved in determining the said processes, they will need to ensure that their registered auditors comply with the independent standards, monitoring and disciplinary processes.

Auditors' powers

In accordance with s 8 of the 2004 Act (in force from 6 April 2005, amends s 389A, CA 1985 and introduces s 389B, CA 1985), auditors are given greater powers in respect of gathering information. An auditor may require the following persons to provide information and explanations:

- an officer or employee of the company;
- a person holding or accountable for any of the company's books, accounts or vouchers;
- a subsidiary company incorporated in Great Britain (and any officer, employee, or person holding or accountable for any of the subsidiary's books, accounts or vouchers).

Persons falling within one of the above categories who subsequently leave the employment of the company may also be required to provide information and explanations if the same are relevant to the auditor's investigations. Although persons cannot be compelled to provide information subject to legal professional privilege, in other cases a person will commit a criminal offence if he/she fails to comply with the auditor's request for information, or if he/she knowingly or recklessly provides information that is false in a significant manner. The offence carries a maximum sentence of two years' imprisonment and/or an unlimited fine; or, on summary conviction, imprisonment of up to 12 months and/or a fine up to the statutory maximum (currently £5000). These penalties give teeth to the auditor's powers and may serve as a positive deterrent to those directors who may otherwise have pondered the possibility of providing false or misleading returns.

Under s 7 of the 2004 Act (in force from 1 October 2005, introduced by s 390B, CA 1985), companies, other than small and medium-sized enterprises (SMEs), will, subject to the publication of future regulations, be required in the annual accounts to comply with more prescriptive disclosure requirements in respect of the services provided by auditors (previously, s 390A, CA 1985 did not require disclosure of amounts paid to auditors in respect of non-audit work). (From January 2004, the Companies Act 1985 (Accounts of Small and Medium-Sized Enterprises and Audit Exemption) (Amendment) Regulations 2004 (SI 2004/16) deem that the upper limit on qualifying conditions for medium-sized companies includes satisfying two or more of the following requirements: (a) a turnover not more than £22.8 million, (b) a balance sheet total not more than £11.4 million, (c) the number of employees must not be more than 250. A company is classified as 'small' if two or more of the following requirements are met in a year: (i) turnover is not more than £5.6 million, (ii) the balance sheet total is not more than £2.8 million and the number of employees is not more than 50.)

The draft regulations call for the following disclosures:

- audit of own accounts;
- audit of associates' accounts;
- other statutory services;
- services relating to compliance with tax legislation;
- other tax advisory services;
- further assurance services;
- information technology services relating to financial information;
- internal audit services;
- valuation services;
- litigation services;
- recruitment services;
- other services giving rise to a self-review threat; and
- all other services.

SMEs that are subject to an audit will be required to continue to disclose the fees paid to their auditors.

Section 9 of the 2004 Act (in force from 6 April 2005, inserted as s 234ZA, CA 1985) introduces a new requirement concerning the directors' report, which provides that every individual director of the company (including non-executive directors) must include a statement relating to the disclosure of information to auditors. The provision applies to all companies in which a statutory audit is carried out. An individual director will commit a criminal offence where he/she is aware that the statement made was false, or was reckless as to whether it was false and, knowing or being reckless that it was false, he/she failed to take all reasonable steps to prevent the report from being published.

The Financial Reporting Review Panel

The Financial Reporting Review Panel (FRRP) was established in 1990 as a subsidiary of the Financial Reporting Council with the objective of seeking to ensure that the provision of financial information by public and large private companies complies with relevant accounting requirements. Under ss 11, 12 and 14 of the 2004 Act, the powers of the Financial Reporting Review Panel are increased, albeit that their powers to examine the accounts of companies will apply only in the case of public and large private companies. The FRRP can require auditors, or former auditors, to produce documents or to provide information and explanations. The FRRP may require information if it thinks that the accounts or reports in question do not comply with the requirements of the companies legislation or the accounting requirements of the Listing Rules.

From 6 April 2005, the FRRP is authorised to review periodic accounts and reports required by the Listing Rules (although the Financial Services Authority (FSA) retains responsibility for enforcing the Listing Rules under the Financial Services and Markets Act 2000). Where an auditor refuses to comply with a request for documents, information or explanations, the FRRP can apply to the court for an appropriate compelling order. The FRRP may also demand documents or information and explanations from the company, any officer or employee of the company and anyone who was an officer, employee or auditor of the company at the time to which the document or information relates. In all cases, compliance may be enforced by means of a court order.

Transparency issues – the operating and financial review

In the past, government reporting requirements for companies have concentrated their attention on providing information specific to the financial worth and output of a company. For existing shareholders and potential investors, such figures are crucial in the assessment of a company's performance and its future potential to perform. However, in terms of wider corporate governance issues, the government, in the wake of a more proactive approach to governance, is of the view that corporate performance should not solely be determined on the basis of market performance but should include matters such as the environmental impact of the company, its relations with employees, customers and others, and future risks and opportunities. Indeed, as an aid to the general theme of wishing to encourage companies to engage in corporate governance issues beyond those involved in market performance, on 5 July 2004 the government launched a new dedicated Academy to help forward the aims of corporate social responsibility. The new Academy is for the use of companies of any size and any sector wishing to develop their corporate social responsibility skills.

In following the majority of the recommendations of the CLR and draft clauses of the White Paper (2002) and in seeking to comply with the relevant provisions of the Accounts Modernisation Directive (2003/51/EC), from 1 January 2005, the government, in introducing s 13 of the Companies (Audit, Investigations and Community Enterprise) Act 2004, instituted a regulation-making power for the Secretary of State to give statutory authority to reporting standards to give effect to the inclusion of an operating and financial review (OFR). In accordance with the Modernisation Directive, for company financial years starting on or after 1 January 2005, large companies will be required to provide a balanced and comprehensive analysis of the development and performance of the company's business to include both financial and, where appropriate, non-financial key performance indicators incorporating information relating to environmental and employee matters.

The government's intention is that the OFR should be produced as a separate self-standing report which should not be contained within another report such as the directors' report. To avoid duplication with the Modernisation Directive, the government intends to marry the relevant Directive requirements with the OFR so that quoted companies which prepare an OFR in accordance with the regulations will not need to report separately, in the directors' report.

The regulations

The Companies Act 1985 (Operating and Financial Review and Directors Report) Regulations 2005 (SI 2005/1011) were published on 20 April 2005 and take effect for financial years beginning on or after 1 April 2005. The regulations introduce the OFR as an obligatory requirement for **quoted companies**. Although shareholders of quoted companies are perceived to be the most likely beneficiaries of the OFR, the government recognises that the review will also be relevant to creditors and other stakeholders (including employees) and the wider public interest. The statutory requirement for an OFR will be supported by standards giving guidance on best practice and will aim to ensure that OFRs are prepared to a consistently high standard. Directors of quoted companies will be obliged to state whether their OFR has been prepared in accordance with OFR standards and to explain any departures from such standards. The OFR must reflect the directors' view of the business but directors will also need to pay careful attention to how companies are perceived by customers, employees and the wider community. Matters related to environmental issues or health and safety will need to be included where they constitute a significant external risk to the company, and where the company's impact on others, through its activities, products or services, affects its performance.

The OFR will be subject to a review by the company's auditor. It will be the auditor's responsibility to assess the creditability and propriety of the contents of the OFR. Criminal offences will be introduced to enforce the requirements of the OFR. There will be a criminal offence of knowingly or recklessly approving an OFR that does not comply with the relevant provisions of the legislation. The penalty for this offence will be the same as currently applies for knowing or reckless approval of defective accounts, that is a fine of up to £5000 (in summary proceedings) or an unlimited fine (on conviction on indictment).

Summary

Following the corporate scandals in the USA, issues related to corporate governance have been high on the agendas of most governments. The desire for governments to be seen to be active in the protection of financial markets affords some reassurance to investors and the general stability of the economy. In the UK, the government has reacted to the perceived need for corporate governance measures by updating the Combined Code with a strong shift towards a board structure that will comprise a majority of independent non-executive directors. Although in theory independent directors should keep executive directors in check and prevent the potential for corporate scandals, on the downside the said requirement may inhibit executive directors in the pursuit of high-risk but potentially rewarding ventures. As such the pursuit of risky business activities may be shelved in favour of safer options. This may not necessarily be a bad development but it may result in a reduction in the advancement of business ideas and may potentially inhibit economic growth. The desire to achieve independent regulators of corporate activity also runs through the Companies (Audit, Investigations and Community Enterprise) Act 2004. Coupled with the requirements of the new Combined Code in respect of audit committees, here it is suggested that the government's action is to be welcomed in so far as the previous regulation of and powers associated with the audit of companies was somewhat slack, with an obvious danger that the independence supposedly attributed to the audit procedure was more a desire rather than a positive and workable objective.

However, it is suggested that the OFR requirement simply goes too far and may be described as an example of over-zealous regulation.

Suggested further reading

Recent issues

Baldwin (2004) 67 MLR 351

Solomon (2004) 15 ICCLR 99

McConvill (2005) 62 Co Law 35

General reading

Parkinson *Corporate Power and Responsibility* (Clarendon, 1993)

Milman (ed) *Regulating Enterprise* (Hart, 1999)

Parkinson, Kelly and Gamble (eds) *The Political Economy of the Company* (Hart, 2001)

Solomon and Solomon *Corporate Governance and Accountability* (Wiley, 2003)

MacLeod and Parkinson (eds) *Global Governance and the Quest for Justice*, Vol II (Hart, 2006)

21

THE COMPANY IN GENERAL MEETING

INTRODUCTION

This chapter considers the powers and procedures of the general meeting and future proposals for reform (government proposals for reform were given some prominence in Part 8 of the White Paper (Pt II) (2002), many of the said proposals having been carried forward into the subsequent White Paper (2005)). Historically, the general meeting was perceived as the ultimate source of corporate power. Today its position of power has declined in relation to its influence over the management of corporate affairs. Nevertheless, it is still, in the exercise of its inherent powers, properly regarded as an essential organ of the body corporate. The chapter commences by analysing the classification and requirements relating to general meetings. It moves on to consider the various types of formal resolutions which may be passed at a general meeting. In addition, the chapter includes an analysis of informal types of resolutions.

TYPES OF MEETING

The annual general meeting (AGM)

Except in a situation where a private company resolves to dispense with the holding of an AGM (discussed below), s 366(1) of the Companies Act 1985 provides that a company must hold an AGM once every calendar year, and no more than 15 months must elapse between each AGM (s 366(3), CA 1985). Where an AGM is not held within the prescribed period of time, the Secretary of State may, on an application from a member of the company, order that a meeting be held and, in addition, the company and its officers may be fined in respect of a contravention of the statutory requirement (s 367, CA 1985).

Although the matters dealt with at a company's AGM are dependent upon the business raised by the board or individual members of the company, certain procedural tasks must be addressed at an AGM. The procedural tasks include: the appointment of an auditor and adoption of accounts, the receipt of the directors' report, the election of directors and, in appropriate circumstances, the determination of directors' remuneration.

Notice to members of motions to be presented at the AGM

Section 376 of the Companies Act 1985 provides that members holding not less than one-twentieth of the total voting rights or 100 members holding shares on which an average sum per member of not less than £100 has been paid up, may require the company (at the expense of those seeking the requisition, unless the company otherwise resolves) to give notice of and issue statements relating to motions (not more than 1000 words) which they intend to present at the company's next AGM. The company itself should give members general notice of the effect of any intended motion to be introduced pursuant to s 376 (s 376(4), CA 1985) at the same time (or as near to as possible) as sending out the notice for the AGM (s 376(5)). A requisition of this type (i.e. under s 376) must be deposited at the company's registered office at least six weeks prior to the intended date of the AGM (s 377, CA 1985).

Proposals for reform

It is to be noted that the White Paper (2005) recommends a prescribed default regime for private companies, the effect of which will be that all private companies will no longer be required to hold an AGM (unless there is a contrary intention in the company's constitution) (discussed further below: see 'the elective resolution'). Further, in accordance with the White Paper (2005) public companies will be required to hold their AGM within six months of the end of the financial year.

The extraordinary general meeting

A general meeting, other than an AGM, is called an extraordinary general meeting (EGM). A public company must call an EGM in circumstances where its net assets have fallen to one-half or less of its called-up capital (s 142(1), CA 1985). In other respects, an EGM may be convened, by both public and private companies, at the will of the company's board of directors. Alternatively, the board may be required to convene an EGM where under s 370(3) of the Companies Act 1985 they are requisitioned to do so by two or more members holding not less than ten per cent of the company's paid-up share capital; here the share capital must carry voting rights (s 368(1) and (2), CA 1985). In the case of a company not having a share capital an EGM may be requisitioned by not less than five per cent of the company's members who must hold at least ten per cent of the voting rights. (It is to be noted that Volume II of the White Paper (2002), clause 143, sought to provide a proposed change to this requirement by seeking to replace the current five per cent membership figure with 'one or more members who together represent 10 per cent or more of the total voting rights of members entitled to vote'. This proposal was confirmed by clause D21(2) of the White Paper (2005)).

In accordance with s 368, the membership's statutory right to require the board to convene an EGM exists 'irrespective of anything contained within the company's articles'. It should be noted that the aforementioned provision fails to distinguish between articles that prescribe a higher percentage of members required to requisition an EGM and articles which prescribe a percentage requirement lower than the ten per cent figure stipulated by s 368(1). Where the articles of a company allow its membership a more accessible means of requisitioning EGMs, that is, a lower percentage requirement than stipulated in s 368(1), it would, contrary to a literal interpretation of s 368, seem illogical not to give effect to the lower and less restrictive percentage requirement.

If the directors of a company are requisitioned to call a meeting they should, within 21 days of receiving the requisition, give the membership notice of the meeting: see e.g. *Re Windward Islands (Enterprises Ltd)* (1988) 4 BCC 158. (Note that clause 145 of Volume II of the White Paper (2002) proposed that notice of the meeting should be given within a period of 15 days of receiving the requisition. This proposal was not reproduced in the White Paper (2005): see clause D22.) The meeting must be called no more than 28 days after the notice to convene the meeting is sent out (s 368(8), CA 1985, introduced by Sch 19, para 9, CA 1989). (Note that the White Paper (2002), clause 145 proposed a period of 22 days. This proposal was not reproduced in the White Paper (2005): see clause D22.)

Where, after receiving the requisition, the directors fail to give notice of the meeting within the 21-day period, those seeking the requisition, or any of them representing more than one-half of the total voting rights of all of them, may convene the meeting, provided that the meeting is held before the end of three months from the date on which it was convened (s 368(4), CA 1985).

It is to be noted that the Final Report of the CLR recommended that general meetings should be allowed to be held at more than one location with two-way real time communication between the parties. This would seem a sensible suggestion for large public companies with the membership of the same dispersed in different parts of the country. However, the recommendation was not included in either of the White Papers.

THE COURT'S DISCRETION TO CALL MEETINGS

In accordance with s 371 of the Companies Act 1985, if it is impracticable to call or conduct a meeting of a company by a manner prescribed by either the Companies Act or the company's articles or a shareholders' agreement, the court may, on an application from a director or a member of the company who would otherwise have been entitled to attend and vote at the meeting, order a meeting to be called, to be held and conducted in a manner prescribed by the court. The substance of the provision now contained in s 371 dates back to 1862. Earlier examples of its application include *Re Consolidated Mines Ltd* [1914] 1 Ch 883, *Re El Sombrero Ltd* [1958] Ch 900 and *Re Opera Photographic* [1989] 5 BCC 601. In the latter case, Morritt J directed that a meeting should be held for the purpose of passing a resolution to dismiss one of the two members of the company from his directorship. The meeting was called despite the fact that it would be inquorate, the director against which the dismissal was sought having refused to attend (i.e. the quorum requirement of two members present at the meeting could not be satisfied: see s 370(4), CA 1985, discussed below). In allowing the meeting to proceed, Morritt J prevented the quorum requirement from being used as a device to curb the implementation of a statutory power, namely the ability of the general meeting to pass an ordinary resolution to remove a director from office.

A more recent example of the application of s 371 is found in *Union Music Ltd and Anor* v *Watson and Anor* [2004] BCC 37. Here, the issued share capital of a company was held by two shareholders, W (49 per cent holding) and U (51 per cent holding); both of the shareholders were directors of the company. A shareholders' agreement included a clause which provided that '. . . the company could not without the prior consent of both shareholders hold any meeting or transact any business at such a meeting unless there were present duly authorised representatives or proxies for each shareholder'. Following a serious breakdown in the relationship between W and U, U wished to appoint an additional director to the company. However, W refused to be involved in the said appointment. Given the terms of the shareholder agreement, U applied for an order under s 371 of the Companies Act 1985 with the purpose of seeking the appointment of the additional director. At first instance, Howarth J refused (albeit reluctantly) to make an order under s 371 on the basis that the situation was one of deadlock and the terms of the membership agreement should be adhered to; as such the learned judge proposed that U should seek an alternative remedy, namely a derivative claim or a petition under s 459 of the Companies Act 1985.

In overturning the decision of Howarth J, the Court of Appeal accepted that s 371 was not intended to allow the court to break a deadlock between two equal shareholders. However, in this case the shareholdings were not equal and the shareholders' agreement was not designed to ensure that power should be shared equally. The shareholder agreement could not prevent the court making an order under s 371 where the order was necessary to allow the company to manage its affairs in an effective and proper manner and to permit the right of a majority shareholder to remove or appoint a director in accordance with his/her majority voting power (see also *Vectone Entertainment Holding Ltd* v *South Entertainment Ltd* [2004] BCLC 224). Therefore, the court held that an order under s 371 should be permitted so as to allow a meeting the purpose of which would be limited to a single act relating to the appointment of a new director. Further, it was more efficient and cost effective for U to utilise the procedure afforded by s 371 rather than exploring the other types of remedies so suggested by Howarth J.

However, as stressed by the Court of Appeal, s 371 should not be viewed as an appropriate vehicle for resolving a deadlock between two equal ranking shareholders (see e.g. the decision of the Court of Appeal in *Ross* v *Telford* [1997] BCC 945) or for overriding the class rights of a shareholder (see e.g. *Harman* v *BML Group Ltd* [1994] 1 WLR 893).

Therefore, in a dispute between shareholders the provision will usually be invoked in a situation where a minority shareholder purports to employ quorum tactics to prevent a majority shareholder from exercising the voting rights attached to his shares (see s 371(2)). Section 371 is a procedural provision which was not designed to affect substantive voting rights or to shift the balance of power between shareholders where they agreed that the power should be shared equally and where the potential deadlock was a matter that must be taken to have been expressly or impliedly foreseen as relevant to the protection of each of them. For other examples relating to the application of s 371, see *Re Sticky Fingers Restaurant Ltd* [1992] BCLC 84, *Re Whitchurch Insurance Consultants Ltd* [1994] BCC 51 and *Re British Union for the Abolition of Vivisection* [1995] 2 BCLC 1.

FORMAL REQUIREMENTS FOR MEETINGS

The notice requirement

Notice of an intention to call a general meeting of a company must, unless the articles provide otherwise, be given to every member of the company, irrespective of whether or not the member has the right to attend and vote at the meeting (s 370(2), CA 1985). (Note that the rights attached to a particular type of share will determine the voting rights of a member.) Notice of general meetings must also be given to the company's auditor; the auditor is given a right to attend general meetings (s 387(1), CA 1985).

In respect of an AGM or a meeting at which a motion to pass a special resolution is proposed, a company must give not less than 21 days' notice in writing (s 378(2), CA 1985). For a special resolution the notice period may be reduced providing a majority of the membership, holding not less than 95 per cent in nominal value of shares carrying a right to attend and vote at the meeting, agree to a shorter period of notice (s 378(3)). In all other cases, other than for an adjourned meeting, 14 days' written notice must be given (seven days in the case of unlimited companies). A meeting held in contravention of these rules will be deemed invalid unless s 369 applies (see below). A provision in a company's articles which seeks to shorten the prescribed notice time will be void. However, in respect of an AGM, all the members of a company entitled to attend and vote at the meeting may agree to a shorter period of notice (s 369(1), CA 1985). In the case of a meeting other than an AGM, the notice period may be shortened where a majority of the membership, holding not less than 95 per cent in nominal value of shares carrying a right to attend and vote at the meeting, agree to a shorter period of notice (s 369(3), CA 1985). (Note that private companies may elect to reduce the 95 per cent requirement and also note that clause 149 of Volume II of the White Paper (2002) proposed that the 95 per cent figure should be reduced to 90 per cent for private companies. This proposal is confirmed by clause D25(5) of the White Paper (2005).)

Although a company's accidental failure to give notice to a member will not normally invalidate a meeting (see Table A, art 39), a deliberate act or omission on the part of a company that has the effect of preventing a member from receiving proper and adequate notice of the meeting will render the meeting invalid: see e.g. *Royal Mutual Benefit Building Society* v *Sharman* [1963] 1 WLR 581.

Motions (resolutions) which require special notice

Where a provision of the Companies Act 1985 expressly stipulates that a company must be given special notice of an intention to pass a resolution, s 379(1) of the Companies Act 1985 requires those who propose the motion to give at least 28 days' notice to the company before the meeting at which the resolution is to be moved. On receiving special notice, a company must give its membership at least 21 days' notice prior to the date upon which the meeting is to be held (s 379(2), CA 1985). Providing at least 21 days' notice is given to the membership, a company may nevertheless call the meeting at a date prior to the date on which the 28 days' special notice would have expired (s 379(3), CA 1985). Special notice is required for a resolution to remove a director (s 303, CA 1985), a resolution to remove an auditor (s 388, CA 1985) and one which seeks to elect a director of a public company (or a director of the subsidiary of a public company) in circumstances where the director is aged 70 or over (s 293, CA 1985).

Circulars

When giving notice of a general meeting, it is quite common for a company to issue circulars. The usual purpose of a circular is to inform the membership of the views of the company's board. Although it is possible for dissentient members to issue circulars (i.e. to explain an opposing view to the one taken by the board), the expense of issuing circulars may prove prohibitive, especially in companies with a large membership.

As a company's board is authorised to represent the company's interests, the expense of issuing circulars may be met from the company's funds where the information contained in a notice or circular is designed to benefit the company as a whole. However, the board of directors must not issue information for the purpose of personal gain or advantage, nor must the purpose for the circular be to paint a false and misleading picture of a company's affairs. Where, in giving notice or issuing a circular, a company misrepresents a state of affairs, then, in respect of a meeting for which a misleading notice (and/or circular) was issued and at which a resolution favoured by those responsible for the notice was passed, the resolution may be set aside. The misrepresentation may take the form of an omission to provide accurate information. In *CAS (Nominees) Ltd* v *Nottingham Forest FC plc* [2002] BCC 145, Hart J observed that:

'A circular to shareholders must give a fair, candid, and a reasonably full explanation of the purpose for which the meeting is called.'

An early example of a case involving an inappropriate circular is *Kaye* v *Croydon Tramways Co* [1898] 1 Ch 358. Here a purchase agreement was made between Croydon Tramways Co (C) and the British Electric Traction Co Ltd (B) for the sale of C's business. The agreement also provided that B would pay compensation to C's directors for loss of office. The notice of the meeting convened to consider B's offer failed to mention the offer of compensation made to the directors. It was held that the notice, by failing to refer to the compensation offer, did not fairly disclose the purpose of the meeting. Accordingly, the general meeting's approval of the sale transaction was set aside. (See also *Baillie* v *Oriental Telephone & Electric Co Ltd* [1915] 1 Ch 503.)

Proposals for reform

Volume II of the White Paper (2002) proposed that notice of meetings should be capable (providing the recipient member agrees) of being given, not only in the standard written form or via electronic communications such as e-mail in accordance with the Companies Act 1985 (Electronic Communications) Order 2000 (SI 2000/3373) but also via a website (see clause 149). The said proposal was endorsed by clauses D25 and D26 of the White Paper (2005). In the case of notice posted on a website, it was proposed that a member must be notified that the notice of a meeting is to be posted on the website.

In accordance with the recommendations of the CLR (see Final Report (2001) at para 7.10) it was further recommended that notice periods for all general meetings (including the AGM) should be reduced to 14 days unless a company's articles specify a longer period. This proposal was accepted by the White Paper (2005): see clause D25).

The quorum requirement

Section 370(4) of the Companies Act 1985 states that, unless a company's articles provide otherwise, two members (or proxies) must be present at a general meeting to satisfy the quorum requirement (see Table A, arts 40 and 41, which stipulate a requirement of two members (or proxies)). In the case of single member companies, s 370A of the Companies Act 1985 provides that one member present in person or by proxy shall constitute a quorum. Where at a general meeting the quorum requirement is not satisfied, the meeting will be null and void other than in a situation where the court exercises its power under s 371 (see above).

TYPES OF RESOLUTION

The ordinary resolution

An ordinary resolution is one which is passed by a simple majority of members who are entitled to attend and vote at a company meeting. Unless a contrary intention appears in the companies legislation or within a company's articles, resolutions passed by a company in general meeting are to be effected by an ordinary resolution. It should be noted that a clause in the articles which seeks to alter a specific resolution requirement contained within the companies legislation in respect of a requisite majority will be invalid.

The special resolution

In some instances, the companies legislation or a company's articles (providing the clause in the articles is not contrary to a specific requirement as to the requisite majority so contained within the companies legislation) will specify that a resolution may only be passed by a 75 per cent majority of those members entitled to attend and vote at a company meeting, that is by a special resolution. Where a motion is proposed which, if passed, would take the form of a special resolution, the membership of the company must be given at least 21 clear days' notice of the intended motion (s 378(2), CA 1985). Nevertheless, where 95 per cent of the holders of a company's share capital agree (or in the case of a company not having a share capital members holding not less than 95 per cent of the voting rights agree), a special resolution may be passed at a meeting of which less than 21 days' notice has been given (s 378(3), CA 1985). (Note that a private company may elect to reduce the 95 per cent requirement – see below.)

The extraordinary resolution

As with a special resolution, an extraordinary resolution must be passed by a 75 per cent majority of those members entitled to attend and vote at a company meeting (s 378(1), CA 1985). Notice specifying an intention to propose a motion to pass an extraordinary resolution must be given not less than 14 days prior to the meeting at which the motion is to be heard. Examples of instances whereby the companies legislation requires an extraordinary resolution to be passed include: a resolution to commence a voluntary winding up of a company (s 84(1), IA 1986); and a resolution of a class of members where the company proposes to vary the rights of the class in accordance with the variation procedure (s 125(2)(b), CA 1985).

In accordance with s 380 of the Companies Act 1985, a company is obliged to deliver copies of all special and extraordinary resolutions passed in general meeting to the Registrar of Companies. It is to be noted that the classification of a resolution as an extraordinary resolution (instead of pursuing the matter by a special resolution) was doubted by the CLR.

The informal resolution at common law

At common law, a motion to pass a resolution may be approved, without a formal resolution of the general meeting if the resolution carries the unanimous support of those members who would have been entitled to attend and vote, had the motion been put before a general meeting: see e.g. *Parker & Cooper Ltd* v *Reading* [1926] Ch 975. To a limited extent the articles of companies may reiterate the common law position. For example, Table A, art 53 provides as follows:

'A resolution in writing executed by or on behalf of each member who would have been entitled to vote upon it if it had been proposed at a general meeting at which he was present shall be as effectual as if it had been passed at a general meeting duly convened and held and may consist of several instruments in the like form each executed by or on behalf of one or more members.'

However, while Table A, art 53 requires an informal resolution to be in writing, the common law makes no such demand. For example, in *Re Duomatic* [1969] 2 Ch 365 an informal agreement to authorise directors' remuneration (a matter which would normally require an ordinary resolution of the general meeting) was upheld, despite the fact that the agreement was not in writing. Buckley J stated:

'. . . I proceed upon the basis that where it can be shown that all shareholders who have a right to attend and vote at a general meeting of the company assent to some matter which a general meeting of the company could carry into effect, that assent is as binding as a resolution in general meeting would be.'

It would appear unclear whether any specified notice requirement of an intention to pass an informal agreement must, as with a formal resolution, be sent to all members of the company. Section 370(2) only deals with notice requirements in respect of the calling of general meetings; there is no mention of any notice requirement in relation to the passing of a resolution other than at a formal general meeting. Auditors of companies would also appear to be denied the right to any notice requirement in respect of the passing of an informal agreement.

An informal agreement will be as valid as if the resolution had been passed in general meeting, irrespective of the fact that the informal agreement seeks to approve a matter which would ordinarily have required a vote from either a simple or a 75 per cent majority vote. For example, in *Cane* v *Jones* [1980] 1 WLR 1451 the court approved an alteration to a company's articles by the unanimous but informal agreement of the company's voting members (s 9, CA 1985 requires an alteration to a company's articles to be effected by a special resolution, i.e. 75 per cent majority vote, discussed further in Chapter 4).

There are now many case examples to illustrate the acceptance of the informal resolution: see e.g. *Re Bailey, Hay & Co Ltd* [1971] 3 All ER 693, *Re Home Treat Ltd* [1991] BCC 165, *Atlas Wright (Europe) Ltd* v *Wright and Anor* [1999] BCC 163 and *Euro Brokers Holdings Ltd* v *Monecor (London) Ltd* [2003] BCC 573. Indeed the flexibility of the common law approach (referred to as the *Duomatic* principle) allows the members of a company to reach an agreement without any strict and unnecessary adherence to formal procedures (i.e. no need to establish written confirmation of the resolution) and in a manner which is both sensible and logical in the context of a small business. However, it should be noted that the *Duomatic* principle will apply only in relation to agreements between the registered shareholders of a company; it could not, for example, be relied upon by a beneficial owner of shares. Therefore, a person who has purchased shares in the company but who is not listed on the register of members, or a person who beneficially owns shares but who appoints a nominee as shareholder with the nominee registered as a member, will not be able to rely on the *Duomatic* principle: see e.g. *Domoney* v *Godinho* [2004] BCLC 15.

Although the members of a company, having adopted articles which include Table A, art 53 (informal written resolution), may, by agreeing to an unwritten type of informal resolution, commit a technical breach of s 14 of the Companies Act 1985 – that is by not specifically complying with the 'written requirement' of art 53 (s 14 is discussed in Chapter 3) – the breach would nevertheless be of a procedural nature and could be corrected by the company in general meeting (all the members entitled to vote having agreed to the informal resolution). Therefore, it would be highly unlikely that a court would invalidate an informal unwritten resolution on the basis that it constituted a breach of the articles. As Neuberger J said in *Re Torvale Group Ltd* [2000] BCC 626:

> 'The articles constitute a contract, and if the parties to that contract, or if the parties for whom the benefit of a particular term has been included in that contract, are happy unanimously to waive or vary the prescribed procedure for a particular purpose, then . . . it seems to me that there is no good reason why it should not be capable of applying.' (at p 636)

In *Re Home Treat Ltd* [1991] BCC 165, Harman J went a stage further by suggesting that consent may be found in a situation where the members of a company did not informally agree to the resolution, but merely sought not to oppose it. The learned judge stated:

> '. . . acquiescence by shareholders with knowledge of the matter is as good as actual consent.' (at p 168)

However, it is important to point out that acquiescence will suffice only where there is, on the part of the shareholder(s), actual knowledge of the nature, extent and content of the proposed resolution, that is, there must be full knowledge of what has been waived. Neither will it be sufficient to show that a shareholder's assent would have been given if he/she had actually been asked to give the said assent: see e.g. *EIC Services Ltd and Anor* v *Phipps and Ors* [2003] BCC 931.

It should be noted that it may also be possible for a shareholder agreement to be viewed as an implied mechanism to sanction an informal resolution in circumstances where the subject matter of the resolution in question is specifically dealt with by the terms of the shareholders' agreement and where the agreement comprises the entire membership of the company. However, the terms of a shareholder agreement will not be capable of impliedly sanctioning an informal resolution where the agreement is absent of some material matter, so specified and required by the terms of the resolution: see e.g. *Demite Ltd* v *Proctec Health Ltd* [1998] BCC 638.

Statutory provisions – conflict with the Duomatic *principle*

Where a statutory provision is expressly drafted in terms to enable a company to perform an act by means of a resolution to be passed by the general meeting and the act in question requires or permits an additional requirement other than the actual passing of the resolution (see e.g. s 303, CA 1985 – removal of director), an informal resolution may, in such a case, be ineffective, and if relied upon may be liable to be set aside. In effect, whether or not the *Duomatic* principle can be relied upon in any given situation will depend on the underlying purpose and effect of the additional requirement(s) of the provision and whether formal as opposed to informal compliance with the provision is deemed absolutely necessary.

Generally, the courts adopt a strict approach to the formal requirements laid down by statutory provisions. For example, in *Re R W Peak (King's Lynn) Ltd* [1998] BCC 596, a company was comprised of two shareholders. A written agreement was entered into between one of the shareholders (X) for the sale of his shares to the company; the agreement was signed for and on behalf of the company by the other shareholder (Y) who was also a director of the company. Y subsequently died. X sought an order under s 359 of the Companies Act 1985 to rectify the company's register of members to reinsert his name as the holder of the shares on the basis that the agreement of sale was void because the company was not authorised to purchase its own shares by its articles (so required by s 162, CA 1985). Further, no special resolution had been passed authorising the sale contract before it had been entered into (so required by s 164(1) and (2), CA 1985); nor had a copy of the contract been made available for inspection by the members for at least 15 days preceding any meeting at which the resolution was passed (so required by s 164(6), CA 1985).

The company contended (in accordance with the *Duomatic* principle) that the formalities required by the Act could be waived because the shareholders had unanimously assented to the transaction. Lindsay J held that the *Duomatic* principle could not operate to cure the failure to comply with s 164(2) because the provision required the terms of the agreement to be approved by a special resolution of shareholders **before** the agreement was entered into. Here, that had not been the case; there was an agreement but there was no evidence of approval in advance of its execution. It was insufficient to contend that the resolution had been passed simultaneously with or subsequent to the company entering into the agreement because such a contention did not marry with the terms of the provision. If applied, the *Duomatic* principle would have meant that the shareholders had passed the resolution at the exact moment in time at which the company entered into the agreement, a finding quite contrary to the terms and purpose of s 164(2) (i.e. which requires advance approval).

However, much will depend upon the terms and purpose of the actual provision under consideration. For example, in *Re Home Treat Ltd* [1991] BCC 165, Harman J held that an informal resolution could validly alter a company's objects clause in conjunction with s 4 of the Companies Act 1985. His lordship so found, despite the fact that s 5 of the Companies Act 1985 permits the holders of not less than 15 per cent in nominal value of the company's issued share capital or any class of it, or holders of not less than 15 per cent of the company's debentures, a right to object to the court in respect of the alteration; the right to challenge the alteration continuing for up to a period of 21 days after the special resolution securing the change in objects had been passed. In upholding the validity of the informal resolution, Harman J effectively ignored the procedural requirement of s 5, that is, a special resolution had never been formally passed and as such there was no date from which the 21-day period could run. However, whilst ignoring the procedural requirement, the learned judge acknowledged the purpose behind s 5, namely to safeguard shareholder and creditor interests, having considered such interests prior to his decision to validate the informal resolution.

The decision of Nourse J in *Re Barry Artist Ltd* [1985] BCLC 283 also provides a more flexible, albeit perhaps reluctant, acceptance of the fact that members of a company may, in special circumstances, unanimously pass an informal written resolution instead of the statutory prescribed special resolution to effect a reduction of the company's capital (then in accordance with s 66(1), CA 1948; now s 135, CA 1985). The court was reluctant to accept an informal resolution because the provision states that the court must exercise its discretion in relation to whether or not to approve a special resolution passed in general meeting for the purpose of reducing a company's share capital. In *Re Barry Artist* there had never been a formal resolution which the members could approve or disapprove as no formal special resolution had been passed. However, the informal resolution was accepted because the court was still able to exercise its discretion in respect of whether to permit the reduction of capital (in this instance the reduction was approved). However, as stated, the court's decision was taken with some aversion. Nourse J commented:

> 'My strong inclination has been to adjourn this petition so that a meeting can be held and a special resolution passed, but it has been represented to me that the company has a good reason, into which I need not go, for having the reduction confirmed before the end of this term. In the circumstances, although with great reluctance, I am prepared to accede to the petition today. I would not be prepared to do so in any similar case in the future.'
> (at pp 284–85)

The written resolution

Section 381A of the Companies Act 1985 (introduced by s 113(1), CA 1989) provides, in the case of private companies, that the passing of a resolution in general meeting or at a separate meeting of a specific class of shareholders may be achieved by means of a written resolution. The written resolution takes effect as if agreed by the company in general meeting or by a meeting of the relevant class of members of the company (s 382A, CA 1985). However, unlike a resolution passed by the general meeting, no formal notice requirements are attached to the passing of a written resolution.

A written resolution may be passed by the written assent of those members of the company who, as of the date of the resolution, would have been entitled to attend and vote at a general meeting of the company. Section 381A may be invoked to pass any form of resolution whether ordinary, special, extraordinary or elective. A written resolution is passed when signed by or on behalf of the last voting member of the company to sign.

Section 381A is drafted in a similar but wider manner than Table A, art 53 (discussed above). Indeed, any previous purpose served by art 53 (in so far as s 381A is wider in scope) would at first sight appear to have been extinguished. For example, unlike Table A, art 53, s 381A would appear to be applicable even in a situation where a statutory provision is prohibitive of a company passing a resolution otherwise than in general meeting. For example, the doubts expressed by Nourse J in *Re Barry Artist* appear to have been removed in respect of a private company's ability to pass a written resolution to invoke a reduction of the company's capital. (However, in accordance with s 135, CA 1985, the reduction in capital would still need to be affirmed by the court.)

Section 381A is, nevertheless, subject to an exception in the form of Sch 15A, Companies Act 1985 (introduced by s 114, CA 1989). This schedule provides that a written resolution cannot be employed to pass a resolution under s 303 of the Companies Act 1985 (to remove a director) or under s 391 of the Companies Act 1985 (to remove an auditor).

As originally enacted s 381B(1) required a copy of any proposed written resolution to be sent to the company's auditors. Where the resolution concerned the auditors in their capacity as auditors they had an opportunity, within seven days of receiving a copy of the resolution, to give notice to the company to compel it to have the resolution considered by a formal general meeting or, where appropriate, by a separate meeting of a class of shareholders. A written resolution would not take effect until either the auditors notified the company that the resolution did not concern them or, alternatively, after seven days in a situation where the auditors failed to notify the company of their intention to seek a general meeting. However, proposals were laid before Parliament in October 1995 with the purpose of simplifying the procedure for written resolutions. The effect of the resulting legislation (SI 1996/ 1471) is to eradicate the need for proposed resolutions to be sent to a company's auditors.

In respect of some private companies, the removal of the need to call a general meeting to pass a resolution may ease administrative burdens. However, as the majority of private companies are very small concerns, the management of which may often comprise the entire membership of the company, the burden of calling a general meeting may often be no less than organising the implementation of a written resolution, albeit that the written resolution will no longer invoke the administrative burden of having to be sent to the company's auditors. It is interesting to note that, in *Re Barry Artist Ltd* [1985] BCLC 283, Nourse J, commenting on a comparison between the convenience of a written resolution and a resolution passed at a general meeting of a small private company, stated:

> 'The practical advantages of procuring all four members to sign one document, as opposed to inviting them to sign consents to short notice of the meeting and the necessary proxy forms and then getting two of them to attend a meeting in the company's offices, must have been marginal, to say the least.' (at p 284)

It is to be noted that s 381C(2) provides that ss 381A and 381B have no effect on any enactment or rule of law as to things done otherwise than by passing a resolution or cases in which a resolution is treated as having been passed. Therefore, s 381C(2) is not intended to affect the operation of the *Duomatic* principle, albeit that the *Duomatic* principle cannot make good that which would have been deemed ineffective had a written resolution procedure been adopted.

However, the 1989 Act, in giving its statutory blessing to written resolutions, has created an acceptable class of informal resolution. Indeed, because of the said acceptable standard, it may have been thought that the common law informal unwritten type of unanimous consent agreement would have been given a less than sympathetic hearing by the courts. However, this has not been the case. Nevertheless, it is to be noted that the CLR considered that the common law consent rule (the Duomatic principle) should be codified into the companies legislation so as to provide clarity and guidance in the use of the common law procedure. However, the said recommendation would have destroyed the flexibility of the procedure and would, it is suggested, in the creation of a two-tier statutory system for the regulation of informal resolutions, have caused unnecessary confusion. The recommendation was not included within the draft clauses of the White Paper (2002) or the subsequent White Paper (2005). Accordingly, it is most probable that the unanimous consent rule will remain a common law principle.

In accordance with s 380 of the Companies Act 1985, a company is obliged to deliver copies of all elective resolutions and other resolutions and agreements which, had they been agreed otherwise than in an informal manner, would only have been effective had they been passed as special or extraordinary resolutions.

Proposals for reform (written resolutions)

Volume II of the White Paper (2002), following the recommendations of the CLR, set out proposals for an amendment to the current law in respect of the governance of written resolutions (see clauses 170–177). The 2002 White Paper's proposed regime retained the basic theme of the existing procedures but its intention was to provide greater accessibility and flexibility. As a starting point, the White Paper (2002) proposed that, in addition to the board of directors, a member of the company should be capable of instigating the written resolution procedure. The White Paper (2002) did not specify whether member(s) would be required to hold a prescribed percentage of shares to initiate the procedure as, for example, is the case in relation to a member(s) who wishes to call an EGM (discussed above). In the subsequent White Paper (2005), the aforementioned proposal was accepted: see clause D7(3). In addition clause D11(3) suggests (although the clause applies to a requisition) that a written resolution may be proposed by members holding five per cent of total voting rights of all members who would be entitled to vote on the resolution (or a lower requirement, if the articles so prescribe).

A proposed change of major significance to the existing procedure is the proposal that in passing a written resolution a company will no longer be obliged to obtain the written consent of all its members (i.e. the members who would otherwise have been entitled to vote at a formal meeting). This proposal of the CLR was contained in the White Paper (2002) and endorsed by the White Paper (2005). Clause D3 of the White Paper (2005) provides that the ability of a company to pass a written resolution, in terms of the requisite majority required, should, as a minimum requirement, be determined in the same manner as if the resolution had been passed at a formal meeting (companies would be permitted to adopt a stricter requirement in terms of the requisite majority required to pass the written resolution). Therefore, in terms of the minimum requisite majority, a special resolution could be passed as a written resolution where at least 75 per cent of the members agree to the same in writing. Likewise, an ordinary resolution could be passed where more than 50 per cent of the members agree in writing.

The proposal that the unanimous consent of all members should no longer be a mandatory requirement in passing a written resolution would seem to make much sense, although if the proposal is given effect it will be crucial for members to be aware and have time to consider the terms of a proposed written resolution. With the latter in mind, the White Paper (2005), clauses D10 and D11 impose notice requirements in relation to the circulation of any proposed written resolution to the membership. The White Paper also provides that a date may be set by which time the resolution must be passed; if the date is not met the resolution will lapse (see clauses D10(4) and D15). Where no date is set, the resolution will lapse after 28 days beginning with the date of its circulation. When a written resolution is passed, the earlier White Paper (2002) provided that every member should be given notice of that fact within 15 days from the date when a director or secretary first became aware that the resolution had been passed. The White Paper (2005) imposes no such requirement.

The elective resolution

Section 379A of the Companies Act 1985 (introduced by ss 115 and 116, CA 1989) provides that the members of a private company may unanimously elect, by resolution in general meeting or by a written resolution (s 381A(1)), to dispense with certain resolution requirements prescribed by the Companies Act 1985. An elective resolution may be implemented only if all the members of the company entitled to attend and vote at the meeting vote in favour of it. An elective resolution, once passed, may be revoked by ordinary resolution. As initially enacted by s 379A(2), an elective resolution was not effective unless at least 21 days' notice in writing had been given in respect of the date of the motion to consider the passing of the elective resolution. However, as from 19 June 1996, as a result of s 379A(2A) of the Companies Act 1985 (inserted by the Deregulation (Resolutions of Private Companies)

Order 1996 (SI 1996/1471)), the procedure for passing elective resolutions has been simplified with the effect that a private company may now pass an elective resolution on short notice (before the 21-day period has expired) provided that all the members of the company entitled to vote at the meeting vote in favour of the resolution.

A private company may pass an elective resolution in respect of the following matters:

- to disapply s 80(4) and (5) of the Companies Act 1985, in respect of the giving or renewal of the directors' authority to allot shares in the company for a maximum period of five years. Where ss 80(4) and (5) are disapplied, the directors' authority to allot shares will be governed by s 80A. Section 80A provides that an authority to allot shares must state the maximum amount of relevant securities to be allotted and whether the authority is given for a fixed or indefinite period. The authority may be revoked or varied by the passing of an ordinary resolution. Where the elective resolution ceases to have effect (e.g. if it is revoked by the general meeting), then any authority to allot shares, then in force, will be extinguished in a situation where it had been in operation for five or more years. Where, however, the authority had operated for a period of less than five years, it will, in such circumstances, continue to run from the date when it was first granted, for a maximum of five years (s 80A(7), CA 1985);

- to dispense with the holding of an AGM (s 366A, CA 1985). It should be noted that, in accordance with s 366A(3) of the Companies Act 1985, any member of a company who has elected to dispense with the holding of an AGM may, by notice to the company, not later than three months before the end of the year in which an AGM was scheduled to take place, require that the AGM be held in that year. Where a member of a company asserts his right under s 366A(3), then s 366(1) and (4) of the Companies Act 1985 will be applicable in respect of the calling of the meeting and the consequences attached to any default in the procedure (discussed above);

- to reduce the number of members required to sanction a company meeting at short notice or effect notice of a motion to pass a special resolution from 95 per cent to a number not below 90 per cent (ss 369(4) and 378(3), CA 1985). The percentage of members required may be specified in the elective resolution or subsequently determined by the company in general meeting;

- to dispense with the laying of accounts and reports before general meetings (s 252(1), CA 1985);

- to elect to exempt the annual appointment of auditors (s 386(1), CA 1985).

In introducing a system of elective resolutions, the Companies Act 1989 has undoubtedly made some progress in easing the regulatory burden of legislation in relation to private companies. The 1989 Act has moved towards creating some form of distinction and split between the form of the companies legislation as between private and public companies. It should be noted that, under s 117 of the Companies Act 1989, the Secretary of State has the power to make regulations enabling private companies to pass elective resolutions dispensing with further requirements of the companies legislation.

Proposals for reform (the elective regime)

In Volume II of the White Paper (2002) and following the recommendations of the CLR Final Report 2001, it is proposed that parts of the existing elective regime should be made into a prescribed default regime for private companies (however, it is to be presumed that the content of the existing elective regime will (in its entirety) still be available for private companies). The prescribed regime would allow private companies to dispense with the need to lay financial statements before a general meeting, hold an AGM and annually appoint auditors, although it is to be noted that a member (or auditor) could still serve notice on the company requiring it, for that particular financial year, to hold an AGM and to lay its financial statements (see clause 136). The prescribed regime was not to be obligatory, with private companies given the ability to opt into what the White Paper (2002) rather confusingly terms the 'mandatory scheme' (discussed below). The opt in would have been effected by either giving notice to the Registrar at the time of the company's formation or by subsequently passing an ordinary resolution. The opt in could subsequently, subject to any restriction in the company's constitution, be reversed by means of a special resolution.

In the White Paper (2005) it was decided to adopt the aforementioned 'default scheme'. However, the White Paper (2005) proposes that there should be no opt-out mechanism in relation to the scheme albeit that if a private company wished to continue to lay financial statements before an AGM, hold an AGM and annually appoint auditors, it could choose to do so by incorporating the necessary requirements within the company's constitution.

It is suggested that for private companies the aforementioned reforms in respect of the prescribed default regime are probably unnecessary, given the existing and more extensive elective regime. Although the proposed prescribed regime is obviously (as a 'default' regime) more accessible and more permanent than the current elective regime, it is envisaged that a majority of private companies that choose to adopt an elective regime will prefer the more extensive options presented by the existing regime.

By contrast, the White Paper (2002) provided that public companies would be automatically subject to the 'mandatory scheme' although they would have the option to opt out into the prescribed regime if a resolution to that effect was unanimously approved by the membership. However, that resolution could, at any time, be reversed by any member of the company serving a notice on the company. If a public company opted out of the mandatory scheme, any of its members would be allowed to serve notice requiring it to hold an AGM and to lay the financial statements for that financial year. The suggested reform in respect of public companies discarded a suggestion advanced by an earlier CLR consultation document entitled 'Modern Law for a Competitive Economy – General Meetings and Shareholder Communication' (1999), namely to extend generally to plcs the right to dispense with the holding of AGMs by the passing of a special resolution or alternatively by a 90 per cent majority vote of the membership holding voting shares. It is to be observed that neither the recommendation contained in the White Paper (2002) nor the CLR proposal was endorsed by the White Paper (2005): see clause D52 et seq.

For smaller public companies it is suggested that either of the proposed reforms (White Paper (2002) and CLR) may have been advantageous in terms of cost and efficiency. However, in relation to the proposal contained in the White Paper (2002), the ease by which a member may have compelled a return to the mandatory scheme may have rendered any such advantage superfluous.

VOTING PROCEDURE

At general meetings the standard procedure for casting votes in favour/against proposed motions is by the members present at the meeting to vote, by a show of hands. In effect this means that if, for example, a motion was required to be carried by a special resolution and only 100 members out of a total membership of 1000 turned up to the meeting at which the motion was proposed, then the resolution would be carried by just 75 members voting in its favour. Indeed, it is quite a common feature at meetings of companies with a large membership for resolutions to be passed by but a small percentage of the total membership.

Irrespective of the numbers of shares held by a member, a member may, in a vote by the show of hands, cast only one vote. However, unlike a vote decided on by the show of hands, a poll vote entitles members to cast votes in proportion to the number of voting shares held: that is, if a member holds 50 shares each carrying one vote he/she would be entitled to cast 50 votes. A poll vote may, if demanded, be taken instead of, or after, a vote by a show of hands. Section 373(1) of the Companies Act 1985 provides that any provision contained within a company's articles which seeks to exclude the right to demand a poll on any matter other than the election of a chairman or the adjournment of a meeting will be void. (Table A, art 51 does, by implication, allow for a poll to be taken on the election of a chairman or the adjournment of a meeting.) Section 373(1) further provides that any provision contained within a company's articles will be void where it prohibits a poll from being demanded by not less than five members (Table A, art 46 allows a poll to be demanded by two members, or by a member(s) representing not less than one-tenth of the total voting rights of all the members having the right to vote at the meeting, or member(s) holding shares conferring the right to vote on which an aggregate sum has been paid representing not less in total than the sum of one-tenth of the company's existing paid-up capital on shares conferring the right to vote. Table A, art 46 further provides that a poll may be demanded by the chairman of the meeting.) (Further regulations pertinent to procedural aspects of poll votes are contained in Table A, arts 48–53.)

Proxies

A proxy is a person appointed by a member of a company to represent that member's voting interests at a general meeting. Section 372(1) of the Companies Act 1985 provides that any member of a company who is entitled to attend and vote at a general meeting may appoint a proxy to attend in his/her place. The proxy is allowed to vote only on a poll vote. The proxy need not himself be a member of the company. Where a proxy is appointed by a member of a private company (but not a public company) the proxy may speak at the meeting on the member's behalf. However, a member of a private company cannot appoint more than one proxy to attend a meeting unless the company's articles provide otherwise (s 372(2), CA 1985). It should be noted that Table A, art 59 does provide otherwise.

A member who appoints a proxy has no statutory right to demand that the proxy vote be counted on a vote conducted by a show of hands. Nevertheless, a person acting as a proxy may, if permitted by the terms of the company's articles (see above), demand that a poll vote be taken on any motion put before the meeting. The legitimacy of the demand will be determined as if made by the member upon whose behalf the proxy acts (s 373(2), CA 1985). As a member's agent, a proxy should vote in accordance with the wishes of his principal. Nevertheless, where a proxy acts contrary to his principal's instructions, the votes cast will not normally be discounted unless they were considered crucial to the final outcome of the vote: see e.g. *Oliver* v *Dalgleish* [1963] 3 All ER 330.

Proposals for reform

Volume II of the White Paper (2002) (see clauses 153–154), subsequently endorsed by clauses D39–D48 of the White Paper (2005), proposes that the rights of proxies should be the same in both private and public companies and that any member of a company entitled to vote at a general meeting should be permitted to appoint one or more proxies to attend, speak at, vote, and count as a part of the quorum requirement at the meeting. Voting is not to be restricted to a poll vote.

In respect of the voting procedure at AGMs, it is to be noted that the CLR consultation document entitled 'Modern Law for a Competitive Economy – General Meetings and Shareholder Communication' (1999) advanced a quite radical suggestion, namely a delayed voting procedure (a time gap between the hearing of the motion and the time of the vote) so as to provide members with more time to consider the way in which they should vote in respect of the debate advanced for and against motions put forward at AGMs. Although, in theory, a worthwhile proposal, in a practical sense it would have allowed interested parties the time to lobby for support, to the extent that members may have been persuaded to vote in a given way for reasons which may, in some instances, have been unconnected with the merits or otherwise of the motion. Accordingly, this proposal was not included in the White Papers.

Adjournments

In certain circumstances, the necessity may arise for the chairman of a general meeting to adjourn a meeting. In such a case unfinished matters of business will be postponed to a new date. Table A, art 45 states as follows:

> 'The chairman may, with the consent of a meeting at which a quorum is present (and shall if so directed by the meeting), adjourn the meeting from time to time and from place to place, but no business shall be transacted at an adjourned meeting other than business which might properly have been transacted at the meeting had the adjournment not taken place. When a meeting is adjourned for fourteen days or more, at least seven clear days' notice shall be given specifying the time and place of the adjourned meeting and the general nature of the business to be transacted. Otherwise it shall not be necessary to give such notice.'

In exercising the power to adjourn a meeting the chairman must act *bona fide* in the best interests of the company. The decision to adjourn must have been a reasonable one to take in the light of all the relevant circumstances. A meeting must not be adjourned as a means to prevent, delay or handicap the will of the company in general meeting. An example of a chairman's decision to adjourn a meeting which attracted judicial disapproval is to be found in *Byng* v *London Life Association Ltd* [1990] Ch 170. Here, the Court of Appeal considered it impracticable for a chairman to adjourn a meeting for a period of two hours; the meeting was adjourned to a venue located in a different part of London from the one in which the original meeting had taken place (the original meeting was adjourned because the meeting hall was too small). The haste at which the adjourned meeting was rearranged meant that many of the members who attended the original meeting were unable to attend the rescheduled meeting. As a result of the adjournment, a special resolution, which had the support of the board but which had attracted opposition from a strong faction of the membership, was passed; had the original meeting not been adjourned, the outcome of the vote may have been different. The fact that the meeting was rescheduled at such short notice and at a different venue gave rise to a finding that in the circumstances of the case the chairman's decision had been unreasonable. The vote to secure the resolution in question was declared invalid.

Minutes

Every company must keep minutes of the proceedings of its general meetings and meetings of its directors. The minutes must be entered into books kept especially for the purpose of recording minutes. Minutes purporting to be signed by the chairman of a meeting or the chairman of the next succeeding meeting are evidence of the fact that the proceedings of the meeting were conducted in a manner as recorded in the minute book (s 382(1), CA 1985). Provided that minutes have been kept and duly signed, then, unless the contrary is proved, a meeting will be regarded as having been duly held and convened and all resolutions passed at the meeting will be deemed to have been validly approved (s 382(4), CA 1985).

Class meetings

A class meeting is held when it is necessary for a class of shareholders to decide a matter which affects their particular class of share. For example, a class meeting of shareholders holding share type X would be held in accordance with s 125 of the Companies Act 1985 in a situation where the company wished to vary the rights of the holders of share type X (discussed in Chapter 9). Meetings of a particular class of shareholder are regulated in accordance with the terms of a company's articles. The procedure for conducting class meetings is, on the whole, comparable to the procedure which governs general meetings (s 125(6), CA 1985). The standard quorum required at a class meeting is two persons holding or representing by proxy at least one-third in nominal value of the issued share capital of the class in question (s 125(6)(a), CA 1985).

Suggested further reading

Baxter [1976] JBL 323

Prentice [1977] 40 MLR 587

Higginson (1993) 109 LQR 16

Jaffey (1996) 16 LS 27

Grantham (1998) 55 CLJ 554

Goddard [2004] JBL 121

22

THE DIVISION OF A COMPANY'S POWERS BETWEEN THE BOARD AND GENERAL MEETING

INTRODUCTION

This chapter seeks to examine the relationship between the board of directors and the general meeting in respect of the policy and decision-making process of a company. It undertakes a brief historical analysis of the division of powers between the two primary organs of the company before moving on to consider the determination and exercise of corporate powers in more modern times. Although earlier chapters of this book have dealt with the individual characteristics and legal responsibilities of both directors and the general meeting, the purpose here is to consider the relationship between the two organs of the company in terms of their respective influence, determination, control and implementation of corporate powers.

THE HISTORICAL DEVELOPMENT OF THE DIVISION OF CORPORATE POWERS

The registered company was born out of the unincorporated partnership businesses of the nineteenth century (see Chapter 1). Therefore, in many respects, it is not surprising that the power structure of the registered company was originally determined in a manner comparable with principles derived from partnership law. As such, the early statutory regulation of the division of corporate powers was ordained in favour of the collective will of a company's membership, that is, the company in general meeting. A company's board of directors was not, as it now is, considered to be a vital organ of the company, but was merely appointed to carry out the will of the general meeting. Accordingly, conflicts between the board and general meeting were ordinarily resolved to the latter's advantage. Section 90 of the Companies Clauses Consolidated Act 1845 provided, *inter alia*, that the exercise of the board's general powers of management should be:

> '. . . subject also to the control and regulation of any general meeting specifically convened for the purpose*, but not so as to render invalid any act done by the directors prior to any resolution passed by such general meeting.' (emphasis added)

In *Isle of Wight Rly Co v Tahourdin* (1883) 25 ChD 320, Cotton LJ emphasised the ultimate dominance of the general meeting. He stated:

> 'If a shareholder complains of the conduct of the directors while they keep within their powers, the court says to him, "If you want to alter the management of the affairs of the company go to the general meeting, and if they agree with you they will pass a resolution obliging the directors to alter their course of proceeding".' (at p 329)

The ability of the general meeting to supervise and, if necessary, determine corporate policy, persisted throughout the nineteenth century. However, the growth and expansion of the corporate form was, with time, inevitably to result in the general meeting's decline in matters of dictating corporate policy. In many companies expansion brought growth both in terms of wealth and membership numbers. Many shareholders invested in companies for potential profit and not for the capacity to participate in management decisions. In expanding companies of size, the partnership principles on which the corporate form had been founded no longer ruled supreme; membership interest, attendance, and participation at general meetings all declined. This decline was and still is today particularly prevalent in larger companies where commercial reality dictates that the administration of corporate policy demands a consolidation of corporate powers into a centralised body (the board of directors).

THE ARTICLES OF ASSOCIATION AND THE DETERMINATION OF CORPORATE POWER

The decline in the importance of the general meeting as the principal corporate power base has historically been reflected in the reduction of powers afforded to the general meeting by the articles of association. The articles were, and still are considered to this day, to be the dominant factor in determining the division of powers between the board and general meeting. In *Automatic Self-Cleansing Filter Syndicate Co v Cuninghame* [1906] 2 Ch 34 the Court of Appeal recognised that, subject to certain powers reserved to the general meeting by statute, a company's articles were decisive to the extent of powers to be exercised by both the board and general meeting; in effect an acceptance of the quasi-contractual effect of the articles in accordance with what is now s 14 of the Companies Act 1985 (discussed in Chapter 4).

The facts of the *Cuninghame* case were as follows. A dispute arose between the directors and a group of shareholders over the extent of the general meeting's power to subordinate the views of the company's board with the general meeting's own views. The general meeting passed an ordinary resolution instructing the company's board of directors to sell the company's undertaking; the directors having disapproved of the proposed sale. Article 96 of the company's articles was drafted to enable the directors of the company to exercise all corporate powers other than those powers which were expressly reserved to the company in general meeting, subject to such regulations as, from time to time, were made by the general meeting by an extraordinary resolution. The company's articles specifically provided that a decision to sell company property was one to be taken by the board of directors.

The Court of Appeal, in upholding the decision of Warrington J, found that art 96 provided the shareholders with no right to insist that the company's undertaking be sold in accordance with the ordinary resolution passed at the general meeting. In giving effect to the terms of the company's articles, the court held that an alteration of directors' powers in accordance with art 96, could only take place by the passing of an extraordinary resolution (75 per cent majority required).

Subsequent to the decision of the Court of Appeal in *Cuninghame*, the division of corporate powers continues to be determined by a construction of the terms of a company's articles. However, prior to the adoption of the current Table A, art 70 (discussed below), the construction of the standard form Table A articles was the source of much controversy. The 1948 Companies Act, Table A, art 80 (previous Table A articles dealing with a division of powers were written in a similar vein to art 80) provided that:

'The business of the company shall be managed by the directors, and [they] may exercise all such powers of the company as are not by the Companies [legislation] or by these regulations, required to be exercised by the company in general meeting, subject, nevertheless . . . to such regulations being not inconsistent with the aforesaid regulations or provisions, as may be prescribed by the company in general meeting; but no regulation made by the company in general meeting shall invalidate any prior act of the directors which would have been valid if that regulation had not been made.'

(It should be noted that a company incorporated prior to the implementation of the Companies Act 1985, having adopted Table A articles, will still (unless the articles have been altered) have articles based upon the 1948 Table A articles.)

Prima facie, the wording of art 80 is ambiguous. As it provides that the company's directors are to manage the company but subject to any contrary regulations passed by the company in general meeting, it appears to permit conflicts appertaining to the division of corporate powers to be resolved by the general meeting by ordinary resolution. Indeed, to some extent, the first-instance decision of Neville J in *Marshall's Valve Gear Co Ltd* v *Manning, Wardle & Co Ltd* [1909] 1 Ch 267 was supportive of the view that the general meeting had an ultimate authority over the board in a situation of conflict. In *Marshall's* case the court permitted a majority shareholder to commence litigation in the name of the company despite the refusal of a majority of the board to sanction the litigation. The relevant article of the company which determined the division of powers between the board and general meeting was drafted in a similar vein to 1948 Table A, art 80.

Neville J's interpretation of the art 80 type provision suggested that the general meeting's power to interfere with management powers of the board was one untouched by the statutory prescribed method for an alteration of articles, that is, by special resolution. Accordingly, in a situation of conflict between the general meeting and the board the court's ruling in *Marshall's* case was indicative of the view that the art 80 type provision provided the general meeting with an overriding power, by means of an ordinary resolution, to effect a temporary change to the board's powers; as opposed to a permanent change in those powers. To effect a permanent change the company would have been required to alter its articles.

Nevertheless, it is suggested that a contrary explanation of the court's finding in *Marshall's* case may be found in the fact that the litigation in question concerned a matter in which a majority of the directors had a personal interest. As such, it could be contended (although this explanation was not alluded to by Neville J) that the personal-interest factor raised a presumption that the board, in declining to commence litigation, acted otherwise than in the best interests of the company. It would therefore have followed, in accordance with principles related to the exceptions to the rule in *Foss* v *Harbottle* (1843) 2 Hare 461 (discussed in Chapter 23), that it was possible for the majority shareholder (providing the resolution to litigate was sanctioned by the company in general meeting which it of course would have been, i.e. by the majority shareholder) to commence litigation in the name of the company without the need to seek the approval of the board.

In subsequent cases which have dealt with the interpretation of art 80, the courts have been unwilling to accept that the general meeting has an absolute right to interfere in the board's management powers by means of passing an ordinary resolution to effect an alteration in the board's corporate policy: see e.g. *Quinn & Axtens* v *Salmon* [1909] 1 Ch 311, *John Shaw & Sons (Salford) Ltd* v *Shaw* [1935] 2 KB 113 and *Scott* v *Scott* [1943] 1 All ER 582. In *Gramophone and Typewriter Ltd* v *Stanley* [1908] 2 KB 89, Buckley LJ stated:

'. . . even a resolution of a numerical majority at a general meeting of the company cannot impose its will upon the directors when the articles have confided to them the control of the company's affairs. The directors are not servants to obey directions given by the shareholders as individuals; they are not agents appointed by and bound to serve the shareholders as their principals. They are persons who may by the regulations be entrusted with the control of the business, and if so entrusted they can be dispossessed from that control only by the statutory majority which can alter the articles.' (at p 105)

A more recent example is provided by *Breckland Group Holdings Ltd* v *London and Suffolk Properties* [1989] BCLC 100. Here a company (C) had two corporate members: company A (the majority shareholder) and company B. The board of C included two directors appointed by A and one director appointed by B. The corporate members agreed by means of a formal shareholders' agreement that should C wish to commence any form of litigation the matter would first require the approval of one director each, from both company A and B.

In contravention of this agreement, C commenced litigation with the support of A (the majority shareholder). B moved to restrain the action from being commenced in C's name. In denying that A, as the majority shareholder, had a right to overturn the powers properly vested in the board of C, the court refused to accept that, had a general meeting of C been convened to 'rubber stamp' A's decision to commence litigation, the general meeting's authorisation would have been capable of overturning the powers properly vested in the board. The court restrained proceedings until a properly held board meeting could decide whether or not C should commence litigation.

An interesting, although collateral, point arising from this case was whether or not the final decision of the board had to be taken in accordance with the terms of the shareholder agreement. In his judgment, Harman J did not expressly adjudicate on this matter, but his lordship did appear to presume that the shareholder agreement would have been binding. If so, had the majority of the board voted in favour of litigation (company A through its nominees held a majority of the directorships in the company), the decision of the majority would have been overridden by the terms of the shareholder agreement. In effect, the shareholder agreement would have restricted the powers of the board, despite the fact that, in a strict sense, the board, as an organ of the company, was not a party to it. Although the articles of a company bind the membership and the company in a form of contractual agreement, it is surely wrong to assume that the board, acting as an organ of the company, should be bound by the terms of a shareholder agreement. Although individual members of the board can, as members of the company, be bound by such an agreement, they should not be so bound when acting in a capacity other than as members of the company. (Shareholder agreements are discussed further in Chapter 4.)

While the courts, in construing 1948 Table A, art 80 have, with the exception of *Marshall's* case, positively denied that art 80 is permissive of the general meeting's right by ordinary resolution to regulate the management of a company in instances of conflict with the board of directors, it should be noted that where a company's board is unable to carry out its management functions – for example, where directors have been unable to reach a decision because of deadlock or lack of a competent quorum – the courts have been willing to permit the general meeting to act for them: see e.g. *Barron* v *Potter* [1914] 1 Ch 895 and *Foster* v *Foster* [1916] 1 Ch 352.

A compelling reason for denying the general meeting the power, by ordinary resolution, to regulate the management of a company is that to do so would be to allow it to alter the powers afforded to directors (as contained in the articles) other than in a manner normally associated with an ability to alter a company's articles, that is, by the passing of a special resolution (s 9, CA 1985). As Greer LJ stated in *John Shaw & Sons (Salford) Ltd* v *Shaw* [1935] 2 KB 113:

> 'If the powers of management are vested in the directors, they and they alone can exercise these powers. The only way in which the general body of the shareholders can control the exercise of the powers vested by the articles in the directors is by altering their articles.'
> (at p 134)

Indeed, it may be possible to contend that art 80 merely endorses the statutory requirement that an alteration of the board's powers must take place by means of a special resolution. Article 80 provides that where there is inconsistency between the views of the general meeting and the board, in order for the views of the general meeting to prevail, regulations to remove the board's powers must be prescribed. If, in construing art 80, the term 'regulations' is simply interpreted to mean 'articles' (this interpretation is quite possible in that Table A articles are, in the context of companies legislation, referred to as 'Table A Regulations'), then an alteration of the regulations (articles) may only be effected by means of a special resolution.

1985 Table A, art 70

In respect of the current 1985 Table A articles, art 70 provides that the general meeting is afforded a power to effect a temporary change in directors' powers, albeit that the temporary change of power must be exercised by means of a special resolution. Article 70 states:

> 'Subject to the provisions of the Act and the memorandum and the articles and to any directions given by special resolution the business of the company shall be managed by the directors who may exercise all the powers of the company. No alteration of the memorandum or articles and no such direction shall invalidate any prior act of the directors which would have been valid if that alteration had not been given.'

Therefore, Table A, art 70 empowers the general meeting, by direction, to regulate management affairs properly vested in the directors without the need formally to adopt a resolution to alter the articles. By specifying the need for a special resolution,

Table A, art 70 removes the controversy which had previously surrounded the general meeting's capacity to regulate management powers.

Powers of management specifically reserved to the general meeting

The articles of most companies are drafted in compliance with, or are closely aligned to, the standard Table A articles, thereby conferring the majority of the powers of management on the board of directors. Nevertheless, the articles of a company will normally reserve limited powers of management to the general meeting. For example, Table A provides that the election of directors (art 78), the remuneration of directors (art 82) and the declaration of dividends up to an amount recommended by the directors (art 102) are powers to be reserved to the general meeting.

The Companies Act 1985 also reserves certain exclusive powers of management to the general meeting. The powers reserved are few, but are nevertheless quite substantive, being concerned with the constitutional functioning of the company. For example, to alter its principal constitutional documents, namely the memorandum (s 4, CA 1985) and the articles (s 9, CA 1985), a company must seek a special resolution of the general meeting. Also, a company, if permitted to do so by its articles (Table A so permits), may only alter its share capital clause contained within the memorandum by means of an ordinary resolution of the general meeting (s 121, CA 1985).

In addition to the aforementioned powers of management, the general meeting has the right, by ordinary resolution, to remove any director from office. This power is of some significance because where members of a company disagree with the board's management policy they may, if they command sufficient support, either threaten the directors with dismissal or, if that tactic fails, actually enforce s 303 of the Companies Act 1985, so removing the directors from office. The power of the general meeting in respect of s 303 is in theory a very important one; however, much will depend on whether a director is able directly or indirectly to control a bare majority of the membership. Nevertheless, in the hands of an effective and independent membership that possesses sufficient support, s 303 provides an indirect means to challenge the management policy of the directors and does so in a manner which exceeds the powers given to the general meeting by the articles of association.

The duty of the general meeting to act for the benefit of the company as a whole

In exercising its limited powers of management, the general meeting must, in a manner akin to the company's directors, apply its powers for the benefit of the company as a whole. In any given situation, the test to determine whether the general meeting acted for the benefit of the company as a whole may, by analogy with the duties owed to a company by its directors, be said to be dominated by an objective consideration of whether the general meeting's powers were exercised for a proper purpose. However, the interpretation of the test is one which has at times been clouded in some confusion. The confusion over the application of the test as applied to the exercise of corporate powers by the general meeting was evident in the case of *Clemens* v *Clemens Bros Ltd* [1976] 2 All ER 268.

The facts of the *Clemens* case were as follows. The company, Clemens Bros Ltd (C), was a small domestic concern. Its share capital was divided between Miss Clemens (M) and her niece (N). M held 55 per cent of the shares and N the remaining 45 per cent. M was one of five directors; the other four directors were not shareholders in the company. The board of directors proposed a new share issue, the substance of which was to create an employee share scheme and also to allow the four non-shareholding directors to hold a small minority of the company's shares. The effect of the new share issue would have been to reduce M's shareholding interest in C to below 50 per cent; N's holding would have been reduced to below 25 per cent.

M exercised her voting control to pass the new share issue. N objected on the premise that, following the new share issue, the income which she derived from dividend payments would be reduced. In addition, and perhaps of more importance in terms of the outcome of the case, N's proposed new holding of less than 25 per cent would have resulted in the loss of her negative control in C, because she would have been unable to prevent (had she so wished) the passing of a special resolution. The loss of N's negative control was an advantage to M because, prior to the new share issue, N and M had experienced a very poor working relationship.

Foster J, in finding in favour of N's minority action, held that M's majority voting control could not be exercised without questioning whether such votes had been exercised for the benefit of the company as a whole. His lordship took the view that M's motive in assenting to the resolution was primarily the removal of N's voting influence in the company and not a desire to benefit the company's employees and four non-voting directors. Therefore, the learned judge concluded that M had not acted for the benefit of the company as a whole but for her own selfish interests.

Although the actual outcome of the case may be defended, it is nevertheless impossible to decipher the precise principle of law on which the interpretation of the test applied to the 'benefit of the company as a whole' was reached. Foster J was content to leave the reasoning for his decision wrapped up in a number of principles, or, as he put it:

> 'I think that one thing which emerges from the case to which I have referred is that in such a case as the present, Miss Clemens is not entitled to exercise her majority vote in whatever way she pleases. The difficulty is in finding a principle, and obviously expressions such as "bona fide for the benefit of the company as a whole", "fraud on a minority" and "oppressive" do not assist in formulating a principle.' (at p 282)

The decision taken in *Clemens* in relation to the 'the benefit of the company as a whole' is difficult to rationalise in terms of anything other than having been decided on purely equitable considerations. However, was justice really served? Was Miss Clemens' act a purely selfish one? If one objectively considers the effect of the new share issue, it is to be observed that, had it been allowed, M would have lost her majority control in the company. In addition, M's income from dividend payments would also have been reduced. Further, the benefit of the share issue could, in rewarding employees and the non-shareholding directors, have benefited the company as a whole. Indeed, the contention that M acted for her own selfish interests may have been somewhat overstated.

In addition to considering the interests of minority shareholders, a power reserved to the general meeting must not be used where its effect would be to defraud or seriously prejudice creditors (by analogy, in considering the interests of the company as a whole, directors of a company may be obliged to consider the interests of creditors). A case example which illustrates that the general meeting's use of its powers must take account of the interests of creditors, in so far as corporate creditors may fall within the interests expressed within the concept of the company as a whole, is *Re Halt Garage* [1982] 3 All ER 1016. Here the court was called upon to determine the question of whether a company's membership, comprised of a husband and wife team, both of whom held directorships in the company, had, in authorising remuneration payments to themselves as directors, awarded payments which were in reality gratuitous distributions out of capital dressed up as remuneration. The company, which had been put into liquidation, sought, through its liquidator, the return of remuneration payments over a period of three years.

In determining whether the shareholders had authorised remuneration payments in a manner consistent with a proper exercise of their powers, Oliver J formulated the following test:

'I think that in circumstances such as exist in this case where payments are made under the authority of a general meeting acting pursuant to an express power, the matter falls to be tested by reference to the genuineness and honesty of the transaction rather than reference to some abstract standard of benefit . . . As it seems to me, the submission of counsel for the respondents involves the notion that where there is a purported exercise of an express power by a general meeting the court is a slave to whatever form of words the members may have chosen to use in the resolution which they may pass. I do not think that can be so. I agree with counsel for the liquidator that it cannot be right that shareholder directors acting in unison can draw any sum they like out of the company's capital and leave the liquidator and the company's creditors without remedy in the absence of proof of intent to defraud because they choose to dignify the drawing with a particular description . . . the court is not, in my judgment, precluded from examining the true nature of the payments merely because the members choose to call them remuneration.' (at p 1043)

In applying the above test, Oliver J concluded that, while there was no evidence that the husband's level of takings had been excessive or unreasonable, the level of takings paid to the wife had been unreasonably high. The wife had ceased to be active in the employment of the company and therefore was not entitled to remuneration during the period over which the complaint related. Although the company's articles included a power to award remuneration for the mere assumption of the office of director, Oliver J was of the opinion that the awards made to the wife were so out of proportion to any possible value to be attributed to her holding office that the court was justified in not treating them as genuine payments of remuneration but, rather, as dressed-up dividends out of capital. Accordingly, it was held that the payments to the wife had been invalidly authorised by the general meeting. While there was no evidence of any intent/motive on the part of the wife to defraud the company and its creditors, Oliver J remarked that:

'. . . the court must, I think, look at the matter objectively and apply the standard of reasonableness'. (at p 1044)

The general meeting's ability to ratify an irregular act of the directors

Where a company director commits a breach of duty or exceeds his authority in exercising a management power, the irregular act will, in most instances, be voidable. The general meeting may ratify the irregular act, usually by an ordinary resolution. An irregular act will be capable of ratification if the general meeting acts for the benefit of the company as a whole (i.e. without instigating a fraud on minority shareholders; fraud on the minority is discussed in Chapter 23).

Where an irregular act of the directors is liable to cause damage to creditor interests, any purported ratification of the act by the general meeting may be set aside in circumstances which indicate that the general meeting acted without honestly considering the question of whether it was fair and proper to ratify the act: see e.g. the *obiter* comments of Cumming-Bruce and Templeman LJJ in *Re Horsley & Weight Ltd* [1982] 3 All ER 1045. (By analogy see *Re Halt Garage* (above), a case concerned with the exercise of a general meeting's power to award directors' remuneration.)

Although directors are not permitted to exercise powers which are by the terms of a company's articles vested in the general meeting, should such a usurpation of a power occur, the general meeting may nevertheless ratify the abuse of power by ordinary resolution, regardless of the fact that the power use would otherwise have required a special resolution: see e.g. *Grant v United Kingdom Switchback Railways Co* (1888) 40 ChD 135. While, in such a case, the general meeting's power to ratify by ordinary resolution would appear to be contradictory to the manner in which the general meeting could otherwise have exercised the power, in reality the power to ratify affects the approval of an unauthorised act as opposed to an attempt to usurp the terms of the company's articles; ratification does not confer future powers on the directors, whereas an alteration of the articles would have a permanent effect.

However, where an ordinary resolution of the general meeting purports to ratify an irregular act and the act in question contravenes the terms of a company's articles, then, in such a case, the general meeting's attempted ratification would be invalid. For example, in *Boschoek Proprietary Co Ltd v Fuke* [1906] 1 Ch 148, the directors of a company appointed a managing director at a level of remuneration in excess of the amount prescribed in the company's articles and also in contravention of a share qualification clause. The appointment was purportedly ratified by the general meeting. The court concluded that the general meeting could not of itself have appointed or ratified the terms of the appointment in contravention of the terms of the articles and as such the purported ratification was invalid. The articles, until altered, bound the membership in the same way as they bound the board of directors.

Suggested further reading

Goldberg (1970) 33 MLR 177

Sullivan (1977) 93 LQR 569

Mackenzie (1983) 4 Co Law 99

23

SHAREHOLDER ACTIONS – THE PROTECTION OF THE COMPANY'S INTERESTS

INTRODUCTION

This chapter commences by examining the types of action available to an aggrieved share-holder under the common law and in so doing examines the potential conflict between corporate and personal actions. However, the primary purpose of this chapter is to concentrate on minority shareholder actions geared to the protection of the interests of the company as a whole. Accordingly, the principal part of the chapter seeks to examine the ability of a minority shareholder(s) to redress a wrong committed against the company. The availability of such an action seeks to override a fundamental principle of company law which dictates that an action to correct a corporate wrong should be pursued at the will of and by the company. The personal remedies of an aggrieved minority shareholder are dealt with in Chapter 24.

THE TYPES OF ACTION AVAILABLE TO THE MINORITY SHAREHOLDER

The personal action

A personal action may be commenced where a shareholder's legal rights of membership have been abused by an act deemed to be that of the company. The action will be commenced by an individual shareholder against the company. A typical example of a personal action would be where a shareholder sought to commence an action to enforce the terms of a contractual obligation with the company: for example, via s 14 of the Companies Act 1985 (see Chapter 4). However, where a member's legal rights of membership have been adversely affected but the wrong in question also equates to a wrong perpetrated against the company (e.g. a breach of a director's duty), the proper plaintiff to that action will (other than perhaps where the right equates to a membership interest under s 459 of the Companies Act 1985 (discussed in Chapter 24)) be the company and not the aggrieved shareholder: see *Johnson* v *Gore Wood & Co* [2002] 2 AC 1 (discussed below).

The representative action

Where an individual shareholder's legal rights have been infringed, the infringement may also affect other shareholders in the company. In this situation the appropriate action will be a representative one. The action will be commenced by a shareholder on behalf of himself and all other aggrieved shareholders and will be instigated against the company. Any judgment obtained as a result of a representative action will bind all the parties which are made subject to it. The company may defend a representative action by showing that the plaintiff took part or acquiesced in the act which formed the subject matter of the complaint: see e.g. *Nurcombe v Nurcombe* [1985] 1 WLR 370.

The derivative action

In instances where a director or other officer of the company acts in breach of his duties or without due authority and, as such, commits a wrong against the company, the wrongful act will be voidable. The act may be avoided by the passing of an ordinary resolution in general meeting. Where the wrongful act is not avoided, the director or officer concerned may, in accordance with agency principles, be made liable to account to the company for any profit made or loss sustained as a result of entering into the transaction in question. However, it should be noted that any decision to pursue litigation to, for example, recover corporate property which was lost as a consequence of a wrongful act, will normally be a decision which is vested in the board of directors (Table A, art 70): see e.g. *Breckland Group v London & Suffolk Properties* [1989] BCLC 100 (discussed in Chapter 22). Therefore, in theory, it would be possible for the general meeting to sanction litigation, but the pursuit of the action to be refused by the board of directors. However, such a scenario would be most unlikely given that the general meeting could, by the passing of an ordinary resolution, remove any dissenting directors from the board.

Therefore, where a wrong is committed against the company, by a member of a company, the company will be the proper plaintiff to instigate proceedings. An action brought in the company's name without the support of the general meeting will ordinarily be struck out by the court and will render the applicant and his solicitor personally liable to pay the costs of the litigation. Accordingly, if an individual shareholder (or a group of shareholders) wishes to pursue an action on behalf of the company without the support of the general meeting, the action must be in the derivative form. To so proceed, the shareholder(s) must convince the court that the wrong against which the complaint is made was a wrong perpetrated by persons in control of the company's affairs. The wrong must be of a serious nature: 'a fraud on the company'. A shareholder must bring the action on behalf of himself and all other shareholders (save for any shareholders who were party to the alleged wrongdoing). The alleged wrongdoers and the company will be made defendants to the action. (The company is made a defendant to enable it to take the benefit of any court order.) In commencing a derivative action, the court has a discretion to order that a plaintiff's costs be paid by the company, even where the plaintiff's action proves to be unsuccessful: see e.g. *Wallersteiner v Moir (No 2)* [1975] QB 373. It is important to note that an order for costs may be made only where the plaintiff sues in the derivative form: see e.g. *Re Sherborne Park Residents Co Ltd* [1987] BCLC 82.

A PERSONAL OR CORPORATE ACTION?

Occasionally, and quite often justifiably, the courts have found great difficulty in distinguishing between the nature and right of action in circumstances where the wrong in question causes loss to both the company and an individual shareholder(s). Indeed, in circumstances where, for example, the wrongful act directly conflicts with the terms of a company's constitution, thereby affecting both the personal rights of the membership and the rights of the company, the courts have, in the past, permitted an action to be brought in either the corporate (or derivative) form, or as a personal action. An example of this 'dual' type of action was seen in *Simpson* v *Westminster Palace Hotel* (1860) 8 HLC 712, an action to restrain a company from entering into an *ultra vires* activity; and in *Edwards* v *Halliwell* [1950] 2 All ER 1064, an action to restrain a company from passing a resolution by a simple majority vote instead of the prescribed special resolution. However, it should be noted that, following the decision of the House of Lords in *Johnson* v *Gore Wood & Co* [2002] 2 AC 1, it must now be doubted whether a dual type of action would be sustained (discussed below).

Confusion surrounding whether an action should be of a personal or corporate nature is particularly evident in cases where a shareholder suffers an indirect personal loss as a result of a wrong committed against the company: for example, in a situation where the value of a member's shares depreciate following the wrongful act of a third party, or a breach of directors' duty. Here, a shareholder's loss may be particularly striking where the company is in reality little more than the alter ego of the shareholder, whereby a depreciation in the worth of the company may cause great financial harm to the individual shareholder. As is apt in private companies, a shareholder may fail to distinguish between corporate and personal assets, ignoring the separate legal status of the company and so treating the entity, in the expenditure and injection of funds, as but part and parcel of his/her own individual trading identity.

Nevertheless, although a wrongful act inflicted against a company may cause an individual shareholder to suffer personal loss, such losses, being merely a reflection of the overall corporate loss, will not be recoverable, as a contrary conclusion would be unjust, giving rise to double recovery against the wrongdoer. In *Prudential Assurance Co* v *Newman Industries* [1982] Ch 204, the Court of Appeal advanced the following principle of law.

> 'But what [a shareholder] cannot do is to recover damages merely because the company in which he is interested has suffered damage. He cannot recover a sum equal to the diminution in the market value of his shares, or equal to the likely diminution in dividend, because such a "loss" is merely a reflection of the loss suffered by the company. The shareholder does not suffer any personal loss. His only "loss" is through the company, in the diminution in the value of the net assets of the company. . . .' (at p 223)

In more recent times, a number of cases have sought to determine whether an action should be pursued as a corporate or personal action. In *George Fischer (Great Britain) Ltd* v *Multi Construction Ltd* [1995] BCC 310, a holding company, Fischer (F), which conducted its business through wholly owned subsidiaries, sought to recoup the losses incurred by its subsidiaries as a consequence of a third party defaulting on a contract entered into for the benefit of three of F's subsidiary companies. F sued as the sole shareholder of the subsidiaries; the subsidiaries could not pursue an action in their own right as they were not a party to the contract (i.e. no privity of contract). F therefore pursued a personal action for the indirect losses sustained as a result of the losses incurred by its subsidiaries. The nature of the indirect losses caused by the breach of contract were alleged to have resulted in a fall in the value of F's holding in the subsidiaries and a loss in profits sustained by F as a consequence of the said fall in the profits of its subsidiaries.

In allowing F, suing *qua* shareholder, to recover the indirect losses, the Court of Appeal allowed the personal action. However, the *Fischer* case cannot be viewed as opening the floodgates to personal actions involving wrongs which are in essence committed against the company. The wrong, although perpetrated against the subsidiary companies, was incapable of being corrected by the subsidiary companies (i.e. the wrong in question resulted from a breach of contract to which the subsidiary companies were not privy and as such they could not sue on their own account).

The reluctance of the courts to permit a personal action in a situation where the wrong in question stemmed from a corporate loss was emphasised by the Court of Appeal in *Stein* v *Blake* [1998] 1 BCLC 573. The case involved a group of companies (the old companies) in which D held 50 per cent of the group's shares (he was also sole director of these companies). P held the remaining 50 per cent of the shares. D purchased the assets of the old companies and transferred them to another group of companies under his control. The old companies were subsequently placed into liquidation. P contended that the transactions were in breach of D's duty to the group of companies, in so far as D had acquired the assets at an undervaluation. P alleged that his personal rights had been indirectly infringed as a result of D's actions.

P commenced a personal action; he would have been unable to commence a derivative action in so far as the old companies had been put into liquidation. D successfully applied to have the action struck out. The Court of Appeal held that P's loss was in reality a corporate loss. P's loss was not independent or distinct from the corporate loss.

More recently, in *Johnson* v *Gore Wood & Co* [2002] 2 AC 1, the House of Lords upheld the *Prudential* principle to defeat the claim of a company's dominant shareholder. Here the shareholder (P) sought personal damages as a result of a diminution in the value of his shares, a loss of earnings and pension rights; losses flowing from the negligent advice and actions of the defendant solicitors (D). D had advised and acted for both the company and P. The said negligence resulted in the company's demise and caused severe financial hardship to P. The House of Lords sought to explain and expand upon the *Prudential* principle. Lord Bingham, with whom Lord Goff and Lord Millett were in agreement, advanced three propositions, namely:

'(1) Where a company suffers loss caused by a breach of duty owed to it, only the company may sue in respect of that loss. No action lies at the suit of a shareholder suing in that capacity and no other to make good a diminution in the value of the shareholder's shareholding where that merely reflects the loss suffered by the company. A claim will not lie by a shareholder to make good a loss which would be made good if the company's assets were replenished through action against the party responsible for the loss, even if the company, acting through its constitutional organs, has declined or failed to make good that loss. . . .

(2) Where a company suffers loss but has no cause of action to sue to recover that loss, the shareholder in the company may sue in respect of it (if the shareholder has a cause of action to do so), even though the loss is a diminution in the value of the shareholding.

(3) Where a company suffers loss caused by a breach of duty to it, and a shareholder suffers a loss separate and distinct from that suffered by the company caused by breach of a duty independently owed to the shareholder, each may sue to recover the loss caused to it by breach of the duty owed to it but neither may recover loss caused to the other by breach of the duty owed to that other. . . .' (at pp 35–36)

In accordance with the above propositions, if a shareholder suffers a wrong and seeks to pursue a personal action to recover his/her loss and the wrong in question is also a matter which adversely (in an economic sense) affects the company, then it will be most improbable that the shareholder will be able to proceed with the personal action. In reality, a shareholder loss, accountable as a reflection of an economic loss to the company, will not be recoverable, other than where the company is, by law, precluded from maintaining the action or, alternatively, where the shareholder can establish that the defendant's conduct resulted in a breach of a distinct legal duty which was owed to him (the shareholder) personally, under the law. The defendant's conduct must cause personal loss which is separate and distinct from any loss suffered by the company: see e.g. *Shaker* v *Al-Bedrawi* [2003] BCC 465.

The three propositions advanced by Lord Bingham in *Johnson* may be accepted as a benchmark standard for determining issues relating to the standing of a corporate/ personal action (but note the reservations of Lord Hutton and Lord Cooke, especially the latter who, in *Johnson*, sought to distinguish the *Prudential* principle on the premise that (in *Johnson*) the claim concerned a client's (P) action against a solicitor and not an internal action involving a director's breach of duty (as in *Prudential*)). In cases subsequent to *Johnson*, the Court of Appeal has sought to follow Lord Bingham's propositions to the letter: see e.g. *Day* v *Cook* [2002] 1 BCLC 1, *Ellis* v *Property Leeds (UK) Ltd* [2002] 2 BCLC 175, *Shaker* v *Al-Bedrawi* [2003] BCC 465, *Floyd and Ors* v *Fairhurst & Co* [2004] EWCA Civ 604 and *Gardner* v *Parker* [2005] BCC 46.

However, a possible diversion to Lord Bingham's propositions may be found in the Court of Appeal's decision in *Giles* v *Rhind* [2001] 2 BCLC 582 (decided after *Johnson*). Here, G and R held equal proportions of the shares in a company (S) (both held approximately just under 50 per cent of the issued share capital); G and R were the appointed directors of S. The company refinanced with the result that G and R were left with a combined holding of approximately 20 per cent of the issued share capital. The refinance agreement was subject to a shareholders' agreement of which G and R were both parties. The relationship between R and G broke down. R set up a new business, of a type similar to the business pursued by S. R took with him employees of S and a vital contract which had properly belonged to S. S commenced proceedings against R but, before the hearing, S was placed into receivership and then, subsequently, liquidation.

G issued distinct proceedings against R, claiming that R's actions had resulted in personal losses equating to a loss of remuneration and the loss in the value of his shareholding. At first instance, it was accepted that R had used confidential information to divert the contract away from S and had also acted in breach of a contractual duty of confidence, so owed to the parties to the shareholders' agreement. In giving judgment, Blackburne J held that such losses were irrecoverable because, although the company had not been able to pursue such losses, the losses claimed did, in fact, extend to losses that would have been recoverable by the company. (The judgment was given somewhat reluctantly as there had been no double recovery, but the learned judge considered himself bound by *Johnson*.)

In reversing the decision of Blackburne J, the Court of Appeal sought to distinguish *Johnson*. The said distinction was based on two distinct grounds. First, in *Giles*, the company was unable to pursue any action against R due to a lack of funds and as such there would be no double recovery against R. It is submitted that the logic of this distinction is most correct given that it was the wrongdoer (R) who actually disabled the company from pursuing any cause of action. Nevertheless, despite such logic, this first ground would appear to contradict the second proposition advanced in *Johnson*, namely, while the company was unable to pursue the action due to a lack of funds, the company did, nevertheless, have a cause of action.

The second (and valid) ground for the distinction related to G's claim for the loss of future remuneration. While the court accepted that G's claim for the loss of accrued earnings would ordinarily be defeated on the basis of the reflective loss principle (i.e. the loss suffered by G as an employee was reflective of the company's own loss) – therefore if the company had been able to enforce its rights against R, it would have had the funds needed to pay its debts (including loss of accrued earnings) – the question relating to future earnings was a different matter. In this context, the loss suffered by G was not reflective of any loss suffered by the company because it flowed from the termination of G's employment, following the demolition of the company's business. If the company had been able to enforce its rights against R, following the destruction of its business, any damages recoverable by the company would not have compensated G for the loss which flowed from the termination of his employment.

The principles of law emanating from *Prudential* and *Johnson* confirm that a share cannot be viewed as being subject to full and typical property rights because otherwise a shareholder, having suffered a loss to the value of his/her 'property', would have the right to claim damages for that loss, notwithstanding that the shareholder's loss may have also been a reflection of a corporate loss. If a share did carry full property rights, although double recovery would not be possible, damages could be apportioned as between the company and the shareholder. Indeed, the latter conclusion was accepted by the New Zealand Court of Appeal in *Christensen* v *Scott* [1996] 1 NZLR 273 (also see the concurring (*obiter*) comments of the Court of Appeal in *Barings plc* v *Coopers & Lybrand* [1997] 1 BCLC 427). However, it is submitted that the *Christensen* line of authority is incorrect because, while a share constitutes a property right, the said right is limited. A share may, as a reflection of its commercial value, be bought, sold and insured as a species of property and may afford its holder a right to exercise votes attached to the share; however, the said property rights are limited in so far as they are governed and subject to the company's constitution and the overriding interests of the corporate entity.

But what of the position where a shareholder seeks to commence an action, not *qua* shareholder but rather *qua* employee or *qua* creditor of the company? Following *Johnson* the answer must be that the no reflective loss principle will bar any recovery of a personal loss where the substance of the wrong, having resulted in the said loss, was also suffered by the company (*Giles* v *Rhind* can be distinguished on this latter point) irrespective of the capacity in which the shareholder brought the action. In effect, the loss will be regarded as a corporate loss and no other (see, further, the judgment of Neuberger LJ in *Gardner* v *Parker* [2005] BCC 46).

Finally, it is to be noted that in *Re a Company (No 005136 of 1986)* [1987] BCLC 82 (see also *Alexander* v *Automatic Telephone Co* [1900] 2 Ch 56, *Hogg* v *Cramphorn Ltd* [1967] Ch 254 and *Heron International Ltd* v *Lord Grade* [1983] BCLC 244), Hoffmann J held, on a preliminary issue, that it may be possible for a shareholder to commence a personal action following an improper allotment of shares where the purpose of the allotment was to manipulate voting control. The allotment would constitute an unlawful exercise of a director's corporate powers and therefore result in an abuse of the company's constitutional obligations to its shareholders (s 14, CA 1985). While it is perhaps difficult to reconcile the reasoning of Lord Hoffmann (as he now is) with the *Prudential* principle and the interpretation of the same in *Johnson*, it may be possible to contend that in such a scenario the company suffers no loss (a company is not concerned with the identity of its shareholders), whereas the shareholder's property rights (a potential loss of control and influence in the company's affairs) are prejudiced by the wrongful act. It is to be noted that this type of action may be more appropriately commenced under s 459 of the Companies Act 1985 (see Chapter 24).

THE RULE IN *FOSS* V *HARBOTTLE*

In situations where a wrong is allegedly committed against a company, the protection of minority interests is regulated by the rule taken from the judgment of Wigram V-C in the case of *Foss* v *Harbottle* (1843) 2 Hare 461. The rule is prohibitive of the availability of minority actions for, as Wigram V-C made clear in his judgment, every individual shareholder must realise that on becoming a member of a company, majority rule will, as in all other walks of society, prevail. The rule born of *Foss* v *Harbottle* can be stated in the following way:

> An individual shareholder has no absolute right to seek redress for a wrong purportedly committed against the company in which he is a member. The company in such an instance is the proper plaintiff to instigate such an action. Whether the company proceeds with the action will depend upon the will of the company's board of directors and the shareholders in general meeting. Only in exceptional circumstances will the court interfere with a decision taken by the company to sanction the alleged wrongful act.

Justifications for the rule in Foss v Harbottle

The internal management principle

The internal management principle may be defined as confirming a company's right to decide for itself, in accordance with the wishes of its management and the shareholders in general meeting, corporate strategy in respect of decisions appertaining to alleged acts of a wrongful character: see e.g. *Carlen* v *Drury* (1812) 1 Ves & B 154 and, more recently, *Breckland Group Holdings* v *London & Suffolk Properties Ltd* [1989] BCLC 100.

The proper plaintiff principle

To allow a minority shareholder to commence an action on behalf of a company whenever the company has suffered some alleged wrong would be to open the floodgates to many future actions. As such, if a company is allegedly wronged, the company should be viewed as the proper plaintiff to the action; it must, if it so decides, pursue the action in its own name (see e.g. the judgment of Mellish LJ in *MacDougall* v *Gardiner* (1875) 1 Ch 13). Where a minority shareholder purports to commence an action on behalf of the company, it will be the normal procedure of the court to postpone proceedings until the general meeting is convened to determine whether it agrees that proceedings should be commenced in the company's name: see e.g. *Danish Mercantile Co Ltd* v *Beaumont* [1951] Ch 680. Even if the general meeting agrees to authorise proceedings, in theory, the board of directors, in so far as they are vested with the power to instigate litigation on behalf of the company, may refuse to do so: see Table A, art 70 (discussed in Chapter 22).

The ratifiability principle

Where a minority shareholder alleges that the company's directors have acted in a wrongful manner, an action arising from such an allegation may not be pursued in a situation where the wrong in question was capable of being ratified by the general meeting (i.e. the general meeting of the company must be given the opportunity to confirm, validate and sanction the act which forms the subject matter of the complaint).

In voting to ratify a wrongful act, a shareholder may generally vote in a manner beneficial to his own interests: see e.g. *North West Transportation Co Ltd* v *Beatty* [1887] 12 App Cas 589, *Peters American Delicacy Co* v *Heath* (1939) 61 CLR 457 and *Mills* v *Mills* (1938) 60 CLR 150. However, it should be noted that the ability to allow a member to vote in accordance with his self-interests may be overturned if what is considered beneficial to an individual shareholder is nevertheless construed to be detrimental to the interests of the company as a whole (discussed further below).

The irregularity principle

If a mere informality or minor irregularity in the course of the internal management of a company would not have taken place if the correct corporate procedure had been adhered to, then an action challenging the effect of such an irregularity will not be permitted. For example, in *Browne* v *La Trinidad* (1887) 37 ChD 1, a meeting of directors was called, following which it was decided that an extraordinary general meeting of the company should be held to consider a motion to remove one of the directors, a Mr Browne (B). The motion was subsequently passed whereupon B claimed that the resolution had been invalidly passed because he had received inadequate notice of the directors' meeting. The Court of Appeal held that the irregularity (the inadequate notice) was not a significant factor in respect of the vote to oust B from his directorship. The resolution was upheld.

However, where the effect of an irregularity is such that it may potentially alter the outcome of a vote, the court will intervene to render the vote invalid: see e.g. *Pender* v *Lushington* (1877) 6 ChD 70 (discussed further in Chapter 4).

EXCEPTIONS TO THE RULE IN *FOSS* V *HARBOTTLE*

The underlying theme for the protection of minority interests is set against a back-cloth which vests the guardianship of a company's interests in the hands of the board of directors and the majority shareholders. To protect and correct any abuse of this guardianship, the courts must, in appropriate circumstances, depart from the concept of majority rule. However, a court will be reluctant to overturn the wishes of the majority and will do so only where the actions of those in control of the company were patently inspired by motives other than to promote the best interests of the company as a whole.

The courts' ability to override the principle of majority control is itself derived from the case of *Foss* v *Harbottle*. In giving the judgment of the court, Wigram V-C stated:

> 'If a case should arise of injury to a corporation by some of its members, for which no adequate remedy remained, except that of a suit by individual corporators in their private characters, and of asking in such a character the protection of those rights to which in their corporate character they were entitled, I cannot but think that the claims of justice would be found superior to any difficulties arising out of technical rules respecting the mode in which corporators are required to sue.' (at p 492)

Although Wigram V-C spoke of the 'claims of justice', determining whether a minority shareholder may proceed, the justice criteria must be viewed as a double-edged sword in that justice is not solely to be measured in terms of the rights of the minority, but is also to be determined by observing the corresponding rights of the majority. Accordingly, those in control of the company's affairs are generally presumed, as guardians of the company's affairs, to have acted in the best interests of the company as a whole. The presumption is rebuttable, but the controllers of a company may often be able to justify their actions on the premise that the wrong in question was not of a significant nature to merit expensive litigation on the part of the company or that, if the wrong had been litigated, it would have caused a lapse of confidence in the corporate body and possible panic amongst its investors and creditors: see *Prudential Assurance Co Ltd* v *Newman Industries Ltd* (*No 2*) [1982] Ch 204.

To convince the court that a corporate wrong should be righted, an aggrieved minority shareholder must establish that those in control of the company failed to act in the best interests of the company as a whole. Although judicial obscurity masks the exact meaning of the term 'the best interests of the company as a whole', it is clear that a shareholder will not be permitted to commence a derivative action in circumstances where, irrespective of corporate irregularities, the complaint was primarily inspired by an ulterior purpose devoid of any connection to the alleged wrongdoing: see e.g. *Barrett* v *Duckett* [1995] 1 BCLC 243.

The Court of Appeal's decision in *Barrett* v *Duckett* is also indicative of the view that a derivative action should not be available where the complainant had the option of pursuing an alternative remedy. In *Barrett* the alternative remedy in question was the liquidation of the company, a remedy that, in itself, is very much of the last resort. As such, the Court of Appeal took the view that a derivative action is one which should only be pursued in exceptional circumstances. Indeed, if one considers the potentially progressive remedies afforded to shareholders by s 459 of the Companies Act 1985 (discussed in Chapter 24), then, at first sight, it would appear that the pursuit of a derivative action, without recourse to s 459, should be an unlikely occurrence. However, it must be stressed that the underlying motive for pursuing a derivative action is one which seeks to benefit the company as a distinct commercial entity as opposed to one which purports to directly or indirectly benefit the personal interests of a minority shareholder(s), the latter type of action being specifically governed by s 459 of the Companies Act 1985.

Fraud against the company (fraud on the minority)

A corporate act that has not been pursued *bona fide* in the best interests of the company as a whole may be tentatively defined as a corporate act which results in a fraud on the company. Therefore, a minority shareholder of a company may *prima facie* pursue a derivative action in circumstances where the company is the victim of such a fraud. However, it should be stressed from the outset that the interpretation of 'a fraud' extends beyond more than just the common law concept of fraud, exemplified by cases such as *Derry* v *Peek* (1889) 14 App Cas 337. For example, the term 'fraud on the minority' may apply to a breach of fiduciary duty, an act of discrimination, or a negligent abuse of corporate power, without the need to establish any dishonest intent or deception. Indeed, here it is an improbable task to attempt to provide a precise definition of which 'wrongs' may or may not be judicially perceived as constituting 'frauds'. The matter must be determined on a case-by-case basis, albeit within the confines of what may be described as the accepted headings for a fraud on the minority (discussed below).

A derivative action may proceed even if, at the time the fraud was discovered, the plaintiff is no longer a member of the company against which the fraud was perpetrated. Where an individual acquires shares from a member who was a party to a fraud or a member who voted against any action to redress a fraudulent act, it would appear that the wrong in question cannot be pursued by the subsequent holder of the shares: see e.g. *Ffooks* v *South Western Railway Co* (1853) 1 Sm & G 142.

The fraud exception to the rule in *Foss* v *Harbottle* is commonly referred to as 'fraud on the minority shareholder', despite the fact that the wrong will invariably be committed against the company. In allowing a minority shareholder to commence an action on behalf of the company (i.e. to commence a derivative action), the court will need to distinguish the necessity of adhering to one or more of the four justifications for the rule in *Foss* v *Harbottle* (discussed above). The triggering of one of the accepted fraud on the minority exceptions will render any ratification of the alleged wrong ineffective, save, perhaps, where an independent board of directors or a majority of the independent part of the minority (those not involved in the wrongdoing) resolve to rescind from proceeding with an action: see e.g. *Atwool* v *Merryweather* (1868) LR 5 Eq, *Rights and Issues Investment Trust* v *Stylo Shoes*

[1956] Ch 250 and, more recently, *Smith* v *Croft (No 2)* and *(No 3)* [1987] BCLC 206 and [1987] BCLC 355.

Accepted instances of a fraud on the minority (the accepted headings)

An intentional misappropriation of corporate assets

This heading is akin to the common law concept of fraud and involves instances whereby those in control of a company have acted dishonestly by appropriating to themselves corporate property or other assets: see e.g. *Cook* v *Deeks* [1916] 1 AC 554 (see Chapter 17).

A negligent misappropriation of corporate assets

In analysing this particular heading it must be stressed that not every negligent act that results in the loss or devaluation of a corporate asset may be classified as a fraud on the minority: see e.g. *Pavlides* v *Jensen* [1956] Ch 565. However, where those in control of a company personally derive some benefit, at the company's expense, from self-serving negligence, a minority shareholder may, in such an instance, be capable of intervening on behalf of the company to right the wrong via a derivative action. For example, in *Daniels* v *Daniels* [1978] Ch 406, a company's board of directors negligently sold a corporate asset to one of their number at a gross undervaluation. Four years later, the asset was resold and a substantial profit was made. The validity of the transaction was successfully challenged. Templeman J opined that a minority shareholder was capable of commencing an action on behalf of the company in circumstances where directors of a company used their powers in a manner which benefited themselves or one of their number at the expense of the company, irrespective of whether the power had been used intentionally, unintentionally, fraudulently or negligently.

Unfair advantage

The classification of a fraud on the minority based upon facts which establish that the controlling body of a company obtained some unfair advantage at the expense of the company and its minority shareholders is a controversial classification, because the scope of this definition of fraud closely resembles one touched with the notion that justice may have a primary role to play in determining a minority shareholder's ability to pursue a derivative action. Nevertheless, case examples exist to justify the inclusion of a classification based upon unfair advantage: see e.g. *Alexander* v *Automatic Telephone* Co [1900] 2 Ch 56 and *Estmanco* v *Greater London Council* [1982] 1 All ER 437.

In the latter case, a minority shareholder of a company formed by the Greater London Council (GLC) to manage a block of flats, sued the GLC on behalf of the company to enforce an agreement entered into by the tenants of the flats. The agreement provided that the block of flats in question (comprising 60 flats) would be sold privately and that each purchaser would acquire one share in the company; the shares of the individual purchasers did not carry voting rights until all the flats had been sold. After 12 of the flats had been sold, the political constitution of the GLC changed and, as a result, the newly constituted council altered its policy of selling off the flats: instead of being sold privately, the flats were to be rented to needy council tenants. As the GLC retained 48 of the flats (a figure representing the total number of flats unsold), the GLC was able to prevent the company from taking any action to challenge the policy change (i.e. the purchasers of the 12 flats were in the minority and in any case had no voting rights).

Megarry V-C held that the circumstances of the case were such that the Council (in effect the majority shareholders) had acted otherwise than in the best interests of the company as a whole. The Council had gained an unfair advantage by preventing the company from challenging the Council's decision to alter its policy in respect of the sale of the council flats.

Although it is arguable that the decision in *Estmanco* v *Greater London Council* is supportive of a claim that the justice of a case may form the basis for a valid exception to the rule in *Foss* v *Harbottle*, it is submitted that the facts of *Estmanco* indicate that the GLC's decision to depart from its agreement with the flat owners (i.e. a type of shareholder agreement) was clearly detrimental to the interests of the company as a whole, because the GLC's decision was intended to end the very existence of the company.

LIMITING THE INTERPRETATION OF FRAUD

Although the justice of a case may not in itself be regarded as a standard exception to the rule in *Foss* v *Harbottle*, justice does, however, provide the foundation stone upon which all acceptable forms of the exception to the rule in *Foss* v *Harbottle* have been built. Indeed, in at least one case the justice criteria prevailed as the overwhelming factor in the court's decision to afford relief to the claims of a minority shareholder, albeit that the case in question, *Clemens* v *Clemens Bros Ltd* [1976] 2 All ER 268 (discussed in Chapter 19), was not pursued in the derivative form.

However, the availability of an exception to the rule in *Foss* v *Harbottle* based primarily on issues of justice, was strongly refuted by the Court of Appeal in *Prudential Assurance Co Ltd* v *Newman Industries Ltd* (No 2) [1982] Ch 204. The facts of the case were as follows. The plaintiff, a large industrial investor, held three per cent of the share capital in Newman Industries Ltd (N). The plaintiff alleged that two of N's directors had dishonestly purchased the assets of another company in which they held a majority of the shares, and in doing so had defrauded N of some £400 000. The plaintiff maintained that the two directors had misled the general body of shareholders into approving the transaction by issuing tricky and misleading circulars which failed properly to set out the actual amount which had been paid by N to purchase the assets of the other company. The plaintiff commenced a personal and derivative action against the two directors concerned. At first instance, Vinelott J, in allowing the derivative action, implied that an exception to the rule in *Foss* v *Harbottle* could be made out where justice so demanded.

The Court of Appeal disagreed with Vinelott J, in so far as the court was not convinced that the justice of any case could ever be advanced as a practical test to determine the merits of a derivative action. However, in delivering a joint judgment,

Cumming-Bruce, Templeman and Brightman LJJ considered that on the facts of the appeal before them it was unnecessary for the court to attempt to define the exact scope of the exceptions to the rule in *Foss* v *Harbottle* in so far as N, following the High Court proceedings, had agreed to accept the benefit of any order made in the company's favour (i.e. it was no longer necessary for the Court of Appeal to determine the derivative action).

The controlling interest

For a minority shareholder to proceed with a derivative action, in addition to establishing a fraud on the minority, he/she must show that the company was unable to bring an action in its own name (i.e. those persons accused of the alleged wrong-doing were in control of the company and were unwilling to proceed with an action): see e.g. *Birch* v *Sullivan* [1957] 1 WLR 1247.

Where the ratification of a wrongful act rests on a decision of the general body of shareholders, it is somewhat unclear whether the alleged wrongdoers' control of a company can be interpreted as majority voting control in terms of an arithmetic ability (50+ per cent of the voting shares) to secure the passing of an ordinary resolution, or whether *de facto* control will suffice. For example, in large public companies where many shareholders fail to attend meetings or vote by proxy, an alleged wrongdoer, holding, for example, 30 per cent of the share capital may be able to secure the passing of an ordinary resolution to prevent the company pursuing an action (i.e. the alleged wrongdoer may exert *de facto* control).

Although *obiter* comments exist to support the view that, if an alleged wrongdoer has *de facto* control, then such control should be sufficient to establish majority control (see e.g. *Pavlides* v *Jensen* [1956] Ch 565 and Vinelott J in *Prudential Assurance* v *Newman Industries Ltd* [1981] Ch 257), it is to be observed that the Court of Appeal in *Prudential Assurance* v *Newman Industries Ltd* (No 2) ([1982] Ch 204) strongly opposed such reasoning (in *Prudential* the alleged wrongdoers did not hold a majority of the voting shares in the company).

The principal objection of allowing an action to proceed where a person(s) holds *de facto* control is the inability precisely to define the exact meaning of *de facto* control. Basically it is impossible to predict how many shareholders will vote at a given company meeting; *de facto* control may arise where one shareholder holds just 20 per cent of the voting shares, or 30 per cent, 40 per cent, 45 per cent, indeed any figure up to the figure required to pass an ordinary resolution.

The preliminary hearing

In *Prudential Assurance* v *Newman Industries Ltd* (No 2) [1982] Ch 204, the Court of Appeal took the view that to determine whether a potentially long and expensive trial was deemed necessary, a preliminary hearing should be held to assess the merits of any case brought as an exception to the rule in *Foss* v *Harbottle*. The Court of Appeal stated that the preliminary hearing should determine if the wrong against which an action was brought was capable of ratification and whether the supposed wrongdoers were, in fact, in control of the company. Whilst the Court of Appeal's reasoning is theoretically sound, it is suggested that in many cases it will be impossible to determine a prospective plaintiff's standing to commence an action without a full investigation into whether or not the purported action is of a type which can be identified as a fraud on the minority – a view endorsed by the Australian courts (see e.g. the decision of the Supreme Court of Western Australia in *Eromanga Hydrocarbons* v *Australis Mining* (1989) 14 ACLR 486).

PROPOSALS FOR FUTURE REFORM

The statutory derivative action

The difficulty in establishing a derivative action based upon the exceptions to the rule in *Foss* v *Harbottle* has led some commentators to call for the introduction of a statutory derivative action. This call was echoed in the Law Commission Report, 'Shareholder Remedies' (1997, Law Com No 246) and has been endorsed by subsequent reports of the CLR (discussed below).

Indeed, statutory derivative actions are already available in a number of Commonwealth jurisdictions. For example, in Canada (the action was introduced by s 232 of the Canada Business Corporation Act 1974) a complainant may apply to the court to commence a statutory derivative action where the complainant, in seeking to enforce the action, acted in good faith, and the action was construed to be in the best interests of the company. The term 'complainant' is defined, in the context of a stakeholder, to include a party who, at the court's discretion, is considered to have a direct financial interest in how the company is being managed. Therefore, in appropriate circumstances the term 'proper person' is permissive of the right of employees and creditors of the company to apply to the court.

Although the court may take into account, in determining whether to allow the derivative action to proceed, any ratification of the alleged wrong by the company's general meeting, ratification will not be regarded as conclusive in relation to the court's decision to allow or refuse the derivative action. In determining whether an application should proceed by way of a derivative action the court will also consider the constitution of a company's board of directors. Where, for example, a decision of the board concluded that an action should not be pursued on behalf of the company, then in circumstances where the board was divorced from the interests of the alleged wrongdoers (i.e. it was independent) the court will attach importance and weight to the independently constituted board. It should be noted that a statutory derivative action based upon the Canadian system would allow actions to be commenced in the name of and on behalf of the company irrespective of whether fraud or an intentional abuse of corporate power had taken place. Therefore, reckless or negligent abuses of corporate power would fall within the ambit of a potential action. Indeed, the discretion of the court in its determination of whether to permit an action to proceed would, following the Canadian model, be very wide.

Proposals for reform within the UK

In theory, the principal advantage of introducing a statutory derivative action in the UK would be to provide a more accessible route by which a minority shareholder could challenge the ordinance of a corporate wrong. The ability to pursue a derivative action may be especially crucial in public companies in circumstances where a large part of the shareholding body is apathetic to management activities to the extent that corporate malpractice may be hidden and indeed unwittingly approved by the general meeting.

Law Commission proposals

The Law Commission sought the introduction of a statutory derivative action to replace in total the existing derivative action based upon the exceptions to the rule in *Foss* v *Harbottle*. The Law Commission recommended that the new procedure should be available, in the case of an existing member of a company, only in circumstances where the cause of action arose:

> '. . . as a result of an actual or threatened act or omission involving (a) negligence, default, breach of duty or breach of trust by a director of the company, or (b) a director putting himself in a position where his personal interests conflict with his duties to the company. The cause of action may be against the director or another person (or both). We also recommend that, for these purposes, director should include a shadow director.'
> ('Shareholder Remedies' (1997, Law Com No 246), para 6.49)

In relation to the manner in which a derivative action should proceed, the Law Commission recommended the introduction of a case management conference for all derivative actions. The Law Commission advanced five specific matters which it considered the court should take into account, namely: the applicant's good faith; the interests of the company; that the wrong has been, or may be, approved in general meeting; the views of an independent organ (board or general meeting); and the availability of alternative remedies.

With regard to the general meeting's ability to ratify a wrongful act, the Law Commission's proposals were, to say the least, somewhat confusing. While the report sought to abrogate completely the existing common law derivative action, it nevertheless provided that the ratification of a wrongful act should be capable of being discarded in cases involving fraud; but in all other cases, effective ratification should be a complete bar to the continuation of a derivative action. The Law Commission failed to define the concept of fraud, neither did it attempt to limit its definition in a way which would preclude the existing examples of a 'fraud on the minority'. Accordingly, it is probable that the examples of fraud, as expounded in cases involving the common law derivative action, would remain capable, even if ratified, of being brought as a derivative action (i.e. a shareholder's ability to commence a derivative action would still exist, irrespective of the ratification of a wrongful (fraudulent) act). Yet, in such cases, it is to be noted that the Commission recommended that the court should take account of the fact that the company in general meeting had resolved not to pursue the cause of action. Further, the Law Commission recommended that the court should have a power to adjourn a hearing to enable a meeting of shareholders to be convened for the purpose of considering a resolution affecting the claim.

CLR proposals

The CLR approved the Law Commission's recommendation in respect of the need for a statutory derivative action and that such an action should be restricted to actions for a breach of directors' duty, including the duty of care (and, one would assume, a breach of the conflict of interest rule; the latter would in effect be seen as a duty under the CLR proposals for the reform of directors' duties, discussed in Chapter 17). However, the CLR (see e.g. 'Completing the Structure' (2000), paras 5.82–5.90) considered that there should be no distinction, in the procedure to ratify a wrongful act, as between fraudulent and non-fraudulent acts. In all cases involving a wrongful act, the CLR concluded that ratification should be considered valid only in circumstances where it was by the requisite majority of persons who could not be classified as the wrongdoers in relation to the wrongful act in question (or persons who were substantially under the influence of the wrongdoers – note that in practice this latter qualification may be very difficult to establish, a point recognised by the CLR). Where a wrongful act was not ratified in accordance with the above procedure, the CLR recommended that the derivative action should *prima facie* be allowed to proceed but only in circumstances where the court considered the action to be in the best interests of the company, the court paying particular attention to the interests of a majority of the independent members (i.e. members who had no connection with the wrongdoing). Finally it is to be noted that the White Paper (2002) made no reference to the proposed introduction of a statutory derivative action. However, the acceptance of a statutory derivative action is to be found in the subsequent White Paper (2005), albeit there is no draft clause to spell out the way in which the action is to be advanced into legislation.

Comment

Although the advantage of a statutory derivative action would *prima facie* increase the ability of a complainant's right to seek redress for abuses of corporate power, it is nevertheless questionable whether the shift towards the protection of minority interests, by the adoption of a statutory derivative action, is absolutely necessary in the light of the protection already provided by s 459 of the Companies Act 1985 (discussed in Chapter 24). Although s 459 is primarily concerned with personal actions, the provision is nevertheless permissive of an action which affects members generally. A wrong which affects members generally – for example, a breach of a director's duty – will affect the company as a whole and is undoubtably a corporate wrong. Although the common law provides that a corporate wrong must be pursued by the company (or by means of a derivative action), s 461 of the Companies Act 1985 makes specific reference to a remedy which is of a derivative character (i.e. s 461(c) provides that the court may authorise civil proceedings to be brought in the name and on behalf of the company by such person or persons and on such terms as the court may direct). Therefore, could not this form of the statutory derivative action be pursued by establishing conduct unfairly prejudicial to the interests of the members generally, as opposed to the procedures set out by the exceptions to the rule in *Foss* v *Harbottle* (or indeed the procedures and proposed recommendations of the CLR)?

Suggested further reading

No reflective loss principle

Ferran [2001] CLJ 245

Mitchell (2004) 120 LQR 457

Foss v Harbottle – *consequences and exceptions*

Wedderburn [1957] CLJ 194 and [1958] CLJ 93

Prentice (1976) 92 LQR 502

Joffe (1977) 40 MLR 71

Smith (1978) 41 MLR 147

Boyle (1980) 1 Co Law 3

Burridge (1981) MLR 40

Sullivan (1985) 44 CLJ 236

Drury (1986) 45 CLJ 219

Baxter (1987) 38 NILQ 6

Sterling (1987) 50 MLR 468

Prentice (1988) 104 LQR 341

The statutory derivative action

Giggs and Lowry [1994] JBL 463

24

THE STATUTORY PROTECTION OF A MINORITY SHAREHOLDER

INTRODUCTION

The purpose of this chapter is to examine the statutory protection afforded to minority shareholders. The sometimes problematic nature of the judicial interpretation of the statutory provisions will be explored in depth. The focal point of the chapter is the discussion of the unfair prejudice remedy, represented by s 459 of the Companies Act 1985. The chapter also examines s 122(1)(g) of the Insolvency Act 1986, a provision which permits a shareholder to apply to have a company wound up in circumstances where the court considers that remedy to be just and equitable.

THE DEVELOPMENT OF A STATUTORY REMEDY FOR OPPRESSIVE CONDUCT

In 1945, the Cohen Committee (Cmd 6659) considered that it was essential for legislation to be introduced to protect the interests of minority shareholders. The primary reason why legislative intervention was deemed essential was because of the absence of a personal remedy for an aggrieved minority shareholder. Although in appropriate circumstances, a minority shareholder had the right to pursue a derivative action, the ability to pursue the action was severely limited (discussed in Chapter 23) and the character of the remedy was one which sought to protect a corporate as opposed to a personal interest. While a minority shareholder also had the right to seek a winding up order against the company, this alternative was rather a drastic measure of the last resort (discussed below).

In response to the Cohen Committee recommendations, statutory intervention was introduced as s 210 of the Companies Act 1948. This provision provided a remedy against conduct which was considered oppressive to the interests of a part of the membership. However, s 210 did not establish itself as a practical remedy for the minority shareholder. The failings of the provision may be briefly summarised as follows.

- To succeed under s 210, a petitioner had to establish that the factual circumstances of the case would have justified the court in ordering the company to be wound up on just and equitable grounds. If that requirement was established, the petitioner then had to convince the court that a s 210 remedy was more apt as an alternative to the winding up order: see e.g. *Re Bellador Silk Ltd* [1965] 1 All ER 667.

- The judicial interpretation of s 210 in relation to the term 'oppressive conduct' proved to be of an inflexible nature. In *Scottish Co-operative Wholesale Society* v

Meyer [1959] AC 324, Lord Simmonds defined the term to mean 'burdensome, harsh and wrongful'. Such an austere definition was a paramount factor in limiting the successful application of the section to only two actions, namely *Scottish Co-operative Wholesale Society* v *Meyer* and *Re H Harmer Ltd* [1959] 1 WLR 62.

● Further difficulties with the provision included a need on the part of the aggrieved shareholder to establish that the oppressive conduct was of a continuous nature up to the time of the petition and further that the conduct affected the petitioning member, *qua* member, and not in some outside capacity: see e.g. *Ebrahimi* v *Westbourne Galleries Ltd* [1973] AC 360 (discussed below).

THE UNFAIR PREJUDICE REMEDY

The difficulties associated with s 210 were significantly removed by s 75 of the Companies Act 1980. In accordance with the recommendations of the Jenkins Committee 1962, the petitioner's need to establish 'oppressive conduct' was replaced with a more flexible requirement of establishing 'unfairly prejudicial conduct'. In addition, the requirement of a petitioner to establish grounds for a winding up order and that a continuous course of oppression had occurred up to the time of the petition, was removed by the new legislation. With the passing of the Companies Act 1985, s 75 of the Companies Act 1980 became (without any change in its wording) s 459 of the 1985 Act. With the implementation of Sch 19, para 11 to the Companies Act 1989, the wording of s 459 was slightly, although perhaps significantly, altered to extend the ambit of s 459, so that it now also covers a situation where the unfairly prejudicial conduct affects members generally; prior to the implementation of the 1989 Act, an action under s 459 had been limited to a situation whereby the unfairly prejudicial conduct affected but a part of the membership. Therefore, s 459(1) now provides:

> 'A member of a company may apply to the court by petition for an order . . . on the ground that the company's affairs are being or have been conducted in a manner which is unfairly prejudicial to the interests of its *members generally* or some part of its members (including himself) or that any actual or proposed act or omission on the part of the company (including an act or omission on its behalf) is or would be prejudicial.' (*1989 Act amendment*)

The effect of the 1989 Act amendment

Prior to the 1989 Act's amendment of s 459, the interpretation of unfairly prejudicial conduct was limited by the fact that the alleged unfairly prejudicial conduct had to affect but a part of the membership – see e.g. *Re Carrington Viyella plc* (1983) 1 BCC 98, 951 and *Re a Company (No 00370) of 1987* [1988] 1 WLR 1068, where Harman J remarked:

> 'It may be regrettable but, in my view, the statute providing a statutory remedy, although in wide terms in part, does contain the essential provision that the conduct complained of must be conduct unfairly prejudicial to a part of the members, and that cannot possibly mean unfairly prejudicial to all the members . . . I am of the opinion that no s 459 petition could be based on conduct that has had an equal effect on all the shareholders and was not intended to be discriminatory between shareholders.' (at pp 1074–75)

The above interpretation of s 459 supported the view that the provision was inapplicable in circumstances where the conduct in question was objectively viewed as conduct which was applied without any intention to discriminate against the legal rights of a part of the membership. Unfortunately, this interpretation failed to consider the practical consequences of a prejudicial act upon **variable membership** interests, namely, although the prejudicial conduct may have objectively touched all membership interests and was never intended to discriminate against a minority shareholder, in practical terms, the conduct may have seriously affected the interests of a minority shareholder but not the interests of a majority of the membership.

However, in *Re Sam Weller* [1990] BCLC 80, Peter Gibson J strongly opposed the notion that a member's interest should be viewed without recall to the variable nature of shareholding interests. The learned judge firmly believed that where corporate conduct had a prejudicial effect on the legal rights of the entire membership then such a scenario would not in itself present an obstacle to an action on behalf of a part of the membership in circumstances where the said part had been adversely and unfairly affected. Peter Gibson J cited with approval the decision of the House of Lords in *Scottish Co-operative Wholesale Society v Meyer* [1959] AC 324. Although the *Meyer* case was commenced under s 210 of the Companies Act 1948, the wording of s 210 (as with s 459) provided that the conduct in question had to affect 'a part of the membership'. The House of Lords held that conduct which touched the whole of the membership in an oppressive manner could nevertheless substantiate an action by a part of the membership. The House fully endorsed the decisions of the Court of Session (Scotland) from which the *Meyer* appeal originated (1954 SLT 273). The Lord President of the Inner House of the Court of Session expressed the following opinion (at p 277), an opinion quoted by Peter Gibson J in *Re Sam Weller*:

> '... a point is taken with regard to the statutory requirement that the oppression must affect "some part of the members", the suggestion being that s 210 is not available in any case where all the members, as distinguished from a part, are in the same boat ... I have come to think that this is to give too narrow a meaning to this remedial position and to place on the words "some part" an emphasis which they were not intended to bear ... When the section inquires whether the affairs of the company are being conducted in a manner oppressive to some part of the members, including the complainer, that question can still be answered in the affirmative even if, *qua* member of the company, the oppressor has suffered the same or even a greater prejudice.' (at p 86)

As a result of the Companies Act 1989, a petition under s 459 may now be commenced irrespective of whether the prejudicial conduct affects a part of the membership or the members generally. As such, the difficulties encountered by the interpretation of the term 'part of the membership' have *prima facie* been resolved by statutory intervention.

However, in reality it may be unlikely whether prejudicial conduct will ever be deemed to be unfair in respect of members generally. It is difficult to appreciate how corporate conduct may be perceived as affecting the totality of membership interests in an unfairly prejudicial manner. Whilst, objectively, conduct may have a prejudicial effect on the entire membership of a company, it is unlikely that every membership interest will be affected in an unfairly prejudicial manner. After all, membership interests are of a variable nature. For example, is it logical to suppose that those in control of a company would instigate conduct which would have the effect of unfairly prejudicing their own interests? Further, while it is possible to imagine a situation in which those in control of a company may conduct the affairs of a company to the prejudice of all membership interests (e.g. by the board of directors (also shareholders in the company) acting in a negligent manner), it is, in such a situation, unlikely that the conduct of the company's affairs would, in respect of those responsible for the misconduct, be considered unfair (i.e. those responsible for the misconduct could surely not complain of an unfairly prejudicial act which was of their own making).

A further point, although the phrase 'members generally' may have been intended to impart a meaning to be equated with the whole of the membership (so as to overturn the interpretation of 'part' so found in, for example, in *Re a Company (No 00370) of 1987* [1988] 1 WLR 1068), it is arguable that the word 'generally' falls short of such an objective. If conduct affects interests generally, it is arguable that it may only affect a majority of interests, in which case is not a majority of the membership merely a part, albeit a large part, of the total membership? In Commonwealth countries where the oppression/unfair prejudice remedy is employed, it has become commonplace to state that the corporate conduct may affect either a part or the whole of the membership. Accordingly the use of the word 'whole' would surely have been a more emphatic alternative to the use of the word 'generally'.

Defining the concept of unfairly prejudicial conduct

As under s 210 of the Companies Act 1948, under s 459 of the Companies Act 1985, the court employs an objective test to determine whether a particular type of conduct may or may not be classed as unfairly prejudicial. The test to determine unfairly prejudicial conduct may be tentatively expressed in the following manner: 'Would a reasonable bystander regard the conduct, which forms the subject matter of the complaint, as constituting conduct which affected the petitioner's membership interest in an unfairly prejudicial manner?'

According to Hoffmann LJ in *Re Saul D Harrison & Sons plc* [1994] BCC 475 (at p 488), the starting point in any case under s 459 will be to ascertain whether the conduct, which forms the subject matter of the shareholder's complaint, was conduct of a type which transgressed the terms of the company's articles, for within the articles is to be found the contractual terms which govern the relationship between the shareholders and the company. However, as Hoffmann LJ pointed out (at p 489), there will be cases in which a company's articles do not fully reflect the understandings upon which the shareholders are associated, therefore conduct that apparently complies with the terms of a company's articles may still found a petition under s 459.

While it is impossible to give a precise definition of what type of conduct may fall to be defined as unfairly prejudicial, the term 'unfairly prejudicial' does, in some respects, appear synonymous with conduct which may be described as 'unjust and inequitable' (by analogy, see the discussion of the just and equitable winding up order (s 122(1)(g)), discussed below). It should also be noted that, while s 459 provides a primary function in affording statutory protection to a minority shareholder, the section does not in itself preclude the possibility of a majority shareholder commencing an action for unfairly prejudicial conduct. To take a hypothetical example, a majority shareholder may decide that he/she will not interfere in the management decisions of the company's board of directors. As a result of a failure in the management of the company, the petitioner's membership interest is unfairly prejudiced. In this hypothetical situation the majority shareholder may be able to proceed under s 459. (See e.g. *Re Baltic Real Estate Ltd* [1992] BCC 629, *Re Legal Costs Negotiators Ltd* [1999] BCC 547 and *Re Ravenhart Service (Holdings) Ltd* [2004] 2 BCLC 376.)

Prejudicial conduct

Prejudicial conduct is damaging conduct which is caused in a commercial as opposed to an emotional sense: see e.g. the judgment of Harman J in *Re Unisoft Group Ltd (No 3)* [1994] 2 BCLC 609 (at p 611). Accordingly, the conduct in question must adversely affect the property rights afforded to a petitioner's shareholding interest. The most obvious example of a membership interest being subject to prejudice in the commercial sense will be where the conduct of a company's affairs depreciates the monetary value of a member's shareholding interest or where the conduct disturbs or prevents the enjoyment of rights previously associated with the member's shareholding interest. In *Rock Nominees Ltd v RCO (Holdings Ltd) plc* [2004] 1 BCLC 439, the Court of Appeal held that there could be no unfairly prejudicial conduct in circumstances where the petitioner suffered no financial detriment. The court so held, notwithstanding that the transaction which formed the basis of the complaint amounted to conduct properly described as unfair because it had been entered into by the respondent directors in breach of their fiduciary duties.

Further, it is to be noted, following *CAS (Nominees) Ltd v Nottingham Forest plc* [2002] BCC 145, that a decision of a company to circumvent the need to pass a special resolution (in this particular case for the disapplication of pre-emption rights) to achieve a desired outcome (in this case a transfer in the control of the company's subsidiary) may be achieved, providing its execution is by means of a legitimate method, notwithstanding that the effect of the alternative method removes a minority shareholder's capacity to block a desired outcome (i.e. in this case, by defeating the proposed conduct via voting to prevent the special resolution being passed). The denial of a minority shareholder's opportunity to have a matter resolved in accordance with a prescribed statutory procedure (in this case by a special resolution) as a result of the company adopting an alternative but legitimate course of conduct cannot be said to amount to prejudicial conduct, notwithstanding that as a consequence of the company's conduct the minority shareholder may suffer some financial loss. The loss would in effect be as a consequence of the company's decision to pursue a legitimate as opposed to an illegitimate course of conduct.

Unfair conduct

The ability to label conduct as 'unfair' will obviously depend upon the nature and extent of the effect of the conduct. In many cases, whether conduct can be described as unfair will be influenced by the underlying motive behind the pursuit of the particular conduct in question. Certainly, it is clear that in cases where the motive for and/or the effect of prejudicial conduct creates a discriminatory imbalance in relation to the rights and/or interests of a member, then such conduct will amount to conduct which is of an unfair nature.

Indeed, in cases where a petitioner cannot rely on a company's intentional act of discrimination or an intentional but improper exercise of the company's powers, the ability to establish unfairly prejudicial conduct may prove to be a difficult task. For example, where a petitioner's complaint is based upon a company's negligent conduct, it is doubtful whether an act of corporate misjudgment will ever amount to unfair conduct, other than where the conduct is of a type resulting in self-serving negligence. For example, in *Re Elgindata Ltd* [1991] BCLC 959, a case in which a petitioner claimed (in part) that his membership interest had been subjected to unfairly prejudicial conduct as a result of the company's negligent mismanagement, Warner J opined:

'. . . it is not for this court to resolve such disagreements on a petition under s 459. Not only is a judge ill qualified to do so, but there can be no unfairness to the petitioner in those in control of the company's affairs taking a different view from theirs on such matters . . . a shareholder acquires shares in a company knowing that their value will depend in some measure on the competence of the management. He takes the risk that the management may not prove to be of the highest quality. Short of a breach by a director of his duty of skill and care . . . there is prima facie no unfairness to a shareholder . . .' (at p 994)

(See also *Re Blackwood Hodge plc* [1997] 2 BCLC 650.)

However, in accordance with the decision of Arden J in *Re Macro (Ipswich) Ltd* [1994] 2 BCLC 354, it would appear that a petition under s 459 may extend to matters which broaden those identified by Warner J in *Re Elgindata Ltd*. Briefly, the facts of *Re Macro* were as follows. Mr Thompson (T), the majority shareholder and sole director of two independent companies (companies linked, however, in the sense that the share capital of both was divided between two families), failed to adequately supervise the management of properties owned by the two companies. The supervision of the said properties was under the control of an estate agency controlled by T. As a result of the mismanagement of the properties, the value of the shareholding interests depreciated. In concluding that the minority shareholder's interest had been unfairly prejudiced, Arden J held that a s 459 action was sustainable in circumstances where the mismanagement of a company was related to the internal administration of a company's affairs (i.e. as opposed to an instance or instances of commercial misjudgment involving, for example, the purchase or sale of corporate assets). It is also interesting to note that Arden J (in referring to the recommendations of the Cadbury Committee Report, despite the fact that the report was concerned with public and not private companies) regarded the absence of any independent director on the boards of the two companies as unfairly prejudicial to the interests of the minority shareholders. Indeed, it is submitted that this innovative suggestion relating to the deficiencies of the actual board structure of a private company may be taken up in future cases in circumstances where a court is of the opinion that the interests of minority shareholders have been unfairly prejudiced by a situation whereby the control and governance of corporate affairs was vested in the hands of a dominant and inflexible master.

However, perhaps by partial analogy, it should be noted that, following the decision of Jonathan Parker J in *Re Astec (BSR) plc* [1999] BCC 59, it is unlikely whether a public company's non-compliance with corporate governance issues will ever be capable of giving rise to a successful action under s 459. Although the learned judge held that the shareholders of a public company would rightly expect rules relating to corporate governance issues to be complied with, he nevertheless opined that such an expectation could not give rise to an equitable constraint on the exercise of legal rights so contained within the company's constitution. Jonathan Parker J justified his belief on the premise that for the legal rights of the membership to be subject to equitable constraints it would be essential to establish a personal relationship (of mutual trust and understanding) as between the petitioner and the company, a relationship which may be apt to describe the internal workings of a private company but one which would be misplaced in the context of a public company.

Conduct of a company's affairs

As a company's management functions are primarily vested in its board of directors, it is to be expected that the board or individual directors who have been authorised to act by the board will normally be responsible for the conduct of the company's affairs. However, this presumption may be rebutted. For example, in *Nicholas v Soundcraft Electronics Ltd* [1993] BCLC 360, the Court of Appeal found that in a holding company–subsidiary relationship, the holding company could be held responsible for conducting the affairs of its subsidiary (principle confirmed by the decision of the Court of Appeal in *Gross v Rackind* [2004] 4 All ER 735).

The *Nicholas* case concerned an allegation by a minority shareholder of the subsidiary company to the effect that the holding company's policy of withholding payments due to its subsidiary amounted to unfairly prejudicial conduct. While the Court of Appeal concluded that the holding company conducted the affairs of its subsidiary in a prejudicial way, the court nevertheless held that by withholding funds from its subsidiary, the holding company had acted for the greater good of the group (i.e. to secure the survival of the holding company without which the subsidiary company would have perished). As such, it was impossible to argue that the holding company had conducted the affairs of its subsidiary in an unfair manner: see also *Scottish Co-operative Wholesale Society v Meyer* [1959] AC 324 (discussed in Chapter 2).

Although a s 459 action may, in appropriate circumstances, be successfully commenced in the context of a holding company–subsidiary relationship (i.e. where the unfairly prejudicial conduct of the subsidiary's affairs was instigated as a consequence of its holding company's *de facto* control), it is, by analogy, nevertheless improbable whether a majority shareholder of a company could, *qua* shareholder, ever be found to have conducted the company's affairs, other than where he controlled the constitution of the company's board in a manner akin to that of a shadow director: see e.g. *Re Astec (BSR) plc* [1999] BCC 59. However, where the subject matter of an allegation under s 459 is founded on conduct emanating from a resolution of the general meeting, it would appear logical that the responsibility for conducting the company's affairs would fall on the general meeting as an organ of the company, or the majority who sanctioned the offending resolution.

The effect of the conduct

To substantiate a finding of unfairly prejudicial conduct, a petitioner must show that the conduct of the company's affairs resulted in more than a mere trivial assault on his/her membership interest: see e.g. *Re Saul D Harrison & Sons plc* [1994] BCC 475. However, although conduct which forms the subject matter of the petitioner's complaint may objectively be construed as trivial, the effect of that conduct may still be deemed to have been unfair in respect of the petitioner's membership interest. For example, a small and technical breach of a director's duty may cause little if any harm in relation to the financial standing of a company, but the very fact of the breach of duty may result in a loss of trust and confidence resulting in a deadlock situation between the membership. Although the conduct may have been trivial, the effect of that conduct may have a very damaging effect on the relationship of the members. In such a case, a petition under s 459 may be sustained: see e.g. *Re Baumler (UK)* [2005] 1 BCLC 92.

Where, however, the evidence to support a s 459 petition is considered inadequate, the alleged wrongdoers may apply to the court to strike out the petition. For example, in *Re a Company, ex parte Burr* [1992] BCLC 724, a petition under s 459 was dismissed on the premise that the alleged misconduct, namely a decision of the company's board of directors to continue to trade the business to protect the directors' own interests, could not be corroborated by documentary evidence. In dismissing the petition, Vinelott J remarked thus:

> 'In my judgment, the petitioner has not adduced any evidence which, if accepted at trial would support the allegations in the petition and justify the relief sought. The petitioner's case in substance is that something might be revealed on discovery in the course of cross examination of the directors that could be relied on as justifying the petition. That is not a proper ground for presenting a petition. The damaging effect which the presentation of the petition may have on the business of the company, even if it is not advertised, has often been the subject of judicial comment. A petition should not be presented unless it can be supported by evidence which, if accepted at the trial, would found a claim for relief.' (at p 736)

(See also *Re a Company (No 008699 of 1985)* [1986] BCLC 382.)

The definition of a member for the purposes of section 459

To pursue a petition under s 459, the petitioner must be a member of the company, and as a member he/she must petition *qua* member (i.e. the action must be concerned with a membership interest as opposed to some other collateral interest). The definition of 'a member of a company' is provided by s 22 of the Companies Act 1985. Section 22(1) states:

> 'The subscribers of a company's memorandum are deemed to have agreed to become members of the company, and on its registration shall be entered as such on its register of members.'

Section 22(2) provides that:

> 'Every other person who agrees to become a member of a company, and whose name is entered in its register of members, is a member of the company.'

A mere promise to transfer shares to a third party is insufficient to enable the third party to claim that he/she has agreed to become a member: see e.g. *Re a Company (No 003160 of 1986)* [1986] BCLC 391. However, in *Re Nuneaton Borough AFC Ltd* [1989] BCLC 454, it was held that the phrase 'agrees to become a member' would be satisfied where a person claiming to be a member of a company actually assented to become a member, even if such an assent was not confirmed by the signing of a contractual document.

In accordance with s 22(2), the member's name must be entered in the register of members. Providing a person's name is entered in the register of members, that person is capable of presenting a petition under s 459, notwithstanding that the person in question acts as a nominee shareholder: see e.g. *Lloyd* v *Casey* [2002] 1 BCLC 454, *Rock (Nominees) Ltd* v *RCO Holdings plc (in liq)* [2004] BCC 466, and *Re Brightview Ltd* [2004] BCC 542. However, following this latter case, the membership interests attributed to the nominee shareholder must be capable of including the economic and contractual interests of the beneficial owner of the shares (i.e. the interests of the nominee are for the purposes of the petition co-extensive with the interests of the beneficial owner).

In relation to a past member's ability to present a petition under s 459, it would appear that on a literal construction of the section no such capacity exists (i.e. it is impossible to construe a past member as 'a member of the company'). However, in *Re a Company (No 005287 of 1985)* [1986] 1 WLR 281, Hoffmann J suggested that there should be no such bar to a past member presenting a petition under s 459. It is suggested (despite the literal interpretation of s 459 and despite the contrary recommendations of the Law Commission and CLR, discussed below) that where the prejudicial conduct which forms the subject matter of a complaint under s 459 was instigated at a time when a petitioner was a member of the company, albeit that the nature of the wrongdoing may have been unknown to the petitioner at that time, an action under s 459 should be possible. Surely, it is unreasonable and inequitable to deny a past shareholder the right to seek redress especially where the effect of the misconduct may, for example, actively have influenced either the shareholder's decision to dispose of his shareholding interest, or the value of the interest at the time of its disposal.

However, it should be noted that s 459(2) does provide a remedy to non-members of a company in circumstances where shares have been transferred or transmitted by operation of law: for example, in the case of personal representatives or trustees in bankruptcy (see e.g. *Re Quickdome Ltd* [1988] BCLC 370).

While a past member's standing to present a petition under s 459 may be doubtful, it is clear that a past member of a company may be held responsible for the unfairly prejudicial conduct of a company's affairs in a situation where the conduct was instigated by that past member, prior to the disposal of his shareholding interest: so held in *Re a Company (No 005287 of 1985)* [1986] 1 WLR 281. Indeed, if any person is likely to be affected by any order made by the court as a consequence of a petition under s 459, the court may deem that the said party be made a respondent to the petition, irrespective of whether he/she had been involved in the conduct giving rise to the petition: see e.g. the decision of Lindsay J in *Re Little Olympian Each*

Ways Ltd [1994] 2 BCLC 420, also the decision of Vinelott J in *Re a Company (No 007281 of 1986)* [1987] BCLC 593.

The definition of membership interests for the purposes of section 459

To substantiate an action under s 459, the unfairly prejudicial conduct must affect a membership interest or, as in *Re Kenyon Swansea Ltd* [1987] BCLC 514, there must be evidence to establish the likelihood of a threatened act (i.e. an act which, if it was implemented, would constitute unfairly prejudicial conduct). Where a petition is sought to restrain a threatened act, there must be positive as opposed to speculative evidence of a future intention to instigate the conduct in question. However, an action under s 459 may be sustainable even in circumstances where the immediate threat of employing the conduct has momentarily passed.

The phrase 'membership interests' includes the legal rights of membership, that is rights protected by the companies legislation and rights attached to the memorandum and articles (e.g. a failure to comply with the terms of a valuation clause contained within the articles: see the Court of Appeal's decision in *Re Benfield Greig Group plc* [2002] BCC 256). However, the distinction between membership rights and membership interests is obscure and, as one might therefore expect, the judicial interpretation of the term 'interests' has had moments of vagueness.

In *Re Carrington Viyella plc* [1983] 1 BCC 98, 951, Vinelott J opined that a membership interest was no more than a membership right. On the other hand, in *Re a Company (No 008699 of 1985)* [1986] BCLC 382, Hoffmann J considered that a membership interest encompassed a wider concept than a membership right and that, coupled with the word 'unfair', s 459 permitted the court to consider the legitimate expectations of the membership of a company. For example, Hoffmann J believed that in a small domestic type company, a legitimate expectation could exist in a situation where a person became a shareholder on the premise that he would be allowed to participate in the management of the company (under s 14 of the CA 1985 no such expectation would be enforceable in so far as it would amount to an outsider right, discussed in Chapter 4).

The conclusion of Hoffmann J as to the possibility of a member of a company having a legitimate expectation to participate in the management of the company was echoed by the decision of the Privy Council in *Tay Bok Choon v Tahansan Sdn Bhd* [1987] 3 BCC 132 and the judgment of Mummery J in *Re a Company (No 00314 of 1989)* [1991] BCLC 154. Indeed, it is now firmly established that a member of a small domestic/quasi-partnership private company may have a legitimate expectation to participate in the management of the company in circumstances where the membership interest was related to some form of express or implied understanding confirming that member's expectation to participate in the management of the company's affairs: see e.g. *R & H Electrical Ltd v Haden Bill Electrical Ltd* [1995] BCC 958, *Quinlan v Essex Hinge Co Ltd* [1996] 2 BCLC 417 and *Re Eurofinance Group Ltd* [2001] BCC 551.

However, it must be stressed that exclusion from management is in itself insufficient to justify a successful petition under s 459; the exclusion must be of an unfairly prejudicial nature. For example, a member's exclusion from management may be justified on the basis that he/she failed to participate in management issues or that he/she was unhelpful or unreasonably hostile to other board members. In other words, although an exclusion from management may be viewed to be prejudicial to a member's interest, it may, in appropriate circumstances, still be construed as fair conduct: see e.g. *Re John Reid & Sons (Strucsteel) Ltd* [2003] 2 BCLC 319 and *Baker* v *Bellevue Garages Ltd* [2004] EWHC 1422 (Ch).

In *Re J E Cade & Son Ltd* [1991] BCC 360, Warner J equated the concept of a membership interest with the interpretation afforded to 'interests' so used to determine an action brought under the just and equitable winding up provision (i.e. s 122(1)(g) of the Insolvency Act 1986; this provision is discussed below). The facts of the case were as follows.

The petitioner (P) claimed relief under s 459 and in the alternative sought a winding up order on the just and equitable ground. P had granted a licence to his brother (R) to occupy and farm land which was in P's ownership. The licence had in fact been granted to a company in which R was the majority shareholder; P held a minority shareholding in the company. The licence was granted for a five-year period and on terms which included an option for R to purchase the farm and P's shares in the company at any time during the five-year period. P contended that an underlying feature of the agreement was that, if the option was not exercised, the farm would be sold. P claimed this as a legitimate expectation of membership. After the end of the five-year period the option had not been exercised and R (and therefore the company) refused to give up the occupation of the farm.

P commenced an action under s 459 and s 122(1)(g). Warner J refused to grant relief under both heads of the petition (criticism of this decision is discussed below in the context of s 122(1)(g)). The learned judge held that, although a court could give effect to equitable considerations, such considerations arose only where a petitioner pursued his interests as a member of the company. According to Warner J, here the petitioner had pursued his interests as the owner of the freehold and as such the petitioner's claim had not been based upon an interest which was linked to a membership right.

Although Warner J did not believe that a petitioner's claim had necessarily to be based upon the strict legal rights of membership, the learned judge contended that a shareholder's interest in a company could not be subject to expectations founded on a general concept of fairness (i.e. expectations which were unrelated to the legal rights of membership). For the purpose of construing the scope of a membership interest, the learned judge maintained that the interpretation was the same under both s 459 and s 122(1)(g). Accordingly, the learned judge concluded that the definition of a membership interest should be strictly confined to rights or obligations that were related to strict legal rights: for example, the terms of a company's constitution, a director's service contract, or an express shareholder agreement. While Warner J accepted that equitable considerations should be examined, the learned judge believed that considerations unconnected to the strict legal rights of membership could not, for the purposes of s 459 (and s 122(1)(g), IA 1986), found appropriate grounds upon which relief could be sought. Warner J stated that there could be:

'. . . no such third tier of rights and obligations. The court, exercising its jurisdiction to wind up a company on the just and equitable ground or jurisdiction conferred by s 459 . . . has a very wide discretion, but it does not sit under a palm tree.' (at p 372)

From the decision of Rattee J in *Re Leeds United Holdings Ltd* [1996] 2 BCLC 545, it would also appear to be an essential requirement of a s 459 petition to ensure that the membership interest which is central to the petitioner's case is specifically derived and related to the conduct of a company's affairs as opposed to, for example, personal rights afforded to the petitioner by the terms of a shareholder agreement. However, here Rattee J would seem to have been at odds with the earlier judgment of Warner J in *Re J E Cade* (discussed above). Rattee J was of the opinion that:

'In my judgment, the legitimate expectation which the court has held in other cases can give rise to a claim for relief under s 459 must, having regard to the purpose of the section as expressed in s 459(1), be a legitimate expectation relating to the conduct of the company's affairs, the most obvious and common example being an expectation of being allowed to participate in decisions as to such conduct. An expectation that a shareholder will not sell his shares without the consent of some other or other shareholders does not relate in any way to the conduct of the company's affairs and, therefore, cannot, in my judgment, fall to be protected by the court under s 459.' (at pp 559–60)

Proper boundaries must be drawn to limit the concept of a membership interest thereby preventing a membership interest from being defined in terms quite unrelated to the proper functioning of a company. For example, it would be wrong to allow a member of a company who owned land adjacent to a proposed extension of the company's premises, to petition under s 459 where the subject matter of the complaint was that the extension would devalue the member's land. Clearly, this example illustrates a purely personal interest as opposed to a membership interest: that is, a membership interest must relate to the internal and external functioning of the company's affairs.

However, the suggestion that a membership interest must always be linked to a strict legal right or indeed a right flowing from the conduct of a company's affairs (as opposed to the conduct between members of the company) is perhaps to endanger the very essence of the distinction between a membership interest and membership right. Support for this view may be found in the words of Sir Donald Nicholls V-C in *Re Tottenham Hotspur plc* [1994] 1 BCLC 655, namely:

'In deciding whether and how to exercise its wide powers under s 459, the court will have regard not only to the company's constitution but also to equitable considerations arising from expectations created by the dealings between members. The court will do what is just and equitable in all the circumstances.' (at p 659)

The above passage is particularly apt to counteract the restrictive stance taken by Rattee J in *Re Leeds United Holdings Ltd*. Indeed, following the judgment of Lord Hoffmann in *O'Neill v Phillips* [1999] 1 WLR 1092 (discussed below), it is contended that terms of a legally binding membership agreement may satisfy the requirements of a 'membership interest' under s 459.

The interpretation of a 'membership interest' so expounded by Warner J in *Re J E Cade* would now appear to be settled as the acceptable norm in construing s 459.

This view was confirmed in *O'Neill* v *Phillips*, the first case under s 459 to be considered by the House of Lords. The facts of the case were as follows.

P controlled a company involved in the construction industry. P owned the company's entire share capital and acted as its sole director. A company employee (O) proved himself to be invaluable to the company and was rewarded with a gift of a 25 per cent holding of the company's shares, a directorship in the company and half of the company's profits (some of which he left in the company). O acted as the company's *de facto* managing director and his personal involvement and commitment to the company was such that he guaranteed the company's bank overdraft; this was secured by a charge over O's principal residence. As a result of O's involvement in the company, P gave O an informal promise (although no formal agreement was ever signed) to the effect that, if certain targets were met, O would be given a 50 per cent holding in the company (50 per cent voting rights).

With O at its helm, the company prospered. However, a decline in the growth of the construction industry led to a gradual but sustained fall in the company's fortunes, to the extent that P became extremely concerned about the company's performance and O's involvement in the management of its affairs. P's concern was such that he returned to head the management of the company. Subsequently, O was informed that he would no longer be paid 50 per cent of the profits and that he would only be paid his salary and dividends in respect of his 25 per cent holding in the company.

O left the employment of the company and petitioned under s 459. O claimed he had a legitimate expectation of acquiring a 50 per cent holding in the company and an expectation of continuing to receive 50 per cent of the company's profits. Further, O claimed that P's actions and poor treatment of him had forced him to leave the company's employment.

At first instance (heard by Judge Paul Baker QC), O failed in his action, in so far as P had never entered into any formal agreement with O in respect of the alleged share issue nor had there been any formal promise to pay O 50 per cent of the company's profits (i.e. there was no legal right to which any legitimate expectation could attach). In reversing the first instance decision, the Court of Appeal (heard as *Re a Company No 00709 of 1992 – Re Pectel Ltd* [1997] 2 BCLC 739) held that, irrespective of the absence of any formal agreement, O did have a legitimate expectation of receiving 50 per cent of the profits and 50 per cent of the shares (i.e. when agreed targets had been met). Nourse LJ stated:

> 'I am, with respect to the judge, unable to accept his assessment of the position. On 29 January 1985, less than two years after he had started to work for the company, Mr O'Neill [O] became both a member and a director of it. It is true that he did not subscribe for his shares and did not bring any capital into the company. But that is immaterial. From the end of January 1985, or at any rate from May of that year when the understanding as to an equal sharing of profits was come to, the company represented an association continued on the basis of a personal relationship involving mutual confidence between Mr Phillips and Mr O'Neill, with an understanding that Mr O'Neill should participate in the conduct of the business and restrictions on share transfers. All three typical elements of a quasi-partnership were present. At all times thereafter Mr O'Neill had a legitimate expectation that he would receive 50 per cent of the profits. By the beginning of 1991 he

had a legitimate expectation, subject to meeting the £500 000 and £1 000 000 targets respectively, that he would receive 50 per cent of its voting shares.' (at p 769)

The House of Lords overturned the decision of the Court of Appeal. Lord Hoffmann, previously a judge renowned for a liberal/radical approach to the construction of s 459, delivered the leading judgment of the House. Although the most lucid of judgments, it is submitted that its content was of a surprisingly conforming and conservative nature. In his judgment, Lord Hoffmann emphasised the significance of the legal characteristics of the relationship between a company and its membership; the terms of that association being found within the articles of association and additionally via the relationship between members of the company – for example, as found within a distinct shareholder agreement. Derived from principles applicable to the law of partnership, Lord Hoffmann explained that a company was subject to equitable principles, the role of which:

'. . . was to restrain the exercise of strict legal rights in certain relationships in which it considered that this would be contrary to good faith.' (at p 1098)

His lordship emphasised that a member of a company would have grounds to complain of unfairly prejudicial conduct where there had been a breach of the legal rules which governed the manner in which the affairs of the company should be conducted. Alternatively, but more exceptionally, a member of a company could make a complaint in circumstances where equitable considerations made it necessary to abandon the application of strict legal rights so as to prevent unfairness. Lord Hoffmann identified unfairness in the following manner:

'Thus unfairness may consist in a breach of the rules or in using the rules in a manner which equity would regard as contrary to good faith . . .' (at p 1099)

However, in seeking to protect the principle of legal certainty, his lordship considered it necessary to limit the extent by which the equitable principles could apply, finding that such principles could not stand as an indefinite notion of fairness. In seeking to identify this limitation, Lord Hoffmann analysed the term 'legitimate expectations', a term he used in *Re Saul D Harrison & Sons plc* and which, thereafter, had been regularly applied by the courts as one appropriate to the identification of a membership interest. His lordship admitted that perhaps it had been a mistake to use the expression 'legitimate expectations'. He explained his reservations such:

'The concept of a legitimate expectation should not be allowed to lead a life of its own, capable of giving rise to equitable restraints in circumstances to which the traditional equitable principles have no application . . . I think that the Court of Appeal may have been misled by the expression "legitimate expectation". The real question is whether in fairness or equity [O] had a right to the shares.' (at p 1102)

Lord Hoffmann's anxiety over the use of the term 'legitimate expectations' was born of the fear that an 'expectation' may be considered 'legitimate' even though unrelated to one derived from a legal right. Accordingly, in *O'Neill* v *Phillips*, his lordship considered that O's expectations could not be equated with a membership interest because the expectations relied upon had never been subject to any formal legal agreement. In respect of the said expectations, Lord Hoffmann remarked:

'On this point, one runs up against what seems to me the insuperable obstacle of the judge's finding that [P] never agreed to give them. He made no promise on the point. From which it seems to me to follow that there is no basis, consistent with established principles of equity, for a court to hold that [P] was behaving unfairly in withdrawing from the negotiation. This would not be restraining the exercise of legal rights. It would be imposing upon [P] an obligation to which he never agreed. Where, as here, parties enter into negotiations with a view to a transfer of shares on professional advice and subject to a condition that they are not to be bound until a formal document has been executed, I do not think it is possible to say that an obligation has arisen in fairness or equity at an earlier stage. The same reasoning applies to the sharing of profits. The judge found as a fact that [P] made no unconditional promise about the sharing of profits.' (at p 1103)

Therefore, the position after *O'Neill* v *Phillips* is that a s 459 action cannot ordinarily be sustained where the alleged membership interest is not linked to an enforceable legal right. Where a legally binding agreement fails to incorporate a member's expectation, it may be possible to imply the expectation (term) as under the general law of contract, or subject the legal right to equitable considerations. However, it is most improbable that equitable considerations will extend to expectations which cannot be linked to a legal right other than where, in exceptional circumstances, the nature of the company in question demands that an implied expectation be taken into account.

Accordingly, in *O'Neill* v *Phillips*, the petitioner's expectation of participating in an equal share of the profits and an equal shareholding in the company could not be enforced as a membership interest because such expectations were not subject to any binding agreement or legal right (i.e. an agreement covering the distribution of profits or shares simply did not exist). Further, there could be no implied expectation relating to a share in profits and the shares because the nature and structure of the company was not a typical quasi-partnership type company.

The decision of the House of Lords in *O'Neill* v *Phillips* does create a substantive degree of certainty in respect of the definition of a membership interest. However, it clearly blurs the distinction between a membership interest and a membership right. Following *O'Neill*, other than in the quasi-partnership type of company, equitable considerations would appear to be irrelevant where they are indicative of matters detached from any legal agreement. Although there may be positive evidence (as in *O'Neill* v *Phillips*: e.g. the fact that O personally guaranteed the company's debts) to suggest that a member's claim was justified, giving rise to a defined interest, the said evidence will be immaterial and irrelevant in respect of determining the existence of a membership interest for the purpose of substantiating a petition under s 459. From *O'Neill* it may be concluded that a s 459 petition will fail other than where the evidence of a case can link the member's expectation to a legal right or, alternatively, in the case of a quasi-partnership company, an enforceable implied expectation/right which flows from the commonly held expectations of the membership of the company. Here, a petitioner, in seeking to establish a membership interest must therefore convince the court that the membership interest, which he/she relies upon, was commonly and universally recognised by the entire membership. For example, in *Phoenix Office Supplies Ltd* v *Larvin* [2003] BCC 11, L, who held one-third of the company's issued share capital, decided to resign as a director of the company; the resignation was on personal grounds and had nothing to do with the substance of the subsequent s 459 petition. L had been the pivotal force behind the company's success and sought a fair valuation for his shareholding, contending that the company's two other shareholders had breached a common understanding, namely that in a quasi-partnership company of this type, a shareholder would, if he left the company, be entitled to one-third of the company's net asset value.

The defendants (the company's two other shareholders) had offered to purchase L's shares at a discounted rate to reflect L's minority holding. The company's articles contained no right of pre-emption in the event of a shareholder seeking to dispose of his shares. The Court of Appeal rejected L's claim. The valuation procedure, in discounting a minority interest, was not unfair because L had no equitable entitlement to expect more (i.e. there had not been a breach of any legal right or formal understanding between the parties as to an alternative valuation procedure). Although the company was a quasi-partnership concern, it was not, in this case, possible to impart a finding of any agreement or understanding (implied expectation/right) between the shareholders to confirm a share valuation procedure in accordance with L's expectations.

Finally, and to return to *O'Neill* v *Phillips*, if one accepts the definition of a membership interest as per *O'Neill*, it is at first sight difficult to explain how and why a member/director of a company should be able to rely on s 459 to protect his/her management position in the company. A membership interest must ordinarily be related to a legal right; a legal right may then be subject to equitable considerations. But what legal right exists to protect a member in relation to the retention of a management role? Clearly no such legal right exists. The legal right in relation to the removal from office is contained in s 303 of the Companies Act 1985 and as such it must be this legal right to which equitable considerations apply. Yet this is a statutory provision, not a contractual provision or common law rule. Yes, it is a legal right but it is still difficult to comprehend how and why equitable principles should provide a remedy for a minority shareholder/director in effect to usurp a **statutory right** to remove the director under s 303 of the Companies Act 1985.

Possibly, an alternative answer to justify a member/director's ability to protect him or herself from removal from office may be that the right to petition under s 459 is an example of an enforceable implied expectation/right derived from the nature and type of company under consideration so that an ability to retain a management position will be dependent upon the principles of fairness, mutual trust, confidence and the expectations of the entire membership of the company.

Of course, the difficulty with identifying so called implied expectations/rights is the nature and classification of such rights. Basically, a classification of the same is impossible because the existence of the implied right will need to be ascertained on a case by case basis, to be determined more as a jury question than one based upon predetermined categories. However, case examples (as in the case of a director's exclusion from office) may establish some form of guidance in relation to the identification of such rights. The decision of the Court of Appeal in *Jones* v *Jones* [2003] BCC 226 may provide another example of a type of implied right within a quasi-partnership type company. Here, on a preliminary point, it was held that an informal agreement in relation to the voting structure of the company's board of directors may constitute a membership interest with the effect that where the company's shares were controlled and split equally between two shareholder/directors then, in accordance with the implied right, a third appointed director (related to the defendant shareholder) and one who held no shares in the company, should not, at board meetings, be permitted to exercise a casting vote on issues of substance.

Public companies

The s 459 provision is generally applicable to the shareholders of private companies and, more especially, those of a type often referred to as quasi-partnership/domestic companies (i.e. companies founded on the principles of mutual trust and confidence). The practical application of s 459 to shareholders of public companies would appear doubtful. In *Re Astec (BSR) plc* [1999] BCC 59, Jonathan Parker J opined that it would be a misconception to assume that any form of legitimate expectation could properly attach to the shares of a public company. The learned judge stated:

> 'In my judgment, as the authorities stand today, the concept of "legitimate expectation" as explained by Hoffmann LJ in *Saul D Harrison* can have no place in the context of public listed companies. Moreover, its introduction in that context would, as it seems to me, in all probability prove to be a recipe for chaos. If the market in a company's shares is to have any credibility, members of the public dealing in that market must it seems to me be entitled to proceed on the footing that the constitution of the company is as it appears in the company's public documents, unaffected by any extraneous equitable considerations and constraints.' (at p 88)

The above passage is clearly apt in relation to a director/member of a public company (i.e. the director will have no equitable right to be maintained in a management position: see e.g. *Re Blue Arrow plc* [1987] BCLC 585 and *Re a Company (No 003096 of 1987)* [1988] 4 BCC 80). A contrary view would preclude future shareholders in a public company from asserting their wishes in respect of determining the persons best suited to participate in the management of the company.

However, although the composition of the membership of a public company will be less predictable and stable than in a private company and the rights and equitable expectations of shareholders in private and public companies will differ, clearly the legal rights of shareholders in public companies deserve the same protection as those afforded to the shareholders of private companies. Here, the 'legal' right as opposed to the 'equitable right' of the shareholder must be stressed. For example, if a shareholder in a public company claims that the company is in breach of the terms of its constitution (a breach of a legal right) with the effect that the shareholder is prejudiced in a manner which is deemed unfair in the context of his/her membership interest, why should the shareholder be precluded from seeking recourse under s 459, if the breach of that right would enable him/her to, for example, pursue an action under the often more troublesome and less flexible (in terms of remedy) s 14 of the Companies Act 1985?

To take the argument a radical step further, why should members of public companies not have the ability to pursue an action under s 459 in circumstances where the wrong is **related** to a strict legal right as opposed to constituting an absolute legal right? In answer, Jonathan Parker J remarked that a member of a public company should be precluded from pursuing an action under s 459 on the premise that the availability of the action would destroy the creditability in the market for the company's shares. Yet surely, existing and potential shareholders of a public company would not be completely distracted from dealing in shares by the potential availability of the s 459 provision? Indeed in certain circumstances they may welcome that right. Further, following the judgment of Lord Hoffmann in *O'Neill* v *Phillips* and therein the limitation of equitable considerations to matters related to a member's legal rights, the potential scope of actions under s 459 is limited and as such it is perhaps no longer pertinent to describe (as Jonathan Parker J so described) the scope of rights actionable under s 459 as 'extraneous equitable considerations and constraints'.

The interests of the company as a whole?

Where a company's affairs have been conducted in the best interests of the company as a whole, is it nevertheless possible that such conduct could still give rise to a minority action for unfairly prejudicial conduct? Is an individual member's interest independent from an interest which serves the greater good of a company? If affirmative answers are given to such questions, logic would seem to dictate that the notion of majority rule is but a theoretical myth.

Yet, in *Re D R Chemicals Ltd* [1989] 5 BCC 39 Peter Gibson J may be seen to suggest that an individual member's interest is quite independent from considerations relating to the interests of the company as a whole. The learned judge observed:

> '**I do not doubt that if the objective bystander observes unfairly prejudicial conduct by a respondent the fact that the respondent had a proper motive will not prevent the conduct from falling within the section.**' (at p 46)

However, notwithstanding the above comment, is it correct to assert that fairness, in relation to a course of conduct, should be measured only in terms of an individual shareholder's interests without further consideration of any potential benefits or good motives in respect of the company as a whole? For example, a company may make a rights issue at a fair and reasonable price so as to inject more capital into the company. A member may nevertheless complain that because of his poor financial position he cannot afford to participate in the issue. His interest in the company would be diluted if other members subscribed for shares; his membership interest would be prejudiced. Yet, if the shares were issued for a proper purpose and the issue was objectively determined to benefit the company as a whole, surely it would be a radical and improper distortion of the balance of corporate power, as between shareholders and the management of the company, to allow the prejudiced member to claim unfair prejudice and succeed in an action under s 459. (See *Nicholas* v *Soundcraft Electronics Ltd* [1993] BCLC 360, discussed above.)

Naturally, in the above example, the position would be quite different if a company was aware of a member's inability to take up shares, and such knowledge was a factor in the company's decision to issue shares. In such a case the conduct may be unfairly prejudicial in so far as the share issue would not have been for a proper purpose: see e.g. *Re Cumana Ltd* [1986] BCLC 430.

Can a section 459 action be sustained where the conduct complained of is capable of giving rise to a corporate action?

Where a member of a company purports to commence an action under s 459 on the premise that the company's affairs have been conducted in a manner which is unfairly prejudicial to his/her membership interest and the said conduct is of a type that would also give rise to a corporate action (i.e. it incorporates a wrong perpetrated against the company), should not the company be the proper plaintiff to the action, or, if the company declines to pursue the action, should it not be pursued as a derivative action? Following the case of *Johnson* v *Gore Wood & Co* [2002] 2 AC 1 (discussed in Chapter 23) it would appear that a shareholder has no personal right of action where the wrong in question adversely affects the company, giving rise to the potential for a corporate action.

However, s 459 is a statutory claim for relief and not, as in *Johnson* v *Gore Wood & Co*, one concerned with a conflict as to claims arising from a breach of contract or tort. Therefore, can *Johnson* v *Gore Wood & Co* be relied upon in this context to defeat the claims of a minority shareholder under s 459?

Further, as s 459 permits a petition in circumstances where the unfairly prejudicial conduct affects 'members generally', then conduct giving rise to the complaint is likely to have an adverse affect on the interests of the company as a whole (i.e. it is likely to involve a wrong against the company). Therefore, if a petition under s 459 was denied in circumstances incorporating a corporate wrong, would this not defeat the purpose of the provision in the use of the term 'members generally'?

In *Re Brightview Ltd* [2004] BCC 542, Jonathan Crow (sitting as a deputy judge of the High Court) gave a classic example of conduct affecting members generally that would also constitute a corporate wrong, namely asset stripping. However, the learned deputy judge was clear that in such a case a petition under s 459 could be sustained:

> '. . . where a company's assets are stripped out for the benefit of some transferee. Any such stripping out will inevitably involve conduct (or possibly omissions) of the company, acting (or possibly not acting) through its directors. Their conduct (or inaction) in facilitating such a transfer would in all probability amount to a breach of their duties to the company. To suggest that, in such a case, s 459 is powerless would in my judgment be to deprive the amendment of much of its value.' (at para 61)

Nevertheless, contrary to the opinion voiced by Jonathan Crow, may it not be possible to contend that, while s 459 is a statutory provision, the adoption of the term 'membership interest' asserts an absolute requirement that indeed the interest in question must be a distinct membership interest as opposed to one which also belongs to the company and that, in circumstances where there is a dual type of interest, recourse should be made to the common law to determine the standing of the parties? Indeed, if this latter view was to be adopted, then, given the dual nature of the interest, the corporate action should prevail and the petition under s 459 should be denied.

However, many previous cases under s 459 have proceeded on the basis of allowing a minority shareholder to petition where the action in question also incorporates a wrong against a company, most ordinarily a breach of a director's duty: see e.g. *Re a Company (No 005287 of 1985)* (1985) 1 BCC 99, 586, *Re a Company, ex parte Burr* [1992] BCLC 724, *Re Little Olympian Each Ways Ltd* [1994] 2 BCLC 420, *Re Macro (Ipswich) Ltd* [1994] 2 BCLC 354, *Anderson v Hogg* [2002] BCC 923 and *Re Baumler Ltd* [2005] BCC 181, to name but a few. In the light of *Johnson v Gore Wood & Co*, can it be contended that the said cases should no longer be followed, or should the precedent of *Johnson v Gore Wood & Co* be restricted to the common law, having no place in the statutory interpretation of the phrase 'membership interest' in the context of s 459?

A company's involvement in a section 459 action

As is the norm, a dispute which gives rise to a petition under s 459 is essentially an action between different sections of the shareholders. As such, the court may prevent the management of a company from causing the company's money to be spent on financing the defence of the action: see e.g. *Re Milgate Developments Ltd* [1991] BCC 24, *Re a Company (No 004502 of 1988), ex parte Johnson* [1991] BCC 234 and *Corbett v Corbett* [1998] BCC 93. Accordingly, although a company will necessarily be included in a s 459 petition, the inclusion will often be as a nominal respondent to the action.

However, according to the judgment of Lindsay J in *Re a Company (No 1126 of 1992)* [1994] 2 BCLC 146, a presumption that a company should not be responsible for financing the defence of a s 459 petition involving a dispute between the majority and minority shareholders of the company may not be viewed as an absolute rule and accordingly may be subject to an exception where, for example, the defence of the action is viewed to be beneficial to the company as a whole (but here should not the company litigate?). According to Lindsay J, the onus of establishing that the defence would benefit the company should fall upon the board of directors. However, where the court is of the opinion that corporate funds were improperly used to finance the defence, the board, in such an instance, may be made personally liable to account to the company.

THE AVAILABLE REMEDIES TO AN ACTION UNDER SECTION 459

Where a petitioner succeeds in convincing the court that a company's affairs have been conducted in a manner which is unfairly prejudicial to the interests of a part of the membership or the membership generally, the court may make an order under s 461 of the Companies Act 1985. However, it should be noted that even where a petitioner establishes unfairly prejudicial conduct, the court may nevertheless decide that an order under s 461 would be inappropriate. The court may also come to the conclusion that a more convenient alternative remedy is available. For example, in *Re Full Cup International Trading Ltd* [1995] BCC 682, Ferris J considered that the petitioner's interest would be better served if the company in question was subjected to a winding up order (a decision subsequently approved by the Court of Appeal [1997] 2 BCLC 419).

The courts have a very wide discretion in determining the nature of the relief under s 461(1) and, in accordance with this section, may make 'an order as it thinks fit'. A list of some examples of the type of orders which are available is given in s 461(2). The section provides that, without prejudice to the generality of subs (1), the court's order may:

(a) regulate the conduct of the company's affairs in the future;

(b) require the company to refrain from doing or continuing an act complained of by the petitioner or to do an act which the petitioner has complained it has omitted to do;

(c) authorise civil proceedings to be brought in the name and on behalf of the company by such person or persons and on such terms as the court may direct;

(d) provide for the purchase of the shares of any members of the company by other members or by the company itself and, in the case of a purchase by the company itself, authorise the reduction of the company's capital.

Section 461(3) and (4) further provide that the court has the power to restrain the company from making any alterations to the company's memorandum and articles or conversely that the court may make any alterations to the company's memorandum or articles as it sees fit.

The most common type of order sought is the one provided for by example (d), namely the purchase of the petitioner's shares. In such cases the valuation of shares will be of paramount importance. The underlying theme in determining the value of shares is that of fairness. As such, the actual moment in time at which the valuation is to be calculated is apt to vary from case to case (i.e. the fairness of a particular valuation procedure and the date at which the valuation is to take place will depend upon the individual circumstances of a case). Accordingly, depending upon the circumstances of a case, the valuation of shares may be based upon the share value:

- at a time prior to the petition,
- at the date of the petition, or
- at the actual date of the hearing.

In *Re London School of Electronics Ltd* [1986] Ch 211, it was suggested that the valuation procedure should normally take place at the actual date of the hearing (see also *Re D R Chemicals Ltd* (1989) 5 BCC 39). However, this presumption is rebuttable. Indeed, in *Re London School of Electronics Ltd*, it was decided that the valuation procedure should be as of the date of the petition, in so far as the company's fortunes had improved in the period between the petition and the hearing. It was considered to be unfair to allow the petitioner to reap the benefit of the company's improved position.

However, as stated, much will depend upon the individual circumstances of the case. For example, in *Scottish Co-operative Society* v *Meyer* [1959] AC 324 (heard under s 210, CA 1948), the House of Lords valued the company's shares prior to the date of the hearing on the basis that the time of valuation should be at a moment in time prior to the date when the offending conduct may have had an effect on the value of the shares. In *Re Cumana Ltd* [1986] BCLC 430, Lawton LJ also put forward an example of a situation (see also *Re OC (Transport) Services* [1984] BCLC 251) which would warrant the court in valuing shares prior to the commencement of the petition, namely:

> 'If, for example, there is before the court evidence that the majority shareholder deliberately took steps to depreciate the value of shares in anticipation of a petition being presented, it would be permissible to value the shares at a date before such action was taken.' (at p 436)

Guidance as to the position of arriving at an early valuation date was given and neatly summarised by Robert Walker LJ in *Profinance Trust SA v Gladstone* [2002] 1 WLR 1024. His lordship opined:

> 'i) Where a company has been deprived of its business, an early valuation date (and compensating adjustments) may be required in fairness to the claimant (see, *Meyer*).
>
> ii) Where a company has been reconstructed or its business has changed significantly, so that it has a new economic identity, an early valuation date may be required in fairness to one or both parties (see, *OC Transport*, and to a lesser degree *London School of Electronics*). But an improper alteration in the issued share capital, unaccompanied by any change in the business, will not necessarily have that outcome (see, *DR Chemicals*).
>
> iii) Where a minority shareholder has a petition on foot and there is a general fall in the market, the court may in fairness to the claimant have the shares valued at an early date, especially if it strongly disapproves of the majority shareholder's prejudicial conduct (*Re Cumana*).
>
> iv) But a claimant is not entitled to what the deputy judge called a one-way bet, and the court will not direct an early valuation date simply to give the claimant the most advantageous exit from the company, especially where severe prejudice has not been made out (see, *Re Elgindata*).
>
> v) All these points may be heavily influenced by the parties' conduct in making and accepting or rejecting offers either before or during the course of the proceedings (see, *O'Neill v Phillips*).' (at para 61)

Method of valuation

In accordance with *Re Castleburn* (1989) 5 BCC 652, it would appear that where the articles of association provide a mechanism for a fair and independent valuation of shares, the court should not ordinarily interfere with the independent valuation procedure, unless the said mechanism is not properly adhered to or where the procedure is itself considered to be unjust. An example of the court departing from the valuation procedure contained within a company's articles is to be found in *Re Abbey Leisure* [1990] BCC 60 (discussed further below); also see *Re a Company (No 00330 of 1991), ex parte Holden* [1991] BCLC 597.

In determining the value of shares, the court will normally discount the value of a minority holding. However, for the purposes of s 461, no universal rule exists whereby a minority holding must be valued at a discount and indeed, where the petitioner is not in any way at fault, the court will tend to favour an undiscounted valuation: see e.g. the comments of Lord Hoffmann in *O'Neill v Phillips* [1999]

1 WLR 1092 at pp 1105–08. However, by contrast, see *Phoenix Office Supplies Ltd v Larvin* [2003] BCC 11.

The determining factor for the valuation process is to achieve justice between the parties to the petition. In cases where the petitioner's interest is affected in an extreme and oppressive manner, the court's desire to achieve justice may also incorporate an award of an implied form of compensation: see e.g. *Re Bird Precision Bellow* [1986] 1 Ch 658 and *Quinlan v Essex Hinge Co Ltd* [1996] 2 BCLC 417.

In most cases involving a share purchase order, the order will be to the effect that the majority purchase the petitioner's shares. Nevertheless, it is possible for the court to decide that the minority shareholder should be permitted to purchase the majority's holding: see e.g. *Re Brenfield Squash Racquets Club* [1996] 2 BCLC 184 and *Re Nuneaton Borough AFC Ltd (No 2)* [1991] BCC 44 (discussed below). However, it should be noted that in *Re Ringtower Holdings plc* (1989) 5 BCC 82, Peter Gibson J opined that an order for the purchase of the shares of the majority was an inappropriate one to make where the majority opposed the sale and the minority held less than five per cent of the company's share capital.

A decision which highlights the power of the courts to exercise their discretion in the making of an order under s 461 is provided by the case of *Re Nuneaton Borough AFC Ltd (No 2)* [1991] BCC 44. The unusual facts of the case resulted in a decision to allow a minority shareholder (P) to purchase a controlling interest in the company (from R). However, as R had given substantial loans to the company, Harman J declared that it would be inequitable to force R to surrender his majority control without being able to recoup the money loaned to the company. Accordingly, his lordship ordered that, as a condition of the purchase of R's shares, P should also be required to repay the amount of the loan on behalf of the company. This potential scope of the decision is extreme in that the minority shareholder, in whose favour the s 459 petition was decided, was ultimately made responsible for the company's debts. It is submitted that where, as in this case, a creditor is unable to enforce a loan agreement against a company, the court, in exercising its very wide powers under s 461, should not readily overturn the principle that a company in its guise as a separate legal entity should be accountable for its own debts. In this case P was not the company; a company is, of course, a separate and distinct legal entity.

Other orders under section 461

As to the other s 461 orders, an excellent example of the type of situation which would invoke an order under s 461(a) is provided by the case of *Re Harmer Ltd* [1959] 1 WLR 62. This case (decided under s 210, CA 1948) involved a domestic type company, the voting control of which was in the hands of the company's founder (H). H also held the post of 'governing director' (akin to the post of managing director). H, whilst retaining voting control of the company, nevertheless gifted a greater proportion of the company's shares to his sons, who also held directorships in the company. H (who was 88 years old) imposed his will against the wishes of the other members of the company and was apt to ignore the wishes of the board by, for example, entering into contracts without the board's approval. As a result of H's attitude, the business of the company suffered greatly.

The sons pursued an action under s 210 of the Companies Act 1948. The Court of Appeal, in approving the decision of Roxburgh J, ordered that H should be stripped of his control in the company. This was achieved by removing H's executive powers. H was made a life president of the company, a title given in recognition of H's past services to the company, but one which carried no power or authority in relation to the management of the company's affairs.

An example of a s 461(b) type of order would be where a minority shareholder of a company sought to prevent the company from engaging in an act which, if instigated, would constitute conduct which was unfairly prejudicial to the interests of the shareholders. An example of a case illustration of this type of order is to be found in *Re Kenyon Swansea Ltd* (1987) 3 BCC 259.

Section 461(c) is, in effect, a statutory alternative to the derivative action (discussed in Chapter 23). Under s 461(c), the court has a power to order civil proceedings to be brought in the name and on behalf of the company. In avoiding the hurdles imposed by the procedural requirements of the rule in *Foss v Harbottle* (i.e. establishing a fraud on the minority), a s 461(c) order may be sought where a petitioner establishes that the company's affairs were conducted in a manner unfairly prejudicial to the interests of the company as a whole (members generally). Section 461(c) is not a commonly sought remedy because of the potential inability of a petitioner to obtain a *Wallersteiner*-type order for costs. However, it should be noted that in *Re a Company (No 005136 of 1986)* [1987] BCLC 82 (sub nom *Re Sherbourne Park Residents Co Ltd*), Hoffmann J suggested that, where a derivative action was brought by way of a s 459 petition, the petitioner would be entitled to an indemnity from the company for his/her costs in line with *Wallersteiner v Moir (No 2)* [1975] QB 373 (a view impliedly confirmed by the Court of Appeal in *Clark v Cutland* [2003] 2 BCLC 393).

It should be stressed that, under s 461, the court may make any order it sees fit and as such is not bound to prescribe an order of the type represented by s 461(a)–(d). For example, in *Wilton Davies v Kirk* [1997] BCC 770, the court concluded that, as a result of an irretrievable breakdown in the relationship between the company's shareholders, either the plaintiff or respondent should purchase the shares of the other. However, to preserve the assets of the company during the interim period, the court, exercising its jurisdiction under s 37 of the Supreme Court Act 1981, and in accordance with the petitioner's application, ordered the appointment of a receiver to oversee the company's affairs.

The relationship between section 459 and the rule in Foss v Harbottle

First, it should be pointed out that while the theoretical remnants of the exceptions to the rule in *Foss v Harbottle* remain, in practice, the extent to which s 459 actions now dominate the law relating to the protection of minority shareholders, reflects and continues to give effect to a rapid decline in actions brought on the basis of the fraud on the minority exception. Although actions commenced under s 459 are primarily designed as personal claims pursued against those responsible for the conduct of a company's affairs, a strict adherence to the distinction between personal claims and those actions seeking to right a corporate wrong (the rule and exceptions to *Foss v Harbottle*) have not been observed in the interpretation of s 459. Matters which, in accordance with the rule in *Foss* v *Harbottle*, should only be commenced by the company (other than where a fraud on the minority was established) have been capable of being commenced via s 459.

Additionally, although a minority shareholder would, in commencing a s 459 action, ordinarily be concerned with a personal remedy (i.e. a remedy other than one which seeks to redress a wrong to the company), it is nevertheless possible that an underlying motive for the action may be one which seeks to protect the company's interests. Indeed, it may be possible under s 461 for a remedy to be couched in terms which would give effect to both a petitioner's interests and the interests of the company as a whole. For example, in *Clark* v *Cutland* [2003] 2 BCLC 393, the Court of Appeal accepted that the relief sought under s 461 of the Companies Act could also be sought for the benefit of the company (but note here the complexities of a potential conflict with the rule in *Johnson* v *Gore Wood & Co* [2002] 2 AC 1).

PROPOSALS FOR FUTURE REFORM

The Law Commission's proposals

In its consultation paper entitled, 'Shareholder Remedies' (1997, Law Com No 246), the Law Commission advanced proposals aimed at improving the efficiency of actions commenced under s 459. The final recommendations of the Commission may be summarised as follows.

The length and cost of proceedings

The Commission recommended that the problems associated with the excessive length and cost of many proceedings brought under s 459 should primarily be dealt with by active case management by the courts. In this respect, the Commission recommended that greater use be made of the power to direct that preliminary issues be heard, or that some issues be tried, before others. Further, the Commission recommended that the courts be given the power to dismiss any claim or part of a claim or defence thereto which, in the opinion of the court, had no realistic prospect of success at full trial. In respect of costs, the Commission recommended that the court should have a greater flexibility in its ability to make costs orders so as to reflect the manner in which the successful party conducted the proceedings and the outcome of individual issues.

A presumption of unfairly prejudicial conduct

In the case of a private company limited by shares, the Commission recommended a presumption of unfairly prejudicial conduct in a situation where, immediately prior to a petitioner's exclusion from management, the petitioner:

(a) held ten per cent or more of the company's voting shares; and

(b) all or substantially all of the company's members were directors.

The Commission considered that the presumption should be rebuttable; the burden of establishing that it should not apply would be on the respondent. Accordingly, it would be open to the respondent to show, for example, that the petitioner had no legitimate expectation of being able to continue to participate in the management of the company, or that the exclusion was justified by the petitioner's conduct. It is to be observed that the Commission recommended that the presumption should be based on 'structural' factors (for example, the percentage of shares held by the petitioner) rather than the expectations of the parties. However, the Commission noted that if a case did not satisfy the conditions for the presumption to arise, then it should not necessarily be precluded from being heard under s 459.

The Commission believed the above recommendations would be advantageous in so far as they would provide some degree of certainty in respect of the outcome of proceedings relating to the exclusion of a director. Further, the Commission considered that the implementation of the recommendations would result in cases being dealt with more quickly following the issue of the proceedings.

Limitation period

The Commission recommended the creation of a limitation period in respect of claims under the section. This recommendation was advanced on the premise that, on many occasions, allegations made in s 459 proceedings involved conduct which spanned a time period going back over a number of years. Accordingly, investigations into such cases increased the length and cost of the proceedings.

Winding up as an available remedy

The Commission further recommended that the winding up of a company should be added to the available remedies under s 461 because, while s 459 remedies are very wide, they did not expressly include the power to order the company to be wound up. Accordingly, the Commission considered that it was desirable to have a single remedy (incorporating winding up) which would give the court the maximum flexibility to deal with the matters before it. However, in an attempt to prevent claims for a winding up order from being used as a means of 'blackmail', the Commission recommended that a petitioner should seek the court's leave to apply for winding up under s 461. On an application for leave, the court would then, for example, determine whether the petitioner was seeking to exert unjustified pressure on the respondents by pursuing a claim to have the company wound up. It is to be observed that the Commission stressed that winding up should still remain a remedy of last resort and that s 122(1)(g) of the Insolvency Act 1986 should remain as a distinct provision.

Exit rights

The Commission recommended that a draft regulation be included in Table A so as to encourage parties to resolve areas of potential dispute at the outset of their difficulties, thereby avoiding the need to commence legal proceedings. Accordingly, the Commission recommended the introduction of exit rights, to be conferred by ordinary resolution. In respect of the authorising resolution, the Commission recommended that every shareholder who was to have or was to be subject to exit rights should be named in the resolution and consent to it, and that the terms of the resolution should set out the events which would trigger the operation of the exit rights. In circumstances where an exit right was operative, the Commission recommended that the shareholder who was entitled to the right could require other shareholders named in the conferring resolution to buy his/her shares at a 'fair price'; the shares to be shares held when the resolution was passed or shares acquired in right of them. In relation to determining the 'fair price', the conferring resolution was to provide a mechanism for its calculation.

The CLR proposals

The CLR's response to the proposals advanced by the Law Commission were somewhat mixed. As a starting point, the CLR (Final Report 2001) accepted the effect of the ruling in *O'Neill* v *Phillips*, albeit that the CLR considered that the effect of the case was one which would 'restrict the ability of members to take action for unfair prejudice under s 459 . . .' (para 2.26). The CLR's approval and acceptance of *O'Neill* was born of a desire to limit the scope of s 459 with the objective of preventing lengthy and expensive proceedings, proceedings which the CLR considered may, in some instances, destroy small companies. In seeking generally to avoid costly litigation the CLR also recommended the greater pursuit of alternative dispute resolution (ADR). Indeed, and not surprisingly, the said recommendation was adopted by the government's White Paper (2002), albeit that there was no mention of this proposal in the subsequent White Paper (2005).

The CLR report, 'Developing the Framework' (2000), came out against proposals advanced by the Law Commission (see above) in respect of allowing specific types of conduct (e.g. exclusion from management) to raise an automatic presumption of unfairly prejudicial conduct. The 2000 report also opposed the introduction of exit rights. In relation to an 'automatic presumption' it is suggested that the CLR's reaction was understandable given that the circumstances giving rise to a petitioner's exclusion from management may not necessarily give rise to a finding of unfair prejudice and indeed are very much dependent upon the individual facts of any given case.

The CLR also rejected the Law Commission proposal that winding up should be made a remedy under the s 459 provision. However, it is submitted that the CLR's rejection of this idea was perhaps misguided in the sense that the evidence to substantiate both provisions is ordinarily the same. Further, the practice of pleading s 459 and s 122(1)(g) of the Insolvency Act 1986 in the alternative would have been rendered redundant, thus possibly facilitating a reduction in litigation costs.

Finally, it is to be noted that the Government White Papers (2002) and (2005) contain no mention of any type of reform in respect of the s 459 provision, other than the proposal to encourage shareholder arbitration schemes through ADR (but only mentioned in the 2002 White Paper).

THE JUST AND EQUITABLE WINDING UP PROVISION

Section 122(1)(g) of the Insolvency Act 1986 is often referred to as a remedy of the last resort, in so far as a company against which a s 122(1)(g) order is invoked will be wound up (i.e. its existence will end). Under s 122(1)(g), a company may be wound up on the premise that its liquidation would provide a just and equitable remedy. Prior to the implementation of the unfair prejudice remedy, the just and equitable winding up provision was often seen as the only alternative to the problematic remedies afforded to shareholders at common law.

Section 124 of the Insolvency Act 1986 allows any contributory to petition for the equitable winding up order, provided that the proposed petitioner's shares were either originally allotted to him or held by him and registered in his name for at least six months during the 18 months prior to the presentation of a petition. A contributory is defined by s 79 of the 1986 Act as 'every person liable to contribute to the assets of the company in the event of it being wound up'. Although the Insolvency Act 1986 fails to mention the availability of an action under s 122(1)(g) for members whose shares in the company have been fully paid up, the courts have allowed such petitions. However, in all cases, the courts will require the member concerned to have a tangible interest in the winding up of the company.

Tangible interest

For a member of a company to establish a tangible interest, the member must show that the company is solvent. However, even where a company is *prima facie* solvent, a winding up order may still be refused if, after paying its creditors, the company would have no available surplus assets for distribution amongst its membership: see e.g. *Re Expanded Plugs Ltd* [1966] 1 WLR 514.

Further, a petitioner must not, in commencing an action under s 122(1)(g), seek to have the company wound up for a collateral purpose. Therefore, a member must not seek a winding up order where, for example, the purpose of the order is to benefit a competing company in which the petitioning member has an interest.

The qua *member requirement*

A member must petition in his capacity as a member, i.e. *qua* member and not in some other capacity. For example, in *Re J E Cade & Son Ltd* [1991] BCC 360 the petitioner claimed relief under s 459 (discussed above) and in the alternative sought a winding up order on the just and equitable ground. Warner J refused to grant relief under both heads of the petition. The learned judge held that, although a court could give effect to equitable considerations, such considerations arose only where a petitioner pursued his interests as a member of the company. According to Warner J, the petitioner had pursued his interests as the owner of the freehold and not as a member of the company.

Just and equitable considerations

In *Re J E Cade & Son Ltd* [1991] BCC 360 Warner J took the view that, to satisfy the requirements of ss 459 and 122(1)(g), a petitioner's claim had to be based upon an interest which was linked to a legal right of membership. Although Warner J did not believe that a petitioner's claim had necessarily to be based upon the strict legal rights of membership, his lordship nevertheless contended that a shareholder's interest in a company was not subject to expectations which were founded on a general concept of fairness (i.e. expectations which were unrelated to the legal rights of membership). For the purpose of interpreting the scope of a membership interest, the learned judge maintained that the interpretation was the same under both provisions.

As was previously suggested in the context of the discussion of this case in respect of s 459, Warner J's interpretation of a membership interest would appear to be too narrow. It is asserted that, whilst the term 'membership interest' does indeed have the same meaning for both ss 459 and 122(1)(g), the meaning must surely go beyond the interpretation ascribed to it by Warner J. Indeed, in the leading case on the interpretation of the just and equitable winding up provision, namely the House of Lords' decision in *Ebrahimi* v *Westbourne Galleries* [1973] AC 360, Lord Wilberforce stated, regarding the interpretation of the words 'just and equitable':

> 'If there is any respect in which some of the cases may be open to criticism it is that the courts may sometimes have been too timorous in giving them full force.' (at p 379)

The facts of *Ebrahimi* were as follows. A partnership business was incorporated with a share capital split equally between two shareholders (E and N). Both E and N became directors of the company. Subsequently, N's son became a director with one-fifth of both E and N's shares transferred to him. The company prospered until there was a serious and irreconcilable difference of opinion between E and N; E alleged that N had made secret profits at the expense of the company.

An extraordinary general meeting was called by N at which E was removed from his directorship, the votes of N and his son being sufficient to pass the required ordinary resolution to enforce E's dismissal. As a result of being dismissed from office, E lost his right to claim directors' remuneration and, as the company was not in the practice of declaring dividends (the company's profits were distributed via directors' remuneration), E, whilst holding two-fifths of the share capital was, in effect, deprived of any return on his shareholding investment.

In reversing the decision of the Court of Appeal, the House of Lords held that E was entitled to a winding up order on the just and equitable ground. In delivering the leading judgment of the House, Lord Wilberforce stressed that the court should not be restricted to the enforcement of strict legal rights in a situation where it was established that there was a special underlying obligation between the membership of the company. (Note the comparison between the use of 'underlying obligation' and the use of the term 'legitimate expectation' as used in s 459 cases.) In such circumstances, the court could, if it was just and equitable to do so, enforce such an obligation to the extent that, where the obligation had been broken, the company could be dissolved. Lord Wilberforce suggested that the circumstances in which a court could depart from adhering to the strict legal rights of the membership might arise where one or more of the following elements were present:

(a) where a company was formed or continued on the basis of a personal relationship which involved mutual confidence;

(b) if there was an agreement or understanding that all or some of the members of the company would be responsible for the management of the company;

(c) where there was a restriction on the transfer of a member's interest in a company with the consequence that a member who had lost confidence in the running of the company's affairs or had been removed from management would be unable to dispose of his shares.

In the majority of cases where the just and equitable provision has been applied, the category of company made subject to a winding up order has been the quasi-partnership or domestic type of company. For a petition for the just and equitable winding up of a company to succeed, it will be necessary to establish what Lord Wilberforce described as an 'underlying obligation or agreement between the shareholding parties'. In the decided cases this obligation has arisen as a result of either:

(a) an implied agreement on the part of the shareholders to conduct the company's business in a certain manner: see e.g. *Re Crown Bank Ltd* (1890) 44 ChD 634 and *Loch v John Blackwood Ltd* [1924] AC 783;

(b) an implied understanding as to a shareholder's right to participate in the management of the company: see e.g. *Re A & BC Chewing Gum Ltd* [1975] 1 WLR 579, *Re R A Noble Clothing Ltd* [1983] BCLC 273 and *Re Zinotty Properties Ltd* [1984] 1 WLR 1249);

(c) an implied duty on the part of the directors to consider the distribution and proper payment of dividends to the company's shareholders: see e.g. *Re a Company (No 00370 of 1987)* [1988] 1 WLR 1068.

A comparison between section 459 and section 122(1)(g)

Unfairly prejudicial conduct and conduct justifying a court in concluding that a company should be wound up on the just and equitable ground will, in most cases, be indistinguishable. Section 459 and s 122(1)(g) are provisions couched in very similar terms. Both provisions are primarily concerned with quasi-partnership companies, both require the petitioner to establish a membership interest which may, in special circumstances, extend beyond the strict legal rights of membership, a membership interest that must be affected by conduct which destroys a previous relationship of mutual trust and confidence; the very foundation stone of the company's incorporation. Indeed, in the vast majority of cases, the conduct that forms the subject matter of the complaint will equate to conduct that would substantiate either a petition under s 459 or s 122(1)(g); the choice of provision being dependent upon the remedy sought (discussed below).

Accordingly, there would seem little point in a petitioner seeking to plead both s 459 and s 122(1)(g) together. Indeed, *Practice Direction No 1 of 1990* ([1990] 1 WLR 1089) stipulates that s 122(1)(g) should not ordinarily be pleaded as an alternative to an action under s 459. The direction provides that an action under s 122(1)(g) should only be sought as an alternative to an action under s 459 in circumstances where it is established that the relief under s 122(1)(g) would be preferred, or where it is considered that it may be the only form of relief available: see *Re Copeland & Craddock Ltd* [1997] BCC 294.

In *Re Guidezone Ltd* [2001] BCC 692, Jonathan Parker J opined that:

'. . . it would in my judgment be extremely unfortunate, and inconsistent with the approach and the reasoning of Lord Hoffmann in *O'Neill* v *Phillips*, if, given the two parallel jurisdictions, conduct which is not "unfair" for the purposes of s 459 should nevertheless be capable of founding a case for a winding-up order on the "just and equitable" ground. As to Nourse J's decision in *Re Noble (R A) & Sons (Clothing) Ltd* [1983] BCLC 273, in so far as that decision is authority for the proposition that conduct which is not unfair for the purposes of s 459 can nevertheless found a case for a winding up on the just and equitable ground it is in my judgment inconsistent with *O'Neill* v *Phillips*.'
(at p 721)

However, the similarity between the provisions is not as absolutely clear cut as the words of Jonathan Parker J may suggest. There is a subtle difference between the two provisions. Indeed, in *Re Noble (R A) & Sons (Clothing) Ltd* [1983] BCLC 273 and *Jesner* v *Jarrad Properties Ltd* [1992] BCC 807, it was held that conduct, although not classified as unfairly prejudicial, could, in a quasi-partnership type of company, still result in a breakdown of mutual confidence so as to substantiate an action under s 122(1)(g) (e.g. where there was a deadlock situation between two controlling parties but neither party was necessarily at fault). Indeed, in *Re Jayflex Construction Ltd* [2004] 2 BCLC 145, Sir Donald Rattee (sitting as a judge of the High Court) found that, notwithstanding that there had been a mutual breakdown of trust and confidence between the parties, the conduct, the subject matter of the petition under s 459, could not be described as conduct of an unfair nature. In this case, a winding up order, in accordance with s 122(1)(g) had not been sought (other than at the last moment without the matter being subject to argument). However, it is suggested that if a winding up order had been applied for from the start of the proceedings, then it would have succeeded, given that the conduct, however trivial or absent of unfairness, did result in a deadlock situation.

Therefore, while it is accepted that there will be few cases in which a petitioner will be granted a winding up order on the just and equitable ground instead of being obliged to seek an alternative remedy under s 459 – especially as s 125(2) of the Insolvency Act 1986 provides that a winding up order may be struck out if the court is of the opinion that it was unreasonable for the petitioner not to have pursued an alternative course of action (i.e. where another form of remedy was available) – there may be exceptional cases where the nature of the prejudicial conduct meets the requirements of s 122(1)(g) but not those of s 459.

Although the nature, extent and identification of the conduct giving rise to the implementation of s 122(1)(g) and s 459 may often be identical, an aggrieved shareholder may decide to pursue his/her case under s 122(1)(g) in circumstances where this provision affords the most equitable remedy. An example of where a just and equitable winding up order would be the more appropriate remedy is in a situation where a petitioner contends that a company's conduct was indicative of the fact that it was formed to defraud minority shareholders and the investing public. In such circumstances, where the petitioner's claim is proved, it would be improper to allow the company to continue its existence: see, generally, *Re Millennium Advanced Technology* [2004] 2 BCLC 77.

An equitable winding up order would also be a more appropriate type of remedy in circumstances similar to those that arose in *Re Abbey Leisure* [1990] BCC 60. In this case, the petitioner based his action on an implied understanding between the shareholders of the company to the effect that the company had been formed for the sole purpose of acquiring, refurbishing and managing a nightclub. The nightclub in question was acquired but subsequently sold. The petitioner argued that, as the principal purpose in forming the company had failed (i.e. the nightclub had been sold), the company should be wound up. The Court of Appeal, in determining whether to grant the winding up order, had to consider whether the petitioner had been unreasonable in not seeking some other form of remedy (i.e. under s 459). The respondents contended that the petitioner should have petitioned under s 459 and as such obtained an order under s 461 for the purchase of his shares at a fair price. The valuation procedure to ascertain the fair price was, in accordance with the company's articles, to be determined by an independent valuer.

The Court of Appeal, in reversing the first instance judgment of Hoffmann J, held that the winding up order was, in the circumstances of the case, the most appropriate remedy. Relying to a large extent on Lord Wilberforce's comments in *Ebrahimi*, the court opined that the strict legal rights of the petitioner, represented by the valuation procedure within the company's articles, should be made subject to equitable considerations. In so far as the petitioner would gain a greater financial benefit in having the company wound up, rather than if he sold his shares in accordance with the valuation procedure, the court concluded that the just and equitable provision could be employed to override the strict legal rights contained within the company's articles. Here, the circumstances of the case vindicated the application of the just and equitable winding up order.

Suggested further reading

Section 459

Prentice (1988) 8 OJLS 55

Bouchier [1991] JBL 132

Griffin (1993) 14 Co Law 64

Lowry [1995] LMCLQ 337

Roberts and Poole [1999] JBL 38

Hirt (2003) 24 Co Law 100

Alternative dispute resolution and section 459

Corbett and Nicholson (2002) 23 Co Law 274

Section 122(1)(g)

Prentice (1973) 89 LQR 107

Chesterman (1973) 36 MLR 129

25

DEPARTMENT OF TRADE AND INDUSTRY INVESTIGATIONS

INTRODUCTION

The protection of minority interests is enhanced by the availability of Department of Trade and Industry (DTI) investigations. Sections 21–24 of the Companies (Audit, Investigations and Community Enterprise) Act 2004 increase the powers afforded to investigations. The aim of this chapter is briefly to outline the powers and procedures associated with the conduct of DTI investigations. The chapter also considers the role of the Serious Fraud Office.

THE NEED FOR DTI INVESTIGATIONS

In the case of a public company or large private company, the size and scale of business activity may preclude a minority shareholder from obtaining evidence of a suspected abuse of corporate power by the company's management. To police the activities of such companies and to collate evidence of any suspected abuse of corporate powers, the Secretary of State for the DTI may appoint inspectors, through the DTI's Companies Investigation Branch (CIB), to investigate a company's affairs.

Inspectors may be CIB staff but often private sector inspectors are appointed: for example, lawyers or accountants or persons who possess other professional skills which may be relevant to a particular case. Inspectors may also be appointed in circumstances where the pursuit of certain corporate activities is considered contrary to the public interest, irrespective of the fact that the company involved may have the full support of its shareholders. Examples of recent reported investigations include the report into Queens Moat Houses plc and the report into Mirror Group Newspapers plc (reports available from the DTI website: www.dti.gov.uk).

Inspections under section 447, Companies Act 1985

The vast majority of all company investigations are commenced under s 447 of the Companies Act 1985 (as amended by s 63, CA 1989). More recently, as from 6 April 2005 and as a consequence of the implementation of the Companies (Audit, Investigations and Community Enterprise) Act 2004, s 447 is subject to amendment by s 21 of the 2004 Act. The s 447 type of investigation is of a pre-emptive nature, usually lasting for a period of three to four months. The s 447 type investigation is limited to the inspection of documents and related information. As a consequence of the Companies Act 1989, the term 'document' is defined to include recorded material: for example, a computer disk is now included within the general definition of a document.

Investigations under s 447 are confidential and allow suspicions of misconduct to be looked into without the risk of publicly harming the company (i.e. if the inquiries were published, the company could be wrongly prejudiced). Therefore, the DTI does not announce such investigations; neither will it respond to enquiries as to whether a particular company is under investigation. The Secretary of State has unlimted discretion to direct a company to produce documents or information (see s 21 of the 2004 Act).

In accordance with s 23 of the 2004 Act and the Companies Act 1985 (Power to Enter and Remain on Premises: Procedural) Regulations 2005 (SI 2005/684), new ss 453A and 453B are inserted into the Companies Act 1985 to provide and regulate the powers of inspectors in their ability to have access to all the 'relevant premises' of the company under investigation. These provisions enhance the inspectors' previous powers, which were limited by the fact that inspectors were required to obtain the consent of the company prior to entering the company's business premises. Further, the use of the term 'relevant premises' extends the ambit of an inspector's access to all premises linked with the company's business operations (this may include private dwellings and the premises of associated businesses). However, the power to have access to 'relevant premises' does not include the right to search the premises without first having obtained a relevant search warrant.

Where a s 447 type of investigation produces evidence of corporate misconduct, a full investigation into the company's affairs may then be ordered. Prior to the 2004 Act it was a criminal offence, punishable by a fine, for a person to fail to produce documents which were legitimately requested by an inspector. As a result of the 2004 Act, this offence has been repealed. The offence is replaced with a new certification procedure whereby an investigator or the Secretary of State certifies to the court that there has been a failure to comply with a request for documents or information. A court hearing will determine the matter. If the court finds that there was no reasonable excuse for non-compliance, the court may find the defendant guilty of a contempt of court. However, the defendant may escape punishment if, at the request of the court, he/she provides documents/information as specifically required by the court.

Any present or past officer or employee of the company may be requested to provide an explanation for the contents of documents which have been requested for inspection: see e.g. *Re Attorney-General's Reference (No 2 of 1998)* [1999] BCC 590.

Investigations under section 431, Companies Act 1985

The Secretary of State may, at his/her discretion, order a s 431 investigation in the following circumstances:

(a) where the investigation is demanded by a company;

(b) in the case of a company with a share capital, where shareholders holding at least 200 shares in the company or holding ten per cent of the issued share capital apply for an investigation;

(c) in the case of a company not having a share capital, where not less than 20 per cent of the company's members apply for an investigation.

Shareholders must establish reasonable grounds for an investigation to proceed, shareholders who instigate an investigation may be liable for its cost and the Secretary of State may ask the applicants to give a security of up to £5000. The investigation will normally be conducted by two inspectors.

Investigations under section 432, Companies Act 1985

The Secretary of State must appoint inspectors where the court declares that a company's affairs should be investigated (s 432(1)). Further, in accordance with s 432(2), the Secretary of State may, at his/her discretion, order an investigation where grounds exist to substantiate a finding of at least one of the following matters:

(a) the company's affairs are, or have been, conducted with an intent to defraud creditors, or the company's affairs have been conducted for some other fraudulent or unlawful purpose, or in a manner which is, or which might result in unfairly prejudicial conduct to any part of its members; or

(b) any actual or proposed act or omission of the company (including an act or omission on its behalf) is, or would be, prejudicial, or that the company was formed for any fraudulent or unlawful purpose; or

(c) persons connected with the company's formation or management have been guilty of fraud, misfeasance or other misconduct towards the company or its members; or

(d) shareholders have not been given all the information with respect to the management of a company's affairs, which they might reasonably have expected to be given.

In relation to the negligent conduct of a company's affairs, such conduct will not normally give the Secretary of State a right to order an investigation: see e.g. *SBA Properties Ltd* v *Cradock* [1967] 1 WLR 716. However, as the Secretary of State is not obliged to disclose why an investigation was ordered (see e.g. *Norwest Holst Ltd* v *Secretary of State for Trade* [1978] Ch 201), it is not inconceivable that the negligent conduct of a company's affairs may be the catalyst for the instigation of an investigation. It should be noted that the Secretary of State may exercise his power to instigate an investigation even where a company is in the process of being voluntarily wound up (s 432(3), CA 1985).

Specific reasons for an investigation

Ownership or control

In accordance with ss 442–445 of the Companies Act 1985, an inspector has the power to investigate the ownership of shares and debentures and may impose certain restrictions upon the internal structure of a company in relation to its securities: for example, restrictions upon the rights of certain shareholders to vote and/or receive dividend payments (discussed further in Chapter 9).

Share dealings

An inspector may investigate dealings in a company's securities (s 446, CA 1985).

Related companies

An inspector appointed to investigate a company may also investigate the company's related companies (i.e. the company's holding company or subsidiary companies). A related company may be investigated whether it is incorporated in the UK or overseas (s 433, CA 1985).

Powers associated with an investigation

In accordance with s 434 of the Companies Act 1985, where inspectors are appointed under ss 431 or 432, it is the duty of the officers and agents of the company under investigation and other officers and agents of any other related companies privy to the investigation, to produce corporate documents which are requested by the inspectors. Persons requested to attend before the inspectors must do so and such persons must offer any other form of assistance as required by the inspectors.

In accordance with s 434(2), an inspector may require a director of a company under investigation to produce any document in his custody where that document is considered relevant to the investigation and may order a director to comply with matters specified in s 434(1). An inspector may, for the purposes of the investigation, examine any person on oath. An answer given by a person to a question put to him may be used in evidence against that person: see e.g. *London & County Securities Ltd* v *Nicholson* [1980] 3 All ER 861 (s 434(5), CA 1985). Any person who withholds information may be reported to the court and may be punished for contempt of court.

Inspectors may examine documents relating to bank accounts into or out of which moneys have been paid (i.e. where a bank account is connected with alleged corporate misconduct). An inspector may also require the production of documents relating to corporate finances where such finances should have been disclosed in the company's accounts but, for whatever reason, were not so disclosed.

The report of an investigation

A copy of the report of an investigation is admissible in any legal proceedings as evidence of the opinion of the inspectors in respect of any matter contained within the report (s 441, CA 1985). It is not, however, save under s 8 of the Company Directors Disqualification Act 1986, admissible as evidence of fact: see e.g. *Savings and Investment Bank Ltd* v *Gasco Investments* [1984] 1 All ER 296.

As a result of the implementation of s 55 of the Companies Act 1989, incorporated into the Companies Act 1985 as s 432(2A), the Secretary of State has the power to appoint inspectors on the understanding that their report will not be published (i.e. made available to the general public). This provision may be seen as an extension of s 437 of the Companies Act 1985, which deems that a report does not have to be published unless the Secretary of State thinks fit. The implementation of the Secretary of State's power under s 432(2A) removes the danger of criticism and any controversy surrounding a decision not to publish under s 437. A positive and welcomed consequence of the power not to publish a report is that non-publication will reduce the time taken to complete the investigation. Nevertheless, on the negative side, a report's non-disclosure may obviously be subject to criticism on the basis of being overprotective in relation to the non-divulgence of any suspected corporate malpractice.

The consequences attached to an investigation

If, as a result of an investigation, the Secretary of State believes that it is in the public interest to dissolve a company, he may present a winding up petition on the just and equitable ground. Alternatively, he may order civil proceedings to be taken on behalf of and in the company's name (s 438, CA 1985) or bring proceedings under s 460 of the Companies Act 1985 on the premise that the company's affairs have been conducted in an unfairly prejudicial manner against a part of the membership. (It should be noted that the power to commence proceedings on the basis of unfairly prejudicial conduct does not, unlike s 459, CA 1985, expressly extend to a situation whereby the company's affairs have been conducted in a manner that was unfairly prejudicial to members generally. This omission is somewhat odd given the misconduct in question may often affect the company as a whole.) The Secretary of State may also apply to the court for a disqualification order to be made against a company director(s) under s 8 of the Company Directors Disqualification Act 1986: see e.g. *Re Aldermanbury Trust plc* [1993] BCC 598. In appropriate circumstances, criminal proceedings may also be commenced against an individual.

During the course of an investigation, a person called upon to answer the questions of the inspectors is obliged to answer all questions, unless in the particular circumstances of a case it is unreasonable to expect him to do so: see e.g. *Re Mirror Group Newspapers plc* [1999] 1 BCLC 691. A person to whom the inspectors have put questions is not allowed to attend or be represented when another witness is giving evidence, nor is he allowed to see a transcript of that evidence or challenge it; in this respect there is no right of appeal against the inspectors' findings: see e.g. *Re Pergamon Press Ltd* [1971] Ch 388. The inspectors' right to compel persons under investigation to provide answers and information is not in contravention of Art 6 of the European Convention on Human Rights (which is concerned with a person's right to a fair trial – incorporated into UK law by the Human Rights Act 1998): see *Fayed* v *UK* (1994) 18 EHRR 393.

However, the European Convention on Human Rights (Human Rights Act) will have relevance where the evidence taken from the investigation is used in subsequent criminal law proceedings. The compelled testimony of a person may not be used in a subsequent trial other than where the testimony was introduced into the proceedings by the said person: see *Guinness* v *Saunders* [1998] 1 BCLC 362. This reverses the previous position whereby compelled evidence given to inspectors could be used in subsequent proceedings: see e.g. *R* v *Lord Spens* [1992] 1 WLR 148. However, it should be noted that any evidence from an investigation which is in the form of documents or other materials (but not a record of testimony) may be used in a subsequent criminal prosecution. Finally, it should be noted that a person, in providing information in relation to an investigation, may be protected from legal liability for any breach of confidence or contract, following a 'relevant disclosure' (new s 448A, CA 1985, inserted by s 22 of the 2004 Act).

THE SERIOUS FRAUD OFFICE

The Serious Fraud Office (SFO) was set up under the Criminal Justice Act 1987 (CJA 1987) following the recommendations of the Fraud Trials Committee Report, more commonly known as 'the Roskill Report' (1986). The SFO commenced operations in April 1988. The purpose for its creation was to investigate any suspected offence involving serious or complex fraud. The SFO is made up of lawyers, accountants and police representatives. Section 1(3) of the CJA 1987 empowers the SFO to investigate any suspected offence where it has reasonable grounds to believe that the offence involves serious or complex fraud. In determining whether to investigate and expend (limited) resources on an allegation of fraudulent conduct, the SFO will determine the matter by considering the following questions:

- Does the value of the alleged fraud exceed £1 million?
- Is there a significant international dimension?
- Is the case likely to be of widespread public concern?
- Does the case require highly specialised knowledge, e.g. of financial markets?
- Is there a need to use the SFO's powers?

The powers of the officers of the SFO are similar to those of the DTI inspectors, save that the powers of the SFO are not limited to companies and extend to the investigation of any person. Following the enactment of the Criminal Justice Act 2003, search powers have now been afforded to civilian inspectors when accompanying police officers in executing searches, thus giving specialist staff of the SFO a more effective role in gathering evidence. Under s 2 of the CJA 1987, the SFO may compel a person or other body – for example, a bank – to answer questions and provide information and documents that may subsequently be used to convict an individual. Although a bank or other financial institution may owe a duty of confidence to their clients, the said duty is overridden by s 2.

A person may be compelled to provide information even after he has been charged with an offence: so held by the House of Lords in *R* v *Director of Serious Fraud Office, ex parte Smith* [1993] AC 1. It is a criminal offence, without reasonable excuse, to refuse to provide the requisite information: see e.g. *Re Mirror Group Newspapers plc* [1999] 1 BCLC 691. However, answers to questions required under s 2 may not be used as evidence in criminal proceedings against the person who provides them, unless the trial is in relation to an offence of providing misleading information under s 2, or where the testimony was introduced into the proceedings by the person himself.

Suggested further reading

Lidbetter *Company Investigations and Public Law* (Hart, 1999)

Fraser (1971) 34 MLR 260

Instone [1978] JBL 121

Chaikin (1982) 3 Co Law 115

Sheikh (2002) 13 ICCLR 228

Griffiths (2005) 155 NLJ 198

Serious Fraud Office

Frommel (1994) 15 Co Law 227

Sarker (1995) 16 Co Law 56 212 and (ii) Sarker (1995) 16 Co Law 213

Wright (2003) 11 JFC 10

INDEX